VOLUME II

THE WEST
ENCOUNTERS & TRANSFORMATIONS
SECOND CUSTOM EDITION FOR OREGON STATE UNIVERSITY

Brian Levack ● **Edward Muir** ● **Meredith Veldman**

Note to students:

The material in this book has been specifically selected by your instructors. They have chosen to eliminate some material which is not critical to your course, and in doing so the price of this book has been adjusted to reflect the content removed.

Please note because content has been removed from your text, you will see some breaks in the page numbering.

Taken From:

The West: Encounters & Transformations, Combined Volume, Third Edition
by Brian Levack, Edward Muir, and Meredith Veldman

Learning Solutions

New York Boston San Francisco
London Toronto Sydney Tokyo Singapore Madrid
Mexico City Munich Paris Cape Town Hong Kong Montreal

Cover Art: Courtesy of PhotoDisc/Getty Images

Taken from:

The West: Encounters & Transformations, Combined Volume, Third Edition
by Brian Levack, Edward Muir, and Meredith Veldman
Copyright © 2011, 2007, 2004 by Pearson Education, Inc.
Published by Longman
New York, New York 10036

Pearson Learning Solutions, 501 Boylston Street, Suite 900, Boston, MA 02116
A Pearson Education Company
www.pearsoned.com

Printed in the United States of America

1 2 3 4 5 6 7 8 9 10 V0FB 15 14 13 12 11 10

000200010270653962

SD

ISBN 10: 0-558-92034-9
ISBN 13: 978-0-558-92034-0

BRIEF CONTENTS

DETAILED CONTENTS

MAPS

PREFACE

We wrote this textbook to answer questions about the identity of the civilization in which we live. Journalists, politicians, and scholars often refer to our civilization, its political ideologies, its economic systems, and its cultures as "Western" without fully considering what that label means and why it might be appropriate. The classification of our civilization as Western has become particularly problematic in the age of globalization. The creation of international markets, the rapid dissemination of ideas on a global scale, and the transmission of popular culture from one country to another often make it difficult to distinguish what is Western from what is not. *The West: Encounters & Transformations* offers students a history of Western civilization in which these issues of Western identity are given prominence. Our goal is neither to idealize nor to indict that civilization, but to describe its main characteristics in different historical periods.

The West: Encounters & Transformations gives careful consideration to two basic questions. The first is, how did the definition of the West change over time? In what ways did its boundaries shift and how did the distinguishing characteristics of its cultures change? The second question is, by what means did the West—and the idea of the West—develop? We argue that the West is the product of a series of cultural encounters that occurred both outside and within its geographical boundaries. We explore these encounters and the transformations they produced by detailing the political, social, religious, and cultural history of the regions that have been, at one time or another, a part of the West.

DEFINING THE WEST

What is the West? How did it come into being? How has it developed throughout history? Many textbooks take for granted which regions or peoples of the globe constitute the West. They treat the history of the West as a somewhat expanded version of European history. While not disputing the centrality of Europe to any definition of the West, we contend that the West is not only a geographical realm with ever-shifting boundaries, but also a cultural realm, an area of cultural influence extending beyond the geographical and political boundaries of Europe. We so strongly believe in this notion that we have written the introductory essay "What Is the West?" to encourage students to think about their understanding of Western civilization and to guide their understanding of each chapter. Many of the features of what we call Western civilization originated in regions that are not geographically part of Europe (such as North Africa and the Middle East), while ever since the fifteenth century various social, ethnic, and political groups from non-European regions (such as North and South America, eastern Russia, Australia, New Zealand, and South Africa) have identified themselves, in one way or another, with the West. Throughout the text, we devote considerable attention to the boundaries of the West and show how borderlines between cultures have been created, especially in eastern and southeastern Europe.

Considered as a geographical and cultural realm, *the West* is a term of recent origin, and the civilization to which it refers did not become clearly defined until the eleventh century, especially during the Crusades, when western European Christians developed a distinct cultural identity. Before that time we can only talk about the powerful forces that created the West, especially the dynamic interaction of the civilizations of western Europe, the Byzantine Empire, and the Muslim world.

Over the centuries Western civilization has acquired many salient characteristics. These include two of the world's great legal systems (civil law and common law), three of the world's monotheistic religions (Judaism, Christianity, and Islam), certain political and social philosophies, forms of political organization (such as the modern bureaucratic state and democracy), methods of scientific inquiry, systems of economic organization (such as industrial capitalism), and distinctive styles of art, architecture, and music. At times one or more of these characteristics has served as a primary source of Western identity: Christianity in the Middle Ages, science and rationalism during the Enlightenment, industrialization in the nineteenth and twentieth centuries, and a defense of individual liberty and democracy in the late twentieth century. These sources of Western identity, however, have always been challenged and contested, both when they were coming into prominence and when they appeared to be most triumphant. Western culture has never been monolithic; even today references to the West imply a wide range of meanings.

CULTURAL ENCOUNTERS

The definition of the West is closely related to the central theme of our book, which is the process of cultural encounters. Throughout *The West: Encounters & Transformations*, we examine the West as a product of a series of cultural encounters both outside the West and within it. We show that the West originated and developed through a continuous process of inclusion and exclusion resulting from a series of encounters among and within different groups. These encounters can be described in a general sense as external, internal, or ideological.

External Encounters

External encounters took place between peoples of different civilizations. Before the emergence of the West as a clearly defined entity, external encounters occurred between such diverse peoples as Greeks and Phoenicians, Macedonians and Egyptians, and Romans and Celts. After the eleventh century, external encounters between Western and non-Western peoples occurred mainly during periods of European exploration, expansion, and imperialism. In the sixteenth and seventeenth centuries, for example, a series of external encounters took place between Europeans on the one hand and Africans, Asians, and the indigenous people of the Americas on the other. Two chapters of *The West: Encounters & Transformations* (Chapters 13 and 18) and a large section of a third (Chapter 24) explore these external encounters in depth and discuss how they affected Western and non-Western civilizations alike.

Internal Encounters

Our discussion of encounters also includes similar interactions between different social groups *within* Western countries. These internal encounters often took place between dominant and subordinate groups, such as between lords and peasants, rulers and subjects, men and women, factory owners and workers, masters and slaves. Encounters between those who were educated and those who were illiterate, which recurred frequently throughout Western history, also fall into this category. Encounters just as often took place between different religious and political groups, such as between Christians and Jews, Catholics and Protestants, and royal absolutists and republicans.

Ideological Encounters

Ideological encounters involve interaction between comprehensive systems of thought, most notably religious doctrines, political philosophies, and scientific theories about the nature of the world. These ideological conflicts usually arose out of internal encounters, when various groups within Western societies subscribed to different theories of government or rival religious faiths. The encounters between Christianity and polytheism in the early Middle

Ages, between liberalism and conservatism in the nineteenth century, and between fascism and communism in the twentieth century were ideological encounters. Some ideological encounters had an external dimension, such as when the forces of Islam and Christianity came into conflict during the Crusades and when the Cold War developed between Soviet communism and Western democracy in the second half of the twentieth century.

* * *

The West: Encounters & Transformations illuminates the variety of these encounters and clarifies their effects. By their very nature encounters are interactive, but they have taken different forms: They have been violent or peaceful, coercive or Cooperative. Some have resulted in the imposition of Western ideas on areas outside the geographical boundaries of the West or the perpetuation of the dominant culture within Western societies. More often than not, however, encounters have resulted in a more reciprocal process of exchange in which both Western and non-Western cultures, or the values of both dominant and subordinate groups, have undergone significant transformation. Our book not only identifies these encounters, but also discusses their significance by returning periodically to the issue of Western identity.

COVERAGE

The West: Encounters & Transformations offers both comprehensive coverage of political, social, and culture history and a broader coverage of the West and the world.

Comprehensive Coverage

Our goal throughout the text has been to provide comprehensive coverage of political, social, and cultural history and to include significant coverage of religious and military history as well. Political history defines the basic structure of the book, and some chapters, such as those on Hellenistic civilization, the age of confessional divisions, absolutism and state building, the French Revolution, and the coming of mass politics, include sustained political narratives. Because we understand the West to be a cultural as well as a geographical realm, we give a prominent position to cultural history. Thus, we include rich sections on Hellenistic philosophy and literature, the cultural environment of the Italian Renaissance, the creation of a new political culture at the time of the French Revolution, and the atmosphere of cultural despair and desire that prevailed in Europe after World War I. We also devote special attention to religious history, including the history of Islam as well as that of Christianity and Judaism. Unlike many other textbooks, our coverage of religion continues into the modern period.

The West: Encounters & Transformations also provides extensive coverage of the history of women and gender. Wherever possible the history of women is integrated into the broader social, cultural, and political history of the period. But there are also separate sections on women in our chapters on classical Greece, the Renaissance, the Reformation, the Enlightenment, the Industrial Revolution, World War I, World War II, and the postwar era.

The West and the World

Our book provides broad geographical coverage. Because the West is the product of a series of encounters, the external areas with which the West interacted are of major importance. Three chapters deal specifically with the West and the world.

- Chapter 13, "The West and the World: The Significance of Global Encounters, 1450–1650"
- Chapter 18, "The West and the World: Empire, Trade, and War, 1650–1815"
- Chapter 24, "The West and the World: Cultural Crisis and the New Imperialism, 1870–1914"

These chapters present substantial material on sub-Saharan Africa, Latin America, the Middle

East, India, and East Asia. Our text is also distinctive in its coverage of eastern Europe and the Muslim world, areas that have often been considered outside the boundaries of the West. These regions were arenas within which significant cultural encounters took place. Finally, we include material on the United States and Australia, both of which have become part of the West. We recognize that most American college and university students have the opportunity to study American history as a separate subject, but treatment of the United States as a Western nation provides a different perspective from that usually given in courses on American history. For example, this book treats America's revolution as one of four Atlantic revolutions, its national unification in the nineteenth century as part of a broader western European development, its pattern of industrialization as related to that of Britain, and its central role in the Cold War as part of an ideological encounter that was global in scope.

What's New to This Edition?

- In preparing this edition we have thoroughly revised every chapter to ensure that we include the most recent research in the field and to make it even more accessible to students. Most significantly, we have reduced the length of each chapter by approximately 20 to 25 percent.
- We have written separate chapters on Hellenistic civilization and the Roman Republic. In the second edition we had included both subjects in the same chapter because Rome was a part of the Hellenistic world and absorbed large doses of Greek culture. Separate chapters, however, allow us not only to devote more space to each topic, but also to clarify the ways in which republican Rome developed a distinctive brand of Hellenism.
- The discussion of ancient Egypt, which was divided between Chapters 1 and 2 in the second edition, has been consolidated into Chapter 1 for ease of teaching. Discussion of the ancient Hebrews, now in Chapter 2, has been expanded.

- Instead of including three separate primary source documents in each chapter we have included two documents that present different and often contradictory positions on the same person, event, or development. These documents, which are followed by questions for discussion, appear in the "Different Voices" feature in each chapter.
- We have written new "Encounters and Transformations" features in Chapters 2, 5, 6, 11, and 12, and new "Justice in History" features for Chapters 2, 4, 13, and 14.

FEATURES AND PEDAGOGICAL AIDS

In writing this textbook we have endeavored to keep both the student reader and the classroom instructor in mind at all times. The text includes the following features and pedagogical aids, all of which are intended to support the themes of the book.

"What Is the West?"

The West: Encounters & Transformations begins with an essay to engage students in the task of defining the West and to introduce them to the notion of cultural encounters. "What Is the West?" guides students through the text by providing a framework for understanding how the West was shaped. Structured around the six questions of What? When? Where? Who? How? and Why?, this framework encourages students to think about their understanding of Western civilization. The essay serves as a blueprint for using this textbook.

"Encounters and Transformations"

These features, which appear in about half the chapters, illustrate the main theme of the book by identifying specific encounters and showing how they led to significant

ENCOUNTERS AND TRANSFORMATIONS

The Introduction of the Table Fork: The New Sign of Western Civilization

Sometime in the sixteenth century, western Europeans encountered a new tool that initiated a profound and lasting transformation in Western society: the table fork. Before the table fork, people dined in a way that, to our modern sensibilities, seems disgusting. Members of the upper classes indulged themselves by devouring meat in enormous quantities. Whole rabbits, lambs, and pigs roasted on a spit were placed before diners. A quarter of veal or venison or even an entire roast beef, complete with its head, might be heaved onto the table. Diners used knives to cut off a piece of meat that they then ate with their hands, allowing the juices to drip down their arms. They used the long sleeves of their shirts to wipe meat juices, sweat, and spittle from their mouths and faces. These banquets celebrated the direct physical contact between the body of the dead animal and the bodies of the diners themselves who touched, handled, chewed, and swallowed it.

During the sixteenth century, puritanical reformers who were trying to abolish the cruder aspects of popular culture also promoted new table manners.

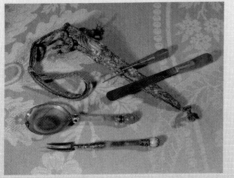

THE INTRODUCTION OF THE TABLE FORK
During the late sixteenth century the refinement of manners among the upper classes focused on dining. No innovation was more revolutionary than the spread of the use of the table fork. Pictured here is the travel cutlery, including two table forks, of Queen Elizabeth I.

transformations in the cultures of the West. These features show, for example, how camels enabled encounters among nomadic tribes of Arabia, which led to the rapid spread of Islam; how the Mayans' interpretation of Christian symbols transformed European Christianity into a hybrid religion; how the importation of chocolate from the New World to Europe changed Western consumption patterns and the rhythms of the Atlantic economy; and how Picasso's encounter with African art contributed to the transformation of modernism. Each of these essays concludes with questions for discussion.

"Justice in History"

Found in every chapter, this feature presents a historically significant trial or episode in which different notions of justice (or injustice) were debated and resolved. The "Justice in History" features illustrate cultural encounters

within communities as they try to determine the fate of individuals from all walks of life. Many famous trials dealt with conflicts over basic religious, philosophical, or political values, such as those of Socrates, Jesus, Joan of Arc, Martin Luther, Charles I, Galileo, and Adolf Eichmann. Other "Justice in History" features show how judicial institutions, such as the ordeal, the Inquisition, and revolutionary tribunals, handled adversarial situations in different societies. These essays, therefore, illustrate the way in which the basic values of the West have evolved through attempts to resolve disputes and conflict.

Each "Justice in History" feature includes two pedagogical aids. "For Discussion" helps students explore the historical significance of the episode just examined. These questions can be used in classroom discussion or as student essay topics. "Taking It Further" provides the student with a few references that can be consulted in connection with a research project.

JUSTICE IN HISTORY

The *Auto-da-Fé:* The Power of Penance

Performed in Spain and Portugal from the sixteenth to eighteenth centuries, the *auto-da-fé* merged the judicial processes of the state with the sacramental rituals of the Catholic Church. An *auto* took place at the end of a judicial investigation conducted by the inquisitors of the Church after the defendants had been found guilty of a sin or crime. The term **auto-da-fé** means "act of faith," and the goal was to persuade or force a person who had been judged guilty to repent and confess. Organized through the cooperation of ecclesiastical and secular authorities, autos-da-fé brought together an assortment of sinners, criminals, and heretics for a vast public rite that dramatized the essential elements of the sacrament of penance: *contrition,* by which the sinner recognized and felt sorry for the sin; *confession,* which required the sinner to admit the sin to a priest; and *satisfaction* or *punishment,* by which the priest absolved the sinner and enacted some kind of penalty. The auto-da-fé transformed penance, especially confession and satisfaction, into a spectacular affirmation of the faith and a manifestation of divine justice.

The *auto* symbolically anticipated the Last Judgment. By suffering bodily pain in this life the soul

miters or hats
their sin, four
devils, and th
their necks to
tives. The sinr
sent their lack
escaped arres
sion by effigie
who had died
carried in thei
appeared befc
zens stripped
dressed only i
Among them
mous *sanbeni*
yellow strip d
painted with
the unrepenta

The proces
platform on w
lic penances a
their knees, pr
and to plead f
church. For th
announced fro
from the pains
auto. The sent
tial procession

"Different Voices"

Each chapter contains a new feature consisting of two primary source documents that present different and often opposing views regarding a particular person, event, or development. An introduction to the documents provides the necessary historical context, identifies the authors of the documents and suggests the different perspectives they take. A set of questions for discussion follows the two documents.

DIFFERENT VOICES WERE THERE REALLY WITCHES?

Even during the height of the witch-hunt the existence of witches was controversial. Most authorities assumed that the devil worked evil on earth and that hunting witches, therefore, was an effective means of defending Christians. These authorities used the church and secular courts to interrogate alleged witches, sometimes supplemented by torture, to obtain confessions and the identities of other confederate witches. These authorities considered the hunting of witches part of their duty to protect the public from harm. Others accepted the reality of witchcraft but doubted the capacity of judges to determine who was a witch. A few doubted the reality of witchcraft altogether.

Johann Weyer (1515?–1588) was a physician who argued that most witches were deluded old women who suffered from depression and need medical help rather than legal punishment. The devil deceived them into thinking they had magical powers, but because Weyer had a strong belief that only God had power over nature, he did not credit the devil or witches with any special powers. No one else during the sixteenth century disputed the reality of the powers of witches as systematically as he. Jean

permission and
and storms, he
them to use th
when the troub
witches are cor
have caused it.
make hail and
deluded and bl
whom they hav
they think that
storms. Not on
godless lives sh
severely....

Our witches
phantasy by th
they have done
pen or caused
did not take pla
cially under tor
causing many t
them and for ar
them when the
themselves to t

Chapter Review and Questions for Discussion

This edition of *The West* offers three different sets of questions in each chapter.

- Each of the major sections of the chapter begins with the main question that the section addresses. These questions are printed in blue. These section questions appear once again at the end of the chapter under the heading "Chapter Questions."
- At the end of each chapter a set of questions under the heading "Taking It Further" ask the student to think about some

of the more specific issues discussed in the chapter.
- Each Justice in History and Different Voices feature is followed by a set of questions under the heading "For Discussion."

Maps and Illustrations

Artwork is a key component of our book. We recognize that many students often lack a strong familiarity with geography, and so we have taken great care to develop maps that help sharpen their geographic skills. Complementing the book's standard map program, we include maps focusing on areas outside the borders of Western civilization. More than 300 images of fine art and photos tell the story of Western civilization and help students visualize the past: the way people lived, the events that shaped their lives, and how they viewed the world around them.

Chronologies

Each chapter includes a varying number of chronologies that list in tabular form the events relating to a particular topic discussed in the text. Chronologies present the sequence of events and can be helpful for purposes of review.

CHRONOLOGY: SPAIN AND THE NETHERLANDS, 1568–1648	
1568	Edict against Morisco culture
1580	King Philip II inherits Portugal and the Portuguese Empire
1584	Assassination of William the Silent
1588	Defeat of the Spanish Armada, failed Spanish invasion of England; the seven northern provinces of the Netherlands becomes a republic
1609	Expulsion of the Moriscos from Spain
1648	Treaty of Westphalia recognizes independence of the Netherlands

Key Terms and Glossary

We have sought to create a work that is accessible to students with little prior knowledge of the basic facts of Western history or geography. Throughout the book we have explained difficult concepts at length. For example, we present in-depth explanations of the concepts of Zoroastrianism, Neoplatonism, Renaissance humanism, the various Protestant denominations of the sixteenth century, capitalism, seventeenth-century absolutism, nineteenth-century liberalism and nationalism, fascism, and modernism. We have identified these concepts as key terms by printing them in bold in the text. Key terms for each chapter are listed at the end of each chapter, and all key terms are listed in alphabetical order, together with their definitions, in the Glossary at the end of the book.

Suggested Readings

An annotated list of suggested readings for all the chapters appears at the end of the book. The items listed there are not scholarly works for the benefit of the instructor, but suggestions for students who wish to explore a topic in greater depth or to write a research paper. References to books or articles relevant to the subject of the "Justice in History" feature appear in each chapter under the heading "Taking it Further."

A Note About Dates and Transliterations

In keeping with current academic practice, *The West: Encounters & Transformations* uses B.C.E. (before the common era) and C.E. (common era) to designate dates. We also follow the most current and widely accepted English transliterations of Arabic. *Qur'an*, for example, is used for *Koran; Muslim* is used for *Moslem*. Chinese words appearing in the text for the first time are written in pinyin, followed by the older Wade-Giles system in parentheses.

ANCILLARY MATERIALS

The ancillary materials that accompany *The West: Encounters and Transformations,* Third Edition, are designed to reinforce and enliven the richness of the past and inspire students with the excitement of studying the history of Western Civilization.

For Instructors

THE INSTRUCTOR'S RESOURCE CENTER (www.pearsonhighered.com) Text-specific materials, such as the instructor's manual, and the test item file, are available for downloading by adopters.

INSTRUCTOR'S RESOURCE MANUAL/TEST ITEM FILE The Instructor's Manual contains chapter outlines, summaries, key points and vital concepts, and information on audio-visual resources that can be used in developing and preparing lecture presentations. The Test Item File includes 1,200 multiple-choice and essay test questions. **Available on the Instructor's Resource Center: www.pearsonhighered.com/irc/**

MyTest   MyTest is an online test management program. The program allows instructors to select items from the Test Item File in order to create tests. It also allows for online testing. **Available on the Instructor's Resource Center: www.pearsonhighered.com/irc/**

Digital Transparency Masters and Power-Points   The Digital Transparency Masters are full-color PDFs containing high-resolution images of all the maps and line art that appear in the text. These files are suitable for both printing to acetate or electronic display. The PowerPoints contain chapter outlines and full-color images of maps and line art. Both are text specific and available for download from the Instructor's Resource Center. **Available on the Instructor's Resource Center: www. pearsonhighered.com/irc/**

For Instructors and Students

MyHistoryLab   (www.myhistorylab.com) **Save time. Improve results.** MyHistoryLab is a

dynamic website that provides a wealth of resources geared to meet the diverse teaching and learning needs of today's instructors and students. MyHistoryLab's many accessible tools will encourage students to read their text and help them improve their grade in their course.

Here are some of the features that will help you and your students save time and improve results:

■ Pearson eText—Just like the printed text, students can highlight and add their own notes. Students save time and improve results by having access to their book online.
■ Gradebook—Students can follow their own progress and instructors can monitor the

work of the entire class. Automated grading of quizzes and assignments helps both instructors and students save time and monitor their results throughout the course.
■ History Bookshelf—Students may read, download, or print 100 of the most commonly assigned history works like Homer's *The Iliad* or Machiavelli's *The Prince*.
■ MySearchLab—This website provides students access to a number of reliable sources for online research, as well as clear guidance on the research and writing process.

CourseSmart Textbooks Online   www.coursesmart.com. provides students an inexpensive alternative to purchasing the print textbook by subscribing to the same text online. Features include search, online note-taking, a print option and bookmarking.

For Students

Please contact your Pearson Arts and Sciences representative for ordering information.

Lives and Legacies: Biographies in Western Civilization, Second Edition   Extensively revised, *Lives and Legacies* includes brief, focused biographies of 60 individuals whose lives provide insight into the key developments of Western civilization. Each biography includes an introduction, pre-reading questions, and suggestions for additional reading.

Volume One: **ISBN-10: 0205649157 | ISBN-13: 9780205649150**
Volume Two: **ISBN-10: 0205649149 | ISBN-13: 9780205649143**

A variety of Penguin-Putnam texts are available at a discounted prices when bundled with *The West: Encounters & Transformations*, Third Edition. The complete list of titles is available at www.pearsonhighered.com/penguin

THE PRENTICE HALL ATLAS OF WEST-ERN CIVILIZATION, SECOND EDITION Produced in collaboration with Dorling Kindersley, the leader in cartographic publishing, the updated second edition of *The Prentice Hall Atlas of Western Civilization* applies the most innovative cartographic techniques to present western civilization in all of its complexity and diversity. Copies of the atlas can be bundled with *The West: Encounters & Transformations*, Third Edition, for a nominal charge. Contact your Pearson Arts and Sciences sales representative for details. **ISBN-10: 0136042465 | ISBN-13: 9780136042464**

A GUIDE TO YOUR HISTORY COURSE: WHAT EVERY STUDENT NEEDS TO KNOW Written by Vincent A. Clark, this concise, spiral-bound guidebook orients students to the issues and problems they will face in the history classroom. Available at a discount when bundled with *The West: Encounters & Transformations*, Third Edition. **ISBN-10: 0131850873 | ISBN-13: 9780131850873**

A SHORT GUIDE TO WRITING ABOUT HISTORY, SEVENTH EDITION Written by Richard Marius, late of Harvard University, and Melvin E. Page, Eastern Tennessee State University, this engaging and practical text helps students get beyond merely compiling dates and facts. Covering both brief essays and the documented resource paper, the text explores the writing and researching processes, identifies different modes of historical writing, including argument, and concludes with guidelines for improving style. **ISBN-10: 0205673708 | ISBN-13: 9780205673704**

ACKNOWLEDGMENTS

We wish to thank Michael Maas, whose contributions to the second edition have been incorporated into Chapters 1–8 of this edition. We are also grateful to Priscilla McGeehon, for her support during the production of all three editions of the book; Janet Lanphier, for helping us plan the third edition; Gerald Lombardi, for his editorial comments on the first eight chapters; and Charles Cavaliere, who guided us through the long process of preparing the third edition.

We would also like to thank the following friends and colleagues for their valuable advice and suggestions: Gabor Agoston, Catherine Clinton, Catherine Evtuhov, Wojciech Falkowski, Andrzej Kaminski, Adam Kozuchowski, Christopher Lazarski, David Lindenfeld, John McNeill, Suzanne Marchand, John Merriman, James Miller, Daria Nalecz, Karl Roider, and Mark Steinberg. Finally, we wish to thank Graham Nichols for telecommunications assistance and expertise.

ABOUT THE AUTHORS

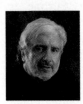

Brian Levack grew up in a family of teachers in the New York metropolitan area. From his father, a professor of French history, he acquired a love for studying the past, and he knew from an early age that he too would become a historian. He received his B.A. from Fordham University in 1965 and his Ph.D. from Yale in 1970. In graduate school he became fascinated by the history of the law and the interaction between law and politics, interests that he has maintained throughout his career. In 1969 he joined the history department of the University of Texas at Austin, where he is now the John Green Regents Professor in History. The winner of several teaching awards, Levack teaches a wide variety of courses on British and European history, legal history, and the history of witchcraft. For eight years he served as the chair of his department, a rewarding but challenging assignment that made it difficult for him to devote as much time as he wished to his teaching and scholarship. His books include *The Civil Lawyers in England, 1603–1641: A Political Study* (1973), *The Formation of the British State: England, Scotland and the Union, 1603–1707* (1987), *The Witch-Hunt in Early Modern Europe* (3rd edition, 2006), and *Witch-Hunting in Scotland: Law, Politics, and Religion* (2008).

His study of the development of beliefs about witchcraft in Europe over the course of many centuries gave him the idea of writing a textbook on Western civilization that would illustrate a broader set of encounters between different cultures, societies, and ideologies. While writing the book, Levack and his two sons built a house on property that he and his wife, Nancy, own in the Texas hill country. He found that the two projects presented similar challenges: It was easy to draw up the design, but far

more difficult to execute it. When not teaching, writing, or doing carpentry work, Levack runs along the jogging trails of Austin and has recently discovered the pleasures of scuba diving.

Edward Muir grew up in the foothills of the Wasatch Mountains in Utah, close to the Emigration Trail along which wagon trains of Mormon pioneers and California-bound settlers made their way westward. As a child he loved to explore the broken-down wagons and abandoned household goods left at the side of the trail and from that acquired a fascination with the past. Besides the material remains of the past, he grew up with stories of his Mormon pioneer ancestors and an appreciation for how the past continued to influence the present. During the turbulent 1960s, he became interested in Renaissance Italy as a period and place that had been formative for Western civilization. His biggest challenge is finding the time to explore yet another new corner of Italy and its restaurants.

Muir received his Ph.D. from Rutgers University, where he specialized in the Italian Renaissance and did archival research in Venice and Florence, Italy. He is now the Clarence L. Ver Steeg Professor in the Arts and Sciences at Northwestern University and former chair of the history department. At Northwestern he has won several teaching awards. His books include *Civic Ritual in Renaissance Venice* (1981), *Mad Blood Stirring: Vendetta in Renaissance Italy* (1993 and 1998), *Ritual in Early Modern Europe* (1997 and 2005), and *The Culture Wars of the Late Renaissance: Skeptics, Libertines, and Opera* (2007). His books have also been published in Italian.

Some years ago Muir began to experiment with the use of historical trials in teaching and discovered that students loved them. From that experience he decided to write this textbook, which employs trials as a central feature. He lives beside Lake Michigan in Evanston, Illinois. His twin passions are skiing in the Rocky Mountains and rooting for the Chicago Cubs, who manage every summer to demonstrate that winning isn't everything.

Meredith Veldman grew up in the western suburbs of Chicago, where she learned to love winter and the Cubs—which might explain her preference for all things improbable and impractical. Certainly that preference is what attracted her to the study of history, filled as it is with impractical people doing the most improbable things. Veldman majored in history at Calvin College in Grand Rapids, Michigan, and then earned a Ph.D. in modern European history, with a concentration in nineteenth-and twentieth-century Britain, from Northwestern University in 1988.

As an associate professor of history at Louisiana State University, Veldman teaches courses in nineteenth- and twentieth-century British history and twentieth-century Europe, as well as the second half of "Western Civ." In her many semesters in the Western Civ. classroom, Veldman tried a number of different textbooks but found herself increasingly dissatisfied. She wanted a text that would convey to beginning students at least some of the complexities and ambiguities of historical interpretation, introduce them to the exciting work being done in cultural history, and, most important, tell a good story. The search for this textbook led her to accept the offer made by Levack and Muir to join them in writing *The West: Encounters & Transformations.*

An award-winning teacher, Veldman is also the author of *Fantasy, the Bomb, and the Greening of Britain: Romantic Protest, 1945–1980* (1994). She and her family ride out the hurricanes in Baton Rouge, Louisiana. She remains a Cubs fan and she misses snow.

The West

What Is the West?

Many of the people who influence public opinion—politicians, teachers, clergy, journalists, and television commentators—refer to "Western values," "the West," and "Western civilization." They often use these terms as if they do not require explanation. But what *do* these terms mean? The West has always been an arena within which different cultures, religions, values, and philosophies have interacted; any definition of the West will inevitably arouse controversy.

The definition of the West has always been disputed. Note the difference in the following two poems, the first by Rudyard Kipling (1865–1936), an ardent promoter of European imperialism who wrote "The Ballad of East and West" at the height of the British Empire:

> OH, East is East, and West is West, and never the twain shall meet,
> Till Earth and Sky stand presently at God's great Judgment Seat....

The second, "East/West Poem," is by a Chinese-American living in Hawaii, Wing Tek Lum (1946–), who expresses the confusion caused by terms that designate both cultural traits and directions around the globe:

> O
> East is East
> and
> West is West.
> but
> I never did
> understand
> why
> in Geography class
> the East was west
> and
> the West was east
> and that no
> one ever
> cared
> about the difference.

This textbook cares about the difference. It also shows that East and West have, in contrast to Kipling's view, often "met." These encounters created the idea of the East and the West and helped identify the ever shifting borders between the two.

THE SHIFTING BORDERS OF THE WEST

The most basic definition of the West is of a place. Western civilization is now typically thought to comprise the regions of Europe, the Americas, Australia, and New Zealand. However, this is a contemporary definition of the West. The inclusion of these places in the West is the result of a long history of European expansion through colonization and conquest.

This textbook begins about 10,000 years ago in what is now Iraq; the final chapter returns to discuss the Iraq War, but in the meantime the Mesopotamian region is only occasionally a concern for Western history. The history of the West begins with the domestication of animals, the cultivation of the first crops, and the establishment of long-distance trading networks in the Tigris, Euphrates, and Nile River valleys. Cities, kingdoms, and empires in those valleys gave birth to the first civilizations in the West. By about 500 B.C.E., the civilizations that were the cultural ancestors of the modern West had spread from southwestern Asia and north Africa to include the entire Mediterranean basin—areas influenced by Egyptian, Hebrew, Greek, and Roman thought, art, law, and religion. The resulting Greco-Roman

THE TEMPLE OF HERA AT PAESTUM, ITALY:

Greek colonists in Italy built this temple in the sixth century B.C.E. Greek ideas and artistic styles spread throughout the ancient world, both from Greek colonists, such as those at Paestum, and from other peoples who imitated the Greeks.

culture created the most enduring foundation of the West. By the first century C.E. the Roman Empire drew the map of what historians consider the heartland of the West: most of western and southern Europe, the coastlands of the Mediterranean Sea, and the Middle East.

For many centuries, these ancient foundations defined the borders of the West. During the last century, however, the West came to be less about geography than about culture, identity, and technology. When Japan, an Asian country, accepted human rights and democracy after World War II, did it become part of the West? Most Japanese might not think they have adopted "Western" values, but the thriving capitalism and stable democracy of this traditional Asian country

that was never colonized by a European power complicates the idea of what is the West. Or consider the Republic of South Africa, which the white minority—people descended from European immigrants—ruled until 1994. The oppressive white regime violated human rights, rejected full legal equality for all citizens, and jailed or murdered those who questioned the government. Only when democratic elections open to blacks replaced that government did South Africa fully embrace what the rest of the West would consider Western values. To what degree was South Africa part of the West before and after these developments?

Or how about Russia? Russia long saw itself as a Christian country with cultural, economic,

WHERE IS THE WEST?

The shifting borders of the West have moved many times throughout history, but they have always included the areas shown in this satellite photo. These include Europe, north Africa, and the Middle East.

CHANGING IDENTITIES WITHIN THE WEST

In addition to being a place, the West is the birthplace of Western civilization, a civilization that encompasses a cultural history—a tradition stretching back thousands of years to the ancient world. Over this long period the civilization we now identify as Western gradually took shape. The many characteristics that identify it emerged over this time: forms of governments, economic systems, and methods of scientific inquiry, as well as religions, languages, literature, and art.

Throughout the development of Western civilization, the ways in which people identified themselves changed as well. People in the ancient world had no such idea of the common identity of the West, only of being members of a tribe, citizens of a town, or subjects of an empire. But with the spread of Christianity and Islam between the first and seventh centuries, the notion of a distinct civilization in these "Western" lands subtly changed. People came to identify themselves less as subjects of a particular empire and more as members of a community of faith—whether that community comprised followers of Judaism, Christianity, or Islam. These communities of faith drew lines of inclusion and exclusion that still exist today. Starting about 1,600 years ago, Christian monarchs and clergy began to obliterate polytheism (the worship of many gods) and marginalize Jews. From 1,000 to 500 years ago, Christian authorities fought to expel Muslims from Europe. Europeans developed definitions of the West that did not include Islamic communities, even though Muslims continued to live in Europe, and Europeans traded and interacted with the Muslim world. The Islamic countries themselves erected their own barriers, seeing themselves in opposition to the Christian West, even as they continued to look back to the common cultural origins in the ancient world that they shared with Jews and Christians.

During the Renaissance in the fifteenth century, these ancient cultural origins became an alternative to religious affiliation for thinking

and political ties with the rest of Europe. The Russians have intermittently identified with their Western neighbors, especially during the reign of Peter the Great (1682–1725), but their neighbors were not always sure about the Russians. After the Mongol invasions of the thirteenth and fourteenth centuries much of Russia was isolated from the rest of the West, and during the Cold War from 1949 to 1989 Western democracies considered communist Russia an enemy. When was Russia "Western" and when not?

Thus, when we talk about where the West is, we are almost always talking about the Mediterranean basin and much of Europe (and later, the Americas). But we will also show that countries that border "the West," and even countries far from it, might be considered Western in many aspects as well.

about the identity of the West. From this Renaissance historical perspective Jews, Christians, and Muslims descended from the cultures of the ancient Egyptians, Hebrews, Greeks, and Romans. Despite their differences, the followers of these religions shared a history. In fact, in the late Renaissance a number of Jewish and Christian thinkers imagined the possibility of rediscovering the single universal religion that they thought must have once been practiced in the ancient world. If they could just recapture that religion, they could restore the unity they imagined had once prevailed in the West.

The definition of the West has also changed as a result of European colonialism, which began about 500 years ago. When European powers assembled large overseas empires, they introduced Western languages, religions, technologies, and cultures to many distant places in the world, making Western identity a transportable concept. In some of these colonized areas—such as North America, Argentina, Australia, and New Zealand—the European newcomers so outnumbered the indigenous people that these regions became as much a part of the West as Britain, France, and Spain. In other European colonies, especially on the Asian continent, Western cultures failed to exercise similar levels of influence.

As a result of colonialism Western culture sometimes merged with other cultures, and in the process, both were changed. Brazil, a South American country inhabited by large numbers of indigenous peoples, the descendants of African slaves, and European settlers, epitomizes the complexity of what defines the West. In Brazil, almost everyone speaks a Western language (Portuguese), practices a Western religion (Christianity), and participates in Western political and economic institutions (democracy and capitalism). Yet in Brazil all of these features of Western civilization have become part of a distinctive culture in which indigenous, African, and European elements have been blended. During Carnival, for example, Brazilians dressed in indigenous costumes dance in African rhythms to the accompaniment of music played on European instruments.

MARINER'S COMPASS

The mariner's compass was a navigational device intended for use primarily at sea. The compass originated in China; once adopted by Europeans, it enabled them to embark on long ocean voyages around the world.

WESTERN VALUES

For many people today, the most important definition of the West involves adherence to "Western" values. The values typically identified as Western include democracy, individualism, universal human rights, toleration of religious diversity, ownership of private property, equality before the law, and freedom of inquiry and expression. These values, however, have not always been part of Western civilization. In fact, they describe ideals rather than actual realities; these values are by no means universally accepted throughout the West. Thus, there is nothing inevitable about these values; Western history at various stages exhibited quite different ones. Western societies seldom prized legal or political equality until quite recently. In ancient Rome and throughout most of medieval Europe, the wealthy and the powerful enjoyed more protection under the law than did slaves or the poor. Most medieval Christians were completely convinced of the virtue of making war against Muslims and heretics and curtailing the actions of Jews. Before the end of the eighteenth century, few Westerners questioned the practice of slavery, a social hierarchy of birth that remained powerful in the West through the nineteenth century; in addition, most women were excluded from equal economic and educational opportunities until well into the twentieth century. In many places women still do not have equal opportunities. In the twentieth century, millions of Westerners followed leaders who stifled free inquiry, denied basic human rights to many of their citizens, made terror an instrument of the state, and censored authors, artists, and journalists.

The values that define the West have not only changed over time, they also remain fiercely contested. One of the most divisive political issues today, for example, is that of "gay marriage." Both sides in this debate frame their arguments in terms of "Western values." Supporters of the legalization of same-sex marriages highlight equality and human rights: They demand that all citizens have equal access to the basic legal protections afforded by marriage. Opponents emphasize the centrality of the tradition of monogamous heterosexual marriage to Western legal, moral, and religious codes. What this current debate shows us is that no single understanding of "Western values," or of the West itself, exists. These values have always been contended, disputed, and fought over. In other words, they have a history. This text highlights and examines that history.

ASKING THE RIGHT QUESTIONS

So how can we make sense of the West as a place and an identity, the shifting borders and definitions of the West, and Western civilization in general? In short, what has Western civilization been over the course of its long history—and what is it today?

Answering these questions is the challenge this book addresses. There are no simple answers to any of these questions, but there is a method for finding answers. The method is straightforward. Always ask the *what, when, where, who, how,* and *why* questions of the text.

The "What" Question

What is Western civilization? The answer to this question will vary according to time and place. In fact, for much of the early history covered in this book, "Western civilization" did not exist. Rather, a number of distinctive civilizations emerged in the Middle East, northern Africa, and Europe, each of which contributed to what later became Western civilization. As these cultures developed and intermingled, the idea of Western civilization slowly began to form. Thus, the understanding of Western civilization will change from chapter to chapter. The most extensive change in the place of the West was through the colonial expansion of the European nations between the fifteenth and twentieth centuries. Perhaps the most significant cultural change came with acceptance of the values of scientific inquiry for solving human and philosophical problems, an approach that did not exist before the seventeenth century but became one of the distinguishing characteristics of Western civilization. During the late eighteenth and nineteenth centuries, industrialization became the engine that drove economic development in the West. During the twentieth century, industrialization in both its capitalist and communist forms dramatically gave the West a level of economic prosperity unmatched in the nonindustrialized parts of the world.

The "When" Question

When did the defining characteristics of Western civilization first emerge, and for how long did they prevail? Dates frame and organize the content of each chapter, and numerous short chronologies are offered. These resources make it possible to keep track of what happened when. Dates have no meaning by themselves, but the connections *between* them can be very revealing. For example, dates show that the agricultural revolution that permitted the birth of the first civilizations unfolded over a long span of about 10,000 years—which is more time than was taken by all the other events and developments covered in this textbook. Wars of religion plagued Europe for nearly 200 years before Enlightenment thinkers articulated the ideals of religious toleration. The American Civil War—the war to preserve the union, as President Abraham Lincoln termed it—took place at exactly the same time as wars were being fought for national unity in Germany and Italy. In other words, by paying attention to other contemporaneous wars for national unity, the American experience seems less peculiarly an American event.

By learning *when* things happened, one can identify the major causes and consequences of events and thus see the transformations of Western civilization. For instance, the production of a surplus of food through agriculture and the domestication of animals were prerequisites for the emergence of civilizations. The violent collapse of religious unity after the Protestant Reformation in the sixteenth century led some Europeans to propose the separation of church and state two centuries later. And during the nineteenth century many Western countries—in response to the enormous diversity among their own

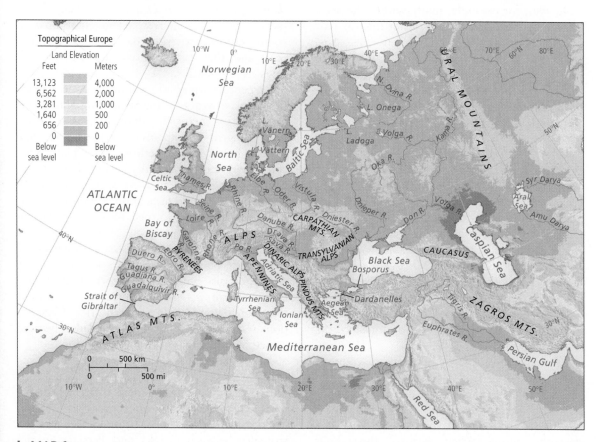

MAP 1

Core Lands of the West

These are the principal geographical features that will appear recurrently throughout this book.

peoples—became preoccupied with maintaining or establishing national unity.

The "Where" Question

Where has Western civilization been located? Geography, of course, does not change very rapidly, but the idea of where the West is does change. By tracing the shifting relationships between the West and other, more distant civilizations with which it interacted, the chapters highlight the changing "where" of the West. The key to understanding the shifting borders of the West is to study how the peoples within the West thought of themselves and how they identified others as "not Western." During the Cold War, for example, many within the West viewed Russia as an enemy rather than as part of the West. In the previous centuries, Australia and North America came to be part of the West because the European conquerors of these regions identified themselves with European cultures and traditions and against non-European values.

The "Who" Question

Who were the people responsible for making Western civilization? Some were anonymous, such as the unknown geniuses who invented the mathematical systems of ancient Mesopotamia. Others are well-known—saints such as Joan of Arc, creative thinkers such as Galileo Galilei, or generals such as Napoleon. Most were ordinary. Humble people, such as the many millions who migrated from Europe to North America or the unfortunate millions who suffered and died in the trenches of World War I, also influenced the course of events.

Perhaps most often this book encounters people who were less the shapers of their own destinies than the subjects of forces that conditioned the kinds of choices they could make, often with unanticipated results. During the eleventh century when farmers throughout Europe began to employ a new kind of plow to till their fields, they were merely trying to do their work more efficiently. They certainly did not recognize that the increase in food they produced would stimulate the enormous population growth that made possible the medieval civilization of thriving cities and magnificent cathedrals. Answering the *who* question requires an evaluation of how much individuals and groups of people were in control of events and how much events controlled them.

The "How" Question

How did Western civilization develop? This is a question about processes—about how things change or stay the same over time. This book identifies and explores these processes in several ways.

First, woven throughout the story is *the theme of encounters and transformations*. What is meant by encounters? When the Spanish *conquistadores* arrived in the Americas some 500 years ago, they came into contact with the cultures of the Caribs, the Aztecs, the Incas, and other peoples who had lived in the Americas for thousands of years. As the Spanish fought, traded with, and intermarried with the natives, each culture changed. The Spanish, for their part, borrowed from the Americas new plants for cultivation and responded to what they considered serious threats to their worldview. Many native Americans, in turn, adopted European religious practices and learned to speak European languages. At the same time, Amerindians were decimated by European diseases, illnesses to which they had never been exposed. The native Americans also witnessed the destruction of their own civilizations and governments at the hands of the colonial powers. Through centuries of interaction and mutual influence, both sides became something other than what they had been.

The European encounter with the Americas is an obvious example of what was, in fact, a continuous process of encounters with other cultures. These encounters often occurred between peoples from different civilizations, such as the struggles between Greeks and Persians in the ancient world or between Europeans and Chinese in the nineteenth century. Other encounters took place among people living in the same civilization. These include interactions between lords and peasants, men and women, Christians and Jews, Catholics and Protestants, factory owners and workers, and capitalists and communists. Western civilization developed and changed, and still does, through a series of external and internal encounters.

Second, *features in the chapters* formulate answers to the question of how Western civilization developed. For example, each chapter contains an essay titled "Justice in History." These essays discuss a trial or some other episode involving questions of justice. Some "Justice in History" essays illustrate how Western civilization was forged in struggles over conflicting values, such as the discussion of the trial of Galileo, which examines the conflict between religious and scientific concepts of truth. Other essays show how efforts to resolve internal cultural, political, and religious tensions helped shape Western ideas about justice, such as the essay on the *auto da fé*, which illustrates how authorities attempted to enforce religious conformity.

Some chapters include another feature as well. The "Encounters and Transformations" features show how encounters between different groups of people, technologies, and ideas were not abstract historical processes, but events that brought people together in a way that transformed history. For example, when the Arabs encountered the camel as an instrument of war, they adopted it for their own purposes. As a result, they were able to conquer their neighbors very quickly and spread Islam far beyond its original home in Arabia.

The "Different Voices" feature in each chapter includes documents from the period that represent contrasting views about a particular issue important at the time. These conflicting voices demonstrate how people debated what mattered to them and in the process formulated what have become Western values. During the Franco-Algerian War of the 1950s and early 1960s, for example, French military officers debated the appropriateness of torture when interrogating Algerian prisoners alleged to be insurgents. The debate about the use of torture against terrorist suspects continues today, revealing one of the unresolved conflicts over the appropriate values of the West.

The "Why" Question

Why did things happen in the way they did in history? This is the hardest question of all, one that engenders the most debate among historians. To take one persistent example, why did Hitler initiate a plan to exterminate the Jews of Europe? Can it be explained by something that happened to him in his childhood? Was he full of self-loathing that he projected onto the Jews? Was it a way of creating an enemy so that he could better unify Germany? Did he really believe that the Jews were the cause of all of Germany's problems? Did he merely act on the deeply seated anti-Semitic tendencies of the German people? Historians still debate the answers to these questions.

Such questions raise issues about human motivation and the role of human agency in historical events. Can historians ever really know what motivated a particular individual in the past, especially when it is so notoriously difficult to understand what motivates other people in the present? Can any individual determine the course of history? The *what, when, where, who,* and *how* questions are much easier to answer; but the *why* question, of course, is the most interesting one, the one that cries out for an answer.

This book does not—and cannot—always offer definitive answers to the *why* question, but it attempts to lay out the most likely possibilities. For example, historians do not really know what disease caused the Black Death in the fourteenth century that killed about one-third of the population in a matter of months. But they can answer many questions about the consequences of that great catastrophe. Why were there so many new universities in the fourteenth and fifteenth centuries? It was because so many priests had died in the Black Death, creating a huge demand for replacements. The answers to the *why* questions are not always obvious, but they are always intriguing; finding the answers is the joy of studying history.

1

The Beginnings of Civilization, 10,000–1150 B.C.E.

- Defining Civilization, Defining Western Civilization
- Mesopotamia: Kingdoms, Empires, and Conquests
- Egypt: The Empire of the Nile

IN 1991 HIKERS TOILING ACROSS A GLACIER IN THE ALPS BETWEEN AUSTRIA AND Italy made a startling discovery: a man's body stuck in the ice. They alerted the police, who soon turned the corpse over to archaeologists. The scientists determined that the middle-aged man had frozen to death about 5,300 years ago. Ötzi the Ice Man (his name comes from the Ötztal Valley where he perished) quickly became an international celebrity. The scientists who examined Ötzi believe that he was a shepherd leading flocks of sheep and goats to mountain pastures when he died. Grains of wheat on his clothing suggested that he lived in a farming community. Copper dust in his hair hinted that Ötzi may also have been a metal-worker, perhaps looking for ores during his journey. An arrowhead lodged in his back indicated a violent death, but the circumstances remain mysterious.

Ötzi's gear was state-of-the-art for his time. His possessions showed deep knowledge of the natural world. He wore leather boots insulated with dense grasses chosen for protection against the cold. The pouch around his waist contained stone tools and fire-lighting equipment. The wood selected for his bow offered strength and flexibility. In his light wooden backpack, Ötzi carried containers to hold burning embers and dried meat and seeds to eat on the trail. The arrows in his quiver featured a natural adhesive that tightly bound bone and wooden points to the shafts. The most noteworthy find among Ötzi's possessions was his axe. Its handle was made of wood, but its head was copper, a remarkable innovation at a time when most tools were made of stone. Ötzi was ready for almost anything—except the person who shot him in the back.

Ötzi lived at a transitional moment, at the end of what archaeologists call the **Neolithic Age,** or "New Stone Age," a long period of revolutionary change lasting from about 10,000 to about 3000 B.C.E. in which many thousands of years of human interaction with nature led to food production through agriculture and the domestication of animals. This chapter begins with this most fundamental encounter of all—that between humans and the natural world.

The achievement of food production let humans develop new, settled forms of communities—and then civilization itself. The growth of civilization also depended on constant interaction among communities that lived far apart. Once people were settled in a region, they began trading for commodities that were not available in

religious life and by the forms of monotheism each practiced. In Byzantium the Greek language and Orthodox Christianity with its elaborate ceremonies defined the culture. By the end of the Umayyad caliphate in 750, the Arabic language and many Islamic beliefs and practices were becoming standard over a wide area. In western Europe, many languages were spoken, but Latin became the universal language of the Church and government.

The end of the Umayyad caliphate saw the limit of Muslim expansion in western Europe and central Asia. After that the Byzantine Empire struggled for survival. In Chapter 9 we will see how the kingdom of the Franks arrested Muslim incursions into western Europe. However, the very survival of many western European kingdoms was put to the test during the ninth and tenth centuries by yet more invasions and migrations from the Eurasian steppes and Scandinavia. By the end of the eleventh century, Latin Christianity had gathered sufficient cohesion and military strength to launch a vast counterstroke against Islam in the form of the Crusades.

KEY TERMS

icons
iconoclasm
Macedonian
   Renaissance

mosque
Pillars of Islam
caliphate
Spanish Reconquest

CHAPTER QUESTIONS

1. How did the Roman Empire's eastern provinces evolve into the Byzantine Empire? (page 234)
2. How did Islam develop in Arabia, and how did its followers create a vast empire so quickly? (page 243)

TAKING IT FURTHER

1. How did the Byzantine Empire manage to hold off so many enemies for so long?
2. Why did Islam split between Sunni and Shi'ites?
3. Should Muslim countries be considered part of the West?

✓ Practice on **MyHistoryLab**

9

Medieval Empires and Borderlands: The Latin West

■ The Birth of Latin Christendom ■ The Carolingians
■ Invasions and Recovery in the Latin West
■ The West in the East: The Crusades

ONE GRAY DAY IN CENTRAL GERMANY IN 740, AN ENGLISH MONK named Boniface swung his axe at an enormous oak tree. This was the sacred Oak of Thor, where German men and women had prayed for centuries to one of their mightiest gods. Some local Christians cheered and applauded the monk. But an angry crowd of men and women gathered as well, cursing Boniface for attacking their sacred tree. Then something extraordinary occurred. Though Boniface had only taken one small chop, the entire tree came crashing down, split neatly into four parts. Boniface's biographer, a monk named Willibald, explained the strange event as God's judgment against "pagan" worshipers. In Willibald's account of the incident, the hostile crowd was so impressed by the miracle that they immediately embraced Christianity. As the news spread, more and more Germans converted, and Boniface's fame grew. According to Willibald, "The sound of Boniface's name was heard through the greater part of Europe. From the land of Britain, a great host of monks came to him—readers, and writers, and men trained in other skills."[1]

Boniface played a leading role in spreading Christianity among the peoples of northern Europe. The Christian missionaries who traveled to lands far beyond the Mediterranean world brought Latin books and established monasteries. Through Christianity and the literacy disseminated from these monastic centers, the monks established cultural ties among the new Germanic converts to Roman learning. Historians refer to the Christianized Germanic kingdoms on the continent and Britain as Latin Christendom because they celebrated the Christian **liturgy** in Latin and accepted the authority of the pope in Rome. Even though they no longer celebrate the liturgy in Latin as they did in the Middle Ages, Roman Catholics today continue to revere the pope and the traditions of medieval Latin Christianity.

As discussed in Chapter 8, Latin Christianity and Orthodox Christianity gradually grew apart during the Middle Ages, primarily over theological differences and disputes about who held the ultimate authority in the Church. For most Christians, however, the crucial differences were over liturgy and language. The liturgy consists of the forms of worship—prayers, chants, and rituals. In the Middle Ages there was a great deal of variety in the Christian liturgy, and a number of languages were used, but followers of the Roman church gradually came to identify themselves with the Latin liturgy and the Latin language. As a result, the diverse peoples of medieval western Europe began to be called the "Latin people."

THE IMAGE OF A MAN
(*IMAGO HOMINIS*)

In this eighth-century manuscript, the image of a man symbolizes the Evangelist Matthew. The other three evangelists, Mark, Luke, and John, were symbolized by a lion, bull, and eagle, all fixed signs of the zodiac, created by ancient polytheist astronomers. The adaptation of Christianity to pagan symbolism conveyed the message that Christianity represented the fulfillment of ancient wisdom.

The Latin Christendom that came to dominate western Europe joined the Greek Orthodox and Arabic Muslim civilizations that constituted the three pillars of the West during the Middle Ages. Recurrently pressing across the frontiers of the Greek Orthodox and Latin Christian civilizations were wave after wave of barbarian peoples coming from the Eurasian steppes and Scandinavia. The Avars, Slavs, Rus, and Bulgars who threatened Byzantium became Orthodox Christians. The raiders and invaders who entered the western half of the Roman Empire—the Germanic tribes, the Magyars, and the Vikings—eventually became Latin Christians. Their conversions took place through missionary efforts and military expeditions that forced the conquered to convert. By the end of the eleventh century few polytheists could still be found in Europe. With the exception of the Muslim pockets in Spain and Sicily and isolated communities of Jews, Christianity had become the dominant faith.

In this crucial phase in forming Western civilization from about 350–1100, new political formations in western Europe made possible greater political cohesion that brought together ethnically and linguistically diverse peoples under obedience to an emperor or king. As in Byzantium and the Islamic caliphates, the empires and kingdoms of the Latin West enforced or encouraged uniformity of religion, spread a common language among the ruling elite, and instituted systematic principles for governing. The Carolingian Empire, which lasted from 800 to 843 and controlled much of western Europe, reestablished the Roman Empire in the West for the first time in more than 300 years and sponsored a revival of interest in Roman antiquity called the Carolingian Renaissance. The Carolingian Empire's collapse was followed by a period of anarchy as Europe faced further incursions of hostile invaders. During the eleventh century, however, the Latin West recovered in dramatic fashion. By the end of the century the Latin kingdoms were strong enough to engage in a massive counterassault against Islam, in part in defense of fellow Christians in Byzantium. These campaigns against Islam, known as the Crusades, produced a series of wars in the Middle East and North Africa that continued throughout the Middle Ages. But the ideals of the crusaders lasted well into modern times, long after the active fighting ceased. The transformations in this period raised this question: How did Latin Christianity help strengthen the new kingdoms of the Latin West so that they were eventually able to deal effectively with both barbarian invaders and Muslim rivals?

THE BIRTH OF LATIN CHRISTENDOM

■ How did Latin Christendom—the new kingdoms of western Europe—build on Rome's legal and governmental legacies and how did Christianity spread in these new kingdoms?

By the time the Roman Empire collapsed in the West during the fifth century, numerous Germanic tribes had settled in the lands of the former empire. These tribes became the nucleus for the new Latin Christian kingdoms that emerged by 750 (see **Map 9.1**).

Germanic Kingdoms on Roman Foundations

The new Germanic kingdoms of Latin Christendom created a new kind of society. They borrowed from Roman law while establishing government institutions, but they also relied on their own traditional methods of rule. Three elements helped unify these kingdoms. First, in the Germanic kingdoms personal loyalty rather than

legal rights unified society. Kinship obligations to a particular clan of blood relatives rather than citizenship, as in the Roman Empire, defined a person's place in society and his or her relationship to rulers. Second, Christianity became the dominant religion in the kingdoms. The common faith linked rulers with their subjects. And third, Latin served as the language of worship, learning, and diplomacy in these kingdoms. German kingdoms based on Roman foundations appeared in Anglo-Saxon England, Frankish Gaul, Visigothic Spain, and Lombard Italy.

ANGLO-SAXON ENGLAND Roman civilization collapsed more completely in Britain during the fifth century than it did on the European continent, largely because of Britain's long distance from Rome and the small number of Romans who had settled there. About 400, the Roman economic and administrative infrastructure of Britain fell apart, and the last Roman legions left the island to fight on the continent. Raiders from the coast of the North Sea called Angles and Saxons (historians referred to them as Anglo-Saxons) took advantage of Britain's weakened defenses and launched invasions. They began to probe the island's southeast coast, pillaging the small villages they found there and establishing permanent settlements of their own.

Because the small bands of Anglo-Saxon settlers fought as often among themselves as they did against the Roman Britons, the island remained fragmented politically during the first few centuries of the invaders' rule. But by 750, three warring kingdoms managed to seize enough land to coalesce and dominate Britain: Mercia, Wessex, and Northumbria.

FRANKISH GAUL Across the English Channel from Britain lay the Roman province of Gaul. From the third to the seventh century the kingdom of the Franks, centered in Gaul, produced the largest and most powerful kingdom in western Europe. One family among the Franks, called the Merovingians, gradually gained preeminence. A crafty Merovingian war chief named Childeric ruled a powerful band of

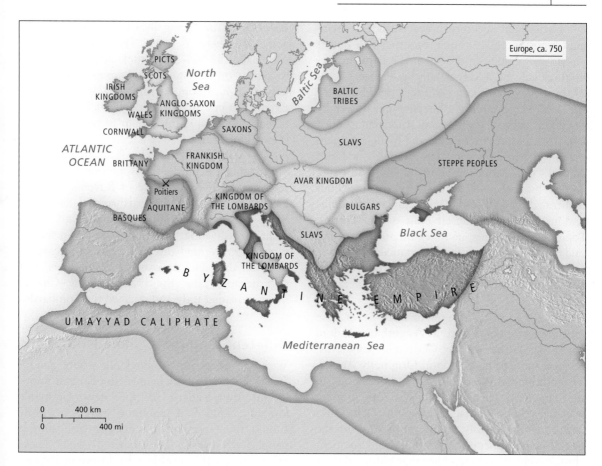

MAP 9.1

Europe, ca. 750

By about 750 the kingdom of the Franks had become the dominant power in western Europe. The Umayyad caliphate controlled Spain, and the Lombard kingdom governed most of Italy. The Byzantine Empire held power in Greece, as well as its core lands in Asia Minor.

Franks from about 460 until his death in 481. With the support of his loyal soldiers, Childeric laid the foundation for the Merovingian kingdom. His energetic and ruthless son Clovis (r. 481–511) made the Franks one of the leading powers in the western provinces of the old Roman Empire. Clovis aggressively expanded his father's power base through the conquest of northern Gaul and neighboring territories. He murdered many of his relatives and other Frankish chieftains whom he considered rivals. In 486 Clovis overcame the last Roman stronghold in northern Gaul.

Around 500 the polytheist Clovis converted to Latin Christianity. About 3,000 warriors, the core of his army, joined their king in this change to the new faith. Clovis had a practical reason to convert. He intended to attack the Visigothic kingdom in southern Gaul. The Visigoths followed Arian Christianity, but their subjects, the Roman inhabitants of the region, were Latin Christians. By converting to Latin Christianity, Clovis won the support of many of the Visigoths' subjects. With their help, he crushed the Visigothic king Alaric II in 507. Clovis now controlled almost all of Gaul as far as Spain.

In the eighth century, however, the Merovingian kings became so ineffectual that real power passed to the man in charge of the royal household called the "Mayor of the Palace." One of these mayors, Charles Martel "the Hammer" (r. 719–741), established his personal power by regaining control over regions that had slipped away from Merovingian rule and by defeating an invading Muslim army at Poitiers in 732. Martel's son, Pepin the Short (r. 741–768), succeeded his father as Mayor of the Palace, but dethroned the last of the Merovingian monarchs and in 751 made himself king of the Franks. Pepin relied on the pope to legitimize his coup, and in exchange the Franks guaranteed the pope's safety. Thus, began the vital alliance between the Frankish monarchy and the popes in Rome.

VISIGOTHIC SPAIN   The Franks were never able to conquer Spain, where a Visigothic kingdom emerged. As in all the Germanic kingdoms, religion unified the kingdom. Originally Arians, Visigoth kings converted to Latin Christianity in the late sixth century, and Visigothic Spain became a Latin Christian kingdom. The kings began to imitate the Byzantine emperors with the use of elaborate court ceremonies and frequent church councils as assemblies that enforced their will. Thus, the key to their success was the ability to employ the spiritual authority of the Church to enhance the secular authority of the king. However, the autocratic instincts of the Visigoth kings alienated many of the substantial landowners who were easily lured by the promises of Muslim invaders to treat them more favorably.

In 711 invading armies of Muslims from North Africa vanquished the last Visigothic king. As a result, most of Spain became part of the Umayyad caliphate. Many Christians from the upper classes converted to Islam to preserve their property and offices. Some survivors of the Visigoth kingdoms held on in the northwest of Spain, where they managed to keep Christianity alive.

LOMBARD ITALY   Between 568 and 774, a Germanic people known as the Lombards controlled most of northern and central Italy. They were called *Langobardi*, or "Long Beards," from which the name *Lombard* derives. The Lombard king, Alboin (r. ca. 565–572), took advantage of the weakness of the Byzantine Empire and invaded Italy in 569. Alboin's army contained soldiers of different ethnic backgrounds. That lack of unity made it impossible for Alboin to build a strong, lasting kingdom.

The Lombard kings also faced two formidable external enemies—the Byzantine forces who remained in the Exarchate of Ravenna and the Franks. In 751 the Lombards' ruler defeated the Exarchate, leading to the Byzantine abandonment of Ravenna. Internal political disputes, however, prevented the Lombards from capitalizing on their victory over the Byzantines. Just two decades later the Frankish king Charlemagne invaded Italy and crushed the Lombards.

Different Kingdoms, Shared Traditions

With the exception of England, where Anglo-Saxon invaders overwhelmed the Roman population, the leaders of the new Germanic kingdoms faced a common problem: How should the Germanic minority govern subject peoples who vastly outnumbered them? These rulers solved this problem by blending Roman and Germanic traditions. For example, kings served as administrators of the civil order in the style of the Roman emperor, issuing laws and managing a bureaucracy. They also served as war leaders in the Germanic tradition, leading their men into battle in search of glory and loot. As the Germanic kings defined new roles for themselves, they discovered that Christianity could bind all their subjects together into one community of believers. The merging of Roman and Germanic traditions could also be traced in the law, which eventually erased the distinctions between Romans and Germans, and in the ability of women to own property, a right far more common among the Romans than the Germans.

CIVIL AUTHORITY: THE ROMAN LEGACY   In imitation of Roman practice, the monarchs of Latin Christendom designated themselves the source of all law and believed that they ruled with God's approval. Kings controlled all appointments to civil, military, and religious office. Accompanied by troops and administrative assistants, they also traveled throughout their lands to dispense justice, collect taxes, and enforce royal authority.

Frankish Gaul provides an apt example of how these monarchs adopted preexisting Roman institutions. When Clovis conquered the Visigoths in Gaul, he inherited the nearly intact Roman infrastructure and administrative system that had survived the collapse of Roman imperial authority. Merovingian kings (as well as Visigoth rulers in Spain and Lombards in Italy) found it useful to maintain parts of the preexisting system and kept the officials who ran them. For instance, Frankish kings relied on the bishops and counts in each region to deal with local problems. Because Roman aristocrats were literate and had experience in Roman administration on the local level, they often served as counts. Based in cities, these officials presided in local law courts, collected revenues, and raised troops for the king's army. Most bishops also stemmed from the Roman aristocracy. In addition to performing their religious responsibilities, bishops aided their king by providing for the poor, ransoming hostages who had been captured by enemy warriors from other kingdoms, and bringing social and legal injustices to the monarch's attention. Finally, the kings used dukes, most of whom were Franks, to serve as local military commanders, which made them important patrons of the community. Thus, the civil and religious administration tended to remain the responsibility of the Roman counts and bishops, but military command fell to the Frankish dukes.

War Leaders and Wergild: The Germanic Legacy The kingdoms of Latin Christendom developed from war bands led by Germanic chieftains. By rewarding brave warriors with land and loot taken in war, as well as with revenues skimmed from subject peoples, chieftains created political communities of loyal men and their families, called **clans** or **kin groups.** Though these followers sometimes came from diverse backgrounds, they all owed military service to the clan chiefs. Because leadership in Germanic society was hereditary, networks of loyalty and kinship expanded through the generations. The various political communities gradually evolved into distinct ethnic groups led by a king. These ethnic groups, such as the Lombards and the Franks, developed a sense of shared history, kinship, and culture.

Kinship-based clans stood as the most basic unit of Germanic society. The clan consisted of all the households and blood relations loyal to the clan chief, a warrior who protected them and spoke on their behalf before the king on matters of justice. Clan chieftains in turn swore oaths of loyalty to their kings and agreed to fight for him in wars against other kingdoms. The clan leaders formed an aristocracy among the Germanic peoples. Like the Roman elites before them, the royal house and the clan-based aristocracy consisted of rich men and women who controlled huge estates. The new Germanic aristocrats intermarried with the preexisting Roman elites of wealthy landholders, thus maintaining control of most of the land. These people stood at the very top of the social order, winning the loyalty of their followers by giving gifts and parcels of land. Under the weight of this new upper class, the majority of the population, the ordinary farmers and artisans, slipped into a deepening dependence. Most peasants could not enter into legal transactions in their own name, and they had few protections and privileges under the law. Even so, they were better off than the slaves who toiled at society's very lowest depths. Valued simply as property, these men, women, and children had virtually no rights in the eyes of the law.

Though this social hierarchy showed some similarities to societies in earlier Roman times, the new kingdoms' various social groups were defined by law in a fundamentally different way. Unlike Roman law, which defined people by citizenship rights and obligations, the laws of the new kingdoms defined people by their **wergild.** A Germanic concept, *wergild* referred to what an individual was worth in case he or she suffered some grievance at the hands of another. If someone injured or murdered some-one else, wergild was the amount of compensation in gold that the wrongdoer's family had to pay to the victim's family.

In the wergild system, every person had a price that depended on social status and perceived usefulness to the community. For example, among the Lombards service to the king increased a free man's worth—his wergild was higher than that of a peasant. In the Frankish kingdom, if a freeborn woman of childbearing age was murdered, the killer's family had to pay 600 pieces of gold. Noble women and men had higher wergild than peasants, while slaves and women past childbearing age were worth very little.

UNITY THROUGH LAW AND CHRISTIANITY Within the kingdoms of Latin Christendom, rulers tried to achieve unity by merging Germanic and Roman legal principles and by accepting the influence of the Church. Religious diversity among the peoples in their kingdoms made this unity difficult to establish. As discussed in Chapter 7, many of the tribes that invaded the Roman Empire during the fifth century practiced Arian Christianity. They kept themselves apart from the Latin Christians by force of law. For example, they declared marriage between Arian and Latin Christians illegal.

These barriers began to collapse when Germanic kings converted to the Latin Christianity of their Roman subjects. Some converted for reasons of personal belief or because their wives were Latin Christians. Others decided to become Latin Christians to gain wider political support. For instance, when Clovis converted about 500, laws against intermarriage between Arians and Latin Christians in Gaul disappeared. More and more Franks and Romans began to marry one another, blending the two formerly separate communities into one and reinforcing the strength of the Latin Church. By 750 most of the western European kingdoms had officially become Latin Christian, though substantial pockets of polytheist practice survived and communities of Jews were allowed to practice their faith.

Germanic kings adopted Latin Christianity, but they had no intention of abandoning their own Germanic law, which differed from Roman law on many issues, especially relating to the family and property. Instead, they offered their Roman subjects the opportunity to live under the Germanic law that governed the king. Clovis's *Law Code* or *Salic Law,* published sometime between 508 and 511, illustrated this development. The *Law Code* applied to Franks and to any other non-Roman peoples in his realm who chose to live according to Frankish law. Because the Romans dwelling in the Frankish kingdom technically still followed the laws of Byzantium, Clovis did not presume to legislate for them. Romans could follow their own law if they wished, or they could follow his laws and become Franks. By 750, however, most Romans had chosen to abandon their legal identity as Romans and live according to Frankish law, and the distinction between Roman and Frank lost all meaning. A similar process occurred in the other Germanic kingdoms. This unification of peoples under one law happened without protest, a sign that various groups had blended politically, religiously, and culturally.

WOMEN AND PROPERTY Roman law influenced more than just local administration in Latin Christendom. It also prompted Germanic rulers to reconsider the question of a woman's right to inherit land. In the Roman Empire, women had inherited land without difficulty. Indeed, perhaps as much as 25 percent of the land in the entire empire had been owned by women. In many Germanic societies, however, men could inherit land and property far more easily than women. Attitudes about female inheritance began to shift when the Germanic settlers established their homes in previously Roman provinces—and began to marry Roman women who owned property.

By comparing the law codes of the new kingdoms over time, historians have detected the impact of Roman customs on Germanic inheritance laws. By the late eighth century, women in Frankish Gaul, Visigothic Spain, and Lombard

Italy could inherit land, though often under the restriction that they had to eventually pass it on to their sons. Despite these limitations, the new laws transformed women's lives. A woman who received an inheritance of land could live more independently, support herself if her husband died, and have a say in the community's decisions.

The Spread of Latin Christianity in the New Kingdoms of Western Europe

As Latin Christianity spread as the official religion through the new kingdoms, churchmen decided that they had a moral responsibility to convert all the people of these kingdoms and beyond. They sent out missionaries to explain the religion to nonbelievers and challenge the worship of polytheist gods.

Meanwhile, bishops based in cities directed people's spiritual lives, instilling the moral and social conventions of Christianity through sermons delivered in church. Monks such as Boniface, who introduced this chapter, traveled from their home monasteries in Ireland, England, and Gaul to spread the faith to Germanic tribes east of the Rhine. Monasteries became centers of intellectual life, and monks replaced urban aristocrats as the keepers of books and learning.

THE GROWTH OF THE PAPACY In theory, the Byzantine emperors still had political authority over the city of Rome and its surrounding lands during this violent time. However, strapped for cash and troops, these distant rulers proved unequal to the task of defending the city from internal or external threats. In the resulting power vacuum, the popes stepped in to manage local affairs and became, in effect, princes who ruled over a significant part of Italy.

Gregory the Great (r. 590–604) stands out as the most powerful of these popes. The pragmatic Gregory wrote repeatedly to Constantinople, pleading for military assistance that never came. Without any relief from the Byzantines, Gregory had to look elsewhere for help. Through clever diplomacy, Gregory successfully cultivated the good will of the Christian communities of western Europe by offering religious sanction to the authority of friendly kings. He negotiated skillfully with his Lombard and Frankish neighbors to gain their support and establish the authority of the Roman church. He encouraged Christian missionaries to spread the faith in England and Germany. In addition, he took steps

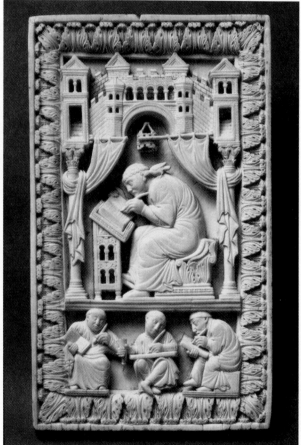

POPE GREGORY THE GREAT AND THREE SCRIBES

In this tenth-century ivory depicting the influential sixth-century Pope Gregory, writing symbolizes his power and influence. During early Middle Ages, the church alone kept literacy and writing alive in the West.

Source: St. Gregory writing with scribes, Carolingian, Franco-German School, c. 850–875 (ivory). Kunsthistorisches Museum, Vienna, Austria/Bridgeman Art Library

to train educated clergymen for future generations, in this way securing Christianity's position in western Europe.

Gregory set the stage for a dramatic increase in papal power. As his successors' authority expanded over the next few centuries, relations between Rome and the Byzantine emperors slowly soured, especially during the Iconoclastic Controversy discussed in Chapter 8. By the early eighth century the popes abandoned the fiction that they were still subject to the Byzantines and sought protection from the Frankish kings.

CONVERTING THE IRISH   Though the Romans had conquered most of Britain during the imperial period, they never attempted to bring Ireland into their empire. Thus, the island off Britain's west coast had had only minimal contact with Christianity. Little is known of how Christianity came to Ireland. There were probably missionaries who traveled with traders from the Roman Empire, but the earliest firm date is 431 when Palladius was supposedly sent to administer to those in Ireland who were already Christians. The figure of Patrick (d. ca. 492 or 493) dominates the subsequent missionary history of Ireland, largely because his later biographers improbably gave him credit for converting all the Irish to Christianity. A ninth-century record describes Patrick's capture from a Roman villa in Britain by Irish raiders, who sold him into slavery in Ireland. He managed to escape and return to Britain, where he was ordained into the priesthood and sent back to Ireland as a missionary. A great deal of confusion exists regarding Patrick's life; some scholars argue that the traditional story of Patrick actually merges the experiences of the two missionaries Palladius and Patrick. Nevertheless, by the end of the fifth century, Christianity had a firm foothold in Ireland.

But Ireland was still an entirely rural place. Elsewhere in the West, Christianity spread out into the countryside from cities, with bishops administering the local church from their city cathedrals. Ireland, however, lacked cities in which to build churches and housing for bishops. No one living in Ireland knew Latin, Greek, or any of the other languages into which the Bible had been translated. And no schools existed where churchmen might teach the Gospel to new converts.

Irish churchmen found solutions to these problems in monasteries, places where priests could receive training and men and women from the surrounding homesteads and hamlets could learn to read Latin and absorb the basics of Christian education. The Irish scholars produced by these monasteries gained a high reputation for their learning across western Europe. They produced magnificently illustrated manuscripts in their libraries. These books brought Irish art to all the lands where Irish missionaries traveled.

THE BOOK OF KELLS

The Book of Kells consists of an ornately illustrated manuscript produced by Irish monks about 800 C.E. The book contains the four gospels of the New Testament in Latin and is one of the masterpieces of early medieval art. This highly decorated page shows two Greek letters, Chi and Rho, the first two letters of Christ in Greek.

Source: The Board of Trinity College, Dublin, Ireland

CONVERTING THE ANGLO-SAXONS Irish missionaries established new monasteries in England and on the European continent. Columba (521–597), for instance, founded one on the island of Iona, off Scotland's western coast. From this thriving community missionaries began to bring Christianity to the peoples of Scotland. The offshoot monastery of Lindisfarne in northern England also became a dynamic center of learning and missionary activity. During the seventh century, missionaries based there carried Christianity to many other parts of England. They also began converting the people of Frisia on the North Sea, in the area of the modern Netherlands.

Pope Gregory the Great (r. 590–604) understood that the first step in creating new Christian communities was to convert as many people as possible to the faith. Deep learning about the religion could come later. To that end he instructed missionaries to permit local variations in worship and to accommodate harmless vestiges of pre-Christian worship practices. "Don't tear down their temples," Gregory advised, "put a cross on the roofs!"

Following Gregory's pragmatic suggestion, missionaries in England accepted certain Anglo-Saxon calendar conventions that stemmed from polytheist worship. For example, in the Anglo-Saxon calendar, the weekdays took their names from old gods: Tuesday derived from Tiw, a war god; Wednesday from Woden, king of the gods; Thursday from Thor, god of thunder; and Friday from Freya, goddess of agriculture. Anglo-Saxon deities eventually found their way into the Christian calendar as well. Eostre, for example, a goddess whose festival came in April, gave her name to the Christian holiday Easter.

Despite their common commitment to Latin Christianity, the Irish and Roman monks working throughout England disagreed strongly about proper Christian practice. For instance, they argued over how to perform baptism, the ritual of anointing someone with water to admit him or her into the Christian community. They bickered about how monks should shave the tops of their heads to show their religious vocation, and they squabbled about the correct means of calculating the date of Easter. These disputes threatened to create deep divisions among England's Christians. The overall conflict finally found resolution in 664 in the Anglo-Saxon kingdom of Northumbria, where monastic life flourished. At a council of monks and royal advisers called the Synod of Whitby, the Northumbrian monarch commanded that the Roman rather than Irish version of Christianity would prevail in his kingdom. His decision eventually was accepted throughout England.

MONASTIC INTELLECTUAL LIFE The missionaries from Rome were members of the vigorous monastic movement initiated by Benedict of Nursia (ca. 480–547) from his monastery at Monte Cassino in Italy (see Chapter 7). These monks followed Benedict's *Rule*, a guidebook for the management of monastic life and spirituality. In the *Rule*, Benedict had written that individual monks should live temperate lives devoted to spiritual contemplation, communal prayer, and manual labor. So that their contemplations might not depart from the path of truth, Benedict had encouraged monks to seek guidance in the Bible, in the writings of the renowned theologians, and in works of spiritual edification. For Benedict, contemplative reading constituted a fundamental part of monastic life. Thus, monks had to be literate in Latin. They needed training in the Latin classics, which required books.

Medieval monasteries set aside at least two rooms—the **scriptorium** and the library—to meet the growing demand for books. In the scriptorium, scribes laboriously copied Latin and Greek manuscripts as an act of religious devotion. Monastery libraries were small in comparison with the public libraries of classical Rome, but the volumes were cherished and carefully protected. Because books were precious possessions, these libraries set forth strict rules for their use. Some librarians chained books to tables to prevent theft. Others pronounced a curse against anyone who failed to return a borrowed book. Nevertheless, librarians also generously lent books to other monasteries to copy.

CHRONOLOGY: THE BIRTH OF LATIN CHRISTENDOM

481–511	Clovis reigns; Frankish kingdom divided at his death
529	Benedict founds monastery at Monte Cassino
568	Lombards invade Italy
587	Visigothic king of Spain converts to Latin Christianity; Columbanus travels to Gaul from Ireland
ca. 700	Lombards accept Latin Christianity
732	Charles Martel defeats Muslims at Poitiers
751	Pepin overthrows last Merovingian king; Exarchate of Ravenna falls to Lombards

Monks preferred to read texts with a Christian message, so these books were the most frequently copied. In many monasteries, however, monks preserved non-Christian texts as well. By doing so, they helped to keep knowledge of Latin and classical learning alive. Indeed, many of the surviving works by authors of the Classical Age were copied and passed on by monks in the sixth and seventh centuries. Without the monasteries and scriptoria, knowledge today of the literature of the classical world would be greatly reduced.

Monks did far more than merely copy ancient texts, however. Some wrote original books of their own. At the English monastery at Jarrow, for example, Bede (d. 735) became the most distinguished scholar in eighth-century Europe. He wrote many books, including the *History of the English Church and People*. This work provided an invaluable source of information about the early Anglo-Saxon kingdoms.

Monks carried books with them when they embarked on missionary journeys. They also acquired new books during their travels. For instance, Benedict Biscop, the founder of the monasteries of Wearmouth (674) and Jarrow (682) in England, made six trips to Italy. Each time he brought back crates of books on all subjects, including works written by classical authors whom monks studied with interest. Other Anglo-Saxon missionaries transported this literary heritage to the monasteries they founded in Germany during the eighth century. As monks avidly read, copied, wrote, and transported books of all sorts, knowledge and intellectual discourse flourished in the monasteries.

Monks shared their expanding knowledge with Christians outside the monastery walls. They established schools at monasteries where boys (and, in some places, girls) could learn to read and write. In Italy some public schools survived from antiquity, but elsewhere most of the very few literate people who lived between 550 and 750 gained their education at monastery schools. The men trained in these schools played an important role in society as officials and bureaucrats. Their skills in reading and writing were necessary for keeping records and writing business and diplomatic letters.

THE CAROLINGIANS

■ How did the Carolingian Empire contribute to establishing a distinctive western European culture?

Among the successor kingdoms to the Roman Empire in the West, discussed in the previous section, none was more powerful militarily than the Merovingian kingdom of the Franks. The Merovingian dynasty, however, was plagued by factions, royal assassinations, and do-nothing kings. When Pepin the Short deposed the last of the Merovingian kings in 751, he made himself king of the Franks and inaugurated the Carolingian dynasty.

Both the weak Merovingians and the strong Carolingians illustrated how the problem of succession from one king to another could destabilize early medieval monarchies. The kingdom was considered the private property of the royal family, and according to Frankish custom, a father was obliged to divide his estates among all his legitimate sons. As a result, whenever a king of the Franks died, the kingdom was divided up. When Pepin died in 768, the kingdom was divided between his sons, Charlemagne and Carloman. When Carloman died suddenly in 771, Charlemagne ignored the inheritance rights of Carloman's sons and may even have had them killed, making himself the sole ruler of the Franks.

The Leadership of Charlemagne

Charlemagne's (r. 768–814) ruthlessness with his own nephews epitomized the leadership that made him the mightiest ruler in western Europe and gave him the nickname of Charles the Great. An unusually tall and imposing figure, Charlemagne was a superb athlete and swimmer, a lover of jokes and high living, but also a deeply pious Christian. One of his court poets labeled him "The King Father of Europe." No monarch in European history has enjoyed such posthumous fame.

During his reign, Charlemagne engaged in almost constant warfare, especially against polytheistic Germanic tribes that he compelled to accept Christianity after their defeat. He went to war 18 times against the Saxons, whose forced conversion only encouraged subsequent rebellions. Three factors explain Charlemagne's persistent warfare. He believed he had an obligation to spread Christianity. He also needed to protect his borders from incursions by hostile tribes. Perhaps most important, however, was his need to satisfy his followers, especially the members of the aristocracy, by providing them with opportunities for plunder and new lands. As a result of his many wars, Charlemagne established a network of subservient kingdoms that owed tribute to him (see **Map 9.2**).

The extraordinary expansion of the Carolingian Empire represented a significant departure from the small, loosely governed kingdoms that had prevailed after the Roman Empire's collapse.

Charlemagne's empire covered all of western Europe except for southern Italy, Spain, and the British Isles. His military ambitions brought the Franks into direct confrontation with other cultures—the polytheistic German, Scandinavian, and Slavic tribes, the Orthodox Christians of Byzantium, and the Muslims in Spain. These confrontations were usually hostile and violent, characterized as they were by the imposition of Frankish rule and Latin Christian faith.

CORONATION OF CHARLEMAGNE AS EMPEROR On Christmas Day 800 in front of a large crowd at St. Peter's Basilica in Rome, Pope Leo III (r. 795–816) presided over a ceremony in which Charlemagne was crowned emperor. Historians have debated exactly what happened, but according to the most widely accepted account, the assembled throng acclaimed Charlemagne emperor, and the pope prostrated himself before the new emperor in a public demonstration of submission. Charlemagne's biographer Einhard later stated that the coronation came as a surprise to the king. Certainly there were dangers in accepting the imperial crown because the coronation was certain to antagonize Byzantium, where there already was a Roman emperor. To the Byzantines, Charlemagne was nothing more than a barbarian usurper of the imperial crown. In their minds the pope had no right to crown anyone emperor. Instead of reuniting the eastern and western halves of the ancient Roman Empire, the coronation of Charlemagne drove them further apart. Nevertheless, Charlemagne became the first Roman emperor in the West since the fifth century.

The coronation exemplified two of the most prominent characteristics of the Carolingians. The first was the conscious imitation of the ancient Roman Empire, especially the Christian empire of Constantine. Charlemagne conquered much of the former territory of the western Roman Empire, and the churches built during his reign were modeled after the fourth- and fifth-century basilicas of Rome. The second characteristic of Carolingian rule was the obligation of the Frankish kings to protect

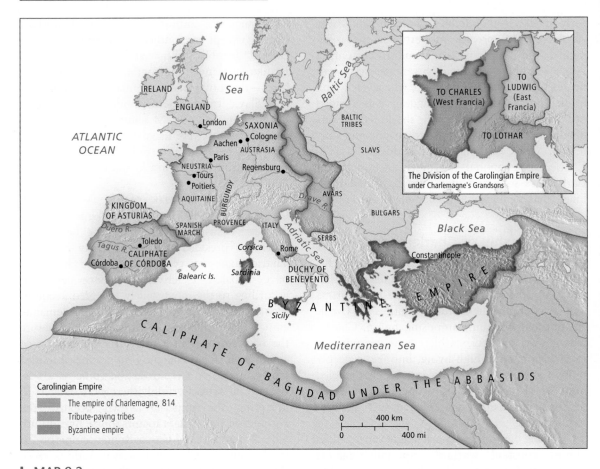

MAP 9.2

Carolingian Empire

Charlemagne's conquests were the greatest military achievement of the Early Middle Ages. The Carolingian armies successfully reunified all western European territories of the ancient Roman Empire except for southern Italy, Spain, and Britain. However, the empire was fragile due to Frankish inheritance laws that required all legitimate sons to inherit lands from their father. By the time of Charlemagne's grandsons the empire began to fragment.

the Roman popes, an obligation that began under Charlemagne's father Pepin. In exchange for Frankish protection, the popes offered the Carolingian monarchs the legitimacy of divine sanction.

CAROLINGIAN RULERSHIP Even under the discerning and strong rulership of Charlemagne, the Carolingian Empire never enjoyed the assets that had united the ancient Roman Empire for so many centuries. The Carolingians lacked a standing army and navy, professional civil servants, properly maintained roads, regular communications, and a money economy—a stark contrast with Byzantium and the Muslim caliphates, which could also boast splendid capital cities of Constantinople, Damascus, Baghdad, and Córdoba. However, Charlemagne governed very effectively without a capital, spending much of his time ruling from the saddle.

Such a system of government depended more on personal than institutional forms of rule. Personal loyalty to the Carolingian monarch, expressed in an oath of allegiance, provided the strongest bonds unifying the realm, but betrayals were frequent. The Carolingian system required a monarch with outstanding personal abilities and unflagging energy, such as Charlemagne possessed, but a weak monarch threatened the collapse of the entire empire. Until the reign of Charlemagne, royal commands had been delivered orally, and there were few written records of what decisions had been made. Charlemagne's decrees (called "capitularies") gradually came to be written out. The capitularies began to strengthen and institutionalize governmental procedures. In addition, Charlemagne's leading adviser, Alcuin, insisted that all official communications be stated in the appropriate Latin form, which would help prevent falsification because only the members of Charlemagne's court were well enough educated to know these proper forms.

One of the weaknesses of the previous Merovingian dynasty had been the decentralization of power, as local dukes appropriated royal resources and public functions for themselves. To combat this weakness, Charlemagne followed his father's lead in reorganizing government around territorial units called **counties**, each administered by a count. The counts were rewarded with lands from the king and sent to areas where they had no family ties to serve as a combined provincial governor, judge, military commander, and representative of the king. Traveling circuit inspectors reviewed the counts' activities on a regular basis and remedied abuses of office. On the frontiers of their sprawling kingdom, the Franks established special territories called **marches,** which were ruled by margraves with extended powers necessary to defend vulnerable borders.

In many respects, however, the Church provided the most vital foundations for the Carolingian system of rulership. As discussed in Chapter 7, during the last years of the ancient Roman Empire the administration of the Church was organized around the office of the bishop.

By the late seventh century this system had almost completely collapsed, as many bishoprics were left vacant or were occupied by royal favorites and relatives who lacked qualifications for church office. Because Carolingian monarchs considered themselves responsible for the welfare of Christianity, they took charge of the appointment of bishops and reorganized church administration into a strict hierarchy of archbishops who supervised bishops who, in turn, supervised parish priests. Pepin and Charlemagne also revitalized the monasteries and endowed new ones, which provided the royal court with trained personnel—scribes, advisers, and spiritual assistants. Most laymen of the time were illiterate, so monks and priests wrote the emperor's letters for him, kept government records, composed histories, and promoted education—all essential for Carolingian rule.

THE CAROLINGIAN RENAISSANCE In addition to organizing an efficient political administration, Charlemagne sought to make the royal court an intellectual center. He gathered around him prominent scholars from throughout the realm and other countries. Under Charlemagne's patronage, these scholars were responsible for the flowering of culture that is called the Carolingian Renaissance.

The **Carolingian Renaissance** ("rebirth") was one of a series of revivals of interest in ancient Greek and Latin literature. Charlemagne understood that both governmental efficiency and the propagation of the Christian faith required the intensive study of Latin, which was the language of the law, learning, and the Church. The Latin of everyday speech had evolved considerably since antiquity. During Charlemagne's time, spoken Latin had already been transformed into early versions of the Romance languages of Spanish, Italian, Portuguese, and French. Distressed that the poor Latin of many clergymen meant they misunderstood the Bible, Charlemagne ordered that all prospective priests undergo a rigorous education and recommended the liberal application of physical punishment if a pupil was slow in his lessons. The lack of properly educated teachers, however, ensured that the Carolingian reforms did not penetrate very far into the lower levels of the clergy, who taught by rote the rudiments of Christianity to the illiterate peasants.

Charlemagne's patronage was crucial for the Carolingian Renaissance, which took place in the monasteries and the imperial court. Many of the heads of the monastic scriptoria wrote literary works of their own, including poetry and theology. The Carolingian scholars developed a beautiful new style of handwriting called the Carolingian minuscule, in which each letter was carefully and clearly formed. Texts collected by Carolingian librarians provided the foundation for the laws of the Church (called **canon law**) and codified the liturgy, which consisted of the prayers offered, texts read, and chants sung on each day of the year.

The man most fully responsible for the Carolingian Renaissance was the English poet and cleric Alcuin of York (ca. 732–804), whom Charlemagne invited to head the palace school in Aachen. Charlemagne himself joined his sons, his friends, and his friends' sons as a student, but Charlemagne struggled as a student. Despite many years of practice he still could not learn to form letters. Nevertheless, under Alcuin's guidance the court became a lively center of discussion and exchange of knowledge. They debated issues such as the existence of Hell, the meaning of solar eclipses, and the nature of the Holy Trinity. After 15 years at court, Alcuin became the abbot of the monastery of St. Martin at Tours, where he expanded the library and produced a number of works on education, theology, and philosophy.

A brilliant young monk named Einhard (ca. 770–840), who studied in the palace school, quickly became a trusted friend and adviser to Charlemagne. Based on 23 years of service to Charlemagne and research in royal documents, Einhard wrote the *Life of Charlemagne* (830–833), which describes Charlemagne's family, foreign policy, conquests, administration, and personal attributes. In Einhard's vivid Latin prose, Charlemagne comes alive as a great leader, a lover of hunting and fighting, who unlike his rough companions possessed a towering sense of responsibility for the welfare of his subjects and the salvation of their souls. In Einhard's biography, Charlemagne appears as an idealist, the first Christian prince in medieval Europe to imagine that his role was not just to acquire more possessions but to better humankind.

Charlemagne's rule and reputation have had lasting significance for western Europe. Around 776 an Anglo-Saxon monk referred to the vast new kingdom of the Franks as the Kingdom of Europe, reviving the Roman geographical term *Europa*. Thanks to the Carolingians, Europe became more than a geographical expression. It became the geographical center of a new Christian civilization that supplanted the Roman civilization of the Mediterranean and transformed the culture of the West.

The Division of Western Europe

None of Charlemagne's successors possessed his personal skills, and without a permanent institutional basis for administration, the empire was vulnerable to fragmentation and disorder. When Charlemagne died in 814, the imperial crown passed to his only surviving son, Louis the Pious (r. 814–840). Louis's most serious problem was dividing the empire among his own three sons, as required by Frankish inheritance laws. Disputes among Louis's sons led to civil war, even before the death of their father; while they were fighting, the administration of the empire was neglected.

After years of fighting, the three sons—Charles the Bald (d. 877), Lothair (d. 855), and Louis the German (d. 876)—negotiated the Treaty

CHRONOLOGY: THE CAROLINGIAN DYNASTY	
751	Pepin the Short deposes last Merovingian king
800	Charlemagne crowned emperor in Rome
843	Treaty of Verdun divides Frankish kingdom
987	Death of the last Carolingian king

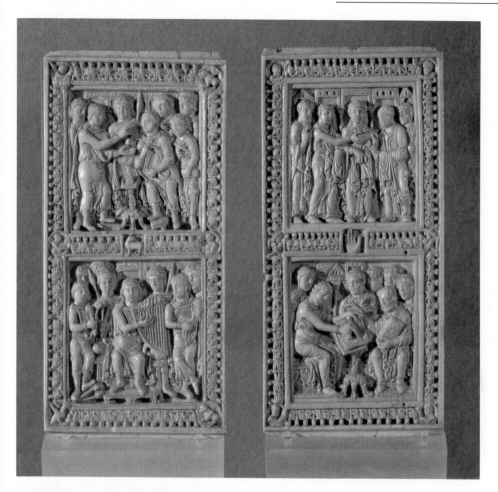

CAROLINGIAN RENAISSANCE ART

This exquisitely carved book cover for the Psalter of Dagulf was made for Pope Hadrian (d. 795) in the workshops of Charlemagne's palace. In the upper left side panel, King David orders the psalms be written down. In the lower left he sings them. In the upper right the pope orders Saint Jerome to edit the psalms for inclusion in the Bible, which he does in the lower right.

of Verdun, which divided the Carolingian Empire. Charles the Bald received the western part of the territories, the kingdom of West Francia. Louis the German received the eastern portion, the kingdom of East Francia. Lothair obtained the imperial title as well as the central portion of the kingdom, the "Middle Kingdom," which extended from Rome to the North Sea (see Map 9.2). In succeeding generations, the laws of inheritance created further fragmentation of these

kingdoms, and during the ninth and tenth centuries the descendants of Charlemagne died out or lost control of their lands. By 987 none were left.

The Carolingian Empire lasted only a few generations. Carolingian military power, however, had been formidable, providing within the Frankish lands an unusual period of security from hostile enemies, measured by the fact that few settlements were fortified. After the empire's collapse, virtually every surviving community in western

Europe required fortifications, represented by castles and town walls. Post-Carolingian Europe became fragmented as local aristocrats stepped into the vacuum created by the demise of the Carolingians—and it became vulnerable, as a new wave of raiders from the steppes and the North plundered and carved out land for themselves.

INVASIONS AND RECOVERY IN THE LATIN WEST

- After the collapse of the Carolingian Empire, how did the western kingdoms consolidate in the core of the European continent and how did Latin Christianity spread to its periphery?

Despite Charlemagne's campaigns of conquest and conversion, the spread of Christianity throughout western Europe remained uneven and incomplete. By 900, Latin Christianity was limited to a few regions that constituted the heartland of western Europe—the Frankish lands, Italy, parts of Germany that had been under Carolingian rule, the British Isles, and a fringe in Spain. Moreover, the heartland was vulnerable because during the ninth and tenth centuries, hostile polytheistic tribes raided deep into the tightly packed Christian core of western Europe (see **Map 9.3**). Despite these attacks Christianity survived, and the polytheist tribes eventually accepted the Christian faith. These conversions were not always the consequence of Christian victories in battle, as had often been the case during late antiquity and the Carolingian period. More frequently they resulted from organized missionary efforts by monks and bishops.

The Polytheist Invaders of the Latin West

Some of the raiders during the eighth to eleven centuries plundered what they could from the Christian settlements of the West and returned home. Others seized lands, settled down, and established new principalities. The two groups who took advantage of the weakness of the Latin West most often during this period were the Magyars and Vikings.

The original homeland of the Magyars, later known as the Hungarians, was in the central Asian steppes. Gradually driven by other nomads to the western edge of the steppes, the Magyars crossed en masse in 896 into the middle of the Danube River basin, occupying sparsely settled lands that were easily conquered. Mounted raiding parties of Magyars ranged far into western Europe. Between 898 and 920 they sacked settlements in the prosperous Po River valley of Italy and then descended on the remnant kingdoms of the Carolingian Empire. Wherever they went they plundered for booty and took slaves for domestic service or sale. The kings of western and central Europe were powerless against these fierce raiders, who were unstoppable until 955 when the Saxon king Otto I destroyed a band of marauders on their way home with booty. After 955, Magyar raiding subsided.

The definitive end of Magyar forays, however, may have had less to do with Otto's victory than with the consolidation of the Hungarian plain into its own kingdom under the Árpád dynasty. Both Orthodox and Latin missionaries vied to convert the Magyars, but because of western political alliances they accepted Latin Christianity. On Christmas Day 1000, the Árpád king Stephen I (r. 997–1038) received the insignia of royalty directly from the pope and was crowned king. To help convert his people, King Stephen laid out a network of bishoprics and lavishly endowed monasteries.

The most devastating of the eighth- to eleventh-century invaders of western European settlements were the Vikings, also called Norsemen or Northmen. During this period, Danish, Norwegian, and Swedish Viking warriors sailed on long-distance raiding expeditions from their homes in Scandinavia. Every spring the long Viking dragon ships sailed forth, each carrying 50–100 warriors avid for loot. Propelled by a

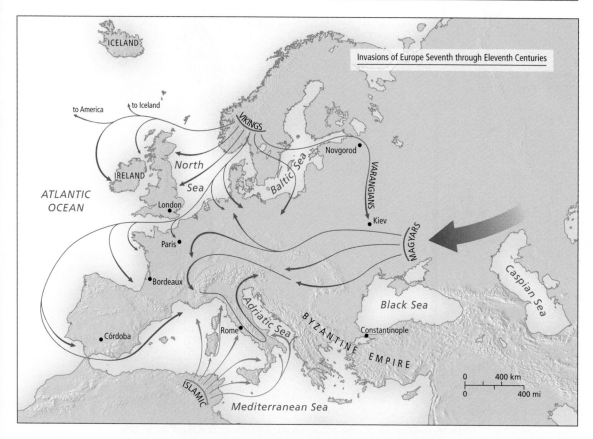

MAP 9.3

Invasions of Europe, Seventh Through Eleventh Centuries

After the division of the Carolingian empire, Britain and northern France, in particular, came under severe pressure from invading Viking bands from Scandinavia. The Varangians were a Viking tribe that invaded Kievan Rus and the territories of the Novgorod. From the east came the Magyars, who eventually settled in the vast Hungarian plain. From the south there were persistent raids and conquests from various Islamic states, some of which established a rich Muslim civilization in Europe. (For these, see Chapter 8.)

single square sail or by oarsmen when the winds failed or were blowing in the wrong direction, Viking ships were unmatched for seaworthiness and regularly sailed into the wild seas of the North Atlantic. The shallow-draft vessels could also be rowed up the lazy rivers of Europe to plunder monasteries and villages far into the interior.

Historians continue to debate the causes for the enormous Viking onslaught. Higher annual temperatures in the North may have stimulated a spurt in population that encouraged raiding and

eventually emigration. But the primary motive seems to have been an insatiable thirst for silver, which was deemed the essential standard of social distinction in Scandinavian society. As a result, monasteries and cathedrals with their silver liturgical vessels were especially prized sources of plunder for Viking raiding parties. In 793, for example, Vikings pillaged the great English monastery at Lindisfarne for its silver—and largely destroyed it in the process.

By the middle of the ninth century, the Vikings began to maintain winter quarters in

VIKING SHIP

This reconstructed Viking ship, discovered at Oseberg, Norway, dates from ca. 800. It would have been propelled by a single square sail or rowed by oarsmen. Horses and warriors crowded into the ship. The tiller was mounted on the starboard side toward the stern. Stern-mounted rudders, which gave the helmsman much greater control of the direction of the ship, were gradually introduced during the twelfth century.

the British Isles and on the shores of the Carolingian kingdoms—locations that enabled them to house and feed ever-larger raiding parties. These raiders soon became invading armies that took land and settled their families on it. As a result, the Vikings moved from disruptive pillaging to permanent occupation, which created a lasting mark on Europe. Amid the ruins of the Carolingian Empire, Viking settlements on the Seine River formed the beginnings of the duchy of Normandy ("Northman land"), whose soldiers in the eleventh century would conquer England, Sicily, and much of southern Italy.

The most long-lasting influence of the Vikings outside Scandinavia was in the British Isles and North Atlantic. In 865 a great Viking army conquered large parts of northeastern England, creating a loosely organized network of territories known as the Danelaw. The Danish and Norse conquests in the British Isles left deep cultural residues in local dialects, geographical names, personal names, social structure, and literature. The most enduring example in Old English, the earliest form of spoken and written English, remains the epic of *Beowulf*, which recounts the exploits of a great Scandinavian adventurer in combat with the monster Grendel, Grendel's mother, and a fiery dragon.

In the North Atlantic, Vikings undertook long voyages into the unknown across cold rough seas. Beginning about 870, settlers poured into unsettled Iceland. Using Iceland as a base, they ventured farther and established new colonies in Greenland. In Iceland the adventures of these Viking warriors, explorers, and settlers were celebrated in poetry and sagas. The sagas of Erik the Red and the Greenlanders recount hazardous voyages to the coasts of Canada. These Europeans arrived in North America 500 years before Christopher Columbus. In 930 the fiercely independent Icelanders founded a national parliament, the *althing*, an institution at which disputes were adjudicated through legal procedures rather than combat.

After the mid-ninth century, the kings of Scandinavia (Norway, Denmark, and Sweden) began to assert control over the bands of raiders who had constituted the vanguard of the Viking invasions. By the end of the tenth century, the great age of Viking raiding by small parties ended. The Scandinavian kings established firm hold over the settled population and converted to Christianity, bringing their subjects with them into the new faith. Hence, the descendants of the Viking raiders settled down to become peaceable farmers and shepherds.

The Rulers in the Latin West

As a consequence of the disintegration of the Carolingian order and the subsequent invasions, people during the ninth and tenth centuries began to seek protection from local warlords who assumed responsibilities once invested in royal authorities. Some of these warlords became the founders of what would become the kingdoms of the Latin West. They provided protection and a modicum of order in a period of anarchy caused by weak or failed governments.

LORDS AND VASSALS The society of warlords derived from Germanic military traditions in which a great chief attracted followers who fought alongside him. The relationship was voluntary and egalitarian. By the eighth century, however, the chief had become a **lord** who dominated others, and his dependents were known as **vassals.**

The bond of loyalty between lord and vassal was formalized by an oath. In the Carolingian period the vassal proved his loyalty to the lord by performing an act of homage, which made the vassal the "man" of the lord. The act of homage was a ritual in which the kneeling vassal placed his clasped hands between the hands of the lord and made a verbal declaration of intent, usually something such as, "Sir, I become your man." In return for the vassal's homage or fealty, as it came to be called, the lord swore to protect the vassal. The oath established a personal relationship in which the lord reciprocated the vassal's loyalty and willingness to obey the lord with protection and in some cases with a land grant called a **fief.** Lords frequently called on their vassals for military assistance to resist invaders or to fight with other lords. The fief supplied the vassal with an income to cover the expenses of armor and weapons and of raising and feeding horses, all of which were necessary to be an effective mounted soldier, known by the twelfth century as a **knight.** Historians called this connection between lord-vassal relations and the holding of a fief **feudalism.** The privileges for lords and vassals and their hold on fiefs lasted for many centuries, well into the eighteenth century in some parts of Europe. The long persistence of feudalism was one of the most important themes in the history of the West.

During the ninth and tenth centuries, after the collapse of public authority during the invasions

Revealing the Truth: Oaths and Ordeals

No participant in a lawsuit or criminal trial today would dream of entering the courtroom without an accompanying pile of documents to prove the case. In modern society we trust written over oral evidence because we are aware of how easily our memories can be distorted. In an early medieval court, however, the participants usually arrived with nothing more than their own sworn testimony and personal reputations to support their cause. Papers alleging to prove one thing or another meant little in a largely illiterate society. Unable to read and perhaps aware that the few who could read might deceive them, most people trusted what they had personally seen and heard. Count Berthold of Hamm expressed the opinion of many when, after being presented with documents opposing his claim to a piece of land, he "laughed at the documents, saying that since anyone's pen could write what they liked, he ought not to lose his rights over it."

To settle disputes, medieval courts put much more faith in confession or in eyewitness testimony than in documents. In 1124 Pope Calixtus II pronounced that "we put greater faith in the oral testimony of living witnesses than in the written word."

Under normal trial procedures, a man would give his oath that what he was saying was true. If he was an established and respected member of the community, he would also have a number of "oath-witnesses" testify for his reliability, although not to the truth or falsehood of his evidence. The court would also hear from witnesses in the case. This system worked well enough when two local men, known in the community, were at odds. But what happened when there was a trial involving a person who had a bad reputation, was a known liar, or was a stranger? What would happen in a case with no witnesses?

In these instances, medieval courts sometimes turned to trial by ordeal—subjecting the accused to a painful test—to settle the matter. The judicial ordeal was used only as a last resort, as a German law code of 1220 declared: "It is not right to use the ordeal in any case, except that the truth may be known in no other way." The wide range of situations and people handed over to the ordeal makes clear that in the eyes of the medieval courts, the ordeal was a fallback method when all else failed to reveal the truth.

There were several types of trial by ordeal. The most common was trial by fire. The accused would plunge his or her arm into a cauldron of boiling water to retrieve a coin or a jewel, or alternately would pick up a red-hot iron and walk nine paces. A variation of this method was to walk over hot coals or red-hot plowshares. After the accused suffered this ordeal, his or her hand or foot would be bound for three days and then examined. If the wound was healing "cleanly," meaning without infection, the accused was declared innocent. If not, he or she was adjudged guilty. Another common form of the ordeal was immersion in cold water, or "swimming," made famous in later centuries by its use in witch trials. The accused would be thrown into a river or lake. If the water "rejected" her and she floated, then she was guilty. If the water "embraced" her and she sank, then she was innocent. The obvious complication that a sinking person, even though innocent, may have also been a drowning person did not seem to deter use of trial by water.

The ordeal was especially widespread in judging crimes such as heresy and adultery and in assigning paternity. In 1218, Inga of Varteig carried the hot iron to prove that her son, born out of wedlock, was the son of deceased King Hakon III, which if true would change the line of succession in Norway. The ordeal was also used to decide much more pedestrian matters. In 1090, Gautier of Meigné claimed a plot of land from the monks of Saint Auban at Angers, arguing that he had traded a horse in return for the property. He too carried a hot iron to prove his claim.

The belief that an ordeal could effectively reveal guilt or innocence in a judicial matter was based on the widespread conviction that God constantly and actively intervened in earthly affairs and that his judgment could be seen immediately. To focus God's attention on a specific issue, the participants performed the ordeal in a ritual manner. A priest was usually present to invoke God's power and to bless the implements employed in the ordeal. In one typical formula, the priest asked God "to bless and sanctify this fiery iron, which is used in the just examination of doubtful issues." Priests would also inform the accused, "If you are innocent of this charge...you may confidently receive this iron in your hand and the Lord, the just judge, will free you." The ritual element of the judicial ordeal emphasized the judgment of God over the judgment of men.

During the eleventh and twelfth centuries, the use of the ordeal waned. The recovery of Roman law, the rise of literacy and written documents in society at large, and a greater confidence in the power of courts to settle disputes all contributed to the gradual replacement of the ordeal with the jury trial or the use of torture to elicit a confession from the accused. In England the common law began to entrust the determination of the truth to a jury of peers who listened to and evaluated all the testimony. The jury system valued the opinions of members of the community over the reliability of the ordeal to reveal God's judgment. These changes mark a shift in medieval society toward a growing belief in the power of secular society to organize and police itself, leaving divine justice to the afterlife. But the most crucial shift came from within the Church itself, which felt its spiritual mission compromised by the involvement of priests in supervising ordeals. In 1215 the Fourth Lateran Council forbade priests from participating, and their absence made it impossible for the ordeal to continue as a formal legal procedure.

For Discussion

1. Why was someone's reputation in the community so significant for determining the truth in a medieval trial? How do reputations play a role in trials today?

TRIAL BY ORDEAL
This fifteenth-century painting by Dieric Bouts (ca. 1415–1475), was commissioned by the city of Louvain in 1468 for a large project on the theme of the Last Judgment.

2. What do oaths and the trial by ordeal reveal about the relationship between human and divine justice during the Middle Ages?

Taking it Further
Bartlett, Robert. *Trial by Fire and Water: The Medieval Judicial Ordeal.* 1986. Associates the spread of the trial by ordeal with the expansion of Christianity. The best study of the ordeal.

van Caenegen, R. C. *An Historical Introduction to Private Law.* 1992. A basic narrative from late antiquity to the nineteenth century that traces the evolution of early medieval trial procedures.

and the dissolution of the Carolingian Empire, the lords often became the only effective rulers in a particular locality. Lords came to exercise many of the powers of a king, such as adjudicating disputes over property or inheritance and punishing thieves and murderers. (See *Justice in History* in this chapter.)

The mixture of personal lord-vassal obligations, property rights conveyed by the fief, and legal jurisdiction over communities caused endless complications. The king's vassals were also lords of their own vassals, who in turn were lords over lesser vassals down to the level of simple knight. In theory such a system created a hierarchy of authority that descended down from the king, but reality was never that simple. In France, for example, many of the great lords possessed as much land as the king, which made it very difficult for the king to force them to enact his will. Many vassals held different fiefs from different lords, which created a confusion of loyalties, especially when two lords of the same vassal went to war against one another.

Women could inherit fiefs and own property of their own, although they could not perform military services. They often managed royal and aristocratic property when men were absent or dead, decided how property would be divided up among heirs, and functioned as lords when receiving the homage of male vassals. The lineage and accomplishments of prominent ladies enhanced their husbands' social prestige. A number of aristocratic families traced their descent from the female line, if it was more prestigious than the male line, and named their children after the wife's illustrious ancestors.

Lord-vassal relationships infiltrated many medieval social institutions and practices. Because most vassals owed military service to their lords, medieval armies were at least partially composed of vassal-knights who were obliged to fight for their lord for a certain number of days (often 40) per year. Vassals were required to provide their lord with other kinds of support as well. When summoned, they had to appear at the lord's court to offer advice or sit in judgment of other vassals who were their peers. When the lord traveled, his vassal was required to provide food and shelter in the vassal's castle, sometimes for a large entourage of family and retainers who accompanied the lord. Vassals were obliged to pay their lord certain fees on special occasions, such as the marriage of the lord's daughter. If the lord was captured in battle, his vassals had to pay the ransom.

THE WESTERN EUROPEAN KINGDOMS AFTER THE CAROLINGIANS   At a time when the bonds of loyalty and support between lords and vassals were the only form of protection from invaders and marauders, lordship was a stronger social institution than the vague obligations all subjects owed to their kings. To rule effectively, a king was obliged to be a strong lord, in effect to become the lord of all the other lords, who in turn would discipline their own vassals. Achieving this difficult goal took several steps. First, the king had to establish a firm hand over his own lands, the royal domain. With the domain supplying food, materiel, and fighting men, the king could attempt the second step—establishing control over lords who lived outside the royal domain. To hold sway over these independent-minded lords, kings sometimes employed force but frequently offered lucrative rewards by giving out royal prerogatives to loyal lords. These prerogatives included the rights to receive fines in courts of law, to collect taxes, and to perform other governmental functions. As a result, some medieval kingdoms, such as France and England, began to combine in the hands of the same people the personal authority of lordship with the legal authority of the king, creating feudal kingship.

The final step in the process of establishing royal authority was to emphasize the sacred character of kingship. With the assistance of the clergy, kings emulated the great Christian emperors of Rome, Constantine and Justinian. Medieval kings became quasi-priests who received obedience from their subjects because commoners believed kings represented the majesty of God on Earth. The institution of sacred kingship gave kings an additional weapon for persuading the nobles to recognize the king's superiority over them.

Under the influence of ancient Roman ideas of rulership, some kings began to envision their kingdoms as something grander than private property. As the Germanic king and later emperor Conrad II (r. 1024–1039) put it, "If the king is dead the kingdom remains, just as the ship remains even if the helmsman falls overboard."[2] The idea slowly began to take hold that the kingdom had an eternal existence separate from the mortal person of the king and that it was superior to its component parts—its provinces, tribes, lords, families, bishoprics, and cities. This profound idea reached its fullest theoretical expression many centuries later. Promoting the sacred and eternal character of kingship required monarchs to patronize priests, monks, writers, and artists who could formulate and express these ideas.

EAST FRANCIA: THE GERMAN EMPIRE The kingdoms of East and West Francia, which arose out of the remnants of the Carolingian Empire, produced kings who attempted to expand the power of the monarchy and enhance the idea of kingship. East Francia largely consisted of Germanic tribes, each governed by a Frankish official called a duke. After 919 the dukes of Saxony were elected the kings of East Francia, establishing the foundations for the Saxon dynasty. With few lands of their own, the Saxon kings maintained their power by acquiring other duchies and controlling appointments to high church offices, which went to family members or loyal followers. The greatest of the Saxon kings, Otto I the Great (936–973), combined deep Christian piety with formidable military ability. More than any other tenth-century king, he supported the foundation of missionary bishoprics in polytheist Slavic and Scandinavian lands, thereby pushing the boundaries of Christianity beyond what they had been under Charlemagne. The pope crowned Otto emperor in 962, reviving the Roman Empire in the West, as Charlemagne had done earlier. Otto and his successors in the Saxon dynasty attempted to rule a more restricted version of the western empire than had Charlemagne. By the 1030s the Saxon kingdom had become the German Empire, consisting of most of the Germanic duchies, north-central Italy, and Burgundy. In later centuries these regions collectively came to be called the Holy Roman Empire.

As had been the case under Charlemagne, effective rulership in the new German Empire included the patronage of learned men and women who enhanced the reputation of the monarch. Otto and his able brother Bruno, the archbishop of Cologne, initiated a cultural revival, the **Ottonian Renaissance**, which centered on the imperial court. Learned Irish and English monks, Greek philosophers from Byzantium, and Italian scholars found positions there. Among the many intellectuals patronized by Otto, the most notable was Liutprand of Cremona (ca. 920–972), a vivid writer whose unabashed histories reflected the passions of the troubled times. For example, his history of contemporary Europe vilified his enemies and was aptly titled *Revenge*.

WEST FRANCIA: FRANCE Like East Francia, West Francia included many groups with separate ethnic and linguistic identities, but the kingdom had been Christianized much longer because it had been part of the Roman Empire. Thus, West Francia, although highly fragmented, possessed the potential for greater unity by using fully established Christianity to champion the authority of the king.

Strengthening the monarchy became the crucial goal of the Capetian dynasty, which succeeded the last of the Carolingian kings. Hugh Capet (r. 987–996) was elevated as king of West Francia in an elaborate coronation ceremony in which the prayers of the archbishop of Reims offered divine sanction to the new dynasty. The involvement of the archbishop established an important precedent for the French monarchy: Thereafter, the monarchy and the church hierarchy were closely entwined. From this mutually beneficial relationship, the king received ecclesiastical and spiritual support while the upper clergy gained royal protection and patronage. The term *France* at first applied only to Capet's feudal domain, a small but rich region around Paris, but through the persistence of the Capetians, West Francia became so unified that the name France came to refer to the entire kingdom.

The Capetians were especially successful in soliciting homage and services from the great lords of the land—despite some initial resistance. Hugh and his successors distinguished themselves by emphasizing that unlike other lords, kings were appointed by God. Shortly after his own coronation, Hugh had his son crowned—a strategy that ensured the succession of the Capetian family. Hugh's son, Robert II, the Pious (r. 996–1031), was apparently the first to perform the "king's touch": curing certain skin diseases with the power of his touch. The royal coronation cult and the king's touch established the reputation of French kings as miracle workers.

ANGLO-SAXON ENGLAND Anglo-Saxon England had never been part of the Carolingian Empire, but because it was Christian, England shared in the culture of the Latin West. England suffered extensive damage at the hands of the Vikings. After England was almost overwhelmed by a Danish invasion during the winter of 878–879, Alfred the Great (r. 871–899) finally defeated the Danes as spring approached. As king of only Wessex (not of all England), Alfred consolidated his authority and issued a new law code. Alfred's successors cooperated with the nobility more effectively than the monarchs in either East or West Francia and built a broad base of support in the local units of government, the hundreds and shires. The Anglo-Saxon monarchy also enjoyed the support of the Church, which provided it with skilled servants and spiritual authorization.

During the late ninth and tenth centuries, Anglo-Saxon England experienced a cultural revival under royal patronage. King Alfred proclaimed that the Viking invasions had been God's punishment for the neglect of learning, without which God's will could not be known. Alfred accordingly promoted the study of Latin. He also desired that all men of wealth learn to read the language of the English people. Under Alfred a highly sophisticated literature appeared in Old English. This literature included poems, sermons,

commentaries on the Bible, and translations of important Latin works. The masterpiece of this era was a history called the *Anglo-Saxon Chronicle*. It was begun during Alfred's reign but maintained over several generations.

During the late tenth and early eleventh centuries, England was weakened by another series of Viking raids and a succession of feeble kings. In 1066 William, the duke of Normandy and a descendant of Vikings who had settled in the north of France, defeated King Harold, the last Anglo-Saxon king. William seized the English throne. William the Conqueror opened a new era in which English affairs became deeply intertwined with those of the duchy of Normandy and the kingdom of France.

The Conversion of the Last Polytheists

As the core of the Latin West became politically stronger and economically more prosperous during the tenth and eleventh centuries, Christians made concerted attempts to convert the invaders, especially the polytheistic tribes in northern and eastern Europe. Through conversion, Latin Christianity dominated northern Europe up to the Kievan Rus border where Orthodox Christianity adopted from Byzantium triumphed.

Among the polytheistic tribes in Scandinavia, the Baltic Sea region, and parts of eastern Europe, the first Christian conversions usually took place when a king or chieftain accepted Christianity. His subjects were expected to follow. Teaching Christian principles and forms of worship required much more time and effort, of course. Missionary monks usually arrived after a king's conversion, but these monks tended to take a tolerant attitude about variations in the liturgy. Because most Christians were isolated from one another, new converts tended to practice their own local forms of worship and belief. Missionaries and Christian princes discovered that the most effective way to combat this localizing tendency was to found new bishoprics. Especially among the formerly polytheist tribes in northern and eastern Europe, the foundation of bishoprics created cultural centers of considerable prestige

CHRISTIAN CHURCH IMITATES POLYTHEIST TEMPLE

The stave church was a type of wooden church built in northern Europe during the Middle Ages. Most of the surviving examples in Scandinavia are generally assumed to be modeled on polytheist temples. The Borgund church in Norway pictured here dates from about 1150.

that attracted members of the upper classes. Those educated under the supervision of these new bishops became influential servants to the ruling families, further enhancing the stature of Christian culture.

Christian conversion especially benefited women through the abandonment of polygamous marriages, common among the polytheist peoples. As a result, aristocratic women played an important role in helping convert their peoples to Christianity. That role gave them a lasting influence in the churches of the newly converted lands, both as founders and patrons of convents and as writers on religious subjects. By the end of the fourteenth century organized polytheistic worship had disappeared in Scandinavia.

From the middle of the tenth century, a line of newly established Catholic bishoprics ensured that the Poles, Bohemians (Czechs), and Magyars (Hungarians) looked to the West and the pope for their cultural models and religious leadership. Poland, especially, favored Latin Christianity, an association that helped create strong political and cultural ties to western Europe. The Poles inhabited a flat plain of forested land with small clearings for farming. First exposed to missionaries tied to Saint Methodius, Poland resisted Christianity until Prince Mieszko (ca. 960–992) created the most powerful of the Slav states and accepted Latin Christianity in 966 in an attempt to build political alliances with Christian princes. Mieszko formally subordinated his country to the Roman pope with the Donation of Poland (ca. 991). Thus, began Poland's long and special relationship with the papacy. At Mieszko's death, the territory of Poland approximated what it is today.

CHRONOLOGY: THE WESTERN EUROPEAN KINGDOMS EMERGE

843–911	Carolingian dynasty in East Francia
843–987	Carolingian dynasty in West Francia
919–1024	Saxon or Ottonian dynasty
955	Otto I defeats Magyars
962	Otto crowned emperor in Rome
987–1328	Capetian dynasty in France
1066	William the Conqueror defeats last Anglo-Saxon king

THE WEST IN THE EAST: THE CRUSADES

■ What were the causes and consequences of the Crusades?

On a chilly November day in 1095 in a bare field outside Clermont, France, Pope Urban II (r. 1088–1099) delivered a landmark sermon to the assembled French clergy and laypeople eager to hear the pope. In stirring words Urban recalled that Muslims in the East were persecuting Christians and that the holy places in Palestine had been ransacked. He called upon the knights "to take up the cross" to defend their fellow Christians in distress.

Urban's appeal for a crusade was stunningly successful. When he finished speaking, the crowd chanted back, "God wills it." The news of Urban's call for a holy war in the East spread like wildfire. All across France and the western part of the German Empire knights prepared for the journey to Jerusalem. Unexpectedly and probably contrary to the pope's intentions, the poor and dispossessed also became enthused about an armed pilgrimage to the Holy Land. The zealous Peter the Hermit (ca. 1050–1115) preached the Crusade among the poor and homeless and gathered a huge unequipped, undisciplined army, which left for Jerusalem well in advance of the knights. Most of the Peter's People's Crusade starved or were enslaved long before they arrived in Constantinople. The Byzantine emperor was unwilling to feed the few who did arrive and

shipped them off to Turkish territory where the Turkish army annihilated nearly all of them.

Urban's call for a crusade gave powerful religious sanction to the western Christian military expeditions against Islam. From 1095 until well into the thirteenth century, recurrent, large-scale crusading operations attempted to take, retake, and protect Christian Jerusalem (see **Map 9.4**), while the idea of going on a crusade lasted long after the thirteenth century into modern times. (See *Different Voices* in this chapter.)

The Origins of Holy War

The original impulse for the **Crusades** was the threat that Muslim armies posed to Christian peoples, pilgrims, and holy places in the eastern Mediterranean. By the middle of the eleventh century the Seljuk Turks, who had converted to Islam, were putting pressure on the Byzantine empire. In 1071, after the Seljuks defeated the Byzantine army at Manzikert, all of Asia Minor lay open to Muslim occupation. Pope Urban's appeal for a crusade in 1095 came in response to a request for military assistance from the Byzantine emperor Alexius Comnenus, who probably thought he would get yet another band of Western mercenaries to help him reconquer Byzantine territory lost to the Seljuks. Instead, he got something utterly unprecedented—a massive volunteer army of perhaps 100,000 soldiers devoted less to cooperating with their Byzantine Christian brethren than to wresting Jerusalem from Muslim hands.

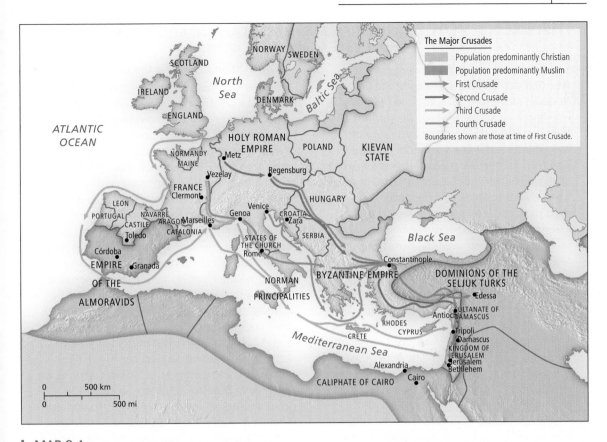

MAP 9.4

The Major Crusades

During the first three Crusades, Christian armies and fleets from western Europe attacked Muslim strongholds and fortresses in the Middle East in an attempt to capture and hold Jerusalem. The Fourth Crusade never arrived in the Middle East, as it was diverted to besiege Constantinople.

Pope Urban made a special offer in his famous sermon at Clermont to remit all penance for sin for those who went on the Crusade. Moreover, a penitential pilgrimage to a holy site such as Jerusalem provided a sinner with a pardon for capital crimes such as murder. Urban's offer muddled the long-standing difference between a pilgrim and a crusader. Until this point, a pilgrim was always unarmed, while a crusader carried weapons and was willing not just to defend other pilgrims from attack, but to launch an assault on those he considered heathens. The innovation of the Crusades was to create the idea of armed pilgrims who received special rewards from the Church. The merger of

a spiritual calling and military action was strongest in the knightly orders—Templars, Hospitallers, and Teutonic Knights. The men who joined these orders were soldiers who took monastic vows of poverty, chastity, and obedience. But rather than isolating themselves to pray in a monastery, they went forth, sword in hand, to conquer for Christ. These knightly orders exercised considerable political influence in Europe and amassed great wealth.

In the minds of crusader-knights, greed probably jostled with fervent piety. Growing population pressures and the spread of primogeniture (passing landed estates on to the eldest male heir) left younger sons with little to antici-

DIFFERENT VOICES CHRISTIAN AND MUSLIM JUSTIFICATIONS FOR HOLY WAR AGAINST THE OTHER

Both Christians and Muslims were convinced that God was on their side during the Crusades. However, leaders on both sides had to find a way to convince people about the justness of their cause and the necessity to take up arms. The problem was to find a way to persuade people to risk their lives and fortunes on behalf of co-religionists and the abstract idea of holy war. Robert the Monk recorded what Pope Urban said to the assembly at the Council of Clermont in 1095. He addressed the crowd as the "race of Franks, race from across the mountains, race beloved and chosen by God." He went on to describe the situation in Jerusalem. Pope Urban's appeal relied a great deal on the idea that the enemy was racially different.

After the First Crusade the gravest threat to the Christians in the Holy Land came from Damascus, Syria, an important Muslim city inland from the crusader states established in what is now Lebanon.

After the Second Crusade (1147–1149) failed to conquer Damascus, an anonymous Muslim author called on all Muslims to resist another Christian attack. In this appeal he calls for a defensive jihad on behalf of fellow Muslims. The passage begins with a quotation from Abu Hamid Al Ghazali (1058–1128), a prominent Muslim scholar, about a Muslim's obligations to take up arms.

I. Pope Urban II Calls for the Crusades

From the confines of Jerusalem and from the city of Constantinople a grievous report has gone forth and has repeatedly been brought to our ears; namely, that a race from the kingdom of the Persians, an accursed race, a race wholly alienated from God, "a generation that set not their heart aright, and whose spirit was not steadfast with God," has violently invaded the lands of those Christians and has depopulated them by pillage and fire. They have led away a part of the captives into their own country, and a part they have killed by cruel tortures. They have either destroyed the churches of God or appropriated them for the rites of their own religion. They destroy the altars, after having defiled them with their uncleanness....

Let hatred therefore depart from among you, let your quarrels end, let wars cease, and let all dissensions and controversies slumber. Enter upon the road to the Holy Sepulcher; wrest that land from the wicked race, and subject it to yourselves. That land which, as the Scripture says, "floweth with milk and honey" was given by God unto the power of the children of Israel. Jerusalem is the center of the earth; the land is fruitful above all others, like another paradise of delights. This spot the Redeemer of mankind has made illustrious by his advent, has beautified by his sojourn, has consecrated by his passion, has redeemed by his death, has glorified by his burial.

pate at home and much to hope for by seeking their fortunes in the Crusades. Nevertheless, crusaders testified to the sense of community they enjoyed by participating in "the common enterprise of all Christians." Fulcher of Chartres recalled the unity displayed by crusaders from so many different countries: "Who has ever heard of speakers of so many languages in one army....If a Breton or a German wished to ask me something, I was utterly without words to reply. But although we were divided by language,

we seemed to be like brothers in the love of God and like near neighbors of one mind." The exhilarating experience of brotherhood in the love of God motivated many crusaders.

Crusading Warfare

The First Crusade (1095–1099) was strikingly successful, but it was as much the result of Muslim weakness as Christian strength. Two factors depleted Arab Muslims' ability to resist the

This royal city, however, situated at the center of the earth, is now held captive by the enemies of Christ and is subjected, by those who do not know God, to the worship of the heathen. She seeks, therefore, and desires to be liberated and ceases not to implore you to come to her aid....Accordingly, undertake this journey eagerly for the remission of your sins, with the assurance of the reward of imperishable glory in the kingdom of heaven.

Source: From *Readings in European History* vol. 1, ed. James Harvey Robinson (Boston: Ginn 1904).

II. A Muslim Appeal for Jihad against the Crusaders

All Muslims who were free, responsible for their acts and capable of bearing arms must march against (the unbelievers) until they form a force large enough to smite them. This war is to glorify the Word of God and to make His religion victorious over its enemies....If the enemy attacks a town (in Syria) that is incapable of self-defense, all the towns in Syria must raise an army that could drive him back....If, however, the soldiers in Syria are insufficient for the task, the inhabitants of the nearer surrounding countries have the duty to assist them, while those of the more remote lands are free from this obligation.

Apply yourself to carry out the precept of jihad! Help one another in order to protect your religion and your brothers! Seize this opportunity and march forth against the unbelievers, for it does not require too great an effort and God has prepared you for it!...Commit jihad to make combat in your soul before committing jihad against your enemies because your souls are worse enemies for you than your foes. Turn your soul away from disobedience to its creator so that you would achieve the much desired victory....Forsake the sins that you insist on committing and then begin to do good deeds....Fight for God as He deserves it!

Source: From *Islam from the Prophet Muhammad to the Capture of Constantinople*, ed. and trans. by Bernard Lewis, Vol. II *Religion and Society* (1987). By permission of Oxford University Press. Copyright © 1974 by Bernard Lewis.

For Discussion

1. Both sides see holy war as defensive. Are there differences in how the Christians and Muslims justify holy war?

2. What is more important in these appeals to war, serving God or defending co-religionists?

3. Since the Crusades, appeals for holy war have been a recurrent feature of relations between Muslims and Christians. How would you argue against the idea of holy war?

crusaders. First, the Arab states that controlled access to Jerusalem were already weakened from fighting the Seljuk Turks. Second, Muslims were divided internally. Theological divisions between Sunni and Shi'ite Muslims prevented the Muslim caliphs from uniting against the Christians.

In 1099, after a little more than a month's siege, the crusaders scaled the walls of Jerusalem and took possession of the city, which was also holy to Muslims and Jews and largely inhabited by them. The triumph of the First Crusade led to the establishment of the Latin principalities, which were devoted to maintaining a Western foothold in the Holy Land. The Latin principalities included all of the territory in contemporary Lebanon, Israel, and Palestine.

The subsequent crusades never achieved the success of the first. In 1144 Muslims captured the northernmost Latin principality, the county of Edessa—a warning to Westerners of the fragility of a defensive system that relied

Jco ut le nef ouerr · t eftes vous vn cheoual blaunch · al ge ster sur as auoun
leaux · t uerreis · t il uige en dreiture · t se combar · ces oils sunt austcome

JESUS CHRIST LEADING THE CRUSADERS

The rider on the white horse is Jesus, who holds the Gospels in his right hand and the sword of righteousness in his teeth. The crusading knights bearing banners and shields emblazoned with the cross follow him. The figure in the upper left-hand corner represents St. John the Evangelist, whose writings were understood to prophesy the Crusades. This manuscript illumination dates from ca. 1310–1325.

on a few scattered fortresses strung along a thin strip of coastline. In response to the loss of Edessa, Christians launched the Second Crusade (1147–1149). This ambitious offensive on several fronts failed in the East where the crusaders gained little ground. In the West, however, it was a great success because northern European crusaders helped the King of Portugal retake Lisbon from the Muslims. In 1187, the sultan of Egypt and Syria, Saladin (1137–1193), recaptured Jerusalem for Islam.

In response to this dispiriting loss, the Third Crusade (1189–1192) assembled the most spectacular army of European chivalry ever seen, led by Europe's three most powerful kings: German emperor Frederick Barbarossa, Philip Augustus of France, and Richard the Lion-Heart of England. Yet the Third Crusade's results were far from spectacular: After Frederick drowned wading in a river en route and Philip went home, Richard the Lion-Heart negotiated a truce with Saladin.

KRAK DES CHEVALIERS

This crusader castle survives in northern Syria in what was once the County of Edessa, a Latin Christian principality constructed to defend the Holy Land. The word *krak* derives from an Arabic word meaning "strong fort."

Source: Dagli Orti/Picture Desk, Inc./Kobal Collection

In 1199, Pope Innocent III called for the Fourth Crusade with the goal of recapturing Jerusalem. However, the Frankish knights and Venetian fleet diverted to intervene in a disputed imperial succession in Byzantium. Rather than fighting Muslims, Christian knights fought fellow Christians. In 1204 they besieged and captured Constantinople. The Westerners then divided the Byzantine Empire, set up a Latin regime that lasted until 1261, and neglected their oaths to reconquer Jerusalem. The Fourth Crusade dangerously weakened the Byzantine Empire by making it a prize for Western adventurers. None of the subsequent Crusades achieved lasting success in the Middle East. (See *Encounters and Transformations* in this chapter.)

The Significance of the Crusades

Despite the capture of Jerusalem during the First Crusade, the crusaders could not maintain control of the city. For more than two centuries, they wasted enormous efforts on what proved to be a futile enterprise. Neither did any of the Latin principalities in the Middle East survive for more than two centuries. The crusaders who resided in these principalities were obliged to learn how to live and trade with their Muslim neighbors, but few of them learned Arabic or took seriously Muslim learning. The strongest Islamic cultural and intellectual influences on Christian Europe came through Sicily and Spain rather than via returning crusaders.

ENCOUNTERS AND TRANSFORMATIONS

Legends of the Borderlands: Roland and El Cid

From the eighth to the fifteenth centuries, Muslim and Latin Christian armies grappled with one another in the borderlands between their two civilizations in the Iberian peninsula, the territory now called Spain. The borderlands, however, were more than just places of conflict. During times of peace, Christians and Muslims traded with and even married one another, and in the confused loyalties typical of the times, soldiers and generals from both faiths frequently switched sides. These borderland clashes produced legends of great heroes, which once refashioned into epic poems created a lasting memory of Muslim and Christian animosity.

The Song of Roland, an Old French epic poem that dates from around 1100, tells a story about the Battle of Roncesvalles, which took place in 779. The actual historical battle had been a minor skirmish between Charlemagne's armies and some local inhabitants in Spain who were not Muslims at all, but *The Song of Roland* transformed this sordid episode into a great epic of Christian-Muslim conflict. In the climax of the poem, the Christian hero Roland, seeking renown for his valor, rejected his companion Oliver's advice to blow a horn to alert Charlemagne of a Muslim attack. The battle was hopeless; when the horn was finally sounded it was too late to save Roland or Oliver. Roland's recklessness made him the model of a brave Christian knight.

In the subsequent Spanish border wars, the most renowned soldier was Rodrigo Díaz de Vivar (ca. 1043–1099), known to history as El Cid (from the Arabic word for "lord"). He is remembered in legend as a heroic knight fighting for the Christian Reconquest of the peninsula, but the real story of El Cid was much more self-serving. El Cid repeatedly switched allegiances to the Muslims. Even when a major Muslim invasion from North Africa threatened the very existence of Christian Spain, El Cid did not come to the rescue and instead undertook a private adventure to carve out a kingdom for himself in Muslim Valencia.

Soon after El Cid's death and despite his inconstant loyalty to Castile and Christianity, he was elevated to the status of the great hero of Christian Spain. The popularity of the twelfth-century epic poem, *The Poem of My Cid,* transformed this cruel, vindictive, and utterly self-interested man into a model of Christian virtue and self-sacrificing loyalty.

THE DEATH OF ROLAND

No legend from the borderlands between Christianity and Islam had a greater influence on European Christian society than that of Roland.

The medieval borderlands created legends of heroism and epic struggles that often stretched the truth. The borderlands were a wild frontier, not unlike the American frontier, into which desperate men fled to hide or to make opportunities for themselves. However, the lasting significance of the violent encounters that took place in these borderlands was not the nasty realities but the heroic models they produced. Poetry transformed reality into a higher truth that emphasized courage and faithfulness. Because these poems were memorized and recited in the vernacular languages of Old French and Castilian (now Spanish), they became a model of aristocratic values in medieval society and over the centuries a source for a national literary culture. Thus, becoming French or Spanish meant, in some respects, rejecting Islam, which has created a lasting anti-Muslim strain in western European culture.

For Discussion

How did transforming the accounts of battles between Christian and Muslims into heroic poems change how these events would be remembered among Christians?

The most important immediate consequence of the Crusades was not the tenuous Western possession of the Holy Land, but the expansion of trade and economic contacts the expeditions facilitated. No one profited more from the Crusades than the Italian cities that provided transportation and supplies to the crusading armies. The Crusades helped transform Genoa, Pisa, and Venice from small ports of regional significance into hubs of international trade. Genoa and Venice established their own colonial outposts in the eastern Mediterranean, and both vied to monopolize the rich commerce of Byzantium. The new trade controlled by these cities included luxury goods such as silk, Persian carpets, medicine, and spices—all expensive, exotic consumer goods found in the bazaars of the Middle East. Profits from this trade helped galvanize the economy of western Europe, leading to an era of exuberant economic growth during the twelfth and thirteenth centuries.

The crusading ideal survived long after Europeans quit going on actual Crusades. When Columbus sailed west in 1492, he imagined he was engaged in a kind of Crusade to spread

CHRONOLOGY: THE CRUSADES

1071	Battle of Manzikert; Seljuk Turks defeat the Byzantine emperor
1095	Council of Clermont; Urban II calls First Crusade
1095–1099	First Crusade
1099	Christians capture Jerusalem
1147–1149	Second Crusade
1189–1192	Third Crusade, led by Emperor Frederick Barbarossa (who drowned), King Philip II of France, and King Richard the Lion-Heart of England
1202–1204	Fourth Crusade, culminates in capture of Constantinople by Western crusaders

Christianity. Even as late as the twentieth century, some Latin American countries continued to collect a tax to finance crusades.

CONCLUSION

An Emerging Unity in the Latin West

The most lasting legacy of the Early Middle Ages was the distinction between western and eastern Europe, established by the patterns of conversion to Christianity. Slavs in eastern Europe, such as the Poles, who were converted to Latin Christianity looked to Rome as a source for inspiration and eventually considered themselves part of the West. Those who converted to Orthodox Christianity, such as the Bulgarians and Russians, remained Europeans certainly but came to see themselves as culturally distinct from their Western counterparts. The southern border of Christian Europe was defined by the presence of the Islamic caliphates, which, despite recurrent border wars with Christian kingdoms, greatly contributed to the cultural vitality of the West during this period.

During this same period, however, a tentative unity began to emerge among western European Christians, just as Byzantium fell into decline and Islam divided among competing caliphates. That ephemeral unity was born in the hero worship of Charlemagne and the resurrection of the Roman Empire in the West, symbolized by his coronation in Rome. The collapse of the Carolingian Empire created the basis for the European kingdoms that dominated the political order of Europe for most of the subsequent millennium. These new kingdoms were each quite distinctive, and yet they shared a heritage from ancient Rome and the Carolingians that emphasized the power of the law on the one hand and the intimate relationship between royal and ecclesiastical authority on the other. The most distinguishing mark of western Europe became the practice of Latin Christianity, a distinctive form of Christianity identifiable by the use of the Latin language and the celebration of the church liturgy in Latin.

In the wake of the Carolingian Empire, a system of personal loyalties associated with lordship and vassalage came to dominate the military and political life of Latin Christendom. All medieval kings were obliged to build their monarchies on the social foundations of lordship, which provided cohesion in kingdoms that lacked bureaucracies and sufficient numbers of trained officials. In addition to the lords and vassals, the Latin kingdoms relied on the support of the Church to provide unity and often to provide the services of local government. By the end of the eleventh century, emerging western Europe had recovered sufficiently from the many destructive invaders and had built new political and ecclesiastical institutions that enabled it to assert itself on a broader stage.

KEY TERMS

liturgy	canon law
clans	lord
kin groups	vassals
wergild	fief
scriptorium	knight
counties	feudalism
marches	Ottonian Renaissance
Carolingian Renaissance	Crusades

CHAPTER QUESTIONS

1. How did Latin Christendom—the new kingdoms of western Europe—build on Rome's legal and governmental legacies and how did Christianity spread in these new kingdoms? (page 264)
2. How did the Carolingian Empire contribute to establishing a distinctive western European culture? (page 272)

3. After the collapse of the Carolingian Empire, how did the western kingdoms consolidate in the core of the European continent and how did Latin Christianity spread to its periphery? (page 278)

4. What were the causes and consequences of the Crusades? (page 288)

TAKING IT FURTHER

1. Why were the kingdoms of Latin Christendom usually so weak?

2. How did the Carolingian Empire rise above those weaknesses? Why did it eventually fall prey to them?

3. Was military conflict between Christians and Muslims inevitable in the Crusades?

✓•—⎡Practice on **MyHistoryLab**

10

Medieval Civilization: The Rise of Western Europe

■ Two Worlds: Manors and Cities ■ The Consolidation of
Roman Catholicism ■ Strengthening the Center of the West
■ Medieval Culture: The Search for Understanding

FRANCIS OF ASSISI (CA. 1182–1226) WAS THE SON OF A PROSPEROUS MERCHANT in a modest-sized town in central Italy. As a young man of 20, Francis joined the Assisi forces in a war with the nearby town of Perugia. Taken prisoner, he spent nearly a year in captivity. After his release he became seriously ill, the first of many painful illnesses that afflicted him throughout his life. During a journey to join another army, he had the first of his many visions or dreams that led him to give up fighting and to convert to a life of spirituality and service to others. Initially he searched about for what to do. He went on a pilgrimage to Rome as a beggar and, although lepers personally disgusted, him he gave them alms and kissed their hands as an act of charity and humility. Then, according to his earliest biographer, while praying in the dilapidated chapel of San Damiano outside the gates of Assisi, he received a direct command from the crucifix above the altar: "Go Francis, and repair my house which, as you see, is nearly in ruins."

At first, Francis understood this command literally and began to repair churches and chapels. To raise money he took some of the best cloth from his father's shop and rode off to a nearby town where he sold the cloth and the horse. Angered by the theft of cloth, his father denounced him to the town's authorities. When Francis refused the summons to court, his father had him brought to the bishop of Assisi for interrogation. Before his father could explain the situation to the bishop, Francis "without a word stripped off his clothing even removing his pants and gave them back to his father." Stark naked, Francis announced that he was switching his obedience from his earthly to his heavenly father. The astonished bishop gave him a cloak, but Francis renounced all family ties and worldly goods to live a life of complete poverty. Henceforth, he seemed to understand the command to "repair my house" as a metaphor for the entire Church, which he intended to serve in a new way.

Dressed in rags, Francis went about town begging for food, preaching repentance in the streets, and ministering to outcasts and lepers. Without training as a priest or license as a preacher, Francis at first seemed like a devout eccentric or even a dangerous heretic, but his rigorous imitation of Jesus began to attract like-minded followers. In 1210 Francis and twelve of his ragged brothers showed up in the opulent papal court of Pope Innocent III to request approval for a new religious order. A less discerning man than Innocent would have sent the strange band packing or thrown them in prison as a danger to established society, but Innocent was impressed by Francis's sincerity and his willingness to profess obedience to the pope. Innocent's provisional approval of the Franciscans was a brilliant stroke, in that it gave the papacy a way to manage the widespread enthusiasm for a life of spirituality and purity.

ST. FRANCIS RENOUNCES HIS WORLDLY GOODS

St. Francis stripped off all his clothing in the town square and renounced his worldly possessions, a spiritual act signifying his rejection of the material world. Francis's angry father, the figure in left center, has to be restrained to prevent him from striking his son with his clenched fist.

Source: Assisi, Upper Church of S. Francesco. Giotto and pupils, "St. Francis Renouncing his Earthly Possessions." Fresco c. 1295–1330. © Canali Photobank, Capriolo, Italy

The life of Francis of Assisi and the religious order he founded, the Friars Minor (Lesser Brothers), known as the Franciscans, epitomized the strengths and tensions of medieval Europe. Francis was a product of the newly prosperous towns of Europe, which began to grow at an unprecedented rate after about 1050. In the streets of towns such as Assisi that thrived on profits from the international cloth trade, the extremes of wealth and poverty were always on display. Rich merchants such as Francis's father lived in splendid comfort and financed an urban building boom that had not been seen in the West for more than a 1,000 years. The most lasting manifestations of that building boom were the vast new cathedrals, the pride of every medieval city. At the same time wretchedly poor people, many of them immigrants from the overpopulated countryside—starving and homeless—lined the steps into the great churches begging for alms. Francis abhorred the immorality of this contrast between

wealth and poverty. His reaction was to reject all forms of wealth, to give away all his possessions, and to disdain money as poison. He and his followers devoted themselves to the poor and abandoned. They became traveling street preachers who relied entirely on the charity of others for food and shelter. Francis's rejection of the material world was not just a protest against the materialist values of his times. It was a total denial of the self, or to put it in modern terms, a rejection of all forms of egotism and pride, combined with a revolutionary commitment to equality.

The late eleventh through thirteenth centuries were revolutionary in other ways. Based on the efforts of the knights who fought in the Crusades, the European merchants, and the great theologians of the Church, the Catholic West began to assert itself militarily, economically, and intellectually both in Byzantium and against the Muslim world. As a result, western Europeans more sharply distinguished themselves from the Orthodox and Muslim worlds. The West became more exclusively Latin and Catholic.

Internal developments within Europe made possible this consolidation of a distinctive Western identity and projection of Western power outside Europe. The agricultural revolution that began in the eleventh century stimulated population growth and urbanization. Fed by more productive farms, the expanding cities began to produce industrial goods, such as woolen cloth, that could be sold abroad in exchange for luxury goods from the Middle East and Asia. A number of vigorous kings created political stability in the West by consolidating their authority through financial and judicial bureaucracies. The most effective of these kings used a variety of strategies to force the most dangerous element in society, the landed aristocrats, to serve the royal interest. At the same time, the West experienced a period of creative ferment unequaled since antiquity. The Roman Catholic Church played a central role in encouraging intellectual and artistic activity, but there was also a flourishing literature in the vernacular languages such as French, German, and Italian. All these developments led to this question: How did western European civilization mature during the eleventh through thirteenth centuries?

TWO WORLDS: MANORS AND CITIES

■ How was medieval western European economy and society organized around manors and cities?

After the end of the destructive Magyar and Viking invasions of the ninth and tenth centuries, the population of western Europe recovered dramatically. Technological innovations created the **agricultural revolution** that increased the supply of food. With more food available, people were better nourished than they had been in more than 500 years, and the population began to grow. In the seventh century all of Europe was home to only 14 million inhabitants. By 1300 the population had exploded to 74 million. From the seventh to the fourteenth centuries, then, the population grew many times over, perhaps as much as 500 percent.

The Medieval Agricultural Revolution

In the year 1000, the vast majority of people lived in small villages or isolated farmsteads. Peasants literally scratched out a living from a small area of cleared land around the village by employing a light scratch plow that barely turned over the soil. The farms produced mostly grain, which was consumed as bread, porridge, and ale or beer. Vegetables were rare; meat and fish, uncommon. Over the course of the century, the productivity of the land was greatly enhanced by a number of innovations that came into widespread use.

TECHNOLOGICAL INNOVATIONS The invention of new labor-saving devices ushered in the agricultural revolution. Farmers used water and windmills to grind grain, but others gradually adapted them to a wide variety of tasks, including turning saws to mill timber. In addition to these mechanical devices, the power of animals began to be used more efficiently. Metal horseshoes (until then, horses' hooves had been bound in cloth) gave horses better footing and traction. Perhaps even more important was the introduction of a new type of horse and ox collar. Older collars put pressure on the throat, which tended to choke the animal. The new collars transferred the pressure to the shoulders. With enhanced animal pulling power, farmers could plow the damp, heavy clay soils of northern Europe much more efficiently.

The centerpiece of the agricultural revolution was the heavy plow, called the *carruca*. It cut deeply and lifted the soil, aerating it and bringing minerals to the surface vital for plant growth. The *carruca*, however, required six or eight horses or oxen to pull it, and no single peasant family in the eleventh century could afford that many draft animals. Farmers had to pool their animals to create plow teams, a practice that required mutual planning and cooperation.

The introduction of the three-field system supplied the final piece in the agricultural revolution. In the three-field system farmers planted one field in the fall with grain and one in the spring with beans, peas, or lentils. The third field lay fallow. They harvested both fall and spring plantings in the summer, after which all the fields shifted. The

A HEAVY *CARRUCA* PLOW

At the center of the two-wheeled plow is a sturdy timber from which the coulter projects just in front of the plowshare, which is hidden by the earth.

created village councils and developed habits of collective decision making that were essential for stable community life. Second, the system produced not only more food, but better food. Beans and other vegetables grown in the spring planting were rich in proteins.

MANORS AND PEASANTS   The medieval agricultural economy bound landlords and peasants together in a unit of management called the **manor.** The lord of the manor usually owned his own large house or stone castle and served as the presiding judge of the villagers in the manor court.

The peasants who worked the land of manors fell into three categories: serfs, freeholders, and cottagers. Lords did not own **serfs,** who were not slaves, but lords tied their serfs to the manor, which they could not leave. Serfs had certain legal rights denied slaves, such as the right to a certain portion of what they produced, but the lord's will was law. Freeholders worked as independent farmers, owned their land outright, and did not have to answer to a lord. At the bottom of rural peasant society struggled numerous impoverished cottagers who had no rights to the land and farmed small, less desirable plots, often as squatters.

No matter what their official status, each family worked the land together with all family members performing tasks suitable to their abilities, strength, and age. The rigors of medieval farm labor did not permit a fastidious division of labor between women and men. Women did not usually drive the heavy plow, but they toiled at other physically demanding tasks. During the critical harvest times, women and children worked alongside men from dawn to dusk. Young girls typically worked as gleaners, picking up the stalks and kernels that the male harvesters dropped or left behind, and girls took responsibility for weeding and cleaning the fields.

three-field system produced extraordinary advantages: the amount of land under cultivation increased; beans planted in the spring rotation returned nitrogen to the soil; and the crop rotation combined with animal manure reduced soil exhaustion from excessive grain planting.

The agricultural revolution had a significant effect on society. First, villagers learned to cooperate—by pooling draft animals for plow teams, redesigning and elongating their fields to accommodate the new plow, coordinating the three-field rotation of crops, and timing the harvest schedule. To accomplish these cooperative ventures, they

THE GREAT MIGRATIONS AND THE HUNGER FOR LAND   After the eleventh century most peasant families were considerably better off than their ancestors had been before the new technological innovations. Due to the agricultural revolution, nutritional levels improved so that famines

TWELFTH-CENTURY MANOR MADE POSSIBLE BY THE HEAVY PLOW
Aerial photograph of the manor of West Whelpington North (England), which was settled in the twelfth century, but whose inhabitants died out during the Black Death of the fourteenth century (see Chapter 11). Outlines of the individual families' farm gardens can be seen in the left center. On the lower right are the ridges and furrows of the elongated fields required by the use of the heavy plow.

decreased, and a "baby boom" led to dramatic population growth.

The effect of the baby boom meant that the amount of land available to farm was insufficient to support the expanding population of the manors. As more and more young people entered the workforce, they either sought opportunities in the cities or searched for land of their own. Both options meant that many young people and whole families had to migrate. The modern phenomenon of mass immigration is hardly new.

Where did all these people go? Migrants seeking to clear new lands for agriculture moved in three directions: Germans into lands of the Slavic tribes to the east, Scandinavians to the far north and the North Atlantic islands, and Christian Spaniards to the south into previously Muslim territories on the Iberian peninsula, slowly creating the outlines of what would become modern Spain. Between 1100 and 1300, these migrants brought as much as 40 percent more land under cultivation in Europe. The vibrant civilization discussed in the rest of this chapter was the direct consequence of the European demographic success.

The Growth of Cities

All across Europe during the twelfth and thirteenth centuries cities exploded in size. Exact population figures are difficult to determine, and by our own modern standards most of these cities were modest in size—numbering in the tens of thousands rather than hundreds of thousands—but there is ample evidence of stunning growth. Between 1160 and 1300 Ghent expanded its city walls five times to accommodate all its inhabitants. During the thirteenth century the population of Florence grew by an estimated 640 percent.

THE CHALLENGE OF FREE CITIES The newly thriving cities proved troublesome for the lords, bishops, and kings who had legal authority over them. As the population grew and urban merchants, such as Francis of Assisi's father, became increasingly rich, the cities in which they lived enjoyed even greater resources in people and money than those available to the rural lords. In many places the citizens of the new enlarged towns attempted to rid themselves of their lords to establish self-rule or, at least, substantial autonomy for their city. In the cities of north-central Italy, for example, townsmen formed sworn defensive associations called **communes** (from *communis* meaning "shared"), which quickly became the effective government of the towns. The communes evolved into city-states, which seized control of the surrounding countryside. Perhaps as many as 100 or more cities in north-central Italy formed communes after 1070.

The Italian communes created the institutions and culture of self-rule. They were not fully democratic, but, nevertheless, in many of them a significant percentage of the male population, including artisans, could vote for public officials, hold office themselves, and have a voice in important decisions such as going to war or raising new taxes. They also emphasized the civic responsibilities of citizens to protect the weakest members of the community, to beautify the city with public buildings and monuments, and to defend it by serving in the militia and paying taxes. These cities created vital community institutions, some of which survive to this day. In the wake of the Crusades several north Italian communes, especially Venice, Genoa, and Pisa,

A MEDIEVAL TOWN

Painted on the wall of the city council chambers in Siena, Italy, this fresco from 1338–1339 depicts how a well-governed medieval town should look. Workers repair buildings, merchants bring goods into the bustling city, and the streets are so safe that young women dance in the streets on their way to a wedding.

became ports of international significance. Sailors from these cities had transported the crusading knights to the Holy Land, Egypt, Syria, and Byzantium. Even after the crusader kingdoms collapsed, these cities kept footholds in the eastern Mediterranean, some of which evolved into colonies. Through these trading cities western Europe became integrated into the international luxury trade, which they carried out with ships crisscrossing the Mediterranean Sea.

THE ECONOMIC BOOM YEARS The cities of the medieval West thrived on an economic base of unprecedented prosperity. What made possible the twelfth- and thirteenth-century economic boom? Four related factors explain the thriving medieval economy. We have already touched on the first two reasons: the agricultural revolution of the eleventh century, which enabled population growth; and the expansion of cities, which both facilitated the commercial boom and allowed city dwellers to be the primary beneficiaries of it.

The other two reasons were just as important: advances in transportation networks and the creation of new business techniques. Trade in grain, woolen cloth, and other bulk goods depended on the use of relatively cheap water transportation for hauling goods. Where there were neither seaports nor navigable rivers, drovers hauled goods cross-country by pack train, a very expensive enterprise. In Europe there were no land transportation routes or pack animals that rivaled the efficiency of the camel in the deserts of North Africa and the steppes of Asia. To address the problem and to facilitate transportation and trade, governments and local lords built new roads and bridges and repaired old Roman roads that had been neglected for 1,000 years.

The most lucrative trade was the international commerce in luxury goods. Because these goods were lightweight and high-priced, they could sustain the cost of long-distance transportation across land. Italian merchants virtually monopolized the European luxury trade. Camel caravans transported raw silk from China and Turkestan across Asia. Merchants sold the silk at trading posts on the shores of the Black Sea and in Constantinople

to Italian merchants who shipped the goods across the Mediterranean, had the raw silk woven into cloth, and then earned enormous profits selling the shimmering fabrics to the ladies and gentlemen of the European aristocracy. Though small in quantity, the silk trade was of great value to international commerce because silk was so highly prized. One ounce of fine Chinese black silk sold on the London market for as much as a highly skilled mason would earn in a week's labor. Even the bulk commodities the Italians brought from the East were valuable enough to sustain the high transportation costs. Known by the generic term "spices," these included hundreds of exotic items: True spices such as pepper, sugar, cloves, nutmeg, ginger, saffron, mace, and cinnamon enhanced the otherwise bland cuisine; for dyeing cloth, blue came from indigo and red from madder root; for fixing the dyes the Genoese imported alum; and for pain relievers were medicinal herbs including opiates. The profits from spices generated much of the capital in European financial markets.

Long-distance trade necessitated the creation of new business techniques. For example, the expansion of trade and new markets required a moneyed economy. Coins had almost disappeared in the West for nearly 400 years during the Early Middle Ages, when most people lived self-sufficiently on manors and bartered for what they could not produce for themselves. The few coins that circulated came from Byzantium or the Muslim caliphates. By the thirteenth century, Venice and Florence minted their own gold coins, which became the medium for exchange across much of Europe.

Merchants who engaged in long-distance trade invented the essential business tools of capitalism during this period. They created business partnerships, uniform accounting practices, merchants' courts to enforce contracts and resolve disputes, letters of credit (used like modern bankers' checks), bank deposits and loans, and insurance policies. The Italian cities established primary schools to train merchants' sons to write business letters and keep accounts—a sign of the growing professional character of business. Two centuries earlier an international merchant had been an itinerant peddler who led pack trains over dusty and muddy tracks to customers in small villages and castles. But by the end of the thirteenth century an international merchant could stay at home behind a desk, writing letters to business partners and ship captains and enjoying the profits from his labors in the bustling atmosphere of a thriving city.

At the center of the European market were the Champagne fairs in France, where merchants from northern and southern Europe met every summer to bargain and haggle (see **Map 10.1**). The Italians exchanged their silk and spices for English raw wool, Dutch woolen cloth, German furs and linens, and Spanish leather. From the Champagne fairs, prosperity spread into previously wild parts of Europe. Cities along the German rivers and the Baltic coast thrived through the trade of raw materials such as timber and iron, livestock, salt fish, and hides. The most prominent of the north German towns was Lübeck, which became the center of the Hanseatic League, a loose trade association of cities in Germany and the Baltic coast. Never achieving the level of a unified government, the league nonetheless provided its members mutual

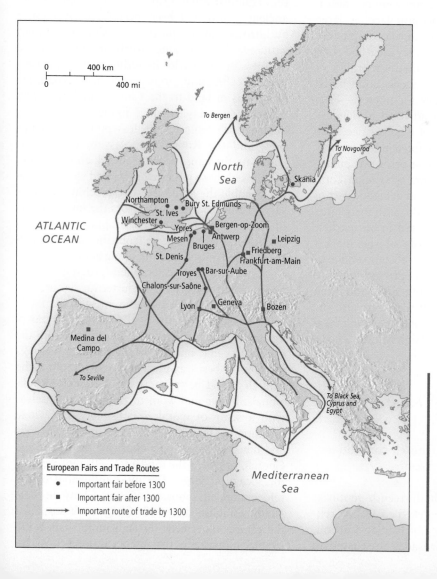

MAP 10.1

European Fairs and Trade Routes

Trade routes crisscrossed the Mediterranean Sea and hugged the Atlantic Ocean, North Sea, and Baltic Sea coastlines. Land routes converged in central France at the Champagne fairs. Other trade routes led to the large market cities in Germany and Flanders.

security and trading monopolies—necessary because of the weakness of the German imperial government.

Urban civilization, one of the major achievements of the Middle Ages, thrived from the commerce of the economic boom. From urban civilization came other achievements. All the cities built large new cathedrals to flaunt their accumulated wealth and to honor God. New educational institutions, especially universities, trained the sons of the urban, commercial elite in the professions. However, the merchants who commanded the urban economy were not necessarily society's heroes. The populace at large viewed them with deep ambivalence, despite the immeasurable ways in which they enriched society. Churchmen worried about the morality of making profits. Church councils condemned usury—the lending of money for interest—even though papal finances depended on it. Theologians promulgated the idea of a "just price," the idea that there should be a fixed price for any particular commodity. The just price was anathema to hardheaded merchants who were committed to the laws of supply and demand. Part of the ambivalence toward trade and merchants came from the inequities created in all market-based economies—the rewards of the market were unevenly distributed, both socially and geographically, as St. Francis's protest demonstrated. The prosperous merchants symbolized disturbing social changes, but they were also the dynamic force that made possible the intellectual and artistic flowering of the High Middle Ages.

THE CONSOLIDATION OF ROMAN CATHOLICISM

■ How did the Catholic Church consolidate its hold over the Latin West?

The late eleventh through thirteenth centuries witnessed one of the greatest periods of religious vitality in the history of Roman Catholicism. Manifest by the Crusades (discussed in Chapter 9), the rise of new religious orders, remarkable intellectual creativity, and the final triumph over the surviving polytheistic tribes of northern and eastern Europe, the religious vitality of the era was due in no small part to the effective leadership of a series of able popes. They gave the Church the benefits of the most advanced, centralized government in Europe.

The Task of Church Reform

As the bishops of the Church accepted many of the administrative responsibilities that in the ancient world had been performed by secular authorities, their spiritual mission sometimes suffered. They became overly involved in the business of the world. In addition, over the centuries wealthy and pious people had made large donations of land to the Church, making many monasteries, in particular, immensely wealthy. Such wealth tempted the less pious to corruption, and the Roman popes were unlikely to eliminate the temptations from which they benefited. Even those popes who wanted to were slow to assemble the administrative machinery necessary to enforce their will across the unruly lands of Roman Catholicism. The impulse for reform derived in many respects from the material success of the Church and the monasteries.

The slow but determined progress of the popes from the eleventh to thirteenth centuries to enforce moral reform is the most remarkable achievement of the medieval papacy. The movement for reform, however, did not begin with the popes. It came out of the monasteries. Monks thought the best way to clean up corruption in the Church would be to improve the morals of individuals. If men and women conducted themselves with a sense of moral responsibility, the whole institution of the Church could be purified. Monks and nuns, who set an example for the rest of the Church, provided the model for self-improvement for society at large. The most influential of the reform-minded monasteries was **Cluny** in Burgundy, established in 910. Cluny itself sustained the reform movement through more than 1,500 Cluniac monasteries throughout Europe.

From the very beginning Cluny was exceptional for several reasons. First, its aristocratic founder offered the monastery as a gift to the pope. As a result, the pope directed the activities of the Cluny monastery from Rome and kept it independent from local political pressures, which so often caused corruption. The Rome connection positioned Cluniacs to assist in reforming the papacy itself. Second, the various abbots who headed Cluny over the years closely coordinated reform activities of the various monasteries in the Cluniac system. Some of these abbots were men of exceptional ability and learning who had a European-wide reputation for their moral stature. Third, Cluny regulated the life of monks much more closely than did other monasteries, so the monks there were models of devotion. To the Cluniacs moral purity required complete renunciation of the benefits of the material world and a commitment to spiritual experiences. The elegantly simple liturgy in which the monks themselves sung the text of the mass and other prayers symbolized Cluniac purity. The beauty of the music enhanced the spiritual experience, and its simplicity clarified rather than obscured the meaning of the words. Because of these attractive traits, the Cluniac liturgy spread to the far corners of Europe.

The success of Cluny and other reformed monasteries provided the base from which reform ideas spread beyond the isolated world of monks to the rest of the Church. The first candidates for reform were parish priests and bishops. Called the *secular clergy* (in Latin *saeculum,* meaning "secular") because they lived in the secular world, they differed from the regular clergy (in Latin *regula,* those who followed a "rule") who lived in monasteries apart from the world. The lives of many secular clergy differed little from their lay neighbors. (*Laypeople* or *the laity* referred to all Christians who had not taken religious vows to become a priest, monk, or nun.) In contrast to celibate monks, who were sexually chaste, many priests kept concubines or were married and tried to bequeath church property to their children. In contrast to the Orthodox Church, in which priests were allowed to marry, the Catholic Church had repeatedly forbidden married priests, but the prohibitions had been ineffective until Cluniac reform stressed the ideal of the sexually pure priest. During the eleventh century bishops, church councils, and reformist popes began to insist on a celibate clergy.

The clerical reform movement also tried to eliminate the corrupt practices of simony and lay investiture. **Simony** was the practice of buying and selling church offices. **Lay investiture** took place when aristocrats, kings, or emperors installed churchmen and gave them their symbols of office ("invested" them). Through this practice, powerful lords controlled the clergy and usurped the property of the Church. In exchange for protecting the Church, these laymen conceived of church offices as a form of vassalage and expected to name their own candidates as priests and bishops. The reformers saw as sinful any form of lay authority over the Church—whether the authority was that of the local lord or the emperor himself. As a result of this controversy, the most troublesome issue of the eleventh century became establishing the boundaries between temporal and spiritual authorities.

THE POPE BECOMES A MONARCH   Religious reform required unity within the Church. The most important step in building unity was to define what it meant to be a Catholic. In the Middle Ages, Roman Catholicism identified itself in two ways. First, the Church insisted on conformity in rites. Rites consisted of the forms of public worship called the liturgy, which included certain prescribed prayers and chants, usually in Latin. Uniform rites meant that Catholics could hear the Mass celebrated in essentially the same way everywhere from Poland to Portugal, Iceland to Croatia. Conformity of worship created a cultural unity that transcended differences in language and ethnicity. When Catholics from far-flung locales encountered one another, they shared something meaningful to them all because of the uniformity of rites. The second thing that defined a Catholic was obedience to the pope. Ritual uniformity and obedience to the pope were closely interrelated because both the ritual and the pope were Roman. There were many bishops in Christianity, but as one monk put it, "Rome is…the head of the world."

Beginning in the late eleventh century the task of the popes became to make this theoretical assertion of obedience real—in short, to make the papacy a religious monarchy. Among the reformers who gathered in Rome was Hildebrand (ca. 1020–1085), one of the most remarkable figures in the history of the Church, a man beloved as saintly by his admirers and considered an ambitious, self-serving megalomaniac by many others. From 1055 to 1073 during the pontificates of some four popes, Hildebrand became the power behind the throne, helping enact wide-ranging reforms that enforced uniformity of worship and establishing the rules for electing new popes by the college of cardinals. In 1073 the cardinals elected Hildebrand himself pope, and he took the name Gregory VII (r. 1073–1085).

Gregory's greatness lay in his leadership over the internal reform of the Church. Every year he held a Church council in Rome where he decreed against simony and married priests. Gregory centralized authority over the Church itself by sending out papal legates, representatives who delivered orders to local bishops. He attempted to free the Church from external influence by asserting the superiority of the pope over all other authorities. Gregory's theory of papal supremacy led him into direct conflict with the German emperor, Henry IV (r. 1056–1106). The issue was lay investiture. During the eighth and ninth centuries weak popes relied on the Carolingian kings and emperors to name suitable candidates for ecclesiastical offices in order to keep them out of the hands of local aristocrats. At stake was not only power and authority, but also the income from the enormous amount of property controlled by the Church, which the emperor was in the best position to protect. During the eleventh century, Gregory VII and other reform-minded popes sought to regain control of this property. Without the ability to name his own candidates as bishops, Gregory recognized that his whole campaign for church reform would falter. When Pope Gregory tried to negotiate with the emperor over the appointment of the bishop of Milan,

Henry resisted and commanded Gregory to resign the papacy in a letter with the notorious salutation, "Henry, King not by usurpation, but by the pious ordination of God to Hildebrand now not Pope but false monk."

Gregory struck back in an escalating confrontation now known as the **Investiture Controversy.** He deposed Henry from the imperial throne and excommunicated him. **Excommunication** prohibited the sinner from participating in the sacraments and forbade any social contact whatsoever with the surrounding community. People caught talking to an excommunicated person or writing a letter or even offering a drink of water could themselves be excommunicated. Excommunication was a form of social death, a dire punishment indeed, especially if the excommunicated person were a king. Both sides marshaled arguments from Scripture and history, but the excommunication was effective. Henry's friends started to abandon him, rebellion broke out in Germany, and the most powerful German lords called for a meeting to elect a new emperor. Backed into a corner, Henry plotted a clever counterstroke.

Early in the winter of 1077 Pope Gregory set out to cross the Alps to meet with the German lords. When Gregory reached the Alpine passes, however, he learned that Emperor Henry was on his way to Italy. In fear of what the emperor would do, Gregory retreated to the castle of Canossa, where he expected to be attacked. Henry surprised Gregory, however, by arriving not with an army, but as a supplicant asking the pope to hear his confession. As a priest Gregory could hardly refuse to hear the confession of a penitent sinner, but he nevertheless attempted to humiliate Henry by making him wait for three days, kneeling in the snow outside the castle. Henry's presentation of himself as a penitent sinner posed a dilemma for Gregory. The German lords were waiting for Gregory to appear in his capacity as the chief justice of Christendom to judge Henry, but Henry himself was asking the pope to act in his capacity as priest to grant absolution for sin. The priest in Gregory won out over the judge, and he absolved Henry.

Even after the deaths of Gregory and Henry, the Investiture Controversy continued to poison relations between the popes and emperors until the Concordat of Worms in 1122 resolved the issue in a formal treaty. The emperor retained the right to nominate high churchmen, but in a concession to the papacy, the emperor lost the ceremonial privileges of investiture that conveyed spiritual authority. Without the ceremony of investiture, no bishop could exercise his office. By refusing to invest unsuitable nominees, the popes had the last word. Gregory VII's vision of papal supremacy over all kings and emperors persevered.

HOW THE POPES RULED The most lasting accomplishment of the popes during the twelfth and thirteenth centuries derived less from dramatic confrontations with emperors than from the humdrum routine of the law. Beginning with Gregory VII, the papacy became the supreme court of the Catholic world by claiming authority over a vast range of issues. To justify these claims, Gregory and his assistants conducted massive research among old laws and treatises. These were organized into a body of legal texts called canon law.

Canon law came to encompass many kinds of cases, including all those involving the clergy, disputes about church property, and donations to the Church. The law of the Church also touched on many of the most vital concerns of the laity including annulling marriages, legitimating bastards, prosecuting bigamy, protecting widows and orphans, and resolving inheritance disputes. Most of the cases originated in the courts of the bishops, but the bishops' decisions could be appealed to the pope and cardinals sitting together in the papal consistory. The consistory could make exceptions from the letter of the law, called dispensations, giving it considerable power over kings and aristocrats who wanted to marry a cousin, divorce a wife, legitimate a bastard, or annul a will. By the middle of the twelfth century, Rome was awash with legal business. The functions of the canon law courts became so important that those elected popes were no longer monks but trained canon lawyers, men very capable in the ways of the world.

The pope also presided over the **curia,** the administrative bureaucracy of the Church.

The cardinals in the curia served as ministers in the papal administration and visited foreign princes and cities as ambassadors or legates. Because large amounts of revenue were flowing into the coffers of the Church, the curia functioned as a bank. Rome became the financial capital of the West.

In addition to its legal, administrative, and financial authority, the papacy also made use of two powerful spiritual weapons against the disobedient. Any Christian who refused to repent of a sin could be excommunicated, as the Emperor Henry IV had been. The second spiritual weapon was the **interdict,** the suspension of the sacraments in a locality or kingdom whose ruler had defied the pope. During an interdict the churches closed their doors, creating panic among the faithful who could not baptize their children or bury their dead. The interdict, which encouraged a public outcry, could be a very effective weapon for undermining the political support of any monarch who ran afoul of the pope.

THE PINNACLE OF THE MEDIEVAL PAPACY: POPE INNOCENT III The most capable of the medieval popes was Innocent III (r. 1198–1216). To him, the pope was the overlord of the entire world. He recognized the right of kings to rule over the secular sphere, but he considered it his duty to prevent and punish sin, a duty that gave him wide latitude to meddle in the affairs of kings and princes.

Innocent's first task was to provide the papacy with a strong territorial base of support so that the popes could act with the same freedom as kings and princes. Historians consider Innocent the founder of the Papal State in central Italy, an independent state that lasted until 1870 and survives today in a tiny fragment as Vatican City.

Innocent's second goal was keeping alive the crusading ideal. He called the Fourth Crusade, which went awry when the crusaders attacked Constantinople instead of conquering Jerusalem. He also expanded the definition of crusading by calling for a crusade to eliminate heresy within Christian Europe. Innocent was deeply concerned about the spread of new heresies, which attracted enormous numbers of converts, especially in the growing cities of southern Europe. By crusading against Christian heretics—the Cathars and Waldensians (see the following discussion)—Innocent authorized the use of military methods to enforce uniformity of belief.

The third objective was to assert the authority of the papacy over political affairs. Innocent managed the election of Emperor Frederick II. He also assumed the right to veto imperial elections. He excommunicated King Philip II of France to force him to take back an unwanted wife. And Innocent placed England under the interdict to compel King John to cede his kingdom to the

papacy and receive it back as a fief, a transaction that made the king of England the vassal of the pope. Using whatever means necessary, he made papal vassals of the rulers of Aragon, Bulgaria, Denmark, Hungary, Poland, Portugal, and Serbia. Through the use of the feudal law of vassalage, Innocent brought the papacy to its closest approximation of a universal Christian monarchy (see **Map 10.2**).

Innocent's fourth and greatest accomplishment was to codify the rites of the liturgy and to define the dogmas of the faith. This monumental task was the achievement of the Fourth Lateran Council, held in Rome in 1215. This council, attended by more than 400 bishops, 800 abbots,

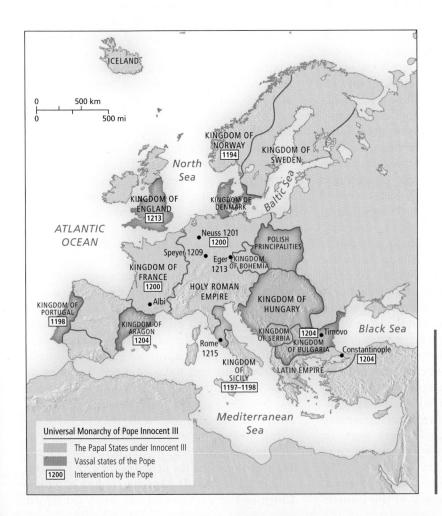

MAP 10.2

Universal Monarchy of Pope Innocent III

Besides his direct control of the Papal States in central Italy, Pope Innocent III made vassals of many of the kings of Catholic Europe. These feudal ties provided a legal foundation for his claim to be the highest authority in Christian Europe.

and the ambassadors of the monarchs of Catholic Europe, issued decrees that reinforced the celebration of the sacraments as the centerpiece of Christian life. They included rules to educate the clergy, define their qualifications, and govern elections of bishops. The council condemned heretical beliefs, and it called for yet another crusade. The council became the guidepost that has since governed many aspects of Catholic practice, especially with regard to the sacraments. It did more than any other council to fulfill the goal of uniformity of rites in Catholicism.

THE TROUBLED LEGACY OF THE PAPAL MONARCHY

Innocent was an astute, intelligent man who in single-minded fashion pursued the greater good of the Church as he saw it. No one succeeded better than he in preserving the unity of the Catholic world in an era of chaos. His policies, however, were less successful in the hands of his less able successors. Their blunders undermined the pope's spiritual mission. Innocent's successors went beyond defending the Papal State and embroiled all Italy in a series of bloody civil wars between the Guelfs, who supported the popes, and the Ghibellines, who opposed them. The pope's position as a monarch superior to all others collapsed under the weight of immense folly during the pontificate of Boniface VIII (r. 1294–1303). His claims to absolute authority combined with breathtaking vanity and ineptitude corroded the achievements of Innocent III.

In 1302 Boniface promulgated the most extreme theoretical assertion of papal superiority over lay rulers. The papal bull, *Unam Sanctum*, decreed that "it is absolutely necessary for salvation that every human creature be subject to the Roman pontiff." Behind the statement was a specific dispute with King Philip IV of France (r. 1285–1314), who was attempting to try a French bishop for treason. The larger issue behind the dispute was similar to the Investiture Controversy of the eleventh century, but this time no one paid much attention to the pope. The loss of papal moral authority had taken its toll. In the heat of the confrontation, King Philip accused Pope Boniface of heresy, one of the few sins of which he was not guilty, and sent his agents to arrest the pope who died shortly after. With Boniface the papal monarchy died as well.

THE RELIGIOUS OUTCASTS: CATHARS AND WALDENSIANS

In its efforts to defend the faith, the Church during the first half of the thirteenth century began to authorize bishops and other clerics to conduct inquisitions (formal inquiries) into specific instances of heresy or perceived heresy. The so-called heretics tended to be faithful people who sought personal purity in religion. During the thirteenth and early fourteenth centuries, inquisitions and systematic persecutions targeted the Cathars and Waldensians, who at first had lived peacefully with their Catholic neighbors and shared many of the same beliefs with them.

The name *Cathar* derives from the Greek word for purity. The Cathars were especially strong in northern Italy and southern France. Heavily concentrated around the French town of Albi, the Cathars were also known as Albigensians. They departed from Catholic doctrine, which held that God created the Earth, because they believed that an evil force had created all matter. To purify themselves, an elite few—known as "perfects"—rejected their own bodies as corrupt matter, refused to marry and procreate, and in extreme cases gradually starved themselves. These purified perfects provided a dramatic contrast to the more worldly Catholic clergy. For many, Catharism became a form of protest against the wealth and power of the Church. By the 1150s the Cathars had

CHRONOLOGY: THE PAPAL MONARCHY

1073–1085	Reign of Pope Gregory VII
1075–1122	The Investiture Controversy
1198–1216	Reign of Pope Innocent III
1215	Fourth Lateran Council
1294–1303	Reign of Pope Boniface VIII

organized their own churches, performed their own rituals, and even elected their own bishops. Where they became deeply rooted, as in the south of France, they practiced their faith openly until Pope Innocent III authorized a crusade against them.

The Waldensians were the followers of Peter Waldo (d. ca. 1184), a merchant of Lyons, France, who like Francis of Assisi had abandoned all his possessions and taken a vow of poverty. Desiring to imitate the life of Jesus and live in simple purity, the Waldensians preached and translated the Gospels into their own language so that laypeople who did not know Latin could understand them. At first the Waldensians' seemed similar to the Franciscans, but because of the Waldensians' failure to obtain licenses to preach as the Franciscans had done, they came to be depicted by Church authorities as heretics. In response, the Waldensians created an alternative church that became widespread in southern France, Rhineland Germany, and northern Italy.

Catholic authorities, who were often the objects of strong criticisms from the Cathars and Waldensians, grew ever more hostile to them. Bishops declared heretics liable to the same legal penalties as those guilty of treason, which authorized the political authorities to proceed against them. In 1208 Pope Innocent III called the Albigensian Crusade, the first of several holy wars launched against heretics in the south of France. The king of France was only too happy to fight the Albigensian Crusade because he saw it as a means of expanding royal power in a region of France where his authority was weak. To eradicate the remaining Cathars and Waldensians, several kings and popes initiated inquisitions. By the middle of the thirteenth century, Catholic authorities had either converted or exterminated the Cathars except for a few isolated pockets in the mountains. Inquisitorial campaigns nearly wiped out the Waldensians, but scattered groups have managed to survive to this day, mostly by retreating to the relative safety of

the high Alps and later to the Americas. (See *Justice in History* in this chapter.)

Discovering God in the World

Even before the First Crusade, Catholic Europe began to experience an unprecedented spiritual awakening. The eleventh-century papal campaign to reform the morals of the clergy helped make priests both more respectable and better educated. A better-educated clergy in turn educated the laity more effectively. In large numbers Catholic Christians began to internalize the teachings of the Church. The most devout were drawn to dedicating their lives to religion. In England, for example, the number of monks increased tenfold from the late eleventh century to 1200. The newly expanding cities built loyalty and encouraged peaceable behavior through the veneration of civic patron saints. The most vital indication of spiritual renewal was the success of new religious orders, which satisfied a widespread yearning to discover the hand of God in the world.

THE PATRON SAINTS   Saints are holy people whose moral perfection gives them a special relationship with the sacred. Ordinary Christians venerated saints to gain access to supernatural powers, protection, and intercession with God.

The relationship between Christian believers and the saints was profoundly intimate and intertwined with many aspects of life: Parents named their children after saints who became special protectors; every church dedicated itself to a saint; every town and city adopted a patron saint. And even entire peoples cherished a patron saint. For example, the Irish adopted Saint Patrick, who supposedly brought Christianity to the island.

A city gained protection from a patron saint by obtaining the saint's relics, the corpse or skeleton or part of the skeleton or some object associated with the saint. These relics, verified by miracles, served as contacts between Earth and Heaven. The belief in the miraculous powers of relics created an enormous demand for them in the thriving medieval cities. But because the remains of the martyrs and early saints of the church were spread across the Middle East and Mediterranean from Jerusalem to Rome, someone had first to discover the saint's relics and then transfer them to new homes in the churches of the growing western and northern European cities. Relics were bought or stolen, and there was ample room for fraud in passing off unauthentic bones to gullible buyers. During the Crusades the supply of relics greatly increased because the knights had access to the tombs of early Christian saints and martyrs.

During the twelfth and thirteenth centuries public veneration of saints began to undergo a subtle shift away from the cults of the local patron saints toward more universal figures such as Jesus and the Virgin Mary. The patron saints had functioned almost like the family deities of antiquity who served the particular needs of individuals and communities, but the papal monarchy encouraged uniformity throughout Catholicism.

Christians had always honored the Virgin Mary, but beginning in the twelfth century her immense popularity provided Catholics with a positive female image that contradicted the traditional misogyny and mistrust associated with Eve. Clerics and monks had long depicted

MOSAICS IN THE BASILICA OF ST. MARK IN VENICE

Pilgrims learned of Venice's intimate association with its patron St. Mark from the magnificent mosaics that adorned the basilica's ceilings and walls. This scene shows a miracle that occurred after St. Mark's body was lost during a fire in the basilica. After the leaders of Venice spent days in prayer, shown on the left, St. Mark opened a door in a column shown at the far right to reveal the place where his body was hidden. In between these two scenes, those who witnessed the miracle turn to one another in amazement. The leaders of Venice derived considerable prestige and political authority from their veneration of St. Mark.

women as deceitful and lustful in luring men to their moral ruin. In contrast, the veneration of the Virgin Mary promoted the image of a loving mother who would intervene with her son on behalf of sinners at the Last Judgment. Theologians still taught that the woman Eve had brought sin into the world, but the woman Mary offered help in escaping the consequences of sin.

The popularity of Mary was evident everywhere. The burgeoning cities of Europe dedicated most of the new cathedrals to her. Mary became a model with whom women could identify, presenting a positive image of femininity. In images of her suckling the Christ child, she became the perfect embodiment of the virtue of charity, the willingness to give without any expectation of reward. In contrast to the early Christian saints who were predominantly martyrs and missionaries, during the twelfth and thirteenth centuries saints exhibited sanctity more through nurturing others, especially by feeding the poor and healing the sick. Women embodied the capacity to nurture, and many more women became saints during this period than during the entire first millennium of Christianity. In 1100 fewer than 10 percent of all the saints were female. By 1300 the percentage had increased to 24 percent. During the fifteenth century about 30 percent were women.

THE TWO MARYS: THE MOTHER OF GOD AND THE REPENTANT PROSTITUTE

Medieval thinking about women began with the fundamental dichotomy between Eve, the symbol of women as they are, and Mary, the ideal to which all women strived. Eve brought sin and sex into the world through her disobedience to God. Mary, the Virgin Mother, kept her body inviolate. Into the gap between the two natures of women emerged Mary Magdalene, a repentant prostitute whose veneration reached a pinnacle in the twelfth century. In contrast to the perpetually virginal ideal of Mary, the mother of Christ, Magdalene offered the possibility of redemption to all women.

THE NEW RELIGIOUS ORDERS   By the eleventh century many men attracted to the religious life found the traditional orders too lax in their discipline and too worldly. In 1098 a small group of Benedictine monks removed themselves to an isolated wasteland to establish the Cistercian Order. The Cistercians practiced a very strict discipline. They ate only enough to stay alive. Each monk possessed only one robe. Unlike other orders, such as the Cluniacs, which required monks to attend frequent and lengthy services, the Cistercians spent more time in private prayer and manual labor. Their churches were bare of all decoration. Under the brilliant leadership of Bernard of Clairvaux (1090–1153), the Cistercians grew rapidly, as many men disillusioned with the sinful and materialistic society around them joined the new order. Bernard's asceticism led him to seek refuge from the affairs of the world, but he was also a religious reformer and activist, engaged with the important issues of his time. He even helped settle a disputed papal election and called for a crusade.

The Cistercians established their new monasteries in isolated, uninhabited places where they cleared forests and worked the land so that they could live in complete isolation from the troubled affairs of the world. Their hard work had an ironic result. By bringing new lands under the plow and by employing the latest technological innovations, such as water mills, many of the Cistercian monasteries produced more than was needed for the monks, and the sale of excess produce made the Cistercians rich. The economic success of the Cistercians helped them expand even more rapidly, especially into places previously untouched by monasticism in northeastern Europe. The rapid Cistercian push beyond the frontiers of Latin Europe helped disseminate the culture of Catholic Christianity through educating the local elites and attracting them to join the Cistercians. By recruiting lay brothers, known as *converses*, the Cistercians made important connections with the peasants.

More than a century after the foundation of the Cistercians in France, the Spaniard Dominic and the Italian Francis formulated a new kind of religious order composed of mendicant **friars**. From the very beginning the friars wanted to distinguish themselves from monks. As the opening of this chapter indicated, instead of working in a monastery to feed themselves as did the Cistercians, friars ("brothers") wandered from city to city and throughout the countryside begging for alms (*mendicare* means "to beg"; hence, *mendicant friars*). Unlike monks who remained in a cloister, friars tried to help ordinary laypeople with their problems by preaching and administering to the sick and poor.

The Spaniard Dominic (1170–1221) founded the Dominican Order to convert Muslims and Jews and to combat heresy among Christians against whom he began his preaching mission while traveling through southern France. The ever-perceptive Pope Innocent III recognized Dominic's talents while he was visiting Rome and gave his new order provisional approval. Dominic believed the task of conversion could be achieved through persuasion and argument. To hone the Dominicans' persuasive skills, they created the first multigrade, comprehensive educational system. It connected schools located in individual friaries with more advanced regional schools that offered specialized training in languages, philosophy, and especially theology. Most Dominican friars never studied at a university but enjoyed, nevertheless, a highly sophisticated education that made them exceptionally influential in European intellectual life. Famed for their preaching skills, Dominicans were equally successful in exciting the illiterate masses and debating sophisticated opponents.

The Franciscan Order enjoyed a similar success. Francis of Assisi (1182–1226), whose story opened this chapter, deeply influenced Clare of Assisi (1194–1253), who founded a parallel order for women, the Poor Clares. Like the Franciscans, she and her followers enjoyed the "privilege of perfect poverty," which forbade the ownership of any property even by the community itself.

Both the Dominican and Franciscan Orders spread rapidly. Whereas the successful Cistercians had founded 500 new houses in their first century, the Franciscans established more than 1,400 in their first 100 years. Liberated from the obligation to live in a monastery, the mendicant friars traveled wherever the pope ordered them, making them effective agents of the papal monarchy. They preached crusades. They pacified the poor. They converted heretics and non-Christians through their inspiring preaching revivals. Even more effectively than the Cistercians before them, they established Catholic colonies along the frontiers of the West and beyond. They became missionary scouts looking for opportunities to disseminate Christian culture. In 1254 the Great Khan in Mongolia sponsored a debate on the principal religions of the world. There, many thousands of miles from Catholic Europe, was a Franciscan friar

JUSTICE IN HISTORY

Inquiring into Heresy: The Inquisition in Montaillou

In 1208 Pope Innocent III issued a call for a crusade against the Cathars or Albigensians. Fighting on behalf of French King Philip II, Simon de Montfort decisively defeated the pro-Cathar barons of southern France at Muret in 1213. Catharism retreated to the mountains, where a clandestine network of adherents kept the faith alive. The obliteration of these stubborn remnants required methods more subtle than the blunt instrument of a crusade. It required the techniques of inquisitors adept at interrogation and investigation.

Against the Cathar underground, the inquisition conducted its business through a combination of denunciations, exhaustive interrogations of witnesses and suspects, and confessions. Because its avowed purpose was to root out doctrinal error and to reconcile heretics to the Church, eliciting confessions was the preferred technique. But confessed heretics could not receive absolution until they informed on their friends and associates.

One of the last and most extensively documented inquisition cases against Catharism took place in Montaillou, a village in the Pyrenees Mountains, near the border of modern France and Spain. The Montaillou inquisition began in 1308, a century after the launch of the Albigensian Crusade and long after the heyday of Catharism.

However, the detailed records of the Montaillou inquisitors provide a revealing glimpse into Catharism and its suppression as well as the procedures of the inquisition. The first to investigate Montaillou was Geoffrey d'Ablis, the inquisitor of Carcassone. In 1308 he had every resident over age 12 seized and imprisoned. After the investigation, the villagers suffered the full range of inquisitorial penalties for their Cathar faith. The inquisitor's court sentenced some to life in prison, others to be burned at the stake. It forced many of those who were allowed to return to Montaillou to wear a yellow cross, the symbol of a heretic, sewn to the outside of their garments.

Unfortunately for these survivors, the most fearsome inquisitor of the age, Jacques Fournier, who was later elected Pope Benedict XII, investigated Montaillou again from 1318 to 1325. Known as an efficient, rigorous opponent of heresy, Fournier forced virtually all the surviving adults in Montaillou to appear before his tribunal. When the scrupulous Fournier took up a case, his inquiries were notoriously lengthy and rigorous. Both witnesses and defendants spoke of his tenacity, skill, and close attention to detail in conducting interrogations. If Fournier and his assistants could not uncover evidence through interrogation and confession, they did not hesitate to employ informers and spies to obtain the necessary information. When Pierre Maury, a shepherd the inquisitors sought for many years, returned to the village for a visit, an old friend received him with caution: "When we saw you again we felt both joy and fear. Joy, because it was a long time since we had seen you. Fear, because I was afraid lest the Inquisition had captured you up there: if they had they would have made you confess everything and come back among us as a spy in order to bring about my capture."[1]

Fournier's success in Montaillou depended on his ability to play local factions against each other by encouraging members of one clan to denounce the members of another. Fournier's persistence even turned family members against one another. The clearest example of this convoluted play of local alliances and animosities, family ties, religious belief, and self-interest is the case of Montaillou's wealthiest family, the Clergues.

Bernard Clergue was the count's local representative, which made him a kind of sheriff; his brother Pierre was the parish priest. Together they represented both the secular and religious arms of the inquisition in Montaillou. In his youth, Pierre had Cathar sympathies, and he allegedly kept a heretical book or calendar in his home. Nevertheless, at some time before 1308, he and Bernard betrayed the local Cathars to

BURNING OF THE HERETICAL BOOKS OF THE CATHARS

In this fifteenth-century painting, St. Dominic, the figure with a halo on the left, gives a Catholic book to a Cathar priest dressed in blue. The Cathars attempt to burn the book, which miraculously floats unharmed above the flames.

the inquisition. In the proceedings that followed, they had the power to either protect or expose their neighbors and family members. When the inquisition summoned one of his relatives, Bernard warned her to "say you fell off the ladder in your house; pretend you have broken bones everywhere. Otherwise it's prison for you."[2] Pierre relentlessly used his influence for his own and his family's benefit. A notorious womanizer, Pierre frightened women into sleeping with him by threatening to denounce them to the inquisition. Those he personally testified against were primarily from other prominent Montaillou families who represented a challenge to the Clergues' power. As one resident bitterly testified, "The priest himself cause[s] many inhabitants of Montaillou to be summoned by the Lord Inquisitor of Carcassone. It is high time the people of the priest's house were thrust as deep in prison as the other inhabitants of Montaillou."[3]

Despite the Clergues' attempted misuse of the inquisitorial investigation for their own purposes, the inquisitor Fournier persevered according to his own standards of evidence. In 1320 he finally had Pierre Clergue arrested as a heretic. The sly priest died in prison.

For Discussion

1. How did the methods of the inquisition help create outcasts from Catholic society? How did these methods help consolidate Catholic identity?
2. The primary function of the inquisition was to investigate what people believed. What do you think the inquisitors thought justice to be?

Taking It Further

Lambert, Malcolm. *The Cathars.* 1998. The best place to investigate the Cathar movement in the full sweep of its troubled history.

Le Roy Ladurie, Emmanuel. *Montaillou: The Promised Land of Error.* Translated by Barbara Bray. 1978. The best-selling and fascinating account of life in a Cathar village based on the records of Fournier's inquisition.

Moore, R. I. *The Formation of a Persecuting Society: Power and Deviance in Western Europe, 950–1250.* 1987. Places the harassment of heretics in the broader context of medieval persecutions.

ready to debate the learned men representing Islam, Buddhism, and Confucianism.

THE FLOWERING OF RELIGIOUS SENSIBILITIES During the twelfth and thirteenth centuries the widespread enthusiasm for religion exalted spiritual creativity. Experimentation pushed Christian piety in new directions, not just for aristocratic men, who dominated the Church hierarchy and the monasteries, but for women and laypeople from all social levels.

Catholic worship concentrated on the celebration of the Eucharist. The **Eucharist,** which was the crucial ritual moment during the Mass, celebrated Jesus's last meal with his apostles. The Eucharistic rite consecrated bread and wine as the body and blood of Christ. After the consecration, the celebrating priest distributed to the congregation the bread, called the host. Drinking from the chalice of wine, however, was a special privilege of the priesthood. More than anything else, belief in the miraculous change from bread to flesh and wine to blood, along with the sacrament of baptism, distinguished Christian believers from others. The Fourth Lateran Council in 1215 obligated all Christians to partake of the Eucharist at least once a year at Easter.

As simple as it was as a ritual observance, belief in the Eucharistic miracle presented a vexing and complex theological problem—why the host still looked, tasted, and smelled like bread rather than flesh, and why the blood in the chalice still seemed to be wine rather than blood. After the Fourth Lateran Council, Catholics solved this problem with the doctrine of **transubstantiation.** The doctrine rested on a distinction between the outward appearances (the "accidents" in theological terms) of the object, which the five senses could perceive, and the substance of an object, which they could not. When the priest spoke the words of consecration during the Mass, the bread and wine changed into the flesh and blood of Christ in substance ("transubstantiated"), but not in outward appearances. Thus, the substance of the Eucharist literally became God's body, but the senses of taste, smell, and sight perceived it as bread and wine.

Veneration of the Eucharist enabled the faithful to identify with Christ because believers considered the consecrated Eucharistic wafer to be Christ himself. By eating the host, they had literally ingested Christ, making his body part of their bodies. Eucharistic veneration became enormously popular in the thirteenth century and the climax of dazzling ritual performance. Priests enhanced the effect of the miracle by dramatically elevating the host at the moment of consecration, holding it in upraised hands. Altar screens had special peepholes so that many people could adore the host at the elevation, and the faithful would rush from altar to altar or church to church to witness a succession of host elevations.

Many Christians became attracted to mysticism, the attempt to achieve union of the self with God. To the mystic, complete understanding of the divine was spiritual, not intellectual, an understanding best achieved through asceticism, the repudiation of material and bodily comforts. Both men and women became mystics, but women concentrated on the more extreme forms of asceticism. For example, some women allowed themselves to be walled up in dark chambers to achieve perfect seclusion from the world and avoid distractions from their mystical pursuits. Others had themselves whipped, wore painful scratching clothing, starved themselves, or claimed to survive with the Eucharist as their only food. Female mystics, such as Juliana of Norwich (1342 to ca. 1416), envisioned a holy family in which God the Father was almighty, but the Mother was all wisdom. Some female mystics believed that Christ had a female body because he was the perfect nurturer, and they ecstatically contemplated spiritual union with him.

Mystics, however, were exceptional people. Most Christians contented themselves with the sacraments, especially baptism, penance, and the Eucharist; perhaps a pilgrimage to a saint's

CHRONOLOGY: MEDIEVAL RELIGIOUS DEVELOPMENTS

1098	Founding of Cistercian Order
1208–1213	Albigensian Crusade
1215	Fourth Lateran Council promulgates dogma of transubstantiation
1226	Death of Francis of Assisi
1221	Death of Dominic

shrine; and a final attempt at salvation by making a pious gift to the Church on their deathbed.

STRENGTHENING THE CENTER OF THE WEST

■ How did the western European monarchies strengthen themselves?

During the twelfth and thirteenth centuries, the kingdoms of Catholic western Europe became the supreme political and economic powers in the Christian world, eclipsing Byzantium—an achievement that made them potent rivals to the Islamic states. One reason was stronger political unity. These kingdoms laid the foundations of the modern nation-states, which remain to this day the dominant forms of government around the globe. What happened in France and England during the twelfth and thirteenth centuries, therefore, represents one of the most important and lasting contributions of the West to world history.

The Monarchies of Western Europe

During the High Middle Ages, France and England began to exhibit the fundamental characteristics of unified kingdoms. Stable borders, permanent bureaucracies, sovereignty, and the rule of law were the foundations on which they became the most powerful kingdoms in Europe during the twelfth and thirteenth centuries (see **Map 10.3**).

The kings of France achieved unity through military conquests and shrewd administrative reforms. In the turbulent Middle Ages, dynastic continuity was a key ingredient in building loyalty and avoiding chaos. From Philip I (r. 1060–1108) to Philip IV (r. 1285–1314), France enjoyed not only a succession of extremely effective kings but a consistent policy that guaranteed the borders, built a bureaucracy, expanded the idea of royal sovereignty, and enforced the rule of law. By securing complete military and judicial control of the royal domain, the Ile-de-France, these kings provided the dynasty with a dependable income from the region's abundant farms and the thriving trade of Paris. To administer the domain and lands newly acquired by conquest, the French monarchy introduced new royal officials, the *baillis,* who were paid professionals, some trained in Roman law. Directly responsible to the king, they had full administrative, judicial, and military powers in their districts. The *baillis* laid the foundation for a bureaucracy that centralized French government. Louis IX (r. 1226–1270), who was canonized St. Louis in 1297 for his exemplary piety and justice, introduced a system of judicial appeals that expanded royal justice and investigated the honesty of the *baillis*. Philip IV, the Fair (r. 1285–1314), greatly expanded the king's authority and also managed to bring the Church under his personal control, making the French clergy largely exempt from papal supervision. To pay for his frequent wars, Philip expelled the Jews after stripping them of their lands and

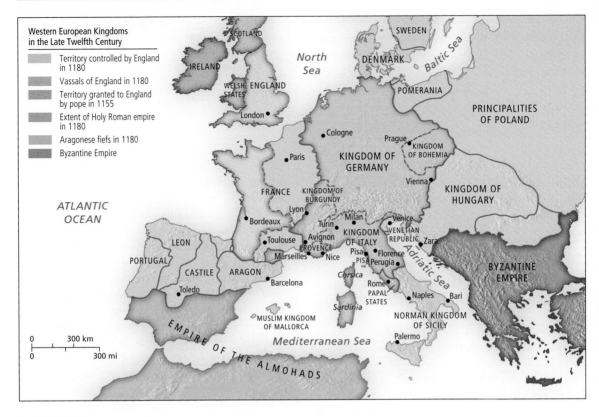

Western European Kingdoms in the Late Twelfth Century

Legend:
- Territory controlled by England in 1180
- Vassals of England in 1180
- Territory granted to England by pope in 1155
- Extent of Holy Roman empire in 1180
- Aragonese fiefs in 1180
- Byzantine Empire

MAP 10.3

Western European Kingdoms in the Late Twelfth Century

The kings of England occupied Ireland as well as much of western France. France itself was consolidated around the Ile-de-France, the area around Paris. The kingdoms of Germany, Bohemia, Burgundy, and Italy were ruled by the German emperors.

goods and then turned against the rich Order of the Knights Templar, a crusader order that had amassed a fortune as the papal banker and creditor of Philip. He confiscated the Templars' lands and tortured the knights to extort confessions to various crimes in a campaign to discredit them. (See *Different Voices* in this chapter.) Philip was perhaps most effective in finding new ways to increase taxation. Under Philip, royal revenues grew tenfold from what they had been in the saintly reign of Louis IX.

England was even better unified than France. When the Duke of Normandy, William I the Conqueror (r. 1066–1087), seized England in 1066, he claimed the crown and all the land for

himself. The new king kept about one-fifth of the land under his personal rule and parceled out the rest to the loyal nobles, monasteries, and the churches. This policy ensured that every land holder in England held his property as a fief, directly or indirectly, from the king, a principle of lordship enforced by an oath of loyalty to the crown required of all vassals. About 180 great lords from among the Norman aristocracy held land directly from the king, and hundreds of lesser nobles were vassals of these great lords. William accomplished what other kings only dreamed about: He had truly made himself the lord of all lords. William's hierarchy of nobles transformed the nature of the English monarchy, giving the Norman kings far greater authority over England than any of the earlier Anglo-Saxon kings had enjoyed.

Building on the legacy of the conquest, King Henry II (r. 1154–1189) reformed the judiciary. His use of sheriffs to enforce the royal will produced the legends of Robin Hood, the bandit who resisted the nasty sheriff of Nottingham on behalf of the poor. But in reality the sheriffs probably did more good than harm in protecting the weak against the powerful. In attempting to reduce the jurisdiction of the nobles, Henry made it possible for almost anyone to obtain a writ that moved a case to a royal court. Henry introduced a system of itinerant **circuit court** judges who visited every shire in the land four times a year. When this judge arrived, the sheriff assembled a group of men familiar with local affairs to report the major crimes that had been committed since the judge's last visit. These assemblies were the origins of the **grand jury** system, which persists to this day as the means for indicting someone for a crime. To resolve disputes over the possession of land, sheriffs collected a group of twelve local men who testified under oath about the claims of the disputants, and the judge made his decision based on their testimony. These assemblies began **trial by jury.** Judges later extended to criminal cases trial by jury, which remains the basis for rendering legal verdicts in common-law countries, including Britain, the United States, and Canada.

Henry also subjected priests alleged to have committed crimes to the jurisdiction of the royal courts. The king wanted to apply a principle of universal justice to everyone in the realm, a principle fiercely opposed by Thomas Becket, the archbishop of Canterbury. Becket insisted the Church must be free of interference from secular authorities. When four knights—believing they were acting on the king's wishes—murdered Becket before the altar of the Canterbury cathedral, the public was outraged and blocked Henry's plan to subject the Church to royal justice. The Church soon canonized Becket, revered as England's most famous saint.

The royal authority Henry asserted foundered under King John (r. 1199–1216), who lost to King Philip II of France the duchy of Normandy, which had been one of the foundations of English royal power since William the Conqueror. The barons of England grew tired of John's requests to pay for wars he lost. In 1215 English barons forced John to sign **Magna Carta** ("great charter," in reference to its size), in which the king pledged to respect the traditional feudal privileges of the nobility, towns, and clergy. Contrary to widespread belief, Magna Carta had nothing to do with asserting the liberty of the common people or guaranteeing universal rights. It addressed only the privileges of a select few rather than the rights of the many. Subsequent kings, however, swore to uphold it, thereby accepting the fundamental principle that even the king must respect the law. After Magna Carta the lord of all lords became less so. King Edward I (r. 1272–1307) began to call the **English Parliament** (from the French "talking together") in order to raise sums of money for his foreign wars. The English Parliament differed from similar assemblies on the Continent. It usually included representatives of the "commons," which consisted of townsmen and prosperous farmers who lacked titles of nobility, but whom the king summoned because he needed their money. As a result, a broader spectrum of the population joined parliament than in most other medieval kingdoms.

To the east the Holy Roman Empire suffered from the division between its principal component parts in Germany and northern Italy. Germany itself was an ill-defined region, subdivided by deep ethnic diversity and powerful dukes who ruled their lands with a spirit of fierce independence. As a result, emperors could not rule Germany directly, but only by demanding homage from the dukes who became imperial vassals. These feudal bonds were fragile substitutes for the kinds of monarchic institutions that evolved in France and England. The emperor's best asset was the force of his personality and his willingness to engage in a perpetual show of force to prevent rebellion. In northern Italy, the other part of the emperor's dominion, he did not even enjoy these extensive ties of vassalage and could rely

DIFFERENT VOICES THE TRIAL OF THE KNIGHTS TEMPLAR

The Knights Templar had been one of the most successful crusading orders, but after the end of the Crusades, their popularity declined. Nevertheless, they retained extensive properties given to finance their crusading expeditions. Deeply indebted to the Knights and in need of cash to finance his wars against England, King Philip IV of France seized upon rumors about a secret Templar initiation rite to justify arresting the prominent French Templars and confiscating their properties. Some Templars confessed under torture but later reversed themselves. The documents below describe the alleged secret rites of the Templars and summarize the testimony of some of those arrested. This notorious case not only illustrates how a ruthless king financed his kingdom, but how unsubstantiated rumors of homosexual practices could be used to destroy personal reputations and the order itself. The Crown burned many Templars at the stake, dissolved their order, and seized their property.

Royal Order for the Arrests of the Templars (September 14, 1307)

Some time ago indeed, we received insistent reports from very reliable people that brothers of the Order of the knights of the Temple, wolves in sheep's clothing, in the habit of a religious order vilely insulting our religious faith, are again crucifying our Lord Jesus Christ in these days, He who was crucified for the redemption of the human race. But they are causing Him greater injuries than those He received on the Cross. When they enter the Order and make their profession, they are confronted with His image, and their miserable or rather pitiful blindness makes them deny Him three times and spit in His face three times. Afterwards, they remove the clothes they wore in the secular world, and naked in the presence of the Visitor or his deputy, who receives their profession, they are kissed by him first on the lower part of the dorsal spine, secondly on the navel and finally on the mouth, in accordance with the profane rite of their Order but to the disgrace of the dignity of the human race.... By the vow of their profession they are unequivocally bound to accept the request of another to perform the vice of that horrible, dreadful intercourse, and this is why the wrath of God has fallen on these sons of infidelity.

only on vague legal rights granted by the imperial title and his ability to keep an army on the scene.

The century between the election of Frederick I (r. 1152–1190), known as Barbarossa or "redbeard," and the death of his grandson Frederick II (r. 1212–1250) represented the great age of the Holy Roman Empire, a period of relative stability preceded and followed by disastrous phases of anarchy and civil war. In the case of both of these emperors, lofty ambitions contrasted with the flimsy base of support and the failure to sustain judicial reforms, which prevented the centralization that took place in France and England. After Frederick II's death, his successors lost their hold on both Italy and Germany.

During the twelfth and thirteenth centuries, Spain and Poland, both of which would later become major European powers, were broken into small, weak principalities.

MEDIEVAL CULTURE: THE SEARCH FOR UNDERSTANDING

■ What made western European culture distinctive?

Medieval intellectuals vastly expanded the range of Western culture. The most important cultural encounters came when thinkers read the books of ancient philosophers and faced challenging ideas that did not fit easily into their view of the world. The greatest medieval

Deposition of Templar, Geoffrey of Charney (October 21, 1307)

He said on oath that after he had been received and the mantle placed on his shoulders, there was brought to him a certain cross bearing the image of Jesus Christ, and the said receptor told him not to believe in the one whose image was portrayed there since he was a false prophet and was not God. And then the said receptor made him deny Jesus Christ three times, but he claimed to have done this only with his tongue and not with his heart.

Asked whether he had spat on the said image, he swore that he could not remember and believed that this was due to the fact that they were acting in haste.

Examined about the kiss, he swore on oath that he kissed the receiving master on the navel, and he heard it said . . . to the brothers present at a chapter he was holding, that it was better to have sex between brothers of the Order than to assuage their lust with women, but he claimed never to have done this or even to have been asked.

Deposition of James of Molay, Grand Master (October 24, 1307)

Asked if, when he vowed chastity, anything was said to him about homosexual practices with the brothers, he said on oath that this was not the case and that he had never done this.

Source: Malcolm Barber and Keith Bate (eds.), *The Templars* (Manchester and New York: Manchester University Press, 2002), 245, 251, 253. Reprinted by permission.

For Discussion

1. Historians now consider the charges against the Templars fabrications. Why would these particular kinds of accusations rather than others be fabricated to destroy the Templars?

2. Which allegation seem worse, the denial of Christ or homosexual practices? Under torture, why might defendants confess they had denied Christ, but not admit to homosexual practices?

---

thinkers attempted to reconcile the reason of the ancients and the faith of the Christians by creating new philosophical systems. Lawyers began to look back to ancient Roman law for guidance about how to settle disputes, adjudicate crimes, and create governmental institutions. Muslim influences reinvigorated the Christian understanding of the sciences. Themes found in Persian love poetry found their way into the Christian notion of courtly love. Catholic western Europe experienced a cultural flowering through the spread of education, the growing power of Latin learning, and the invention of the university. Distinctively western forms developed in literature, music, drama, and above all the Romanesque and Gothic architecture of Europe's great cathedrals.

Revival of Learning

Some simple statistics reveal the magnitude of the educational revolution in medieval western Europe. In 1050 less than one percent of the population of Latin Christian Europe could read, and most of these literate people were priests who knew just enough Latin to recite the offices of the liturgy. Four hundred years later, as much as 40 percent of men living in cities were literate. Europeans embraced learning on a massive scale. How did this come about?

In 1050 only monasteries and cathedral schools provided an education. The curriculum was very basic, usually only reading and writing. Monastic education trained monks to read the books available in their libraries as an aid to contemplating the mysteries of the next world. In contrast, the cathedral schools, which trained members of the ecclesiastical hierarchy, emphasized the practical skills of rational analysis that would help future priests, bishops, and royal advisers solve the problems of this world.

By 1100 the number of cathedral schools had grown significantly and the curriculum expanded to include the study of the ancient Roman masters, Cicero and Virgil, who became models for clear Latin composition. These schools met the demand for trained officials from various sources—the thriving cities, the growing church bureaucracy, and the infant bureaucracies of the western kingdoms.

SCHOLASTICISM: A CHRISTIAN PHILOSOPHY In the cathedral schools the growing need for training in logic led to the development of scholasticism. **Scholasticism** refers to the use of logic learned from Aristotle to interpret the meaning of the Bible and the writings of the Church Fathers, who formulated Christian theology in its first centuries. The principal method of teaching and learning in the cathedral schools was the lecture. In the classroom the lecturer recited a short passage in Latin, presented the comments of other authorities on it, and drew his own conclusions. He then moved on to another brief passage and repeated the process. In addition to listening to lectures, students engaged in disputations in which they presented oral arguments for or against a particular thesis, a process called dialectical reasoning. The lecturers evaluated student disputants on their ability to investigate through logic the truth of a thesis. Disputations required several skills—verbal facility, a prodigious memory to produce apt citations on the spot, and the ability to think quickly. The process we know today as debate originated with these medieval disputations. Lectures and disputations became the core activities of the scholastics, who considered all subjects, however sacred, as appropriate for reasoned examination.

None of the scholastic teachers was more influential than the acerbic, witty, and daring Peter Abelard (1079–1142). Students from all over Europe flocked to hear Abelard's lectures at the cathedral school of Paris. Abelard's clever criticisms of the ideas of other thinkers delighted students. In *Sic et Non* ("Yes" and "No"), Abelard boldly examined some of the foundations of Christian truth. Employing the dialectical reasoning of a disputation, he presented both sides of 150 theological problems discussed by the Church Fathers. He left the conclusions open in order to challenge his students and readers to think further, but his intention was to point out how apparent disagreements among the experts masked a deeper level of agreement about Christian truth.

UNIVERSITIES: ORGANIZING LEARNING From the cathedral schools arose the first universities. The University of Paris evolved from the cathedral school where Abelard once taught. Initially the universities were little more than guilds (trade associations), organized by either students or teachers to protect their interests. As members of a guild, students bargained with their professors, as would other tradesmen, over costs and established minimum standards of instruction. The guild of the law students at Bologna received a charter in 1158, which probably made it the first university. Some of the early universities were professional schools, such as the medical faculty at Salerno, but true to their origins as cathedral schools, most emphasized theology over other subjects.

The medieval universities formulated the basic educational practices still in place today. They established a curriculum, examined students, conferred degrees, and conducted graduation ceremonies. Students and teachers wore distinctive robes, which are still worn at graduation ceremonies. Teachers were clergymen—that is, they "professed" religion, hence, the title of *professor* for a university instructor. In their first years students pursued the liberal arts curriculum, which consisted of the *trivium* (grammar, rhetoric, and logic) and the *quadrivium* (arithmetic, geometry, astronomy, and music). Arts and sciences faculties and distribution requirements in modern universities are vestiges of the medieval liberal arts curriculum.

Medieval universities did not admit women because the Church barred women from the priesthood and most university students trained to become priests. (Women did not attend universities in significant numbers until the nineteenth century.) The few women who did receive advanced educations relied on a parent or a private tutor, such as Abelard who tutored the young Heloise. But tutoring had its own dangers. The relationship of Abelard and Heloise resulted in a love affair, a pregnancy, and Abelard's castration at the hands of Heloise's relatives.

THE ANCIENTS: RENAISSANCE OF THE TWELFTH CENTURY   The scholastics' integration of Greek philosophy with Christian theology represented a key facet of the **Twelfth-Century Renaissance,** a revival of interest in the ancients comparable in importance to the Carolingian Renaissance of the ninth century and the Italian Renaissance of the fifteenth. Between about 1140 and 1260, new Latin translations of the Greek classics arrived from Sicily and Spain, where Christians had close contacts with Muslims and Jews. Muslim philosophers translated into Arabic the Greek philosophical and scientific classics, which were readily available in the Middle East and North Africa. Jewish scholars who knew both languages then translated these Arabic versions into Latin. Later a few Catholic scholars traveled to Byzantium, where they learned enough Greek to make even better translations from the originals.

As they encountered the philosophy of the ancients, Muslim, Jewish, and Christian thinkers faced profoundly disturbing problems. The philosophical methods of reasoning found in Greek works, especially those by Aristotle, were difficult to reconcile with the principles of faith revealed in the Qur'an of Islam and the Hebrew and Christian Bibles. Religious thinkers recognized the superiority of Greek thought and worried that the power of philosophical reasoning undermined religious truth. As men of faith they challenged themselves to demonstrate that philosophy did not, if properly understood, contradict religious teaching. Some of them went even further to employ philosophical reasoning to demonstrate the truth of religion. They always faced opposition within their own religious faiths, however, especially from people who thought philosophical reason was an impediment to religious faith.

The most perceptive Muslim thinker to confront the questions raised by Greek philosophy was Averroës (1126–1198), who rose to become the chief judge of Córdoba and an adviser to the caliph. In *The Incoherence of the Incoherence* (1179–1180), Averroës argued that the aim of philosophy was to explain the true, inner meaning of religious revelations. This inner meaning, however, was not to be disclosed to the unlettered masses, who had to be told only the simple, literal stories and metaphors of Scripture. Although lively and persuasive, Averroës's defense of philosophy failed to stimulate additional philosophical speculation within Islam. Once far superior to that of the Latin Christian world, Islamic philosophy and science declined as Muslim thinkers turned to mysticism and rote learning over rational debate. In fact, Averroës received a more sympathetic hearing among Jews and Catholics than among Muslims.

Within Judaism, Moses Maimonides (1135–1204)—a contemporary of Averroës, also from Córdoba—was the most prominent thinker. His most important work in religious philosophy, *The Guide for the Perplexed* (ca. 1191), synthesized Greek philosophy, science, and Judaism. Widely read in Arabic, Hebrew, and Latin versions, the book stimulated both Jewish and Christian philosophy.

For medieval Catholic philosophers, one of the most difficult tasks was reconciling the biblical account of the divine creation with Aristotle's teaching that the universe was eternal. Even in this early clash between science and religion, creationism was the sticking point. Thomas Aquinas (1225–1274), whose philosophy is called **Thomism,** most effectively resolved the apparent conflict between faith and philosophy. A Dominican friar, Aquinas spent most of his career developing a school system for the Dominicans in Italy, but he also spent two short periods teaching at the University of Paris.

Aquinas avoided distracting controversies and academic disputes to concentrate on his two great summaries of human knowledge—the *Summary of the Catholic Faith Against the Gentiles* (1261) and the *Summary of Theology* (1265–1274). In both of these massive scholastic works, reason fully confirmed Christian faith. Encyclopedias of knowledge, both books rigorously examined whole fields through dialectical reasoning.

Building on the works of Averroës, Aquinas solved the problem of reconciling philosophy and religion by drawing a distinction between *natural truth* and *revealed truth*. For Aquinas, natural truth meant the kinds of things anyone can know through the operation of human reason. Revealed truth referred to the things that one can know only through revelation, such as the doctrines of the Trinity and the incarnation of Christ. Aquinas argued that these two kinds of truths could not possibly contradict one another because both came from God. Apparent contradictions could be accommodated by an understanding of a higher truth. On the issue of Creation, for example, Aquinas argued that Aristotle's understanding of the eternal universe was inferior to the higher revealed truth of the Bible that God created the universe in seven days.

The most influential of the scholastic thinkers, Aquinas asserted that to achieve religious truth one should start with faith and then use reason to reach conclusions. He was the first to understand theology systematically in this way, and in doing so he raised a storm of opposition among Christians threatened by the difficulty of philosophical thinking. The theological faculties in universities at first prohibited Aquinas's writings. Nevertheless, his method remains crucial for Catholic theology to this day.

Just as scholastic theologians looked to ancient Greek philosophy as a guide to reason, jurists revived ancient Roman law, especially at the universities of Bologna and Pavia in Italy. In the law faculties, students learned the legal work of the Emperor Justinian—the text of the *Corpus Juris Civilis,* together with the commentaries on it. The systematic approach of Roman law provided a way to make the legal system less arbitrary for judges, lawyers, bureaucrats, and advisers to kings and popes. Laws had long consisted of a contradictory mess of municipal regulations, Germanic customs, and feudal precepts. Under Roman law, judges had to justify their verdicts according to prescribed standards of evidence and procedure. The revival of Roman law in the twelfth century made possible the legal system that still guides most of continental Europe.

Courtly Love

In addition to the developments in philosophy, theology, and the law, the Twelfth-Century Renaissance included a remarkable literary output of romances in the vernacular languages, the tongues spoken in everyday life. Poets called **troubadours** wrote romances—poems of love, meant to be sung to music—which reflected an entirely new sensibility about the relationships between men and women. Their literary movement is called **courtly love** or chivalry. The troubadours composed their poems in Provençal, one of the languages of southern France, and the princely courts of southern France provided the first audience. These graciously elegant poems show influences from Arabic love poetry and from Muslim mystical literature in which the soul, depicted as feminine, seeks her masculine God/lover. The troubadours secularized this theme of religious union by portraying the ennobling possibilities of the love between a woman and a man. In so doing, they popularized the idea of romantic love, one of the most powerful concepts in all of Western history, an ideal that still dominates popular culture to this day.

The ideal male depicted in courtly love poems was the knight-errant, a warrior who roamed in search of adventure. He was poor and free of ties to home and family, a man who lived a life of perfect freedom, but whose virtue led him to do the right thing. Knights took vows in the name of ladies, revealing that the courtly love ideal included a heavy dose of erotic desire. Besides self-denial, the most persistent chivalric fantasy was the motif of the young hero who liberates a virgin, either from a dragon or from a rioting mob of peasants.

The courtly love poems of the troubadours idealized women. The male troubadours, such as Chrétien de Troyes (1135–1183), placed women on a pedestal and treated men as the "love vassals" of beloved women to whom they owed loyalty and service. Female troubadours, such as Marie de France (dates unknown), did not place women on a pedestal but idealized emotionally honest and open relationships between lovers. From southern France, courtly love spread to Germany and elsewhere throughout Europe.

The Center of Medieval Culture: The Great Cathedrals

When tourists visit European cities today, they usually want to see the cathedrals. Mostly built between 1050 and 1300, these imposing structures symbolize the soaring ambitions and imaginations of their largely unknown builders. During the great medieval building boom, cities built hundreds of new cathedrals and thousands of other churches, sparing no expense and reflecting the latest experimental techniques in architectural engineering and artistic fashion. These buildings became multimedia

centers for the arts—incorporating architecture, sculpture, stained glass, and painting and providing a setting for the performance of music and drama. The medieval cathedrals took decades, sometimes centuries, to build at great cost and sacrifice.

The **Romanesque** style of cathedral-building spread throughout western Europe during the eleventh century and the first half of the twelfth century because the master masons who understood sophisticated stone construction techniques traveled from one building site to another, bringing with them a uniform style. The principal innovation of the Romanesque was the arched stone roofs, which were more aesthetically pleasing and less vulnerable to fire than the flat roofs they replaced. The rounded arches of these stone roofs, called barrel vaults, looked like the inside of a barrel. Romanesque churches employed transepts, which fashioned the church into the shape of a cross if viewed from above, the vantage point of God. The high stone vaults of Romanesque churches and cathedrals required the support of massive stone pillars and thick walls. As a result, windows were small slits that imitated the slit windows of castles.

The religious experience of worshiping in a Romanesque cathedral had an intimate, almost familiar quality to it. In such a building, God

FLYING BUTTRESSES OF CHARTRES CATHEDRAL

The flying buttress did more than hold up the thin walls of Gothic cathedrals. The buttress created an almost lacelike appearance on the outside of the building, magnifying the sense of mystery evoked by the style.

ROMANESQUE CATHEDRAL ARCHITECTURE

The rounded arches, the massive columns, the barrel vaults in the ceilings, and the small windows were characteristic of the Romanesque style. Compare the massiveness of this interior with the Gothic style of the Abbey Church of St. Denis in the next illustration.

Source: Dagli Orti/Picture Desk, Inc./Kobal Collection

GOTHIC VAULTS

The delicately ribbed ceiling vaults and vast expanses of stained glass in the Abbey Church of St. Denis, France, contrast with the heavy barrel vaults of the Romanesque Cathedral in Vezelay.

became a fellow townsman, an associate in the grand new project of making cities habitable and comfortable.

During the late twelfth and thirteenth centuries, the **Gothic** style replaced the Romanesque. The innovation of this style was the ribbed vault and pointed arches, which superseded the barrel vault of the Romanesque. These narrow pointed arches drew the viewer's eye upward toward God and gave the building the appearance of weightlessness that symbolized the Christian's uplifting reach for heaven. The neighborly solidity of the Romanesque style disappeared for a mystical appreciation of God's utter otherness, the supreme divinity far

above mortal men and women. The Gothic style also introduced the innovation of the flying buttress, an arched construction on the outside of the walls that redistributed the weight of the roof. This innovation allowed for thin walls pierced by windows much bigger than possible with Romanesque construction techniques.

The result was stunning. The stonework of a Gothic cathedral became a skeleton to support massive expanses of stained glass, transforming the interior spaces into a mystical haven from the outside world. At different times of the day, the multicolored windows converted sunlight into an ever-changing light show that offered sparkling hints of the secret truths of God's Creation. The light that passed through these windows symbolized the light of God. The windows themselves contained scenes that were an encyclopedia of medieval knowledge and lore. In addition to Bible stories and the lives of saints, these windows depicted common people at their trades, animals, plants, and natural wonders. Stained-glass windows celebrated not only the promise of salvation, but all the wonders of God's creation. They drew worshipers out of the busy cities in which they lived and worked toward the perfect realm of the divine.

In France, Germany, Italy, Spain, and England, cities made enormous financial sacrifices to construct new Gothic cathedrals during the economic boom years of the thirteenth century. Because costs were so high, many cathedrals, such as the one in Siena, Italy, remained unfinished, but even the incomplete ones became vital symbols of local identity.

CONCLUSION

Asserting Western Culture

During the twelfth and thirteenth centuries, western Europe matured into its own self-confident identity. Less a semi-barbarian backwater than it had been even in the time of Charlemagne, western Europe cultivated modes of thought that revealed an almost limitless capacity for creative renewal and critical self-examination. That capacity, first evident during the Twelfth-Century Renaissance, especially in scholasticism, is what has most distinguished the West ever since. These critical methods repeatedly caused alarm among some believers. However, this tendency to question basic assumptions is among the greatest achievements of Western civilization. The western European university system, which was based on teaching methods of critical inquiry, differed from the educational institutions in other cultures, such as

Byzantium or Islam, that were devoted to passing on received knowledge. This distinctive critical spirit connects the cultures of the ancient, medieval, and modern West.

KEY TERMS

agricultural revolution	circuit court
manor	grand jury
serfs	trial by jury
communes	Magna Carta
Cluny	English Parliament
simony	scholasticism
lay investiture	Twelfth-Century
Investiture Controversy	Renaissance
excommunication	Thomism
curia	troubadours
interdict	courtly love
friars	Romanesque
Eucharist	Gothic
transubstantiation	

CHAPTER QUESTIONS

1. How was medieval western European economy and society organized around manors and cities? (page 300)
2. How did the Catholic Church consolidate its hold over the Latin West? (page 306)
3. How did the western European monarchies strengthen themselves? (page 319)
4. What made western European culture distinctive? (page 322)

TAKING IT FURTHER

1. What was the role of theology and philosophy in allowing the West to assert itself more forcefully?
2. Why was kingship the most effective form of political organization in the Middle Ages?
3. By the end of the thirteenth century what distinguished Christian from Muslim culture?

✓• Practice on MyHistoryLab

11

The Medieval West in Crisis

■ A Time of Death ■ A Cold Wind from the East ■ Economic Depression
and Social Turmoil ■ An Age of Warfare ■ A Troubled Church
and the Demand for Religious Comfort ■ The Culture of Loss

THE FOURTEENTH CENTURY DAWNED WITH A CHILL. IN 1303 AND THEN again during 1306–1307, the Baltic Sea froze over. No one had ever heard of that happening before, and the freezings foretold worse disasters. The cold spread beyond its normal winter season, arriving earlier in the autumn and staying later into the summer. Then it started to rain and did not let up. The Caspian Sea began to rise, flooding villages along its shores. In the summer of 1314 all across Europe, crops rotted in sodden fields. The meager harvest came late, precipitating a surge in prices for farm produce and forcing King Edward II of England to impose price controls. But capping prices did not grow more food.

In 1315 the situation got worse. In England during that year, the price of wheat rose 800 percent. Preachers compared the ceaseless rains to the great flood in the Bible, and floods did come, overwhelming dikes in the Netherlands and England, washing away entire towns in Germany, turning fields into lakes in France. Everywhere crops failed.

Things got much worse. Torrential rains fell again in 1316, and for the third straight year the crops failed, creating the most severe famine in recorded European history. The effects were most dramatic in the far north. In Scandinavia agriculture almost disappeared, in Iceland peasants abandoned farming and turned to fishing and herding sheep, and in Greenland the European settlers began to die out. Already malnourished, the people of Europe became susceptible to disease and famine. Desperate people resorted to desperate options. They ate cats, rats, insects, reptiles, animal dung, and tree leaves. Stories spread that some ate

their own children. In Poland the starving were said to cut down criminals from the gallows for food.

By the 1340s, nearly all of Europe west of Poland was gripped by a seemingly endless cycle of disease and famine. Then came the deadliest epidemic in European history, the Black Death, which killed at least one-third of the total population. The economy collapsed. Trade disappeared. Industry shriveled. Hopeless peasants and urban workers revolted against their masters, demanding relief for their families. Neither state nor church could provide it. The two great medieval kingdoms of France and England became locked in a struggle that depleted royal treasuries and wasted the aristocracy in a series of clashes that historians call the Hundred Years' War. The popes left the dangerous streets of Rome for Avignon, France, where they were obliged to extort money to survive. After the pope returned to Rome, a group of French cardinals refused to go and elected a second pope, leading to the Great Schism when Europe was divided by allegiances to two different popes.

During the twelfth and thirteenth centuries the West had asserted itself against Islam through the Crusades and spread Catholic Christianity to the far corners of Europe. During the fourteenth and early fifteenth centuries, however, the West drew into itself due to war, epidemics, and conflicts with the Mongol and Ottoman Empires. As an additional shock, the Byzantine Empire, once the bastion of Orthodox Christianity, fell to the Muslim armies of the Ottomans. This chapter explores these encounters with death and turmoil, and asks this question: How did the death and

THE OTTOMAN SULTAN

In 1478 the Venetian painter, Gentile Bellini, went to Constantinople to paint the portrait of Sultan Mehmet II, who had conquered the Byzantine Empire. Hence, encounters between the Christian Europe and the Turks became one of the most important themes in the history of West.

turmoil of fourteenth- and fifthteenth-century Europe transform the identity of the West?

A TIME OF DEATH

■ What caused the deaths of so many Europeans?

The magnitude of Europe's demographic crisis is evident from the raw numbers. In 1300 the population of Europe was about 74 million—roughly 15 percent of its current population. Population size can be an elementary measure of the success of an economy to keep people alive, and by this measure Europe had been very successful up to about 1300. It had approximately doubled its population over the previous 300 years. After the 1340s, however, Europe's ability to sustain its population evaporated. Population fell to just 52 million. The demographic crisis of the fourteenth century was the greatest natural disaster in Western civilization since the epidemics of antiquity. How did it happen?

Famine

Widespread famine, caused by a crisis in agricultural production, began during the decade of 1310–1320. The agricultural revolution of the eleventh century had made available more food and more nutritious food, triggering the growth of the population during the Middle Ages. During the twelfth and thirteenth centuries, vast tracks of virgin forests were cleared for farming, especially in eastern Europe. After all the good bottomland was cleared, farmers moved to clear the more marginal land on hills and mountainsides. These clearings created soil erosion that contributed to the devastating floods of the 1310s. Thus, human actions facilitated the ecological catastrophe. By the fourteenth century no more virgin land was available for clearing, which meant that a still-growing population tried to survive on a fixed amount of farming land. Because of the limitations of medieval agriculture, the ability of farmers to produce food could not keep up with unchecked population growth. The propensity for famine was especially acute in heavily populated western Europe. In eastern Europe the lower population and better balance between agriculture, animal husbandry, and fishing meant the population remained better fed and less susceptible to famine and disease.

At the same time there was probably a change in climate, known as the "Little Ice Age." The mean annual temperatures dropped just enough to make it impossible to grow crops in the more northerly parts of Europe and at high elevations such as the Alps. Before the fourteenth century, for example, grapes were grown in England to produce wine, but with the decline in temperatures, the grape vineyards ceased to produce. Growing grapes in England became possible again only with global warming in the twenty-first century. The result of the Little Ice Age was twofold. First, there was less land available for cultivation as it became impossible to grow crops in marginal areas. Second, a harsher climate shortened the growing season, which meant that even where crops could still grow, they were less abundant.

The imbalance between food production and population set off a dreadful cycle of famine and disease. Insufficient food resulted in either malnutrition or starvation. Those who suffered from prolonged malnutrition were particularly susceptible to epidemic diseases, such as typhus, cholera, and dysentery. By 1300, children of the poor faced the probability of extreme hunger once or twice during the course of their childhood. In Pistoia, Italy, priests kept the *Book of the Dead*, which recorded the pattern: famine in 1313, famine in 1328–1329, famine and epidemic in 1339–1340 that killed one-quarter of the population, famine in 1346, famine and epidemic in 1347, and then the killing hammer blow—the Black Death in 1348 (see **Map 11.1**).

The Black Death

Following on the heels of the Great Famine, the **Black Death** arrived in Europe in the spring of 1348 with brutal force. In the lovely hilltop city of Siena, Italy, all industry stopped, carters refused to bring produce and cooking oil in from the countryside, and on June 2 the daily records of the city council and civil courts abruptly ended, as if the city fathers and judges had all died or rushed home in panic. A local chronicler, Agnolo di Tura, wrote down his memories of those terrible days:

> Father abandoned child, wife husband, one brother another; for this illness seemed to strike through the breath and sight. And so they died. And none could be found to bury the dead for money or friendship. Members of a household brought their dead to a ditch as best they could, without priest, without divine offices. Nor did the [death] bell sound. And in many places in Siena great pits were dug and piled deep with the multitude of dead....And I, Agnolo di Tura, called the Fat, buried my five children with my own hands. And there were also those who were so sparsely covered with earth that the dogs dragged them forth and devoured many bodies throughout the city.[1]

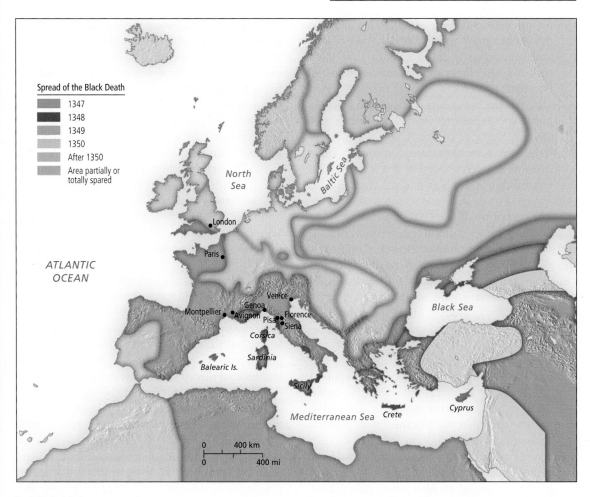

MAP 11.1

Spread of the Black Death

After the Black Death first appeared in the ports of Italy in 1348, it spread relentlessly throughout most of Europe, killing at least 20 million people in Europe alone.

During the summer of 1348 more than half of the Sienese died. The construction of Siena's great cathedral, planned to be the largest in the world, stopped and was never resumed due to a lack of workers. In fact, Siena, once among the most prosperous cities in Europe, never fully recovered and lost its economic preeminence.

No disease left more distinctive and disturbing signs on the body than the Black Death. According to one quite typical contemporary description: "all the matter which exuded from their bodies let off an unbearable stench; sweat, excrement, spittle, breath, so fetid as to be overpowering; urine turbid, thick, black or red...."[2] In the introduction to *The Decameron*, Giovanni Boccaccio described what he had witnessed of the symptoms:

In the year 1348 after the fruitful incarnation of the Son of God, that most beautiful of Italian cities, noble Florence, was attacked by deadly plague....The symptoms...began both in men and women with certain swellings in the groin or under the armpit. They grew to the size of a small apple or an egg, more or less, and were vulgarly called tumors. In a short space of time these tumors spread from the two parts named [to] all over the body. Soon after this the symptoms changed and black or purple spots appeared on the arms or thighs or any other part of the body, sometimes a few large ones, sometimes many little ones. These spots were a certain sign of death, just as the original tumor had been and still remained.[3]

The fear of the Black Death and the inability to discern its causes focused the attention of contemporaries on the bodies of the sick. Almost any discoloration of the skin or glandular swellings could be interpreted as a sign of the Black Death's presence. Physicians and surgeons, of course, were the experts in reading the signs of the body for disease. As victims and their distraught families soon discovered, however, physicians did not really know what the glandular swellings and discolorations of the skin meant. Boccaccio reported that "No doctor's advice, no medicine could overcome or alleviate this disease....Either the disease was such that no treatment was possible or the doctors were so ignorant that they did not know what caused it, and consequently could not administer the proper remedy."[4]

In the absence of an alternative, government officials resorted to quarantines to stop the spread of the disease. They locked up infected households for 40 days, which was especially hard on the poor who needed to work to eat. To maintain quarantines and bury the dead, city councils created public health bureaucracies, complete with their own staff physicians, grave diggers, and police force. The extraordinary powers granted to the public health authorities helped expand the authority of the state over its citizens in the name of pursuing the common good. The expansion of governmental bureaucracy that distinguished modern from medieval states was partly the result of the need to keep human bodies under surveillance and control—a need that began with the Black Death.

Experts still dispute the cause of the Black Death, but there is growing doubt about the validity of the traditional theory that the bubonic plague was the most likely culprit. The dispute about the cause of the Black Death is a revealing example of the difficulty of interpreting evidence from the distant past. According to the traditional theory the bubonic plague can appear in two forms. In the first form it is usually transmitted to humans by a flea that has bitten a rodent infected with the *Yersinia pestis* bacillus, usually a rat. The infected flea then bites a human victim. The infection enters the bloodstream, causing inflamed swellings called buboes (hence, "bubonic" plague) in the glands of the groin or armpit, internal bleeding, and discoloration of the skin, symptoms similar to those Boccaccio described, which is why some historians have thought that the "Black Death" was the bubonic plague. The second form of plague was the pneumonic type, which infected the lungs and spread by coughing and sneezing. Either form could be lethal, but the complex epidemiology of bubonic plague meant that the first form could not be transmitted directly from one person to another. According to the traditional theory, after being infected, many victims probably developed pneumonia as a secondary symptom, which then spread quickly to others. As one contemporary physician put it, one person could seemingly infect the entire world. In some cases, the doctor caught the illness and died before the patient did.

The visitations of the bubonic plague in the late nineteenth and twentieth centuries, which have been observed by physicians trained in modern medicine, formed that basis for the traditional theory linking the Black Death to the bubonic plague. Alexandre Yersin discovered the bubonic plague bacillus in Hong Kong in 1894 and traced its spread through rats and fleas. For more than a century, most historians and epidemiologists have thought that something similar to this must have happened in 1348.

However, there are problems with this traditional theory. The Black Death spread much more rapidly from person to person and place to place than the bubonic plague does in modern epidemics. For example, rats do not travel very far very fast, and in modern examples the bubonic plague has rarely spread more than twelve miles per year. In 1348, however, the Black Death traveled as far in a day as rat-borne bubonic plague does in a year. Many of the reported symptoms from the fourteenth century do not match the symptoms observed in modern plague victims. Moreover, the Black Death, unlike the bubonic plague, seems to have had a long incubation period before the first symptoms appeared. Because of the long incubation, those who had the disease transmitted it to others before they knew they were sick, which helps explain why the disease was so lethal despite attempts to quarantine those afflicted with it. The most recent research suggests that the Black Death may have been caused by an unidentified virus that produced bleeding similar to the Ebola virus that has appeared in Africa in recent years.

In Europe about 20 million people died, with the deaths usually clustered in a matter of a few weeks or months after the disease first appeared in a particular locale. The death toll, however, varied erratically from place to place, ranging from about 20 to 90 percent. So great was the toll in southern and western Europe that entire villages were depopulated or abandoned. Paris lost half its population, Florence as much as four-fifths, and Venice two-thirds. In the seaport of Trapani, Italy, everyone apparently died or left. Living in enclosed spaces, monks and nuns were especially hard hit. All the Franciscans of Carcassonne and Marseille in France died. In Montpellier, France, only 7 of the 140 Dominicans survived. In isolated Kilkenny, Ireland, Brother John Clyn found himself left alone among his dead brothers, and he began to write a diary of what he had witnessed because he was afraid he might be the last person left alive in the world. (See *Different Voices* in this chapter.)

THE TRIUMPH OF DEATH

A detail from Francesco Traini's fresco, *The Triumph of Death*, in the Camposanto, Pisa, ca. 1350. Frescoes such as this reflect the horror of the Black Death.

Source: Cemetery, Pisa, Italy/Canali PhotoBank, Milan/SuperStock

DIFFERENT VOICES THE BLACK DEATH FORETELLS THE END OF THE WORLD

Christianity had a long tradition, rooted in the Bible, of prophecies about the end of the world. The most common theology of the end is called millenarianism, the belief that there would be definitive signs in human events of the coming of the end. These prophecies took various forms. One form predicted the reign of Antichrist, who would rule for a 1,000 years before the second coming of Christ. The prophetic tradition encouraged people to look for signs of the Antichrist, and the appearance of the Black Death seemed to be one of those signs. Another form popular in Germany depicted the return from the dead of the Emperor Frederick II, who would cleanse the earth in preparation for Christ's return. The first document reports rumors from Rome in 1349 sent to a friar in England.

There are various prophets in the regions around Rome, whose identity is still secret, who have been making up stories like this for years. They say that this very year, 1349, Antichrist is aged ten, and is a most beautiful child, so well educated in all branches of knowledge that no one now living can equal him. And they also say that there is another boy, now aged twelve and living beyond the land of the Tartars [Mongols], who has been brought up as a Christian and that this is the one who will destroy the Saracens [Muslims] and become the greatest man in Christendom, but his power will be quickly brought to an end by the coming of Antichrist.

These prophets also say, among a great deal else, that the present pope will come to a violent end, and that after his death there will be more revolutions in the world than there have ever been before. But after that another pope will arise, a good and just man, who will appoint God-fearing cardinals, and there will be almost total peace in his time. And after him there will be no other pope, but Antichrist will come and reveal himself.

Source: *The Black Death* trans. and ed. Rosemary Horrox (Manchester and New York: Manchester University Press, 1994), 154. Reprinted by permission.

The second source by Johann von Winterthur, a Franciscan friar, reports events from the time of the Black Death in 1348. Winterthur is decidedly skeptical of the millenarian prophecies.

In these times it was freely spread abroad among men of various races, indeed of every race, that the Emperor Frederick II...would return in the full might of his power to reform the corrupt church completely. The men who believed this also added that it was inevitable that he would return, even if he had been cut into a thousand pieces, or burnt to ashes, because it had been foretold that this would happen and it could not possibly be otherwise....After resuming a power more just and a rule more glorious than before, he will cross the seas with a large army and will resign his power on the Mount of Olives or at the dry tree [that is in Jerusalem].

I do not cease to be amazed by this false belief; that anyone could hope for or believe in the revival of a man dead 80 years, who was emperor for 30 years. The men who hold this false belief have been deceived just like the Jews, who believe that King David will be raised up by the Lord to reign again over Israel as he did in the past. They believe it on the basis that the Lord, speaking through the prophets, said: "I will raise up my

The Black Death kept coming back. In the Mediterranean basin where the many port cities formed a network of contagion, the plague reappeared between 1348 and 1721 in one port or another about every 20 years. Some of the later outbreaks were just as lethal as the initial 1348 catastrophe. Florence lost half its population in 1400; Venice lost a third in 1575–1577 and a third again in 1630–1631.

Less exposed than the Mediterranean, northern Europe suffered less and saw the last of the dread disease in the Great Plague of London of 1665–1666. Most of Poland escaped without any signs of the disease, and east-central Europe in general was far less severely hit than western Europe, probably because the sparse population made the spread of contagion less likely.

FLAGELLANTS

During the Black Death many people believed God was punishing them for their sins. In order to expiate those sins some young men practiced flagellation, a practice once reserved for monks who whipped themselves as a form of penance. In order to control the practice among laymen, confraternities were formed in which collective flagellation was organized. The flagellants depicted here wear the white robes of a confraternity and cover their faces to remain anonymous.

Source: Dagli Orti/Picture Desk, Inc./Kobal Collection

faithful servant David." ...But these and other similar authorities are to be understood as referring to Christ or to another of the race of David.

Source: *The Black Death* translated and edited by Rosemary Horrox (Manchester and New York: Manchester University Press, 1994), 155–156. Reprinted by permission.

For Discussion

1. Why might people want to believe in these prophecies? How does Winterthur go about refuting them?

A COLD WIND FROM THE EAST

■ How did forces outside Europe, in particular the Mongol and Ottoman Empires, influence conditions in the West?

During the same period the West was suffering from deadly microbes, it also faced the mounted warriors of the distant Mongol tribes, whose relentless conquests drove them from Outer Mongolia across central Asia toward Europe. The Mongols and Turks were nomadic peoples from central Asia. Closely related culturally but speaking different languages, these peoples exerted an extraordinary influence on world history despite a rather small population. **Map 11.2** shows the place of origin of the Mongols and Turks and where

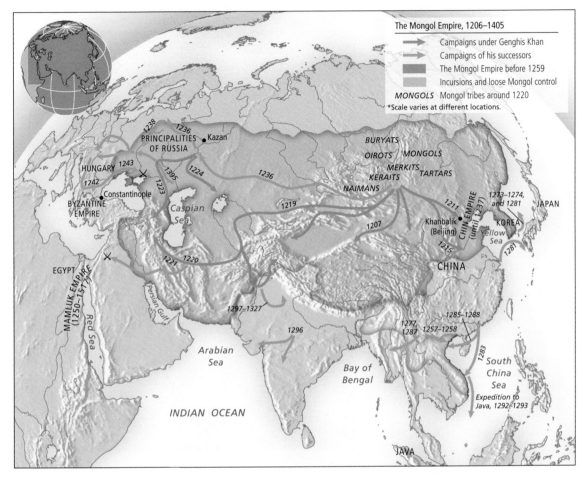

MAP 11.2

The Mongol Empire, 1206–1405

The Mongols and Turks were nomadic peoples who spread out across Asia and Europe from their homeland in the region of Mongolia. The Mongol armies eventually conquered vast territories from Korea to the borders of Hungary and from the Arctic Ocean to the Arabian Sea.

they spread across a wide belt of open, relatively flat steppe land stretching from the Yellow Sea between China and the Korean peninsula to the Baltic Sea and the Danube River basin in Europe. Virtually without forests and interrupted only by a few easily traversed mountain ranges, the broad Eurasian steppes have been the great migration highway of world history from prehistoric times to the medieval caravans and the modern trans-Siberian railway.

As the Mongols and Turks charged westward out of central Asia on their fast ponies, they put pressure on the kingdoms of the West. Mongol armies hobbled Kievan Rus, and Turks destroyed Byzantium. As a consequence, the potential Orthodox allies in the East of the Catholic Christian West were weakened or eliminated. Converts to Islam, the Ottomans pushed into the Balkans. In contrast to the era of the twelfth-century Crusades, Catholic Europe found itself on the defensive against a powerful Muslim foe.

The Mongol Invasions

Whereas the Europeans became successful sailors because of their extensive coastlines and close proximity to the sea, the Mongols became roving horsemen because they needed to migrate several times a year in search of grass and water for their ponies and livestock. They also became highly skilled warriors because they competed persistently with other tribes for access to the grasslands.

Between 1206 and 1258, the Mongols transformed themselves from a collection of disunited tribes with a vague ethnic affinity to create the most extensive empire in the history of the world. The epic rise of the previously obscure Mongols was the work of a Mongol chief named Temujin, who succeeded in uniting the various quarreling tribes and transforming them into a world power. In 1206 Temujin was proclaimed Genghis Khan (ca. 1162–1227)

("Very Mighty King"), the supreme ruler over all the Mongols. Genghis broke through the Great Wall of China, destroyed the Jin (Chin) empire in northern China, and occupied Beijing. His cavalry swept across Asia as far as Azerbaijan, Georgia, northern Persia, and Kievan Rus. Genghis Khan ordered that after his death his empire would be divided into four principalities or khanates for his sons and grandsons. They continued Mongol expansion. Eventually, Mongol armies conquered territories that stretched from Korea to Hungary and from the Arctic Ocean to the Arabian Sea.

The Mongol success was accomplished through a highly disciplined military organization, tactics that relied on extremely mobile cavalry forces, and a sophisticated intelligence network. During the campaign against the Rus in the winter of 1223, the Mongol cavalry moved with lightning speed across frozen rivers. Although the Rus forces

MONGOL HORSEMAN

Unlike the fourteenth-century European representations of the Mongols, this contemporary Chinese illustration accurately depicts the appearance, dress, and equipment of a Mongol Archer on horseback.

ENCOUNTERS AND TRANSFORMATIONS

The Silk Road

Nothing better facilitated encounters between East and West than the Silk Road. The label actually refers to a network of caravan trails connecting China with western Asia and Europe through the Taklimakan, one of the most inhospitable deserts on earth. Travelers had little choice but to pick their way from oasis to oasis across central Asia. On the eastern and western edges of this vast territory the civilizations of China and the West developed, and the Silk Road connected them.

Many highly valuable commodities were transported along these routes besides silk, including ivory, gold, jewels, iron, furs, and ceramics (hence, the term "fine China" for the most precious ceramics). None of these commodities, however, captured the imagination of the West as much as silk, which had been transported from China across the Silk Road since Roman times (see Chapter 6). The importance of the Silk Road required peaceful political conditions to thrive, lest caravans be plundered. Perhaps the greatest era for the Silk Road came under the Chinese T'ang Dynasty (618–907), which provided stability that allowed commerce to flower along the road. After the T'ang dynasty collapsed, the road was unsafe until the Mongol invasions in the thirteenth century.

The Mongol invasions completely altered the composition of Asia and much of eastern Europe—economically, politically, and ethnically. Once the Mongols had conquered new territories, they established the Mongol Peace by reopening the Silk Road across the Asian steppes, making trans-Eurasian trade possible and guaranteeing the safety of merchants. Thanks to the Mongols, European Christians began to traverse the Silk Road to China and to encounter directly the civilizations of the East. The Mongols were tolerant of religious diversity and welcomed the first Christian missionaries into China. A Roman Catholic archbishopric was founded in Beijing in 1307.

The most famous of the many merchants who traversed the Silk Road during the Mongol Peace were the Venetians from the Polo family, including Marco Polo, who arrived at the court of the Great Khan in China in 1275. Marco Polo's book about his travels offers a vivid and often remarkably perceptive account of the Mongol Empire during the Mongol Peace. It also illustrates better than any other source the cultural engagement of the Christian West with the Mongol East during the late thirteenth century. Although Marco Polo was a merchant who traveled to make a profit, his book brought a great store of cultural information, some accurate, some fanciful that stimulated the western imagination about the East. Perhaps most revealing were his discussions of religion. Marco classified peoples according to their religion and evaluated religions with the eye of a western European Catholic. He was harshest about Muslims, but seemed more tolerant of "idolaters," that is Buddhists and Hindus, whose practices he found intriguing. He also reported on magical practices and reports of miracles. Because of the popularity of his book, Marco Polo's views of Asia became the principle source of knowledge in the West about the East until the sixteenth century.

For Discussion

What were the advantages and disadvantages of the Mongol Peace for the West?

CHRONOLOGY: THE MONGOLS

1206–1227	Reign of Genghis Khan
1206–1258	Mongol armies advance undefeated across Eurasia
1260	Defeat in Syria of Mongols by Mamluks of Egypt
1369–1405	Reign of Tamerlane

outnumbered the Mongol armies and had superior armor, they were crushed in every encounter with the Mongols.

The Mongol armies employed clever tactics. First, they unnerved enemy soldiers with a hail of arrows. Then they would appear to retreat, only to draw the enemy into false confidence before the Mongol horsemen delivered a deadly final blow. European chroniclers at the time tried to explain their many defeats at the hands of the Mongols by reporting that the Mongol "hordes" had overwhelming numbers, but evidence clearly shows that their victories were the result not of superior numbers, but of superior discipline and the sophistication of the Mongol intelligence network.

Mongol power climaxed in 1260. In that year the Mongols suffered a crushing defeat in Syria at the hands of the Mamluk rulers of Egypt, an event that ended the Mongol reputation for invincibility. Conflicts and succession disputes among the various Mongol tribes made them vulnerable to rivals and to rebellion from their unhappy subjects. The Mongol Empire did not disappear overnight, but its various successor khanates never recaptured the dynamic unity forged by Genghis Khan. During the fourteenth century the Mongol Peace sputtered to an end.

In the wake of these upheavals, a warrior of Mongol descent known as Tamerlane (r. 1369–1405) created an army composed of Mongols, Turks, and Persians, which challenged the established Mongol khanates. Tamerlane's conquests rivaled those of Genghis Khan, but with very different results. His armies pillaged the rich cities that supplied the caravan routes. Thus, in his attempt to monopolize the lucrative trans-Eurasian trade, Tamerlane largely destroyed it. The collapse of the Mongol Peace broke the thread of commerce across Eurasia and stimulated the European search for alternative routes to China that ultimately resulted in the voyages of Christopher Columbus in 1492. (See *Encounters and Transformations* in this chapter.)

The Rise of the Ottoman Turks

The Mongol armies were never very large, so the Mongols had always augmented their numbers with Turkish tribes. The result was that outside Mongolia, Turks gradually absorbed the Mongols. Turkish replaced Mongolian as the dominant language, and the Turks took over the government of the central Asian empires that had been scraped together by the Mongol conquests. In contrast to the Mongols, many of whom remained Buddhists, the Turks became Muslims and created an exceptionally dynamic, expansionist society of their own (see **Map 11.3**).

Among the Turkish peoples, the most successful state builders were the Ottomans. Named for Osman I (r. 1281–1326), who brought it to prominence, the Ottoman dynasty endured for more than 600 years, until 1924. The nucleus of the Ottoman state was a small principality in Anatolia (a portion of present-day Turkey), which in the early fourteenth century began to expand at the expense of its weaker neighbors, including the Byzantine Empire. The Ottoman state was built not on national, linguistic, or ethnic unity, but on a purely dynastic network of personal and military loyalties to the Ottoman prince, called the sultan. Thus, the vitality of the empire depended on the energy of the individual sultans. The Ottomans thought of themselves as *ghazis*,

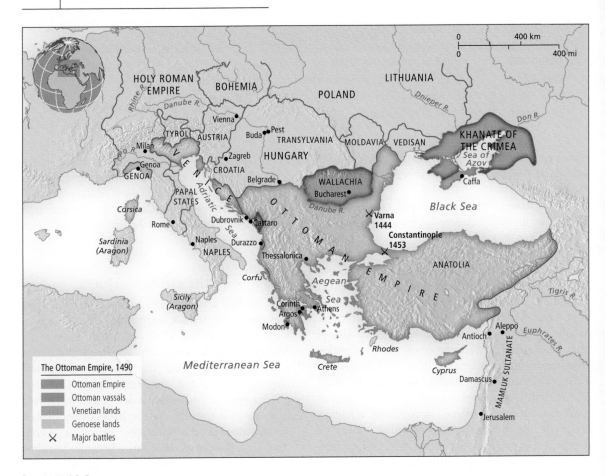

MAP 11.3

The Ottoman Empire

The Ottoman state expanded from a small principality in Anatolia, which is south of the Black Sea. From there the Ottomans spread eastward into Kurdistan and Armenia. In the West they captured all of Greece and much of the Balkan peninsula.

warriors for Islam devoted to destroying polytheists, including Christians. (To some Muslims, the Christian belief in the Trinity and veneration of numerous saints demonstrated that Christians were not true monotheists.) During the fourteenth century, incessant Ottoman guerilla actions gradually chipped away at the Byzantine frontier.

The Byzantine Empire in the middle of the thirteenth century was emerging from a period of domination by Frankish knights and Venetian merchants who had conquered Constantinople during the Fourth Crusade in 1204. In 1261, the Byzantine emperor, Michael VIII Palaeologus (r. 1260–1282), recaptured the great city. The revived Byzantine Empire, however, was a pale vestige of what it once had been, and the Palaeologi emperors desperately sought military assistance from western Europe to defend themselves from the Ottomans. Dependent on mercenary armies and divided by civil wars, the Byzantines offered only pathetic resistance to the all-conquering Ottomans.

From their base in Anatolia, the Ottomans raided far and wide, launching pirate fleets into the Aegean and gradually encircling Constantinople after they crossed over into Europe in 1308. By 1402 Ottoman territory had grown to 40 times its size a century earlier. During that century of conquests, the frontier between Christianity and Islam shifted. The former subjects of the Byzantines in the Balkans fell to the Ottoman Turks. Fragile Serbia, a bastion of Orthodox Christianity in the Balkans, broke under Ottoman pressure. First unified in the late twelfth century, Serbia established political independence from Byzantium and autonomy for the Serbian church. Although the Serbs had taken control over a number of former Byzantine provinces, they fell to the invincible Ottomans at the Battle of Kosovo in 1389. Lamenting the Battle of Kosovo has remained the bedrock of Serbian national identity to this day.

Serbia's western neighbors, the kingdoms of Bosnia and Herzegovina, deflated under Ottoman pressure during the late fifteenth century. Unlike Serbia, where most of the population remained loyal to the Serbian Orthodox Church, in Bosnia and Herzegovina the Serbian-speaking land-holding classes converted to Islam to preserve their property. The subjugated peasants, also Serbian-speaking, remained Orthodox Christians who turned over one-third of everything they raised to their Muslim lords, which created considerable resentment and religious tensions. The Ottomans allowed the Bosnians to keep their territorial identity and name, a unique situation among conquered provinces of the Ottoman Empire.

When Mehmed II, "The Conqueror" (r. 1451–1481), became the Ottoman sultan, he began to obliterate the last remnants of the Byzantine Empire. During the winter of 1451–1452, the sultan ordered the encirclement of Constantinople, a city that had once been the largest in the world but now was reduced from perhaps a million people to fewer than 50,000. The Ottoman siege strategy was to bombard Constantinople into submission with daily rounds from enormous cannons. The largest was a monster cannon, 29 feet long, that could shoot 1,200-pound stones. It required a crew of 200 soldiers and 60 oxen to handle it, and each firing generated so much heat

that it took hours to cool off before it could be fired again. The siege was a gargantuan task because the walls of Constantinople, which had been built, repaired, and improved over a period of a 1,000 years, were formidable. However, the new weapon of gunpowder artillery had rendered city walls a military anachronism. Brought from China by the Mongols, gunpowder had gradually revolutionized warfare. Breaching city walls in sieges was merely a matter of time as long as the heavy metal cannons could be dragged into position. Quarrels among the Christians also hampered the defense of Constantinople's walls. Toward the end, the Byzantine emperor was forced to melt down church treasures so "that from them coins should be struck and given to the soldiers, the sappers and the builders, who selfishly cared so little for the public welfare that they were refusing to go to their work unless they were first paid."[5]

The final assault came in May 1453 and lasted less than a day. When the city fell, the Ottoman army spent the day plundering, raping, and enslaving the populace. The last Byzantine emperor, Constantine XI, was never found amid the multitude of the dead. The fall of Constantinople ended the Christian Byzantine Empire, the continuous remnant of the ancient Roman Empire. But the idea of Rome was not so easily snuffed out. The first Ottoman sultans residing in Constantinople continued to be called "Roman emperors."

Although the western European princes had done little to save Byzantium, its demise shocked them. Now they were also vulnerable to the Ottoman onslaught. For the next 200 years the Ottomans used Constantinople as a base to threaten Christian Europe. Hungary and the eastern Mediterranean empire of Venice remained the last lines of defense for the West, and at various times in succeeding centuries the Ottomans launched expeditions against Europe, including two sieges of Vienna (1529 and 1683) and several invasions of Italy.

Hundreds of years of attacks by the Mongol and Ottoman Empires redrew the map of the West. Events in Europe did not and could not

CHRONOLOGY: THE CONQUESTS OF THE OTTOMAN TURKS

1281–1326	Reign of Osman I
1308	Ottoman Empire advances into Europe
1389	Battle of Kosovo; Serbia becomes vassal state of the Ottomans
1451–1481	Reign of Mehmed II, "The Conqueror"
1453	Fall of Constantinople and death of last Byzantine emperor

take place in isolation from the eastern pressures and influences. The Mongol conquest finished off Kievan Rus. Although Mongols burned down Moscow in the winter of 1238 and pillaged it in 1293, its remote, forested location offered some security from further attacks and occupation. As a result, Moscow and the Republic of Novgorod, which escaped the Mongol attacks entirely, replaced Kiev as the centers of power in what would become Russia. The Ottoman conquests also created a lasting Muslim presence within the borders of Europe, especially in Bosnia and Albania. In succeeding centuries Christian Europe and the Muslim Ottoman Empire would be locked in a deadly competitive embrace, but they also benefited from innumerable cultural exchanges and regular trade. Hostility between the two sides was recurrent but never inevitable and was broken by long periods of peaceful engagement. In fact, the Christian kingdoms of western Europe went to war far more often with one another than with the Turks.

ECONOMIC DEPRESSION AND SOCIAL TURMOIL

■ How did disturbances in the rudimentary global economy of the Middle Ages precipitate almost complete financial collapse and widespread social discontent in Europe?

Adding insult to injury in this time of famine, plague, and conquest, the West began to suffer a major economic depression during the fourteenth century. The economic boom fueled by the agricultural revolution and the revitalization of European cities during the eleventh century and the commercial prosperity of the twelfth and thirteenth centuries petered out in the fourteenth. The causes of this economic catastrophe were complex, but the consequences were obvious. Businesses went bust, banks collapsed, guilds were in turmoil, and workers rebelled.

At the same time, the effects of the depression were unevenly felt. Eastern Europe, which was less fully integrated into the international economy, fared better than western Europe. The economic conditions for many peasants actually improved because there was a labor shortage in the countryside due to the loss of population. Forced to pay their peasants more for their labor and crops, landlords saw their own fortunes decline. Finding it harder to pay the higher prices for food, urban workers probably suffered the most because their wages did not keep up with the cost of living.

The Collapse of International Trade and Banking

After the break up of the Mongol Empire and the conquests of Tamerlane, trade between Europe and Asia dwindled. The entire financial infrastructure of medieval Europe was tied to this international trade in luxury goods. The successful, entrepreneurial Italian merchants who dominated the luxury trade deposited their enormous profits in Italian banks. The Italian bankers lent money to the aristocracy and royalty of northern Europe to finance the purchases of exotic luxuries and to fight wars. The whole system was mutually reinforcing, but it was very fragile. With the disruption of supply sources for luxury goods, the financial networks of Europe collapsed, precipitating a major depression. By 1346, all the banks in Florence, the banking center of Europe, had crashed.

The luxury trade that brought exotic items from Asia to Europe represented only half of the economic equation. The other half was the raw materials and manufactured goods that Europeans sold in exchange, principally woolen cloth. The production of woolen cloth depended on a sophisticated economic system that connected shepherds in England, the Netherlands, and Spain with woolen cloth manufacturers in cities. The manufacture of cloth and other commodities was organized by **guilds**, which were professional associations devoted to protecting the special interests of a particular trade or craft and to monopolizing production and trade in the goods the guild produced.

There were two types of guilds. The first type, merchant guilds, attempted to monopolize the local market for a particular commodity. There were spice guilds, fruit and vegetable guilds, and apothecary guilds. The second type, craft guilds, regulated the manufacturing processes of artisans such as carpenters, bricklayers, woolen-cloth manufacturers, glass blowers, and painters. These guilds were dominated by master craftsmen, who ran their own shops. Working for wages in these shops were the journeymen, who knew the craft but could not yet afford to open their own shops. Under the masters and journeymen were apprentices, who worked usually without pay for a specific number of years to learn the trade.

In many cities the guilds expanded far beyond the economic regulation of trade and manufacturing to become the backbone of urban society and politics. The masters of the guilds constituted part of the urban elite, and guild membership was often a prerequisite for holding public office. One of the obligations of city government was to protect the interests of the guildsmen, who in turn helped stabilize the economy through their influence in city hall. Guilds often organized festivals and sports competitions, endowed chapels, and provided funeral insurance for their members and welfare for the injured and widows of masters.

When the economy declined during the fourteenth century, the urban guilds became lightning rods for mounting social tension. Guild monopolies produced considerable conflict, provoking anger among those who were blocked from joining guilds, young journeymen who earned low wages, and those who found themselves unemployed due to the depression. These tensions exploded into dangerous revolts.

Workers' Rebellions

Economic pressures erupted into rebellion most dramatically among woolen-cloth workers in the urban centers in Italy, the Netherlands, and France. The most famous revolt involved the Ciompi, the laborers in the woolen-cloth industry of Florence, Italy, where guilds were the most powerful force in city government. The Ciompi, who performed the heaviest jobs such as carting and the most noxious tasks such as dyeing, had not been allowed to have their own guild and were therefore deprived of the political and economic rights of guild membership.

Fueling the Ciompi's frustration was the fact that by the middle of the fourteenth century woolen-cloth production in Florence dropped by two-thirds, leaving many workers unemployed. In 1378 the desperate Ciompi rebelled. A crowd chanting, "Long live the people, long live liberty," broke into the houses of prominent citizens, released political prisoners from the city jails, and sacked the rich convents that housed the pampered daughters of the wealthy. Over the course of a few months, the rebels managed to force their way onto the city council, where they demanded tax and economic reforms and the right to form their own guild. The Ciompi revolt is one of the earliest cases of workers demanding political rights. The disenfranchised workers did not want to eliminate the guilds' monopoly on political power. They merely wanted a guild of their own so that they could join the regime. That was not to be, however. After a few weeks of success, the Ciompi were divided and defeated.

Shortly after the Ciompi revolt faded, troubles broke out in the woolen-cloth centers of Ghent and Bruges in Flanders and in Paris and Rouen in France. In these cases, however, the revolt spread beyond woolen-cloth workers to voice the more generalized grievances of urban workers. In Ghent and Bruges the weavers attempted to wrest control of their cities from the local leaders who dominated politics and the economy. In Paris and Rouen in 1380, social unrest erupted in resistance to high taxes and attacks by the poor on the rich.

Like urban workers, many rural peasants also rebelled during the troubled fourteenth century. In France in 1358 a peasant revolt broke out called the *Jacquerie*. Filled with hatred for the aristocracy, the peasants indulged in pillaging, murder, and rape, but they offered no plan for an alternative social system or even for their own participation in the political order, so their movement had no lasting effects. They were quickly defeated by a force of nobles.

Unlike the French Jacquerie, the peasants who revolted in England in 1381 had a clear political vision for an alternative society. The English rebels demanded the abolition of new taxes, lower rents, higher wages, and the end of serfdom, but to these they added a class-based argument against the aristocracy. Influenced by popular preachers, who told them that in the Garden of Eden there had been no aristocracy, the English rebels imagined an egalitarian society without ranks or hierarchy. However, the greatest peasant rebellion in medieval English history ended with broken promises and no tangible achievements.

CHRONOLOGY: ECONOMIC DEPRESSION AND SOCIAL TURMOIL

1310–1320	Famines begin
1348	Arrival of Black Death in Europe
1358	Jacquerie revolt in France
1378	Ciompi revolt in Florence
1379–1385	Urban revolts in Flanders and France
1381	Peasants revolt in England

None of the worker or peasant revolts of the fourteenth century met with lasting success. However, the rebellions revealed for the first time in the West a widespread impulse among the lower classes to question and protest the existing social and economic order. The tradition of worker protest became common and recurrent during subsequent centuries.

AN AGE OF WARFARE

■ How did incessant warfare transform the most powerful medieval states?

Prolonged war between its two largest and previously most stable kingdoms, England and France, further weakened western Europe during the fourteenth century. The **Hundred Years' War** (1337–1453) was a struggle over England's attempts to assert its claims to territories in France. The conflict drained resources from the French and English aristocracies, deepening and lengthening the economic depression.

The Fragility of Monarchies

Medieval monarchies depended on the king to maintain stability. Despite the remarkable legal reforms and bureaucratic centralization of monarchies in England and France during the twelfth and thirteenth centuries (see Chapter 10), weak or incompetent kings were all too common during the fourteenth. Weak kings created a perilous situation made worse by disputed successions. The career of Edward II (r. 1307–1327) of England illustrates the peril. Edward was unable to control the vital judicial and financial mechanisms of royal power. He continued the policy of his father, Edward I, by introducing resident justices of the peace who had replaced the inadequate system of itinerant judges who traveled from village to village to hear cases. In theory, these justices of the peace should have prevented the abuses of justice typical of aristocratic jurisdictions, but even though they were royal officials who answered to the king, most of those appointed were also local landowners who were deeply implicated in many of the disputes that came before them. As a result, justice in England became notoriously corrupt and the cause of discontent. Edward II was so incompetent to deal with the consequences of corrupted justice that he provoked a civil war in which his own queen joined his aristocratic enemies to depose him.

The French monarchy was no better. In fact, the French king was in an even weaker constitutional position than the English monarch. In France the king had effective jurisdiction over only a small part of his realm. Many of the duchies and counties of France were quasi-independent principalities paying only nominal allegiance to the king, whose will was ignored with impunity. In these regions the administration of justice, the collection of taxes, and the recruitment of soldiers all remained in the hands of local lords. To explain why he needed to raise taxes, Philip IV, "The Fair" (r. 1285–1314), created a representative assembly, the Estates General, which met for the first time in 1302, but he still had to negotiate with each region and town individually to collect the taxes. Given the difficulty of raising taxes, the French kings resorted to makeshift solutions that hurt the economy, such as confiscating the property of vulnerable Jewish and Italian merchants and debasing the coinage. Such a system made the finances of the kingdom of France especially shaky because the king lacked a dependable flow of revenue.

The Hundred Years' War

The Hundred Years' War revealed the fragility of the medieval monarchies. The initial cause of the war involved disputes over the duchy of Aquitaine. The king of England inherited the title of duke of Aquitaine, who was a vassal of the French crown, which meant that the English kings technically owed military assistance to the French kings whenever they asked for it. A long succession of English kings had reluctantly paid homage as dukes of Aquitaine to the king of France, but the unusual status of the duchy held by the king of England was a continuing source of contention.

The second cause of the war derived from a dispute over the succession to the French crown. When King Charles IV died in 1328, his closest surviving relative was none other than the arch-enemy of France, Edward III (r. 1327–1377), king of England. To the barons of France, the possibility of Edward's succession to the throne was unthinkable, and they excluded him because his relation to the French royal family was through his mother. Instead the barons elected to the throne a member of the Valois family, King Philip VI (r. 1328–1350). At first Edward reluctantly accepted the decision. However, when Philip started to hear judicial appeals from the duchy of Aquitaine, Edward changed his mind. He claimed the title of king of France for himself, sparking the beginning of more than a century of warfare (see **Map 11.4**).

The Hundred Years' War (1337–1453) was not a continuous formal war, but a series of occasional pitched battles, punctuated by long truces and periods of general exhaustion. Nineteenth-century historians invented the term *Hundred Years' War* to describe the prolonged time of troubles between the two countries. France, far richer and with three times the population, held the advantage over sparsely populated England, but the English were usually victorious because of superior discipline and the ability of their long-bows to break up cavalry charges. As a rule, the English avoided open battle, preferring raids, sieges of isolated castles, and capturing French knights for ransom. For many Englishmen the objective of fighting in France was to get rich by looting. Because all the fighting took place on French soil, France suffered extensive destruction and significant civilian casualties from repeated English raids.

FROM ENGLISH VICTORIES TO FRENCH SALVATION In the early phases of the war, the English enjoyed a stunning series of victories. At the Battle of Sluys in 1340, a small English fleet of 150 ships carrying the English invasion forces ran into a French blockade of more than 200

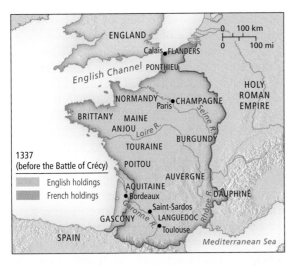

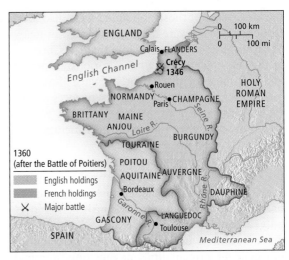

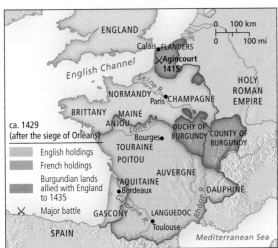

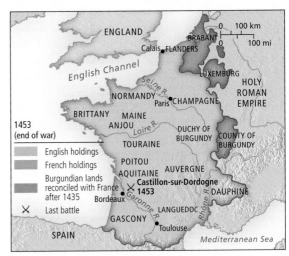

MAP 11.4

The Hundred Years' War

This map illustrates four phases of the Hundred Years' War. In the first phase (1337), England maintained a small foothold in the southwest of France. In the second phase (1360), England considerably expanded the territory around Aquitaine and gained a vital base in the north of France. In the third phase (ca. 1429), England occupied much of the north of France, and England's ally Burgundy established effective independence from French authority. In the fourth phase at the end of the war (1453), England had been driven from French soil except at Calais, and Burgundy maintained control over most of its scattered territories.

ships. In the heavy hand-to-hand combat, the English captured 166 French ships and killed some 20,000 men, so many that it was later said, "If fish could talk, they would speak French." At Agincourt in 1415, King Henry V (r. 1413–1422) and England's disease-racked

army of 6,000 were cut off by a French force of about 20,000, yet in the ensuing battle the English archers repelled a hasty French cavalry charge and the fleeing, terrified horses trampled the French men-at-arms as they advanced. The English lost only a few hundred, but the French

ENGLISH LONGBOW ARCHERS

English archers use the longbow at the Battle of Crecy in 1346. The English longbow archers on the right are massacring the French crossbowmen on the left. Because of the cumbersome process of cranking back the bowstring between shots, the crossbow had a much slower shooting rate than a longbow.

suffered nearly 10,000 casualties. After Agincourt, the French never again dared challenge King Henry in open battle, and were forced to recognize him as the heir to the French throne.

English victory appeared complete, but by 1422 Henry V was dead, leaving two claimants to the French throne. The English asserted the rights of the infant King Henry VI of England, son of King Henry V. Most of the French defended the claim of the Dauphin (the title of the heir to the throne) Charles, the only surviving son of the late King Charles VI of France. The Hundred Years' War entered a new phase with factions of the French aristocracy supporting the two rivals in a bloody series of engagements. The war was now as much a civil war as one between kingdoms.

By 1429 the English were again on the verge of final victory. They occupied Paris and Rheims, and their army was besieging Orleans. The Dauphin Charles was penniless and indecisive. Even his own mother denied his legitimacy as the future king. At this point, a 17-year-old illiterate peasant from Burgundy, Joan of Arc (Jeanne d'Arc, ca. 1412–1431), following "divine voices," went to Orleans to lead the French armies. Under her inspiration Orleans was relieved, French forces began to defeat the English, much of the occupied territory was regained, and the Dauphin was crowned King Charles VII (r. 1429–1461) in the cathedral of Rheims. After Joan failed to recapture Paris, however, her successes ceased. (See *Justice in History* in this chapter.) The final victory of the French came from the leadership of King Charles and the general exhaustion of the English forces.

Charles VII reorganized the French army and gradually chipped away at the English holdings in France, eventually taking away Aquitaine in 1453. The English lost all their possessions in France except Calais, which was finally surrendered in 1558. There was no peace treaty, just a fading away of war in France, especially after England stumbled into civil war—the War of the Roses (1455–1485).

The Trial of Joan of Arc

After only 15 months as the inspiration of the French army, Joan of Arc fell into the hands of the English, who brought her to trial at Rouen in 1431 for witchcraft. The English needed to stage a show trial to demonstrate to their own demoralized forces that Joan's remarkable victories resulted from witchcraft rather than military superiority. In the English trial, Joan testified that she was merely responding to spiritual voices she heard that commanded her to wear men's clothing. On the basis of her cross dressing, the ecclesiastical tribunal declared her a witch and a relapsed heretic. The court sentenced her to be burned at the stake.

From the beginning of her emergence onto the political scene, the voices Joan's heard guided her every move. Joan claimed that she heard the voices of St. Catherine, St. Margaret, and the Archangel Michael. To Joan, these voices carried the authority of divine commands. The problem the English judges faced was to demonstrate that the voices came from the Devil rather than from God. If they could prove that, then they had evidence of witchcraft and sorcery. Following standard inquisitorial guidelines, the judges knew that authentic messages from God would always conform to church dogma. Any deviation from official doctrines would constitute evidence of demonic influence. Thus, during Joan's trial the judges demanded that she make theological distinctions that were alien to her. When they wanted to know if the voices were those of angels or saints, Joan seemed perplexed and responded, "This voice comes from God....I am more afraid of failing the voices by saying what is displeasing to them than answering you."[6] The judges kept pushing, asking if the saints or angels had heads, eyes, and hair. Exasperated, Joan simply replied, "I have told you often enough, believe me if you will."

The judges reformulated Joan's words to reflect their own rigid scholastic categories and concluded that her "veneration of the saints seems to partake of idolatry and to proceed from a pact made with devils. These are less divine revelations than lies invented by Joan, suggested or shown to

her by the demon in illusive apparitions, in order to mock at her imagination while she meddled with things that are beyond her and superior to the faculty of her condition."[7] In other words, Joan was just too naive and uneducated to have authentic visions. But the English judges were on dangerous ground because during the previous 50 years there had been a number of notable female mystics, including St. Catherine of Siena and St. Bridget of Sweden, whose visions the pope had accepted as authentic. The English could not take the chance that they were executing a real saint. So they changed tactics.

If they could not convict her for bad theology, the English needed evidence for superstitious practices. In an attempt to do that, they drew up 70 charges against Joan. Many of these consisted of allegations of performing magic, such as chanting spells, visiting a magical tree at night, and invoking demons. They attempted to prove bad behavior by insinuating that a young man had refused to marry her on account of her immoral life. They asserted that her godmother was a notorious witch who had taught her sorcery. None of these ploys worked, however, because Joan consistently denied the charges. She did, however, admit to one allegation: she dressed as a man.

Some of the charges against her and many of the judges' questions concerned how she dressed:

> The said Joan put off and entirely abandoned women's clothes, with her hair cropped short and round in the fashion of young men, she wore shirt, breeches, doublet, with hose joined together, long and fastened to the said doublet by twenty points, long leggings laced on the outside, a short mantle reaching to the knee, or thereabouts, a close-cut cap, tight-fitting boots or buskins, long spurs, sword, dagger, breastplate, lance and other arms in the style of a man-at-arms.[8]

The judges explained to her that "according to canon law and the Holy Scriptures" a woman dressing as a man or a man as a woman is "an abomination before God."[9] She replied simply and consistently that "everything that I have done, I did by command of the voices" and that wearing male dress "would be for the great good of France."[10] When they asked her to put on a woman's dress in order to take the Eucharist on Easter Sunday, she refused, saying the miracle of the Eucharist did not depend on whether she wore a man's or a woman's clothing. On many occasions she had been asked to put on a woman's dress and refused. "And as for womanly duties, she said there were enough other women to do them."[11]

After a long imprisonment and psychological pressure from her inquisitors, Joan confessed to charges of witchcraft, signed a recantation of her heresy, and agreed to put on a dress. She was sentenced to life imprisonment on bread and water. Why did she confess? Some historians have argued that she was tricked into confessing because the inquisitors really wanted to execute her but could not do so unless she was a *relapsed* heretic. To be relapsed she had to confess and then somehow return to her heretical ways. If that were the inquisitors' intention, Joan soon obliged them. After a few days in prison, Joan threw off the women's clothes she had been given and resumed dressing as a man.

Joan was willing to be burned at the stake rather than disobey her voices. Why? Historians will never know for sure, but dressing as a man may have been necessary for her to fulfill her role as a military leader. In her military career, Joan had adopted the masculine qualities of chivalry: bravery, steadfastness, loyalty, *and* a willingness to accept pain and death. She made herself believable by dressing as a knight. Joan's condemnation was much more than another example of men's attempt to control women. Joan's transgressive gender identity threatened the whole system of neat hierarchical distinctions upon which Christian theology rested. To the theologians, everything in God's Creation had its own proper place and anyone who changed his or her divinely ordained position in society presented a direct affront to God.

JOAN OF ARC

There are no contemporary portraits of Joan, and this image is clearly a generalized one of a young woman rather than a portrait taken from the real Joan.

Source: Marc Charmet/Picture Desk, Inc./Kobal Collection

For Discussion

1. In medieval ecclesiastical trials such as this one, what kinds of evidence were presented and what kind of justice was sought?

2. What did Joan's claim that she heard voices reveal about her understanding of what constituted the proper authority over her life?

Taking It Further

Joan of Arc. *In Her Own Words,* Translated by Willard Trask. 1996. The record of what Joan reputedly said at her trials.

Warner, Marina. *Joan of Arc: The Image of Female Heroism.* 1981. A highly readable feminist reading of the Joan of Arc story.

THE HUNDRED YEARS' WAR IN PERSPECTIVE The Hundred Years' War had broad consequences. First, nearly continuous warfare between the two most powerful kingdoms in the West exacerbated other conflicts as well. Scotland, the German princes, Aragon, Castile, and most importantly Burgundy were drawn into the conflict, making the English-French brawl a European-wide war at certain stages. The squabble between France and England also made it much more difficult to settle the Great Schism that split the Church during the same period. Second, the war devastated France, which eventually regained control of most of its territory but still suffered the most from the fighting. During the century of war, the population dropped by half, due to the ravages of combat, pillage, and plague. Third, the deaths of so many nobles and destruction of their fortunes diminished the international luxury trade. Merchants and banks as far away as Italy went broke. In addition, the war disrupted the Flemish woolen industry causing further economic damage. Finally, the war helped make England more English. Before the war the Plantagenet dynasty in England was more French than English. The monarchs possessed extensive territories in France and were embroiled in French affairs. English aristocrats also had business in France, spoke French, and married their French cousins. After 1450 the English abandoned the many French connections that had stretched across the English Channel since William the Conqueror sailed from Normandy to England in 1066. Henceforth, the English upper classes cultivated English rather than French language and culture.

The Military Revolution

The "military revolution" first became evident during the Hundred Years' War but lasted well into the seventeenth century. It refers to changes in warfare that marked the transition from the late medieval to the early modern state. The heavily armored mounted knights, who had dominated European warfare and society since the Carolingian period, were gradually supplanted by foot soldiers as the most effective fighting unit in battle. Infantry units were composed of men who fought on foot in disciplined ranks, which allowed them to break up cavalry charges by concentrating firepower in deadly volleys. Infantry soldiers could fight on a greater variety of terrains than mounted knights, who needed level ground and plenty of space for their horses to maneuver. The effectiveness of infantry units made battles more ferocious but also more decisive, which was why governments favored them. Infantry, however, put new requirements on the governments that recruited them. Armies now demanded large numbers of well-drilled foot soldiers who could move in disciplined

CHRONOLOGY: AN AGE OF WARFARE

1285	Philip IV, "The Fair," succeeds to the throne of France
1307	Edward II succeeds to the throne of England
1327	Edward III succeeds to the throne of England
1328	Philip VI succeeds to the throne of France
1337	Hundred Years' War begins
1340	Battle of Sluys
1413	Henry V succeeds to the throne of England
1415	Battle of Agincourt
1429	Charles VII succeeds to the throne of France
1455–1485	War of the Roses in England

ranks around a battlefield. Recruiting, training, and drilling soldiers made armies much more complex organizations than they had been, and officers needed to possess a wide range of management skills. Governments faced added expenses as they needed to arrange and pay for the logistical support necessary to feed and transport those large numbers. The creation of the highly centralized modern state resulted in part from the necessity to maintain a large army in which infantry played the crucial role.

Infantry used a variety of weapons. The English demonstrated the effectiveness of longbowmen during the Hundred Years' War. Capable of shooting at a much more rapid rate than the French crossbowmen, the English longbowmen at Agincourt protected themselves behind a hurriedly erected stockade of stakes and rained a shower of deadly arrows on the French cavalry to break up charges. In the narrow battlefield, which was wedged between two forests, the French cavalry had insufficient room to maneuver; when some of them dismounted to create more room, their heavy armor made them easy to topple over and spear through the underarm seam in their armor. Some English infantry units deployed ranks of pikemen who created an impenetrable wall of sharp spikes.

The military revolution of the fourteenth and fifteenth centuries also introduced gunpowder to European warfare. Arriving from China with the Mongol invasions, gunpowder was first used in the West in artillery. Beginning in the 1320s besieging armies shot stone or iron against fortifications from huge wrought-iron cannons. By the early sixteenth century bronze muzzle-loading cannons were used in field battles. With the introduction during the late fifteenth century of the handgun and the harquebus (a predecessor to the musket), properly drilled and disciplined infantrymen could deliver destructive firepower. Gunshots pierced plate armor, whereas arrows bounced off. The slow rate of fire of these guns, however, necessitated carefully planned battle tactics. Around 1500 the Spanish introduced mixed infantry formations that pursued "shock" and "shot" tactics. Spanish pikemen provided the shock, which was quickly followed by gunshot or missile fire. This combination of technology and technique enabled Spanish infantry formations to defeat cavalry even in the open field without defensive fortifications, an unprecedented feat. By the end of the fifteenth century, every army included trained infantry.

The military revolution precipitated a major shift in European society. The successful states were those that created the financial base and bureaucratic structures necessary to field a professional army composed of infantry units and artillery. Superior armies required officers capable of drilling infantry or understanding the science of warfare to serve as an artillery officer.

A TROUBLED CHURCH AND THE DEMAND FOR RELIGIOUS COMFORT

■ Why did the Church fail to provide leadership and spiritual guidance during these difficult times?

In reaction to the suffering and widespread death during the fourteenth century, many people turned to religion for spiritual consolation and for explanations of what had gone wrong. But the spiritual authority of the Church was so dangerously weakened during this period that it failed to satisfy the popular craving for solace. The moral leadership that had made the papacy such a powerful force for reform during the eleventh through thirteenth centuries evaporated in the fourteenth. Many laypeople found their own means of religious expression, making the Later Middle Ages one of the most religiously creative epochs in Christian history.

The Babylonian Captivity of the Church and the Great Schism

Faced with anarchy in the streets of Rome as local aristocrats engaged in incessant feuding, seven consecutive popes chose to reside in the relative calm of Avignon, France. This period of voluntary papal exile is known as the **Babylonian Captivity of the Church** (1305–1378), a biblical reference recalling the captivity of the Jews in Babylonia (587–539 B.C.E.). The popes' presumed subservience to the kings of France during this period dangerously politicized the papacy, destroying its ability to rise above the petty squabbles of the European princes and to serve as a spiritual authority to all. Even though these French popes residing in France were never the French kings' lackeys, the enemies of the kings of France did not trust them. The loss of revenues from papal lands in Italy lured several popes into questionable financial schemes, which included accepting kickbacks from appointees to church offices, taking bribes for judicial decisions, and selling **indulgences,** certificates that allowed penitents to atone for their sins and reduce their time in Purgatory.

When Pope Urban VI (r. 1378–1389) announced his intention to reside in Rome, a group of disgruntled French cardinals returned to Avignon and elected a rival French pope. The Church was then divided over allegiance to Italian and French claimants to the papal throne, a period called the **Great Schism** (1378–1417). Toward the end of the schism there were actually four rival popes. During the Great Schism the kings, princes, and cities of Europe divided their allegiances between the rival candidates. Competing political alliances, not doctrinal differences, split the Church.

The **Conciliar Movement** attempted to create a mechanism for ending the Schism. The conciliarists, however, also sought to restrict the theoretical and practical authority of the papacy. They argued that a general meeting or *council* of the bishops of the Church had authority over the pope. A king could call such a council to undertake reforms, pass judgment on a standing pope, or order a conclave to elect a new one. Several general councils convened during the early fifteenth century to resolve the schism and initiate reforms, but the intertwining of political and Church affairs made solutions were difficult to achieve. The Council of Constance (1414–1417) finally succeeded in

restoring unity to the Church and also in formally asserting the principle that a general council was superior to the pope and should be called frequently. The Council of Basel (1431–1449) approved a series of necessary reforms, but Pope Eugene IV (r. 1431–1447), who opposed conciliarism, never implemented them. The failure of even the timid reforms of the Council of Basel opened the way for the more radical rejection of papal authority during the Protestant Reformation of the sixteenth century.

The Search for Religious Alternatives

The popes' loss of moral authority during the Babylonian Captivity and the Great Schism opened the way for a remarkable variety of reformers, mystics, and preachers. Most of these movements were traditional in their doctrines, but some were heretical. The weakened papacy was unable to control them, as it had successfully done during the thirteenth-century crusade against the Albigensians.

PROTESTS AGAINST THE PAPACY: NEW HERESIES   For most Catholic Christians during the fourteenth century, religious life consisted of witnessing or participating in the seven sacraments, the formal rituals celebrated by duly consecrated priests usually within the confines of churches. After baptism, which was universally performed on infants, the most common sacraments for lay adults were penance and communion. Both of these sacraments emphasized the authority of the clergy over the laity and therefore were potential sources for resentment. The sacrament of penance required the layperson to confess his or her sins to a priest, who then prescribed certain penalties to satisfy the sin. At communion, it was believed, the priest changed the substance of an unleavened wafer of bread, called the Eucharist, into the body of Christ and a chalice of wine into Christ's blood, a miraculous process of transubstantiation (see Chapter 10). Priests and lay recipients of communion both ate the wafer, but the chalice was reserved for the priest alone. More than anything else, the reservation of the chalice for priests profoundly symbolized the privileges of the clergy. Because medieval Catholicism was primarily a sacramental religion, reformers and heretics tended to concentrate their criticism on sacramental rituals.

The most serious discontent about the authority of the popes, the privileges of the clergy, and the efficacy of the sacraments appeared in England and Bohemia (a region in the modern Czech Republic). An Oxford professor, John Wycliffe (1320–1384), criticized the power and wealth of the clergy, played down the value of the sacraments for encouraging ethical behavior, and exalted the benefits of preaching, which promoted a sense of personal responsibility. During the Great Schism, Wycliffe rejected the authority of the rival popes and asserted instead the absolute authority of the Bible, which he wanted to make available to the laity in English rather than in Latin, which most laypeople could not understand.

Outside England Wycliffe's ideas found their most sympathetic audience among a group of reformist professors at the University of Prague in Bohemia, where Jan Hus (1369–1415) regularly preached to a large popular following. Hus's most revolutionary act was to offer the chalice of consecrated communion wine to the laity, thus symbolically diminishing the special status of the clergy. When Hus also preached against indulgences, which he said converted the sacrament of penance into a cash transaction, Pope John XXIII excommunicated him. Hus attended the Council of Constance to defend his ideas. Despite the promise of a safe-conduct from the Holy Roman emperor (whose jurisdiction included Bohemia and Constance) that should have made him immune from arrest, Hus was imprisoned, his writings were condemned, and he was burned alive as a heretic.

Wycliffe and Hus started movements that survived their own deaths. In England Wycliffe's followers were the Lollards and in Bohemia the Hussites carried on reform ideas. Both groups were eventually absorbed into the Protestant Reformation in the sixteenth century.

IMITATING CHRIST: THE MODERN DEVOTION   In the climate of religious turmoil of the fourteenth and fifteenth centuries, many Christians sought deeper spiritual solace than the institutionalized Church could provide. By stressing individual piety, ethical behavior, and intense religious education, a movement called the **Modern Devotion** built on the existing traditions of spirituality and became highly influential. Promoted by the Brothers of the Common Life, a religious order established in the Netherlands, the Modern Devotion was especially popular throughout northern Europe. In the houses for the Brothers, clerics and laity lived together without monastic vows, shared household tasks, joined in regular prayers, and engaged in religious studies. (A similar structure was devised for women.) The lay brothers continued their occupations in the outside world, thus influencing their neighbors through their pious example. The houses established schools that prepared boys for church careers through constant prayer and rigorous training in Latin. Many of the leading figures behind the Protestant Reformation in the sixteenth century had attended schools run by the Brothers of the Common Life.

The Modern Devotion also spread through the influence of the best-seller of the late fifteenth century, the *Imitation of Christ,* written about 1441 by a Common Life brother, probably Thomas à Kempis. By emphasizing frequent private prayer and moral introspection, the *Imitation* provided a manual to guide laypeople in the path toward spiritual renewal that had traditionally been reserved for monks and nuns. There was nothing especially reformist about the *Imitation of Christ,* which emphasized the need for regular confession and communion. However, its popularity helped prepare the way for a broad-based reform of the Church by turning the walls of the monastery inside out, spilling out a large number of lay believers who were dedicated to becoming living examples of moral purity for their neighbors.

CHRONOLOGY: TROUBLES IN THE CHURCH

1305–1378	Babylonian Captivity of the Church; popes reside in Avignon
1320–1384	John Wycliffe
1369–1415	Jan Hus
1378–1417	Great Schism; more than one pope
1414–1417	Council of Constance
1431–1449	Council of Basel
ca. 1441	*Imitation of Christ*

THE CULTURE OF LOSS

■ How did European culture offer explanations and solace for the otherwise inexplicable calamities of the times?

During the fourteenth and early fifteenth centuries, the omnipresence of violence and death provoked widespread anxiety. This anxiety had many manifestations. Some people went on long penitential pilgrimages to the shrines of saints or to the Holy Land. During the fourteenth century the tribulations of the pilgrim's travels became a metaphor for the journey of life itself, stimulating creative literature. Still others tried to find someone to blame for calamities. The search for scapegoats focused on minority groups, especially Jews and Muslims.

Reminders of Death

In no other period of Western civilization has the idea of death so pervaded popular cultures as during the fourteenth and fifteenth centuries. The Reminders of Death was a theme found in religious books, literary works, and the visual arts. A contemporary book of moral guidance advised the reader that "when he goes to bed, he should imagine not that he is putting himself to bed, but that others are laying him in his grave."[12] Reminders of Death became the everyday theme of preachers, and popular woodcuts represented death in simple but disturbing images. The Reminder of Death tried to encourage ethical behavior in this life by showing that in everyone's future was neither riches, nor fame, nor love, nor pleasure, but only the decay of death.

The most famous Reminder of Death was the Dance of Death. First appearing in a poem of 1376, the Dance of Death evolved into a street play, performed to illustrate sermons that called for repentance. It also appeared in church murals, depicting a procession led by a skeleton that included representatives of the social orders, from children and peasants to pope and emperor. All danced to their inevitable deaths. At the Church of the Innocents in Paris, the inscription that accompanies the mural depicting the Dance of Death reads:

> Advance, see yourselves in us, dead, naked, rotten and stinking. So will you be....To live without thinking of this risks damnation....Power, honor, riches are nothing; at the hour of death only good works count....Everyone should think at least once a day of his loathsome end [in order to escape] the dreadful pain of hell without end which is unspeakable.[13]

In earlier centuries, tombs had depicted death as serene: On top of the tomb rested an effigy of the deceased, dressed in the finest clothes with hands piously folded and eyes open to the promise of eternal life. In contrast, during the fourteenth century, tomb effigies began to depict putrefying bodies or naked skeletons, symbols of the futility of human status and achievements. These tombs were disturbingly graphic Reminders of Death. Likewise, poems spoke of the disgusting smell of rotting flesh, the livid color of plague victims, and the cold touch of the dead.

DANCE OF DEATH

This late-fifteenth century painted engraving illustrates the widespread preoccupation with death during the period. The skeletons dance and play musical instruments. The cadaver on the right holds his own entrails.

Late medieval society was completely frank about the unpleasant process of dying, unlike modern societies that hide the dying in hospitals and segregate mourning to funeral homes. Dying was a public event, almost a theatrical performance. The last rites of the Catholic Church and the Art of Dying served to assist souls in their final test before God and to separate the departed from their kin. According to the Art of Dying, outlined in numerous advice books and illustrations, the sick or injured person should die in bed, surrounded by a room full of people, including children. Christians believed that a dying person watched a supernatural spectacle visible to him or her alone as the heavenly host fought with Satan and his demon minions for the soul. The Art of Dying compared the deathbed contest to a horrific game of chess in which the Devil did all he could to trap the dying person into a checkmate just at the moment of death. In the best of circumstances, a priest arrived in time to hear a confession, offer words of consolation, encourage the dying individual to forgive his or her enemies and redress any wrongs, and perform the last rites.

Pilgrims of the Imagination

During the Middle Ages, a pilgrimage offered a religiously sanctioned form of escape from the omnipresent suffering and peril. Pious Christians could go on a pilgrimage to the Holy

Land, Rome, or the shrine of a saint, such as Santiago de Compostela in Spain, Canterbury in England, or Częstochowa in Poland. The usual motive for a pilgrimage was to fulfill a vow or promise made to God, or to obtain an indulgence, which exempted the pilgrim from some of the time spent in punishment in Purgatory after death. The pilgrimage became the instrument for spiritual liberation and escape from difficulties. As a result, going on a pilgrimage became a compelling model for creative literature, especially during the fourteenth century. Not all of these great works of literature were fictional pilgrimages, but many evoked the pilgrim's impulse to find a refuge from the difficulties of daily life or to find solace in the promise of a better life to come.

TOMB EFFIGY OF A KNIGHT

This effigy above the tomb of Jean d'Alluy shows the deceased as if he were serenely sleeping, still dressed in the armor of his worldly profession.

Source: Tomb Effigy of Jean d'Alluye. Mid-thirteenth Century. From France, Touraine, Loire Valley. Limestone, 83 1/2 × 34 1/4 in. (212.1 × 87 cm). The Cloisters Collection, 1925 (25.120.201). Image copyright © The Metropolitan Museum of Art/Art Resource, NY

DANTE ALIGHIERI AND *THE DIVINE COMEDY* In *The Divine Comedy* an Italian poet from Florence, Dante Alighieri (1265–1321), imagined the most fantastic pilgrimage ever attempted, a journey through Hell, Purgatory,

DECOMPOSING CADAVER

The tomb effigy of Jean de Lagrange.

Source: Musee du Petit Palais, Avignon, France

THE ART OF DYING

In this death scene, the dying man receives extreme unction (last rites) from a priest. A friar holds a crucifixion for him to contemplate. Above his head a devil and angel compete for his soul, while behind him Death lurks waiting for his moment.

and Paradise. A work of astounding originality, *The Divine Comedy* remains the greatest masterpiece of medieval literature. Little is known about Dante's early life except that somehow he acquired expertise in Greek philosophy, scholastic theology (the application of logic to the understanding of Christianity, discussed in Chapter 10), Latin literature, and the newly fashionable poetic forms in Provençal, the language of southern France. Dante's involvement in the dangerous politics of Florence led to his exile under pain of death if he ever returned. During his exile Dante wandered for years, suffering grievously the loss of his home: "Bitter is the taste of another man's bread and...heavy the way up and down another man's stair" (*Paradiso*, canto 17). He sustained himself by writing his great poetic vision of human destiny and God's plan for redemption.

In the poem Dante himself travels into the Christian version of the afterlife. Dante's trip, initially guided by the Latin poet Virgil, the epitome of ancient wisdom, starts in Hell. As he travels deeper into Hell's harsh depths, a cast of sinful characters who inhabit the world of the damned warn Dante of the harmful values of this world. In Purgatory his guide becomes Beatrice, Dante's deceased beloved, who stands for the Christian virtues. In this section of the poem, he begins the painful process of spiritual rehabilitation in which he comes to accept the Christian image of life as a pilgrimage. In Paradise he achieves spiritual fulfillment by speaking with figures from the past who have defied death. Although the poem is deeply Christian, it displays numerous non-Christian influences. The passage through Hell, for example, derived from a long Muslim poem reconstructing Muhammad's *miraj,* a night journey to Jerusalem and ascent to heaven.

The lasting appeal of this long and difficult poem is a wonder. Underlying the appeal of *The Divine Comedy* is perhaps its optimism, which expresses Dante's own cure to his depressing condition as an exile. The power of Dante's poetry established the form of the modern Italian language. Even in translation the images and stories can intrigue and fascinate.

GEOFFREY CHAUCER AND *THE CANTERBURY TALES* Geoffrey Chaucer (ca. 1342–1400) was the most outstanding English poet prior to William Shakespeare. As a courtier and diplomat, Chaucer was a trusted adviser to three successive English kings. But he is best known for his literary output, including *The Canterbury Tales.*

In *The Canterbury Tales* a group of 30 pilgrims tell stories as they travel on horseback to the shrine at Canterbury. Chaucer's use of the pilgrimage as a framing device for telling the stories allowed him to bring together a collection of people from across the social spectrum, including a wife, indulgence hawker, miller, town magistrate, clerk, landowner, lawyer, merchant, knight, abbess, and monk. The variety of characters who told the tales allowed Chaucer to experiment with many kinds of literary forms, from a chivalric romance to a sermon. The pilgrimage combined the considerations of religious morality with the fun of a spring vacation. Many pilgrims were more concerned with the pleasures of

this world than preparing for the next, which was the avowed purpose of going on a pilgrimage. In this intertwining of the worldly and the spiritual, Chaucer brought the abstract principles of Christian morality down to a level of common understanding.

CHRISTINE DE PISAN AND THE DEFENSE OF FEMALE VIRTUE The work of the poet Christine de Pisan (1364–1430) was not a spiritual pilgrimage like Dante's or Chaucer's but a thoughtful and passionate commentary on the tumultuous issues of her day. At age 15 Pisan married a notary of King Charles V of France, but by age 25 she was a widow with three young children. In order to support her family, she turned to writing and relied on the patronage of the royalty and wealthy aristocrats of France, Burgundy, Germany, and England.

Christine de Pisan championed the cause of women in a male-dominated society. Following the fashion of the times, she invented a new chivalric order, the Order of the Rose, whose members took a vow to defend the honor of women. She wrote a defense of women for a male readership and an allegorical autobiography. But she is most famous for the two books she wrote for women readers, *The Book of the City of Ladies* and *The Book of Three Virtues* (both about 1407). In these she recounted tales of the heroism and virtue of women and offered moral instruction for women in different social roles. In 1415 she retired to a convent where in the last year of her life she wrote a masterpiece of ecstatic lyricism that celebrated the early victories of Joan of Arc. Pisan's book turned the martyred Joan into the heroine of France.

Defining Cultural Boundaries

During the Later Middle Ages, systematic discrimination against certain ethnic and religious groups increased markedly in Europe. As European society enforced ever-higher levels of religious uniformity, intolerance spread in the ethnically mixed societies of the European periphery. Intolerance was marked in three areas: Spain with its mixture of Muslim, Jewish, and Christian cultures; the German borderlands in east-central Europe, where Germans mingled with Slavs; and Ireland and Wales, where Celts came under the domination of the English. Within the heartland of Europe were other areas of clashing cultures—Switzerland, for example, where the folk culture of peasants and shepherds living in the isolated mountains collided with the intense Christian religiosity of the cities.

RELIGIOUS COMMUNITIES IN TENSION The Iberian peninsula was home to thriving communities of Muslims, Jews, and Christians. Since the eleventh century the aggressive northern Christian kingdoms of Castile and Aragon had engaged in a protracted program of Reconquest (*Reconquista*) against the Muslim states of the peninsula. By 1248 the Reconquest was largely completed, with only a small Muslim enclave in Granada holding out until 1492. The Spanish Reconquest placed former enemies in close proximity to one another. Hostilities between Christians and Muslims ranged from active warfare to tense stalemate, with Jews working as cultural intermediaries between the two larger communities.

During the twelfth and thirteenth centuries Muslims, called the Mudejars, who capitulated to the conquering Christians, received guarantees that they could continue to practice their own religion and laws. During the fourteenth century, however, Christian kings gradually reneged on these promises. In 1301 the king of Castile decreed that the testimony of any two Christian witnesses could convict a Jew or Muslim, notwithstanding any previously granted privileges that allowed them to be tried in their own courts. The Arabic language began to disappear in Spain as the Mudejars suffered discrimination on many levels. By the sixteenth century, the practice of Islam became illegal, and the Spanish state adopted a systematic policy to destroy Mudejar culture by prohibiting Muslim dress, customs, and marriage practices.

The Jews also began to feel the pain of organized, official discrimination. Christian preachers accused Jews of poisonings, stealing Christian babies, and cannibalism. When the Black Death arrived in 1348, the Jews of Aragon were accused of having poisoned the wells, even though Jews were dying just like Christians. Beginning in 1378, a Catholic prelate in Seville, Ferrant Martínez, commenced an anti-Jewish preaching campaign by calling for the destruction of all 23 of the city's synagogues, the confinement of Jews to a ghetto, the dislodging of all Jews from public positions, and the prohibition of any social contact between Christians and Jews. His campaign led to an attack on the Jews of Seville in 1391. Violence spread to other cities throughout the peninsula and the nearby Balearic Islands. Jews faced a stark choice: conversion or death. After a year of mob violence, about 100,000 Jews had been murdered and an equal number had gone into hiding or fled to more tolerant Muslim countries. The 1391 pogroms led to the first significant forced conversions of Jews in Spain. A century later in 1492, on the heels of the final Christian victory of the Reconquest, all remaining Jews in Spain were compelled to either leave or convert.

Violence against religious minorities occurred in many places, but besides Spain it was most systematic in German-speaking lands. Between November 1348 and August 1350, violence against Jews occurred in more than 80 German towns. Like the allegations in Aragon, the fear that Jews poisoned the wells led to massacres in German lands even *before* plague had arrived in these communities. The frequent occurrence of violence on Sundays or feast days suggests that preachers consciously or unconsciously encouraged the rioting mobs.

Jews had already been expelled from England in 1290 and France in 1306. The situation for Jews was better in Italy where the small population of Jews signed contracts with local towns offering them protection. This pattern of friction among ethnic communities was largely absent in Poland, however, where King Casimir III the Great (1333–137) granted Jews special privileges and welcomed Jewish immigrants, many of them fleeing persecution elsewhere.

ETHNIC COMMUNITIES IN TENSION   Other regions with diverse populations also witnessed discrimination and its brutal consequences. During the population boom of the twelfth and thirteenth centuries, German-speaking immigrants had established colonial towns in the Baltic and penetrated eastward, creating isolated pockets of German culture in Bohemia, Poland, and Hungary. During the fourteenth and fifteenth centuries, hostilities between the native populations and the colonizing Germans arose, particularly in Bohemia. One Czech prince offered 100 silver marks to anyone who brought him 100 German noses. The Teutonic Knights, who had been the vanguard of the German migrations in the Baltic, began to require German ancestry for membership. In German-speaking towns along the colonized borderlands of east-central Europe, city councils and guilds began to use ethnicity as a qualification for holding certain offices or joining a guild. The most famous example was the "German Paragraph" in guild statutes, which required candidates for admission to a guild to prove German descent. As the statutes of a bakers' guild put it, "Whoever wishes to be a member must bring proof to the councilors and the guildsmen that he is born of legitimate, upright German folk." Others required members to be "of German blood and tongue," as if language were a matter of biological inheritance.[14] German guildsmen were also forbidden to marry non-Germans.

In the Celtic fringe of the British Isles, too, discrimination became far more evident in the fourteenth century. In Ireland the ruling English promulgated laws that attempted to protect the cultural identity of the English colonists. The English prohibited native Irish from citizenship in town or guild membership. The Statutes of Kilkenny of 1366 attempted to legislate ethnic purity: They prohibited intermarriage between English and Irish and required English colonists to speak English, use English names, wear English clothes, and ride horses in the English way. They also forbade the English to play Irish games or listen to Irish music. A similar pattern appeared in Wales, where the lines dividing the Welsh and English communities hardened as the English community attempted to prevent its absorption into the majority culture.

CONCLUSION

Looking Inward

Unlike the more dynamic, outward-looking thirteenth century, Europeans during the fourteenth and early fifteenth centuries turned their attention inward to their own communities and their own problems. Europe faced one calamity after another, each crisis compounding the misery. The process of changing Western identities during this period can be seen in two ways.

First, as a result of the Western encounters with the Mongol and Ottoman Empires, the political and religious frontiers of the West shifted. These two empires redrew the map of the West by ending the Christian Byzantine Empire. With the Mongol invasions, the eastward spread of Christianity into Asia ended. The Ottoman conquests left a lasting Muslim influence inside Europe, particularly in Bosnia and Albania. The Ottoman Empire remained hostile to and frequently at war with the Christian West for more than 200 years.

Second, most Europeans reinforced their identity as Christians and became more self-conscious of the country in which they lived. At the same time Christian civilization was becoming eclipsed in parts of the Balkans, it revived in the Iberian peninsula, where the Muslim population, once the most extensive in the West, suffered discrimination and defeat. The northern Spanish kingdoms, for example, began to unify their subjects around a militant form of Christianity that was overtly hostile to Muslims and Jews. In many places in the West, religious and ethnic discrimination against minorities increased. A stronger sense of self-identification by country can be most dramatically seen in France and England as a consequence of the Hundred Years' War.

Except for the very visible military conquests of the Mongols and the Ottomans, the causes of most of the calamities of the fourteenth century were invisible or unknown. No one recognized a climate change or understood the dynamics of the population crisis. No one understood the cause of the epidemics. Only a few merchants grasped the role of the Mongol Empire in the world economy or the causes for the collapse of banking and trade. Unable to distinguish how these forces were changing their lives, Europeans only witnessed their consequences. In the face of these calamities, European culture became obsessed with death and with finding scapegoats to blame for events that could not be otherwise explained. However, calamity also bred creativity. The search for answers to the question, "Why did this happen to us?" produced a new spiritual sensibility and a rich literature. Following the travails of the fourteenth century, moreover, there arose in the fifteenth a new, more optimistic cultural movement—the Renaissance. Gloom and doom were not the only responses to troubles. As we will see in the next chapter, during the Renaissance some people began to search for new answers to human problems in a fashion that would transform the West anew.

KEY TERMS

Black Death
guilds
Hundred Years' War
Babylonian Captivity
  of the Church

indulgences
Great Schism
Conciliar Movement
Modern Devotion

CHAPTER QUESTIONS

1. What caused the deaths of so many Europeans? (page 331)
2. How did forces outside Europe, in particular the Mongol and Ottoman Empires, influence conditions in the West? (page 337)
3. How did disturbances in the rudimentary global economy of the Middle Ages precipitate almost complete financial collapse and widespread social discontent in Europe? (page 344)
4. How did incessant warfare transform the most powerful medieval states? (page 347)
5. Why did the Church fail to provide leadership and spiritual guidance during these difficult times? (page 353)
6. How did European culture offer explanations and solace for the otherwise inexplicable calamities of the times? (page 356)

TAKING IT FURTHER

1. Many of the responses to the calamities of the fourteenth century seem "irrational" to modern eyes. Why might people have reacted in these ways? If one-third of the population of the United States were to die from a mysterious disease in a matter of a few months, how do you think people would react today?
2. Calamities provoked fear. Who were the most likely victims of widespread fear?
3. How could the Church have better helped Christians deal with their suffering during this period?

✓•⎡Practice on **MyHistoryLab**

The Italian Renaissance and Beyond: The Politics of Culture

- The Cradle of the Renaissance: The Italian City-States
- The Influence of Ancient Culture
- The Early Modern European State System

NICCOLÒ MACHIAVELLI (1469–1527) IS BEST KNOWN AS THE FATHER OF MODERN POLITICAL THOUGHT. His little book, *The Prince* (1513), became a classic because it unmasked the realities of political life. For 15 years he worked as a diplomat and political adviser, at the center of the action in his hometown of Florence. But in 1512 the regime there changed. Distrusted by the new rulers and suspected of involvement in an assassination plot, he was imprisoned, tortured, and exiled to his suburban farm. Impoverished, and miserable, Machiavelli survived by selling lumber from his woods to his former colleagues, who cheated him. To help feed his family he snared birds. For entertainment he played cards with the local innkeeper, a butcher, a miller, and two bakers. As he put it, "caught this way among these lice I wipe the mold from my brain (by playing cards) and release my feeling of being ill-treated by Fate."

In the evenings, however, Machiavelli transformed himself. He put on the elegant robes he had worn as a government official. And then, "dressed in a more appropriate manner I enter into the ancient courts of ancient men and am welcomed by them kindly." Machiavelli was reading the works of the ancient Greek and Roman historians, but he described it as a conversation: He asked the ancients

about the reasons for their actions, and he found answers in their books. He recorded their answers in *The Prince.* For four hours, "I feel no boredom, I dismiss every affliction, I no longer fear poverty nor do I tremble at the thought of death: I become completely part of them."

Renaissance means "rebirth," and historians use the word to describe a movement that sought to imitate and understand the culture of antiquity. Machiavelli's evening conversations with the ancients perfectly expressed the sensibility of the Italian Renaissance. This bored, unhappy, disillusioned man found in the ancients the stimulating companions he missed in life. For him, the ancient past was more alive than the present. In this sense Machiavelli was very much a Renaissance man, because feeling part of antiquity is what the Renaissance was all about. Ancient examples of leadership promised to be a cure for the ills of a troubled time.

As we discussed in Chapter 11, during the fourteenth and fifteenth centuries, many Europeans experienced a sense of loss, a preoccupation with death, and pessimism about the human capacity for good. Yet in Florence during this same period, a cultural movement we call the Renaissance began to express a more optimistic view of life. The Renaissance

THE IDEALIZED BODY

Michelangelo's statue of the biblical warrior King David transformed the young boy who slew the giant Goliath into a kind of superman whose physical bearing was greater than any normal man. Michelangelo wanted to improve upon nature by altering the proportions of a natural man, making the head and hands significantly larger than normal.

emphasized the responsibilities of humans to improve their communities through social welfare, to beautify their cities, and to devote themselves to the duties of citizenship. Machiavelli—despite the bleak circumstances of his later life—was one of the Renaissance thinkers who thought the world could be set right through concerted political action. Like medieval thinkers he was pessimistic about human nature, but he believed that strong leadership and just laws could counteract human weakness. In this respect he differed from the medieval writers who thought the contemplative life of the monk was the highest calling to which a person could aspire.

The Renaissance came alive in Italy because the political structures of its city-states encouraged cultural experimentation. The idea that society could be reengineered according to the principles that made ancient Greece and Rome

great first appeared in the early 1400s in Italy, but by 1500, the Renaissance had spread to much of western Europe.

The Italian Renaissance was not the first time the West experienced a revival of ancient learning and thought. In the ninth century, members of the Emperor Charlemagne's court had reinvigorated education in Latin (Chapter 9). And in the twelfth century, a European-wide intellectual movement had led to the foundation of the universities, the reintroduction of Roman law, and the spread of scholastic philosophy and theology (Chapter 10). But unlike these earlier rediscoveries of classical learning, the Italian Renaissance helped refashion the concept of Western civilization. From the fifth to the fourteenth centuries, the West identified itself primarily through conformity to Latin Christianity or Roman Catholicism, which meant the celebration of uniform religious rituals in Latin and obedience to the pope. The Renaissance added a new element to this identity. Although by no means anti-Christian, Renaissance thinkers began to think of themselves as the heirs of pre-Christian cultures—Hebrew, Greek, and Roman. They began to imagine Western civilization identified by more than Christianity. Western civilization became the history of a common culture dating back to Antiquity. Through reading the texts and viewing the works of art of the long-dead ancients, people during the Italian Renaissance gained historical and visual perspective on their own world and cultivated a critical attitude about both the past and their own culture. How then did the encounter during the Renaissance with the philosophy, literature, and art of the Ancient world transform the way Europeans thought?

THE CRADLE OF THE RENAISSANCE: THE ITALIAN CITY-STATES

■ How did the political and social climate of the Italian city-states help create Renaissance culture?

Compared with the rest of Europe and other world civilizations, Renaissance Italy had many politically autonomous city-states. The Netherlands and parts of the Rhine valley were as thoroughly urbanized, but only in Italy did cities have so much political power.

The evolution of the Italian city-states went through two distinct phases. The first phase established the institutions of self-government, the procedures for electing officials, and the theory of republicanism. During the eleventh and twelfth centuries, about 100 Italian towns became independent republics, also known as communes because they practiced a "communal" form of government. They developed the laws and institutions of self-government. The male citizens of these tiny republics gathered on a regular basis in the town square to debate important issues. To conduct the day-to-day business of government, they elected city officials from among themselves.

The governmental practices of these city-states produced the political theory of **republicanism,** which described a state in which government officials were elected by the people or a portion of the people. The theory of republicanism was first articulated in the Middle Ages by Marsilius of Padua (1270–1342) in *The Defender of the Peace,* a book that relied on the precedents established by the ancient Roman republic. Marsilius recognized two kinds of government—principalities and republics. Principalities relied upon the idea that political authority came directly from God and trickled down through kings and princes to the rest of humanity. According to this principle, government's job was to enforce God's laws. Marsilius, however, suggested that laws derive not from God, but from the will of the people, who freely choose their own form of government and can change it. In Marsilius's theory, citizens regularly expressed their will through voting.

In the second phase of the evolution, which occurred during the fourteenth century, most city-states abandoned or lost their republican institutions and came to be ruled by princes. This transformation was related to the economic and demographic turmoil created by the international economic collapse and the Black Death (see Chapter 11). Two of the largest republics, however, Florence and Venice survived without losing their liberty to a prince. The Renaissance began in these two city-states (see **Map 12.1**). Their survival as republics helps explain the origins of the Renaissance. Renaissance culture, at least at first, required the freedom of a city-republic.

The Renaissance Republics: Florence and Venice

In an age of despotic princes, Florence and Venice were keenly aware of how different they were from most other cities, and they feared they might suffer the same fate as their neighbors if they did not defend their republican institutions and liberty. In keeping alive the traditions of republican self-government, these

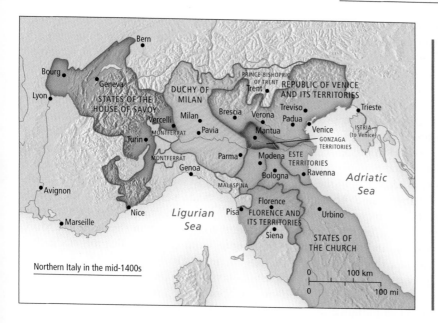

MAP 12.1

Northern Italy in the Mid-Fifteenth Century

During the Renaissance the largest city-states, such as Milan, Venice, and Florence, gained control of the surrounding countryside and smaller cities in the vicinity, establishing regional territorial states. Among the large states, only Venice and Florence remained republics. Milan and Savoy were ruled by dukes. The Gonzaga family ruled Mantua and the Este family Modena and Ferrara. The states of the Church were ruled by the pope in Rome.

two cities created an environment of competition and freedom that stimulated creative ingenuity. Although neither of these cities were democracies or egalitarian, they were certainly more open to new ideas than cities ruled by princes. In both Florence and Venice, citizens prized discussion and debate, the skills necessary for success in business and politics. By contrast, in the principalities all cultural activity tended to revolve around and express the tastes of the ruler, who monopolized much of the wealth. In Florence and Venice a few great families called the *patriciate* controlled most of the property, but these patricians competed among themselves to gain recognition and fame by patronizing great artists and scholars. This patronage by wealthy men and women made the Renaissance possible. Because the tastes of these patricians dictated what writers and artists could do, understanding who these patricians were helps explain Renaissance culture.

FLORENCE UNDER THE MEDICI The greatest patron during the early Renaissance was the fabulously rich Florentine banker Cosimo de' Medici (1389–1464). Based on his financial power,

Cosimo effectively took control of the Florentine republic in 1434, ushering in a period of unprecedented peace in the city and artistic splendor called the Medicean Age (1434–1494). Cosimo's style of rule was clever. Instead of making himself a prince, which most of the citizens of Florence would have opposed, he managed the policies of the republic from behind the scenes. He seldom held public office, but he made himself the center of Florentine affairs through shrewd negotiating, quiet fixing of elections, and generous distribution of bribes, gifts, and jobs. Cosimo's behind-the-scenes rule illustrated a fundamental value of Renaissance culture—the desire to maintain appearances. In this case, the appearance of a republic was saved, even as the reality of liberty was compromised.

Cosimo's patronage of intellectuals and artists mirrored a similar ambition to maintain appearances. It helped make him appear a great statesman similar to those of the ancient Roman republic, such as the orator and senator Cicero. Cosimo appreciated intelligence and merit wherever he found it. He frequented the discussions of prominent scholars, some of whom became his friends. He financed the acquisition of manuscripts of ancient Latin and Greek literature and philosophy. In return for his financial support, many Florentine scholars dedicated their works to Cosimo. His artistic patronage helped create the image of an open-handed and benevolent godfather for his community. Because he had not been elected to rule Florence, he needed to find a way to create a proper image that would justify his power. To do that, he decorated the private chapel in his palace with frescoes that depicted him accompanying the Magi, the wise men or kings who according to the Bible brought gifts to the baby Jesus. Thus, Cosimo made himself appear similar to those ancient kings who first recognized the divinity of Christ. This image of great wisdom and religious piety helped Cosimo justify the fact that he controlled elections and dictated policies.

Cosimo's grandson Lorenzo the Magnificent (r. 1469–1492) expanded Medici dominance in Florentine politics through "veiled lordship." Although Lorenzo never took the title of prince, he behaved like one by intervening publicly in the affairs of state. Unlike Cosimo's public patronage, Lorenzo's interest in the arts concentrated on building villas, collecting precious gems, and commissioning small bronze statues, things that gave him private pleasure rather than a public reputation. Although a fine poet and an intellectual companion of the most renowned scholars of his age, Lorenzo ignored the republican sensibilities of the Florentines with his princely style of rule and undermined public support for the Medici.

VENICE, THE COSMOPOLITAN REPUBLIC Venice was more politically stable than Florence. Situated in the midst of a vast lagoon, Venice's main streets consisted of broad channels in which great seagoing merchant ships were moored and canals choked with private boats for local transportation. To protect their fragile city from flooding, the Venetians recognized that they had to cooperate among themselves, and thus the imperative for survival helped create a republic that became a model of stability and ecological awareness. The Venetians, for example, created the world's first environmental regulatory agencies, which were responsible for hydrological projects, such as building dikes and dredging canals, and for forestry management to prevent soil erosion and the consequent silting up of the lagoon.

Venice was among the first European powers to possess overseas colonies. To guarantee its merchant ships access to the eastern Mediterranean and Constantinople, Venice conquered a series of ports along the Adriatic and in Greece. Its involvement in international trade and its distant colonies made Venice unusually cosmopolitan. Many Venetian merchants spent years abroad, and some settled in the colonies. Moreover, people from all over Europe flocked to Venice—Germans, Turks, Armenians, Albanians, Greeks, Slavs, and Jews—each creating their own neighborhoods and institutions. Venetian households owned Russian, Asian, Turkish, and African slaves, all of whom contributed to the diversity of the city.

The most influential foreign group in Venice consisted of the Greeks. Venice had long maintained close commercial and cultural ties with the Greek world. Many of Venice's churches were modeled after the huge basilicas of Constantinople, and many Venetian merchants spoke Greek. After the fall of the Byzantine Empire to the Ottoman Turks in 1453, Greek Christian refugees found a home in Venice and other Italian cities, including scholars who reintroduced Greek philosophy and literature to eager Italian readers. One of these scholars was John Bessarion (1403–1472), a Byzantine archbishop who compiled a library of Greek manuscripts that he left to the republic of Venice. Venice also became the leading center in western Europe for the publication of Greek books.

The defining characteristics of Venetian government were its social stability and liberty, traits that made it the envy of more troubled cities in Italy and republican-minded reformers throughout Europe, especially in England, the Netherlands, and Poland. Whereas the Florentine republic was notoriously unstable and subject to subversion by the Medici, Venice's republican constitution lasted from 1297 to 1797, making it the longest-surviving republic in history. It was, however, an exclusive republic. Out of a total population of nearly 150,000, only the political elite of 2,500 nobles could vote or hold high office. This elite and Venice's many wealthy religious institutions patronized Renaissance thinkers and artists.

At the top of Venetian society was the *doge*, a member of the nobility who was elected to the office for life. The most notable Renaissance doge was Andrea Gritti (r. 1523–1538). Gritti sometimes bent the laws in his favor, but he never manipulated elections or managed Venice's affairs as completely as Cosimo de' Medici did in Florence a century before. Like the Medici, however, Gritti used his own financial resources and his personal influence to transform his city into a major center of Renaissance culture.

Gritti hired some of the most prominent European artists, musicians, and poets to come to Venice. These included the architect and sculptor Jacopo Sansovino (1486–1570). As official architect of the city, Sansovino transformed its appearance with his sculptures, palaces, and churches that imitated the styles of classical Greece and Rome. One of his most notable buildings is the Marciana Library, which was begun in 1537 to house Bessarion's collection of Greek manuscripts.

Princes and Courtiers

Although the Renaissance began in the relative freedom of republics, such as Florence, it soon spread to the Italian principalities. In contrast to the multiple sources of support for the arts and

THE MARCIANA LIBRARY

Built by the architect Jacopo Sansovino, the Marciana Library was built to house the collection of Greek manuscripts given to the Republic of Venice by the exiled Greek archbishop John Bessarion. The Marciana, the oldest public library in the world, is still housed in this building and is open to scholars and university students.

learning in the republics, patronage in the principalities was more constricted, confined to the ruler and members of his court. The term *prince* refers to rulers who possessed formal aristocratic titles, such as the Marquis of Mantua, the Duke of Milan, or the King of Naples. Most Renaissance princes came from local families who seized control of the government by force. Some, however, had been soldiers of fortune who had held on to a city as a spoil of war or had even overthrown a government that had once employed them to defend the city. Regardless of how a prince originally obtained power, his goal was to establish a dynasty, that is, to guarantee the rights of his descendants to continue to rule the city. Some dynasties—such as that of the d'Este family, which ruled Ferrara from 1240 to 1597—were well established and popular.

THE IDEAL PRINCE   Federico II da Montefeltro (1422–1482), Duke of Urbino, achieved the glorious reputation that so many princes craved. Although he was illegitimate, his father sent him to study at the most fashionable school in Italy and to apprentice as a soldier under a renowned mercenary captain. In Renaissance Italy, an illegitimate boy could not inherit his father's property. Thus, he usually had two career options: He could become a priest to obtain a living from the church, or he could become a mercenary and take his chances at war. Federico became a mercenary. From among the peasants of Urbino he recruited an army that he hired out to the highest bidder. He soon earned a European-wide reputation for his many victories and enriched the duchy with the income from mercenary contracts and plunder. When his half-brother was assassinated in 1444, Federico became the ruler of Urbino; by 1474 he obtained from the pope the title of duke. Federico epitomized the ideal Renaissance prince—a father figure to his subjects, astute diplomat, brilliant soldier, generous patron, avid collector, and man of learning.

Federico's rule was stern but paternalistic. He personally listened to his subjects' complaints and judged their disputes. His conquests tripled the size of his duchy and financed his building projects and collection of Latin manuscripts. Federico's personal library surpassed that of any contemporary university in Europe, and his wide-ranging reading showed his openness to the latest developments in learning. His greatest achievement, however, was the building of a vast palace, the best example of Renaissance architectural ideals. Because of Federico, the small mountainous duchy of Urbino acquired a cultural importance far greater than its size of 18,000 inhabitants warranted.

THE IDEAL PRINCESS   Isabella d'Este (1474–1539), the Marchioness of Mantua, was the ideal Renaissance princess, known during her lifetime as "the first lady of the world." Enjoying an education that was exceptional for a woman in the fifteenth century, she grew up in the court at Ferrara, where she was surrounded by painters and poets and where she cultivated ambassadors and intellectuals. But her influence went far beyond that. When her husband was absent and after his death, she ruled Mantua by herself, earning a reputation as a negotiator and diplomat. An avid reader and collector, she knew virtually all the great artists and writers of her age.

THE IDEAL COURTIER   The Renaissance republics developed a code of conduct for the ideal citizen that encouraged citizens to devote their time and energies to public service: to hold public office, pay taxes honestly, and beautify the city through patronage of the arts.

The Renaissance principalities also created a code for the ideal courtier. A courtier was a man or woman who lived in or regularly visited the palace of a prince. Courtiers performed all kinds of services for princes, such as taking care of the family's wardrobe, managing servants, educating children, providing entertainment, keeping accounts, administering estates, going on diplomatic missions, and fighting battles. To best serve the princely family, a courtier needed to cultivate many skills. Men trained in horsemanship, swordplay, and athletics to stay in shape for war. Women learned to draw, dance, play musical

ISABELLA D'ESTE, THE IDEAL PRINCESS
The Marchioness of Mantua, Isabella d'Este, was the most famous woman of the early sixteenth century. She set the fashions for all of Europe, but most important, she was a brilliant negotiator and ruler in her husband's absence.

Source: Titian (c. 1488–1576). Portrait Isabella d'Este (1474–1539), Margravine of Mantua, wife of Francesco Gonzaga, Margrave of Mantua. 1534. Oil on canvas, 102 × 64 cm. Kunsthistorisches Museum, Vienna, Austria. © Erich Lessing/Art Resource, NY

instruments, and engage in witty conversation. Both men and women needed to speak foreign languages to converse with visitors and diplomats. Men, and some of the women, also learned Latin and Greek, which were the foundations of a formal education.

The courtiers performed many of the essential functions in the princely states that elected officials did in the republics. To preserve the peace of the state, princes needed to prevent conflicts among the courtiers. Baldasar Castiglione (1478–1529), who wrote the most influential guide to how a courtier should behave, *The Book of the Courtier*, maintained that two general principles governed all courtly manners—nonchalance and ease:

> I have found quite a universal rule which...seems to me valid above all others, and in all human affairs whether in word or deed: and that is to avoid affectation in every way possible as though it were some very rough and dangerous reef; and...to practice in all things a certain nonchalance, so as to conceal all art and make whatever is done or said appear to be without effort and almost without any thought about it....
>
> Therefore we may call that art true art which does not seem to be art; nor must one be more careful of anything than of concealing it, because if it is discovered, this robs a man of all credit and causes him to be held in slight esteem.[1]

In other words, Castiglione praised the ability to appear to be natural and effortless while doing something that required training and effort. The need to maintain appearances, which we saw in the disguised ruler of Cosimo de' Medici in Florence, became a distinguishing trait of Italian Renaissance culture. *The Book of the Courtier* translated the ideals of civility so admired in Renaissance culture into a plan for human comportment. By using courtly manners, human beings governed the movements of the body according to an almost mathematical ideal of proportion.

By studying *The Book of the Courtier* and its many imitators, which were translated into Latin, English, French, and Spanish, any literate young man or woman of talent and ambition could aspire to act and speak like an aristocrat. Many of its precepts of the courtly ideal were incorporated into the curriculum of schools.

THE PAPAL PRINCE   The Renaissance popes combined the roles of priests and princes. They were

COURTIERS WAITING ON A PRINCELY FAMILY

On the right side of this fresco male courtiers pose while waiting around in the court of the Gonzaga in Mantua. These elegant gentlemen epitomized the nonchalance and ease idealized in Baldasar Castiglione's *The Book of the Courtier*. On the left, the prince they serve receives a letter from a messenger. Other courtiers surround the prince, princess, and their family.

the heads of the Church. They also had jurisdiction over the Papal States in central Italy. The Papal States were supposed to supply the pope with the income to run the Church, but when the popes had resided in Avignon (France) from 1305 to 1378 and during the Great Schism of 1378–1417, they had lost control of the Papal States. To reassert their control, popes had to force rebellious lords and cities into obedience. Julius II (r. 1503–1513) took his princely role so seriously that he donned armor and personally led troops in battle. The popes also fought with neighboring Italian states that had taken advantage of the weakness of the papacy.

These military adventures undermined the popes' ability to provide moral leadership. In addition, Pope Alexander VI (r. 1492–1503) ignored his priestly vows of celibacy and fathered four children by his favorite mistress. He financed his son Cesare Borgia's attempts to carve out a principality for himself in Italy. He also married off his daughter, Lucrezia Borgia, in succession to Italian princes who were useful allies in the pope's military ambitions. The enemies of the Borgia family accused them of all kinds of evil deeds, including poisoning one of Lucrezia's husbands, incest, and conducting orgies in the Vatican. Many of these allegations were false or exaggerated, but the papacy's reputation suffered.

Despite their messy engagement with politics, several Renaissance popes gained lasting fame as builders and patrons of the arts. They were embarrassed by the squalor of the city of Rome, which had become a neglected ruin. They sought to create a capital they felt worthy for Christendom. During the reign of Leo X (1513–1521), a son of Lorenzo the Magnificent, Rome became a center of Renaissance culture. Leo's ambition for the city can best be measured in his project to rebuild St. Peter's Basilica as the largest church in the world. He tore down the old basilica, which had been a major pilgrimage destination for more than 1,000 years, and planned the great church that still dominates Rome today.

The Contradictions of the Patriarchal Family

The princes and even the popes justified their authority, in part, on the principle that men should rule. Governments were based on the theory of the patriarchal family in which husbands and fathers dominated women and children. (See *Justice in History* in this chapter.) In advice books on family management, such as Leon Battista Alberti's *Four Books on the Family* (written in the 1430s), patriarchs were the sources of social order and discipline for all society. Although mothers or marriage brokers might arrange marriages, by law fathers or male guardians had to approve the arrangement. They sought beneficial financial and political alliances with other families. This gave older men an advantage in the marriage market because they were usually better off financially than younger ones. As a result, husbands tended to be much older than wives. In Florence in 1427, for example, the typical first marriage was between a 30-year-old man and an 18-year-old woman. Husbands were encouraged to treat their spouses with a kindly but distant paternalism. All women were supposed to be kept under strict male supervision. The only honorable role for an unmarried woman was as a nun.

However, reality often contradicted patriarchal theory. First, death from epidemic diseases, especially the Black Death, and separations due to marital strife, which were common even though divorce was not possible, made family life insecure. Second, the wide age gap meant that husbands were likely to die long before their wives. Thus many women became widows at a relatively young age with children still to raise. Third, many men, especially international merchants and migrant workers, were away from their families for long periods. So regardless of the patriarchal theory that fathers should be in control, in reality they were often absent or dead. Mothers who were supposed to be modest, obedient to their husbands, and invisible to the outside world not only had to raise children alone but often had to manage their dead or absent husbands' business and political affairs. By necessity, many resilient, strong, and active women were involved in worldly affairs, and

CHRONOLOGY: THE CRADLE OF THE RENAISSANCE, THE ITALIAN CITY-STATES

ca. 1070	Founding of first city republics or communes
1324	Marsilius of Padua publishes *The Defender of the Peace*
1434	30-year long rule of Cosimo de' Medici in Florence begins
1444	40-year long rule of Federico II da Montefeltro, Duke of Urbino, begins
1469	Rule of Lorenzo, the Magnificent, de' Medici in Florence begins
1474	Birth of Isabella d'Este, Marchioness of Mantua
1492	Alexander VI becomes pope
1503	Pontificate of Julius II begins
1508	Baldasar Castiglione begins writing *The Book of the Courtier*
1513	Pontificate of Leo X begins
1523	Rule of Andrea Gritti, Doge of Venice, begins

JUSTICE IN HISTORY

Vendetta as Private Justice

During the fourteenth and fifteenth centuries, the official justice the law courts provided competed with the private justice of revenge. Private justice was based on the principle of retaliation. When someone was murdered or assaulted, the victim's closest male relatives were obliged to avenge the injury by harming the perpetrator or one of his relatives to a similar degree. A son was obliged to avenge the death of his father, a brother the injury of his brother. Because governments were weak, the only effective justice was often private justice or, as the Italians called it, *vendetta*. As the most significant source of disorder during the Renaissance, vendetta was a practice that all governments struggled to eradicate.

While criminals tried to cover their tracks, vendetta avengers committed their acts openly and even bragged about them. An act of revenge was carried out in public, so there would be witnesses, and often in a highly symbolic way to humiliate the victim. Private justice always sought to deliver a message.

An episode of revenge from the most sophisticated city in Europe on the eve of the Renaissance illustrates the brutality of private justice, especially the need to make a public example of the victim. After a period of disorder in 1342, the Florentines granted extraordinary judicial powers to a soldier of fortune, Walter of Brienne, known as the Duke of Athens. But Walter offended many Florentines by arresting and executing members of prominent families. In September 1342 a crowd led by these families besieged the government palace in Florence and captured the duke's most hated henchmen, the "conservator" and his son. An eyewitness reported what happened next:

> The son was pushed out in front, and they cut him up and dismembered him. This

done, they shoved out the conservator himself and did the same to him. Some carried a piece of him on a lance or sword throughout the city, and there were those so cruel, so bestial in their anger, and full of such hatred that they ate the raw flesh.[2]

Another account from nearly 200 years later tells of the murder of Antonio Savorgnan, a nobleman who had killed a number of his enemies. Rather than attempting to have Antonio arrested as they could have, the murderers avenged their dead relatives through private justice. One eyewitness recounted that Antonio was attacked while leaving church, and then, "It was by divine miracle that Antonio Savorgnan was wounded: his head opened, he fell down, and he never spoke another word. But before he died, a giant dog came there and ate all his brains, and one cannot possibly deny that his brains were eaten."[3] This time a dog did the avengers' work for them.

In both of these accounts, the writers wanted readers to believe that the victim had been eaten, by humans or by a dog. The eating of a victim signaled that avengers were killing as an act of private justice, a legitimate act of revenge for the murder of close relatives. To convey that message, avengers had to confront their opponent in broad daylight before witnesses. There had to be the appearance, at least, of a fair fight. And to symbolize their revenge, murderers butchered the corpses as if they were the prey of a hunt and fed the remains to hunting dogs or even ate it themselves.

Governments, whether of a tiny city-state or a great monarchy, tried to substitute public justice for private justice, but the violent tradition was strong. Violent crime rates were extremely high during the Renaissance.

By some estimates the murder rate was ten times higher than in the inner cities of the United States today. As governments sought to control violence and the values of moderation spread, a different kind of private justice appeared—the duel. Traditionally, the duel had been a means for knights to resolve disputes, but during the sixteenth century, duels became more common, even among men who had never been soldiers. Duelists had to conform to elaborate rules: There had to be legitimate causes for a challenge to a duel, the combatants had to recognize each other as honorable men, the fight took place only after extensive preparations, judges who were experts on honor had to serve as witnesses, and the combatants had to swear to accept the outcome and not to fight one another again.

Dueling, in effect, civilized private justice. The complexity of the rules of dueling limited the violence and meant that fewer fights took place. Although dueling was always against the law, princes tended to wink at duels because they kept conflicts among their own courtiers under control. But governments became far less tolerant of other forms of private justice, especially among the lower classes. They attempted to abolish feuds and vendettas and insisted that all disputes be submitted to the courts.

For Discussion

1. Why was private justice a challenge to the emerging states of the Renaissance?
2. How did private justice reflect Renaissance values, such as the value of keeping up appearances?

Taking it Further

Muir, Edward. *Mad Blood Stirring: Vendetta in Renaissance Italy.* 1998. A study of the most

PRIVATE JUSTICE

In Titian's painting *The Bravo* (ca. 1515/1520), a man wearing a breastplate and hiding a drawn sword behind his back grabs the collar of his enemy before assaulting him. To enact honorable revenge the attacker could not stab his enemy in the back, but had to give him a chance in a fair fight.

extensive and long-lasting vendetta in Renaissance Italy. It traces the evolution of vendetta violence into dueling.

Weinstein, Donald. *The Captain's Concubine: Love, Honor, and Violence in Renaissance Tuscany.* 2000. An engaging account of an ambush and fight between two nobles over a woman who was the concubine of the father of one of the fighters and the lover of the other. It reveals the relationship between love and violence in Renaissance society.

mothers had much more direct influence on children than fathers. Despite the theory of patriarchy, the families of Renaissance Italy were matriarchies in which mothers ruled.

The contradictions of family life and the tenuous hold many families had on survival encouraged examinations of family life in the culture of Renaissance Italy. Making fun of impotent old husbands married to unfulfilled young wives became a major theme in comic drama. Given the demographic ravages of the Black Death, preachers showed particular concern for the care of children; the chubby little cherubs that seem to fall from the sky in many Renaissance paintings show the universal craving for healthy children.

THE INFLUENCE OF ANCIENT CULTURE

■ How did ancient culture influence the Renaissance?

The need in Renaissance Italy to provide effective models for how citizens, courtiers, and families should behave stimulated a reexamination of ancient culture. The civilizations of ancient Greece and Rome had long fascinated the educated classes in the West. In Italy, where most cities were built among the ruins of the ancient past, antiquity was particularly seductive. During the fourteenth and fifteenth centuries Italian thinkers and artists attempted to foster a rebirth of ancient cultures. At first they merely tried to imitate the Latin of the best Roman writers. Then contact with Greek-speaking refugees from Byzantium led scholars to do the same thing with Greek. Artists trekked to Rome to sketch ancient ruins, sculptures, and medallions. Wealthy collectors hoarded manuscripts of ancient philosophy, built libraries to house them, bought every ancient sculpture they could find, and dug up ruins to find more antiquities to adorn their palaces. Patrons demanded that artists imitate the styles of the ancients and display similar concern for rendering natural forms. They especially prized lifelike representations of the human body.

Patrons, artists, and scholars during the Renaissance also began to understand the enormous cultural distance between themselves and the ancients, which gave them a sense of their place in history The leaders in the reexamination of ancient cultures were the **humanists,** scholars who studied ancient Greek and Latin texts. The humanists developed techniques of literary analysis to determine when a text had been written and to differentiate authentic texts from ones that copyists' mistakes had corrupted. Humanists devoted themselves to grammar, rhetoric, history, poetry, and ethics. The modern university disciplines in the Humanities are the descendants of the Renaissance humanists.

The Humanists

The first humanist was Francesco Petrarca (1304–1374), known in English as Petrarch. Petrarch and his follower Lorenzo Valla (1407–1457) developed critical methods by editing classical texts to establish the original words, a method different from the medieval scribe's temptation to alter or improve a text as he saw fit. Petrarch's method was called **philology,** the study of the meaning of words in a specific historical context. The meaning of many Latin words had changed since the fall of Ancient Rome, and Petrarch attempted to trace the changes in meaning. He strived to get the words right because he wanted to understand exactly what an ancient author had meant. This concern with finding original texts and the meaning of words gave Petrarch and his followers insight into the individuality of writers who lived and wrote many centuries before.

An interest in the meaning of words led Petrarch to study **rhetoric,** the art of persuasive or emotive speaking and writing. He came to think that rhetoric was superior to philosophy because he preferred a good man over a wise one, and rhetoric offered examples worthy of imitation rather than abstract principles subject to debate. Petrarch wanted people to behave morally. And he believed that the most efficient way to inspire his readers to do the right thing was to write moving rhetoric. (See *Encounters and Transformations* in this chapter.)

ENCOUNTERS AND TRANSFORMATIONS

Encounters with the Ancient World: Petrarch Writes a Letter to Cicero's Ghost

Petrarch was famous for his poetry, in both his native Italian and Latin. To improve his Latin style, he was always watching for anything by the Roman orator Cicero (106–43 B.C.E.). In 1345 Petrarch discovered a previously unknown collection of letters Cicero had written to his friend Atticus.

As Petrarch read the letters, however, he suffered a shock. Cicero had a reputation as the greatest Roman sage, a model of Latin style, philosophical sophistication, and ethical standards. But in the letters Petrarch found not sage moral advice, but gossip, rumors, and crude political calculations. Cicero looked like a scheming politician, a man of crass ambition rather than grand philosophical wisdom. Although Petrarch could never forgive Cicero for failing to live up to his philosophical ideals, he had discovered a man so human he could imagine having a conversation with him.

And a conversation was precisely what Petrarch set out to have. Cicero, however, had been dead for 1,388 years. So Petrarch wrote a letter to his ghost. Adopting Cicero's own elegant Latin, Petrarch attacked the Roman for going against the moral advice he had given others. Petrarch quoted Cicero back to Cicero, asking how he could be such a hypocrite: "I long had known how excellent a guide you have proved for others; at last I was to learn what sort of guidance you gave yourself.... Now it is your turn to be the listener."[4]

Petrarch lectured Cicero for his corruption and moral failures. The point of the exercise of writing a letter to a dead man was in part to practice good Latin style, but also to compare the ideals Cicero had avowed in his philosophical work and the way he really lived. Making comparisons is an elementary critical technique, and it became the hallmark of Petrarch's analysis. His letter made the ancients seem like other men who made mistakes and told lies. No longer a repository of timeless truths, the ancient world became a specific time and place. After his letter to Cicero, Petrarch wrote letters to other illustrious ancients in which he revealed their human qualities and shortcomings.

Petrarch's encounter with the ancients changed how he understood the past and humanity. The ancients were history in the most literal sense. They were long dead. But they were also human, capable of brave deeds and vulnerable to temptations, just the way Petrarch and his contemporaries were.

For Discussion

How did Petrarch's encounter with Cicero transform his view of his own culture? How can an encounter with another culture change how you view your own?

Renaissance humanists sought to resurrect a form of Latin that had been dead for more than 1,000 years and was distinct from the living Latin used by the Church, law courts, and universities—which they thought inferior to ancient Latin. In this effort, humanists acquired a difficult but functional skill that opened many employment opportunities to them and gave them public influence. They worked as schoolmasters, secretaries, bureaucrats, official historians, and ambassadors. Many other humanists were wealthy men who did not need a job but were fascinated with the way the new learning could be used to persuade other people to do what they wanted them to do.

Because humanists could be found on different sides of almost all important questions, the significance of their work lies less in what they said than in how they said it. They wrote about practically everything: painting pictures, designing buildings, planting crops, draining swamps, raising children, managing a household, and educating women. They debated the nature of human liberty, the virtues of famous men, the vices of wicked ones, the meaning of Egyptian hieroglyphics, and the cosmology of the universe.

How did the humanists' use of Latin words and grammar influence the understanding of this vast range of subjects? Each language organizes experience according to the needs of the people who speak it, and all languages make arbitrary distinctions, dividing up the world into different categories. People who study a foreign language run across these arbitrary distinctions when they learn that some expressions can never be translated exactly. When humanists read classical Latin texts, they encountered unfamiliar words, sentence patterns, and rhetorical models—the linguistic leftovers of ancient experience and culture. Humanists' recovery of what can be called the *Latin point of view* often altered their own perceptions and shaped their own cultural experiences in subtle ways.

For example, when a fifteenth-century humanist examined what the ancient Romans had written about painting, he found the phrase *ars et ingenium*. *Ars* referred to skills that could be learned by following established rules and adhering to models provided by the best painters. Thus, the ability of a painter to draw a straight line, to mix colors properly, and to identify a saint with the correct symbol were examples of *ars* or what we would call craftsmanship. The meaning of *ingenium* was more difficult to pin down, however. It referred to the inventive capacity of the painter, to his or her ingenuity. The humanists discovered that the ancients had made a distinction between the craftsmanship and the ingenuity of a painter. As a result, when humanists and their pupils looked at paintings, they began to make the same distinction and began to admire the genius of artists whose work showed ingenuity as well as craftsmanship. Ingenuity came to refer to the

ability of the painter to arrange figures in a novel way, to employ unusual colors, or to create emotionally exciting effects that conveyed piety, sorrow, or joy as the subject demanded. So widespread was the influence of the humanists that the most ingenious artists demanded higher prices and became the most sought after. In this way, creative innovation was encouraged in the arts, but it all started very simply with the introduction of new words into the Latin vocabulary of the people who paid for paintings. A similar process of establishing new categories altered every subject the humanists touched.

The humanist movement spread rapidly during the fifteenth century. Leonardo Bruni (ca. 1370–1444), who became the chancellor of Florence (the head of the government's bureaucracy), created **civic humanism** to defend the republican institutions and values of the city. By reading the ancient writers, Bruni rediscovered the ethics of public service. Civic humanists argued that the ethical man should devote himself to active service to his city rather than to passive contemplation in scholarly retreat or monastic seclusion.

Lorenzo Valla employed humanist scholarship to undermine papal claims to authority over secular rulers. The pope's theoretical authority depended on the so-called Donation of Constantine, according to which the Emperor Constantine had transferred his imperial authority in Italy to the pope in the fourth century. By using philology, Valla demonstrated that many of the Latin words found in the Donation could not have been written before the eighth century. For example, the document used the word *satrap*, which Valla was confident a Roman at the time of Constantine would not have known. Thus, he proved that this famous document was a forgery. Valla's analysis of the Donation was one of the first uses of philology and historical analysis of documents to serve a political cause. As a result, many rulers and especially the popes saw the need to hire a humanist to defend their own interests.

The intellectual curiosity of the humanists led them to master many topics. This breadth of accomplishment contributed to the ideal of the "Renaissance Man (or "Renaissance Woman"), a person who sought excellence in everything he or she did. No one came closer to this ideal than Leon Battista Alberti (1404–1472). As a young man, Alberti wrote Latin comedies and satirical works that drew on Greek and Roman models, but as he matured he tackled more serious subjects. Although he was a bachelor and thus knew nothing firsthand about marriage, he drew upon the ancient writers to create the most influential Renaissance book on the family, which included sections on relations between husbands and wives, raising children, and estate management. He composed the first grammar of the Italian language. He dabbled in mathematics and wrote on painting, law, the duties of bishops, love, horsemanship, dogs, agriculture, and flies. He mapped the city of Rome and wrote the most important fifteenth-century work on the theory and practice of architecture. His interest in architecture, moreover, was not just theoretical. In the last decades of his life, Alberti dedicated much of his spare time to building projects that included restoring an ancient church in Rome, designing Renaissance façades for medieval churches, and erecting a palace for his most important patron. One of his last projects was the first significant work for making and deciphering secret codes in the West.

The humanists guaranteed their lasting influence through their innovations in education. Humanist education did not seek to train specialists or professionals, such as the theologians, lawyers, and physicians. Instead, humanists aimed to create well-rounded men (women were not usually accepted in humanist schools), critical thinkers who could tackle any problem that life presented. The curriculum emphasized the study of Greek and Latin and the best authors in those ancient languages. Command of good grammar, the ability to write and speak effectively, knowledge of history, and an appreciation for virtuous behavior were the goals of humanist education. It was a curriculum well suited for the active life of civic leaders, courtiers, princes, and churchmen. The influence of the humanist curriculum persists in the general education requirements of modern American universities, which require students, now of both sexes, to obtain intellectual breadth before they specialize in narrow professional training.

Historians have identified a few female humanists from the Renaissance. Because they were so unusual, learned humanist women were often ridiculed. Jealous men accused the humanist Isotta Nogarola (1418–1466) of promiscuity and incest, and other women insulted her in public. A famous male schoolmaster said that Isotta was too feminine in her writings and should learn how to find "a man within the woman."[5] Laura Cereta (1475–1506), who knew Greek as well as Latin and was adept at mathematics, answered the scorn of a male critic with rhetorical insult:

> I would have been silent, believe me, if that savage old enmity of yours had attacked me alone....But I cannot tolerate your having attacked my entire sex. For this reason my thirsty soul seeks revenge, my sleeping pen is aroused to literary struggle, raging anger stirs mental passions long chained by silence. With just cause I am moved to demonstrate how great a reputation for learning and virtue women have won by their inborn excellence, manifested in every age as knowledge, the [purveyor] of honor. Certain, indeed, and legitimate is our possession of this inheritance, come to us from a long eternity of ages past.[6]

These few humanist women were among the first feminists. They advocated female equality and female education but also urged women to take control of their lives. Cereta maintained that if women paid as much attention to learning as they did to their appearances, they would achieve equality. But despite the efforts of female humanists, progress in women's education was slow. The universities remained closed to women until late in the nineteenth century. The first woman to earn a degree from a university only did so in 1678. It took another 200 years before many others could follow her example. (See *Different Voices* in this chapter.)

The humanists educated generations of wealthy young gentlemen whose appreciation of Antiquity led them to collect manuscripts of

DIFFERENT VOICES THE BATTLE OF THE SEXES

Abusive writing about women was pervasive in Western literature. However, during the Renaissance the "women's question" raised the issue of whether education could improve women's lot in life. What distinguished this debate during the Renaissance was the active role women took in defending their own interests.

Although they wrote in the seventeenth century, Ferrante Pallavicino (1618–1644) and Arcangela Tarabotti (1604–1652) represented the culmination of the Italian Renaissance debate about women. Pallavicino pulled out the usual litany of the anti-woman argument. Tarabotti answered Pallavicino on every point.

Ferrante Pallavicino, Letter addressed to "Ungrateful Woman"

I know how you mock my scorn: a woman never grieves unless she weeps tears of blood, and her normal tears are pure deceit in liquid form, the holding back of pretense....

Your ingratitude has reached the limit in bad manners; it has taught me that there is nothing human in a woman but her face, with which she lies even when silent and warns how there is nothing to expect but falsity from a being who deceives at first sight. She shares the same genus of animal with man, appropriating for herself, however, all the bestial qualities that ensure, while differing from man in that she simply has no reason whatsoever: as a consequence, she acts like a brute animal....

Unfortunate women are those without men to provide the support that remedies their own weakness! Without men they could not avoid being flung down at every moment, like the blind and the mad, into a thousand chasms. The women of Tartary (Mongolia and Turkey) understood this well: it was their custom never to allow their head to be covered by a more precious headdress than the form of a human foot, to signify that woman, brainless and witless, finds her greatest glory in her subjection to man. Representing themselves in the act of being trodden underfoot, they paid homage to their noblest part; they were not foolish like other women, adorning their heads with treasures from robbed tombs or weighed down with braided chains dotted with gems.

---

ancient literature, philosophy, and science. These patrons also encouraged artists to imitate the ancients. What began as a narrow literary movement became the stimulus to see human society and nature through entirely new eyes. Some humanists, especially in northern Europe, applied the techniques of humanist scholarship with revolutionary results to the study of the Bible and the sources of Christianity.

Understanding Nature: Moving Beyond the Science of the Ancients

The humanists' initial concern was to imitate the language of the ancients. Most of them preferred to spend time reading rather than observing the world. In fact, their methods were ill-suited to understanding nature: When they wanted to explain some natural phenomenon such as the movement of blood through the body or the apparent movements of the planets and stars, they looked to ancient authorities for answers rather than to nature itself. Renaissance scientists searched for ancient texts about nature, and then debated about which ancient author had been correct. The humanists' most prominent contributions to science consisted of recovering classical texts and translating the work of ancient Greek scientists into the more widely understood Latin. The Renaissance approach contrasted to the scientific method of today, in which scientists form a hypothesis and then determine whether it is correct by experimenting and observing the natural world as directly as possible.

Arcangela Tarabotti, "Misognynists Named and Unnamed Are Condemned" from *Paternal Tyranny*

(Divine Omnipotence) wills (women) supreme authority over the male sex to be made manifest, as he is unworthy of any other treatment but prison and stripes (scars from whipping). So it is simply not true that man, like staves to the vine, supports the woman who otherwise would fall spineless; rather he approaches her to induce her to fall by countless ploys and be supported by him.

A clever mind wishing to operate in a sinister fashion easily manages to invent chimeras (an absurd creation of the imagination) that distort the true nature of things and force the strangest meanings from bits of arcane learning. And thus our most astute author wrongly interprets the custom of women of Tartary, who bore on their heads as their most precious ornament a human foot. The correct meaning is that woman, as quick and ready for noble deeds, runs with many feet along the path of virtue, keeping one united with her mind so she can walk securely on her way, without stumbling. She needs the extra assistance so as not to fall into the snares and traps set for her innocent nature without end by the cursed "genius" of the male sex, who is always opposed to doing good.

His interpretation, therefore, that there is no greater glory for a woman, a mindless creature with no sense, than to be subject to the male is obviously false. The contrary is true: that her greatest torment and suffering is to find herself subjected to the tyranny and inhumane whims of men.

Source: Arcangela Tarabotti, *Paternal Tyranny*, edited and translated by Letizia Panizza. (Copyright © 2004 by The University of Chicago. Reprinted by permission of the University of Chicago Press.) 146–149, 158–162.

For Discussion

1. Do Pallavicino and Tarabotti argue through rhetoric or logic? What is the difference between the two ways of arguing?

2. How would you refute Pallavicino? How would you refute Tarabotti?

The texts rediscovered and translated during the Renaissance, nevertheless, broadened the discussion of two subjects crucial to the scientific revolution of the late sixteenth and seventeenth centuries—astronomy and anatomy. In 1543 the Polish humanist Nicolaus Copernicus (1473–1543) resolved the complications in the system of the second-century astronomer Ptolemy. Whereas Ptolemy's writings had placed Earth at the center of the universe, Copernicus cited other ancient writers who put the sun in the center. Thus, the first breakthrough in theoretical astronomy was achieved not by making new observations, but by comparing ancient texts. Nothing was proven, however, until Galileo Galilei (1564–1642) turned his newly invented telescope to the heavens in 1610 to observe the stars through his own eyes rather than through an ancient text (see Chapter 17).

Andreas Vesalius (1514–1564) built upon recently published studies in anatomy from ancient Greece to write a survey of human anatomy, *On the Fabric of the Human Body* (1543), a book that encouraged dissection of corpses and anatomical observations. With Vesalius, anatomy moved away from relying exclusively on the authority of ancient books to encouraging medical students and physicians to examine the human body with their own eyes. Building upon Vesalius's work, Gabriele Falloppio (ca. 1523–1562) made many original observations of muscles, nerves, kidneys, bones, and most famously the "fallopian tubes," which lead from the ovaries to the uterus in the female reproductive system, which he described for the first time.

Besides recovering ancient scientific texts, the most important Renaissance contributions to science came secondhand from developments in the visual arts and technology. Florentine artists during the early fifteenth century applied mathematics to paintings. The goal was to make paintings more accurately represent reality by creating the visual illusion of the third dimension of depth on a two-dimensional rectangular surface, a technique known as linear perspective (see the next section, "Antiquity and Nature in the Arts"). These artists contributed to a more refined understanding of how the eye perceives objects, which led to experiments with glass lenses. A more thorough knowledge of optics made possible the invention of the telescope and microscope.

Invented in the 1450s the printing press combined with the availability of cheap paper led to the printing revolution, which rapidly expanded the availability of books. Scientific books accounted for only about 10 percent of the titles of the first printed books, but the significance of printing for science was greater than the sales figures would indicate. Print meant that new discoveries and ideas reached a wider audience, duplication of scientific investigation could be avoided, illustrations were standardized, and scientists built upon each other's work. With the invention of the printing press, scientific work became closely intertwined with publishing, so that published scientific work advanced science, and scientific work that was not published went largely unnoticed. Leonardo da Vinci (1452–1519), the greatest Renaissance observer of nature, contributed nothing to science because he failed to publish his findings. Because he hid the drawing he made of an airplane in a secret notebook, he had no influence on the development of air travel. The fundamental principle of modern science and, in fact, of all modern scholarship is that research must be made available to everyone through publication.

Antiquity and Nature in the Arts

More than any other age in Western history, the Italian Renaissance is identified with the visual

LEONARDO INVENTS A FLYING MACHINE AND PARACHUTE

Leonardo da Vinci's notebooks are filled with numerous examples of his unprecedented inventions. In his drawings on the top he designed a flying machine similar to a modern helicopter and a parachute. On the bottom are modern models based on his drawings. Leonardo kept his inventions in his secret notebooks, which meant no one could follow up on his ideas.

arts. The unprecedented numbers of brilliant artists active in a handful of Italian cities during the fifteenth and sixteenth centuries overshadow any other contribution of Renaissance culture.

Under the influence of the humanists, Renaissance artists began to imitate the sculpture, architecture, and painting of the artists from classical Greece and Rome. At first they merely tried to copy ancient styles and poses. Just as humanists recaptured antiquity by collecting, translating, and analyzing the writings of classical authors, so Renaissance artists made drawings of classical medals, sculpture, and

CHRONOLOGY: INFLUENCE OF ANCIENT CULTURE

1345	Francesco Petrarca (Petrarch), first humanist, discovers Cicero's letters to Atticus
1402	Leonardo Bruni, chancellor of Florence, begins to write about civic humanism
1404–1472	Leon Battista Alberti, humanist and architect
1418–1466	Isotta Nogarola, first female humanist
1440	Lorenzo Valla begins circulating his critique of the Donation of Constantine
ca. 1454	Johannes Gutenberg begins printing books
1475–1506	Laura Cereta, humanist
1543	Nicolaus Copernicus publishes new cosmological theory
	Andreas Vesalius publishes on human anatomy
1561	Gabriele Falloppio publishes his *Anatomy*
1610	Galileo Galilei, astronomer, publishes discoveries made possible by the telescope

architecture. Because artists believed that classical art was superior to their own, these sketches became valuable models from which other artists could learn. Two of the most influential Florentine artists, the architect Filippo Brunelleschi (1377–1446) and the sculptor Donatello (1386–1466), probably went to Rome together as young men to sketch the ancient monuments.

Renaissance artists, however, wanted not only to copy ancient styles, they also wanted to understand how the ancients had made their figures so lifelike. That led them to observe nature itself more directly, especially the anatomy of the human body. Renaissance art, then, was driven by the passionate desire of artists and their patrons to imitate both ancient works and nature. These twin desires produced a creative tension in their work because the ancients, whose works of art often depicted gods and goddesses, had idealized and improved on what they observed in nature. Renaissance artists sought to depict simultaneously the ideal and the real—an impossible goal, but one that sparked remarkable creativity.

The work of the most important painter of the early Renaissance in Florence, Masaccio (1401–ca. 1428) exemplified this blending of the idealized and the natural. In the Brancacci chapel, Masaccio depicted street scenes from Florence complete with portraits of actual people, including himself. These were examples of naturalism. On other figures in the scene called *The Tribute Money* (shown on the next page)—Jesus, St. Peter, and St. John—he placed heads copied from ancient sculptures of gods. These were examples of idealized beauty, which were especially suitable for saints. The realistic figures helped viewers identify with the subject of the picture by allowing them to recognize people they actually knew. The idealized figures represented the saintly, whose superior moral qualities made them appear different from average people.

The Renaissance style evolved in Masaccio's hometown of Florence early in the fifteenth century. In 1401 the 24-year-old Brunelleschi entered a competition to design bronze panels depicting the biblical account of Abraham's willingness to sacrifice his son Isaac for the north doors of the Baptistery of Florence's cathedral. He lost to Lorenzo Ghiberti (1378–1455). Look at the illustrations on page 385. Ghiberti's panel shown on the right reveals the two characteristic elements of the early Renaissance style: idealization and naturalism. The head of Isaac is modeled after a classical Roman sculpture, and the figures and horse on the left of his panel are depicted as realistically as possible. In these elements, Ghiberti was imitating both antiquity and nature.

Ghiberti worked on the north doors for 21 years. He won such fame that when he finished he was immediately offered a new commission to

THE TRIBUTE MONEY: COMBINING NATURAL AND IDEALIZED REPRESENTATIONS

In this detail of a fresco of Christ and his apostles, Masaccio mixed naturalism and idealized beauty. The figure on the right with his back turned to the viewer is a tax collector, who is depicted as a normal human being. The head of the fourth figure to the left of him, who represents one of the apostles, was copied from an ancient statue that represents ancient ideals of beauty.

Source: Dagli Orti/Picture Desk, Inc./Kobal Collection

complete panels for the east doorway. These doors, begun in 1425, took 27 years to finish. In the east doors, Ghiberti substituted a simple square frame for the Gothic frame of the north doors, thereby liberating his composition. In the illustration on page 386, which depicts the biblical story of the brothers Jacob and Esau, the background architecture of rounded arches and classical columns creates the illusion of depth. This illusion is achieved through **linear perspective,** that is, the use of geometrical principles to depict a three-dimensional space on a flat, two-dimensional surface. Linear perspective, a method for imitating the way nature appears to

the human eye, was an achievement of the Renaissance, something never perfected before. In the panels of the east doors, Ghiberti created the definitive Renaissance interpretation of the ancient principles of the harmony produced by geometry. Michelangelo said that the doors were fit to serve as the "gates of paradise."

Most humanist theorists of painting linked artistic creativity with masculinity. By the sixteenth century, however, these theorists were proved wrong, as female painters rose to prominence. The most notable was Sofonisba Anguissola (ca. 1532–1625). Born into an aristocratic family, she received a humanist education along

THE COMPETITION PANELS OF THE SACRIFICE OF ISAAC

These two panels were the finalists in a competition to design the cast bronze doors on the north side of the Baptistery in Florence. Each demonstrates a bold new design that attempted to capture the emotional trauma of the exact moment when an angel arrests Abraham's arm from sacrificing his son Isaac (Genesis 22:1–12). Both artists went on to be closely associated with the new style of the Renaissance. The panel on the left, by Filippo Brunelleschi, lost to the one on the right, by Lorenzo Ghiberti. Notice how the Ghiberti relief better conveys the drama of the scene by projecting the elbow of Abraham's upraised arm outward toward the viewer. As a result, the viewer's line of sight follows the line of the arm and knife directly toward Isaac's throat.

with her five sisters and brother. As a woman, she was prohibited from studying anatomy or drawing male models. So she specialized in portraits, often of members of her family, and self-portraits. She developed a distinctive style of depicting animated faces as in the portrait of her sisters playing chess shown on page 387. Her fame was so great that King Philip II of Spain hired her as his official court painter. Her example inspired other aristocratic women to take up painting.

The Renaissance Patron

All the Renaissance arts displayed the influence of patrons, the wealthy people who controlled the city-states and had been educated in humanist schools. Until the end of the sixteenth century, all painters, sculptors, and even poets worked for a patron. A patron, who could be an individual or a group, such as a religious order or a government, commissioned a work of art, such as an altar painting, portrait bust, statue, or palace. Patron and artist would agree on a contract, which might specify exactly what the artist was to do, what kinds of materials he was to use (almost all Renaissance artists were men), how much they could cost, how much he could rely on assistants, how much he had to do himself, and even how he was to arrange figures in the work. Michelangelo Buonarroti (1475–1564) sculpted *David*, which has become the most famous work of Renaissance art, to fulfill a contract that had been debated in a

LINEAR PERSPECTIVE

In these square panels Ghiberti explored the full potential of the newly discovered principles of linear perspective.

committee meeting of the government of Florence. Regardless of their talent, artists could never do whatever they wanted.

Some patrons supported the career of an artist for an extended time. Princes, in particular, liked to take on an artist—give him a regular salary and perhaps even an official title—in exchange for having him do whatever the prince wanted. Thus, Duke Lodovico Sforza (1451–1508) brought Leonardo da Vinci to Milan, where Leonardo painted a portrait of the duke's mistress, devised plans for a giant equestrian statue of the duke's father, designed stage sets and carnival pageants, painted the interior decorations of the castle, and did engineering work.

Most patrons supported the arts to enhance their own prestige and power. Some, such as Pope Julius II, had exceptional influence on artists. He persuaded Michelangelo, who saw himself as a sculptor, to paint the ceiling of the Sistine Chapel.

The Spread of the Renaissance

The Renaissance spread as other Europeans encountered the culture of Italy. Princes and aristocrats who studied or fought in Italy were the

PORTRAITS IN RENAISSANCE ART

Sofonisba Anguissola excelled at portrait painting. In this collective portrait of her three sisters and their nurse, she rejected the traditional props associated with women, such as pets or needlework, to show them engaged in the challenging intellectual game of chess. In this way Anguissola subverted female stereotypes.

first to export Italian art and artists abroad. King Philip of Spain was just one of many sixteenth-century monarchs who lured Italian artists to his court. Leonardo da Vinci spent his last years living in a great chateau given him by the king of France. Perhaps no country was more enthralled with the Italian Renaissance than Poland where many aristocrats who had studied in Italy built

CHRONOLOGY: ANTIQUITY AND NATURE IN THE ARTS

1401	Lorenzo Ghiberti and Filippo Brunelleschi compete for commission to make the door panels on the Florentine baptistery
1404–1407	Donatello, Florentine sculptor, and Filippo Brunelleschi go to Rome to investigate Antiquities
ca. 1425	Filippo Brunelleschi, Florentine sculptor and architect, demonstrates the use of linear perspective
1452–1519	Leonardo da Vinci, Florentine painter and inventor
1504	Michelangelo Buonarroti, Florentine sculptor, painter, architect, poet, completes his statue of David
ca. 1532–1625	Sofonisba Anguissola, painter

palaces and whole planned towns in imitation of Renaissance ideals. Even the Kremlin in Moscow was designed by Italian architects.

After the collapse of the Italian city-states during the Italian Wars (1494–1530), the growing power of the western European monarchies facilitated the spread of Renaissance culture outside of Italy. As we discuss next, the French invaded the Italian peninsula at the end of the fifteenth century and sparked years of warfare in Italy; however, King Francis I (r. 1515–1547) was impressed by what he saw. He had the first Renaissance-style chateau built in France and hired Italian artists, including Leonardo da Vinci, to bring Renaissance culture to his kingdom.

THE EARLY MODERN EUROPEAN STATE SYSTEM

■ How did the monarchies of western Europe become more assertive and effective during the late fifteenth and early sixteenth centuries?

The civic independence that had made the Italian Renaissance possible was challenged during the Italian Wars when France, Spain, and the Holy Roman Empire attempted to carve up the peninsula for themselves. The wars started in 1494 when the French king attempted to seize the kingdom of Naples. His invasion of Italy drew in rival monarchs from Spain and the Holy Roman Empire who could not tolerate French control of wealthy Italy and pitted the Italian city-states against one another as they attempted to save themselves from foreign conquest. These wars were a disaster for Italy. For nearly 40 years wave after wave of foreign armies crossed the Alps and turned Italy into a battle ground. The low point was the sack of Rome in 1527 when German mercenaries plundered the city, destroyed works of art, and imprisoned the Medici pope. By 1530 the king of Spain had defeated his rival in France for control of Italy. All of the large cities except Venice came under Spanish domination.

The surrender of the rich city-states of Italy was the first sign of a transformation in the European system of states. Only the large monarchies of the West, such as France, Spain, and England, could muster the materiel and manpower necessary to put and keep a large army in the field. The Italian Wars revealed the outlines of the early modern European state system, which was built on the power of large countries ruled by kings. These kings amassed unprecedented resources that not only crushed Italy, but also enabled Europe to dominate much of the globe through colonies in the Americas, Asia, and Africa (see Chapter 13).

The Origins of Modern Historical and Political Thought

The revival of the monarchies of western Europe and the loss of the independence of the Italian city-states forced a rethinking of politics. As in so many other fields, the Florentines led the way. To understand their own troubled city-state, they analyzed politics by comparing one kind of government with another and observing current events.

The shock of the Italian Wars that began in 1494 stimulated a quest for understanding the causes of Italy's fall and prompted a new kind of history writing that went beyond the medieval chronicles. There had been critical histories during the Middle Ages, such as Jean Froissart's account of France during the Hundred Years' War and Jan Dlugosz's history of the kings of Poland. The new Renaissance history, however, set new standards for criticizing evidence and borrowed from the rhetorical precepts of the humanists to make arguments. The first person to write a successful history in the new vein was Francesco Guicciardini (1483–1540). Born to a well-placed Florentine family, educated in a humanist school and experienced as a diplomat, governor, and adviser to the Medici, Guicciardini combined literary skill and practical political experience. Besides collecting information about contemporary events, he kept a record of how his own thoughts and values evolved in response to what he observed. One of the hallmarks of his work was that as he analyzed the motives of others, he engaged in self-scrutiny and self-criticism. His masterpiece, *The History of Italy* (1536–1540), was the first account of events that occurred across the entire Italian peninsula. Guicciardini saw human causes for historical events rather than the hidden hand of God. He suggested, for example, that emotions mattered more than rational calculation and noted that nothing ever turns out as anticipated.

Just as Guicciardini examined the causes of historical change, Niccolo Macchiavelli explored the dynamics of effective rule. In *The Prince* Machiavelli encouraged rulers to understand the underlying principles of political power, which differed from the personal morality expected of those who were not rulers. A prince had to appear to be a moral person, but Machiavelli pointed out that the successful prince might sometimes have to be immoral to protect the state. How would the prince know when this might be the case?

Machiavelli's answer was that "necessity" forced political decisions to override normal morality. The prince "must consider the end result," which meant that his highest obligation was preserving the existence of the state that had been entrusted to him and providing security for all its citizens. This obligation took precedence even over his religious duty.

Through Guicciardini's analysis of human motivations and Machiavelli's attempt to discover what made certain actions necessary, historical and political thought moved in a new direction. The key to understanding history and politics was in the details of human events. To Guicciardini, these details provided clues to the psychology of leaders. To Machiavelli, they revealed the hidden mechanisms of chance and planning that governed not just political decisions, but all human events.

Monarchies: The Foundation of the State System

The European state system was one of the most lasting achievements of the Renaissance. By the state system, historians referred to a complex of interrelated changes. First, governments established standing armies. As a result of the military revolution that brought large numbers of infantry to the field of battle and gunpowder cannons to besiege cities and castles, governments had to modernize their armies or face defeat. Since the ninth century, kings had relied on feudal levies in which soldiers were recruited to fulfill their personal obligation to a lord, but by the late fifteenth century, governments began to organize standing professional armies. These armies, however, were expensive because the soldiers had to be regularly paid and the new artillery was costly. Moreover, fortifications had to be improved to withstand the artillery. As a result, kings were desperate for new revenues.

The need for revenues led to the second development, the growth of taxation. Every European state struggled with the problem of taxation. The need to tax efficiently produced the beginnings of a bureaucracy of tax assessors and collectors. People resisted the new taxes, creating tension with the monarch.

This tension led to the third development. Monarchs attempted to weaken the resistance by abolishing the tax exemptions of local communities and ignoring regional assemblies and parliaments that were supposed to approve new taxes. During the twelfth and thirteenth centuries, effective government was local government, and kings could seldom interfere in the affairs of towns and regions. During the fifteenth century, however, to raise taxes and impose their will throughout the realm, kings everywhere tried to eliminate or erode the independence of towns and parliaments.

Fourth, monarchs tried to reduce the independence of the aristocracy and the Church. In the kingdoms of western Europe, the most significant threats to the power of the king were the aristocrats. Kings struggled to co-opt these aristocrats or force them to submit. Most monarchs also sought to oblige churchmen to become agents of government policy. Monarchs were most successful in reducing the power of the aristocrats and the Church in France, England, and Spain. In eastern Europe, despite the attempts by kings to accomplish what their western cousins had done, the aristocracy remained in control. In Poland, Bohemia, and Hungary, the aristocrats elected the kings and kept royal power in check.

The fifth development in the evolution of the Renaissance Europe state system was the institution of resident ambassadors. During the Italian Wars, the kings of Europe began to exchange ambassadors who resided at foreign capitals and were responsible for informing their sovereign about conditions in the host country and representing their rulers' interests abroad. Resident ambassadors became the linchpins in a sophisticated information network that provided intelligence about the intentions and capabilities of other kings, princes, and cities. These ambassadors typically enjoyed a humanist education, which helped them adapt to strange and unpredictable situations, understand foreign languages, negotiate effectively, and speak persuasively. Ambassadors cultivated courtly manners, which smoothed over personal conflicts. For the new state system, gathering reliable information became as important as maintaining armies and collecting taxes. Although the Italian city states were the first in many of these developments, they were soon outstripped by the larger monarchies of the West.

France, with the largest territory and population (more than 16 million) in western Europe, had the potential to become the most powerful state in Europe. Under King Charles VII (r. 1422–1461), France created its first professional army. Equally important, the **Pragmatic Sanction of Bourges** (1438) guaranteed the virtual autonomy of the French Church from papal control, enabling the French king to interfere in religious affairs and exploit Church revenues for government purposes. A third important weapon in the development of the French national monarchy was the *taille*, an annual direct tax. During the final years of the Hundred Years' War, which ended in 1453, the Estates General (France's parliament) granted the king the right to collect the *taille*. After the war, Louis XI (r. 1461–1483) turned it into a permanent source of revenue for himself and his successors. Armed with the financial resources of the *taille*, Louis and his successors expanded the reach of the French monarchy.

In contrast to France, the kingdoms of Spain had never been major players in European affairs during the Middle Ages. The Iberian peninsula was home to several small kingdoms—Portugal, Castile, Navarre, and Aragon, which were all Christian, and Granada, which was Muslim. Each kingdom had its own laws, political institutions, customs, and language. Unlike France, these Christian kingdoms were poor, underpopulated, and preoccupied with the reconquest, the attempt to drive the richer Muslims from the peninsula. There was little reason to assume that this region would become one of the greatest powers in Europe, the rival of France. The Renaissance made that possible.

That rise to power began with a wedding. In 1469 Isabella, who later would become queen of Castile (r. 1474–1504), married Ferdinand, who later would be king of Aragon (r. 1479–1516). The objective of this arranged marriage was to solidify an alliance between the two kingdoms, not to unify them, but in 1479 Castile and Aragon were combined into the kingdom of Spain. Of the two, Castile was the larger, with a population of perhaps six million, and wealthier. Together Isabella and Ferdinand, each still ruling their own kingdoms, at least partially subdued the rebellious aristocracy and built up a bureaucracy of well-educated middle-ranking lawyers and priests to manage the government.

The Christian kings of Iberia had long wanted to make the entire peninsula Christian. In 1492 the armies of Isabella and Ferdinand defeated the last remaining Iberian Muslim kingdom of Granada. While celebrating the victory over Islam, the monarchs made two momentous decisions. The first was to rid Spain of Jews as well as Muslims. Isabella and Ferdinand decreed that within six months all Jews had to either convert to Christianity or leave. To enforce conformity to Christianity among the converted Jews who did not leave, the king and queen authorized an ecclesiastical tribunal, the Spanish Inquisition, to investigate the sincerity of conversions. The second decision was Isabella's alone. She financed a voyage by a Genoese sea captain, Christopher Columbus, to sail west into the Atlantic in an attempt to reach India and China. Isabella seemed to have wanted to outflank the Muslim kingdoms of the Middle East and find allies in Asia. As we shall see in the next chapter, Columbus's voyage had consequences more far-reaching than Isabella's intentions, adding to the crown of Castile immense lands in the Americas.

Despite the diversity of their kingdoms, Isabella and Ferdinand made Spain a great power and established the framework for the diplomatic relations among European states for the next century and a half (see **Map 12.2**). They married their children into the royal houses of England, Portugal, Burgundy, and the Holy Roman Empire, creating a network of alliances that isolated France. As a result of these marriage alliances, their grandson, Charles V, succeeded to the Habsburg lands of Burgundy, inherited the crown of Spain, was elected Holy Roman Emperor, which included all of Germany, ruled over the Spanish conquests in Italy, and was the Emperor of the Indies, which included all of Spanish Central and South America and the Philippines. This was the greatest accumulation

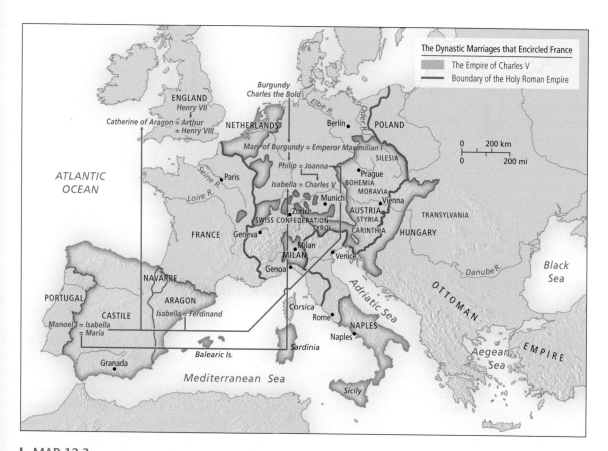

MAP 12.2

The Dynastic Marriages That Encircled France

Through skillfully arranging the marriages of their sons and daughters, Ferdinand of Aragon and Isabella of Castile managed to completely surround the rival kingdom of France with a network of alliances.

CHRONOLOGY: THE EARLY MODERN EUROPEAN STATE SYSTEM

1422	Charles VII succeeds to the throne of France
1455	Wars of the Roses in England underway
1461	Louis XI succeeds to the throne of France
1474	Isabella succeeds to the throne of Castile
1479	Ferdinand succeeds to the throne of Aragon
1479	Unification of Castile and Aragon
1485	Henry VII succeeds to the throne of England; Wars of Roses ends
1492	Conquest of Granada; expulsion of the Jews from Spain; voyage of Christopher Columbus
1494	The Italian Wars begin with the French invasion of Naples
1515	Francis I succeeds to the throne of France
1516	Charles V succeeds to the throne of Spain

of territories by a European ruler since Charlemagne in the ninth century.

Unlike Spain, England had been one of the great medieval powers, but at the end of the Hundred Years' War in 1453, the English crown was defeated and England exhausted. Thousands of disbanded mercenaries flooded England and enlisted in feuds among aristocratic families. The mercenaries brought to England the violence they had practiced in the wars with France. Under the tensions caused by defeat and revolt, the royal family fractured into the two rival branches of Lancaster and York, which fought a vicious civil war, now known as the Wars of the Roses (1455–1485) from the red and white roses used to identify members of the opposing sides.

When Henry Tudor finally ended the civil wars and became King Henry VII (r. 1485–1509), there was little reason to believe that England could again become a major force in European events. Henry took years to become safe on his own throne. He revived the Court of Star Chamber as an instrument of royal will to punish unruly nobles who had long bribed and intimidated their way out of trouble with the courts. Because his own hand-picked councilors served as judges, Henry could guarantee that the court system became fairer and more obedient to his wishes. He confiscated the lands of rebellious lords, thereby increasing his own income,

and he prohibited all private armies except those that served his interests. By managing his administration efficiently, eliminating unnecessary expenses, and staying out of war, Henry governed without the need to call on Parliament for increased revenues.

England was still a backward country with fewer than three million people. But by nourishing an alliance with newly unified Spain, Henry brought England back into European affairs. When his son Henry VIII succeeded to the throne, the Tudor dynasty was more secure than any of its predecessors and England more stable than it had ever been.

CONCLUSION

The Politics of Culture

The Renaissance began as an attempt to imitate the style of the best ancient Latin authors and orators. Within a generation, however, humanists and artists pushed this narrow literary project into a full-scale attempt to refashion human society on the model of ancient cultures. Reading about the ancients and looking at their works of art provoked comparisons with contemporary Renaissance society. The result was the development of a critical approach to the past and present. The critical approach fostered an enhanced historical sensibility, which transformed the idea of the West from one defined primarily by religious identification with Christianity to one forged by a common historical experience.

During the sixteenth century, western Europeans absorbed the critical-historical methods of the Renaissance and turned them in new directions. In northern Europe scholars used the critical historical methods of the humanists to better understand the historical sources of Christianity, especially the Bible. With that development, Christianity began to take on new shades of meaning, and many Christians attempted to make the practices of the Church conform more closely to the Bible. The humanist approach to religion led down a path that permanently divided Christian camps over the interpretation of Scripture. As we will see in Chapter 14, the sixteenth-century Reformation shattered the hard-won unity of the Catholic West.

As the next chapter shows, however, in the century before the Reformation Spanish and Portuguese sailors encountered previously unknown cultures in the Americas and only vaguely known ones in Africa and Asia. Because of the Renaissance, those who thought and wrote about these strange new cultures did so with the perspective of antiquity in mind.

KEY TERMS

Renaissance
republicanism
humanists
philology
rhetoric

civic humanism
linear perspective
Pragmatic Sanction of
    Bourges

CHAPTER QUESTIONS

1. How did the political and social climate peculiar to the Italian city-states help create Renaissance culture? (page 366)
2. How did ancient culture influence the Renaissance? (page 376)
3. How did the monarchies of western Europe become more assertive and effective during the last half of the fifteenth and early sixteenth centuries? (page 388)

TAKING IT FURTHER

1. How did rhetoric influence different kinds of Renaissance activities, such as humanism, visual arts, and political theory?
2. How did the political turmoil of the Italian Wars stimulate new thinking about history and politics?
3. How was the Italian Renaissance encounter with the culture of the ancient world similar to other encounters discussed in this book? How was it different?

✓●—[Practice on MyHistoryLab

13

The West and the World: The Significance of Global Encounters, 1450–1650

■ Europeans in Africa   ■ Europeans in the Americas   ■ Europeans in Asia
■ The Beginnings of the Global System

ON A HOT OCTOBER DAY IN 1492, CHRISTOPHER COLUMBUS AND HIS MEN, dressed in heavy armor, clanked onto the beach of an island in the Bahamas. The captain and his crew had been at sea sailing west from the Canary Islands for five weeks, propelled by winds they thought would take them straight to Asia. As the ships under Columbus's command vainly searched among the islands of the Caribbean for the rich ports of Asia, Columbus thought he must be in India and thus called the natives he met "Indians." At another point he thought he might be among the Mongols of central Asia, which he described in his journal as the "people of the Great Khan." Both of Columbus's guesses about his location were incorrect, but they have left a revealing linguistic legacy: "Indians" for native Americans, and both "cannibals" and "Caribbean" from Columbus's inconsistent spellings of Khan. Columbus believed that the people he called the Cannibals or Caribs ate human flesh. But he got that information—also incorrect—from their enemies. Thus began one of the most lasting misunderstandings from Columbus's first voyage. Historians know very little about the natives' first thoughts of the arrival of their foreign visitors, largely because within a few generations the Caribs almost completely died out. By the time someone was interested in hearing it, no one was left to pass down their story.

Western civilization at the end of the fifteenth century hardly seemed on the verge of encircling the globe with outposts and colonies. Its kingdoms had barely been able to reorganize themselves sufficiently for self-defense, let alone world exploration and foreign conquest. The Ottoman threat was so great that all of southern and eastern Europe was on the defensive. The hostilities between Turks and Christians blocked the traditional trade routes to Asia, which had stimulated the great medieval economic expansion of Europe. In comparison with the Ottoman Empire or Ming China, Europe's puny, impoverished states seemed more prone to quarreling among themselves than to seeking expanded horizons.

Nevertheless, by 1500 Europeans could be found fighting and trading in Africa, the Americas, and Asia. A mere 50 years later, Europeans had destroyed the two greatest civilizations in the Americas, begun the forced migration of Africans to the Americas through the slave trade, and opened trading posts throughout South and East Asia.

Before 1492 the West, identified by its languages, religions, agricultural technology, literature, folklore, music, art, and common intellectual tradition that

CHRISTOPHER COLUMBUS

This near contemporary portrait of the mariner depicts him as a well-dressed Renaissance gentleman.

stretched back to pre-Christian antiquity, was largely confined to Europe and the Middle East. Barely a century after Columbus's voyages, Western culture could be found in many distant lands, and western European languages and forms of Christianity were adopted by or forced upon other peoples. The West was now more of an idea than a place, a certain kind of culture that thrived in many different environments. As western Europeans came under the influence of the far-flung peoples they visited, they were themselves transformed as they began to discover the principle of cultural relativity and tolerate human differences. The European voyages integrated the globe biologically and economically. Microbes, animals, and plants that had once been isolated were now transported throughout the world. Because the Europeans possessed the ships for transport and the guns for coercion, they became the dominant players in international trade, even in places thousands of miles from the European homeland. The question raised by this first phase of the European global encounters is, how were both the West and the rest of the world transformed?

EUROPEANS IN AFRICA

■ Why did the European incursions into sub-Saharan Africa lead to the vast migration of Africans to the Americas as slaves?

Medieval Europeans had accumulated a substantial knowledge about North Africa, but except for Ethiopia they were almost completely ignorant of the region south of the Sahara desert. By the fifteenth century, Muslim contacts with sub-Saharan Africa made it clear that the region was a source of gold and slaves. In search of these, Europeans, especially the Portuguese, began to journey down the west coast of Africa.

Sub-Saharan Africa Before the Europeans Arrived

For centuries highly developed, prosperous kingdoms had governed the interior of sub-Saharan Africa. During the fifteenth and sixteenth centuries when European contacts with the sub-Sahara dramatically expanded, however, the once-strong kingdoms were either in decline or engaged in protracted struggles with regional rivals. The Europeans arrived at precisely the moment when they could take advantage of the weaknesses produced by internal African conflicts.

The Muslim kingdom of Mali, a landlocked empire between the Upper Senegal and Niger Rivers, had long had a monopoly of the gold caravans that carried the coveted metal from the fabled city of Timbuktu across the Sahara to the gold-greedy Mediterranean. During the European Middle Ages Mali was the greatest empire in sub-Saharan Africa, but by 1400 it was in decline. Internal power struggles had split apart the once-vast empire. In 1482, when the Portuguese founded a gold-trading post at Elmina, they found the rulers of Mali much weaker than they had been 100 years before (see the trade routes and towns on **Map 13.1**).

Influenced by Mali, the forest kingdoms of Guinea were built on a prosperous urban society and extensive trading networks. European travelers compared the great city of Benin favorably with the principal European cities of the time. The towns of Guinea held regular markets, similar to the periodic fairs of Europe, and carefully scheduled them so they would not compete with each other. The staples of the long-distance trade routes in this region were high-value luxury goods, especially imported cloth, kola nuts (a mild stimulant popular in Muslim countries), metalwork such as cutlasses, ivory, and of course gold. However, civil wars weakened these kingdoms during the sixteenth century, opening the way for greater European influence.

Unlike the kingdoms of the western sub-Sahara, which tended to be Muslim, mountainous Ethiopia was predominantly Christian. In fact, Europeans saw Ethiopians as potential allies against Islam. Diplomatic contacts between Rome and Ethiopia intensified at the time of the Council of Florence in 1439, which attempted to unify all Christians in defense against Ottoman Turks. Learned Ethiopian churchmen became known in western Europe and created the impression that Ethiopia was an abundant land peopled by pious Christians. Portuguese visitors were duly impressed by the splendor of the emperor of Ethiopia, the Negus, who traveled with 2,000 attendants and 50,000 mules to carry provisions and tents. By the early sixteenth century, however, the Ethiopian kingdom had become overextended. In the 1520s and 1530s Muslims attacked deep into the Ethiopian heartland, raiding and burning the wealthy Ethiopian monasteries. The raids severely weakened the power of the Negus. Ethiopia survived, but competing Christian warlords weakened the central authority.

European Voyages Along the African Coast

Gold brought Europeans to sub-Saharan Africa. European merchants traded European silver for African gold in the Maghreb, the collective name for the present-day regions of Morocco, Algeria, and Tunisia. The Maghreb was the northern terminus of the gold caravans from Mali. European merchants made handsome profits from the gold trade, but they recognized they could make even greater profits if they could cut out the middlemen of the Maghreb. The Europeans had little hope, however, of using the camel caravan routes across the Sahara because of the hostility of Muslim inhabitants who were wary about foreign interlopers, especially Christian ones.

The alternative for Europeans was to outflank the Muslims by a sea route. As early as the thirteenth century, European voyagers ventured down the west coast of Africa into uncharted waters, but such voyages soon ran into trouble. Adapted to the calm waters of the Mediterranean,

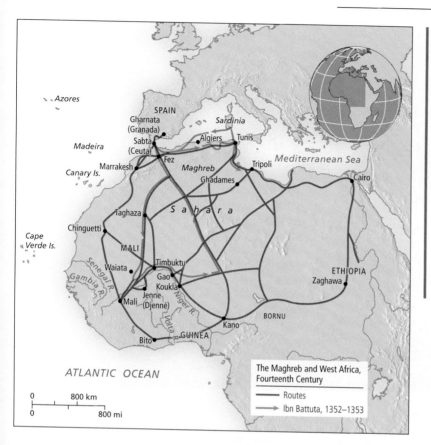

MAP 13.1

The Maghreb and West Africa, Fourteenth Century

Long before the arrival of the Portuguese via sea routes, caravans of camels criss-crossed the Sahara desert during the fourteenth century, linking the sources of gold in Mali with the Maghreb (the coast of north-west Africa) and the seaports of the Mediterranean. The greatest medieval Arabic traveler, Ibn Battuta (1304–1368/69), crossed the Sahara and spent more than a year in Mali. He left the most extensive account of medieval West Africa.

European galleys were ill-suited for voyaging on the heavy seas of the Atlantic. Such ships were not only easily swamped, they also required the feeding of large crews of oarsmen. In addition, the long coastline of West Africa lacked protective harbors for refuge from storms. For Europeans to gain direct access to the gold of Mali, they needed to develop new kinds of ships.

NEW MARITIME TECHNOLOGY During the fifteenth century changes in the technology of ocean sailing surmounted the disadvantages of Mediterranean galleys. The location of the Iberian peninsula (the land of present-day Portugal and Spain) made possible the building of a hybrid ship that combined features of Mediterranean and Atlantic designs.

The new ship was the **caravel.** Iberians modified the older cog design, the dominant ship in the Atlantic, by adding extra masts and creating a new kind of rigging that combined the square sails of Atlantic ships, suitable for sailing in the same direction as the wind was blowing, with the triangular "lateen" sails of Mediterranean galleys, which permitted sailing into the wind. The result was a ship that could sail in a variety of winds, carry large cargoes, be managed by a small crew, and be defended by guns mounted in the castle superstructure. These hybrid three-mast caravels first appeared about 1450; for the next 200 years Europeans sailed ships of this same basic design on long ocean voyages to the very ends of the Earth.

Other late-medieval innovations also assisted European navigators. The compass, originally from China, provided an approximate indicator of direction. The astrolabe, borrowed from Muslim mariners, and naked-eye celestial

FIFTEENTH-CENTURY CARAVEL

The caravel was typical of the hybrid ship developed during the fifteenth century on the Iberian peninsula. The two sails toward the bow are square rigged, the two at the stern are lateen. This ship is an exact replica of the Niña, one of the ships on Columbus's first voyage.

navigation made it possible to estimate latitudes. Books of sailing directions, called portolanos, many of which were adapted from Islamic sources, included charts of ports and recorded the location of dangerous shoals and safe harbors for future voyages.

Technology alone, however, does not explain why Europeans set sail around the globe in this era. There had been great ocean navigating efforts before. For centuries, Polynesians successfully navigated their way across the Pacific Ocean in open canoes. The Vikings regularly crossed the North Atlantic from the tenth to fourteenth centuries, and the Chinese engaged in extensive exploratory voyages throughout the Indian Ocean earlier in the fifteenth century. The desire to profit from an expanded trade network

and to outflank the Muslims who blocked the eastern trade routes motivated European voyages in the fifteenth and sixteenth centuries.

NEW COLONIALISM   The search for greater profits created new kinds of colonies. Mediterranean colonies established during the Crusades of the twelfth and thirteenth centuries had relied on native inhabitants to produce commodities that the colonizers expropriated. These were either aristocratic colonies in which a few warriors occupied castles to dominate the native population or mercantile colonies built around a trading post for foreign merchants.

During the fifteenth century, Castile and Portugal founded colonies in the Canary Islands, the Madeira archipelago, the Azores, and the

Cape Verde Islands. The climate of these islands was similar to that of the Mediterranean and invited the cultivation of typical Mediterranean crops, such as grains and sugar cane, but the islands lacked a native labor force for either an aristocratic or a mercantile colony. When Europeans arrived, the Canaries had few inhabitants and the other islands were uninhabited. In response to the labor shortage, two new types of colonies emerged, both of which were later introduced into the Americas.

The first new type of colony was the **settler colony.** The settler colony derived from the medieval, feudal model of government, in which a private person obtained a license from a king to seize an island or some part of an island. The king supplied financial support and legal authority for the expedition. In return, the settler promised to recognize the king as his lord and occasionally to pay a fee after the settlement was successful. The kings of Castile and Portugal issued such licenses for the exploitation of the Atlantic islands. The actual expeditions to colonize these islands were private enterprises, and adventurers from various parts of Europe vied for a license from any king who would grant them one. For example, the first European settlement in the Canary Islands was led by a Norman-French knight, who could not obtain sufficient support from the king of France and thus switched loyalties to the king of Castile.

After the arrival of the Europeans, all the natives of the Canaries, called the Guanches, were killed or died off from European diseases, creating the need for settler families from Europe to till the land and maintain the Castilian claim on the islands. These European peasants and artisans imported their own culture. They brought with them their traditional family structures, customs, language, religion, seeds, livestock, and patterns of cultivation. Wherever settler colonies were found, whether in the Atlantic islands or the New World, they remade the lands in the image of the Old World.

The second new type of colony was the **plantation colony.** Until the occupation of the Cape Verde Islands in the 1460s, the Atlantic island colonies had relied on European settlers for labor. However, the Cape Verdes attracted few immigrants, and yet the islands seemed especially well-suited for growing the lucrative sugar cane crop. The few permanent European colonists there tended to be exiled criminals who were disinclined to work. Because there was no indigenous population to exploit on the Cape Verdes, the Europeans began to look elsewhere for laborers. They voyaged to the African coast, where they bought slaves who had been captured by African slavers from inland villages. These slaves worked as agricultural laborers in the Cape Verdes sugar cane fields.

Thus, in the Cape Verdes began the tragic conjunction between African slavery and the European demand for sugar. When sugar began to replace honey as the sweetener of choice for Europeans, sugar cultivated by slaves in plantation colonies, first in the Atlantic islands and later in the West Indies and American mainland, met the almost insatiable demand. Over the next 300 years, this pattern for plantation colonies was repeated for other valuable agricultural commodities, such as indigo for dyes, coffee, and cotton, which were grown to sell in European markets. The first loop of what would eventually become a global trading circuit was now completed.

THE PORTUGUESE IN AFRICA The Portuguese launched the first European voyages along the African coast during the fifteenth century. The sponsor of these voyages was Prince Henry the Navigator (1394–1460). As governor of Algarve, the southernmost province of Portugal, Henry financed numerous exploratory voyages. Although the many voyages of Henry's sailors did not fulfill his dreams of conquest and enormous riches, his sailors discovered bases near the Senegal and Gambia Rivers for the Malinese gold trade. He and other members of his family also helped colonize Madeira and the Azores. As a source of sugar, Madeira became a valuable colony (see Maps 13.1 and **13.2**).

After Henry's death, Portuguese exploration of the African coast accelerated. In only six years, a private merchant of Lisbon commissioned voyages

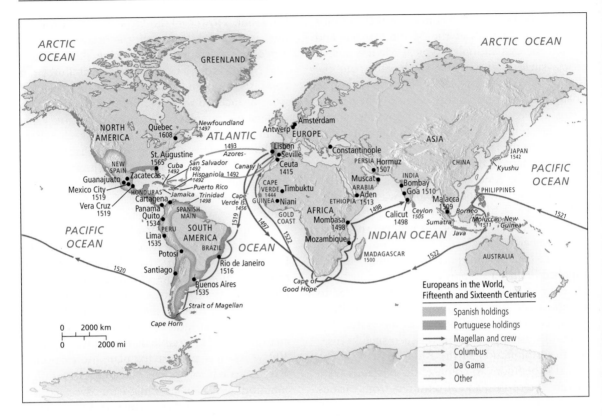

MAP 13.2

Europeans in the World, Fifteenth and Sixteenth Centuries

During the fifteenth and sixteenth centuries European sailors opened sea lanes for commerce across the Atlantic, Pacific, and Indian Oceans. Dates indicate first arrival of Europeans.

that added 2,000 miles of coastline to what was known to the Portuguese. In 1482 the Portuguese royal family took control of trade with Africa and transformed what had been a loose and haphazard enterprise under private contractors into a lucrative source of revenue for the monarchy. The monarchy required that all sailings be authorized and all cargoes inventoried. To protect the trade, the Por-

CHRONOLOGY: EUROPEANS IN AFRICA

1270	Beginnings of the Ethiopian kingdom
1316	Papal delegation sent to Ethiopia
1394–1460	Life of Prince Henry the Navigator of Portugal
1450s	Appearance of new European ship design, the caravel
ca. 1450	European slave trade in Africa begins
1460s	Occupation of Cape Verde Islands
1482	Portuguese gold-trading post founded at Elmina
1520–1530s	Muslim attacks against Ethiopian kingdom

tuguese built a permanent fortress at Elmina near the mouth of the Volta River in modern Ghana in West Africa. Rather than establishing new settler or plantation colonies, the Portuguese on the African coast relied on **trading posts** that supplied gold, ivory, pepper, and slaves.

EUROPEANS IN THE AMERICAS

■ How did the arrival of Europeans in the Americas transform native cultures and life?

The first European voyagers to the Americas also coveted gold and sought an alternative route to India and China. Europeans relied on Asian sources for medicines, spices, and all kinds of luxury goods that were unavailable elsewhere. The desire to profit from this trade impelled men to take great risks to find an alternative route around the Ottoman Empire to East Asia. In the short run, the Americas proved to be an impediment because the two continents stood in the way of getting to Asia. But in the long run, the European voyages to the Americas brought consequences unimaginable to those who first began to sail west from Europe.

The Americas Before the Conquistadores

Prior to their contact with Europeans, the peoples of the Americas displayed remarkable cultural variety. Nomadic hunters spread across the sub-Arctic regions, western North America, and the Amazon jungles, while farming settlements prevailed in much of South America and eastern North America. Some of these North American cultures, such as the Anasazi and Iroquois, developed highly sophisticated forms of political organization, but none matched the advanced civilizations of Mesoamerica and the central Andes to the south. On the eve of the arrival of Europeans, two great civilizations, the Aztecs of central Mexico and the Incas of highland Peru, had built extensive empires that dominated their neighbors.

THE AZTEC EMPIRE OF MEXICO   Mesoamerica (the region known today as Mexico and Central America) had been the home of a series of highly urbanized, politically centralized cultures: the Mayas (300–900), the Toltecs (900–1325), and finally the Aztecs (1325 to the Spanish conquest in 1522). The Aztecs found safety from incessant warfare with neighboring tribes on an island in Lake Texcoco, where they established the city of Tenochtitlán, now Mexico City. From their base at Tenochtitlán the Aztecs followed a brilliantly successful policy of divide and conquer, first allying with powerful neighbors to attack weaker groups, then turning against former allies. With the riches gained from conquest, the Aztecs transformed Tenochtitlán from a dusty town of mud houses to a great imperial capital built of stone with a grand botanical garden that displayed plants taken from various climates.

The Aztecs excelled in the perpetual state of war that had long been the dominant fact of life in Mexico, and as a result, they attributed great religious value to war. They practiced the "flowery war," a staged occurrence during which states agreed to a predetermined time and place for a battle, the only objective of which was to take prisoners for temple sacrifice. Sustaining the gods' hunger for human sacrifices became the most notorious feature of Aztec religion. The Aztecs attributed their military successes to their tribal god, Huitzilpochti, the giver of light and all things necessary for life, but Huitzilpochti could be nourished only with human blood, creating the need among the Aztec faithful to acquire human captives.

The rituals of sacrifice permeated Aztec society. An estimated 10,000 victims were sacrificed each year, with the number rising to 50,000 on the eve of the Spanish conquest. From the very first encounters, the paradox of Aztec culture baffled Europeans. Despite their practice of human sacrifice, the Aztecs displayed refined

THE AZTEC RITE OF HUMAN SACRIFICE

An Aztec priest in a cape prepares to cut the heart out of a sacrificial victim as assistants hold him down.

manners, a sensitivity to beauty, and a highly developed religion. Whatever biases the Europeans brought with them about the "savages" of the New World, it was obvious that the Aztecs had created a great civilization.

THE INCAN EMPIRE OF THE ANDES At about the same time the Aztecs were thriving in Mexico, the Incas expanded their empire in Peru. Whereas the Aztecs created a loosely linked empire based on tribute payments, the Incas employed a more direct form of rulership. Around 1438 the first Incan emperor spread his rule beyond the valley of Cuzco. By the end of the fifteenth century, the Incas had begun to integrate by force the distinctive cultures of the various conquered regions. In this way, they created a mountain empire 200 miles wide and 2,000 miles long, stretching from modern Chile to Ecuador and comprising a population of about ten million. From his capital at Cuzco, the Incan emperor lived in luxury and established an elaborately hierarchic political structure. His authority was carried through layers of aristocrats down to officials who were responsible for every ten families in every village. These families supplied food and tribute for the empire, worked on roads and bridges, and served in the army. State-owned warehouses of food guaranteed the peasants freedom from starvation and provided for the sick and elderly. A superb network of roads and bridges covered more than 18,000 miles and made it possible to communicate with relays of runners who could cover as much as 140 miles a day. Troops could also be quickly dispatched to trouble spots via these roads.

Despite this well-organized imperial system, the Incan Empire became overly centralized because decisions could only be made by the emperor himself. Emperor Huayna Capac (r. 1493–1525) founded a second capital further south at Quito in an attempt to decentralize the overextended empire, but at his death a bitter civil war broke out between the northern and southern halves of the empire, led respectively by his rival sons. This war weakened Incan unity on the eve of the Spanish conquest.

The Mission of the European Voyagers

The European arrival in the Americas was the result of Christopher Columbus's (1451–1506) epic miscalculation. Born in Genoa to an artisan family, Columbus followed the destiny of so many of his compatriots by becoming a sailor. "From a very small age," he reported late in life, "I went sailing upon the sea."[1] He spent more than 40 years sailing everywhere sailors went. Columbus certainly had extensive experience as a seaman, but more crucial to understanding his mistake was his religious devotion. Columbus believed that he had been predestined to fulfill biblical prophecies. If he could reach China, he could outflank the Ottoman Turks and recapture Jerusalem from the Muslims who had held it since 1187. Columbus believed that the recapture of the Holy City would usher in the Second Coming of Christ. To persuade Queen Isabella of Castile to finance his voyage to China by sailing west, Columbus later admitted that he ignored navigational data and, instead, relied "entirely on holy, sacred Scripture and certain prophetic texts by certain saintly persons, who by divine revelation have had something to say on this matter."[2]

Europeans had long recognized that it was theoretically possible to reach China by sailing west. Most educated people, and certainly all those influenced by the Renaissance humanists, agreed the world was round. Sailors knew the world was round because they could see that the hull of a ship disappeared on the horizon before its masts did. The problem was not a theoretical one about the shape of the Earth but a practical one about getting around it. During Columbus's life the most widely accepted authority on the circumference of the Earth was the ancient Greek geographer Ptolemy, who had estimated that the distance across the Atlantic Ocean from Europe to Asia was more than 10,000 miles. No ship in Columbus's day could hope to sail that far without landfalls along the way for finding provisions and making repairs. In fact, Ptolemy had underestimated the size of the Earth by 25 percent.

Columbus, however, decided that Ptolemy had overestimated the distance. He also claimed that the wealthy islands of Japan lay farther east of the Asian continent than they actually do, thus further minimizing the distance of the voyage. When Columbus first proposed sailing west to Asia, King John II of Portugal consulted a committee of experts who quite correctly pointed out Columbus's miscalculations, which seem to have been more the result of wishful thinking and religious fervor than geographical expertise.

King John's rejection led Columbus to seek patronage elsewhere. Columbus applied to Queen Isabella of newly unified Spain, whose own advisers at first recommended against the voyage for the same reasons the Portuguese experts had rejected the plan. When the Spanish defeated the Muslim kingdom of Granada in 1492, which completed the Christian reconquest of the Iberian peninsula, Isabella succumbed to the religious enthusiasm of the moment and relented. She offered Columbus a commission for the voyage in the hope that it would ensure a final Christian victory over Islam.

On August 3, 1492, Columbus set sail with three small ships—the Niña, Pinta, and Santa Maria—and a crew of 90 men and boys. After refitting in the Canary Islands, the modest convoy entered unknown waters guided only by Columbus's faith in finding China, which was, in fact, thousands of miles farther west than he thought it would be. At two in the morning on the moonlit night of October 12, a lookout spied land, probably Watling Island in the Bahamas.

In all, Columbus made four voyages across the Atlantic (1492, 1493, 1498, 1502), exploring the Caribbean Islands, the coast of Central America, and part of the coast of South America. He never abandoned the belief that he had arrived in Asia. His four voyages were filled with adventures. On the third voyage, he was arrested by the newly appointed Spanish governor of Hispaniola on false charges and sent home in chains for trial; on the fourth he was marooned for nearly a year on Jamaica after worms weakened the timbers of his ships. He garnered considerable wealth in gold found on his voyages, but he never received the titles and offices that Queen Isabella had promised him before his first voyage. (See *Justice in History* in this chapter.)

Soon after Columbus returned to Spain from his first voyage, the Spanish monarchs who had sponsored him tried to obtain a monopoly to explore the western Atlantic. They appealed to Pope Alexander VI, who was himself a Spaniard and sympathetic to their request. The pope ordered a line of demarcation drawn along a north-south line 100 leagues (about 300 miles)

JUSTICE IN HISTORY

The Trial of Christopher Columbus

On October 12, 1998, a court put Christopher Columbus on trial in Tegucigalpa, Honduras. The Honduran jury, which included two Catholic priests, found Columbus guilty on ten charges, including kidnapping, rape, enslavement, invasion of peaceful lands, murder, torture, and genocide against the natives of the Americas. A life-size painting of the handcuffed explorer stood in for the defendant, who had been dead for nearly 500 years. The trial took place before a crowd of about 2,000 people, many from the indigenous Lenca people. According to the two priests on the jury, the original plan for the show trial had been to find Columbus guilty and then hold him prisoner until the Spanish government made reparation payments. However, as the jury began to deliberate, the crowd started chanting, demanding he receive capital punishment. Complying with the demands of the people, two Lenca warriors executed Columbus by firing a dozen arrows into the painting.

The Honduran trial was not the only one that has questioned Columbus's reputation in recent years. In the United States elementary school teachers have organized their classes for mock trials of the famous explorer. In New York City a fourth grade class charged Columus with land theft, enslavement, torture, and murder. After a lively mock trial the class unanimously sentenced Columbus to jail time and ordered he undergo psychotherapy. In response, several Italian-American associations launched a campaign to preserve the Italian explorer's image as a hero. The figure of Columbus remains a powerful symbol of the encounters, so often violent and deadly, between the the Europeans and the native peoples of the Americas.

A controversial figure even in his own time, Columbus was, in fact, arrested and put on trial by a royal judge on the island of Hispaniola in 1500. Columbus was an intrepid explorer, but even he admitted he was a poor administrator. He had established a Spanish colony on the island of Hispaniola (Haiti and Domican Republic today), but after six years of his governorship, the island suffered recurrent rebellions, not only from the Indians but from the colonists as well. Part of the problem was that Columbus promised the colonists far more than he could deliver. He depicted the island as offering abundant gold that could be virtually picked off the ground and compliant Indians who would do the setters' work for them. As a result, the colony attracted idlers and former convicts who quickly discovered that the island had a difficult environment and was inhabited by self-reliant Indians who were quite unwilling to become slaves of the Spaniards. When Columbus returned to Hispaniola on his third voyage in 1498, he discovered widespread abuse of the Indians and open rebellion against his governorship by the settlers on the southern part of the island. The arbitrary rule of Columbus and his brothers, who had been in charge during his absence, enraged the rebels. The rebels demanded the right to appeal to the Crown, a demand that raised a fundamental issue about how a colony so far from Spain could be ruled with respect to the law. Columbus himself recognized he was neither suited to be an administrator nor properly educated to act as a judge. He requested one be sent from Spain to help quell the rebellion and bring justice to the island.

Ferdinand and Isabella responded by appointing Francisco de Bobadilla, an aristocratic lawyer, to put down the rebellion and to investigate the numerous charges against Columbus. Bobadilla arrived in Hispaniola with a poor opinion of Columbus based on conversations in Spain with numerous men who had returned from the New World. Bobadilla arrived with the authority to take over the government of Hispaniola if he thought there was a legitimate case against

Ex *Ferdinandus intellectis discordijs quæ oborta inter Columbum & Rola...*

THE ARREST OF CHRISTOPHER COLUMBUS BY BOBADILLA

This image represents what was one of the most famous incidents in the Columbus saga. The engraving shows Bobadilla, the figure in the center-left, wielding a baton, which symbolized his royal authority. In the center right is Columbus gesturing his dismay as irons are fitted to his ankles. Behind Bobadilla the rebels are shown welcoming Bobadilla as he crosses a gang plank. In the far right soldiers load Columbus onto a small boat to be towed out to the caravel anchored at sea ready to transport him back to Spain.

Columbus. Columbus's son Ferdinand reported what happened next:

On his arrival, Bobadilla, who was most anxious to remain in office, neither held a hearing nor took any evidence. Instead, early in October, 1500, he put the Admiral [Columbus] and his brother Diego in chains aboard ship under a strong guard; he forbade anyone publicly to mention them, on pain of very severe penalties.

He then held a farcical inquest, taking testimony from their open enemies, the rebels, and showing public favor to and even egging on all who wished to speak ill of the prisoners. From the wicked and shameless things these people said, one had to be blind not to see that they were guided by prejudice rather than truth.[3]

Columbus considered himself a martyr. On board ship the captain offered to remove the chains, but Columbus refused, wanting to keep them on so that he could embarrass the king and queen when he arrived in their presence. Aboard ship he wrote a series of letters in which he reflected on his humiliation and its causes. He admitted he had exceeded his authority by arbitrarily hanging colonists accused of rebellion, but he justified himself by arguing that he was attempting to bring order to a frontier inhabited by savages. Whereas after his first voyage he had depicted the Indians as peace loving and naturally good, he now changed his mind. The Indians, he said, were warlike and wild, incapable of conforming to civilized society. They were people of the Devil. He blamed them even more than the Spanish rebels who had actually caused his downfall. Ferdinand and Isabella freed Columbus from his shackles and the charges against him, but he never fully regained his authority as the governor of Hispaniola.

The trial of Columbus marked a moment of transformation in the European experience in the New World. Even Columbus had to admit he had not discovered a paradise, but an impoverished land whose inhabitants could barely feed themselves, let alone support invaders unwilling to work. His own attitudes toward the native inhabitants switched to match the bigotry of the other settlers who treated the Indians with contempt. The creaky Spanish legal system showed how ill equipped it was for bringing justice to a distant colony. The experience of 1499–1500 on Hispaniola would be repeated time and again in the Spanish conquests in America. The most brutal men in Spanish society found ways to disregard authority, to abuse the natives, and to subvert justice largely because there was no one capable of stopping them. The fantasy world of a terrestrial paradise Columbus had created in his mind began to collapse around him.

For Discussion

1. What issues were at stake in the trial of Columbus on Hispaniola?

2. What do Columbus's troubles reveal about the strengths and weaknesses of the Spanish colonial system?

3. What do mock trials of historical figures such as Columbus seek to accomplish? Are they successful?

Taking It Further

Felipe Fernández-Armesto, *Columbus*. 1991. Among the many studies of Columbus this may be the most trustworthy and balanced.

The Life of the Admiral Christopher Columbus by his Son Ferdinand. Translated and Annotated by Benjamin Keen. 1959. A fascinating account of events from Columbus's point of view.

---

west of the Azores and Cape Verde Islands. Spain received all lands to the west of the line; Portugal obtained the lands to the east. This line of demarcation seemed to limit the Portuguese to Africa, which alarmed them and led to direct negotiations between the Portuguese and the Spaniards. The result of the negotiations was the Treaty of Tordesillas in 1494, which moved the line of demarcation to 370 leagues (about 1,110 miles) west of the Cape Verde Islands, a decision that granted to Portugal all of Africa, India, and Brazil.

Despite Columbus's persistent faith that he had found a route to the East Indies, other voyagers began to suspect, even before Columbus's death, that he had not found Asia at all and that other routes had to be explored. Another Italian, the Florentine Amerigo Vespucci (1454–1512), met Columbus, helped him prepare for the third voyage, and later made at least two voyages of his

SPANISH CONQUISTADORES LAND ON AN ISLAND IN THE NEW WORLD
The armored Spaniards are met by the naked inhabitants who offer them jewels and gold. As one of their first acts, the Spaniards erect a cross, symbolizing the Christian conquest of the New World.

own across the Atlantic. From his voyages, Vespucci recognized something of the immensity of the South American continent and was the first to use the term *New World*. Because he coined the term and because the account of his voyages got into print before Columbus's, Vespucci's given name, Amerigo (America), came to be attached to the New World rather than Columbus's. By the 1520s, Europeans had explored the Americas extensively enough to recognize that the New World was nowhere near India or China.

Explorers followed two distinct strategies for finding a sea route to East Asia. The first strategy was the Portuguese pursuit of routes to the south and east around Africa. Between 1487

and 1488, Bartholomew Dias (ca. 1450–1500) reached the Cape of Good Hope at the southern tip of the African continent. This discovery made it evident that passage to India could be achieved by sailing south, rounding the tip of Africa, and crossing the Indian Ocean. Political and financial problems in Portugal, however, prevented a follow-up to Dias's voyage for ten years. Between 1497 and 1499, Vasco da Gama (ca. 1460–1524) finally succeeded in sailing from Lisbon to India around the Cape of Good Hope. As a consequence of the route opened by da Gama, the Portuguese were the first Europeans to establish trading posts in Asia. They reached the Malabar Coast of India in 1498 and soon found their way to the Spice Islands and China. By the middle of the sixteenth century, the Portuguese had assembled a string of more than 50 trading posts and forts from Sofala on the east coast of Africa to Nagasaki in Japan.

The second strategy for reaching Asia consisted of Spanish attempts to pursue Columbus's proposed route west. The problem faced by those sailing under the Spanish flag was to find a way around the barrier presented by the American continents. A Portuguese sailor named Ferdinand Magellan (ca. 1480–1521) persuaded the king of Spain to sponsor a voyage to Asia sailing west around South America. That venture (1519–1522), which began under Magellan's command, passed through the strait named after him at the tip of South America and crossed the Pacific in a voyage of extreme hardship. His men suffered from thirst and hunger and died of scurvy. Magellan himself was killed by natives in the Philippines. After three years at sea, 18 survivors from the original 240 in Magellan's fleet reached Seville, Spain, having sailed around the world for the first time. Contemporaries immediately recognized the epic significance of the voyage, but the route opened by Magellan was too long and arduous for the Spanish to employ as a reliable alternative to the Portuguese route around Africa.

In the course of three centuries (about 1480–1780), European navigators linked the previously isolated routes of seaborne commerce, opened all the seas of the world to trade, and encountered many of the cultures and peoples of the world. Within the Indian Ocean and the western Pacific, the Europeans faced stiff competition from Arab and Chinese merchant sailors. But for the first 100 years or so, the Portuguese and Spanish effectively maintained a monopoly over the global trade routes back to Europe. Gradually English, Dutch, and French sailors also made their way around the globe. In the Americas, inadvertently made known to Europeans by Christopher Columbus, the Spanish immediately began settlements and attempted to subdue the indigenous populations.

The Fall of the Aztec and Incan Empires

Following the seafaring captains, such as Columbus and Magellan, came the **conquistadores,** who actually conquered the new-found land. They were Spanish adventurers, usually from impoverished minor noble families, who sought fortune and royal recognition through exploration and conquest. Spain was a poor land with few opportunities for advancement, a bleak situation that made the lands of the New World a powerful lure to many men seeking a fortune. Embroiled in almost continuous warfare in Europe, the Spanish crown was also perennially strapped for cash, which meant the king of Spain was highly motivated to encourage profitable foreign conquests. Many of the conquistadores launched their own expeditions with little or no legal authority, hoping to acquire sufficient riches to impress the king to give them official sanction for additional conquests. Those who did acquire legal authority from the crown received the privilege to conquer new lands in the name of the king of Spain and to keep a portion of those territories for themselves. In return they were obliged to turn over to the king one-fifth— the "royal fifth"—of everything of value they acquired, an obligation enforced by a notary sent along with the conquistadores to keep a record of valuables that were found. The conquistadores also extended Spanish sovereignty over new lands and opened the way for missionaries to bring millions, at least nominally, into the Christian fold.

The king required all conquistadores to read a document, called the **requerimiento,** to the natives before making war on them. Derived from the Muslim declaration of *jihad* or holy war, this Spanish Christian document briefly explained the principles of Christianity and commanded the natives to accept them immediately along with the authority of the pope and the sovereignty of the king of Spain. If the natives refused, the conquistador warned that they would be forced through war to subject themselves "to the yoke and obedience of the Church and of Their Highnesses. We shall take you and your wives and your children, and shall make slaves of them, and as such shall sell and dispose of them as Their Highnesses may command. And we shall take your goods, and shall do you all the mischief and damage that we can."[4] The *requerimiento* revealed the conflicting motives behind the Spanish conquest. On the one hand, the Spanish were sincerely interested in converting the natives to Christianity. On the other, the conquistadores tried to justify their actions by suggesting that the natives had brought the attack on themselves by refusing to obey the Spanish king.

HERNÁN CORTÉS AND THE CONQUEST OF MEXICO

Among the first and most successful of the conquistadores was Hernán Cortés (1485–1547). Cortés arrived on the Yucatán peninsula of present-day Mexico in February 1519, beginning a conquest that culminated in the collapse of the Aztec Empire and the Spanish colonization of Mexico. Cortés followed a policy with the natives of divide and conquer, making alliances with peoples who resented Aztec domination and then using their warriors on the front lines of his battles where they absorbed most of the losses. If after a reading of the *requerimiento* the native chieftains did not immediately surrender, Cortés's men attacked them, breaking through their lines on horses, which the natives had never seen before.

Cortés's greatest achievement was the conquest of the Aztec capital. After a number of bloody battles, he set off with only 450 Spanish troops, 15 horses, and 4,000 native allies to seize Tenochtitlán, a city of at least 300,000 and defended by thousands of warriors. As Cortés approached, Montezuma II was slow to set up a strong defense, because he suspected Cortés might be the white god, Quetzalcóatl, who according to prophecies would arrive one day from the east. The result was disastrous for the Aztecs. Montezuma knew his reign was doomed

unless he could gain the assistance of other gods to drive Quetzalcóatl away. Thus, rather than an ardent military campaign, the king's defense primarily took the form of human sacrifices to please the gods. By the time Tenochtitlán finally surrendered, the shiny jewel that had so impressed the Spanish when they first glimpsed it from the surrounding mountains lay in smoldering ruins.

By 1522 Cortés controlled a territory in New Spain—as Mexico was renamed—larger than Old Spain itself. Aztec culture and its religion of human sacrifice disappeared as Franciscan friars arrived to evangelize the surviving population.

FRANCISCO PIZARRO AND THE CONQUEST OF PERU

A small contingent of Spanish conquistadores also managed to conquer the vast Incan Empire in Peru. In 1531 Francisco Pizarro (ca. 1478–1541) left Panama with a small expedition of 180 men and 30 horses. He sailed to northern Peru and sent out spies who discovered that the Incan emperor, Atahuallpa, could be found in the highland city of Cajamarca. When Pizarro and his forces arrived there, the central square was empty, but Atahuallpa was encamped nearby with a large army. Pizarro invited Atahuallpa to come for a parlay, but instead treacherously took him captive. The news of the capture plunged the overly centralized Incan Empire into a crisis because no one dared take action without the emperor's orders. In an attempt to satisfy the Spaniards' hunger for riches and to win his freedom, Atahuallpa had a room filled with gold and silver for the conquistadores, but the treasure merely stimulated their appetite for more. In July 1533 Pizarro executed the emperor, and by the following November he had captured the demoralized Incan capital of Cuzco.

The conquest of Peru gave the Spanish access to untold wealth. Through the collection of the royal fifth, gold and silver flowed into the royal coffers in Spain. The discovery in 1545 of the fabulous Peruvian silver mine of Potosí (in what is now southern Bolivia) coincided with the introduction of the mercury amalgamation process that separated silver from ore. Mercury

CORTÉS ARRIVES IN MEXICO

The figure on the right is the native woman La Malinche, who served as Cortés's mistress and translator, a position often occupied by native women who served as mediators between the indigenous and Spanish cultures. She is interpreting for the bearded Hernando Cortés at his meeting with Montezuma II (seated on left) at Tenochtitlan in November 1519.

amalgamation enabled the Spaniards to replace surface gathering of silver ore with tunneling for ore, a procedure that led to greatly elevated yields of precious metals. For a century the silver of Peru helped otherwise impoverished Spain become the most powerful kingdom in Europe.

Spanish America: The Transplanting of a European Culture

With the defeat of the Aztec and Incan Empires, the process of transplanting Spanish society to the Americas began in earnest. The arrival of Europeans was a catastrophe for most native peoples, some of whom—in the Caribbean, northern Argentina, and central Chile—completely disappeared through the ravages of conquest and diseases. Spanish became the language of government and education, and Latin the language of religion. Nevertheless, many native languages and cultural traditions survived. Spanish America became not only the first outpost of Western civilization outside of Europe, but also the home of new hybrid cultures and ethnicities.

The basic form of economic and social organization in Spanish America was the **encomienda** system, created as an instrument to exploit native labor. An encomienda was a royal grant awarded

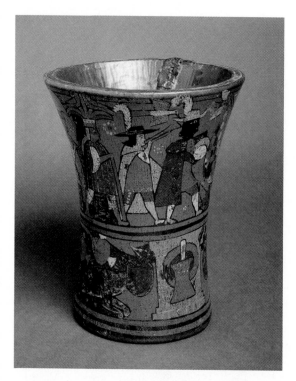

THE ENCOUNTER OF THREE CULTURES
On this wooden bottle painted in the Incan style about 1650, an African drummer leads a procession, followed by a Spanish trumpeter and an Incan official. The mixing of cultures that occurred after the arrival of the Spanish and Portuguese distinguished the Americas from other civilizations.

rose from rags to riches in the New World were so compelling that during the sixteenth century alone more than 200,000 Spaniards migrated there. They came from every part of the Iberian peninsula, from every class except the peasantry, and they practiced a wide variety of trades. There were nobles, notaries, lawyers, priests, physicians, merchants, artisans, and sailors, as well as vagabonds prone to crime and rebellion. In effect, these immigrants duplicated the Spanish Catholic society in the New World, complete with its class divisions and tensions, except that the native population or African slaves substituted for the peasants. Included among the immigrants were an unknown number of Jews who hid their faith and who escaped the rigors of the Spanish Inquisition by fleeing to the Americas, where they were less likely to suffer persecution.

Only one in ten of Spanish immigrants was a woman, and for a long time the colonies suffered from a shortage of Spanish women. Although native Americans were usually excluded from Spanish society, many native women who were the mistresses or wives of Spaniards became partially assimilated to European culture and helped pass it on to their offspring. These women knew both languages, which made them valuable interpreters, and were familiar with both cultures, which enabled them to explain native customs to the Spanish. The progeny of European men and Indian women constituted the *mestizo*, or genetically mixed, population.

The king of Spain was represented in the Americas by two viceroys, the highest colonial officials. One in Mexico City governed the West Indies, the mainland north of Panama, Venezuela, and the Philippines. The other in Lima, Peru, had authority over all of Spanish South America, excluding Venezuela. However, the vast territory of Spanish America and the enormous cultural diversity within it precluded any rigorous centralized control either from Spain or from the viceroys' capitals.

In Spanish America the church was a more effective presence than the state. Driven by the same religious fervor as Columbus, Catholic missionaries trekked into the farthest reaches of Spanish America, converting the native populations to

for military or other services that gave the conquistadores and their successors the right to gather tribute from the Indians in a defined area. In return, the encomendero (the receiver of the royal grant and native tribute) was theoretically obliged to protect the natives and teach them the rudiments of the Christian faith. Because the encomiendas were very large, only a small number of Spanish settlers were actually encomenderos. In greater Peru, which included modern Peru, Ecuador, and Bolivia, there were never more than 500 encomenderos. By the seventeenth century these encomiendas had evolved to become great landed estates called **haciendas.**

There were only a few prosperous encomenderos, but the stories about those who

ENCOUNTERS AND TRANSFORMATIONS

Between Indian and Christian: Creating Hybrid Religion in Mexico

As conquest passed into colonialism during the sixteenth century, Christian missionaries began to exert a profound influence on Indian moral and religious practices. However, as the Indians accepted Christianity they adapted it to meet their needs and to fit into their culture. As a result, native Americans created a new hybrid religion that combined both Christian and Indian elements, as Indian uses of the cross and adoption of flagellation illustrate.

As his army marched across Mexico, Cortés replaced native idols with Christian crosses. Missionaries later placed crosses in churches, encouraged making the sign of the cross a ritual practice, and introduced the wearing of miniature crosses as a kind of personal talisman that offered protection from illness and evil influences. Mayas readily adopted the Christian cross because they already had a symbol similar to it. However, the Maya at first misunderstood what the missionaries meant about the cross and took the example of Christ too literally. Some Maya actually performed crucifixions, usually of children, whose hands were nailed or tied to the cross and whose hearts were torn out in a vestige of pre-Christian practices. There are also reports of pigs and dogs sacrificed on crosses. Even though the Maya had missed the point of Christ's singular sacrifice, they had understood the power behind the Christian symbol, which the Spaniards had used in their conquest of the Maya, and they wanted some of that power for themselves.

When the Franciscan friars arrived in Mexico City in 1524, they introduced the practice of flagellation, which imitated Christ's whipping at the hands of Roman soldiers and served as a means of penance for sins. The friars employed self-flagellation as a tool for impressing the natives. Fray Antonio de Roa encouraged conversions through dramatic flagellations, called "a general discipline." After a collective flagellation in which

HYBRID RELIGION

Here a priest flagellates a naked Incan in Peru. Introduced by Christian missionaries, flagellation became one of the more extreme forms of religious practice among the newly converted Indians.

the Indians who had converted to Christianity imitated Fray Roa, he proceeded out of the church, naked from the waist up, with a cord around his neck, and shoeless. He walked over hot coals, and then delivered a sermon about how much greater the pains of Hell would be than those from the burning coals. After the sermon he doused his whole body with boiling water.

During the sixteenth century the Indians themselves began to practice flagellation, especially during processions conducted during Holy Week (the week before Easter). The natives flogged themselves with such evident enthusiasm that the friars had to intervene to prevent the Indians from seriously harming themselves. On many occasions during the colonial period, the Indians used self-flagellation as a means of rousing their fellows in protest against Spanish domination. Flagellation became not just a form of penance, but a means for arousing the passions of spectators, which could be turned toward rallying Mexicans against the Spanish. Even now flagellation remains the most distinctive feature of the Mexican passion plays. By adapting European Christian rituals for purposes other than those intended by the Christian missionaries, the natives created a new hybrid religious culture that was distinctively Mexican.

For Discussion

How did the native Mexican adaptations of Christianity compare to the popular medieval religious practices discussed in Chapter 11? Had the Mexicans become part of the West by accepting Christianity?

Christianity with much more success than in Africa or Asia. Greed had enticed the conquistadores, but an ardent desire to spread the gospel of Christianity spurred the missionaries. The most zealous missionaries were members of religious orders—Franciscans, Dominicans, and Jesuits—who were distinguished from the parish priests by their autonomy and special training for missionary work.

Church officials generally assumed that it took ten years for the transition to a settled Christian society, a policy that meant that Christianity arrived in two stages. First, members of a religious order evangelized the population by learning the native language, then preaching and teaching in it. They also introduced the celebration of the Catholic sacraments. Once churches were built and Christianity was accepted by the local elite, the missionaries moved on to be replaced, in the second stage, by parish priests who expected to stay in one place for their entire lives. In the border regions, evangelizing never ceased and members of the missionary orders stayed on until the end of colonial times. (See *Encounters and Transformations* in this chapter.)

Portuguese Brazil: The Tenuous Colony

In 1500 Pedro Cabral sighted the Brazilian coast, claiming it for Portugal under the Treaty of Tordesillas. While the Spaniards busied themselves with the conquest of Mexico and Peru, the Portuguese largely ignored Brazil, which lacked any obvious source of gold or temptingly rich civilizations to conquer. Instead, the Portuguese concentrated on developing their lucrative empire in Asia.

The impetus for the further colonization of Brazil was the growing European demand for sugar. The Brazilian climate was perfectly suited for cultivating sugar cane. Between 1575 and 1600, Brazil became the Western world's leading producer of sugar, luring thousands of poor young men from Portugal and the Azores who took native women as wives, thereby producing a distinctive *mestizo* population. Sugar cane production required backbreaking, dangerous labor to clear the land, to weed, and especially to cut the cane. To help work the vast coastal plantations the Portuguese attempted to enslave the Tupí-Guaraní natives, but European diseases soon killed them off.

The Portuguese increasingly looked to Africans to perform the hard labor they were unwilling to do themselves. As a result, the Brazilian demand for slaves intensified the Portuguese presence in West Africa and the African presence in Brazil. In the search for even more slaves, Portuguese slave buyers enlarged their area of operations in Africa south to Angola, where in 1575 they founded a trading post. This post became the embarkation point for slave traders who sailed directly to Brazil and sold slaves in exchange for low-grade Brazilian tobacco, which they exchanged for more slaves when they returned to Angola.

As in Spanish America, Portuguese authorities felt responsible for converting the natives to Christianity. In Brazil, the Jesuits took the lead during the last half of the sixteenth century by establishing a school for the training of missionaries on the site of the present city of São Paulo. Once converted, natives were resettled into villages called **aldeias,** which were similar to Spanish missions. The Jesuits attempted to protect the natives against the white colonists who wanted to enslave them, creating a lasting conflict between the Jesuit fathers and local landowners. Both Jesuits and colonists appealed to the king to settle their dispute. Finally, the king gave the Jesuits complete responsibility for all Indians in aldeias, but he allowed colonists to enslave Indians who had not been converted or who were captured in war. The Portuguese connected Christian conversion with settlement in aldeias, which meant that any unsettled native was, by definition, a heathen. Nevertheless, these restrictions on enslaving Indians created a perceived labor shortage and further stimulated the demand for African slaves.

More rural and more African than Spanish America, Brazil during its colonial history remained a plantation economy in which the few dominant white European landowners were vastly outnumbered by their African slaves. In certain areas a racially mixed population created its own vibrantly hybrid culture that combined native, African, and European elements, especially in the eclectic religious life that fused Catholicism with polytheistic forms of worship. Although Brazil occupied nearly half of the South American continent, until the twentieth century most of the vast interior was unexplored by Europeans and unsettled except by the small native population.

North America: The Land of Lesser Interest

Compared with Central and South America, North America outside Mexico held little attraction for Europeans during the sixteenth century. During the reign of Queen Elizabeth I (r. 1558–1603), English efforts finally turned to establishing colonies in the Americas. Two prominent courtiers, Humphrey Gilbert and his stepbrother, Walter Raleigh, sponsored a series of voyages intended to establish an English colony called Virginia in honor of Elizabeth, "The Virgin Queen." The English interest in colonization was made possible by Elizabeth's success in strengthening the monarchy, building up the fleet, and encouraging investments in New World colonies. In 1585 the first English colonists in the Americas landed on Roanoke Island off the coast of North Carolina, but they were so poorly prepared that this attempt and a second one in 1587 failed. The inexperienced and naive English settlers did not even make provisions for planting crops.

The successful English colonies came a generation later. Learning from past mistakes, the colonists of Jamestown in Virginia, who landed in 1607, brought seeds for planting, built fortifications for protection, and established a successful form of self-government. From these modest beginnings, the English gradually established vast plantations along the rivers of Virginia. There they raised tobacco to supply the new European habit of smoking, which had been picked up from native Americans. In 1620 religious refugees from England settled in Massachusetts Bay, but in contrast to Central and South America, North America by 1650 remained only marginally touched by Europeans and played a very minor role in European economic interests.

EUROPEANS IN ASIA

■ Why was the European encounter with Asian civilizations far less disruptive than those in Africa and the Americas?

India, the Malay peninsula, Indonesia, the Spice Islands, and China were the ultimate goal of the European voyagers during the fifteenth and sixteenth centuries. They were eventually reached by many routes—by the Portuguese sailing around Africa, by the Spanish sailing around

CHRONOLOGY: EUROPEANS IN THE AMERICAS

1438	Founding of Incan Empire in Peru
1492–1493	First two voyages of Christopher Columbus
1498	Third voyage of Columbus
1500	Cabral sights Brazil
1502	Fourth voyage of Columbus
1519–1522	Spanish conquer Mexico
1533	Spanish conquer Peru
1545	Discovery of silver at Potosí
1585	English establish colony on Roanoke Island, North Carolina
1607	English establish colony at Jamestown, Virginia
1620	English establish colony at Massachusetts Bay

South America, and by the Russians trekking across the vastness of Siberia.

Asia Before the European Empires

The greatest potential rival to the Europeans who sought access to Asian trade was Ming China (1368–1644), a highly advanced civilization with maritime technology and organizational capability to launch exploratory voyages far superior to Europe's. Even before the Portuguese began their slow progress down the west coast of Africa, the Chinese organized a series of huge maritime expeditions into the Indian Ocean that reached far down the east coast of Africa. Between 1405 and 1433 the Chinese established diplomatic contacts and demanded tribute in dozens of kingdoms in India and Africa. The size and ambition of these fleets far surpassed anything that sailed from Europe at this time, and the massive crews of as many as 27,500 men (compared to Columbus's crew of 90) included a complement of scholars to communicate with foreign kings and highly skilled technicians to make repairs to the fleet. The Chinese fleets took

trade goods, such as silk, tea, and porcelains, and brought back to China strange animals, hostage kings, and possible trade items. After nearly 30 years of searching the Indian Ocean ports, the Ming emperors concluded that China already possessed all the goods that were available abroad, that China was indeed the center of civilization, and that further investments in oceangoing expeditions were unwarranted.

The European and Chinese voyages of the fifteenth century differed in their objectives and in the motives of the governments that sponsored them. The Europeans were mostly privateers seeking personal profit or captains who enjoyed official government backing in return for a portion of the profits. The economic motive behind the European voyages made them self-sustaining because the Europeans sailed only to places where they could make money. In contrast, the imperial Chinese expeditions were only partially motivated by the desire for economic gain. The official purpose of the Chinese voyages was to learn about the world, and once the Chinese found out what they wanted, they ceased the official voyages. Chinese merchant traders continued to ply the seas on their own, however, and when the Europeans arrived in East Asia, they simply inserted themselves into this already developed Chinese-dominated trade network.

In contrast to the trade in Africa and America, Europeans failed to monopolize trade in Asia. The Europeans were just one among many trading groups, some working under government sponsorship, such as the Portuguese, and others working alone, such as the Chinese.

The Trading Post Empires

For 300 years after establishing the first trading posts in Asia, Europeans had little influence there in comparison to the Americas. In 1497–1499 Vasco da Gama opened the most promising route for the Portuguese around Africa to South and East Asia. But the sailing distances were long, limiting the number of people who could be transported to Asia. In contrast to the Americas, the Asian empires were well equipped to defend themselves against European conquest. Because Europeans lacked the support system, which in the Americas the colonial system provided, few Europeans settled in Asia, and even missionary work proved much more difficult than in the Americas.

Unlike Brazil, where the Portuguese established colonial plantations, in Asia they established trading posts along the coasts of India, China, and the Spice Islands. When the Portuguese first arrived at a location with a safe harbor and easy access to the hinterland, they built a fort and forced, bribed, or tricked the local political authority, usually a chieftain, to cede the land around the post to Portugal. The agents sent to trade in Asia were called *factors* and their trading posts were called **factories.** But they were not factories in the modern sense of sites for manufacturing. They were safe places where merchants could trade and store their merchandise. The factors lived in the factories with a few other Portuguese traders, a small detachment of troops, and servants recruited from the local population. Nowhere did Portuguese authority extend very far into the hinterland. The traditional political structures of local chieftains remained, and the local elites usually went along with the arrangement because they profited by reselling European wares, such as cloth, guns, knives, and many kinds of cheap gadgets. The factors acquired silks, gold, silver, raw cotton, pepper, spices, and medicines. Some of these outposts of the Portuguese Empire survived until late in the twentieth century, but their roots remained exceedingly shallow. Even in places such as East Timor, an island in Indonesia, and Macao on the south China coast, which were Portuguese outposts for more than four centuries, only a small native elite ever learned the Portuguese language or adapted to European culture.

The European trading posts in Asia proved very lucrative. Consider the search for the spice nutmeg. In an account published in 1510, an Italian traveler, Ludovico di Varthema, described the previously unknown nutmeg trees, which he found growing in the Banda Islands, a small archipelago some 1,000 miles east of Java. These were the only places in the world where nutmeg grew. Besides adding flavor to foods, nutmeg was believed to possess powers to cure all kinds of diseases and to induce a hallucinatory euphoria. The demand for nutmeg was so great and the supply so limited that exporting it yielded enormous profits. At one time, nutmeg was the most valuable commodity in the world after gold and silver. In the early seventeenth century the markup on a pound of nutmeg transported from the Banda Islands to Europe was 60,000 percent. It is no wonder European traders were willing to risk their lives on long, dangerous sea voyages to obtain nutmeg and other spices.

In return for raw materials such as nutmeg, European merchants typically traded manufactured goods, and they made every effort to ensure that other European powers were excluded from competing in this trade in Asia. Crucial to enforcing the system was a network of factories and a strong navy, which was primarily used against other European and occasionally Muslim interlopers. Through the trading post empires, commercial rivalries among European states extended abroad to Asia. Competition over these trading posts foreshadowed the beginnings of a global economy dominated by Europeans. It also demonstrated the Europeans' propensity to transform European wars into world wars.

In addition to trade, the Portuguese and other European powers sought to spread Christianity. To accomplish conversions, missionaries resorted to persuasion, because without the backing of a full-scale conquest as in the Americas, resorting to force was usually not an option. The missionaries frequently drew the ire of local rulers, who viewed the converts as traitors—a situation that led to the persecution of some of the new Christians. To accomplish their task of conversion, Christian missionaries had to learn the native languages and something of the native culture and religion. In this effort, the Jesuits were particularly dedicated. They sent members of their order to the Chinese imperial court, where they lived incognito for decades, although they made few converts. Jesuits also traveled to Japan, where they established an outpost of Christianity at Nagasaki. With the exception of the Spanish Philippines, which was nominally converted to Catholicism by 1600, Christian missionaries in Asia were far less successful than in the Americas. Perhaps one million Asians outside the Philippines had been converted during this period, but many of these conversions did not last. Christians were most successful in converting Buddhists and least effective among Muslims, who almost never abandoned their faith.

By the end of the sixteenth century, Portuguese and Spanish shipping in Asian waters faced recurrent harassment from the English, French, and Dutch. The Dutch drove the Portuguese from their possessions in Ceylon, India, and the Spice Islands, except for East Timor. But none of these sixteenth-century European empires was particularly effective at imposing European culture on Asia in a way comparable with the Americas. In the Spanish Philippines, for example, few natives spoke Spanish, and there were fewer than 5,000 Spanish inhabitants as late as 1850. European states competed among themselves for trade and tried to enforce monopolies, but the Europeans remained peripheral to Asian culture until the late eighteenth and early nineteenth centuries, when the British expanded their power in India and colonized Australia and New Zealand.

The expansion of the Russian Empire into Asia depended not on naval power but on cross-country expeditions. The heartland of the Russian Empire was Muscovy, the area around Moscow, but the empire would eventually spread from the Baltic Sea to the Pacific Ocean. After 1552 Russians began to push across the Ural mountains into Siberia, lured by the trade in exotic furs, which were in great demand among the upper classes of northern Europe, both to keep warm and as fashion statements. The Russians' search for furs was equivalent to the Spanish search for gold; like gold, fur attracted adventurous and desperate men. Following the navigable rivers and building strategic forts along the way, expeditions collected furs locally

CHRONOLOGY: EUROPEANS IN ASIA	
1487–1488	Bartholomew Dias reaches Cape of Good Hope
1497–1499	Vasco da Gama reaches India via Cape of Good Hope
1498	Portuguese reach Malabar coast of India
1514	Portuguese reach China
1519–1522	Ferdinand Magellan's crew circumnavigate the globe

and then advanced deeper into the frozen wilds of Siberia. Several of the great aristocratic families of Russia acquired enormous wealth from the Siberian fur trade, which was so lucrative that Russian trappers kept pushing farther and farther east. In this quest for furs, expeditions reached the Pacific coast in 1649, by which time Russia had established a network of trading posts over all of northern Asia.

The significance of the European trading post empires lies less in the influence of Europe on Asia than in the influence of Asia on Europe. Asian products from spices and opium to silk cloth and oriental rugs became commonplace items in middle- and upper-class European households. European collectors became fascinated with Chinese porcelains, lacquered boxes, and screen paintings. At the same time, Asian tourists began to visit Europe, a tradition begun when four Japanese converts to Christianity arrived in Lisbon in 1586 and made a celebrated tour of Europe.

THE BEGINNINGS OF THE GLOBAL SYSTEM

- How was the world tied together in a global biological and economic system?

As a result of the European voyages of the fifteenth and sixteenth centuries, a network of cultural, biological, and economic connections formed along intercontinental trading routes. For many thousands of years, Europe, northern Africa, and Asia had been in contact with one another, but the system that formed during the sixteenth century encompassed most of the globe, including sub-Saharan Africa and the Americas. Unlike earlier international trading systems that linked Europe and Asia, the new global system was dominated by Europeans. Today's global economy, based on cellular telephones, the internet, air transportation, and free trade, is merely an extension and elaboration of the system that first appeared on a global scale during the sixteenth century. This system transformed human society by bringing into contact what had previously been separate and isolated—regional cultures, biological systems, and local economies.

The Columbian Exchange

The most dramatic changes were at first produced by the trade of peoples, plants, animals, microbes, and ideas between the Old and New Worlds—a process known as the **Columbian Exchange**. For the native Americans, the importation of Europeans, Africans, and microbes had devastating consequences—threatening indigenous religions, making native technology irrelevant, disrupting social life, and destroying millions of lives. For Europeans, the discovery of previously unknown civilizations profoundly shook their own understanding of human geography and history. Neither the ancient philosophers nor the Bible, which was understood to be an accurate history of humankind since the creation of the world, had provided a hint about the peoples of the Americas.

THE SLAVE TRADE Slavery and the slave trade had existed long before the Europeans expanded the practice. All of the ancient civilizations had been slave societies with as many as one-third of the population in bondage. During the Middle Ages a small number of slaves were employed as domestic servants and concubines in the Christian cities of the Mediterranean, and in Muslim countries large numbers of slaves were found in harems, used as laborers, and even trained as soldiers. During the wars between Christians and Muslims, victors habitually enslaved captives. In the sixteenth and seventeenth centuries Barbary pirates in the Mediterranean captured approximately 850,000 white Europeans during sea raids and forced them into slavery in Muslim North Africa. Large-scale transportation of black Africans began during the ninth and tenth centuries, when Muslim traders took tens of thousands from the island of Zanzibar off the east coast of Africa to lower Iraq, where they performed the heavy labor of draining swamps and cutting sugar cane. Slavery was also widespread in Islamic West Africa. Mali depended heavily on slave labor, and in Muslim Ghana slaves constituted about one-third of the population. Thus, the enslavement of Africans by Africans was well established when the Europeans arrived.

The slave trade flourished only when and where it was profitable. The necessary conditions for profitability were a strong demand for labor-intensive agricultural commodities, a perceived shortage of local labor, a supply of people who could be captured elsewhere, and a moral and legal climate that permitted slavery. These conditions were all present in the late fifteenth and sixteenth centuries. The population of Europe developed a taste for exotic products such as sugar, tobacco, coffee, and indigo dye. The European colonizers who sought to supply the demand for these goods needed agricultural workers, first for the colonies in the Atlantic islands and then for plantations in the Americas where European diseases decimated the indigenous population, creating a labor shortage. Europeans also found it difficult to enslave the native peoples, who knew the territory and could easily escape.

The flourishing demand for labor was supplied by the population of Africa. Once Europeans started to buy up slaves in the coastal trading posts, enterprising African chieftains sent out slave-hunting expeditions. As a consequence, the slave-trading states of the Guinea coast gained power at the expense of their neighbors and spread the web of the slave trade deep into the African interior. The slave hunters sold captives to the Europeans for transportation across the Atlantic. Following the Portuguese in the trade came the Dutch, English, French, and Danes, who eventually established their own trading posts to obtain slaves.

In addition to the economic incentive for slavery, both Christianity and Islam provided a moral justification and legal protection for it. Enslaving others was considered legitimate punishment for unbelievers. Of all the Western religions, only Judaism demonstrated a consistent moral resistance to the slave trade because Jewish identity depended heavily on remembering the biblical account of the enslavement of the ancient Hebrews in Egypt. Notable exceptions were the few Jewish plantation owners in Surinam, who did use slave labor. The problem for Christian and Muslim slavers was that when a slave converted to Christianity or Islam, the pretext for enslavement disappeared. To solve this problem, Christians created a new rationalization by connecting slavery to race. As the African slave trade expanded during the seventeenth and eighteenth centuries, Europeans began to associate slavery with "blackness," which was considered inferior to "whiteness." Among Muslims, the justification for enslavement remained a religious one, and when a slave converted to Islam he or she was, at least theoretically, supposed to be freed.

Due to slavery large parts of the Americas were transformed into outposts of sub-Saharan African cultures. Blacks came to outnumber native Americans and constituted the majority of the colonial population in most of the Caribbean and broad parts of coastal Central America, Venezuela, Guyana, and Brazil. Much of the male population of Angola was transported directly to Brazil, a forced migration that resulted in a dramatic excess of females over males in the most heavily depopulated areas of Angola. During the nearly 400 years of the European slave trade (ca. 1519–1867),

about eleven million Africans were shipped to the Americas.

The slave ships that sailed the infamous Middle Passage across the Atlantic were so unhealthy, with Africans "stacked like books on a shelf," that a significant portion of the human cargo died en route. The physical and psychological burdens that slavery placed on its victims can scarcely be imagined, in large part because few slaves were ever allowed to learn to read and write, and thus direct records of their experiences are rare. Documents from ship surgeons, overseers, and slave masters, however, indicate that slaves were subjected to unhealthy living conditions, backbreaking work, and demoralization. Despite these crushing hardships and even within the harsh confines of white-owned plantations, black slaves created their own institutions, family structures, and cultures.

BIOLOGICAL EXCHANGES How did a few thousand Europeans so easily conquer the civilizations of the Americas, populated by millions of people? After all, the Aztecs, Incas, and others put up a stubborn resistance to the conquistadores, and yet the Europeans triumphed time after time. The answer: epidemics. Along with their gunpowder weapons, the conquistadores' most effective allies were the invisible microbes of Old World diseases, such as smallpox. A native of the Yucatán peninsula recalled the better days before the conquest:

> There was then no sickness; they had no aching bones; they had then no high fever; they had then no smallpox; they had then no burning chest; they had then no abdominal pain; they had then no consumption; they had then no headache. At that time the course of humanity was orderly. The foreigners made it otherwise when they arrived here.[5]

The toll that epidemic disease had on the natives soon after their initial contact with Europeans stunned nearly every chronicler of the New World conquests. Between 1520 and 1600, Mexico suffered 14 major epidemics, and Peru 17. By the 1580s the populations of the

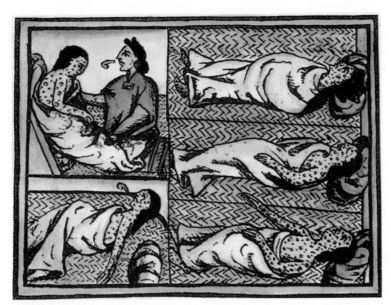

BIOLOGICAL EXCHANGES

A medicine man treats dying Aztecs during a smallpox epidemic in Mexico.

Caribbean islands, the Antilles, and the lowlands of Mexico and Peru had almost completely died off. Historians estimate the deaths in the tens of millions. The pre-conquest population of Mexico, which has been estimated at about 19 million, dropped in 80 years to 2.5 million. Even the infrequent contacts between European fishermen and fur traders with natives on the coast of what is now Canada led to rapid depopulation.

The most deadly culprit was smallpox, but measles, typhus, scarlet fever, and chicken pox also contributed to the devastation. All of these were dangerous and even life-threatening to Europeans and Africans alike, but from exposure, people of the Old World had either died young or survived the illness with a resistance to infection from the disease. However, native Americans had never been exposed to these diseases and as a population completely lacked immunities to them. As a result, all it took was for one infected person to arrive from the Old World to kill off many millions in the New World. After Cortés's men were first driven from Tenochtitlán, a Dominican friar reported that a new ally appeared: "When the Christians were

exhausted from war, God saw fit to send the Indians smallpox, and there was a great pestilence in the city...."[6] The Spaniards' immunity to the very diseases that killed off so many Indians reinforced the impression that the Europeans were favored agents of the gods or gods themselves.

In exchange, the New World gave the Old World syphilis, or at least contemporary Europeans thought so. Historians and epidemiologists have long debated what they call the **Columbian question** about the origins of syphilis. Some argue that syphilis or a venereal disease that might be classified as its ancestor came back from the New World with Columbus's sailors, but others assert that syphilis was widespread in the Old World long before 1492. Scholars still do not know the answer to the Columbian question, but it is true that after 1492 there were epidemic outbreaks of sexually transmitted diseases, leading many to assume an American origin.

The exchange of other forms of life was less obviously disastrous. Following the European settlers came a flood of European animals and plants. With the conquistadores came pigs, cattle, goats, sheep, donkeys, and horses—all previously unknown in the New World. Pigs that escaped from the first Spanish ships to land in Florida were the ancestors of the ubiquitous wild razorback pigs of the southern United States. Vast areas of Mexico and Peru depopulated of humans were repopulated with enormous herds of sheep. The cattle herded by the present-day gauchos of Argentina derive from Iberian stock. The characteristic Latin American burro came from Europe as did the horse, which came to be so prized by the plains Indians of North America. Sheep, cattle, and horses, in particular, completely changed the way of life of the native American peoples.

From Europe came the lucrative plantation crops of sugar, cotton, rice, and indigo, crops that required a large supply of field hands. European varieties of wheat, grapes, and olives soon appeared as major crops in Mexico and elsewhere. In exchange, the Americas offered new crops to the Old World such as tobacco, cocoa, paprika, American cotton, pumpkins, beans, tomatoes, maize (corn), and potatoes. European peasant farmers discovered that maize and the potato provided an attractive substitute for wheat. In many places, the potato replaced wheat as the staple in the diet of the poor. By yielding more calories per acre than wheat or virtually any other traditional grain, the potato made it possible to support more people on a given amount of land. With the spread of the potato as a food source, European populations began to increase rapidly, a trend that created population pressures, which in turn stimulated additional European migrations to the Americas.

THE PROBLEM OF CULTURAL DIVERSITY Before Columbus sailed west, Europeans possessed two systems of thought that seemed to explain everything to them—the Aristotelian and the Christian. The ancient Greek philosopher Aristotle and his commentators provided a systematic explanation of geography and cosmology based on what they knew of the world. They had named the continents, described their peoples, and estimated the size of the globe. Particularly in the European universities, Aristotle was still considered practically infallible, the primary source of all human knowledge. But Aristotle had not even imagined the Americas, and that fact raised the possibility that he was wrong on other matters as well. He knew nothing of the llama, the potato, or syphilis—common knowledge to even the most ignorant conquistador. Aristotle had assumed that the heat of the equatorial zone was so great that no one could live there, but the Spanish had found great civilizations thriving astride the equator. In 1570, when Joseph de Acosta felt a chill in the tropics on his way to America, he

observed, "what could I else do then but laugh at Aristotle's Meteors and his Philosophy."[7] Travelers to the New World began to realize that the ancients had not known half the truth about the world.

For Jews and Christians, the Bible remained the unchallenged authority on the origins of the whole world, but the New World created numerous problems for biblical interpretation. The book of Genesis told of the Creation and the great flood, which had destroyed all people and all animals except those saved in Noah's ark. The New World brought into question that vision of a single creation and cleansing flood simply because it could not explain why the plants and animals of the Americas were so different. If the only animals on Earth were those Noah preserved, then why were they different on the two sides of the Earth? About the New World a French writer asked, "How falls it out that the nations of the world, coming all of one father, Noah, do vary so much from one another, both in body and mind?"[8] Thinkers argued either that there must have been more than one creation or that the great flood must not have covered the entire Earth. However, these solutions tacitly recognized that a literal reading of the words of Scripture could not produce a satisfactory account of the history of the world.

The greatest conceptual challenges to Christian Europe were the New World peoples themselves. If these people were not the children of God's Creation, then how did they get there? If they were God's children, then why were they so different from Europeans? In the terms available to sixteenth-century thinkers, there were three possible ways to answer these questions. One was to assume that the native Americans were subhumans, demons, or some strange form of animal life. This answer was the most convenient one to those who sought to exploit the natives. Often with little or no foundation, these Europeans believed that the natives practiced devil worship, incest, sexual promiscuity, polygamy, sodomy, and cannibalism—all signs of their demonic nature.

DIFFERENT VOICES DEBATE OVER THE TREATMENT OF INDIANS

Bartolomé de las Casas and Juan Ginés de Sepúlveda engaged in a famous debate in Valladolid, Spain, in 1550 over the legitimacy of the Spanish conquest of the Americas. Emperor Charles V organized the debate to determine whether the Indians were capable of self-government. Las Casas had actual experience in the New World, having served as a bishop in Mexico. Lacking any personal experience in the Americas, Sepúlveda relied on the reports of others. Las Casas was shocked by the brutal treatment of the natives and argued the Indians needed protection. Instead of enslaving Indians, Las Casas advocated enslaving Africans, an argument he later regretted. In contrast, Sepúlveda argued the Indians were "natural slaves."

Bartolomé de las Casas, *A Short Account of the Destruction of the Indies* (1542)

God made all the peoples of this area, many and varied as they are, as open and as innocent as can be imagined. The simplest people in the world—unassuming, long-suffering, unassertive, and submissive—they are without malice or guile, and are utterly faithful and obedient both to their own native lords and to the Spaniards in whose service they now find themselves. Never quarrelsome or belligerent or boisterous, they harbour no grudges and do not seek to settle old scores; indeed, the notions of revenge, rancour, and hatred are quite foreign to them....

They are innocent and pure in mind and have a lively intelligence, all of which makes them particularly receptive to learning and understanding the truths of our Catholic faith and to being instructed in virtue; indeed, God has invested them with fewer impediments in this regard than any other people on earth. Once they begin to learn of the Christian faith they become so keen to know more, to receive the Sacraments, and to worship God, that the missionaries who instruct them do truly have to be men of exceptional patience and forbearance; and over the years I have time and again met Spanish laymen who have been so struck by the natural goodness that shines through these people that they frequently can be heard to explain: "These would be the most blessed people on earth if only they were given the chance to convert to Christianity."

Source: Bartolomé de las Casas, *A Short Account of the Destruction of the Indies*, edited and Translated by Nigel Griffin, copyright 1991 by Nigel Griffin, introduction by Anthony Pagden (Penguin Classics 1992). Trans. and notes copyright © 1992 by Nigel Griffin. Introduction copyright © 1992 by Anthony Pagden. Reproduced by permission of Penguin Books Ltd.

Juan Ginés de Sepúlveda, *The Second Democrates* (1547)

The man rules over the woman, the adult over the child, the father over his children. That is to say, the most powerful and most perfect rule over the weakest and most imperfect. This same relationship exists among men, there being some who by nature are masters and others who by nature are slaves. Those who surpass the rest in prudence and intelligence, although not in

In this extreme form of European belief, the natives did not even possess a human soul and were neither capable of converting to Christianity nor worthy of human rights.

A second answer to why the peoples of the New World were so different sprung from a belief that the natives were complete innocents. The native peoples lived in a kind of earthly Paradise, unspoiled by the corruption of European society. Some of the early English explorers of Virginia found the natives "most gentle, loving and faithful, void of any guile or treason," and one missionary found them "all the more children of God owing to their very lack of capacity and skill."[9] A tiny number of unconventional theological thinkers hypothesized that the native Americans had been created before the Hebrews as reported in the

physical strength, are by nature the masters. On the other hand, those who are dim-witted and mentally lazy, although they may be physically strong enough to fulfill all the necessary tasks, are by nature slaves. It is just and useful that it be this way. We even see it sanctioned in divine law itself, for it is written in the Book of Proverbs: "He who is stupid will serve the wise man." And so it is with the barbarous and inhumane peoples (the Indians) who have no civil life and peaceful customs. It will always be just and in conformity with natural law that such people submit to the rule of more cultured and humane princes and nations. Thanks to their virtues and the practical wisdom of their laws, the latter can destroy barbarism and educate these (inferior) people to a more humane and virtuous life. And if the latter reject such rule, it can be imposed upon them by force of arms. Such a war will be just according to natural law....

And you must realize that prior to the arrival of the Christians, they did not live in that peaceful kingdom of Saturn (the Golden Age) that the poets imagine, but on the contrary they made war against one another continually and fiercely, with such fury that victory was of no meaning if they did not satiate their monstrous hunger with the flesh of their enemies.... These Indians are so cowardly and timid that they could scarcely resist the mere presence of our soldiers. Many times thousands upon thousands of them scattered, fleeing like women before a very few Spaniards, who amounted to fewer than a hundred....

Until now we have not mentioned their impious religion and their abominable sacrifices, in which they worship the Devil as God, to whom they thought of offering no better tribute than human hearts.... Interpreting their religion in an ignorant and barbarous manner, they sacrificed human victims by removing the hearts from the chests. They placed these hearts on their abominable altars. With this ritual they believed that they had appeased their gods. They also ate the flesh of the sacrificed men....

War against these barbarians can be justified not only on the basis of their paganism but even more so because of their abominable licentiousness, their prodigious sacrifice of human victims, the extreme harm that they inflicted on innocent persons, their horrible banquets of human flesh, and the impious cult of their idols.

Source: From Pike, Frederick B. *Latin American History: Select Problems*, 1/e. Copyright © 1969 Wadsworth, a part of Cengage Learning, Inc. Reproduced by permission. www.cengage.com/permissions.

For Discussion

1. How did las Casas and Sepúlveda differ in their understanding of the basic nature of the Indians? How did these differing understandings shape their opposing arguments?
2. How reliable are these accounts of the native peoples of the Americas?
3. What was at stake for the definition of the West in these debates?

Bible, and, therefore, had not been subject to the Fall of Man and still lived in the earthly Paradise.

The most influential spokesman during the sixteenth century for this idea of native innocence was the powerful advocate of human rights Bartolomé de Las Casas (1474–1566). Throughout his career, Las Casas forcefully argued against the enslavement and ill treatment of the native Americans, which he chronicled in his most important published work, *A Short Account of the Destruction of the Indies* (1542). He saw the natives as innocents who needed to be guided rather than forced to accept Christianity and should not be enslaved. (See *Different Voices* in this chapter.)

The third response to the question of how to explain the New World peoples neither

MUTILATION OF NATIVE AMERICANS

In this illustration for one of Bartholomew de Las Casas's books condemning Spanish policy in America, a conquistador is shown terrorizing the natives with vicious dogs, a frequently employed technique. The conquistador dangles two infants while the dogs bite them. To the left a priest baptizes a young child whose mother has been hanged.

who tried to make sense of the new discoveries. Perplexed by the cultural diversity he had observed in the New World, Peter Martyr D'Anghiera (1457–1526), a pious priest and astute historian of Spanish explorations, noted that different peoples made judgments on the basis of different criteria: "The Ethiopian thinks the black color to be fairer than the white, and the white man thinks otherwise. The bearded man supposes he is more comely than he that wants a beard. As appetite therefore moves, not as reason persuades, men run into these vanities, and every province is ruled by its own sense...."[10] What others thought fundamental moral truths, Martyr considered manifestations of superficial cultural differences. The discovery in the New World that non-Christians could lead moral lives, love their families, practice humility and charity, and benefit from highly developed religious institutions shook the complacent sense of European superiority.

dehumanized them nor assumed them innocent but simply recognized their differences as the natural consequence of human diversity. Advocates of this position proposed toleration. Deciding whether a particular people were bad or good raised questions about the criteria for making such judgments, and these questions introduced the principle of cultural relativism. **Cultural relativism** recognized that many (but not necessarily all) standards of judgment are specific to particular cultures rather than fixed truths established by natural or divine law. Cultural relativists attempt to understand why other people think and act the way they do. Such an approach can be traced to a small group of sixteenth-century European thinkers

CONCLUSION

The Significance of the Global Encounters

The world was forever changed by the European voyages from about 1450 to 1650. The significance of these encounters lay not so much in the Europeans' geographical discoveries as in the scale of permanent contact these voyages made possible among previously isolated peoples of the world. The European voyages of the fifteenth and sixteenth centuries created the global capitalist system.

As a result of the European slaving enterprises on the coast of West and Central Africa, millions of Africans were uprooted, transported in chains to a strange land, and forced to toil in subhuman conditions on plantations. There they grew crops for the increasingly affluent European consumers and generated profits often used to buy more slaves in Africa, parts of which became depopulated in the process. Until well into the nineteenth century, every cup of coffee, every puff of tobacco, every sugar candy, and every cotton dress of indigo blue came from the sweat of a black slave.

Many of the native Americans lost their lives, their land, and their way of life as a result of European encounters. In the Americas, native peoples suffered from the invasion of Old World microbes even more than from the invasion of Old World conquerors. The destruction of the Aztec and Incan Empires were certainly the most dramatic, but everywhere native peoples struggled to adapt to an invasion of foreign beings from a foreign world.

Asia was far less altered by contact with Europeans. The most thorough European conquest in Asia—the Russians in Siberia—was of the least populated region of the entire continent. European civilization remained on the cultural periphery of Asia. But European access to Asian luxury goods remained a crucial component in the expanding global economy that became one of the first fruits of European capitalism.

Coming to terms with the variety of world cultures became a persistent and absorbing problem in Western civilization. Most Europeans retained confidence in the inherent superiority of their civilization, but the realities of the world began to chip away at that confidence, and economic globalization profoundly altered Western civilization itself. Westerners began to confront the problem of understanding "other" cultures and in so doing changed themselves. The West came to mean less a place in Europe than a certain kind of culture that was exported throughout the world through conversion to Christianity, the acquisition of Western languages, and the spread of Western technology.

KEY TERMS

caravel	haciendas
settler colony	aldeias
plantation colony	factories
trading posts	Columbian Exchange
conquistadores	Columbian question
requerimiento	Cultural relativism
encomienda	

CHAPTER QUESTIONS

1. Why did the European incursions into sub-Saharan Africa lead to the vast migration of Africans to the Americas as slaves? (page 395)
2. How did the arrival of Europeans in the Americas transform native cultures and life? (page 401)
3. Why was the European encounter with Asian civilizations far less disruptive than those in Africa and the Americas? (page 414)
4. How was the world tied together in a global biological and economic system? (page 417)

TAKING IT FURTHER

1. What motivated the European voyagers and conquistadores to take such great risks?
2. Compare and contrast the European treatment of Africans with that of the natives of the New World.
3. The European global encounters of the fifteenth and sixteenth centuries produced one of the greatest disasters in human history. Agree or disagree. What are your reasons?

✓ Practice on MyHistoryLab

The Reformations of Religion

- Causes of the Reformation
- The Diversity of Protestantism
- The Lutheran Reformation
- The Catholic Reformation

ACCORDING TO A POWERFULLY EVOCATIVE STORY THAT MAY OR MAY NOT BE TRUE, THE REFORMATION BEGAN ON HALLOWEEN, OCTOBER 31, 1517. An obscure monk-turned-university-professor nailed to the door of the cathedral in Wittenberg, Germany, an announcement containing 95 theses or debating propositions. Martin Luther had no hint of the ramifications of this simple act—as common then as posting an announcement for a lecture or concert on a university bulletin board now. But Luther's seemingly harmless deed sparked a revolution. Whether or not he ever posted the theses on the cathedral door, he certainly did have copies printed. Within weeks, all Germany was ablaze over Luther's daring attack on the pope. Within a few short years Wittenberg became the European center for a movement to reform the Church. As the pope and high churchmen resisted Martin Luther's call for reform, much of Germany and eventually most of northern Europe and Britain broke away from the Catholic Church. The **Protestant Reformation** dominated European affairs from 1517 until 1560.

Martin Luther succeeded because he expressed in print what many felt in their hearts—that the Church was failing in its most fundamental obligation to help Christians achieve salvation. In contrast, many Catholics considered the Protestants dangerous heretics whose errors made salvation impossible. Moreover, for the many Catholics who had long recognized the need for reforms in the Church and been diligently working to achieve them, the intemperate Martin Luther only made matters worse.

The division between Protestants and Catholics split the West into two distinctive religious cultures. The result was that the hard-won unity of the West, which had been achieved during the Middle Ages through the expansion of Christianity to the most distant corners of the European continent and through the leadership of the papacy, was lost. Catholics and Protestants continued to share a great deal of the Christian tradition, but fateful issues divided them: their understanding of salvation, the function of the sacraments in promoting pious behavior, the celebration of the liturgy in Latin, and obedience to the pope.

The fundamental conflict during the Reformation was about religion, but religion can never be entirely separated from politics or society. The competition among the kingdoms and the social tensions within the cities of central and northern Europe magnified religious controversies. The Reformation raised this question: How did encounters between Catholics and Protestants permanently transform religious unity into religious division in the West?

THE IMITATION OF CHRIST

In Albrecht Dürer's self-portrait at age 28, he literally shows himself imitating Christ's appearance. The initials AD are prominently displayed in the upper left-hand corner. They stand for Albrecht Dürer, but also for *anno domini*, "the year of our Lord."

Source: Albrecht Duerer, "Self-Portrait". 1500. Oil on Panel. 26 1/4" × 19 1/4" (66.7 × 49 cm). Alte Pinakothek, Munich. SCALA/Art Resource, NY

CAUSES OF THE REFORMATION

■ What caused the religious rebellion that began in German-speaking lands and spread to much of northern Europe?

The Protestant Reformation was the culmination of nearly 200 years of turmoil within the Church. During the fourteenth and fifteenth centuries the contradiction between the Church's divine mission and its obligations in this world hampered its moral influence. On the one hand, the Church taught that its mission was otherworldly, the source of spiritual solace and the guide to eternal salvation. On the other hand, the Church was thoroughly of this world. It owned vast amounts of property, maintained a far-reaching judicial bureaucracy to enforce canon (Church) law, and was headed by the pope, who was also the territorial prince of the Papal State in central Italy. Whereas from the eleventh to the thirteenth centuries the popes had been the source of moral reform and spiritual renewal in the Church, by the fifteenth century the popes had become part of the problem. The problem was not so much that they had become corrupt, but they were unable to respond effectively to the demands of ordinary people who were increasingly concerned with their own salvation and the effective government of their communities.

Three developments, in particular, contributed to the demand for religious reform: the search for the freedom of private religious expression; the print revolution; and the northern Renaissance interest in the Bible and other sources of Christian knowledge.

The Search for Freedom

As we saw in Chapter 11, a series of events during the fourteenth century weakened the authority of the popes and led believers to look elsewhere for spiritual leadership and consolation. Between 1305 and 1378 seven popes in a row abandoned Rome and chose to reside in the relative calm of Avignon, France. The period came to be called the Babylonian Captivity of the Church, a pejorative term that reflected the widespread opinion outside France that the popes had become subservient to the kings of France and were financially corrupt. During the Great Schism (1378–1417), rival Italian and French popes divided the Church and eroded papal authority even further.

While the papacy's moral authority declined, lay Christians were drawn to new forms of worship. Particularly influential was the Modern Devotion, encouraged by the *Imitation of Christ* written about 1441. The Modern Devotion channeled believers' desire to transcend this world of evil and pain by emphasizing frequent private prayer and moral introspection. The *Imitation*

provided a kind of spiritual manual that helped laypeople follow the same path toward spiritual renewal that traditionally had been reserved for monks and nuns. The goal was to imitate Christ so thoroughly that Christ entered the believer's soul. In a self-portrait influenced by the Modern Devotion (shown on page 427), Albrecht Dürer (1471–1528) resembles Christ himself.

The religious fervor that drew many Christians to such profound forms of religious expression further alienated many from the papacy. They began to see the pope as a thieving foreigner who extorted money that could be better spent locally. German communities, in particular, protested against the financial demands and the questionable practices of the pope and higher clergy. Some bishops neglected their duties regarding the spiritual guidance of their flock. Some never resided in their dioceses (the district under the bishop's care), knew nothing of the problems of their people, and were concerned only with retaining their incomes and lavish living standards. Living amid the pleasures of Rome, these high clergymen were in no position to discipline parish priests, some of whom also ignored their moral responsibilities by living openly with concubines and even selling the sacraments. Although immorality of this sort was probably not widespread, a few notorious examples bred enormous resentment among the laity.

In an effort to assert control over the church in their own communities, city officials known as magistrates attempted to stem the financial drain and end clerical abuses. They restricted the amount of property ecclesiastical institutions could own, tried to tax the clergy, made priests subject to the town's courts of law, and eliminated the churchmen's exemption from burdensome duties, such as serving in the town militia or providing labor for public works. On the eve of the Reformation—especially in the cities of Germany and the Netherlands—magistrates had already begun to assert local control over the Church, a tendency that prepared the way for the Protestants' efforts. For many laypeople, the overriding desire was to obtain greater spiritual and fiscal freedom from the Church hierarchy.

The Print Revolution

Until the mid-fifteenth century, the only way in the West to reproduce any kind of text—a short business record or a long philosophical book—was to copy it laboriously by hand. As medieval scribes made copies on parchment, however, they often introduced errors or "improved" the original text as they saw fit. Thus, two different copies of the same text could read differently. Parchment books were also very expensive; a book as long as the Bible might require the skins of 300 sheep to make the parchment sheets and hundreds of hours of labor to copy the text. The high cost meant that books were limited to churchmen and to the very rich. Few Christians ever actually read the Bible simply because Bibles—like all books—were so rare.

Two fifteenth-century inventions revolutionized the availability of books. First, movable metal type was introduced around 1450, and after that time printed books first began to appear. Perhaps the very first was a Bible printed by Johannes Gutenberg (ca. 1398–1468) in Mainz, Germany. Equally important, cheap manufactured paper replaced expensive sheepskins. These two developments reduced the cost of books to a level that made them available even to artisans of modest incomes.

The demand for inexpensive printed books was astounding. During the first 40 years of print, more books were produced than had been copied by scribes during the previous 1,000 years. By 1500, presses in more than 200 cities and towns had printed six million books. Half of the titles were on religious subjects, and because the publishing industry (then as now) produced only what people wanted to buy, the predominance of religion reveals what was on the minds of the reading public.

The buyers of printed books included, of course, the traditionally literate classes of university students, churchmen, professionals, and aristocratic intellectuals. Remarkably, however, there was also an enormous demand among people for whom books had previously been an unimaginable luxury. During the fourteenth and fifteenth centuries literacy rates had steadily risen, although they varied a great deal across Europe. The knowledge of what was in books, however, spread widely beyond the literate few because reading for most people in the fifteenth and sixteenth centuries was an oral, public activity. In parish churches, taverns, and private houses the literate read books out loud to others for their entertainment and edification.

The expansion of the university system during this period also created more demand for books. Between 1300 and 1500 the number of European universities grew from 20 to 70. The universities also developed a new way of reading. During the fifteenth century the Sorbonne in Paris and Oxford University decreed that libraries were to be quiet places, an indication of the spread of silent reading among the most highly educated classes. Compared with the tradition of reading aloud, silent reading was faster and more private. The silent reader learned more quickly and also decided independently the meaning of what had been read. Once many cheap books were available to the silent readers among the best educated, the interpretation of texts, especially the notoriously difficult text of the Bible, could no longer be easily regulated.

It is difficult to imagine that the Reformation could have succeeded without the print revolution. Print culture radically changed how information was disseminated and gave people new ways to interpret their experiences. Between 1517 and 1520, Martin Luther wrote some 30 tracts, mostly in a riveting colloquial German. Three hundred thousand copies were printed and distributed throughout Europe. No other author's ideas had ever spread so fast to so many.

The Northern Renaissance and the Christian Humanists

As discussed in Chapter 12, the humanists were devoted to rediscovering the lost works of antiquity and imitating the style of the best Greek and Latin authors of the ancient world. As the humanists examined these ancient texts, they developed the study of philology, of how the meanings of words change over time. These endeavors stimulated a new kind of approach to the sources of Christianity. The humanist Lorenzo Valla (ca. 1407–1457), for example, questioned the accuracy of the Vulgate, the Latin translation of the Bible accepted by the Church.

The humanists who specialized in subjecting the Bible to philological study were called the **Christian humanists.** In examining the sources of Christianity, their goal was not to criticize Christianity or the Church but to understand the precise meaning of its founding texts, especially the Bible and the writings of the Church fathers, who wrote in Greek and Latin and commented on the Bible during the early centuries of Christianity. The Christian humanists first sought to correct what they saw as mistakes in interpreting Christian doctrine. Their second goal was to improve morals. They believed that the path to personal morality and to Church reform lay in imitating "the primitive church," which meant the practices of Christianity at the time of Jesus and the apostles. Most of the Christian humanists came from northern Europe. They constituted the most influential wing of the **northern Renaissance,** a movement that built on the foundations of the Italian Renaissance. Through their efforts, the Christian humanists brought the foundations of Christianity under intense scrutiny during the early sixteenth century.

Exploiting the potential of the relatively new printing industry, the Dutchman, Desiderius Erasmus (ca. 1469–1536), became the most influential and inspiring of the Christian humanists. During times of war, Erasmus eloquently called for peace. He also published a practical manual for helping children develop a sense of morality, and he laid out easy-to-follow guidelines for spiritual renewal in the *Handbook for the Militant Christian.* The artist Albrecht Dürer transformed the theme of that book into a visual allegory shown on page 431. Erasmus's penchant for moral criticism reached the level of high satire in his masterpiece, *The Praise of Folly* (1514). In it he attacked theologians preoccupied by silly questions, such as whether the Resurrection could take place at night; he lampooned corrupt priests who took money from dying men to read the last rites; he ridiculed gullible pilgrims who bought phony relics as tourist souvenirs; and he parodied the vanity of monks who thought the color of their robes more important than helping the poor. Erasmus also translated the Greek New Testament into a new Latin version. His critical studies were the basis of many new translations of the Hebrew and Greek Bible into vernacular languages, including the popular English translation, the King James Bible.

Erasmus's friend, the Englishman Thomas More (1478–1535), is best known for his book *Utopia* (1516). More's little book established the genre of utopian fiction, which described imaginary, idealized worlds. It depicted an imaginary island found in the New World, "Utopia," a double entendre in Greek meaning both "nowhere" and "good place." The Utopians were monotheists who, although not Christians, intuitively understood pure religion and lived a highly regulated life. Utopia represented More's understanding of how a society that imitated the primitive church might appear. In particular he promoted communism based on the passage in Scripture that states believers in Christ "were of one heart and soul, and no one claimed private ownership of any possessions, but everything they owned was held in common" (Acts 4:32). More shared some of Erasmus's ideas about the critical study of Scripture and a purer Church, but unlike Erasmus he was no pacifist.

Erasmus and More remained loyal Catholics, but as a chancellor of the English government, More ruthlessly persecuted Protestants. Nevertheless, the work of these two men helped popularize some of the ideas that came to be associated with the Protestant reformers. To them, the test for the legitimacy of any religious practice was twofold. First, could it be found in the Bible? Second, did it promote moral behavior? By focusing attention on the sources of Christianity, the Christian humanists emphasized the deep disparity they perceived between the Christianity of the New Testament and the state of the Church in their own time.

ALBRECHT DÜRER, *THE KNIGHT, DEATH, AND THE DEVIL*

This engraving of 1513 illustrates Erasmus's *Handbook for the Militant Christian* by depicting a knight steadfastly advancing through a frightening landscape. A figure of death holds an hourglass, indicating that the knight's time on Earth is limited. A devil follows behind him threateningly. His valiant horse and loyal dog represent the virtues that a pious Christian must acquire.

Source: Albrecht Dürer, "Knight, Death and the Devil". Engraving. (MM14997 B). The Metropolitan Museum of Art, Harris Brisbane Dick Fund, 1943. (43.106.2)

THE LUTHERAN REFORMATION

■ How did the Lutheran Reformation create a new kind of religious culture?

The Protestant Reformation began with the protests of Martin Luther against the pope and certain Church practices. Like Erasmus and

More, Luther used the Bible as the litmus test of what the Church should do. If a practice could not be found in the Bible, Luther thought, then it should not be considered Christian. But unlike Erasmus and More, he also introduced theological innovations that made compromise with the papacy impossible.

Luther and his followers, however, would not have succeeded without the support of local political authorities who had their own grievances against the pope and the Holy Roman Emperor, a devout defender of the Catholic faith. The Lutheran Reformation first spread in Germany with the assistance and encouragement of those local authorities—the town magistrates and the territorial princes. Under the sponsorship of princes and kings, Lutheranism spread from Germany into Scandinavia.

Martin Luther and the Break with Rome

Martin Luther (1483–1546) suffered a grim childhood and uneasy relationship with his father, a miner who wanted his son to become a lawyer. During a break from the University of Erfurt, where he was studying law, Luther was thrown from his horse in a storm and nearly died. That frightening experience impelled him to become a monk, a decision that infuriated his father because it meant young Luther abandoned a promising professional career. By becoming a monk, Luther replaced the control of his father with obedience to his superiors in the Augustinian Order. They sent him back to the University of Erfurt for advanced study in theology and then transferred him from the lovely garden city of Erfurt to Wittenberg in Saxony, a scruffy town "on the edge of beyond," as Luther described it. At Wittenberg Luther began to teach at an undistinguished university, far from the intellectual action. Instead of lamenting his isolation, Luther brought the world to his university by making it the center of the religious reform movement.

As a monk, Luther had been haunted by a deep lack of self-worth:

> In the monastery, I did not think about women, or gold, or goods, but my heart trembled, and doubted how God could be gracious to me. Then I fell away from faith, and let myself think nothing less than that I had come under the Wrath of God, whom I must reconcile with my good works.[1]

Obsessed by the fear that no amount of charitable good works, prayers, or religious ceremonies would compensate for God's contempt of him, Luther suffered from anxiety attacks and prolonged periods of depression. He understood his psychic turmoil and shaky faith as any monk would—the temptations of the Devil, who was a very powerful figure for Luther.

Over several years, while preparing and revising his university lectures on St. Paul, Luther gradually worked out a solution to his own spiritual crisis by reexamining the theology of penance. The sacrament of penance provided a way to confess sins and receive absolution for them. If a penitent had lied, for example, he could seek forgiveness for the sin by feeling sorry about it, confessing it to a priest, and receiving a penalty, usually a specified number of prayers. Penance took care of only those penalties the Church could inflict on sinners. God's punishment for sins would take place in Purgatory (a place of temporary suffering for dead souls) and at the Last Judgment. But Catholic theology taught that penance in this world would reduce punishment in the next. In wrestling with the concept of penance, Luther long meditated on the meaning of a difficult passage in St. Paul's epistle to the Romans (1:17): "The just shall live by faith." Luther came to understand this passage to mean that eternal salvation came not from performing the religious good works of penance, but from faith, which was a gift from God. That gift was called "grace" and was completely unmerited. Luther called this process of receiving God's grace **justification by faith** alone, because the ability to

have faith in Christ was a sign that one had received God's grace.

Luther's emphasis on justification by faith alone left no room for human free will in obtaining salvation, because Luther believed that faith could come only from God's grace. This did not mean that God controlled every human action, but it did mean that humans could not will to do good. They needed God's help. Those blessed with God's grace would naturally perform good works. This way of thinking about God's grace had a long tradition going back to St. Augustine, the Church father whose work profoundly influenced Luther's own thought. In fact, many Catholic thinkers embraced a similar position, but they did not draw the same conclusions about free will that Luther did. Luther's interpretation of St. Augustine on free will separated Lutheran from Catholic theology. Based on his rejection of free will, Luther condemned all but two of the Church sacraments as vain works that deluded people into thinking they could earn salvation by performing them. He retained communion and baptism because they were clearly authorized by the Bible, but disputes over the meaning of these two sacraments created divisions within the Protestant Reformation movement itself. Luther and other Protestants, moreover, changed the ceremonies of communion, allowing the laity to partake of the wine, which the Catholics had reserved for priests alone. The woodcut on page 433 by Lucas Cranach illustrates the Lutheran ritual of communion.

For Luther this seemingly bleak doctrine of denying the human will to do good was liberating. It freed him from his persistent fears of damnation. He no longer had to worry whether he was doing enough to please God or could muster enough energy to fight the Devil. All he had to do was trust in God's grace. After this breakthrough, Luther reported that "I felt myself to be born anew, and to enter through open gates into paradise itself. From here, the whole face of the Scriptures was altered."[2]

THE 95 THESES In 1517 Luther became embroiled in a controversy that led to his and his followers' separation from the Roman Catholic

COMMUNION IN BOTH KINDS

In this woodcut by Lucas Cranach the Elder, Lutheran ministers offer both the communion wine and bread to the laity. Catholics reserved the wine for the priests, which set them apart from the laity. Changes in the rituals of the Eucharist or communion were among the most divisive issues separating Catholic from Protestant.

Church. In order to finance the building of a new St. Peter's Basilica in Rome, Pope Leo X had issued a special new "indulgence," a particular form of penance whereby a sinner could remove years of punishment in Purgatory after death by performing a good work here on Earth. For example, pilgrims to Rome or Jerusalem often received indulgences, concrete measures of the value of their penances. Indulgences formed one of the most intimate bonds between the Church and the laity because they offered a means for the forgiveness of specific sins.

During the fourteenth century popes in need of ready cash had begun to sell indulgences. But Pope Leo's new indulgence went far beyond the promise of earlier indulgences by offering a one-time-only opportunity to escape penalties in Purgatory for all sins. Moreover, the special indulgence could apply not only to the purchaser, but to the dead already in Purgatory. The new indulgence immediately made all other indulgences worthless because it removed all penalties for sin whereas others removed only some.

Frederick the Wise, the Elector of Saxony (a princely title indicating that he was one of those who elected the emperors of the Holy Roman Empire) and the patron of Martin Luther's university, prohibited the sale of Pope Leo's special indulgence in Electoral Saxony, but it was sold just a few miles away from Wittenberg, across the border in the domain of Archbishop Albrecht of Mainz. Albrecht needed the revenues that the sale of indulgences would bring because he was in debt. He had borrowed enormous sums to bribe Pope Leo to allow him to hold simultaneously three ecclesiastical offices—a practice that was against Church law. To help Albrecht repay his debts, the pope allowed Albrecht to keep half of the revenue from the indulgence sale in his territories. Wittenbergers began to trek over the border to Albrecht's lands to listen to the sales pitch of a shameless indulgence hawker, the Dominican John Tetzel (1470–1519). Tetzel staged an ecclesiastical version of a carnival barker's act in which he harangued the crowd about their dead parents who could be immediately released from the flames of Purgatory for the sacrifice of a few coins. He allegedly ended his sermons with the notorious jingle,

> As soon as the coin in the coffer rings,
> Right then the soul to heaven springs.[3]

A group of the Wittenbergers who heard Tetzel asked Martin Luther for his advice about buying the indulgence. Luther responded less as a pastor offering comforting advice to his flock than as a university professor keen for debate. He prepared in Latin 95 theses—arguments or talking points—about indulgences that he announced he was willing to defend in an academic disputation. Luther had a few copies printed and, as we saw at the beginning of this chapter, probably posted one on the door of Wittenberg Cathedral. The **95 theses** were hardly revolutionary in themselves. They argued a simple point that salvation could not be bought and sold, a proposition that was sound, Catholic theology, and they explicitly accepted the authority of the pope even as they set limits on that authority. On that point, Luther followed what the Church councils of the fifteenth century had decreed. Luther's tone was moderate. He simply suggested that Pope Leo may have been misled in issuing the new indulgence. No one showed up to debate Luther, but someone translated the 95 theses into German and printed them. Within a few weeks, the previously unknown professor from an obscure university was the talk of the German-speaking lands.

The Dominicans counterattacked. Tetzel himself drew up opposing theses, which provoked a public clamor that Luther had tried to avoid. In 1519 at Leipzig before a raucous crowd of university students, Luther finally debated the theses and other issues with Johann Eck, a professor from the University of Ingolstadt. When Eck cleverly backed him into a logical corner, Luther refused to retreat. He insisted that the Bible was the sole guide to human conscience, and he questioned the authority of both popes and councils when they departed from the Bible. This was the very teaching for which earlier heretics had been burned at the stake. At this point Luther had no choice but to abandon his allegiance to the Church to which he had dedicated his life. By this time, Luther also had a large following in Wittenberg and beyond. The core of this group, who called themselves "evangelicals," consisted of university students, younger humanists, and well-educated, reform-minded priests and monks.

THE PATH TO THE DIET OF WORMS   In the wake of the Leipzig debate, Luther abandoned his moderate tone and launched an inflammatory pamphlet campaign. All were available in Luther's acerbic German prose, which delighted readers.

Freedom of a Christian (1520) argued that the Church's emphasis on good works had distracted Christians from the only source of salvation— God's grace, which was manifest in the faith of the Christian. It proclaimed the revolutionary doctrine of the **priesthood of all believers,** which reasoned that those of pure faith did not need a priest to stand between them and God, a doctrine that undermined the authority of the

33. Ego sum Papa! (Ich bin der Papst!)
Anonyme, zeitgenössische Karikatur des lasterhaften Papstes Alexander VI.
Nach einem französischen Holzschnitt

ANTI-CATHOLIC PROPAGANDA

This woodcut, titled *I Am the Pope,* satirizes the papacy by depicting Pope Alexander VI as a monster. Alexander was infamous for allegedly conducting orgies in the Vatican. This kind of visual propaganda was an effective way to undermine support for the papacy.

Catholic clergy over the laity. The most inspirational pamphlet, *To the Christian Nobility of the German Nation* (1520), called upon the German princes to reform the Church and to defend Germany from exploitation by the corrupt Italians who ran the Church in Rome. When Pope Leo ordered Luther's books burned and demanded Luther retract his writings, Luther responded with a defiant demonstration in which he and his students burned the pope's decree and all of the university library's books of Church law. The die was cast.

The pope demanded that Luther be arrested, but Luther's patron, the Elector Frederick, answered by defending the professor. Frederick refused to make the arrest without first giving Luther a hearing at the Imperial Diet (parliament), which was set to meet at the town of Worms in 1521. Assembled at the Diet of Worms were haughty princes, grave bishops, and the resplendent young emperor Charles V (r. 1519–1558), who was presiding over his first Imperial Diet. The emperor ordered Luther to disavow his writings, but Luther refused to do so. For several days the Diet was in an uproar, divided by friends and foes of Luther's doctrines. Just before he was to be condemned by the emperor, Luther disappeared, and rumors flew that he had been assassinated. For days no one knew the truth. The truth was that Frederick the Wise had kidnapped Luther for his own safety and hid him in the castle at Wartburg, where for nearly a year he labored in quiet seclusion translating Erasmus's version of the New Testament into German (See *Justice in History* in this chapter).

The Appeal of Luther's Message

In its early phases the Reformation spread most rapidly among the educated urban classes. During the sixteenth century, 50 of the 65 German imperial cities, at one time or another, officially accepted the Protestant Reformation. Most of the 200 smaller German towns with a population of more than 1,000 also experienced some form of the Protestant movement. During the 1520 and 1530s, the magistrates (mayors and other officeholders) of these towns took command of the Reformation movement by seizing control of the local churches. The magistrates implemented Luther's reform of worship, disciplined the clergy, and stopped the drain of revenues to irresponsible bishops and the distant pope.

The German princes of the Holy Roman Empire had their own reasons to resent the power of the Church. They wanted to appoint their own nominees to ecclesiastical offices and to diminish the legal privileges of the clergy. Despite his steadfast Catholicism, Emperor Charles V was in no position to resist their demands. During most of his reign, Charles faced a two-front war—against France and against the Ottoman Turks. Charles desperately needed the German princes' military assistance. At the first Imperial Diet of Speyer in 1526, Charles allowed the princes to decide whether they would enforce the edict of the Diet of Worms against Luther and his followers. To preserve the empire from external enemies, the emperor was forced to allow its internal division along religious lines.

Luther's message especially appealed to women. In the early days of the movement, many women felt that Luther's description of "the priesthood of all believers" included them. Women understood Luther's phrase "the freedom of a Christian" as freeing them from the restrictive roles that had traditionally kept them silent and at home. Moreover, Luther and the other major reformers saw positive religious value in the role of wife and mother. Abandoning the Catholic Church's view that celibate monks and nuns were morally superior to married people, Luther declared marriage holy and set an example by taking a wife, the ex-nun Katherina von Bora. In countless popular images of them, Martin and Luther became the model married couple as shown on page 438. The wives of the reformers often became partners in the Reformation, taking particular responsibility for organizing charities and ministering to the poor.

In the early phases of the Reformation, women preached and published on religious

JUSTICE IN HISTORY

Here I Stand: Luther at the Diet of Worms

The Elector Frederick the Wise chose to defend Martin Luther, saving him from arrest and possible execution. Nevertheless, Frederick probably did not fully agree with Luther's positions. He claimed to have never exchanged more than 20 words with Luther. For Frederick, the issue was a matter of law and his own personal authority not of religion, even though he was a pious man. As Luther's lord and the patron of the University of Wittenberg, Frederick felt the obligation to protect his own subject from outside interference, especially from distant Rome.

Luther's case had already been lost in the papal court of Rome with the issuing of a formal ban against him, but Frederick saw some hope by appealing to the new emperor, Charles V, who would be presiding over the Imperial Diet when it met at the city of Worms. The oath the emperor had taken at his coronation obligated him to follow the letter of the law. Two clauses in the imperial constitution, which was revised for Charles's coronation, applied to the Luther case. One guaranteed that no German could be tried outside of Germany. The other stated that no one could be condemned without just cause and a formal hearing. No matter what the emperor's personal views, as a constitutional monarch he could neither pack Luther off to Rome in chains nor refuse to grant a review of the charges against him.

In addition, the old jurisdictional conflicts between the emperor and the pope, which went back to the Investiture Controversy of the eleventh century (see Chapter 10), prevented Charles from accepting too readily the pope's authority in the case. For the same reason the papal party, led by Rome's representative to the Diet of Worms, Aleander, rejected the very idea that Luther should receive a judicial hearing before the Diet. Aleander argued that Emperor Charles should simply implement the Church's decision to condemn the wayward professor. The inexperienced young emperor faced violently conflicting advice from those for and against Luther, but after considerable deliberation he accepted Frederick's position. Luther deserved a hearing. Martin Luther set off for Worms with the full expectation that he was going to his own execution.

When Luther arrived in Worms in a two-wheeled cart with a few companions, he was met by a huge crowd of 2,000 partisans who accompanied him through the streets. The city of Worms was tense. Posters defending Luther were plastered everywhere, and rough-looking Spanish soldiers swaggered about intimidating Luther's followers. The day after his arrival the imperial marshal brought Luther before the electors, members of the Diet, and the emperor, who declared, "That fellow will never make a heretic of me." Piled on a table in front of the emperor were Luther's books. An official named Eck (but not the same Johann Eck of the Leipzig debate) conducted the interrogation. He asked the monk if the books were his. Luther said they were and that he had written even more. "Do you defend them all, or do you care to reject a part?" To everyone's surprise the combative theology professor asked for more time to think things over.

Late the following afternoon Luther returned and Eck put the question to him again. This time he had an answer: "Most serene emperor, most illustrious princes, most clement lords, if I have not given some of you your proper titles I beg you to forgive me. I am not a courtier, but a monk. You asked me yesterday whether the books were mine and whether I would repudiate them. They are all mine, but as for the second question, they are not all of one sort."

Luther had made a clever distinction, one that gave him the opportunity to make a speech rather than answer simply yes or no. First, he pointed out that some of the books quoted Scripture and dealt with fundamental Christian truths. He could hardly damn himself by reputiating what all Christians held true. A second group of books complained about "the desolation of the Christian world by the evil lives and teaching of the papists." To this provocative statement, the emperor blurted out, "No." Luther went on to decry the "incredibile tyranny" to which the papacy had subjected Germany. This appeal to German nationalist sentiment awakened many in the Diet to his cause even if they disagreed with him on doctrinal matters. The third group of books attacked individuals, and although Luther admitted his attacks may have crossed a line for a university professor, he insisted that he could not repudiate these writings either without encouraging future tyrants. Finally, he declared that if he could be convinced of his errors on the grounds of Scripture he would be the first to throw his books into the flames. Eck, however, was not satisfied and demanded a plain answer, "Do you or do you not repudiate your books and the errors which they contain?"

Luther's recorded reply became one of the great moments in the history of religious liberty: "Since then Your Majesty and your lordships desire a simple reply, I will answer.... Unless I am convicted by Scripture and plain reason—I do not accept the authority of popes and councils, for they have contradicted each other—my conscience is captive to the Word of God. I cannot and I will not recant anything, for to go against conscience is neither right nor safe. God help me. Amen."The first printed account of Luther's speech added a final phrase, "Here I stand, I can do no other." Whether he ever spoke it or not, "Here I stand," became the motto of the Lutheran defiance of papal and imperial authority.[4]

The Diet of Worms issued an edict condemning Luther and his writings, making future compromises impossible. Luther himself, however, had managed to ignite the national fervor of the Germans, and it was they who kept Luther and the movement he started alive.

For Discussion

1. What were the legal issues involved in Luther's hearing before the Diet of Worms?

LUTHER BEFORE THE EMPEROR AT THE DIET OF WORMS IN 1521

Luther's courageous stand at the Imperial Diet became one of the most dramatic moments in the Luther story. The young Emperor Charles V is seated on a throne at the left, flanked by the Electors and cardinals. In front of him is a table containing Luther's books. The image captures the episode when Luther was asked whether he would repudiate his books or not.

2. Did the law of the empire serve justice in the case of Luther?
3. What did the ruling imply for the future relationship between church and state on religious questions?

Taking It Further

Roland H. Bainton, *Here I Stand: A Life of Martin Luther*. 1950. Although dated the book is still useful for an account of the legal issues involved in Luther's trial.

Hieko A. Oberman, *Luther: Man between God and the Devil*. Translated by Eileen Walliser-Schwarzbart. 1989. Less detailed on the trial than Bainton, it is the best overall biography of the reformer.

KATHERINA VON BORA AND MARTIN LUTHER
For many pious Lutherans the images of Luther and his wife, herself a former nun, replaced the images of the Virgin Mary and the saints favored by the Catholics.

During the early years of the Reformation, there were many marriages in which one spouse followed the old faith and the other the new. But if the woman converted and her husband did not, the Protestant reformers counseled that she should obey her husband even if he forced her to act contrary to God's will. She could pray for his conversion but could not leave or divorce him. Most women were forced to remain married regardless of their feelings. A few exceptional women left their husbands anyway and continued to proclaim their religious convictions to the world. One such woman, Anne Askew from England, was tortured and executed for her beliefs.

THE GERMAN PEASANTS' REVOLT The Reformation also appealed to many peasants because it offered them a simplified religion and, most important, local control of their churches. The peasants of Wendelstein, a typical South German village, had been complaining about the conduct of its priests for some time. In 1523, they hired a "Christian teacher" and told him in no uncertain terms: "We will not recognize you as a lord, but only as a servant of the community. We will command you, not you us, and we order you to preach the gospel and the word of God purely, clearly, and truthfully—without any human teachings—faithfully and conscientiously."[6] These villagers understood the Reformation to mean that they could take control of their local church and demand responsible conduct from the minister they hired. However, other peasants understood the Reformation in more radical terms as licensing social reforms that Luther himself never supported.

matters. These women demanded to be heard in churches and delivered inspiring sermons. Marie Dentière, a former abbess of a French convent who joined the Reformation cause, asked, "Do we have two Gospels, one for men and the other for women?...For we [women] ought not, any more than men, hide and bury within the earth that which God has...revealed to us women?"[5] Most women were soon disappointed because their preaching and writing threatened the male authorities. In some places laws were passed that prohibited women from discussing religious questions. In England, women were even prevented from reading the Bible aloud to others. The few women who were able to speak and act openly in public were either queens or the wives of prominent reformers. Most women confined their participation in the Reformation to the domestic sphere, where they instructed children, quietly read the Bible, and led prayer circles.

One of the attractions of Protestantism was that it allowed divorce, which was prohibited by Catholic Church law. However, the reform leaders were quite reluctant to grant women the same rights as their husbands in obtaining a divorce.

In June 1524 a seemingly minor event sparked a revolt of peasants in many parts of Germany. When an aristocratic lady demanded that the peasants in her village abandon their grain harvest to gather snails for her, they rebelled and set her castle on fire. Over the next two years, the rebellion spread as peasants rose up against their feudal lords to demand the adoption of Lutheran reforms in the Church, a reduction of feudal privileges, the abolition of serfdom, and the self-government of their communities. Their rebellion was unprecedented. It was the largest and best-organized peasant movement ever in Germany, a measure of the powerful effect of the Protestant reform message. Like the Reformation, the revolt was the culmination of a long period of discontent, but unlike the Reformation, it was a tragic failure.

These peasants were doing exactly what they thought Luther had advocated when he wrote about the "freedom of the Christian." They interpreted his words to mean complete social as well as religious freedom. However, Luther had not meant anything of the sort. To him, the freedom of the Christian referred to inner, spiritual freedom, not liberation from economic or political bondage. Instead of supporting the rebellion begun in his name, Luther and nearly all the other reformers backed the feudal lords and condemned in uncompromising terms the violence of the peasant armies. In *Against the Thieving, Murderous Hordes of Peasants* (1525), Luther expressed his own fear of the lower classes and revealed that despite his acid-tongued attacks on the pope, he was fundamentally a conservative thinker who was committed to law and order. He urged that the peasants be hunted down and killed like rabid dogs. And so they were. Between 70,000 and 100,000 peasants died, a slaughter far greater than the Roman persecutions of the early Christians. To the peasants, Luther's conservative position on social and economic issues felt like betrayal, but it enabled the Lutheran Reformation to retain the support of the princes, which was essential for its survival.

LUTHERAN SUCCESS   Soon after the crushing of the Peasants' Revolt, the Lutheran Reformation faced a renewed threat from its Catholic opponents. In 1530 Emperor Charles V bluntly commanded all Lutherans to return to the Catholic fold or face arrest. Enraged, the Lutherans refused to comply. The following year the Protestant princes formed a military alliance, the Schmalkaldic League, against the emperor. Renewed trouble with France and the Turks prevented a military confrontation

between the league and the emperor for 15 years, giving the Lutherans enough breathing space to put the Reformation on a firmer basis in Germany by training ministers and educating the laity in the new religion. In the meantime Lutheranism spread beyond Germany into Scandinavia, where it received support from the kings of Denmark and Sweden as it had among the princes of northern Germany.

After freeing himself from foreign wars, Charles V turned his armies against the Protestants. However, in 1552 the Protestant armies defeated him, and Charles was forced to relent. In 1555 the **Religious Peace of Augsburg** established the principle of *cuius regio, eius religio*, which means "he who rules determines the religion of the land." Protestant princes were permitted to retain all church lands seized before 1552 and to enforce Protestant worship, but Catholic princes were also allowed to enforce Catholic worship in their territories. Those who disagreed with their ruler's religion would not be tolerated. Their options were to change religion or to emigrate elsewhere. With the Peace of Augsburg the religious division of the Holy Roman Empire became permanent.

The following year, Emperor Charles, worn out from ceaseless warfare, the anxieties of holding his vast territories together, and nearly 40 years of trying to stamp out Protestantism, abdicated his throne and retired to a monastery, where he died in 1558.

THE DIVERSITY OF PROTESTANTISM

■ How and why did Protestant denominations multiply to such an extent in northern Europe and Britain?

The term *Protestant* originally applied only to the followers of Luther who *protested* the decisions of the second Imperial Diet of Speyer in 1529, which attempted to force them back into the Catholic fold, but the term came to describe much more than that small group. Protestantism encompassed innumerable churches and sects, all of which refused to accept the authority of the pope. Many of these have survived since the Reformation, some disappeared in the violence of the sixteenth century, and others have sprung up since, especially in North America, where Protestantism has thrived.

The varieties of Protestantism can be divided into two types. The first was the product of the **Magisterial Reformation,** which refers to the churches that received official government sanction. These included the Lutheran churches (Germany and Scandinavia); the Reformed and Calvinist churches (Switzerland, Scotland, the Netherlands, and a few places in Germany); and the Anglican Church (England, Wales, parts of Ireland, and later in England's colonies). The second was the product of the **Radical Reformation** and included the movements that failed to gain official recognition and were at best tolerated, at worst persecuted. This strict division into Magisterial and Radical Protestantism broke down in eastern Europe, where the states did not enforce religious conformity (see **Map 14.1**).

The Reformation in Switzerland

The independence of Switzerland from the Holy Roman Empire meant that from the beginning of the Reformation local authorities could cooperate

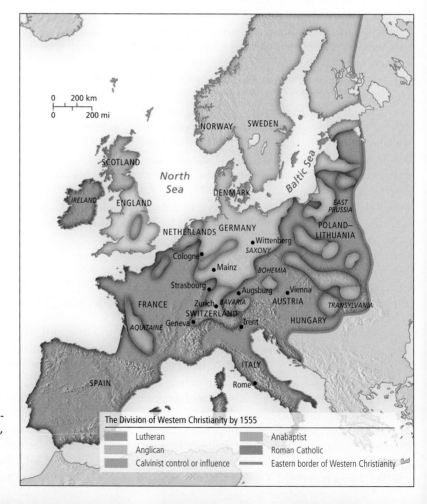

MAP 14.1

The Division of Western Christianity by 1555

The West, which had been culturally unified by Christianity for more than 1,000 years, split apart during the sixteenth century. These religious divisions persist to this day.

with the reformers without opposition from the emperor. The Swiss Confederation bound together 13 fiercely proud regions, called cantons. Except for the leading cities of Zürich, Basel, and Geneva, Switzerland remained an impoverished land of peasants who could not fully support themselves from the barren mountainous land. To supplement their meager incomes, young Swiss men fought as mercenaries in foreign armies, often those of the pope. Each spring, mercenary captains recruited able-bodied Swiss men from the mountain villages. The Swiss men left the women behind to tend the animals and farms. By summer, the villages were emptied of all men except the old and invalid. Each fall at the end of the fighting season, the survivors of that season's campaign trudged home, always bringing bad news to a fresh group of widows. The strain created by the mercenary's life stimulated the desire for sweeping reforms in Switzerland.

ZWINGLI'S ZÜRICH Ulrich Zwingli (1484–1531) had served as a chaplain with the Swiss mercenaries under the pope in Italy. In 1520, after being named the People's Priest of Zürich, Zwingli criticized his superior bishop for recruiting local young men to die in the papal armies. That same year he began to call for reform of the Church, advocating the abolition of the Roman Catholic mass, the marriage of priests, and the closing of monasteries. One of the novel features of Zwingli's reform was the strict emphasis on preaching the Word of Scripture during Church services, in contrast with the emphasis on ritual in the traditional Catholic liturgy. Zwingli ordered the removal of all paintings and statues from churches because they distracted parishioners from concentrating on the preaching. The Zwinglian Reformation began independently of the Lutheran Reformation and created a separate reform center from which reform ideas spread throughout Switzerland, southern Germany, and England.

Two features distinguished the Zwinglian from the Lutheran Reformation. One was Zwingli's desire to have reformed ministers participate in governmental decisions. In Lutheran Germany, church and state supported each other, but they remained legally separate, and the prince alone had the authority to determine the religion of the land. In Zürich, the moral Christian and the good citizen were one and the same, and Zwingli worked with the magistrates of the city council, who step-by-step legalized the Reformation and enforced conformity through its police powers.

Luther and Zwingli also differed in their understanding of the nature of the Eucharist, the communion sacrament that reenacted Christ's Last Supper with his apostles. Luther believed that Christ's body was spiritually present in the communion bread. "You will receive," as he put it, "as much as you believe you receive."[7] This emphasis on the inner, spiritual state of the believer was very characteristic of Luther's introspective piety. In contrast to Luther, Zwingli could not accept the idea of the presence of Almighty God in a humble piece of bread. To Zwingli, the Eucharistic bread was just a symbol that stood for the body of Christ. The problem with the symbolic interpretation of the Eucharist was that the various reformers could not agree with Zwingli

CHRONOLOGY: THE LUTHERAN REFORMATION

1517	Luther posts the 95 theses
1519	Luther debates Johann Eck at Leipzig; election of Charles V as Holy Roman Emperor
1521	Diet of Worms
1524–1525	German peasants revolt
1531	Formation of the Schmalkaldic League
1555	The Religious Peace of Augsburg

on exactly what the Eucharist symbolized. As early as 1524, it became evident that each reformer was committed to a different interpretation, and these different interpretations became the basis for different Protestant churches.

CALVIN'S GENEVA In the next generation the momentum of the Reformation shifted to Geneva, Switzerland, under the leadership of John Calvin (1509–1564). Trained as a lawyer and exiled from his home in France in 1533 for his reformist views, Calvin spent several years wandering, searching for a quiet retreat, and collaborating with other reformers. After he settled in Geneva in 1536, Calvin spent the rest of his life transforming the town into the City of God. The linchpin of the Genevan reform was the close cooperation between the magistrates of the city council and the clergy in enforcing the moral discipline of the citizens.

Calvin's theology extended the insights of Luther and Zwingli to their logical conclusions. This pattern is most obvious in Calvin's understanding of justification by faith. Luther had argued that the Christian could not earn salvation through good works and that faith came only from God. Calvin reasoned that if an all-knowing, all-powerful God knew everything in advance and caused everything to happen, then the salvation of any individual was predetermined or, as Calvin put it, "predestined." Calvin's doctrine of **predestination** was not new. In fact, it had long been discussed among Christian theologians. But for Calvin two considerations made it crucial. First was Calvin's certainty that God was above any influence from humanity. The "majesty of God," as Calvin put it, was the principle from which everything else followed. Second, Calvin and other preachers had noticed that in a congregation attending a sermon, only a few paid attention to what was preached, while the vast majority seemed unable or unwilling to understand. The reason for this disparity seemed to be that only the Elect, as the Bible decreed, could truly follow God's Word. The Elect were those who had received God's grace and would be saved. The Elect were known only to God, but Calvin's theology encouraged the

converted to feel the assurance of salvation and to accept a "calling" from God to perform his will on Earth. God's **calling** gave Calvinists a powerful sense of personal direction, which committed them to a life of moral activity, whether as preacher, wife, or shoemaker.

Calvin composed an elegant theological treatise, the *Institutes of the Christian Religion,* first published in six chapters in 1535 but constantly revised and expanded until it reached 80 chapters in the definitive 1559 edition. Calvin the lawyer wrote a tightly argued and reasoned work, like a trial attorney preparing a case. In Calvin's theology the parts fit neatly together like a vast, intricate puzzle. Calvin's work aspired to be a comprehensive reformed theology that would convince through reasoned deliberation, and it became the first systematic presentation of Protestant doctrine. Whereas Luther spun out his sometimes contradictory ideas in a series of often polemical pamphlets, Calvin devoted himself to perfecting his comprehensive theology of Protestantism. (See *Different Voices* in this chapter.)

Given its emphasis on building a holy community, Calvinism helped transform the nuclear family into a social unit for training and disciplining children. Because women were responsible for educating children, they had to be literate. Calvinist women and men were both disciplined and liberated—disciplined to avoid physical and material pleasures, liberated from the necessity to do good works but guided by God's grace to do them anyway. Calvinism spread far beyond its Swiss home, becoming the dominant form of Protestantism in France, the Netherlands, Scotland, and New England.

The Reformation in Britain

Great Britain, as the island kingdom is known today, did not exist in the sixteenth century. The Tudor dynasty, which began in 1485 with Henry VII (see Chapter 12), ruled over England, Wales, and Ireland, but Scotland was still a separate kingdom with its own monarch and church institutions. These countries had distinctive political traditions, cultures, and languages, and as a

ICONOCLASM IN THE NETHERLANDS

Protestants sometimes initiated reform by vandalizing churches through acts of iconoclasm—the removing, breaking, or defacing of religious statues, paintings, and symbols such as crucifixes. In this engraving the men on the left of the church haul down statues. Note that one statue is already lying on the ground. On the right side of the church, men are breaking the stained glass windows with clubs. Reformers justified iconoclasm because the money for images could be better spent feeding the poor and because they thought paintings and sculptures distracted parishioners from listening to preaching.

result their Reformation experiences differed considerably. The Tudors imposed the Reformation as a matter of royal policy, and they were mostly successful in England and Wales. But they hardly made a dent in the religious culture of Ireland, which was a remarkable exception to the European pattern of conformity to the religion of the ruler. There the vast majority of the population remained Catholic. Scotland, also an exception to the rule, wholeheartedly accepted the Protestant Reformation against the will of its Catholic queen and most of the clergy.

THE TUDORS AND THE ENGLISH REFORMATION In 1527 the rotund, self-absorbed, but crafty King Henry VIII (r. 1509–1547) announced that he had come to the pious conclusion that he had gravely sinned by marrying his brother's widow, Catherine of Aragon. By this time the couple had been married for 18 years, their only living child was the princess Mary, and at age 42 Catherine was unlikely to give birth to more children. Henry let it be known that he wanted a son to secure the English throne for the Tudor dynasty. He also had his eye on the most engaging woman of the court, Anne Boleyn, who was less than half Catherine's age. In the past, popes had usually been cooperative when a powerful king needed an annulment, but Pope Clement VII (r. 1523–1534) was in no position to oblige Henry. At the time of the marriage, the papal curia had issued a dispensation for Henry to marry his brother's widow, a practice that is prohibited in the Bible. In effect, Henry was asking the papacy to admit it had made a mistake.

DIFFERENT VOICES A CATHOLIC CARDINAL CHALLENGES JOHN CALVIN

In 1539 Cardinal Jacopo Sadoleto wrote a letter to the magistrates and citizens of Geneva inviting them to return to the Catholic Church. A few months later the reformer John Calvin replied to Sadoleto. Although both letters are polemical in tone, they isolate the significant differences between the two faiths. In these excerpts from the two letters, Sadoleto and Calvin show how Catholics and Protestants had a very different understanding of what constituted "the Church."

Sadoleto's Letter to the Genevans, March 18, 1539

The point in dispute is whether is it more expedient for your salvation, and whether you think you will do what is more pleasing to God, by believing and following what the Catholic Church throughout the whole world, now for more than 1,500 years, or (if we require clear and certain recorded notice of the facts) for more than 1,300 years approves with general consent; or innovations introduced within these 25 years, by crafty or, as they think themselves, acute men; but men certainly who are not themselves the Catholic Church? For, to define it briefly, the Catholic Church is that which in all parts, as well as at the present time in every region of the world, united and consenting in Christ, has been always and everywhere directed by the one Spirit of Christ; in which Church no dissension can exist; for all its parts are connected with each other, and breathe together. But should any dissension and strife arise, the great body of the Church indeed remains the same, but an abscess is formed by which some corrupted flesh, being torn off, is separated from the spirit which animates the body, and no longer belongs in substance to the body ecclesiastic. I will not here descend to the discussion of single points, or load your ears with a multitude of words and arguments.... [Then he proceeds to do just that] I will say nothing of the Eucharist, in which we worship the most true body of Christ.... Nor will I speak of confession of sins to a priest, in which confession that which forms the strongest foundation of our safety, viz., true Christian humility, has both been demonstrated by Scripture, and established and enjoined by the Church; this humility these men have studied calumniously to evade, and presumptuously to cast away. Nor will I say anything either of the prayers of the saints to God for us, or of ours for the dead, though I would fain know what these same men would be at when they despise and deride them. Can they possibly imagine that the soul perishes along with its body? This they certainly seem to insinuate, and they do it still more openly when they strive to procure for themselves a liberty of conduct set loose from all ecclesiastical laws, and a license for their lusts.

In addition, at the moment when Henry's petition for divorce arrived, Clement was under the control of Catherine's nephew, the Emperor Charles V, whose armies had recently captured and sacked the city of Rome. In 1531 Henry gave up trying to obtain papal approval and divorced Catherine anyway. Eighteen months later he secretly married Anne. England's compliant Archbishop Thomas Cranmer (1489–1556) pronounced the marriage to Catherine void and the one to Anne valid. But the marriage to Anne did not last. When she failed to produce a male heir, Henry had her arrested, charged with incest with her brother and adultery with other men. She was convicted and beheaded.

The English separation from the Roman Catholic Church took place in 1534 through the Acts of Supremacy and Succession. The separation has often been understood as a by-product of Henry's capricious lust and the plots of his brilliant minister, Thomas Cromwell (ca. 1485–1540). It is certainly true that Henry's desire to rid himself of Catherine led him to reject papal authority and to establish himself as the head of the Church of England. It is also certainly true that Henry was an

Calvin's Reply to Sadoleto, September 1, 1539

You are mistaken in supposing that we desire to lead away the people from that method of worshipping God which the Catholic Church always observed. You either labor under a delusion as to the term *church*, or, at least, knowingly and willingly give it a gloss. I will immediately show the latter to be the case, though it may also be that you are somewhat in error. First, in defining the term, you omit what would have helped you in no small degree to the right understanding of it. When you describe it as that which in all parts, as well as at the present time in every region of the earth, being united and consenting in Christ, has been always and everywhere directed by the one Spirit of Christ, what comes of the Word of the Lord [i.e., the Bible], that clearest of all marks, and which the Lord himself, in pointing out the Church, so often recommends to us? For seeing how dangerous it would be to boast of the Spirit without the Word, He declared that the Church is indeed governed by the Holy Spirit, but in order that that government might not be vague and unstable, He annexed it to the Word. For this reason Christ exclaims that those who are of God hear the Word of God—that His sheep are those which recognize His voice as that of their Shepherd, and any other voice as that of a stranger (John X. 27). For this reason the Spirit, by the mouth of Paul declares (Eph. ii. 20) that the Church is built upon the foundation of the Apostles and Prophets. Also, that the Church is made holy to the Lord, by the washing of water in the Word of life. In short, why is the preaching of the gospel so often styled the kingdom of God, but because it is the scepter by which the heavenly King rules His people?

Source: From *A Reformation Debate:* John Calvin and Jacopo Sadoleto. Ed. by John C. Olin (NY: Fordham University Press, 2000), copyright © 2000, Fordham University Press.

For Discussion

1. How do the definitions of the Church in these two writers differ?

2. What is at stake in the differences between these definitions? In other words, who gains and who loses from the Catholic versus the Calvinist definition?

3. Notice how Sadoleto suggests the Calvinists "imagine the soul perishes along with its body." What does this mean? If true what would it mean for the Christian notion of eternal salvation?

4. Notice how often Calvin refers to the Word, that is Scripture. What does he achieve by emphasizing Scripture over all other sources of authority?

---

inconstant husband: Of his six wives, two were divorced and two beheaded. However, historians do not explain the English Reformation simply as the consequence of royal whim or the machinations of a single minister.

The English Reformation began as a declaration of royal independence from papal supervision rather than an attempt to reform the practices of the Church. Under Henry VIII the English Reformation could be described as Catholicism without the pope. Protestant doctrine, at first, had little role in the English Reformation, and Henry himself had sharply criticized Martin Luther in a treatise probably ghost-written by Thomas More. Royal supremacy established control over the Church by granting to the king supervising authority over liturgical rituals and religious doctrines. Thomas Cromwell, who worked out the practical details for parliamentary legislation, was himself a Protestant, and no doubt his religious views emboldened him to reject papal authority. But the principal theorist of royal supremacy was a Catholic, Thomas

Starkey (ca. 1499–1538). A sojourn in Italy had acquainted Starkey with Italian Renaissance political theory, which emphasized concepts of civic liberty. In fact, many English Catholics found royal supremacy acceptable as long as it meant only abandoning submission to the pope in distant Rome. Those who opposed cutting the connection to Rome suffered for their opposition, however. Bishop John Fisher (ca. 1469–1535) and Sir Thomas More, the humanist author of *Utopia* and former chancellor of England, were executed for their refusal to go along with the king's decision.

With this display of despotic power, Henry seized personal control of the English church and then closed and confiscated the lands of the monasteries. He redistributed the monastic lands to the nobility in an effort to purchase their support and to make money for the crown. Henry's officials briefly flirted with some Protestant reform but largely avoided theological innovations. On the local level many people embraced the Reformation for their own reasons, often because it gave them a sense of control over the affairs of their community. Others went along simply because the power of the king was too strong to resist.

Henry's six wives bore three surviving children. As each succeeded to the throne, the official religion of England gyrated wildly. Because his youngest child, Edward, was male, Henry designated him successor to the throne. His two daughters, Mary and Elizabeth, were to succeed only if Edward died without an heir, which he did. Only ten years old when he followed his father to the throne, King Edward VI (r. 1547–1553) was the pawn of his Protestant guardians, some of whom pushed for a more thorough Protestant Reformation in England than Henry had espoused. After Edward's premature death, his half-sister, Queen Mary I (r. 1553–1558), daughter of Henry and Catherine of Aragon, attempted to bring England back to obedience to the pope. Her unpopular marriage to Philip II of Spain and her failure to retain the support of the nobles, who were the foundation of Tudor government, damaged the Catholic cause in England.

Mary's successor and half-sister, Elizabeth Tudor, the daughter of Henry and Anne Boleyn, was an entirely different sort. Queen Elizabeth I (r. 1558–1603), raised as a Protestant, kept her enemies off balance and her quarrelsome subjects firmly in hand with her charisma and shrewd political judgments. Elizabeth became one of the most successful monarchs ever to reign anywhere. Without the considerable talents of Elizabeth, England could easily have fallen into civil war over religion—as the Holy Roman Empire and France did and as England itself did some 40 years after her death.

Between 1559 and 1563, Elizabeth repealed the Catholic legislation of Mary and promulgated her own Protestant laws, collectively known as the Elizabethan Settlement, which established the Church of England, known as the Anglican Church (Episcopalian in the United States). Her principal adviser, William Cecil (1520–1598), implemented the details of the reform through reasonable debate and compromise rather than by insisting on doctrinal purity and rigid conformity. The touchstone of the Elizabethan Settlement was the 39 Articles (finally approved by Parliament in 1571), which articulated a moderate version of Protestantism. It retained the ecclesiastical hierarchy of bishops as well as an essentially Catholic liturgy translated into English.

The Church of England under Elizabeth permitted a wide latitude of beliefs, but it did not tolerate "recusants," those who as a matter of principle refused to attend Church of England services. These were mostly Catholics who set up a secret network of priests to serve their sacramental needs and whom the government considered dangerous agents of foreign powers. Many others were militant Protestants who thought the Elizabethan Settlement did not go far enough in reforming religion. The most vocal and influential of the Protestant dissenters were the Puritans, Calvinists who demanded a church purified of what they thought were remnants of Roman Catholicism.

SCOTLAND: THE CITADEL OF CALVINISM   While England groped its way toward moderate Protestantism, neighboring Scotland became one of the most thoroughly Calvinist countries in Europe. In 1560 the parliament of Scotland overthrew Roman

Catholicism against the will of Mary Stuart, Queen of Scots (1542–1587). The wife of the French king, Mary was absent in France during the crucial early phases of the Reformation and returned to Scotland only after her husband's death in 1561. Despite her Catholicism, Mary proved remarkably conciliatory toward the Protestants by putting royal funds at the disposal of the new Reformed Kirk (Church) of Scotland. But the Scottish Calvinists never trusted her, and their mistrust would bring about her doom when they rebelled against her and drove her into exile in England. There Queen Elizabeth had her imprisoned and eventually executed because she remained a dangerous symbol for Catholics in England and Scotland.

The Scots Confession of 1560, written by a panel of six reformers, established the new church. John Knox (ca. 1514–1572) breathed a strongly Calvinist air into the church through his many polemical writings and the official liturgy he composed in 1564, the *Book of Common Order*. Knox emphasized faith and individual Christian conscience over ecclesiastical authority. Instead of the episcopal structure in England, which granted bishops the authority over doctrine and discipline, the Scots Kirk established a Presbyterian form of organization, which gave organizational authority to the pastors and elders of the congregations, all of whom had equal rank. As a result the Presbyterian congregations were independent from any central authority.

The Radical Reformation

The magisterial reformers in Germany, Switzerland, England, and Scotland managed to obtain official sanction for their religious reforms, often at the cost of some compromise with governmental authorities. As a result of those compromises, radicals from among their own followers challenged the magisterial reformers and demanded faster, more thorough reform. In most places the radicals represented a small minority, perhaps never more than two percent of all Protestants. But their significance outstripped their small numbers, in part because they forced the magisterial reformers to respond to their arguments

and because their enemies attempted to eradicate them through extreme violence.

The radicals divided into three categories: Anabaptists, who attempted to construct a holy community on the basis of literal readings of the Bible; Spiritualists, who abandoned all forms of organized religion to allow individuals to follow the inner voice of the Holy Spirit; and Unitarians, who advocated a rational religion that emphasized ethical behavior over ceremonies.

ANABAPTISTS: THE HOLY COMMUNITY For Anabaptists, the Bible was a blueprint for reforming not just the church, but all of society. Because the Bible reported that Jesus was an adult when he was baptized, the Anabaptists rejected infant baptism and adopted adult baptism. (**Anabaptism** means to rebaptize.) An adult, they believed, could accept baptism as an act of faith, unlike an oblivious infant. Anabaptists saw the sacraments of baptism and communion as symbols of faith, which had no purpose or meaning unless the recipient was already a person of faith. Adult baptism reserved for the Elect allowed the creation of a pure church, isolated from the sinfulness of the world.

Because they did not want the Elect to have to compromise with the sinful, Anabaptists advocated the complete separation of Church and state. Anabaptists sought to obey only God and completely rejected all established religious and political authorities. They required adherents to refuse to serve in government offices, swear oaths, pay taxes, or serve as soldiers. Anabaptists sought to live in highly disciplined "holy communities," which excommunicated errant members and practiced simple services based on scriptural readings. Because the Anabaptist communities consisted largely of uneducated peasants, artisans, and miners, a dimension of economic radicalism colored the early Anabaptist movement. For example, some Anabaptist radicals advocated the elimination of all private property and the sharing of wealth. On the position of women, however, Anabaptists were staunchly conservative, denying women any public role in religious affairs and insisting that they remain under the strict control of their fathers and husbands. By subordinating women, they thought they were following the Bible, but so did their more egalitarian opponents. Literal readings of the Bible proved slippery.

Because the Anabaptists promoted a radical reorganization of society along biblical lines, they provoked a violent reaction. In Zürich the city council decreed that the appropriate punishment for all Anabaptists was to be drowned in the local river where they had been rebaptizing themselves. By 1529 it became a capital offense in the Holy Roman Empire to be rebaptized; during the sixteenth century perhaps as many as 5,000 Anabaptists were executed for the offense, a persecution that tended to fragment the Anabaptists into isolated, secretive rural communities.

During a brief period in 1534 and 1535, an extremely radical group of Anabaptists managed to seize control of the northern German city of Münster. An immigrant Dutch tailor, John of Leiden, set up a despotic regime in Münster that punished with death any sin, even gossiping or complaining. John of Leiden introduced polygamy and collective ownership of property. He set an example by taking 16 wives, one of whom he beheaded for talking back, stomping on her body in front of the other frightened wives. As the besieging armies closed in, John forced his followers to crown him king and worship him. After his capture, John was subjected to an excruciating torture, and as a warning to others, his corpse was displayed for many years hanging in an iron cage.

The surviving Anabaptists abandoned the radicalism of the Münster community and embraced pacifism and nonviolent resistance. However, even these peaceful souls suffered persecution. "God opened the eyes of the governments by the revolt at Münster," as the Protestant reformer Heinrich Bullinger put it, "and thereafter no one would trust even those Anabaptists who claimed to be innocent."[8] A Dutchman, Menno Simons (1496–1561), tirelessly traveled about the Netherlands and Germany, providing solace and guidance to the isolated survivors of the Münster disaster. His followers, the Mennonites, preserved the noblest features of the Anabaptist tradition of quiet resistance to persecution. Both the Mennonites and the Amish in North America are direct descendants of sixteenth- and seventeenth-century Anabaptist groups. Under Mennonite influence, Thomas Helwys founded the first Baptist church in England in 1612. As the leader of the English Baptists, Helwys wrote an unprecedented appeal for the absolute freedom of religion. In it he defended the religious rights of Jews, Muslims, and even atheists as well as all varieties of Christians. For his views he was imprisoned, where he died.

SPIRITUALISTS: THE HOLY INDIVIDUAL   Whereas the Anabaptists radicalized the Swiss Reformation's emphasis on building a godly community, the **Spiritualists** radicalized Luther's commitment to personal introspection. Perhaps the greatest Spiritualist was the aristocratic Caspar Schwenckfeld (1490–1561), who was a friend of Luther's until he broke with the reformer over what he considered the weak spirituality of established Lutheranism. Schwenckfeld believed that depraved humanity was incapable of casting off the bonds of sin, which only a supernatural act of God could achieve. An intense conversion experience revealed this separation from sinfulness and granted spiritual illumination to the believer. Schwenckfeld called this illumination the "inner Word," which he understood as a living form of the Scriptures that the hand of God wrote directly on the believer's soul. Schwenckfeld also prized the "outer Word," that is, the Scriptures, but he found the emotional experience of the inner Word more powerful than the intellectual experience that came from reading the Bible. Spiritualists reflected an inner peace evident in their calm physical appearance, lack of anxiety, and mastery of bodily appetites—a state Schwenckfeld called the "castle of peace."

The most prominent example of the Spiritualist tendency in the English-speaking world is the Quakers, who first appeared in England a century after the Lutheran Reformation. The Quakers, or Society of Friends, interpreted the priesthood of all believers to mean that God's spirit, which they called the Light of Christ, was given equally to all men and women. This belief led them to abandon a separately ordained ministry and to replace organized worship with meetings in which any man, woman, or child could speak, read Scripture, pray, or sing, as the spirit moved them. The Quakers' belief in the sacredness of all human beings also inclined them toward pacifism and egalitarianism. In no other religious tradition have women played such a prominent role for so long. From the very beginning of the movement, female Friends were prominent in preaching the Quaker gospel. In Quaker marriages, wives were completely equal to their husbands—at least in religious matters.

UNITARIANS: A RATIONALIST APPROACH In the middle of the sixteenth century numerous sects that rejected the divinity of Christ emerged as part of the Radical Reformation. They were called Arians, Socinians, Anti-Trinitarians, or **Unitarians** because of their opposition to the Christian doctrine of the Trinity. Since 325, when the Council of Nicaea established the Trinity as official Christian dogma, Christians had accepted that the one God has three identities: God the Father, God the Son, and God the Holy Spirit. The doctrine of the Trinity made it possible for Christians to believe that at a particular moment in history, God the Son became the human being Jesus Christ. The Church Fathers at Nicaea embraced Trinitarian doctrine in response to Arians who accepted Jesus as a religious leader, but denied that he was fully divine and "co-eternal" with God the Father. During the intellectual tumult of the Reformation, radicals revived various forms of the Arian doctrine. The Italian Faustus Socinus (1539–1604) taught a rationalist interpretation of the Scriptures and argued that Jesus was a divinely inspired man, not God-become-man. Born in Siena, Italy, Socinus's rejection of the doctrine of the Trinity made life dangerous for him in Italy, and he escaped to Poland where he found the freedom to proclaim his views. Socinus's ideas remain central to Unitarianism and form the core theology of the Polish Brethren.

Catholics and magisterial Protestants alike were extremely hostile to Unitarians, who tended to be well-educated humanists and men of letters. Unitarian views thrived in advanced intellectual circles in northern Italy and eastern Europe, but the most famous critic of the Trinity was the brilliant, if eccentric, Spaniard Michael Servetus (1511–1553). Trained as a physician and widely read in the literature of the occult, Servetus published influential anti-Trinitarian works and daringly sent his provocative works to the major Protestant reformers. Based on a tip from the Calvinists in Geneva, the Catholic inquisitor-general in Lyons, France, arrested Servetus, but he escaped from prison during his trial. While passing through Geneva on his way to refuge in Italy, he was recognized while attending a church service and again imprisoned. Although no law in Geneva allowed capital punishment, Servetus was convicted of heresy and burned alive.

The Free World of Eastern Europe

Because eastern Europe offered a measure of religious freedom and toleration unknown elsewhere in sixteenth-century Europe, it attracted refugees from the oppressive princes of western Europe, none of whom tolerated more than one religion in their territories if they could help it. Religious toleration was made possible by the relative weakness of the monarchs in Bohemia, Hungary, Transylvania, and Poland-Lithuania, where the great landowning aristocrats exercised nearly complete freedom on their estates. The Reformation radicalized many aristocrats who dominated the parliaments, enabling Protestantism to take hold even against the wishes of the monarch.

In Bohemia (now in the Czech Republic), the Hussite movement in the fourteenth century had rejected papal authority and some of the sacramental authority of the priesthood long before the Protestant Reformation. After the Lutherans and Calvinists attracted adherents in Bohemia, the few surviving Hussites and the new Protestants formed an alliance in 1575, which made common cause against the Catholics. In addition to this formal alliance, substantial numbers of Anabaptists found refuge from persecution in Bohemia and lived in complete freedom on the estates of tolerant landlords who were desperate for settlers to farm their lands.

The religious diversity of Hungary was also remarkable by the standards of the time. By the end of the sixteenth century, much of Hungary's population had accepted some form of Protestantism. Among the German-speaking city dwellers and the Hungarian peasants in western Hungary, Lutheranism prevailed, whereas in eastern Hungary Calvinism was dominant.

No other country was as tolerant of religious variety as Transylvania (now in Romania), largely because of the weak monarchy, which could not have enforced religious uniformity even if the king had wanted to do so. In Transylvania, Unitarianism took hold more firmly than anywhere else. In 1572 the tolerant ruler Prince István Báthory (r. 1571–1586) granted the Unitarians complete legal equality to establish their own churches along with Catholics, Lutherans, and Calvinists—the only place in Europe where equality of religions was achieved. Transylvania was also home to significant communities of Jews, Armenian Christians, and Orthodox Christians.

The sixteenth century was the golden age of the Polish-Lithuanian Commonwealth, the largest territorial unit in Europe. From the Lutheran cities in the German-speaking north to the vast open plains of Great Poland, religious lines often paralleled ethnic or class divisions: Calvinism took hold among the independent-minded nobility while the vast majority of peasants remained loyal to Orthodoxy or Catholicism. Nevertheless, the Commonwealth escaped the religious wars that plagued the Holy Roman Empire. King Sigismund August (r. 1548–1572) declared to the deputies in the Polish parliament, "I am not king

of your consciences," and inaugurated extensive toleration of Protestant churches. Fleeing persecution in other countries, various Anabaptist groups and Unitarians found refuge in Poland. Jews also began to flock to Poland in the sixteenth century where they would eventually create the largest gathering of Jews in Europe.

THE CATHOLIC REFORMATION

■ How did the Catholic Church respond to the unprecedented threat to its dominance of religious authority in the West?

The Catholic Reformation, also known as the Counter Reformation, profoundly revitalized the Catholic Church. The **Catholic Reformation** was a series of efforts to purify the Church. These were not just a reaction to the Protestant Reformation but evolved out of late medieval spirituality, driven by many of the same impulses that stimulated the Protestants.

The Religious Orders in the Catholic Reformation

The new Catholic religious orders of the sixteenth century exhibited a religious vitality that had little to do with the Protestant threat. In fact, none of the new orders began near the centers of Protestantism, such as Germany. Italy, which remained strongly Catholic, produced the largest number of new orders, followed by Spain and France.

CHRONOLOGY: THE DIVERSITY OF PROTESTANTISM

1520	Zwingli declared the People's Priest in Zürich
1534	Parliament in England passes the Acts of Supremacy and Succession
1534–1535	Anabaptist control of Münster, Germany
1535	Execution of John Fisher and Thomas More; first edition of John Calvin's *Institutes of the Christian Religion*
1559–1563	The Elizabethan Settlement of the Anglican Church
1560	Scots Confession

JESUITS: THE SOLDIERS OF GOD   Officially organized in 1540, the Society of Jesus elected Ignatius Loyola (1491–1556) the first General of the Society. Loyola's dynamic personality and intense spirituality gave the new order its distinctive commitment to moral action in the world. Loyola began his career as a courtier to King Ferdinand of Aragon and a soldier. The Society of Jesus preserved some of the values Loyola had acquired as a courtier-soldier—social refinement, loyalty to authority, sense of duty, and high-minded chivalry.

Loyola's personal contribution to religious literature was the *Spiritual Exercises* (1548), which became the foundation of Jesuit practice. Republished in more than 5,000 editions in hundreds of languages, the *Exercises* prescribe a month-long retreat devoted to a series of meditations in which the participant mentally experiences the spiritual life, physical death, and miraculous resurrection of Christ. Much of the power of the *Exercises* derives from the systematic employment of each of the five senses to produce a defined emotional, spiritual, and even physical response. Participants in the *Exercises* seem to hear the blasphemous cries of the soldiers at Christ's crucifixion, feel the terrible agony of his suffering on the cross, and experience the blinding illumination of his resurrection from the dead. Those who participated in the *Exercises* considered the experience life-transforming and usually made a steadfast commitment to serve the Church. As a result, the Jesuit order grew rapidly. At Loyola's death in 1556 there were about 1,000 Jesuits, but by 1700 there were nearly 20,000, and many young men who wished to join had to be turned away because there were insufficient funds to train them.

The Jesuits, like Franciscans and Dominicans, distinguished themselves from other religious orders by ministering to others. They did not wear clerical clothing, and on foreign missions they devoted themselves to learning the language and culture of the peoples they hoped to convert. Jesuits became famous for their loyalty to the pope, and some took a special fourth vow (in addition to the three traditional vows of poverty, chastity, and obedience) to go on a mission if the pope requested it. Many traveled as missionaries to distant parts of the globe, such as China and Japan. In Europe and the Americas the Jesuits established a vast network of colleges. These colleges offered free tuition, which made them open to the poor, and combined a thorough training in languages, humanities, and sciences with religious instruction and moral guidance. They became especially popular because the Jesuit fathers were much more likely to pay personal attention to their students than professors in the established universities. In Europe the Jesuit college system transformed the culture of the Catholic elite. These colleges attracted the sons of the aristocrats and the wealthy who absorbed from the Jesuit instructors the values of Renaissance humanism and the Catholic Reformation.

WOMEN'S ORDERS: "AS IF THEY WERE DEAD"   Creating a ministry that was active in the world was much more difficult for the female orders than for the Jesuits and the other male orders. Women who sought to reinvigorate old orders or found new ones faced hostility from ecclesiastical and civic authorities, who thought women had to be protected by either a husband or the cloister wall. Women in convents were supposed to be entirely separated from the world, "as if they were dead."

The most famous model for convent reform was provided by Teresa of Avila (1515–1582), who wrote a strict new rule for the Carmelites. The new rule required mortifications of the flesh and complete withdrawal from the world. Teresa described her own mystical experiences in her *Autobiography* (1611) and in the *Interior Castle* (1588), a compelling masterpiece in the literature of mysticism. Teresa advocated a very cautious brand of mysticism, which was checked by regular confession and skepticism about extreme acts of self-deprivation. For example, she recognized that a nun who fell into an apparent rapture after extensive fasting was probably just having hallucinations from the hunger.

Many women who willingly chose the religious life thrived in a community of women where they were liberated from the rigors of childbearing and freed from direct male supervision. These women could devote themselves to

THE ECSTASY OF ST. TERESA

Teresa of Avila eloquently expressed the intimate connection between physical and spiritual experiences that was a common feature of Catholic mysticism. Often afflicted by an intense pain in her side, Teresa reported a vision of an angel who thrust a lance tipped with fire into her heart. This "seraphic vision," which became the subject of Gianlorenzo Bernini's famous sculpture in Santa Maria della Vittoria in Rome (1645–1652), epitomized the Catholic Reformation sensibility of understanding spiritual states through physical feelings. In Teresa's case, her extreme bodily deprivations, paralysis, and intense pain conditioned how she experienced the spiritual side of her nature. Many have seen an erotic character to the vision, which may be true, but the vision best demonstrates a profound psychological awareness that bodily and spiritual sensations cannot be precisely distinguished.

cultivating musical or literary talents to a degree that would have been impossible in the outside world. Nuns created their own distinctly female culture, producing a number of learned women and social reformers who had considerable

influence in the arts, education, and charitable work such as nursing.

Paul III, The First Catholic Reformation Pope

Despite the many earlier attempts at reform and the Protestant threat, the Catholic Church was slow to initiate its own reforms because of resistance among bishops and cardinals of the Church hierarchy. More than 20 years after Luther's defiant stand at the Diet of Worms in 1521, Pope Paul III (r. 1534–1549) finally launched a systematic counterattack. As a member of the powerful Farnese family, who had long treated church offices as their private property, Paul seemed an unlikely reformer. But more than any other pope, Paul understood the necessity to respond to Protestantism. It was Pope Paul, for example, who formally approved the Jesuits and began to employ them as missionary soldiers for the Church. To counter Protestantism, Pope Paul III also used three other tools: the Roman Inquisition, the *Index of Forbidden Books*, and, most importantly, the Council of Trent.

In 1542, on the advice of an archconservative faction of cardinals, Paul III reorganized the Roman Inquisition, called the Holy Office. The function of the Inquisition was to inquire into the beliefs of all Catholics primarily to discover indications of heresies, such as those of the Protestants. Jews, for example, were exempt from its authority, although Jews who had converted or been forced to convert to Christianity did fall under the jurisdiction of the Inquisition. There had been other inquisitions, but most had been local or national. The Spanish Inquisition was controlled by the Spanish monarchs, for example. In contrast, the Holy Office came under the direct control of the pope and cardinals and termed itself the Universal Roman Inquisition. Its effective authority did not reach beyond northern and central Italy, but it set the tone for the entire Catholic Reformation Church. The Inquisition subjected defendants to lengthy interrogations and stiff penalties, including prison sentences and even execution in exceptional cases.

A second effort to stop the spread of Protestant ideas led to the *Index of Forbidden Books,* first drawn up in 1549 in Venice, the capital of the publishing industry in Italy. The *Index* censored or banned many books that the Church considered detrimental to the faith and the authority of the Church. Most affected by the strictures were books about theology and philosophy, but the censors also prohibited or butchered books of moral guidance, such as the works of Erasmus, and classics of literature, such as Giovanni Boccaccio's *The Decameron.* The official papal *Index* of 1559 prohibited translations of the Bible into vernacular languages such as Italian because laypeople required a trained intermediary in the person of a priest to interpret and explain the Bible. The Church's protective attitude about biblical interpretation clearly distinguished the Catholic from the Protestant attitude of encouraging widespread Bible reading. It remained possible to buy certain heretical theological books "under the counter," but possessing such books could be dangerous if agents of the Inquisition conducted a raid.

The Council of Trent

By far the most significant of Pope Paul III's contributions to the Catholic Reformation was his call for a general council of the Church, which began to meet in 1545 in Trent on the border between Italy and Germany. The Council of Trent established principles that guided the Catholic Church for the next 400 years.

Between 1545 and 1563 the council met under the auspices of three different popes in three separate sessions, with long intervals of as much as ten years between sessions. The objective of these sessions was to find a way to respond to the Protestant criticisms of the Church, to reassert the authority of the pope, and to launch reforms to guarantee a well-educated and honest clergy.

THE INQUISITION CRITICIZES A WORK OF ART

This painting, now called the *Supper in the House of Levi,* originally depicted the Last Supper when Christ introduced the mass to his apostles. Because there are many figures in it who are not mentioned in the biblical account and the supper appears as if it were a Renaissance banquet, the Inquisitors asked the artist, Paolo Veronese, to answer questions about his intended meaning. Ordered to remove the offending figures, Veronese instead changed the name of the painting to depict the less theologically controversial supper in the house of Levi.

Source: Paolo Verones, "The Feast in the House of Levi". 1573. Oil on Canvas. 18'2" × 41' (5.54 × 12.8 m). Galleria dell' Accademia, Venice. SCALA/Art Resource, NY

THE DEATH OF THE VIRGIN

The Council of Trent enjoined artists to use their art to teach correct doctrine and to move believers to true piety. Religious art had to convey a message simply, directly, and in terms that unlettered viewers could understand. The best Catholic art employed dramatic theatrical effects in lighting and the arrangement of figures to represent deep emotional and spiritual experiences. The Italian painter Caravaggio (1573–1610) most thoroughly expressed the ideal of dramatic spirituality envisioned by the Council. In this image of the death of Virgin Mary, the overhanging drapery evokes a stage curtain as do the lighting effects. The gestures of the apostles and Mary Magdalen imitate those of actors. However, the realism of the scene went too far and got Caravaggio into trouble. The dead Virgin is dressed in red, the color of prostitutes, not her usual blue, and, in fact, Caravaggio used as his model a dead prostitute who had drowned in the Tiber River. In addition, the realism of the corpse offended many.

The decrees of the Council of Trent, which had the force of legislation for the entire Church, defied the Protestants by refusing to yield any ground on the traditional doctrines of the Church. The decrees confirmed the efficacy of all seven of the traditional sacraments, the reality of Purgatory, and the spiritual value of indulgences. In order to provide better supervision of the Church, bishops were ordered to reside in their dioceses. Trent decreed that every diocese should have a seminary to train priests, providing a practical solution to the problem of clerical ignorance.

CHRONOLOGY: THE CATHOLIC REFORMATION

1534	Pontificate of Pope Paul III begins
1540	Founding of the Society of Jesus
1542	Reorganization of the Roman Inquisition or Holy Office
1545	Council of Trent opens
1548	*Spiritual Exercises* of Ignatius Loyola
1549	*Index of Forbidden Books*
1563	Council of Trent concludes

The Council of Trent represented a dramatic reassertion of the authority of the papacy, the bishops, and the priesthood. Yet it had no effect whatsoever in luring Protestants back into the Catholic fold.

CONCLUSION

Competing Understandings

The Reformation permanently divided the West into two discordant religious cultures of Protestant and Catholic. The religious unity of the West achieved during the Middle Ages had been fruit of many centuries of diligent effort by missionaries, monks, popes, and crusading knights. That unity was lost through the conflicts between, on the one hand, reformers, city magistrates, princes, and kings who wanted to control their own affairs and, on the other, popes who continued to cling to the medieval concept of the papal monarchy. In the West, Christians no longer saw themselves as dedicated to serving God in the same way as all other Christians. Instead, Catholics and Protestants emphasized their differences.

The differences between these two cultures had lasting implications for how people understood and accepted the authority of the Church and the state, how they conducted their family life, and how they formed their own identities as individuals and as members of a larger community. The next Chapter 15 will explore all of these themes.

The division also had tragic consequences. From the late sixteenth century to the late seventeenth century, European states tended to create diplomatic alliances along this ideological and religious divide, allowed disputes about doctrine to prevent peaceful reconciliation, and conducted wars as if they were a fulfillment of God's plan. Even after the era of religious warfare ended, Protestant and Catholic cultures remained ingrained in all aspects of life, influencing not just government policy but painting, music, literature, and education. This division reshaped the West into a place of intense religious and ideological conflict, which by the eighteenth century drove many thoughtful people to reject the traditional forms of Christianity altogether and to advocate religious toleration and the separation of Church and state, ideas that were barely conceivable in the sixteenth century.

KEY TERMS

Protestant Reformation
Christian humanists
northern Renaissance
justification by faith
95 theses
priesthood of all believers
Religious Peace of
   Augsburg

Magisterial Reformation
Radical Reformation
predestination
calling
Anabaptism
Spiritualists
Unitarians
Catholic Reformation

CHAPTER QUESTIONS

1. What caused the religious rebellion that began in German-speaking lands and spread to much of northern Europe? (page 427)
2. How did the Lutheran Reformation create a new kind of religious culture? (page 431)
3. How and why did Protestant denominations multiply to such an extent in northern Europe and Britain? (page 439)
4. How did the Catholic Church respond to the unprecedented threat to its dominance of religious authority in the West? (page 450)

TAKING IT FURTHER

1. How did the critical and historical approach of the humanists alter thinking about religion?
2. Compare Catholic and Protestant religious cultures as they were formulated in the sixteenth century.
3. Why did the Protestant Reformation cause so much opposition and even violence?

✔—Practice on MyHistoryLab

15

The Age of Confessional Division

■ The Peoples of Early Modern Europe   ■ Disciplining the People   ■ Hunting Witches
■ The Confessional States   ■ States and Confessions in Eastern Europe

ON JULY 10, 1584, CATHOLIC EXTREMIST FRANÇOIS GUION, WITH A brace of pistols hidden under his cloak, surprised William the Silent, the Prince of Orange, as he was leaving the dining hall of his palace and shot him at point-blank range. William led the Protestant nobility in the Netherlands, which was in revolt against the Catholic king of Spain. Guion masqueraded as a Protestant for seven years in order to ingratiate himself with William's party, and before the assassination he consulted three Catholic priests who confirmed the religious merit of his plan. Spain's representative in the Netherlands, the Duke of Parma, had offered a reward of 25,000 crowns to anyone who killed William; at the moment of the assassination four other potential assassins were in Delft trying to gain access to the Prince of Orange.

The murder of William the Silent exemplified an ominous figure in Western civilization—the religiously motivated assassin. There had been many assassinations before the late sixteenth century, but those assassins tended to be motivated by the desire to gain political power or to avenge a personal or family injury. Religion hardly ever supplied a motive. In the wake of the Reformation, killing a political leader of the opposing faith to serve God's plan became all too common. The assassination of William illustrated patterns of violence that have since become the *modus operandi* of the political

assassin—the use of deception to gain access to the victim, the vulnerability of leaders who wish to mingle with the public, the lethal potential of easily concealed pistols (a new weapon at that time), the corruption of politics through vast sums of money, and the obsessive hostility of zealots against their perceived enemies. The widespread acrimony among the varieties of Christian faith created a climate of religious extremism during the late sixteenth and early seventeenth centuries.

Religious extremism was just one manifestation of an anxiety that pervaded European society at the time—a fear of hidden forces controlling human events. In an attempt to curb that anxiety, the European monarchs formulated their politics based on the **confessions** of faith, or statements of religious doctrine, peculiar to Catholics or the various forms of Protestantism. During this age of confessional division, European countries polarized along confessional lines, and governments persecuted followers of minority religions, whom they saw as threats to public security. Anxious believers everywhere were consumed with pleasing an angry God, but when they tried to find God within themselves, many Christians seemed only to find the Devil in others.

The religious controversies of the age of confessional division redefined the West. During the Middle Ages, the West came to be identified with

PROCESSION OF THE CATHOLIC LEAGUE

During the last half of the sixteenth century, Catholics and Protestants in France formed armed militias or leagues. Bloody confrontations between these militias led to prolonged civil wars. In this 1590 procession of the French Catholic League, armed monks joined soldiers and common citizens in a demonstration of force.

the practice of Roman Catholic Christianity. The Renaissance added to that identity an appreciation of pre-Christian history going back to Greek and Roman Antiquity. The Reformation of the early sixteenth century eroded the unity of Christian Europe by dividing the West into Catholic and Protestant camps. This division was especially pronounced in western Europe, but less so in eastern Europe because it did not create confessional states. During the late sixteenth and seventeenth centuries, governments reinforced religious divisions and attempted to unify their peoples around a common set of beliefs. How did the encounter between the confessions and the state transform Europe into religiously driven camps?

THE PEOPLES OF EARLY MODERN EUROPE

■ How did the expanding population and price revolution exacerbate religious and political tensions?

During the tenth century if a Rus had wanted to see the sights of Paris—assuming he had even heard of Paris—he could have left Kiev and walked under the shade of trees all the way to France, so extensive were the forests and so sparse the human settlements of northern Europe. By the end of the thirteenth century, the wanderer from Kiev would have needed a hat to protect him on the shadeless journey. Instead of human settlements forming little islands in a sea of forests, the forests were by then islands in a sea of villages and farms, and from almost any church tower the sharp-eyed traveler could have seen other church towers, each marking a nearby village or town. At the end of the thirteenth century, the European continent had become completely settled by a dynamic, growing population, which had cleared the forests for farms.

During the fourteenth century all of that changed. A series of crises—periodic famines, the catastrophic Black Death, and a general economic collapse—left the villages and towns of Europe intact, but a third or more of the population was gone. In that period of desolation, many villages looked like abandoned movie sets, and the cities did not have enough people to fill in the empty spaces between the central market square and the city walls. Fields that had once been put to the plow to feed the hungry children of the thirteenth century were neglected and overrun with bristles and brambles. During the fifteenth century a general European depression and recurrent epidemics kept the population stagnant.

In the sixteenth century the population began to rebound as European agriculture shifted from subsistence to commercial farming.

The sudden swell in human numbers brought dramatic and destabilizing consequences that contributed to pervasive anxiety.

The Population Recovery

During a period historical demographers call the "long sixteenth century" (ca. 1480–1640), the population of Europe began to grow consistently again for the first time since the late thirteenth century. As shown in Figure 15.1, *European Population*, in 1340 on the brink of the Black Death, Europe had about 74 million inhabitants, or 17 percent of the world's total. By 1400 the population of all of Europe had dropped to 52 million or 14 percent of the world's total. Over the course of the long sixteenth century, Europe's population grew to 77.9 million, just barely surpassing the pre–Black Death level.

Figure 15.2, *European Population, 1500–1600*, depicts some representative population figures for the larger European countries during the sixteenth century. Two important facts emerge from these data. The first is the much greater rate of growth in northern Europe compared with southern Europe. England grew by 83 percent, Poland grew by 76 percent, and even the tiny, war-torn Netherlands gained 58 percent. During the same period Italy grew

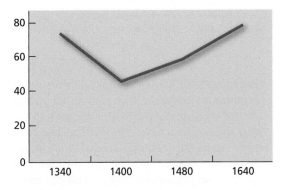

❙ FIGURE 15.1 European Population in Millions

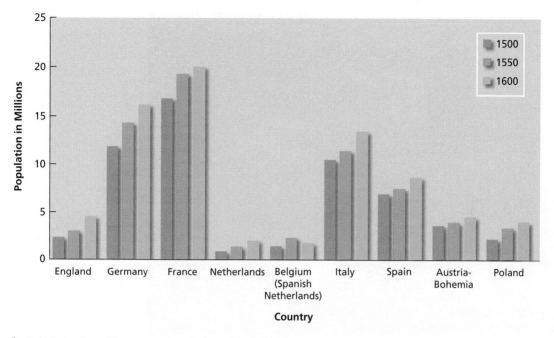

FIGURE 15.2 European Population, 1500–1600

Source: Jan de Vries, "Population," In *Handbook of European History 1400–1600: Late Middle Ages, Renaissance and Reformation,* Vol. 1: *Structures and Assertions,* (eds.) Thomas A. Brady, Jr., Heiko A. Oberman, and James D. Tracy (1994), Table 1, 13. Copyright © 1994 by Brill Academic Publishers. Reproduced with permission of Brill Academic Publishers via Copyright Clearance Center.

by only 25 percent and Spain by 19 percent. These trends signal a massive, permanent shift of demographic and economic power from the Mediterranean countries of Italy and Spain to northern, especially northwestern, Europe. The second fact to note from these data is the overwhelming size of France, which was home to about a quarter of Europe's population. Once France recovered from its long wars of religion, its demographic superiority overwhelmed competing countries and made it the dominant power in Europe, permanently eclipsing its chief rival, Spain.

What explains the growth in the population? To a large extent, the transformation from subsistence to commercial agriculture in certain regions of Europe made it possible. Peasants who practiced subsistence farming consumed about 80 percent of everything they raised, and what little was left over went

almost entirely to the landlord as feudal dues and to the church as tithing—the obligation to give to God one-tenth of everything earned or produced. Peasant families lived on the edge of existence. During the sixteenth century, subsistence agriculture gave way to commercial crops, especially wheat, which was sold in town markets and the great cities such as London, Antwerp, Amsterdam, Paris, Milan, Venice, and Barcelona. As commercial agriculture spread, the population grew because the rural population was better fed and more prosperous.

The amount of land available, however, could not provide enough work for the growing farm population. As a result, the landless were forced to take to the road to find their fortunes. These vagabonds, as they were called, exemplified the social problems that emerged from the uneven distribution of

THE RISE OF COMMERCIAL AGRICULTURE

During the sixteenth century commercial agriculture began to produce significant surpluses for the expanding population of the cities. This scene depicts a windmill for grinding grain and a train of wagons hauling produce from the country to be marketed in a city.

wealth created by the new commerce. Because large-scale migrations to the Americas had not yet begun, except from Spain, the landless had few options other than to seek opportunities in a city.

The Thriving Cities

By the 1480s cities began to grow, but the growth was uneven with the most dramatic growth occurring in the cities of the North, especially London, Antwerp, and Amsterdam. The surpluses of the countryside, both human and agricultural, flowed into the cities during the sixteenth century. Compared with even the prosperous rural villages, the cities seemed incomparably rich. Half-starved vagabonds marveled at shops piled high with food (white bread, fancy pies, fruit, casks of wine, roasting meats); they wistfully passed taverns full of drunken, laughing citizens; and they begged for alms in front of magnificent, marble-faced churches.

Every aspect of the cities exhibited dramatic contrasts between the rich and poor, who lived on the same streets and often in different parts of the same houses. Around 1580 Christian missionaries brought a Native American chief to the French city of Rouen. Through an interpreter he was asked what impressed him the most about European cities, so unlike the villages of North America. He replied that he was astonished that the rag-clad, emaciated men and women who crowded the streets did not grab the plump, well-dressed rich people by the throat.

City officials recognized the social problems caused by the disparities in wealth. Every city maintained storehouses of grain and regulated the price of bread and the size of a loaf so that the poor could be fed. The impulse to feed the poor was less the result of humanitarian motives than fear of a hungry mob. Cities guarded carefully against revolts and crime. Even for petty crime, punishment was swift, sure, and gruesome. The beggar who stole a loaf of bread from a baker's cart had his hand amputated on a chopping block in the market square. A shabbily dressed girl who grabbed a lady's glittering trinket had her nose cut off so that she could never attract a man. A burglar was tortured, drawn, and quartered, with his severed head impaled on an iron spike at the town gate as a warning to others.

However talented or enterprising, new arrivals to the city had very limited opportunities. They could hardly start up their own business because all production was strictly controlled by the guilds, which were associations of merchants or artisans organized to protect their interests. Guilds rigidly regulated their membership and required an apprenticeship of many years. Guilds also prohibited technological innovations, guaranteed certain standards of workmanship, and did not allow branching out into new lines. Given the limited opportunities for new arrivals, immigrant men and women begged on the streets or took charity from the public dole. The men picked up any heavy-labor jobs they could find. Both men and women became servants, a job that paid poorly but at least guaranteed regular meals.

Among the important social achievements of both Protestant and Catholic Reformations were efforts to address the problems of the destitute urban poor, who constituted at least a quarter of the population, even in the best of times. In Catholic countries such as Italy, Spain, southern Germany, and France, there was an enormous expansion of credit banks, which were financed by charitable contributions in order to provide small loans to the poor. Catholic cities established convents for poor young women who were at risk of falling into prostitution and for women who had retired from the sex trade. Catholic and Protestant cities established orphanages, hospitals for the sick, hospices for the dying, and public housing. Both Catholic and Protestant cities attempted to distinguish between the "honest" poor—those who were disabled and truly deserving—and the "dishonest" poor who were thought to be malingerers. Protestant cities established poorhouses, which segregated the poor, subjected them to prisonlike discipline, and forced the able-bodied to work.

The more comfortable classes of the cities enjoyed large palaces and luxurious lifestyles. They hired extensive staffs of servants, feasted on meat and fine wines, and purchased exotic imports such as silk cloth, spices from the East, and, in the Mediterranean cities, slaves from eastern Europe, the Middle East, or Africa. Rich merchants maintained their status by marrying within their own class, monopolizing municipal offices, and educating their children in the newly fashionable humanist schools. The wealthy of the cities were the bastions of social stability. They possessed the financial resources and economic skills to protect themselves from the worst consequences of economic instability, especially the corrosive wave of price inflation that struck the West after about 1540.

The Price Revolution

Price inflation became so pervasive during the last half of the sixteenth century that it contributed to the widespread fear that hidden forces controlled events. After a long period of falling or stable prices that stretched back to the fourteenth century, Europe experienced sustained price increases, beginning around 1540, in what historians called the **Price Revolution**. The inflation lasted a century, forcing major economic and social changes that permanently altered the face of Western society. During this period overall prices across Europe multiplied five- or sixfold.

What caused the inflation? The basic principle is simple. The price paid for goods and services is fundamentally the result of the relationship between *supply* and *demand*. If the number of children who need to be fed grows faster than the supply of grain, the price of bread goes up. This happens simply because mothers who can afford it will be willing to pay a higher price to save their children from hunger. If good harvests allow the supply of grain to increase at a greater rate than the demand for bread, then prices go down. Two other factors influence price. One is the *amount of money in circulation.* If the amount of gold or silver available to make coins increases, there is more money in circulation. When more money is circulating, people can buy more things, which creates the same effect as an increase in demand—prices go up. The other factor is called the *velocity of money in circulation,* which refers to the number of times money changes hands to buy things. When people buy commodities with greater frequency, it has the same effect as increasing the amount of money in circulation or of increasing demand—again, prices go up.

The precise combination of these factors in causing the great Price Revolution of the sixteenth century has long been a matter of considerable debate. Most historians would now agree that the primary cause of inflation was population growth, which increased demand for all kinds of basic commodities, such as bread and woolen cloth for clothing. As Europe's population finally began to recover, it meant that more people needed and desired to buy more things. This explanation is most obvious for commodities that people need to survive, such as grain to make bread. These commodities have what economists call *inelastic demand,* that is, consumers do not have a great deal of discretion in purchasing them. Everybody has to eat. The commodities that people could survive without if the price is too high are said to have *elastic demand,* such as dancing shoes and lace collars. In England between 1540 and 1640 overall prices rose by 490 percent. More telling, however, is that the price of grain (inelastic demand) rose by a stunning 670 percent, whereas the price of luxury goods (elastic demand) rose much less, by 204

percent. Thus, inflation hurt the poor, who needed to feed their children, more than the rich, whose desires were more elastic.

Monetary factors also contributed to inflation. The Portuguese brought in significant amounts of gold from Africa, and newly opened mines in central Europe increased the amount of silver by fivefold as early as the 1520s. The discovery in 1545 of the fabulous silver mine of Potosí (in present-day Bolivia) brought to Europe a flood of silver, which Spain used to finance its costly wars. As inflation began to eat away at royal incomes, financially strapped monarchs all across western Europe debased their currency because they believed, mistakenly, that producing more coins containing less silver would buy more. In fact, the minting of more coins meant each coin was worth less and would buy less. In England, for example, debasement was a major source of inflation during the 1540s and 1550s.

The Price Revolution severely weakened governments. Most monarchs derived their incomes from their own private lands and taxes on property. As inflation took hold, property taxes proved dangerously inadequate to cover royal expenses. Even frugal monarchs such as England's Elizabeth I (r. 1558–1603) were forced to take extraordinary measures, in her case to sell off royal lands. Spendthrift monarchs faced disaster. Spain was involved in the costly enterprise of nearly continuous war during the sixteenth century. To pay for the wars, Charles V resorted to a form of deficit financing in which he borrowed money by issuing *juros,* which provided lenders an annuity yielding between three and seven percent on the amount of the principal. By the 1550s, however, the annuity payments of the *juros* consumed half of the royal revenues. Charles's son, Philip II, inherited such an alarming situation that in 1557, the year after he assumed the throne, he was forced to declare bankruptcy. Philip continued to fight expensive wars and borrow wildly, and thus failed to get his financial house in order. He declared bankruptcy again in 1575 and 1596. Philip squandered

Spain's wealth, impoverishing his own subjects through burdensome taxes and contributing to inflation by borrowing at high rates of interest and debasing the coinage. Although the greatest military power of the sixteenth century, Spain sowed the seeds of its own decline by fighting on borrowed money.

Probably the most serious consequence of the Price Revolution was that the hidden force of inflation caused widespread human suffering. During the late sixteenth and early seventeenth centuries, people felt their lives threatened, but they did not know the source and so they imagined all kinds of secret powers at work, especially supernatural ones. The suspicion of religious differences created by the Reformation provided handy, if utterly false, explanations for what had gone wrong. Catholics suspected Protestants, Protestants suspected Catholics, both suspected Jews, and they all worried about witches. Authorities sought to relieve this widespread anxiety by looking in all the wrong places—disciplining the populace, hunting for witches, and battling against enemies from the opposite side of the confessional divide.

DISCIPLINING THE PEOPLE

■ How did religious and political authorities attempt to discipline the people?

The first generation of the Protestant and Catholic Reformations had been devoted to doctrinal disputes and to either rejecting or defending papal authority. Subsequent generations of reformers faced the formidable task of building the institutions that would firmly establish a Protestant or Catholic religious culture. Leaders of all religious confessions, whether Lutheran, Calvinist, Catholic, or Anglican, attempted to revitalize the Christian community by disciplining nonconformists, enforcing moral rigor, and attacking popular culture. Discipline required cooperation between church and secular authorities, but it was not entirely imposed from above. Many people wholeheartedly cooperated with moral correction and even encouraged reformers to go further. Others actively or resentfully resisted it.

Establishing Confessional Identities

Between 1560 and 1650 religious confessions reshaped European culture. A confession consisted of the adherents to a particular statement of religious doctrine—the Confession of Augsburg for Lutherans, the Helvetic Confessions for Calvinists, the Thirty-Nine Articles for Anglicans, and the decrees of the Council of Trent for Catholics.

The process of establishing confessional identities did not happen overnight. During the second half of the sixteenth century, Lutherans turned from the struggle to survive within the hostile Holy Roman Empire to building Lutheranism wherever it was the chosen religion of the local prince. They had to recruit clergy and provide each clergyman with a university education, which was made possible by scholarship endowments from the Lutheran princes of the empire. Once established, the Lutheran clergy became a branch of the civil bureaucracy, received a government stipend, and enforced the will of the prince. Calvinist states followed a similar process, but where they were in a minority, as in France, Calvinists had to go it alone, and the state often discriminated against them. In those places confessional identities were established in opposition to the state and the dominant confession. Catholics responded with their own aggressive plan of training new clergymen, educating the laity, and reinforcing the bond between church and state. Just as with the Lutheran princes, Catholic princes in the Holy Roman Empire associated conformity to Catholicism with loyalty to themselves, making religion a pillar of the state.

Everywhere in western Europe (except for Ireland, the Netherlands, a few places in the Holy Roman Empire, and for a time France) the only openly practiced religion was the religion of the state. The eastern European states of Poland, Bohemia, Hungary, and Transylvania offered greater religious freedom.

Regulating the Family

One matter on which Calvinists, Lutherans, and Catholics agreed was that the foundation of society should be the authority fathers had over their families. This principle of patriarchy, as discussed in Chapter 12, was a traditional *ideal*. The *reality* of high mortality from disease, however, destabilized family life during the fifteenth and sixteenth centuries. Unstable families often lacked fathers and senior males, making it difficult if not impossible to sustain patriarchy in daily life. The confessions that emerged from the Reformation attempted to combat this trend by reinforcing patriarchy. According to an anonymous treatise published in 1586 in Calvinist Nassau, the three pillars of Christian society were the church, the state, and the household. This proposition made the father's authority parallel to the authority of the clergy and king. To enforce patriarchy, ecclesiastical and secular authorities regulated sexuality and the behavior of children. The authorities' goal seems to have been to encourage self-discipline as well as respect for elders. Self-discipline reached into all aspects of life from sexual behavior to table manners. (See *Encounters and Transformations* in this chapter.)

Despite the near universal acceptance of the theory of patriarchy, the reality of the father's and husband's authority varied a great deal. Since the early Middle Ages in northwestern Europe—in Britain, Scandinavia, the Netherlands, northern France, and western Germany—couples tended to wait to marry until their mid- or late twenties, well beyond the age of sexual maturity. The couple had to be economically independent before they married, which meant both had to accumulate savings or the husband needed to inherit from his deceased father before he could marry. When

they did finally marry, they established their own household separate from either of their parents. Husbands were usually only two or three years older than their wives, and that proximity of age tended to make those relationships more cooperative and less authoritarian than the theory of patriarchy might suggest. By contrast, in southern Europe, men in their late twenties or thirties married teenaged women over whom they exercised authority by virtue of the age difference. In eastern Europe, both spouses married in their teens and resided in one of the parental households for many years, which placed both spouses for extended periods under the authority of one of their fathers.

The marriage pattern in northwestern Europe required prolonged sexual restraint by young men and women until they were economically self-sufficient. In addition to individual self-control, sexual restraint required social control by church and secular authorities. Their efforts seem to have been generally successful. For example, in sixteenth-century Geneva, where the elders were especially wary about sexual sins, the rates of illegitimate births were extremely low. The elders were particularly concerned to discipline women and keep them subservient. In 1584 in another Swiss town, Calvinist elders excommunicated Charlotte Arbaleste and her entire household because she wore her hair in curls, which the elders thought were too alluring.

Northwestern European families also tended to be smaller, as married couples began to space their children through birth control and family planning. These self-restrained couples practiced withdrawal, the rhythm method, or abstinence. When mothers no longer relied on wet nurses and nursed their own infants, often for long periods, they also reduced their chances of becoming pregnant. Thus, limiting family size became the social norm in northwestern Europe, especially among the educated and urban middle classes. Protestant families tended to have fewer children than Catholic families, but Catholics in this region also practiced some form of birth control, even though Church law prohibited all forms except abstinence.

The moral status of marriage also demonstrated regional variations during the early modern period. Protestants no longer considered husbands and wives morally inferior to celibate monks and nuns, and the wives of preachers in Protestant communities certainly had a respected social role never granted to the concubines of priests. But the favorable Protestant attitude toward marriage did not necessarily translate into a positive attitude toward women. In Germany the numerous books of advice, called the Father of the House literature, encouraged families to subordinate the individual interests of servants, children, and the mother to the dictates of the father, who was advised to be fair but who always had to be obeyed. Even if a wife was brutally treated by her husband, she could neither find help from authorities nor expect a divorce.

Discipline also played a large role in raising children. The *Disquisition on the Spiritual Condition of Infants* (1618) pointed out that because of original sin, babies were naturally evil. The godly responsibility of the father was to break the will of his evil offspring, taming them so that they could be turned away from sin toward virtue. The very title of a 1591 Calvinist treatise revealed the strength of the evil-child argument: *On Disciplining Children: How the Disobedient, Evil, and Corrupted Youth of These Anxious Last Days Can Be Bettered.* The treatise advised that the mother's role should be limited to her biological function of giving birth. In order to break the will of their infants, mothers were encouraged to wean them early and turn them over for a strict upbringing by their fathers. It directed fathers to be vigilant so that their wives did not corrupt the children, because women "love to accept strange, false beliefs, and go about with benedictions and witches' handiwork."[1]

THE DOMESTIC IDEAL

During the late sixteenth and seventeenth centuries, idealized depictions of harmonious family life became very popular, especially in the Netherlands. This painting by Pieter De Hooch is a prime example of the simple pleasures of domesticity. A young child opens the door to a bedroom while her mother is making a bed.

Source: Pieter de Hooch (Dutch 1629–1684), "The Bedroom" ca. 1658/1660. Oil on canvas. 20" × 23 1/2" (51.0 × 60.0 cm). Widener Collection. 1942.9.33. Photograph © Board of Trustees, National Gallery of Art, Washington, D.C.

JUSTICE IN HISTORY

The *Auto-da-Fé:* The Power of Penance

Performed in Spain and Portugal from the sixteenth to eighteenth centuries, the *auto-da-fé* merged the judicial processes of the state with the sacramental rituals of the Catholic Church. An *auto* took place at the end of a judicial investigation conducted by the inquisitors of the Church after the defendants had been found guilty of a sin or crime. The term **auto-da-fé** means "act of faith," and the goal was to persuade or force a person who had been judged guilty to repent and confess. Organized through the cooperation of ecclesiastical and secular authorities, autos-da-fé brought together an assortment of sinners, criminals, and heretics for a vast public rite that dramatized the essential elements of the sacrament of penance: *contrition,* by which the sinner recognized and felt sorry for the sin; *confession,* which required the sinner to admit the sin to a priest; and *satisfaction* or *punishment,* by which the priest absolved the sinner and enacted some kind of penalty. The auto-da-fé transformed penance, especially confession and satisfaction, into a spectacular affirmation of the faith and a manifestation of divine justice.

The *auto* symbolically anticipated the Last Judgment. By suffering bodily pain in this life the soul might be relieved from worse punishments in the next. Officers of the Inquisition forced the sinners, convicts, and heretics, now considered penitents, to march in a procession that went through the streets of the city from the cathedral to the town hall or place of punishment. These processions would typically include some 30 or 40 penitents, but in moments of crisis they could be far larger. In Toledo in 1486 there were three *autos*—one parading 750 penitents and two displaying some 900 each.

A 1655 *auto* in Córdoba illustrates the symbolic character of the rites. Soldiers carried torches to light the pyre for those to be burnt. Following them in a procession came three bigamists who wore on their heads conical miters or hats painted with representations of their sin, four witches whose miters depicted devils, and three criminals with harnesses around their necks to demonstrate their status as captives. The sinners carried unlit candles to represent their lack of faith. Criminals who had escaped arrest were represented in the procession by effigies made in their likeness; for those who had died before punishment, effigies were carried in their coffins. The marching sinners appeared before their neighbors and fellow citizens stripped of the normal indicators of status, dressed only in the emblems of their sins. Among them walked a few who wore the infamous *sanbenitos,* a kind of tunic or vest with a yellow strip down the back, and a conical hat painted with flames. These were the *relajados,* the unrepentant or relapsed sinners.

The procession ended in the town square at a platform on which the sinners performed their public penances as on the stage of a theater. Forced to their knees, priests asked the penitents to confess and to plead for readmission into the bosom of the church. For those who did confess, a herald announced the sentence that would rescue them from the pains of Purgatory and the flames of the *auto.* The sentence required them to join a penitential procession for a certain number of Fridays, perform self-flagellation in public, or wear a badge of shame for a prescribed period of time. Those who failed to confess faced a more immediate sentence.

The most horrendous scenes of suffering awaited the *relajados.* If holdouts confessed prior to the reading of the sentence, then the *auto* was a success, a triumph of the Christian faith over its enemies. Therefore, priests attempted everything that they could to elicit confessions, including haranguing, humiliating, and torturing the accused until their stubborn will broke. If the accused finally confessed after the herald read the sentence, then the executioner would strangle them before burning, but if they held out to the very end, the executioner lit the flames while

▌ *AUTO-DA-FÉ* IN LISBON

they were still living. From the ecclesiastics' point of view, the refusal to confess was a disaster for the entire Church because the flames of the pyre opened a window into Hell. They would certainly prefer to see the Church's authority acknowledged through confession than to see the power of Satan manifest in such a public fashion.

Eyewitnesses reported that crowds watched the violence of the autos-da-fé with silent attention in a mood of deep dread, not so much of the inquisitors, it seems, as for the inevitability of the final day of divine judgment that would arrive for them all. The core assumption of the auto-da-fé was that bodily pain could save a soul from damnation. As one contemporary witness put it, the inquisitors removed "through external ritual [the sinners'] internal crimes." Church authorities assumed that the public ritual framework for the sacrament of penance would have a salutary effect on those who witnessed the *auto* by encouraging them to repent before they too faced divine judgment.

For Discussion

1. How did the auto-da-fé contribute to the formation of an individual and collective sense of being a Catholic?

2. In the auto-da-fé, inflicting physical pain was more than punishment. How was pain understood to have been socially and religiously useful?

Taking It Further

Flynn, Maureen. "Mimesis of the Last Judgment: The Spanish *Auto da fé,*" *Sixteenth Century Journal* 22 (1991): 281–297. The best analysis of the religious significance of the auto-da-fé.

Flynn, Maureen. "The Spectacle of Suffering in Spanish Streets," In Barbara A. Hanawalt and Kathryn L. Reyerson (eds.), *City and Spectacle in Medieval Europe* (1994). In this fascinating article Flynn analyzes the spiritual value of physical pain.

ENCOUNTERS AND TRANSFORMATIONS

The Introduction of the Table Fork: The New Sign of Western Civilization

Sometime in the sixteenth century, western Europeans encountered a new tool that initiated a profound and lasting transformation in Western society: the table fork. Before the table fork, people dined in a way that, to our modern sensibilities, seems disgusting. Members of the upper classes indulged themselves by devouring meat in enormous quantities. Whole rabbits, lambs, and pigs roasted on a spit were placed before diners. A quarter of veal or venison or even an entire roast beef, complete with its head, might be heaved onto the table. Diners used knives to cut off a piece of meat that they then ate with their hands, allowing the juices to drip down their arms. They used the long sleeves of their shirts to wipe meat juices, sweat, and spittle from their mouths and faces. These banquets celebrated the direct physical contact between the body of the dead animal and the bodies of the diners themselves who touched, handled, chewed, and swallowed it.

During the sixteenth century, puritanical reformers who were trying to abolish the cruder aspects of popular culture also promoted new table manners.

THE INTRODUCTION OF THE TABLE FORK
During the late sixteenth century the refinement of manners among the upper classes focused on dining. No innovation was more revolutionary than the spread of the use of the table fork. Pictured here is the travel cutlery, including two table forks, of Queen Elizabeth I.

New implements made certain that diners did not come into direct physical contact with their food before they placed it in their mouths. In addition to napkins—which came into widespread use to replace shirt sleeves for wiping the mouth—table forks appeared on upper-class tables. It became impolite to transfer food directly from the common serving plate to the mouth. Food first had to go onto each individual's plate and then be cut into small portions and raised to the mouth. A French treatise of 1672 warned that "meat must never be touched…by hand, not even while eating."[2]

This prohibition had nothing to do with cleanliness because bacteria were not discovered until the end of the nineteenth century. The use of the table fork had more to do with civility than hygiene. Certain foods, such as bread or many fruits such as cherries, were and still are always eaten with the hands. In determining when to use a fork it was not cleanliness that mattered, but the kind of food consumed. Forks enabled sixteenth-century diners to avoid their growing sense of discomfort with the textures and juices of meats that reminded them of an animal's flesh and blood.

Forks, then, enabled cultured people to distance themselves from the dead animal that they were eating. More generally, the spreading use of the fork was part of a set of changes linked to growing revulsion with the more physical aspects of human nature, such as reproduction—or the killing and consumption of animals. Just as sixteenth-century church authorities sought to regulate sexuality, so table manners regulated meat eating.

Paradoxically, the civility that resulted from the use of the table fork both created and eroded social divisions. Eating meat with a fork became one more way for those in the upper social ranks to distinguish themselves from the "uncivilized" masses below. Yet everyone—regardless of their social origins—could learn how to use a fork. A clerk or governess could disguise a humble background simply by learning how to eat properly. Gradually—very gradually—behavior replaced birth as a marker of "good breeding." In the end, the transformations that occurred in Western society because of its encounter with the table fork—the blurring of class distinctions and creation of a universal code of manners—were so gradual and subtle that few of us who use a table fork daily are even aware of its profound significance.

For Discussion

How do manners, both good and bad, communicate messages to other people? Why is it important to have good manners?

HUNTING WITCHES

■ Why did people in the sixteenth century think witches were a threat?

The most catastrophic manifestation of the widespread anxiety of the late sixteenth and seventeenth centuries was the great **witch-hunt**. The judicial prosecution of alleged witches in either church or secular courts dramatically increased about the middle of the sixteenth century and lasted until the late seventeenth, when the number of witchcraft trials rapidly diminished and stopped entirely in most of Europe.

Throughout this period, people accepted the reality of two kinds of **magic.** The first kind was natural magic, such as the practice of alchemy or astrology, which involved the manipulation of occult forces believed to exist in nature. The fundamental assumption of natural magic was that everything in nature is alive. The trained magician could coerce the occult forces in nature to do his bidding. During the Renaissance many humanists and scientific thinkers were drawn to natural magic because of its promise of power over nature. Natural magic, in fact, had some practical uses. Alchemists, for example, devoted themselves to discovering what they called the "philosopher's stone," the secret of transmuting base metals into gold. In practice this meant that they learned how to imitate the appearance of gold, a very useful skill for counterfeiting coins or reducing the content of precious metals in legal coins. Natural magic did not imply any kind of contact with devils. Most practitioners of natural magic desired to achieve good, and many considered it the highest form of curative medicine.

Many people of the sixteenth and seventeenth centuries also believed in a second kind of magic—demonic magic. The practitioner of this kind of magic—usually but not always a female witch—called upon evil spirits to gain access to power. Demonic magic was generally understood as a way to work harm by ritual means. Belief in the reality of harmful magic can be found in the Bible and had been widespread for centuries, but only in the fifteenth century did ecclesiastical and secular authorities, convinced that large groups of people were engaging in such heretical practices, prosecute them in large numbers. By the sixteenth century the Protestants' literal readings of the Bible and the disorienting conflicts of the Reformation contributed to fears about witches.

People in many different places—from shepherds in the mountains of Switzerland to Calvinist ministers in the lowlands of Scotland—thought they perceived the work of witches in human and natural events. The alleged practice of witchcraft took two forms: *maleficia* (doing harm by magical means) and *diabolism* (worshiping the devil). There were many kinds of *maleficia*, including coercing an unwilling lover by sprinkling dried menstrual blood in his food, sickening a pig by cursing it, burning a barn after marking it with a hex sign, bringing wasting diarrhea to a child by reciting a spell, and killing an enemy by stabbing a wax statue of him.

Midwives and women who specialized in healing were especially vulnerable to accusations of witchcraft. The intention behind a particular action they might have performed was often obscure, making it difficult to distinguish between magic designed to bring beneficial results, such as the cure of a child, and *maleficia* designed to bring harmful ones. With the high

infant mortality rates of the sixteenth and seventeenth centuries, performing magical rituals for a sick baby could be very risky. The logic of witchcraft beliefs implied that a bad ending must have been caused by bad intentions.

While some people certainly attempted to practice *maleficia,* the second and far more serious kind of ritual practice associated with demonic magic, diabolism, certainly never took place. The theory behind diabolism was that the alleged witch made a pact with the Devil, by which she received her magical power, and worshiped him as her god.

The most influential witchcraft treatise, *The Hammer of Witches* (1486), had an extensive discussion of the ceremony of the pact. After the prospective witch had declared her intention to enter his service, Satan appeared to her, often in the alluring form of a handsome young man who offered her rewards, including a demonic lover, called an *incubus*. To obtain these inducements, the witch was obligated to renounce her allegiance to Christ, usually signified by stomping on the cross. The Devil then rebaptized the witch, guaranteeing that her soul belonged to him. To signify that she was one of his own, the Devil marked her body in a hidden place, creating a sign, which could easily be confused with a birthmark or blemish. To an inquisitor or judge, a mark on the skin that did not bleed and was insensitive to pain when pierced with a long pin often confirmed the suspicion that she was a witch.

After making the pact witches allegedly gathered in large numbers to worship the devil at nocturnal assemblies known as sabbaths. The devil was believed to have given them the power to fly to these gatherings. At these assemblies, so it was claimed, witches killed and ate babies, danced naked, and had promiscuous sexual relations with other witches and demons. The belief that witches attended sabbaths, which judicial authorities confirmed by forcing them to confess under severe torture, explains why witch-hunting took a high toll in human life. Between 1450 and 1750, approximately 100,000 people in Europe

BURNING OF A WITCH

Authorities burned a young woman accused of witchcraft, Anne Hendricks, in Amsterdam in 1571.

were tried for witchcraft, and about 50,000 were executed. Approximately half of the trials took place in the German-speaking lands of the Holy Roman Empire, where the central judicial authorities exercised little control over the determination of local judges to secure convictions. Prosecutions were also extensive in Switzerland, France, Scotland, Poland, Hungary, and Transylvania. Relatively few witches were executed in Spain, Portugal, Italy, Scandinavia, the Netherlands, England, and Ireland.

The determination of both Catholics and Protestants to discipline deviants of all sorts and to wage war against the Devil intensified the hunt for witches. The great majority of trials occurred between 1560 and 1650, when religious tensions were strong and economic conditions severe. The trials rarely occurred in a steady flow, as one would find for other crimes. In many cases the torture of a single witch would lead to her naming many alleged accomplices, who would then also be tried. This would lead to a witch panic in which scores and sometimes hundreds of witches would be tried and executed. Eighty percent of accused witches were women, especially those who were unmarried or widowed, but men and even young children could be accused of witchcraft as well. The hunts came to an end when judicial authorities recognized that no one was safe, especially during witch panics, and when they realized that legal evidence against witches was insufficient for conviction. The Dutch Republic was the first to ban witch trials in 1608. (See *Different Voices* in this chapter.)

DIFFERENT VOICES WERE THERE REALLY WITCHES?

Even during the height of the witch-hunt the existence of witches was controversial. Most authorities assumed that the devil worked evil on earth and that hunting witches, therefore, was an effective means of defending Christians. These authorities used the church and secular courts to interrogate alleged witches, sometimes supplemented by torture, to obtain confessions and the identities of other confederate witches. These authorities considered the hunting of witches part of their duty to protect the public from harm. Others accepted the reality of witchcraft but doubted the capacity of judges to determine who was a witch. A few doubted the reality of witchcraft altogether.

Johann Weyer (1515?–1588) was a physician who argued that most witches were deluded old women who suffered from depression and need medical help rather than legal punishment. The devil deceived them into thinking they had magical powers, but because Weyer had a strong belief that only God had power over nature, he did not credit the devil or witches with any special powers. No one else during the sixteenth century disputed the reality of the powers of witches as systematically as he. Jean Bodin (1529?–1596) was one of the greatest legal philosophers of the sixteenth century. Although he was once skeptical of the reality of witchcraft, he changed his mind after witnessing several cases in which women voluntarily confessed to performing evil acts under the guidance of Satan. He considered witchcraft a threat to society and condemned Weyer's soft-hearted view.

Johan Weyer's letter to Johann Brenz (1565)

Witches have no power to make hail, storms, and other evil things, but they are deceived by the devil. For when the devil, with the permission and decree of God, can make hail and storms, he goes to his witches and urges them to use their magic and charms, so that when the trouble and punishment come, the witches are convinced that they and the devil have caused it. Thus, the witches cannot make hail and other things, but they are deluded and blinded by the devil himself to whom they have given themselves. In this way they think that they have made hail and storms. Not on that account but for their godless lives should they be punished severely. . . .

Our witches have been corrupted in their phantasy by the devil and imagine often that they have done evil things that didn't even happen or caused natural occurrences that actually did not take place. In their confessions, especially under torture, they admit to doing and causing many things which are impossible for them and for anyone. One should not believe them when they confess that they have bound themselves to the devil, given themselves to his will, promised to follow his evil goals, just as we do not believe their confession that they make hail and storms, disturb and poison the air, and other impossible deeds. . . .

Even if an old woman, in deep depression, gives herself to the devil, one should not immediately condemn her to the fire but instead have regard for her confused, burdened, and depressed spirits and use all possible energy to convert her that she may avoid evil, and give herself to Christ. In this way we may bring her to her senses again, win her soul, and save her from death. . . .

THE CONFESSIONAL STATES

■ How did religious differences provoke violence and start wars?

The Religious Peace of Augsburg of 1555 provided the model for a solution to the religious divisions produced by the Reformation. According to the principle of *cuius regio, eius religio* (he who rules determines the religion of the land), each prince in the Holy Roman Empire determined the religion to be followed by his subjects; those who disagreed were obliged to convert or emigrate. Certainly, forced exile was economically

Jean Bodin, On the Demonic Madness of Witches (1580)

The judgment which was passed against a witch in a case to which I was called on the last day of April, 1578, gave me occasion to take up my pen in order to clarify the subject of witches—persons who seem strange and wondrous to everyone and incredible to many. The witch whom I refer to was named Jeanne Harvillier, a native of Verbery near Compiegne. She was accused of having murdered many men and beasts, as she herself confessed without questioning or torture, although she at first stubbornly denied the charges and changed her story often. She also confessed that her mother presented her at the age of twelve years to the devil, disguised as a tall black man, larger than most men and clothed in black. The mother told him that as soon as her daughter was born she had promised her to him, whom she called the devil. He in turn promised to treat her well and to make her happy. And from then on she had renounced God and promised to serve the devil. And at that instant she had had carnal copulation with the devil, which she had continued to the age of 50, or thereabouts, when she was captured. She said also that [the] devil presented himself to her when she wished, always dressed as he had been the first time, booted and spurred, with a sword at his side and his horse at the door. And no one saw him but her. He even fornicated with her often without her husband noticing although he lay at her side....

Now we have shown that ordinarily women are possessed by demons more often than men and that witches are often transported bodily but also often ravished in an ecstasy, the soul having separated itself from the body, by diabolical means, leaving the body insensible and stupid. Thus, it is completely ridiculous to say that the illness of the witches originates in melancholy, especially because the diseases coming from melancholy are always dangerous.... Thus, Weyer must admit that there is a remarkable incongruity for one who is a doctor, and a gross example of ignorance (but it is not ignorance) to attribute to women melancholy diseases which are as little appropriate for them as are the praiseworthy effects of a tempered melancholy humor. This humor makes a man wise, sober, and contemplative (as all of the ancient philosophers and physicians remark), which are qualities as incompatible with women as fire with water. And even Solomon, who as a man of the world knew well the humor of women, said that he had seen a wise man for every 1,000 men, but that he had never seen a wise woman. Let us therefore abandon the fanatic error of those who make women into melancholics.

Source: Robert M. Kingdon (ed.), *Transition and Revolution: Problems and Issues of European Renaissance and Reformation History* (Minneapolis: Burgess Publishing Company, 1974), 221–232. Reprinted by permission.

For Discussion

1. How can the uncoerced confessions of women to witchcraft be explained?

2. Why would an otherwise intelligent observer such as Jean Bodin be so willing to believe in the reality of the power of witches?

and personally traumatic for those who emigrated, but it preserved what was almost universally believed to be the fundamental principle of successful rulership—one king, one faith, one law. In other words, each state should have only one church. Except in the states of eastern Europe and a few small troubled principalities in the Holy Roman Empire, few thought it desirable to allow more than one confession in the same state.

The problem with this political theory of religious unity was the reality of religious divisions created by the Reformation. In some places there were as many as three active confessions—Catholic, Lutheran, and Calvinist—in addition to the minority sects, such as the Anabaptists and the Jewish communities. The alternative to religious unity would have been religious toleration, but hardly anyone in a position of authority was willing to advocate that. John Calvin expelled advocates of religious toleration, and Martin Luther was aggressively hostile to those who disagreed with him on seemingly minor theological points. After 1542 with the establishment of the Universal Inquisition, the Catholic Church was committed to exposing and punishing anyone who professed a different faith, with the exception of Jews in Italy, who were under papal protection. Geneva and Rome became competing missionary centers, each flooding the world with polemical tracts and specially trained missionaries willing to risk their lives by going behind the enemy lines to console their co-religionists and evangelize for converts.

Religious passions ran so high that during the late sixteenth century a new word appeared to describe a personality type that may not have been entirely new but was certainly much more common—the **fanatic**. Originally referring to someone possessed by a demon, *fanatic* came to mean a person who expressed immoderate enthusiasm in religious matters, a person who pursued a supposedly divine mission, often to violent ends. Fanatics from all sides of the religious divide initiated waves of political assassinations and massacred their opponents. François Guion, the assassin of William the Silent, whose story began this chapter, was in many ways typical of fanatics in his steadfast pursuit of his victim and his willingness to masquerade for years under a false identity. During the sixteenth and seventeenth centuries, no religious community had a monopoly on fanatics. They served the pope as well as the Protestant churches.

Wherever there were significant religious minorities within a state, the best that could be hoped for was a condition of anxious tension, omnipresent suspicion, and periodic hysteria (see **Map 15.1**). The worst possibility was civil war in which religious affiliations and political rivalries intertwined in such complicated ways that finding peaceful solutions was especially difficult. Between 1560 and 1648 several religious civil wars broke out, including the French Wars of Religion, the Dutch revolt against Spain, the Thirty Years' War in Germany, and the English Civil War. (The latter two will be discussed in Chapter 16.)

The French Wars of Religion

When King Henry II (r. 1547–1559) of France died unexpectedly from a jousting accident, he left behind his widow, the formidable Catherine de' Medici (1519–1589), and a brood of young children—including his heir, Francis II (r. 1559–1560), who was only 15. Henry II had been a peacemaker. In contrast, Catherine and her children, including three sons who successively ascended to the throne, utterly failed to keep the peace, and for some 40 years France was torn apart by a series of desperate civil wars.

THE HUGUENOTS: THE FRENCH CALVINIST COMMUNITY
By 1560 Calvinism had made significant inroads into predominantly Catholic France. Pastors sent from Geneva had been especially successful in the larger provincial towns, where their evangelical message appealed to enterprising merchants, professionals, and skilled artisans. One in ten of the French had become Calvinists, or **Huguenots** as French Protestants were called. The political strength of the Huguenots was greater than their numbers might indicate, because between one-third and one-half of the lower nobility professed Calvinism. Calvinism was popular among the French nobility for two reasons. One involved the imitation of social superiors. The financial well-being of any noble depended on his patron, an aristocrat of higher rank who had access to the king and who could distribute jobs and lands to his clients. When a high aristocrat converted to Protestantism, he tended to bring into the new faith his noble clientele, who converted through loyalty to their patron or through the patron's ability to persuade those who were financially dependent on him. As a result of a few aristocratic conversions in southwest France, Calvinism spread through "a veritable religious spider's web,"[3] as one contemporary put it.

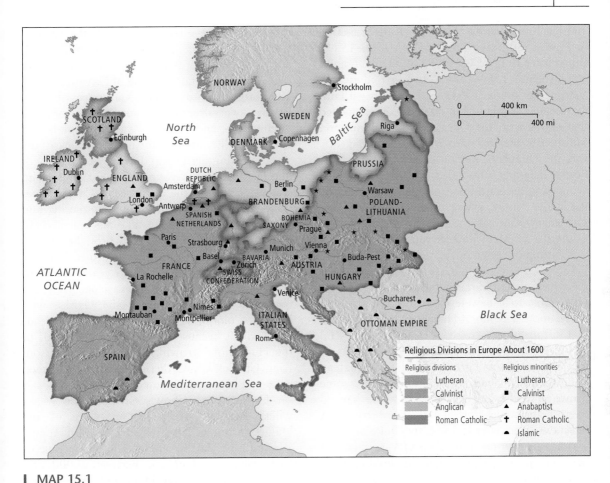

MAP 15.1

Religious Divisions in Europe About 1600

After 1555 the religious borders of Europe became relatively fixed, with only minor changes in confessional affiliations to this day.

A second reason for the spread of Calvinism was the influence of aristocratic women. The sister of King Francis I of France (r. 1515–1547), Marguerite of Angoulême (1492–1549), married the King of Navarre (an independent kingdom situated between France and Spain) and created a haven in Navarre for Huguenot preachers and theologians. Her example drew other aristocratic ladies to the Huguenot cause, and many of the Huguenot leaders during the French Wars of Religion were the sons and grandsons of these early female converts. Marguerite's daughter, Jeanne d'Albret, sponsored Calvinist preachers for several years before she publicly announced her own conversion in 1560. Her son, Henry Bourbon (Henry of Navarre), became the principal leader of the Huguenot cause during the **French Wars of Religion** and the person responsible for eventually bringing the wars to an end.

THE ORIGINS OF THE RELIGIOUS WARS Like all civil wars, the French Wars of Religion exhibited a bewildering pattern of intrigue, betrayal, and treachery. Three distinct groups constituted the principal players. The first group was the royal family, consisting of Queen Catherine de' Medici and her four sons by Henry II—King Francis II (r. 1559–1560), King Charles IX (r. 1560–1574), King Henry III (r. 1574–1589), and Duke Francis of Alençon (1554–1584)—and her daughter, Marguerite Valois (1553–1615). The royal family remained Catholic but on occasion reconciled themselves with the Huguenot opposition, and Marguerite married into it. The second group was the Huguenot faction of nobles led by the Bourbon family who ruled Navarre. The third group was the hard-line Catholic faction led by the Guise family. These three groups vied for supremacy during the successive reigns of Catherine de' Medici's three sons.

During the reign of the sickly and immature Francis II, the Catholic Guise family dominated the government and raised the persecution of the Huguenots to a new level. In response to that persecution, a group of Huguenot nobles plotted in 1560 to kill the Guises. The Guises got wind of the conspiracy and surprised the plotters as they arrived in small groups at the royal chateau of Amboise. Some were ambushed, some drowned in the Loire River, and some hanged from the balconies of the chateau's courtyard. A tense two years later in 1562, the Duke of Guise was passing through the village of Vassy just as a large Huguenot congregation was holding services in a barn. The duke's men attacked the worshipers, killing some 740 of them and wounding hundreds of others.

Following the massacre at Vassy, civil war broke out in earnest. For nearly 40 years religious wars sapped the strength of France. Most of the battles were indecisive, which meant neither side sustained military superiority for long. Both sides relied for support on their regional bases: The Huguenots' strength was in the southwest; the Catholics', in Paris and the north. Besides military engagements, the French Wars of Religion spawned political assassinations and massacres.

MASSACRE OF ST. BARTHOLOMEW'S DAY After a decade of bloody yet inconclusive combat, the royal family tried to resolve the conflict by making peace with the Protestants, a shift of policy

signified by the announcement of the engagement of Marguerite Valois, daughter of Henry II and Catherine de' Medici, to Henry Bourbon, the son of the Huguenot King of Navarre. At age 19, Marguerite—or Queen Margot, as she was known—was already renowned for her brilliant intelligence—and for her wanton morals. To complicate the situation further, on the eve of the wedding Marguerite was having an affair with another Henry, the young Duke of Guise who was the leader of the intransigent Catholic faction. The marriage between Marguerite and Henry of Navarre was to take place in Paris in August 1572, an event that brought all the Huguenot leaders to the heavily armed Catholic capital for the first time in many years. The gathering of all their enemies in one place presented too great a temptation for the Guises, who hatched a plot to assassinate the Huguenot leaders. Perhaps because she had become jealous of the Huguenots' growing influence on her son, King Charles IX, Catherine suddenly switched sides and became implicated in the plot.

Catherine somehow convinced the weak-willed king to order the massacre of the Huguenot nobles gathered in Paris. On August 14, 1572, St. Bartholomew's Day, the people of Paris began a slaughter. Between 3,000 and 4,000 Huguenots were butchered in Paris and more than 20,000 were put to death throughout the rest of France. Henry of Navarre saved his life by pretending to convert to Catholicism, while most of his companions were murdered.

Catherine's attempted solution for the Huguenot problem failed to solve anything. Henry of Navarre escaped his virtual imprisonment in the royal household, set Marguerite up in an isolated castle, returned to Navarre and his faith, and reinvigorated Huguenot resistance.

The wars of religion continued until the assassination of King Henry III, brother of the late Charles IX. Both Charles IX and Henry III had been childless, a situation that made Henry Bourbon of Navarre the rightful heir to the throne, even though he was a Huguenot. Henry Bourbon became King Henry IV (r. 1589–1610). He recognized that predominantly Catholic

and obtain her huge dowry. Affable, witty, generous, and exceedingly tolerant, "Henry the Great" became the most popular king in French history, reuniting the war-torn country by ruling with a very firm hand. With the **Edict of Nantes** of 1598, he allowed the Huguenots to build a quasi-state within the state, giving them the right to have their own troops, church organization, and political autonomy within their walled towns, but banning them from the royal court and the city of Paris.

Despite his enormous popularity, Henry too fell victim to fanaticism. After surviving 18 attempts on his life, in 1610 the king was fatally stabbed by a Catholic fanatic, who took advantage of the opportunity presented when the royal coach unexpectedly stopped behind a cart loading hay. Catholics and Protestants alike mourned Henry's death and considered the assassin mad. Henry's brilliant conciliatory nature and the horrors of the religious wars had tempered public opinion.

ST. BARTHOLOMEW'S DAY MASSACRE

A Protestant painter, François Dubois, depicted the merciless slaughter of Protestant men, women, and children in the streets of Paris in 1572. The massacre was the most bloody and infamous in the French Wars of Religion and created a lasting memory of atrocity.

France would never accept a Huguenot king, and so in 1593 with his famous quip, "Paris is worth a mass," Henry converted to Catholicism. Most Catholic opposition to him collapsed. Once Henry became a Catholic he managed to have the pope annul his childless marriage to Marguerite so that he could marry Marie de' Medici

Philip II, His Most Catholic Majesty

France's greatest rivals were the Habsburgs, who possessed vast territories in the Holy Roman Empire, controlled the elections for emperor, and had dynastic rights to the throne of Spain. During the late sixteenth century, Habsburg Spain took advantage of French weakness to establish itself as the dominant power in Europe. When Emperor Charles V (who had been both Holy Roman Emperor and king of Spain) abdicated his thrones in 1556, the Habsburg possessions in the Holy Roman Empire and the emperorship went to his brother, Ferdinand I, and the balance of his vast domain to his son, Philip II (r. 1556–1598). Philip's inheritance included Spain,

CHRONOLOGY: THE FRENCH WARS OF RELIGION, 1560–1598	
1560	Huguenot conspiracy of Amboise against Catholic Guise family
1572	Massacre of St. Bartholomew's Day, Catholics murder Huguenots
1598	Edict of Nantes granting Huguenots religious toleration

Milan, Naples, Sicily, the Netherlands, scattered outposts on the north coast of Africa, colonies in the Caribbean, Central America, Mexico, Peru, and the Philippines. In 1580 Philip also inherited Portugal and its far-flung overseas empire, which included a line of trading posts from West Africa to the Spice Islands and the vast colony of unexplored Brazil.

This grave, distrustful, rigid man saw himself as the great protector of the Catholic cause and committed Spain to perpetual hostility toward Muslims and Protestants. On the Muslim front he first bullied the Moriscos, the descendants of the Spanish Muslims. The Moriscos had received Christian baptism but were suspected of secretly practicing Islam. In 1568 Philip issued an edict that banned all manifestations of Muslim culture and ordered the Moriscos to turn over their children to Christian priests to educate. The remaining Moriscos were eventually expelled from the country in 1609.

Philip once said he would rather lose all his possessions and die a hundred times than be the king of heretics. (See *Justice in History* in this chapter.) His attitude toward Protestants showed that he meant what he said. Through his marriage to Queen Mary I of England (r. 1553–1558), Philip encouraged her persecutions of Protestants, but they got their revenge. After Mary's death her half-sister, Queen Elizabeth I, refused Philip's marriage proposal and in 1577 signed a treaty to assist the Protestant provinces of the Netherlands, which were in rebellion against Spain. To add insult to injury, the English privateer Sir Francis Drake (ca. 1540–1596) conducted a personal war against Catholic Spain by raiding the Spanish convoys bringing silver from the New World. In 1587 Drake's embarrassing successes culminated with a daring raid on the great Spanish port city of Cadiz, where, "singeing the king of Spain's beard," he destroyed the anchored Spanish fleet and many thousands of tons of vital supplies.

Philip retaliated by building a huge fleet of 132 ships armed with 3,165 cannons, which in 1588 sailed from Portugal to rendezvous with the Spanish army stationed in the Netherlands and launch an invasion of England. As the Invincible Armada, as it was called, passed through the English Channel, it was met by a much smaller English fleet, assembled out of merchant ships refit for battle. Unable to maneuver as effectively as the English in the fluky winds of the channel and mauled by the rapid-firing English guns, the **Spanish Armada** suffered heavy losses and was forced to retreat to the north, where it sustained further losses in storms off the coast of Scotland and Ireland. Barely more than half of the fleet finally straggled home. The defeat severely shook Philip's sense of invincibility.

The reign of Philip II illustrated better than any other the contradictions and tensions of the era. No monarch had at his grasp as many resources and territories as Philip, and yet defending them proved extremely costly. The creaky governmental machinery of Spain put a tremendous burden on a conscientious king such as Philip, but even his unflagging energy and dedication to his duties could not prevent military defeat and financial disaster. Historians remember Philip's reign for its series of state bankruptcies and for the loss of the Dutch provinces in the Netherlands, the most precious jewel in the crown of Spain.

The Dutch Revolt

The Netherlands boasted some of Europe's richest cities, situated amid a vast network of lakes, rivers, channels, estuaries, and tidal basins that periodically replenished the exceptionally productive soil through flooding. The Netherlands consisted of 17 provinces, each with its own distinctive identity, traditions, and even language. The southern provinces were primarily French-speaking; those in the north spoke a bewildering variety of Flemish and Dutch dialects. When Philip II became king of Spain he also inherited all of the Netherlands. With his characteristic bureaucratic mentality, Philip treated Dutch affairs as a management problem rather than a political sore spot, an attitude that subordinated the Netherlands to Spanish interests. Foreign rule irritated the Dutch, who had long enjoyed ancient privileges including the right to raise their own taxes and muster their own troops.

Philip's harsh attitude toward Protestants upset the Netherlands' delicate balance among Catholic, Lutheran, Calvinist, and Anabaptist communities, as did the arrival of Huguenot refugees from the French Wars of Religion. In 1566 Calvinist fanatics occupied many Catholic churches and destroyed paintings and statues.

In response Philip issued edicts against the heretics and strengthened the Spanish Inquisition. The Inquisition in Spain was an arm of the monarchy charged with ensuring religious conformity, but when introduced in the Netherlands, it became an investigating agency devoted to finding, interrogating, and, if necessary, punishing Protestants.

Philip also dispatched 20,000 Spanish troops under the command of the Duke of Alba (1508–1582), a veteran of the Turkish campaigns in North Africa and victories over the Lutheran princes in the Holy Roman Empire. Alba directly attacked the Protestants. He personally presided over the military court, the Council of Troubles, which became so notoriously tyrannical that the people called it the Council of Blood. As an example to others, he systematically razed several small villages where there had been incidents of desecrating Catholic images and slaughtered every inhabitant. Alba himself boasted that during the campaign against the rebels, he had 18,000 people executed, in addition to those who died in battle or were massacred by soldiers. Sixty thousand refugees, about two percent of the population, went into exile.

The Prince of Orange, William the Silent (1533–1584), organized the **Dutch Revolt** to resist to Alba. Within a few short years, William the Silent seized permanent control of the provinces of Holland and Zealand, which were then flooded by Calvinist refugees from the southern provinces.

His policies a failure, Alba was recalled to Spain in 1573. After Alba's departure, no one kept control of the unpaid Spanish soldiers, who in mutinous rage turned against cities loyal to Spain, including Brussels, Ghent, and most savagely Antwerp, the rich center of trade. Antwerp lost 7,000 citizens and one-third of its houses to the "Spanish fury," which permanently destroyed its prosperity.

Alba's replacement, the shrewd statesman and general the Duke of Parma (r. 1578–1592), ultimately subdued the southern provinces, which remained a Spanish colony. The seven northern provinces, however, united in 1579, declared independence from Spain in 1581, and formally organized as a republic in 1588 (see **Map 15.2**). William the Silent became the *stadholder* (governor) of the new United Provinces, and after his assassination in 1584 his 17-year-old son, Maurice of Nassau, inherited the same title.

The Netherlands' struggle for independence transformed the population of the United

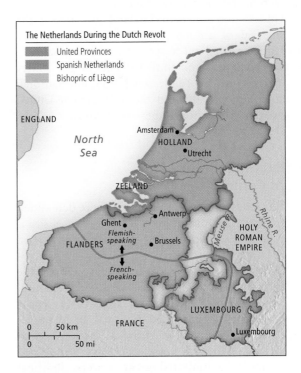

MAP 15.2

The Netherlands During the Dutch Revolt, ca. 1580

During the late sixteenth century the northern United Provinces separated from the Spanish Netherlands. The independence of the United Provinces was not recognized by the other European powers until 1648.

CHRONOLOGY: SPAIN AND THE NETHERLANDS, 1568–1648

1568	Edict against Morisco culture
1580	King Philip II inherits Portugal and the Portuguese Empire
1584	Assassination of William the Silent
1588	Defeat of the Spanish Armada, failed Spanish invasion of England; the seven northern provinces of the Netherlands becomes a republic
1609	Expulsion of the Moriscos from Spain
1648	Treaty of Westphalia recognizes independence of the Netherlands

Provinces from mixed religions to staunch Calvinism. The alliance with England, which provided much-needed financial and moral support, reinforced the Protestant identity of the Dutch, and the failure of the Spanish Armada to land Parma's men in England guaranteed the survival of an independent Netherlands. The Dutch carried on a sporadic and inconclusive war against Spain until the end of the Thirty Years' War in 1648, when the international community recognized the independent United Provinces of the Netherlands, known as the Dutch Republic.

Literature in the Age of Confessional Division

Churches and monarchs everywhere demanded religious conformity in word and deed, a situation that would seem to stifle creativity, and yet the late sixteenth and early seventeenth centuries were one of the most remarkable periods in the history of creative literature. Some literary figures did find their works banned and some had political or personal troubles with their monarch. But the controversies of the day seemed to have stimulated rather than inhibited great writers. Political and religious turmoil led them to rise above the petty religious squabbles that preoccupied so many of their contemporaries and to ask penetrating questions about the meaning of life. And importantly, they did so in their native languages. During this period the native or **vernacular languages** of western Europe

became literary languages, replacing Latin as the dominant form of expression, even for the educated elite.

FRENCH LITERATURE DURING THE RELIGIOUS TURMOIL In France royal decrees in 1520 and 1539 substituted French for Latin in official legal and government documents. A century later, with the founding of the Académie Française, it became government policy to promote, protect, and refine the French language. The greatest masters of French prose during this crucial period were François Rabelais (ca. 1483–1553) and Michel de Montaigne (1533–1592).

Trained as a lawyer, Rabelais became a friar and priest but left the Church under a cloud of heresy to become a physician. Rabelais's satirical masterpiece, a series of novels recounting the fantastic and grotesque adventures of the giants Gargantua and Pantagruel, combined an encyclopedic command of humanist thought with stunning verbal invention that has had a lasting influence on humorous writers to this day. Rabelais's optimistic vision of human nature represented a startling contrast to the growing anxiety provoked by the religious controversies of his time. Rabelais's controversial work was banned, and he was briefly forced into exile.

It is ironic that Montaigne became a master of French prose. His mother was a Catholic of Spanish-Jewish origin, and the young Michel spoke only Latin for the first six years of his life because his German tutor knew no French. After a modestly successful legal career, Montaigne retired to the family chateau to discover himself by writing essays, a literary form well suited to reflective introspection. In his essays, Montaigne struggled with his lasting grief over the premature death from dysentery of a close friend, reflected on his own experience of the intense physical pain of illness, and diagnosed the absurd causes of the French Wars of Religion. Montaigne's essays were a profound series of meditations on the meaning of life and death, presented in a calm voice of reason to an age of violent fanaticism. In one essay, for example, he exposed the presumption of human beings: "The most vulnerable and frail of all creatures is man, and at the same time the most arrogant." Montaigne thought it presumptuous that human beings picked themselves out as God's favorite creatures. How did they know they were superior to other animals? "When I play with my cat, who knows if I am not a pastime to her more than she is to me?"[4] His own skepticism about religion insulated him from the sometimes violent passions of his era. His essay "On Cannibals" pointed to the hypocrisy of Christians who condemned the alleged cannibalism of the native Americans but justified the torture and murder of other Christians over some minor theological dispute. Montaigne argued that the capacity to understand and tolerate cultural and religious differences, not rigid adherence to biblical laws, defined a truly ethical, truly Christian person.

Stirrings of the Golden Age in Iberia The literary tradition in the Iberian peninsula thrived in several languages: Basque, Galician, Portuguese, Castilian, and Catalan. The greatest lyric poet of the peninsula, Luís Vaz de Camões (1524–1580), lost an eye in battle and was sent to the Portuguese East Indies after he killed a royal official in a street brawl. When he returned years later, he completed his epic poem *The Lusiads* (1572), a celebration of Vasco da Gama's discovery of the sea route to India, which became the national poem of Portugal. Camoes modeled this work on the ancient epics, especially the *Aeneid*, the greatest Latin epic of ancient Rome, and even included the gods of Olympus as commentators on the human events of Camões's time. By connecting Portugal directly to the glories of the ancient empires, Camões elevated the adventures of his fellow Portuguese in Asia to an important moment in the history of the world.

The period when Spain was the dominant power in Europe coincided with the Golden Age of Spanish literature. Because Spain was unified around the crown of Castile, the Castilian language became the language we now call Spanish. The greatest literary figure was Miguel de Cervantes Saavedra (1547–1616), an impoverished son of an unsuccessful doctor with little formal education. Like Camões, Cervantes survived many adventures. He lost the use of his left hand at the naval Battle of Lepanto and spent five years languishing in a Turkish prison after his capture by Algerian pirates. The disabled veteran wrote plays for the Madrid theater and worked as a tax collector, but was still imprisoned several times for debts. Desperate to make money, Cervantes published a serial novel in installments between 1605 and 1615. It became the greatest masterpiece in Spanish literature, *Don Quixote*.

The prototype of the modern novel form, *Don Quixote* satirizes chivalric romances. Cervantes presented reality on two levels, the "poetic truth" of the master and dreamer Don Quixote and the "historic truth" of his squire and realist Sancho Panza. Don Quixote's imagination persistently ran away with him as he tilted at windmills, believing they were fierce dragons. It remained to Sancho Panza to point out the unheroic truth. Cervantes pursued the interaction between these two incongruous views of truth as a philosophical commentary on existence. For Cervantes there was no single, objective truth, only psychological truths revealed through the interaction of the characters, an idea that contrasted with the notion of dogmatic religious truth that dominated the time.

THE ELIZABETHAN RENAISSANCE   During the reign of Elizabeth I (r. 1558–1603), the Renaissance arrived in England. The daughter of Henry VIII and Anne Boleyn, Elizabeth faced terrible insecurity as a girl. Her father had her mother beheaded, she was declared illegitimate, and her half-sister Mary imprisoned her in the Tower of London for treason. After she ascended to the throne in 1558, however, she proved to be a brilliant leader. Elizabeth prevented the kind of religious civil wars that broke out in France by establishing a moderate form of Protestantism as the official religion. She presided over the beginnings of England's rise as a major European power. Perhaps most remarkably, she became a patron and inspiration for England's greatest age of literature.

The principal figure of the Elizabethan Renaissance was a professional dramatist, William Shakespeare (1564–1616). In a series of theaters, including the famous Globe on the south side of the Thames in London, Shakespeare wrote, produced, and acted in comedies, tragedies, and history plays. Shakespeare's enormous output of plays, some of which made veiled allusions to the politics of Elizabeth's court, established him not only as the most popular dramatist of his time, but the greatest literary figure in the English language. The power of his plays derives from the subtle understanding of human psychology found in his characters and the stunning force of his language. For Shakespeare, as for Montaigne, the source of true knowledge was self-knowledge, which most people lacked. Pride and human authority prevented people from knowing themselves:

> But man, proud man,
> Drest [dressed] in a little brief authority,

QUEEN ELIZABETH I OF ENGLAND
Carried by her courtiers Elizabeth presided over the greatest age of English literature.

Most ignorant of what he's most assured,
His glassy [dull] essence, like an angry ape,
Plays such fantastic tricks before high
    heaven
  As make the angels weep.
(*Measure for Measure* II, ii, 117)

Unlike most contemporary authors, Shakespeare wrote for a broad audience of paying theater goers that included common workers as well as highly educated members of Elizabeth's court. This need to appeal to a large audience who gave instant feedback helped him hone his skills as a dramatist.

STATES AND CONFESSIONS IN EASTERN EUROPE

■ How did the countries of eastern Europe during the late sixteenth century become enmeshed in the religious controversies that began in western Europe during the early part of the century?

The religious diversity of eastern Europe contrasted with the religious conformity of western Europe's confessional states. Whereas in western Europe the religious controversies stimulated writers to investigate deeply the human condition but made them cautious about expressing nonconforming religious opinions, writers and creative people in eastern Europe during this period were able to explore a wide range of ideas in a relatively tolerant atmosphere. Bohemia and Poland, in particular, allowed levels of religious diversity unheard of elsewhere. During the last decades of the sixteenth century and early decades of the seventeenth, however, dynastic troubles compromised the relative openness of the eastern states, enmeshing them in conflicts among themselves that had an increasingly strong religious dimension. In the Holy Roman Empire, the weakness of the mad Emperor Rudolf permitted religious conflicts to fester, setting the stage for the disastrous Thirty Years' War (1618–1648) that pitted Catholic and Protestant princes against one another.

Around the Baltic Sea, rivalries among Lutheran Sweden, Catholic Poland-Lithuania, and Orthodox Russia created a state of almost permanent war in a tense standoff among three very different political and religious states. The enormous confederation of Poland-Lithuania sustained the most decentralized, religiously diverse state anywhere in Europe. By the end of the century, it remained politically decentralized but had become an active theater of the Catholic Reformation where dynastic policy firmly supported the Roman Church. Russia began to strengthen itself under the authoritarian rule of the tsars, who began to transform it into a major European power.

The Dream World of Emperor Rudolf

In Goethe's *Faust,* set in sixteenth-century Germany, drinkers in a tavern sing:

    The dear old Holy Roman Empire,
    How does it hang together?

Good question. How did this peculiarly decentralized state—neither holy, nor Roman, nor an empire, as Voltaire would later put it—hang together? In the late sixteenth century the empire consisted of one emperor; seven electors; 50 bishops and archbishops, 21 dukes, margraves, and landgraves; 88 independent abbots and assorted prelates of the Church; 178 counts and other sovereign lords; about 80 free imperial cities; and hundreds of free imperial knights. The emperor presided over all, and the Imperial Diet served as a parliament, but the Holy Roman Empire was, in fact, a very loose confederation of semi-independent, mostly German-speaking states, many of which ignored imperial decrees that did not suit them. During the first half of the sixteenth century the empire faced a number of challenges—the turmoil within the empire created by Lutheranism, endless French enmity on the western borders, and the tenacious Ottoman threat on the eastern frontier. Only the universal vision and firm hand of Emperor Charles V kept the empire together. The universal vision and firm hand disappeared in the succeeding generations of emperors to be replaced by petty dynastic squabbles and infirm minds.

The crippling weakness of the imperial system became most evident during the reign of Rudolf II (r. 1576–1612). The Habsburg line had a strain of insanity going back to Joanna "The Mad," the mother of Emperors Charles V (r. 1519–1558) and Ferdinand I (r. 1558–1564), who happened to be Rudolf's two grandfathers, giving him a double dose of Habsburg genes. Soon after his election to the imperial throne, Rudolf moved his court from bustling Vienna to the lovely quiet of Prague in Bohemia. Fearful of noisy crowds and impatient courtiers, stand-offish toward foreign ambassadors who presented him with difficult decisions, paranoid about scheming relatives, and prone to wild emotional gyrations from deep depression to manic grandiosity, Rudolf was hardly suited for the imperial throne. In fact, many contemporaries, who had their own reasons to underrate him, described him as hopelessly insane. Rudolf certainly suffered from moments of profound melancholy and irrational fears that may have had genetic or organic causes, but he was probably unhinged by the conundrum of being the emperor, a position that trapped him between the glorious universal imperial ideal and the ignoble reality of unscrupulous relatives and petty rivalries.

Incapable of governing, Rudolf transmuted the imperial ideal of universality into a strange dream world. In Prague he gathered around him a brilliant court of humanists, musicians, painters, physicians, astronomers, astrologers, alchemists, and magicians. These included an eclectic assortment of significant thinkers—the great astronomers Tycho Brahe and Johannes Kepler, the notorious occult philosopher Giordano Bruno, the theoretical mathematician and astrologer John Dee, and the remarkable inventor of surrealist painting

Giuseppe Arcimboldo. Many of these figures became central figures in the Scientific Revolution, but Rudolf also fell prey to fast-talking charlatans. These included Cornelius Drebber who claimed to have invented a perpetual-motion machine. This weird court, however, was less the strange fruit of the emperor's hopeless dementia than the manifestation of a striving for universal empire. Rudolf sought to preserve the cultural and political unity of the empire, to eradicate religious divisions, and to achieve peace at home. Rudolf's court in Prague was perhaps the only place left during the late sixteenth century where Protestants, Catholics, Jews, and even radical heretics such

EMPEROR RUDOLF II

Among the many creative people in the Emperor Rudolf's court was the Italian surrealist painter Giuseppe Arcimboldo, who specialized in creating images out of fruits, vegetables, flowers, and animals. This is a portrait of the Emperor Rudolf.

as Bruno could gather together in a common intellectual enterprise. The goal of such gatherings was to discover the universal principles that governed nature, principles that would provide the foundations for a single unifying religion and a cure for all human maladies. It was a noble, if utterly improbable, dream.

While Rudolf and his favorite courtiers isolated themselves in their dream world, the religious conflicts within the empire reached a boiling point. Without a strong emperor, confessional squabbles paralyzed the Imperial Diets. In 1607, the Catholic Duke of Bavaria annexed Donauworth—a city with a Lutheran majority—to his own territories. Despite the illegality of the duke's action, Rudolf passively acquiesced, causing fear among German Protestants that the principles of the Religious Peace of Augsburg of 1555 might be ignored. The Religious Peace had allowed princes and imperial free cities, such as Donauworth, to determine their own religion. The Duke of Bavaria's violation of Donauworth's status as a free city jeopardized not only civic liberty but religious liberty. In the following decade, more than 200 religious revolts or riots took place. In 1609 the insane Duke John William of Jülich-Cleves died without a direct heir, and the most suitable claimants to the Catholic duchy were two Lutheran princes. The succession of a Lutheran prince to this Catholic dukedom would have seriously disrupted the balance between Catholics and Protestants in Germany. Religious tensions boiled over. As Chapter 16 will describe, in less than a decade the empire began to dissolve in what became the Thirty Years' War.

The Renaissance of Poland-Lithuania

As the major power in eastern Europe, Poland-Lithuania engaged in a tug-of-war with Sweden over control of the eastern Baltic and almost constant warfare against the expansionist ambitions of Russia (see **Map 15.3**). Nevertheless, during the late sixteenth and early seventeenth centuries, Poland-Lithuania experienced a remarkable cultural and political renaissance inspired by influences from Renaissance Italy linked to strong commercial and diplomatic ties to the Republic of Venice and intellectual connections with the University of Padua. But perhaps the most remarkable achievement of Poland-Lithuania during this contentious time was its unparalleled level of religious toleration and parliamentary rule.

Very loosely joined since 1385, the Kingdom of Poland and the Grand Duchy of Lithuania formally united as the Polish-Lithuanian Commonwealth in 1569. The republican thought from Renaissance Italy directly influenced the political structure and values of the Commonwealth. Polish jurists studied law at the universities of Padua and Bologna where they learned to apply the civic values of Italy to the Polish context. Under these influences, the Polish constitution guaranteed that there would be no changes of the law, no new taxes, and no limitations on freedoms without the consent of the parliament, known as the Sejm. The novel feature of the Commonwealth was how the nobles (*szlachta*) reserved power for themselves through their control of regional assemblies, which in turn dominated the Sejm. The *szlachta* consisted of between 6.6 and 8 percent of the population and nearly 25 percent of ethnic Poles. Elsewhere in Europe, except for Spain, the nobility accounted for no more than 1 to 3 percent of the population. Thus, a much higher percentage of the population of Poland-Lithuania enjoyed political rights than in any other country in Europe. In 1573 the Sejm introduced a highly limited monarchy for Poland. The Sejm elected the king and treated him, at best, as a hired manager. While the rest of Europe moved toward ever more authoritarian monarchies, Poland moved in the opposite direction toward broader political participation.

The Warsaw Confederation of 1573 prohibited religious persecution, making the Commonwealth the safest and most tolerant place in Europe. Poland-Lithuania contained an incomparable religious mixture of Roman

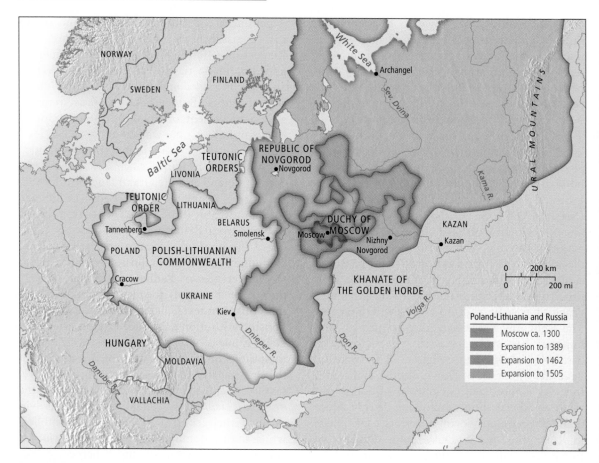

MAP 15.3

Poland-Lithuania and Russia

These countries were the largest in Europe in the size of their territories but were relatively under populated compared to the western European states.

Catholics, Lutherans, Calvinists, Russian Orthodox, Anabaptists, Unitarians, Armenians, and Jews. These communities, however, were strongly divided along geographic and social lines. Lutheranism was a phenomenon of the German-speaking towns, the peasants of Poland remained Catholic, those in Lithuania were Orthodox, and many of the nobles were attracted to Calvinism.

During the late sixteenth century, however, many Protestants in Poland returned or converted

to the Roman Catholic faith. The key to the transformation was the changing attitude of the Polish *szlachta*, who had promoted religious diversity because they believed that religious liberty was the cornerstone of political liberty. The revival of Catholicism owed a great deal to Stanislas Hosius (1504–1579), who had studied in Italy before he returned to Poland to become successively a diplomat, bishop, and cardinal. Imbued with the zeal of the Italian Catholic Reformation, Hosius invited the Society of Jesus (Jesuits) into Poland

and worked closely with the papal *nuncios* (the diplomatic representatives of the pope), who organized a campaign to combat all forms of Protestantism. Between 1565 and 1586, 44 Polish nobles studied at the Jesuit college in Rome. When they returned, they took up the most influential church and government offices in Poland. Jesuit colleges sprouted up in many Polish towns, attracting the brightest sons of the nobility and urban bourgeoisie. A close alliance between the kings of Poland and the Jesuits enhanced the social prestige of Catholicism.

The cultural appeal of all things Italian also helped lure many members of the Polish nobility back to Catholicism. Through the spread of elite education, Catholicism returned to Poland largely through persuasion rather than coercion. But the transformation did not occur without violent repercussions. Lutheran, Calvinist, and Bohemian Brethren churches were burned. In Cracow armed confrontations between Protestant and Catholic militants led to casualties. In 1596 the Polish king and Catholic fanatics imposed Catholicism on the Orthodox in the eastern parts of the Commonwealth. Although allowed to retain their rites, Orthodox believers had to accept the authority of the pope. Despite the growing religious hostility, Poland did not degenerate into civil war, as did France or the Netherlands over much the same issues.

Not all Poles and Lithuanians interpreted the Italian influence as affirming the Catholic Reformation. In 1580 Count Jan Zamoyski (1542–1605) founded the city of Zamość, designed as an ideal Renaissance city on the Italian model. Zamoyski had studied at Padua and returned to Poland determined to build his own Padua. He invited Armenians and Jews to inhabit the new town as citizens. A forceful advocate of civic freedom against royal authority and religious toleration, he built a Roman Catholic Church, a Calvinist chapel, an Armenian Orthodox church, and two synagogues. In Zamoyski's planned town the religions of the West encountered one another on a daily basis

ZAMOŚĆ

One of the finest examples of a Renaissance planned-town, Zamość in eastern Poland imitated the arcaded streets of Padua, Italy.

and exemplified one of the most attractive features of the Polish Renaissance.

Perhaps most remarkable was the position of Jews in Poland. During the early modern period Poland-Lithuania became the center of European Jewish culture. Jews described Vilnius as the "new Jerusalem." Jews had their own parliament and sent nonvoting representatives to the Sejm, a form of unequal citizenship but a guarantee of certain rights without parallel elsewhere in Europe. Unlike other parts of Europe, in Poland-Lithuania Jews were not forced to assimilate or hide and were allowed to develop their own distinctive communities.

The Troubled Legacy of Ivan the Terrible

While Poland experimented with a decentralized confederation dominated by nobles that severely restricted the king's initiative, Russia did the opposite. During the late fifteenth and sixteenth centuries, the grand dukes of Moscow who became the tsars of Russia gradually expanded their power over the **boyars** (the upper-level nobles who dominated Russian society) and challenged Moscow's neighbors—Poland-Lithuania and the Republic of Novgorod.

Although well integrated into the European diplomatic community and engaged in trade with its western neighbors, Russia for more than 300 years had been under the "Tartar Yoke," a term describing the Mongolian tribes that overran the country, pillaging and depopulating it. Ivan III, "The Great" (1462–1505), succeeded in gradually throwing off the Tartar Yoke by refusing to continue to pay tribute to the Mongols.

Ivan's marriage to Zoë, the niece of the last Greek emperor of Constantinople, gave him the basis for claiming that the Russian rulers were the heirs of Byzantium and the exclusive protectors of Orthodox Christianity, the state religion of Russia. Following the Byzantine tradition of imperial pomp, Ivan practiced Byzantine court ceremonies, and his advisers developed the theory of the Three Romes. According to this theory, the authority of the

THE MOSCOW KREMLIN

The Kremlin in Moscow was the seat of government for the Russian tsars until 1712. Originally built in 1156, the present enclosure of the Kremlin dates from the sixteenth century and reflects the influence of Italian architects brought to Moscow as well as traditional Byzantine styles. This view shows the Cathedral of St. Michael the Archangel and Bell Tower of Ivan the Great.

ancient Roman Empire had passed first to the Byzantine Empire, which God had punished with the Turkish conquest, and then to Moscow as the third and last "Rome." Ivan celebrated this theory by assuming the title of tsar (or "Caesar"). With his wife's assistance, he hired Italian architects to rebuild the grand ducal palace, the Kremlin.

With his capture of the vast northern territories of the Republic of Novgorod, Ivan expanded the Russian state north to the White Sea and east to the Urals. In 1478 Ivan sent his army to Novgorod, massacred the population, abolished the parliament, and burned the archive, ending the rich republican tradition of northern Russia. Ivan's invasion of parts of Lithuania embroiled Russia in a protracted conflict with Poland that lasted more than a century. Like his fellow monarchs in western Europe, Ivan began to bring the aristocrats under control by incorporating them into the bureaucracy of the state.

Ivan III's grandson, Ivan IV, "The Terrible" (1533–1584), succeeded his father at age three and became the object of innumerable plots, attempted coups, and power struggles among his mother, uncles, and the boyars. The trauma of his childhood years and a painful disease of the spine made him inordinately suspicious and prone to acts of impulsive violence. When at age 17 Ivan was crowned, he reduced the power of the dukes and the boyars. He obliged them to give up their hereditary estates. In return he redistributed lands to them with the legal obligation to serve the tsar in war. In weakening the boyars, Ivan gained considerable

support among the common people and was even remembered in popular songs as the people's tsar. At first, he was a great reformer who introduced a code of laws and a church council. By setting aside half of the realm as his personal domain, he created a strong financial base for the army, which led to military successes in the prolonged wars against Poland-Lithuania and Sweden.

Nevertheless, Ivan distrusted everyone, and his struggle with the boyars led him to subvert his own reforms. He often arrested people on charges of treason, just for taking trips abroad. In a cruel revenge to his enemies among the boyars, he began a reign of terror in which he personally committed horrendous atrocities. His massacre in 1570 of the surviving inhabitants of Novgorod, whom he suspected of harboring Polish sympathies, contributed to his reputation as a bloody tyrant. During his reign, the Polish threat and boyar opposition to his rule revealed signs of the fragility of Russian unity.

Then, during the **"Time of Troubles"** (1604–1613), Russia fell into chaos. Boyar families struggled among themselves for supremacy, the Cossacks from the south led a popular revolt, and Poles and Swedes openly interfered in Russian affairs. Finally, the Time of Troubles ended when in 1613 the national assembly elected Tsar Michael Romanov, whose descendants ruled Russia until 1917. During the seventeenth century the Romanovs gradually restored order to Russia, eroded the independence of local governments, and introduced serfdom to keep the peasants on the land. By the

CHRONOLOGY: STATES AND CONFESSIONS IN EASTERN EUROPE

1480	Grand Duke and later Tsar Ivan III, "The Great," of Russia refuses to pay tribute to Tartars
1569	Constitutional Union established Polish-Lithuanian Commonwealth
1604–1613	Time of Troubles in Russia
1613	Michael Romanov elected Tsar of Russia

end of the seventeenth century Russia was strong enough to reenter European affairs as a major power.

CONCLUSION

The Divisions of the West

During the late sixteenth and early seventeenth centuries, hidden demographic and economic pressures eroded the confidence and security of many Europeans, creating a widespread sense of unease. Most people retreated like confused soldiers behind the barricades of a rigid confessional faith, which provided reassurance that was unavailable elsewhere. To compensate for the absence of predictability in daily life, societies everywhere imposed strict discipline—discipline of women, children, the poor, criminals, and alleged witches. The frenzy for social discipline displaced the fear of those things that could not be controlled (such as price inflation) onto the most easily controllable people, especially the weak, the subordinate, and those perceived to be different in some way.

The union between religion and political authority in the confessional states bolstered official religious faith with the threat of legal or military coercion. Where different religious confessions persisted within one state—most notably France and the Netherlands—the result was riots, assassinations, and civil war. The West had become divided along religious lines in two ways. The first kind of division was within countries with religiously mixed populations, where distinctive religious communities competed for political power and influence. In these countries religion became the cornerstone to justify patriotism or rebellion, loyalty or disloyalty to the monarch. The second kind of division was international. The confessional states formed alliances, crafted foreign policies, and went to war, with religion determining friend and foe. Over the subsequent centuries, religious differences mutated into ideological differences, but the sense that alliances among states should be linked together by a common set of beliefs has persisted to this day as a legacy from the sixteenth century.

During the period of the middle seventeenth to eighteenth centuries, confessional identity and the fear of religious turmoil led monarchs throughout Europe to build absolutist regimes, which attempted to enforce stability through a strengthened, centralized state. The principles of religious toleration and the separation of church and state were still far in the future. They were made possible only as a consequence of the hard lessons learned from the historical turmoil of the late sixteenth and seventeenth centuries.

KEY TERMS

confessions	French Wars of Religion
Price Revolution	Edict of Nantes
auto-da-fé	Spanish Armada
witch-hunt	Dutch Revolt
magic	vernacular languages
fanatic	boyars
Huguenots	Time of Troubles

CHAPTER QUESTIONS

1. How did the expanding population and price revolution exacerbate religious and political tensions? (page 458)
2. How did religious and political authorities attempt to discipline the people? (page 463)
3. Why did people in the sixteenth century think witches were a threat? (page 469)

4. How did religious differences provoke violence and start wars? (page 472)
5. How did the countries of eastern Europe during the late sixteenth century become enmeshed in the religious controversies that began in western Europe during the early part of the century? (page 483)

TAKING IT FURTHER

1. Why was it so difficult to establish religious toleration in the sixteenth century?

2. A common emotion during the age of confessional division was fear. How do you explain the spread of collective fears?
3. How did religious fanatics perceive the world during this period?

✔•—Practice on **MyHistoryLab**

16

Absolutism and State Building, 1618–1715

- The Nature of Absolutism
- The Absolutist State in France and Spain
- Absolutism and State Building in Central and Eastern Europe
- Resistance to Absolutism in England and the Dutch Republic

IN 1651 THOMAS HOBBES, AN ENGLISH PHILOSOPHER LIVING IN EXILE IN France, was convinced that the West had descended into chaos. As he looked around him, Hobbes saw nothing but political instability, rebellion, and civil war. The turmoil had begun in the late sixteenth century, when the Reformation sparked the religious warfare described in the last chapter. In 1618 the situation deteriorated when another cycle of political strife and warfare erupted. The Thirty Years' War (1618–1648) began as a religious and political dispute in the Holy Roman Empire but soon became an international conflict involving the armies of Spain, France, Sweden, England, and many German states. The war wreaked economic and social havoc in Germany, decimated its population, and forced governments throughout Europe to raise large armies and tax their subjects to pay for them. The entire European economy suffered as a result.

During the 1640s, partly as a result of that devastating conflict, the political order of Europe collapsed. In England a series of bloody civil wars led to the destruction of the monarchy and the establishment of a republic. In France a civil war over constitutional issues drove the royal family from Paris. In Spain the king faced rebellions in four of his territories, while in Ukraine Cossacks staged a military uprising against the Polish-Lithuanian Commonwealth, killing more than one million people.

Hobbes proposed a solution to this multifaceted crisis. In *Leviathan* (1651), a theoretical treatise on the origin of political power, he argued that in the absence of a strong government society would degenerate into a constant state of war. In this dangerous world life would soon become, in Hobbes's famous words, "solitary, poor, nasty, brutish, and short."[1] The only way for people to find political stability would be to agree with their neighbors to form a political society by surrendering their independent power to a ruler who would make laws, administer justice, and maintain order. In this society the ruler would not share power with others. His subjects, having agreed to endow him with such extensive power, could not resist or depose him. The term used to designate the type of government Hobbes was recommending is **absolutism.** In the most general terms, absolutism means a political arrangement in which one ruler possesses unrivaled power.

During the seventeenth and early eighteenth centuries many European monarchs tried to introduce absolutism and increase the wealth and power of the states they ruled. These efforts always met with resistance. In most cases the rulers and their ministers prevailed, and Europe entered the "age of absolutism," which did not end until the outbreak of the French Revolution in 1789. This chapter addresses this question: Why did some European rulers achieve greater success than others in realizing these political objectives?

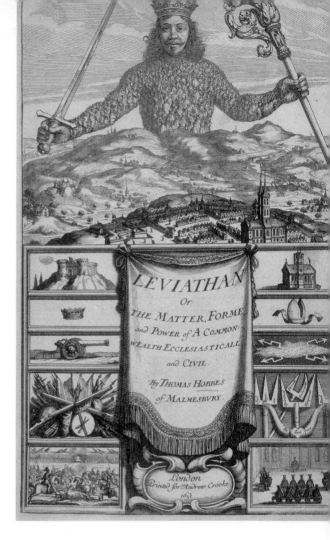

THE FRONTISPIECE OF THOMAS HOBBES'S TREATISE *LEVIATHAN*, PUBLISHED IN LONDON IN 1651

The ruler is depicted as incorporating the bodies of all his subjects, as they collectively authorized him to govern.

THE NATURE OF ABSOLUTISM

■ What did absolutism mean, both as a political theory and as a practical program, and how was absolutism related to the growth of the power of the state?

Seventeenth-century absolutism had both a theoretical and a practical dimension. Theoretical absolutists included writers such as Hobbes who described the nature of power in the state and explained the conditions for its acquisition and continuation. Practical absolutists were the rulers who took concrete political steps to gain control over all other political authorities within the state.

The Theory of Absolutism

When seventeenth-century political writers referred to the monarch's absolute power, they usually meant that he did not share the power to make law with representative assemblies. Hobbes, for example, referred to the absolute ruler as "sole legislator," while the French magistrate Jean Bodin (1530–1596), one of the earliest proponents of absolutist theory, argued in *Six*

Books of a Commonwealth (1576) that the most important power of an absolute ruler was the right to make law by himself.

Absolute rulers also claimed that they were above the law. This meant that when monarchs acted for reason of state, that is, for the benefit of the entire kingdom, they did not have to obey the law of their kingdoms. Nor could they be held legally accountable for their actions because they had no legal superior to judge them. Being above the law, however, did not mean monarchs could act arbitrarily, illegally, or despotically, even though some of them did so from time to time. Absolutist theorists claimed monarchs were obliged to respect the property rights of their subjects whenever they were not acting for reason of state. Under all circumstances monarchs were expected to follow the law of God.

Some absolutist theorists, although not Hobbes, claimed that rulers received their power directly from God. This theory of **divine right** supported royal absolutism, so the theorists claimed, because God would only invest the ruler he appointed with powers that resembled his own. The theory of divine right also supported the absolutist argument that subjects could not resist their monarch under any circumstances.

The Practice of Absolutism

In their quest for absolute power European monarchs employed three strategies. First, they sought to eliminate or weaken national legislative assemblies. In France, which historians consider the most absolutist state in seventeenth-century Europe, the monarchy stopped summoning its national legislature, the **Estates General,** in 1614. In Spain monarchs sought to reduce the powers of the legislative assemblies, the **Cortes,** of their various kingdoms, while in Germany many princes stopped consulting the **diets** of their territorial states.

The second strategy of absolutist rulers was to subordinate the nobility to the king and make them dependent on his favor. Monarchs who aspired to a position of unrivaled power in their kingdoms took steps to keep the nobility in line by suppressing aristocratic challenges to their authority and by appointing men from different social groups as their chief ministers. Yet the king could not afford to alienate these wealthy and high-ranking men, upon whom he still relied for running his government and maintaining order in the localities. Absolute monarchs, therefore, offered nobles special privileges, such as exemption from taxation, positions in the king's government, and freedom to exploit their peasants in exchange for their recognition of the king's absolute authority. In this way, nobles became junior partners in the management of the absolutist state.

The third strategy of absolute monarchs was to control the administrative machinery of the state and use it to enforce royal policy throughout their kingdoms. Absolute monarchs were by nature state builders. They established centralized bureaucracies that extended the reach of their governments down into the smallest towns and villages and out into the most remote regions of their kingdoms. The business conducted by these centrally controlled bureaucracies included the collection of taxes, the recruitment of soldiers, and the operation of the judicial system. Some absolute monarchs used the power of the state to impose and maintain religious conformity. As the seventeenth century advanced, they also used the same power to regulate the price of grain, stimulate the growth of industry, and relieve the plight of the poor. In these ways, absolutist policies had an impact on the lives of all royal subjects, not just noblemen and royal councilors.

Warfare and the Absolutist State

The growth of European states in the seventeenth century was closely related to the conduct of war. During the period from 1600 to 1721, European powers were almost constantly at war. To meet the demands of war, rulers began keeping men under arms at all times. By the middle of the seventeenth century, after the Thirty Years' War had come to an end, most European states had acquired such **standing armies.** These military forces not only served their rulers in foreign wars, but also helped to maintain order and enforce royal policy at home. Standing armies became one of the main props of royal absolutism.

European armies also became larger, in many cases tripling in size. In the 1590s Philip II of Spain had mastered Europe with an army of 40,000 men. By contrast, in the late seventeenth century Louis XIV of France needed an army of 400,000 men to become the dominant power on the continent. The increasing size of these forces partly stemmed from the introduction and extensive use of gunpowder in the fifteenth and sixteenth centuries. Gunpowder led to the widespread use of the musket, a heavy shoulder firearm carried by a foot soldier. The use of the musket demanded the recruitment and equipment of large armies of infantry, who marched in square columns with men holding long pikes (long wooden shafts with pointed metal heads) to protect the musketeers from enemy attacks. As the size of these armies of foot soldiers grew, the role of mounted soldiers, who had dominated medieval warfare, shrank.

Changes in military technology and tactics also necessitated more intensive military training. In the Middle Ages mounted knights had acquired great individual skill, but they did not need to work in precise unison with other men under arms (see "The Military Revolution" in Chapter 11). Seventeenth-century foot soldiers, however, had to learn to march in formation, to coordinate their maneuvers, and to fire without harming their comrades in arms. Therefore, they needed to be drilled. Drilling took place in peacetime as well as during war. The wearing of uniforms, which began when the state assumed the function of clothing its thousands of soldiers, gave further unity and cohesion to the trained fighting force.

The cost of recruiting, training, and equipping these mammoth armies was staggering. In the Middle Ages individual lords often had sufficient financial resources to assemble their own private armies. By the beginning of the seventeenth century the only institution capable of putting the new

armies in the field was the state itself. The same was true for navies, which now consisted of heavily armed sailing ships, each of which carried as many as 400 sailors. To build these large armies and navies, as well as to pay the increasing cost of waging war itself (which rose 500 percent between 1530 and 1630), governments had to identify new methods of raising and collecting taxes. In times of war as much as 80 percent of state revenue went for military purposes.

The equipment and training of military forces and the collection and allocation of the revenue necessary to subsidize these efforts stimulated the expansion and refinement of the state bureaucracy. Governments employed thousands of new officials to supervise the collection of new taxes. To make the system of tax collection more efficient governments often introduced entirely new administrative systems. Some states completely reorganized their bureaucracies to meet the demands of war. They created new departments to supervise the recruitment of soldiers, the manufacture of equipment and uniforms, the building of fleets, and the provisioning of troops in time of war.

THE ABSOLUTIST STATE IN FRANCE AND SPAIN

■ How did France and Spain implement absolutism in the seventeenth century and how powerful did those states become?

The first two European monarchies to become absolutist states were France and Spain. The political development of these two countries, however, followed very different courses. The kingdom of France became a model of state building and gradually emerged as the most powerful country in Europe. The Spanish monarchy, on the other hand, struggled to introduce absolutism at a time when the overall economic condition of the country was deteriorating and its military forces were suffering a series of defeats.

The Foundations of French Absolutism

The first serious efforts to establish absolutism in France took place during the reign of Louis XIII (r. 1610–1643). When Louis was only eight years old, a Catholic assassin killed his father, Henry IV (1589–1610). Louis's mother, Marie de' Medici, assumed the leadership of the government during his youth. This period of **regency**, in which aristocratic factions vied for supremacy at court, exposed the main weakness of the monarchy, which was the rival power of the great noble families of the realm. The statesman who addressed this problem most directly was Louis's main councilor, Cardinal Armand Jean du Plessis de Richelieu (1585–1642), who became the king's chief minister in 1628. Richelieu directed all his energies toward centralizing the power of the French state in the person of the king.

Richelieu's most immediate concern was to bring the independent nobility to heel and subordinate their local power to that of the state. He suppressed several conspiracies and rebellions led by noblemen and restricted the independent power of the provincial assemblies and the eight regional **parlements,** which were the highest courts in the country. Richelieu's great administrative achievement was the strengthening of the system of the **intendants.** These paid crown officials, who were recruited from the professional classes and the lower ranks of the nobility, became the main agents of French local administration. Responsible only to the royal council, they collected taxes, supervised local administration, and recruited soldiers for the army.

Richelieu's most challenging task was increasing the government's yield from taxation, a task

CARDINAL RICHELIEU
Triple portrait of Cardinal Richelieu, who laid the foundations of French absolutism.

that became more demanding during times of war. Levying taxes on the French population was always a delicate process; the needs of the state conflicted with the privileges of various social groups, such as the nobles, who were exempt from taxation, and the estates of individual provinces, such as Brittany, that claimed the right to tax the people themselves. Using a variety of tactics, Richelieu managed to increase the yield from the *taille,* the direct tax on land, as much as threefold during the period from 1635 to 1648. He supplemented the taille with taxes on office-holding. Even then, the revenue was insufficient to meet the extraordinary demands of war.

Richelieu's protégé and successor, Jules Mazarin (1602–1661), continued his policies but was unable to prevent civil war from breaking out in 1648. This challenge to the French state, known as the *Fronde* (a pejorative reference to a Parisian game in which children flung mud at passing carriages), had two phases. The first, the Fronde of the Parlement (1648–1649), began when the members of the Parlement of Paris, the most important of all the provincial parlements, refused to register a royal edict that required them to surrender four years' salary. This act of resistance led to demands that the king sign a document limiting royal authority. The rebels put up barricades in the streets of Paris and forced the royal family to flee the city. The second and more violent phase was the Fronde of the Princes (1650–1653), during which the

Prince de Condé and his noble allies waged war on the government and even formed an alliance with France's enemy, Spain. Only after Condé's military defeat did the entire rebellion collapse.

The Fronde stands as the great crisis of the seventeenth-century French state. It revealed the strength of the local, aristocratic, and legal forces with which the king and his ministers had to contend. In the long run, however, these forces could not destroy the achievement of Richelieu and Mazarin. By the late 1650s the damage had been repaired and the state had resumed its growth.

Absolutism in the Reign of Louis XIV

The man who presided over the development of the French state for the next 50 years was the king himself, Louis XIV (r. 1643–1715), who assumed direct control of his government after the death of Mazarin in 1661. In an age of absolute monarchs, Louis towered over his contemporaries. His reputation as the most powerful ruler of the seventeenth century derives as much from the image he conveyed as from the policies he pursued. Artists, architects, dramatists, and members of his immediate entourage helped the king project an image of incomparable majesty and authority. Paintings and sculptures of the king depicted him in sartorial splendor, holding the symbols of power and displaying expressions of regal superiority that bordered on arrogance. At Versailles, about ten miles from Paris, Louis

CHRONOLOGY: FRANCE IN THE AGE OF ABSOLUTISM	
1598	The Edict of Nantes grants toleration to French Calvinists, known as Huguenots
1610	Assassination of Henry IV of France, who was succeeded by Louis XIII (r. 1610–1643)
1628	Cardinal Richelieu becomes chief minister of Louis XIII of France
1643	Death of Louis XIII of France and accession of Louis XIV; Louis's mother, Anne of Austria, becomes queen regent with Cardinal Mazarin as his minister
1648–1653	The Fronde
1661	Death of Cardinal Mazarin; Louis XIV assumes personal rule
1685	Revocation of the Edict of Nantes
1715	Death of Louis XIV of France; succeeded by his grandson, Louis XV

constructed a lavishly furnished palace that became his main residence and the center of his court. The palace was built in the **baroque** style, which emphasized the size and grandeur of the structure while also conveying a sense of unity and balance among its diverse parts. The sweeping façades of baroque buildings gave them a dynamic quality that evoked an emotional response from the viewer. The baroque style, criticized by contemporaries for its exuberance and pomposity, appealed to absolute monarchs who wished to emphasize their unrivaled position within society and their determination to impose order and stability on their kingdoms.

Court life at Versailles revolved entirely around the king. Court dramas depicted Louis, who styled himself "the sun king," as Apollo, the god of light. The paintings in the grand Hall of Mirrors at Versailles, which recorded the king's military victories, served as reminders of his unrivaled accomplishments. Louis's formal routine in receiving visitors created appropriate distance between him and his courtiers while keeping his subjects in a state of subservient anticipation of royal favor.

Louis's greatest political achievement was securing the complete loyalty and dependence of the old nobility. This he achieved first by requiring the members of these ancient families to come to Versailles for a portion of every year, where they stayed in apartments within the royal palace itself. At Versailles Louis involved them in the elaborate cultural activities of court life and in ceremonial rituals that emphasized their subservience to the king. He also excluded these nobles from holding important offices in the government of the realm, a strategy designed to prevent them from building an independent power

VERSAILLES PALACE, CENTER OF THE COURT OF LOUIS XIV AFTER 1682
The palace was constructed between 1669 and 1686. Its massiveness and grandeur and the order it imposed on the landscape made it a symbol of royal absolutism.

base within the bureaucracy. Instead he recruited men from the mercantile and professional classes to run his government. This policy of taming the nobility and depriving them of central administrative power could work only if they received something in return. Like all the absolute monarchs of western Europe, Louis used the patronage at his disposal to grant members of the nobility wealth and privileges in exchange for their loyalty to the crown. In this way the monarchy and the nobility served each other's interests.

In running the actual machinery of government Louis built upon and perfected the centralizing policies of Richelieu and Mazarin. After the death of Mazarin in 1661, the king, then 23 years old, became his own chief minister, presiding over a council of state that supervised the work of government. An elaborate set of councils at the highest levels of government set policy that department ministers then implemented. The provincial intendants became even more important than they had been under Richelieu and Mazarin, especially in providing food, arms, and equipment for royal troops. The intendants secured the cooperation of local judges, city councils, and parish priests as well as the compliance of the local population. If necessary they could call upon royal troops to enforce the king's policies, but for the most part they preferred to rely on the more effective tactics of negotiation and compromise with local officials. The system, when it worked properly, allowed the king to make decisions that directly affected the lives and beliefs of his 20 million subjects.

In the late seventeenth century the French state also became involved in the economic and financial life of the country. The minister most responsible for this increase in state power was Jean Baptiste Colbert (1619–1683), a protégé of Mazarin who in 1661 became controller general of the realm. Born into a family of merchants, and despised by the old nobility, Colbert epitomized the type of government official Louis recruited into his service. Entrusted with the supervision of the entire system of royal taxation, Colbert increased royal revenues by reducing the cut taken by tax collectors.

Even more important, Colbert exploited the country's economic resources for the benefit of the state. The theory underlying this set of policies was **mercantilism,** which held that the wealth of the state depended on its ability to import fewer commodities than it exported. Its goal was to secure the largest possible share of the world's monetary supply. Colbert increased the size of France's merchant fleet, founded overseas trading companies, and levied high tariffs on France's commercial rivals. To make France economically self-sufficient, he encouraged the growth of the French textile industry, improved the condition of the roads, built canals throughout the kingdom, and reduced some of the burdensome tolls that impeded internal trade.

The most intrusive exercise of the power of the state during Louis XIV's reign was his decision to enforce religious uniformity. In 1598 the Edict of Nantes had given French Calvinists, known as Huguenots, the freedom to practice their religion. Louis considered the existence of this large Huguenot minority within his kingdom an affront to his sense of order. In 1685 therefore Louis revoked the Edict, thereby denying freedom of religious worship to about one million of his subjects. The army enforced public conversions to Catholicism and closed Protestant churches. Large numbers of Huguenots emigrated to the Netherlands, England, Germany, and North America. Few exercises of absolute power in the seventeenth century caused more disruption in the lives of ordinary people than this attempt to realize Louis's ideal of "one king, one law, one faith."

Louis XIV and the Culture of Absolutism

A further manifestation of the power of the French absolutist state was Louis's success in influencing and transforming French culture. Kings had often served as patrons of the arts by providing income for artists, writers, and musicians and endowing cultural and educational institutions. Louis took this type of royal patronage to a new level, making it possible for him to control the dissemination of ideas and the very production of culture itself. During Louis's reign royal patronage, emanating from the court, extended the king's influence over the entire cultural landscape. The architects of the palace at Versailles, the painters of historical scenes that hung in its hallways and galleries, the composers of the plays and operas performed in its theaters, the sculptors who created busts of the king to decorate its chambers, and the historians and pamphlet writers who celebrated the king's achievements in print all benefited from Louis's direct financial support.

Much of Louis's patronage went to cultural institutions. He took over the Academy of Fine Arts in 1661, founded the Academy of Music in 1669, and chartered a theater company, the *Comédie Française,* in 1680. Two great French dramatists of the late seventeenth century, Jean Baptiste Molière (1622–1673), the creator of French high comedy, and Jean Racine (1639–1699), who wrote tragedies in the classical style, benefited from the king's patronage. Louis even subsidized the publication of a new journal, the *Journal des savants,* in which writers advanced their ideas. In 1666 Louis extended his patronage to the sciences with the founding of the *Académie des Sciences,* which had the twofold objective of advancing scientific knowledge and glorifying the king. It also benefited the state by devising improvements in ship design and navigation.

Of all the cultural institutions that benefited from Louis XIV's patronage, the *Académie Française* had the most enduring impact on French culture. This society of literary scholars founded in 1635, sought to standardize the French language and preserve its integrity. In 1694, 22 years after Louis became the academy's patron, the first official French dictionary appeared in print. This achievement of linguistic uniformity, in which words received authorized spellings and definitions, reflected the pervasiveness of Louis's cultural influence as well as the search for order that became the defining characteristic of his reign.

The Wars of Louis XIV, 1667–1714

Colbert's financial and economic policies, coupled with the military reforms of the Marquis de Louvois, laid the foundation for the creation of a formidable military machine. In 1667 Louis XIV began unleashing its full potential. With an army 20 times larger than the French force that had invaded Italy in 1494, Louis fought four separate wars against an array of European powers between 1667 and 1714. His goal in all these wars was territorial acquisition (see **Map 16.1**). In this case Louis set his sights mainly on the German and Spanish territories in the Rhineland along the eastern borders of his kingdom. Contemporaries

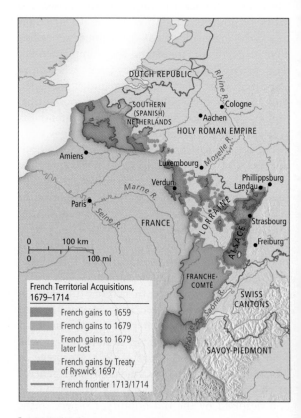

MAP 16.1

French Territorial Acquisitions, 1679–1714

Louis XIV thought of the Rhine River as France's natural eastern boundary, and territories acquired in 1659 and 1697 allowed it to reach that limit.

suggested, however, that he was thinking in grander terms than traditional French dynastic ambition. Propagandists for the king in the late 1660s claimed that Louis harbored visions of establishing a "universal monarchy" or an "absolute empire," reminiscent of the empires of ancient Rome, Charlemagne in the ninth century, and Charles V in the sixteenth century.

Louis never attained the empire of his dreams. After he launched an offensive against German towns along the Rhine River in 1688, Great Britain, the Dutch Republic, Spain, and Austria formed a coalition against him. Finally matched by the combined military strength of these allies, forced to wage war on many different fronts (including North America), and unable to collect enough taxes to pay for the war, France felt compelled to conclude peace in 1697. The Treaty of Ryswick marked the turning point in the expansion of the French state and laid the groundwork for the establishment of a **balance of power** in the next century, an arrangement whereby various countries form alliances to prevent any one state from dominating the others.

The Treaty of Ryswick, however, did not mark the end of French territorial ambition. In 1701 Louis went to war once again, this time as part of an effort to place a French Bourbon candidate, his grandson Duke Philip of Anjou, on the Spanish throne. The impending death of the mentally weak, sexually impotent, and chronically ill King Charles II of Spain (r. 1665–1700) without heirs had created a succession crisis. In 1698 the major European powers had agreed to a treaty that would divide Spanish lands between Louis and the Holy Roman Emperor, both of whom were Charles's brothers-in-law. By his will, however, Charles left the Spanish crown and all its overseas possessions to Philip. This bequest offered France more than it would have received on the basis of the treaty. If the will had been upheld, the Pyrenees Mountains would have disappeared as a political barrier between France and Spain, and France, as the stronger of the two kingdoms, would have controlled unprecedented expanses of European and American territory.

Dreaming once again of universal monarchy, Louis rejected the treaty in favor of King Charles's will. The British, Dutch, and Austrians responded by forming a Grand Alliance against France and Spain. After a long and costly conflict, known as the War of the Spanish Succession (1701–1713), the members of this coalition were able to dictate the terms of the Treaty of Utrecht (1713). Philip, who suffered from fits of manic depression and went days without dressing or leaving his room, remained on the Spanish throne as Philip V (r. 1700–1746), but only on the condition that the French and Spanish crowns would never be united. Spain ceded its territories in the Netherlands and in Italy to the Austrian Habsburg Monarchy and its strategic port of Gibraltar at the entrance to the Mediterranean to the British. Britain also acquired large parts of French Canada, including Newfoundland and Nova Scotia, The treaty thus dashed Louis's hopes of universal monarchy and confirmed the new balance of power in Europe.

The loss of French territory in North America, the strains placed on the taxation system by the financial demands of war, and the weakening of France's commercial power as a result of this conflict made France a less potent state at the time of Louis's death in 1715 than it had been in the 1680s. Nevertheless, the main effects of a century of French state building remained, including a large, well-integrated bureaucratic edifice that allowed the government to exercise unprecedented control over the population and a military establishment that remained the largest and best equipped in Europe.

Absolutism and State Building in Spain

The history of Spain in the seventeenth century is almost always written in terms of failure, as the country endured a long period of economic decline that began in the late sixteenth century. With a precipitate drop in the size of the population, the monarchy became progressively weaker under a series of ineffective kings, To make matters worse,

LOUIS XIV

Portrait of Louis XIV in military armor, with his plumed helmet and his crown on the table to the right. The portrait was painted during the period of French warfare. In the background is a French ship.

Spain, like France, underwent a period of state building during the seventeenth century, and that its government, like that of France, gravitated toward absolutism.

The Spanish monarchy in 1600 ruled more territory than did France, but its many principalities and small kingdoms possessed far more independence than even the most remote and peripheral French provinces. The center of the monarchy was the kingdom of Castile, with its capital at Madrid. This kingdom, the largest and wealthiest territory within the Iberian Peninsula, had been united with the kingdom of Aragon in 1479 when King Ferdinand II of Aragon (r. 1479–1516), the husband of Queen Isabella of Castile (r. 1474–1504), ascended the throne. These two kingdoms, however, continued to exist as separate states after the union, each having its own representative institutions and administrative systems. Each of them, moreover, contained smaller, semiautonomous kingdoms and provinces that retained their own distinctive political institutions. Outside the Iberian Peninsula the Spanish monarchy ruled territories in the Netherlands, Italy, and the New World.

the country suffered a series of military defeats, most of them at the hands of the French. As a result, Spain lost its position as the major European power (see **Map 16.2**). By the early eighteenth century Spain was a shadow of its former self, and its culture reflected uncertainty, pessimism, and nostalgia for its former imperial greatness. None of this failure, however, should obscure the fact that

The only institution besides the monarchy itself that provided any kind of administrative unity to all these Spanish territories in the seventeenth century was the Spanish Inquisition, a centralized ecclesiastical court with a supreme council in Madrid and 21 regional tribunals in different parts of Spain, Italy, and America.

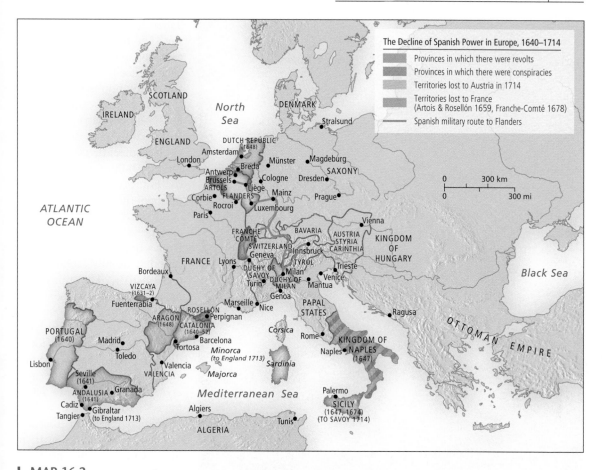

MAP 16.2

The Decline of Spanish Power in Europe, 1640–1714

Revolts in the United Provinces of the Netherlands and Portugal account for two of the most significant losses of Spanish territory. Military defeat at the hands of the French in 1659 and Austria in 1714 account for the loss of most of the other territories.

The great challenge for the Spanish monarchy in the seventeenth century was to integrate the various kingdoms and principalities of Spain into a more highly centralized state and make the machinery of that state more efficient and profitable. The statesman who made the most sustained efforts at realizing these goals was the energetic and authoritarian Count-Duke of Olivares (1587–1645), the contemporary of Richelieu during the reign of the Spanish king Philip IV (1621–1665). Olivares faced a daunting task. As a result of decades of warfare, the Spanish

monarchy in the 1620s was penniless, the kingdom of Castile had gone bankrupt, and the entire country had entered a period of protracted economic decline.

To deal with these deep structural problems Olivares proposed a reform of the entire financial system, the establishment of national banks, and the replacement of the tax on consumption, the *millones*, with proportional contributions from towns and villages in Castile. He also tried to make all the Spanish kingdoms and principalities contribute to the national

DIEGO DE VELÁZQUEZ, PORTRAIT OF THE PRINCE BALTASAR CARLOS, HEIR TO THE SPANISH THRONE

The depiction of the six-year-old prince on a rearing horse was intended to suggest military and political power at a time when the monarchy was losing both. The prince died in 1646, before he could succeed to the throne.

Three factors explain his failure. The first was the opposition he confronted within Castile itself, especially from the cities represented in the Cortes, over the question of taxation. The second, a problem facing Spain throughout the seventeenth century, was military failure. Spanish losses to France during the final phase of the Thirty Years' War aggravated the financial crisis and prevented the monarchy from capitalizing on the prestige that usually attends military victory. The third and most serious impediment was opposition to the policy of subordinating the outlying Spanish regions to the kingdom of Castile. The kingdoms and provinces on the periphery of the country were determined to maintain their individual laws and liberties, especially the powers of their own Cortes. The problem became more serious when Olivares, in the wake of military defeat by the French and Dutch, put more pressure on these outlying kingdoms and provinces to contribute to the war effort. During the tenure of Olivares, Spain faced separatist revolts in Portugal, Catalonia, Sicily, and Naples. With the exception of Portugal, which recovered its sovereignty in 1640, the monarchy managed to retain its provincial and Italian territories, but it failed to bring these areas under central government control.

The relative weakness of the Spanish monarchy became most apparent in the late seventeenth century, the age of Louis XIV. In two important respects the Spanish government failed to match

defense on a proportionate basis. His goal was to unify the entire peninsula in a cohesive Spanish national state, similar to that of France. This policy involved suppression of the historic privileges of the various kingdoms and principalities and the direct subordination of each area to the king. It was, in other words, a policy based on the principles of royal absolutism.

Olivares was unable to match the state-building achievement of Richelieu in France.

CHRONOLOGY: INTERNATIONAL CONFLICT IN THE SEVENTEENTH CENTURY

1609	Truce between the seven Dutch provinces and Spain
1618	Bohemian revolt against Habsburg rule; beginning of the Thirty Years' War
1620	Imperial forces defeat Bohemians at Battle of White Mountain
1648	Treaty of Westphalia, ending the Thirty Years' War; Treaty of Münster, ending the Dutch War of Independence
1667	Beginning of the wars of Louis XIV
1672	William III of Orange-Nassau becomes captain-general of Dutch; beginning of the war against France (1672–1678)
1688–1697	War of the League of Augsburg (Nine Years' War); England and Scotland join forces with Prussia, Austria, the Dutch Republic, and many German states against France
1697	Treaty of Ryswick
1700–1721	Great Northern War in which Russia eventually defeated Sweden; emergence of Russia as a major power
1701–1713	War of the Spanish Succession
1713	Treaty of Utrecht

the achievement of the French. First, Spain could never escape the grip that the old noble families had on the central administration. The unwillingness of the nobility to recruit ministers and officials from the mercantile and professional groups in society (which were small to begin with in Spain) worked against the achievement of bureaucratic efficiency and made innovation almost impossible. Second, unlike the French government during Colbert's ministry, the Spanish government failed to encourage economic growth. The hostility of the aristocratic ruling class to mercantile affairs, coupled with a traditional Spanish unwillingness to follow the example of foreigners (especially when they were Protestants) prevented the country from stemming its own economic decline and the government from solving the formidable financial problems facing it. To make matters worse, the Spanish government failed to make its system of tax collection more efficient.

The mood that prevailed within the upper levels of Castilian society in the seventeenth century reflected the failure of the government and the entire nation. The contrast between the glorious achievements of the monarchy during the reign of Philip II (r. 1555–1598) and the somber realities of the late seventeenth century led most members of the ruling class to retreat into the past, a nostalgia that only encouraged further economic and political stagnation. The work of Miguel de Cervantes (1547–1616), the greatest Spanish writer of the seventeenth century, reflected this change in the Spanish national mood. In 1605 and 1615 Cervantes published (in two parts) *Don Quixote*, the story of an idealistic wandering nobleman who pursued dreams of an elusive military glory. This work, which as we have seen in Chapter 15, explored the relationship between illusion and reality, served as a commentary on a nobility that had lost confidence in itself.

Paradoxically Spanish painting entered its Golden Age at the time the country began to lose its economic, political, and military vitality. Little in the paintings of the great Spanish artist Diego de Velázquez (1599–1660) would suggest the malaise that was affecting Spain and its nobility at the time. Velázquez painted in the baroque style that was in favor in European courts. He depicted his subjects in heroic poses and imbued them with a sense of royal or aristocratic dignity. One of his historical paintings, *The Surrender of Breda* (1634), commemorated a rare Spanish military victory over the Dutch in 1625 and the magnanimity of the Spanish victors toward their captives. All this was intended to reinforce the prestige of the monarchy, the royal family, and Spain itself at a time when the imperial grandeur of the past had faded. Velázquez's painting reflected the ideals of absolutism but ignored the realities of Spanish political and military life.

ABSOLUTISM AND STATE BUILDING IN CENTRAL AND EASTERN EUROPE

■ What was the nature of royal absolutism in central and eastern Europe, and how did the policies of the Ottoman Empire and Russia help to establish the boundaries of the West during this period?

The forces that led to the establishment of absolutism and state building in France and Spain also made an impact on central and eastern Europe. In Germany the Thirty Years' War led to the establishment of two absolutist states, Prussia and the Austrian Habsburg Monarchy. Farther to the east, the Ottoman and Russian Empires developed political systems that shared many of the same characteristics as states in western and central Europe. These policies challenged the traditional European perception that both empires belonged entirely to an Eastern, Asian world.

Germany and the Thirty Years' War, 1618–1648

Before 1648 the main political power within the geographical area known as Germany was the Holy Roman Empire. This large political formation was a loose confederation of kingdoms, principalities, duchies, ecclesiastical territories, and cities, each of which had its own laws and political institutions. The emperor, who was elected by a body of German princes, exercised immediate jurisdiction only in his own dynastic possessions and in the imperial cities. He also convened a legislative assembly known as the *Reichstag,* over which he exercised limited influence. The emperor did not have a large administrative or judicial bureaucracy through which he could enforce imperial law in the localities. The empire was not in any sense a sovereign state, even though it had long been a major force in European diplomacy. It had acquired and maintained that international position by relying on the military and financial contributions of its imperial cities and the lands controlled directly by the Habsburg emperors.

The Thirty Years' War permanently altered the nature of this intricate political structure. That war began as a conflict between Protestant German princes and the Catholic emperor over religious and constitutional issues. The incident that triggered it in 1618 was the so-called Defenestration of Prague, when members of the predominantly Protestant Bohemian legislature, known as the Diet, threw two imperial officials out a castle window as a protest against the religious policies of their recently elected king, the future emperor Ferdinand II. The Diet proceeded to depose Ferdinand, a Catholic, and elect a Protestant prince, Frederick V of the Palatinate, to replace him. The war soon broadened into a European-wide struggle over the control of German and Spanish territory, as the Danes, Swedes, and French successively entered the conflict against the emperor and his Spanish Habsburg relatives. For a brief period in the late 1620s England also entered the conflict against Spain. The war, which was fought mainly on German soil, had a devastating effect on the country. More than one million soldiers marched across German lands, sacking towns and exploiting the resources of local communities. Germany lost up to one-third of its population, while the destruction of property retarded the economic development of the country for more than 50 years.

DEFENESTRATION OF PRAGUE, MAY 23, 1618
The Thirty Years' War was touched off when Protestant nobles in the Bohemian legislature threw two Catholic imperial governors out the window of a castle in Prague.

The political effects of the war were no less traumatic. By virtue of the Treaty of Westphalia, which ended the war in 1648, the empire was permanently weakened, although it continued to function until 1806 (see **Map 16.3**). The individual German territories within the empire developed more institutional autonomy than they had before the war. They became sovereign states, with their own armies, foreign policies, and central bureaucracies. Two of these German states became major European powers and developed their own forms of absolutism. The first was Brandenburg-Prussia, a collection of various territories in northern Germany that was transformed into the kingdom of Prussia at the beginning of the eighteenth century. The second state was the Austrian Habsburg Monarchy, which in the eighteenth century was usually identified simply as Austria. The Habsburgs had long dominated the Holy Roman Empire and continued to secure election as emperors after the Treaty of Westphalia. In the late seventeenth century, however, the Austrian Habsburg Monarchy acquired its own institutional identity, distinct from that of the Holy Roman Empire. It consisted of the lands that the Habsburgs controlled directly in the southeastern part of the empire and other territories, including the kingdom of Hungary, which lay outside the territorial boundaries of the empire.

The Growth of the Prussian State

In 1648, at the end of the Thirty Years' War, Prussia could barely claim the status of an independent state, much less an absolute monarchy. The core of the Prussian state was Brandenburg,

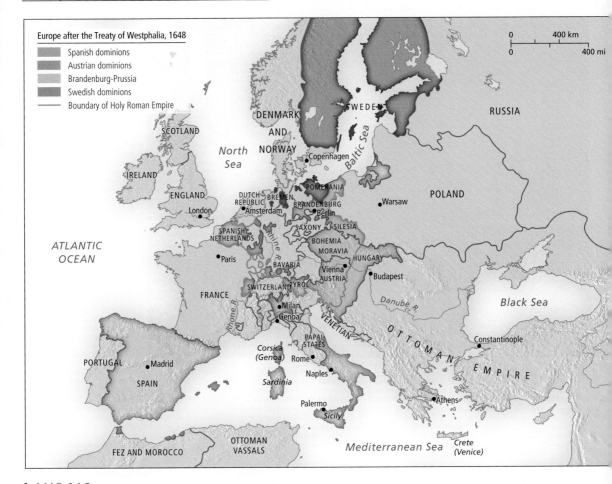

MAP 16.3

Europe after the Treaty of Westphalia, 1648

The Holy Roman Empire no longer included the Dutch Republic, which was now independent of Spain. Some of the lands of the Austrian Habsburg Monarchy and Brandenburg-Prussia lay outside the boundaries of the Holy Roman Empire. Italy was divided into a number of small states in the north, while Spain ruled Naples, Sicily, and Sardinia.

which was an electorate because its ruler cast one of the ballots to elect the Holy Roman Emperor. The Hohenzollern family, which controlled the electorate, held lands that lay scattered throughout northern Germany and stretched into eastern Europe. The largest was Prussia, a Baltic territory lying outside the boundaries of the Holy Roman Empire. As ruler of these disparate and noncontiguous lands, the Elector of Brandenburg had virtually no state

bureaucracy, collected few taxes, and commanded only a small army. Most of his territories, moreover, lay in ruins in 1648, having been devastated by Swedish and imperial troops at various times during the war.

The Great Elector Frederick William (r. 1640–1688) began the long process of turning this ramshackle structure into a powerful and cohesive German state (see **Map 16.4**). His son and grandson, King Frederick I (r. 1688–1713)

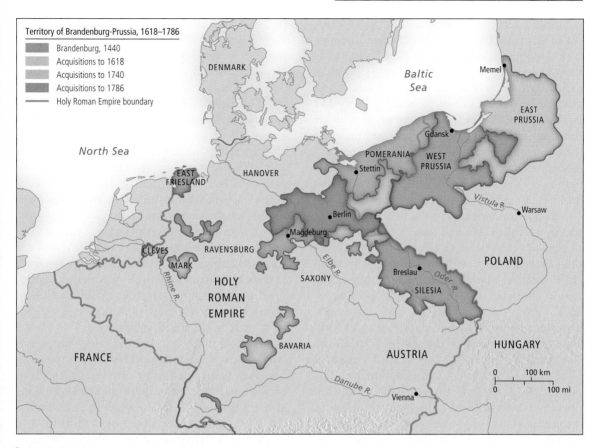

MAP 16.4

The Growth of Brandenburg-Prussia, 1618–1786

By acquiring lands throughout northern Germany, Prussia became a major European power. The process began during the early seventeenth century, but it continued well into the eighteenth century. The Prussian army, which was the best trained fighting force in Europe in the eighteenth century, greatly facilitated Prussia's growth.

and Frederick William I (r. 1713–1740), completed the transformation. The key to their success, as it was for all aspiring absolute monarchs in eastern Europe, was to secure the compliance of the traditional nobility, who in Prussia were known as **Junkers**. The Great Elector Frederick William achieved this end by granting the Junkers a variety of privileges, including exemption from import duties and the excise tax. The most valuable concession was the legal confirmation of their rights over their serfs. During the previous 150 years Prussian peasants had lost their freedom, becoming permanently bound to

the estates of their lords and completely subject to the Junkers' arbitrary brand of local justice. The Junkers had a deeply vested interest in perpetuating this oppressive system of serfdom, and the lawgiver Frederick was able to provide them with the legal guarantees they required.

With the loyalty of the Junkers secure, Frederick William began building a powerful Prussian state with a standing army and a large bureaucracy that superintended military and financial affairs. The army grew rapidly, rising to 30,000 men in 1690 and 80,000 by 1740. It consisted of a combination of carefully recruited volunteers, foreign mercenaries, and, after 1713, conscripts from the general population. Its most famous regiment, known as the Blue Prussians or the Giants of Potsdam, consisted of 1,200 men, each of whom was at least six feet tall. Commanded by officers drawn from the nobility and reinforced by Europe's first system of military reserves, this army quickly became the best trained fighting force in Europe. Prussia became a model military state, symbolized by the transformation of the royal gardens into an army training ground during the reign of Frederick William I.

As this military state grew in size and complexity, its rulers acquired many of the attributes of absolute rule. Most significantly, they became the sole legislators within the state. The main representative assembly in the electorate, the Diet of Brandenburg, met for the last time in 1652. Frederick William and his successors, however, continued to consult with smaller local assemblies, especially in the matter of taxation. The naming of Frederick I as king of Prussia in 1701 marked a further consolidation of royal power. His son's style of rule, which included physical punishment of judges whose decisions displeased him, suggested that the Prussian monarchy not only had attained absolute power, but could occasionally abuse it.

The Austrian Habsburg Monarchy

The Austrian Habsburgs were much less successful than the Hohenzollerns in building a centralized, consolidated state along absolutist lines. The various territories that made up the Austrian Habsburg Monarchy in the late seventeenth century were larger and more diverse than those that belonged to Prussia. **Map 16.3** shows that in addition to the cluster of duchies that form present-day Austria, the Austrian Habsburg monarchy embraced two subordinate kingdoms. The kingdom of Bohemia, lying to the north, had struggled against Habsburg control for nearly a century and included the provinces of Moravia and Silesia. The kingdom of Hungary, lying to the southeast, included the large semiautonomous principality of Transylvania. The Habsburgs

regained Hungary from the Ottoman Empire in stages between 1664 and 1718. In 1713 the monarchy also acquired the former Spanish Netherlands and the Italian territories of Milan and Naples.

The Austrian Habsburg monarchs of the seventeenth and early eighteenth centuries never succeeded in integrating these ethnically, religiously, and politically diverse lands into a unified, cohesive state similar to that of France. The main obstacle was a lack of a unified bureaucracy. The only centralized administrative institutions in this amalgam of kingdoms were the Court Chamber, which superintended the collection of taxes throughout the monarchy, and the Austrian army, which included troops from all Habsburg lands. Even these centralized institutions had difficulty operating smoothly. For all practical purposes, the Habsburgs had to rule their various kingdoms separately.

In governing its Austrian and Bohemian lands, this decentralized Habsburg monarchy nonetheless acquired some of the characteristics of absolutist rule. After defeating the Bohemians at the Battle of White Mountain in 1620 during the Thirty Years' War, Emperor Ferdinand II (r. 1618–1637) strengthened his authority not only in Bohemia, but over all the territories under his direct control. After punishing the rebels and exiling many of the Protestant nobility, he undertook a deliberate expansion of his legislative and judicial powers, and he secured direct control over all his administrative officials.

A policy of severe religious repression accompanied this increase in the emperor's authority. Ferdinand assumed that Protestantism served as a justification for rebellion, and he therefore decided that its practice could not be tolerated. He required that Protestants in all the emperor's territories take a Catholic loyalty oath, and he banned Protestant education.

Habsburgs were not so successful in trying to impose absolutism on Hungary in the late seventeenth and eighteenth centuries. Hungarians had a long tradition of limited, constitutional rule in which the national Diet exercised powers of legislation and taxation, just as Parliament did in England. Habsburg emperors made some limited inroads on these traditions but they were never able to break them. They also were unable to achieve the same degree of religious uniformity that they had imposed on their other territories. In Hungary the Habsburgs encountered the limits of royal absolutism.

The Ottoman Empire: Between East and West

In the seventeenth and early eighteenth centuries the southeastern border of the Habsburg monarchy separated the kingdom of Hungary from the Ottoman Empire. This militarized frontier marked not only the political boundary between two empires, but a deeper cultural boundary between East and West.

As we have seen in previous chapters, the West is not just a geographical area. It is also a cultural area; the people who inhabit this territory share many of the same religious, political, legal, and philosophical traditions. In the eyes of most Europeans, the Ottoman Turks, who posed a recurrent military threat to the Habsburg monarchy, did not belong to this Western world. Because the Ottoman Turks were Muslims, Europeans considered them enemies of Christianity, infidels who were bent on the destruction of Christendom. Ottoman emperors, known as sultans, were reputedly despots who ruled over their subjects as slaves. Western literature also depicted the sultans as cruel and brutal tyrants, the opposite of the ideal Christian prince. One French play of 1612 showed the mother of the sultan Mehmed the Conquerer (r. 1451–1481) drinking the blood of a victim.

These stereotypes of the Turks gave Europeans a sense of their own Western identity. Turks became a negative reference group with whom Europeans could compare themselves. The realities of Ottoman politics and culture, however, were quite different from their representations in European literature. Turkish despotism, the name Europeans gave to the Ottoman system of government, existed only in theory. Ever since the fourteenth century Ottoman writers had claimed for

the sultan extraordinary powers, including the right to seize the landed property of his subjects at will. In practice, however, the sultan never exercised unlimited power. The spirit of Muslim law limited his prerogatives, and he shared power with the grand vizier, his chief executive officer. By the 1660s, when most European states had entered the age of absolutism, the sultan's power had become largely titular. Moreover, the Ottoman practice of tolerating non-Muslim religions within the empire made the sultans less absolutist than most of their seventeenth-century European counterparts. (See *Different Voices* in this chapter.)

Even the Ottoman Empire's high degree of administrative centralization did not extend to all the territories it ruled. Many of its provinces, especially those in the Balkans, enjoyed a considerable measure of autonomy, especially in the seventeenth century. The Balkans, which were geographically part of Europe, never experienced the full force of direct Turkish rule. As in most monarchies of western and central Europe, a complex pattern of negotiation between the central imperial administration and local officials characterized Ottoman rule. In Europe the Ottoman Empire bore the closest resemblance to the Spanish monarchy, which also ruled many far-flung territories. Like Spain, the Ottoman Empire declined in power during the seventeenth century and lost effective control of some of its outlying provinces.

Ottoman Turks and Europeans frequently went to war against each other, but their interactions with the West were not always hostile. The Turks had been involved in European warfare since the fifteenth century, and they had formed diplomatic alliances with the French against the Austrian Habsburgs on a number of occasions. Europeans and Ottomans often acquired military technology and administrative techniques from each other. Trade between European countries and the Ottoman Empire remained brisk throughout this period. Europe supplied hardware and textiles to the Turks while they in turn shipped coffee, tobacco, and tulips to European ports. Communities of Turks and other Muslims lived in European cities, while

DIFFERENT VOICES WESTERN WRITERS EVALUATE THE OTTOMAN TURKS

Western commentators displayed ambivalent feelings toward the Ottoman Turks in the seventeenth century. On the one hand, Westerners were impressed with the power of the Sultan, the size of the Ottoman Empire, the discipline of their soldiers, and the political obedience of their subjects to their sovereign. On the other hand, Westerners considered the Turks barbarous. Richard Knolles (1550–1610) reflected this ambivalence in the preface to his history of the Turks with an analysis of their greatness. He then condemned the ways in which this barbarous people violated international and natural law. Thomas Smith, a clergyman at Oxford University, agreed with Knolles that the Turks were a barbarous nation, but he attributed this trait to their lack of interest in education and their intolerance of other religions.

An English Writer Criticizes the Turks for Violating the Law

But to come nearer unto the causes of the Turks greatness, ... first in them is to be noted an ardent and infinite desire of sovereignty, wherewith they have long since promised unto themselves the monarchy of the whole world, a quick motive unto their so haughty designs. Then, such a rare unity and agreement amongst them, as well in the manner of their religion (if it be so to be called) as in matters concerning their state (especially in all their enterprises to be taken in hand for the augmenting of their Empire) as that thereof they call themselves *Islami*, that is to say, men of one mind, or at peace among themselves; so as it is not to be marveled, if thereby they grow strong themselves, and dreadful to others. Join unto this their courage, conceived by the wonderful success of their perpetual fortune, their notable vigilance in taking the advantage of

every occasion for the enlarging of their monarchy, their frugality and temperateness in their diet and other manner of living, their straight observing of their ancient military discipline, their cheerful and almost incredible obedience unto their princes and Sultans; such, as in that point no nation in the world was to be worthily compared unto them—all great causes why their empire hath so mightily increased and so long continued....

And yet these great ones not contented by such commendable and lawful means still to extend or establish their far spreading empire, if that point once come in question, they stick not in their devilish policy to break and infringe the laws both of nations and nature. Their leagues grounded upon the law of nations, be they with never so strong capitulations concluded, or solemnity of oath confirmed, have with them no longer force than stands with their own profit, serving indeed but as snares to entangle other princes in, until they have singled out him whom they purpose to devour; the rest fast bound still looking on as if their own turn should never come, yet with no more assurance of their safety by their leagues than had the other whom they see perish before their faces. As for the kind law of nature, what can be thereunto more contrary than for the father most unnaturally to embrue his hands in the blood of his own children and the brother to become the bloody executioner of his own brethren, a common matter among the Ottoman emperors? All which most execrable and inhumane murders they cover with the pretended safety of their state, as thereby freed from the fear of all aspiring competitors (the greatest torment of the mighty) and by the preservation of the integrity of their Empire, which they thereby keep whole and entire unto themselves, and so

numerous European merchants resided in territories under Ottoman control.

These encounters between Turks and Europeans suggest that the militarized boundary

between the Habsburgs and the Ottoman Empire was more porous than its fortifications suggested. Military conflict and Western contempt for Turks disguised a complex process of political and

deliver it as it were by hand from one to another, in no part dismembered or impaired. By these and such like means is this barbarous empire (of almost nothing) grown to that height of majesty and power, as that it hath in contempt all the rest, being it self not inferior in greatness and strength unto the greatest monarchies that ever yet were upon the face of the earth, the Roman Empire only excepted.

Source: Richard Knolles, *The General History of the Turks from the First Beginnings of That Nation to the Rising of the Ottoman Family*, 1603.

An English Clergyman Comments on the Learning and Religious Intolerance of the Turks

The Turks are justly branded with the character of a barbarous nation, which censure does not relate either to the cruelty and severity of their punishments…or to want of discipline…or to want of civil behavior among themselves…but to the intolerable pride and scorn wherewith they treat all the world besides.

Their temper and genius, the constitution of their government, and the principles of their education incline them to war, where valor and merit are sure to be encouraged, and have their due reward. They have neither leisure nor inclination to entertain the studies of learning or the civil arts, which take off the roughness and wildness of nature, and render men more agreeable in their conversation. And though they are forced to commend and admire the ingenuity of the Western Christians, when they see any mathematical instrument, curious pictures, map, or sea-charts, or open the leaves of any printed book, or the like; yet they look upon all this as a curiosity, that not only may be spared, but what ought to be

carefully avoided, and kept out of their empire, as tending to soften men's minds, and render them less fit for arms, which they look upon as the best and truest end of life, to enlarge their greatness and their conquests.

But it is not so much their want of true and ingenuous learning which makes them thus intractable and rude to strangers as a rooted and inveterate prejudice against and hatred of all others who are of a different religion. It is not to be expected that where this principle prevails, and is looked upon as a piece of religion and duty, they who embrace it should be guilty of any act of kindness and humanity; except when they are bribed to it with hope of reward and gain, or forced to it by the necessities of state, or wrought upon more powerfully, as it were against their wills by the resentments of some favors and kindnesses received, which may happen now and then in some of better natures and more generous tempers.

Source: Thomas Smith, *Remarks upon the Manners, Religion and Government of the Turks*, 1678.

For Discussion

1. Which characteristics of the Turks given in the two documents did the authors view as positive and which did they view as negative?

2. To what extent do these two descriptions of the Turks support the Western view that the Ottoman Empire was an "oriental despotism"?

3. These two writers based their assessments of the Turks upon reports from travelers. What value do such reports have as historical evidence?

cultural interaction between the two civilizations. Europeans tended to think of the Ottoman Empire as "oriental," but it is more accurate to view it as a region lying between the East and the West.

Russia and the West

The other power that marked the boundary between East and West was the vast Russian Empire, which stretched from its boundary with

Poland-Lithuania in the west to the Pacific Ocean in the east. Until the end of the seventeenth century, the kingdom of Muscovy and the lands attached to it seemed, at least to Europeans, part of the Asiatic world. Dominated by an Eastern Orthodox branch of Christianity, Russia drew very little upon the cultural traditions associated with western Europe. Unlike its Slavic neighbor Poland, Russia had not absorbed large doses of German culture. It also appeared to Europeans to be another example of "oriental despotism," a state in which the ruler, known as the tsar (the Russian word for Caesar), could rule his subjects at will, "not bound up by any law or custom."

During the reign of Tsar Peter I, known as Peter the Great (r. 1682–1725), Russia underwent a process of Westernization, bringing it more into line with the culture of European countries and becoming a major European power. This policy began after Peter visited England, the Dutch Republic, northern Germany, and Austria in 1697 and 1698. Upon his return he directed his officials and members of the upper levels of Russian society to adopt Western styles of dress and appearance, including the removal of men's beards. (Scissors were kept in the customs house for this purpose alone.) Beards symbolized the backward, Eastern Orthodox culture from whose grip Peter hoped to extricate his country. Young Russian boys were sent abroad for their education. Women began to participate openly in the social and cultural life of the cities, in violation of Orthodox custom. Smoking was permitted despite the Church's insistence that Scripture condemned it. The calendar was reformed and books were printed in modern Russian type. Peter's importation of Western art and the imitation of Western architecture complemented this policy of enforced cultural change.

Westernization also involved military and political reforms that changed the character of the Russian state. During the first 25 years of his reign Peter had found himself unable to achieve sustained military success against his two great enemies, the Ottoman Turks to the south and the Swedes to the west. During the Great Northern War with Sweden (1700–1721), Peter introduced

a number of military reforms that eventually turned the tide against his enemy. Having learned about naval technology from the British and Dutch, he built a large navy. He introduced a policy of conscription, giving him a standing army of more than 200,000 men. A central council, established in 1711, not only directed financial administration but also levied and supplied troops.

This new military state also acquired many of the centralizing and absolutist features of western European monarchies. Efforts to introduce absolutism in Russia had begun during the reigns of Alexis (r. 1645–1676) and Fedor (r. 1676–1682), who had strengthened the central administration and brutally suppressed peasant rebellions. Peter built upon his predecessors' achievement. He created a new structure for managing the empire, appointing twelve governors to superintend Russia's 43 separate provinces. He brought the Church under state control. By establishing a finely graded hierarchy of official ranks in the armed forces, the civil administration, and the court, Peter not only improved administrative efficiency, but he also made it possible for men of nonaristocratic birth to attain the same privileged status as the old landowning nobility. He won the support of all landowners by introducing **primogeniture** (inheritance of the entire estate by the eldest son), which prevented the subdivision of their estates, and supporting the enserfment of the peasants. In dealing with his subjects Peter claimed more power than any other absolute monarch in Europe. Muscovites often told foreign visitors that the tsar treated them like slaves, punishing them at will and executing them without due process.[2] During the trial of his own son, Alexis, for treason in 1718, Peter told the clergy that "we have a sufficient and absolute power to judge our son for his crimes according to our own pleasure."[3]

The most visible sign of Peter's policy of westernization was the construction of the port city of St. Petersburg on the Gulf of Finland, which became the new capital of the Russian Empire. One of the main objectives of Russian foreign policy during Peter's reign was to secure access to the Baltic Sea, allowing Russia to open

ENCOUNTERS AND TRANSFORMATIONS

St. Petersburg and the West

The building of a new capital city, St. Petersburg, symbolized the encounter between Russia and the West during the reign of Peter the Great. Peter had seized the land on which the city was located, the marshy delta of the Neva River, from Sweden during the Northern War. The construction of the city, which first served as a fortress and then a naval base, occurred at a tremendous cost in treasure and human life. Using the royal powers he had significantly augmented earlier in his reign, Peter ordered more than 10,000 workers (and possibly twice that number) from throughout his kingdom to realize this ambitious and risky project. The harsh weather conditions, the ravages of malaria and other diseases, and the chronic shortages of provisions in a distant location resulted in the death of thousands of workers. Beginning in 1710 Peter ordered the transfer of central governmental, commercial, and military functions to the new city. The city became the site for Peter's Winter Palace, the residences of Russia's foreign ambassadors, and the headquarters of the Russian Orthodox Church. The Academy of Fine Arts and the Academy of Sciences were built shortly thereafter. During the 1730s Russia's first bourse, or exchange, fulfilled the prophecy of a British observer in 1710 that the city, with its network of canals, "might one day prove a second Amsterdam or Venice." Thus, St. Petersburg came to embody all the modernizing and westernizing achievements of Peter the Great.

The location of the new city and its architecture reflected Russia's encounter with the West. With access to the Baltic Sea, the new city, often described as "a window on the West," looked toward the European ports with which Russia increased its commerce and the European powers that Russia engaged in battle and diplomacy. The architects, stonemasons, and interior decorators that Peter commissioned came from France, Italy, Germany, and the Dutch Republic, and they constructed the buildings in contemporary European styles. The general plan of the city, drawn up by a French architect, featured straight, paved streets with stone paths that are now called sidewalks. St. Petersburg thus became a port through which Western influences entered Russia. The contrast with the old capital, Moscow, which was situated in the center of the country and embodied the spirit of the old Russia that Peter strove to modernize, could not have been clearer.

The construction of St. Petersburg played a central role in transforming Russia from a medieval kingdom on the fringes of Europe into a modern, Western power. It did not, however, eliminate the conflict in Russia between those who held the West up as the cultural standard that Russia should emulate and those who celebrated Russia's cultural superiority over the West. This conflict, which began in the eighteenth century, has continued to the present day. During the period of communism in the twentieth century, when St. Petersburg was renamed Leningrad and Moscow once again became the political capital of the country, the tradition that emphasized Russia's Eastern orientation tended to prevail. It was no coincidence that the collapse of communism and the disintegration of the Union of Soviet Socialist Republics in 1989 led to a renewed emphasis on Russia's ties with the West. The restoration of St. Petersburg's original name in 1991 and the celebration of its 300th anniversary in 2003 were further attempts to integrate Russia more fully into the West.

For Discussion

1. How did the founding of St. Petersburg contribute to the growth of the Russian state?

2. How did Peter the Great's absolute power facilitate the growth of the city?

PICTURE OF ST. PETERSBURG (1815)

This view of St. Petersburg from the quay in front of the Winter Palace reveals the city's Western character. The buildings lying across the Neva River, including the bourse, were designed by European architects. The gondolas, seen in the foreground docking at the quay, enhanced St. Petersburg's reputation as "Venice of the North."

Taking It Further

Russell Bova (ed.), *Russia and Western Civilization: Cultural and Historical Encounters.* (2003).

Lindsey Hughes, *Russia in the Age of Peter the Great.* (1998).

maritime trade with Europe and become a Western naval power. By draining a swamp on the estuary of the Neva River, Peter laid the foundations of a city that became the new capital of his empire. Construction began in 1703, and within 20 years St. Petersburg had a population of 40,000 people. With his new capital city now looking westward, and an army and central administration reformed on the basis of Prussian and French example, Peter could enter the world of European diplomacy and warfare as both a Western and an absolute monarch. (See *Encounters and Transformations* in this chapter.)

RESISTANCE TO ABSOLUTISM IN ENGLAND AND THE DUTCH REPUBLIC

■ Why did absolutism fail to take root in England and the Dutch Republic during the seventeenth century?

Royal absolutism did not succeed in all European states. In Poland-Lithuania and Hungary, for example, where the nobility exercised considerable political power, legislative assemblies continued to meet throughout the seventeenth and eighteenth centuries. Both countries had long traditions of constitutional government, and the Poles elected their kings. In western Europe the kingdom of England and the northern provinces of the Netherlands also resisted efforts to implement royal absolutism. In England this resistance to absolutism resulted in the temporary destruction of the monarchy in the middle of the seventeenth century and the permanent limitation of royal power after 1688. In the northern Netherlands, an even more resounding rejection of absolutism occurred. After winning their independence from absolutist Spain, the Dutch established a republic with a decentralized form of government that lasted the entire seventeenth and eighteenth centuries.

The English Monarchy

At different times in the seventeenth century English monarchs tried to introduce royal absolutism, but the political traditions of the country stood as major obstacles to their designs. The most important of these traditions was that the king could not make law or tax his subjects without the consent of Parliament, which consisted of the House of Lords (the nobility and the bishops) and the House of Commons, an elected assembly that included the lesser aristocracy, lawyers, and townsmen.

In the early seventeenth century some members of the House of Commons feared that this tradition of parliamentary government might come to an end. The first Stuart king, James I (r. 1603–1625), aroused some of these fears as early as 1604 when he called his first parliament. James thought of himself as an absolute monarch, and in a number of speeches and published works he emphasized the height of his independent royal power, which was known in England as the **prerogative.** James's son, Charles I (r. 1625–1649), gave substance to these fears of absolutism by forcing his subjects to lend money to the government during a war with Spain (1625–1629), imprisoning men who refused to make these loans, and collecting duties on exports without parliamentary approval. When

members of the House of Commons protested against these policies, Charles dismissed Parliament in 1629 and decided to rule without summoning it again.

This period of nonparliamentary government, known as the **personal rule,** lasted until 1640. During these years Charles, unable to collect taxes by the authority of Parliament, used his prerogative to bring in new revenues, especially by asking all subjects to pay "ship-money" to support the outfitting of ships to defend the country against attack. During the personal rule the king's religious policy fell under the control of William Laud, who was named archbishop of Canterbury in 1633. Laud's determination to restore many of the rituals associated with Roman Catholicism alienated large numbers of the more zealous Protestants, known as Puritans, and led to a growing perception that members of the king's government were engaged in a conspiracy to destroy both England's ancient constitution and the Protestant religion.

The personal rule might have continued indefinitely if Charles had not once again faced the financial demands of war. In 1636 the king tried to introduce a new religious liturgy in his northern kingdom of Scotland. The liturgy included a number of rituals that the firmly Calvinist Scottish population considered Roman Catholic. The new liturgy so angered a group of women in Edinburgh that they threw their chairs at the bishop when he introduced it. In response to this affront to their religion, the infuriated Scots signed a National Covenant (1638) pledging to defend the integrity of their Church, abolished episcopacy (government of the church by bishops) in favor of a Presbyterian system of church government, and mobilized a large army. To secure the funds to fight the Scots, Charles was forced to summon his English Parliament, thereby ending the period of personal rule.

The English Civil Wars and Revolution

Tensions between the reconvened English Parliament and Charles led to the first revolution of modern times. The Long Parliament, which met in November 1640, impeached many of the king's ministers and judges and dismantled the judicial apparatus of the eleven years of personal rule, including the courts that had been active in the prosecution of Puritans. Parliament declared the king's nonparliamentary taxes illegal and enacted a law limiting the time between the meetings of Parliament to three years.

This legislation did not satisfy the king's critics in Parliament. Their suspicion that the king was conspiring against them and their demand to approve all royal appointments created a poisoned political atmosphere in which neither side trusted the other. In August 1642 civil war began between the Parliamentarians, known as Roundheads because many of the artisans who supported them had close-cropped hair styles, and the Royalists or Cavaliers, who often wore their hair in long flowing locks. Parliament, with the military support of the Scots and a well-trained, efficient fighting force, the New Model Army, won this war in 1646 and took Charles prisoner. The king's subsequent negotiations with the Scots and the English Presbyterians, who had originally fought against him, led to a second civil war in 1648. In this war, which lasted only a few months, the New Model Army once again defeated Royalist forces.

This defeat of the king's forces led to a revolution. Following the wishes of the army, Parliament set up a court that tried and executed the king in January 1649. (See *Justice in History* in this chapter.) Shortly thereafter the House of Commons abolished the monarchy itself, thus making England a republic. This revolutionary change in the form of English government, however, did not lead to the establishment of a democratic regime. Democracy, in which a large percentage of the adult male population could vote, was the goal of the Levellers, a political party that originated in the New Model Army and attracted considerable support in London. The Levellers called for annual parliaments, the separation of powers between the executive and legislative branches of government, and the introduction of universal suffrage for men. The army officers, however, resisted these demands, and after an unsuccessful mutiny in the army, the Leveller party collapsed. The defeat of the Levellers guaranteed that political power in the new English republic would remain in the hands of men who occupied the upper levels of English society, especially those who owned property in land.

The republican government established in 1649 did not last. Tensions between the army and Parliament, fueled by the belief that the

CHRONOLOGY: A CENTURY OF REVOLUTION IN ENGLAND AND SCOTLAND

1603	James VI of Scotland (r. 1567–1625) becomes James I of England (r. 1603–1625)
1625	Death of James I and accession of Charles I (r. 1625–1649)
1629–1640	Personal rule of Charles I
1640	Opening of the Long Parliament
1642–1646	Civil War in England, ending with the capture of King Charles I
1648	Second Civil War
1649	Execution of Charles I of England and the beginning of the Republic
1653	End of the Long Parliament; Oliver Cromwell becomes Protector of England, Scotland, and Ireland
1660	Restoration of the monarchy in the person of Charles II
1685	Death of Charles II and accession of his brother, James II (r. 1685–1688)
1688–1689	Glorious Revolution in England and Scotland
1707	England and Scotland politically joined to form the United Kingdom of Great Britain

JUSTICE IN HISTORY

The Trial of Charles I

In January 1649, after the New Model Army had defeated Royalist forces in England's second civil war and purged Parliament of its Presbyterian members, the few remaining members of the House of Commons voted by a narrow margin to erect a High Court of Justice to try King Charles I. This trial, which resulted in Charles's execution, marked the only time in European history that a monarch was tried and executed while still holding the office of king.

The decision to try the king formed part of a deliberate political strategy. The men who arranged the proceeding knew that they were embarking upon a revolutionary course by declaring that the House of Commons, as the elected representative of the people, was the highest power in the realm. They also knew that the republican regime they were establishing did not command a large body of popular support. By trying the king publicly in a court of law and by ensuring that the trial was reported in daily newspapers (the first such trial in history), they hoped to prove the legitimacy of their cause and win support for the new regime.

The decision to bring the king to justice created two legal problems. The first was to identify a crime upon which the trial would be based. For many years members of Parliament had insisted that the king had violated the ancient laws of the kingdom. The charge read that he had "wickedly designed to erect an unlimited and tyrannical power" and had waged war against his people in two civil wars. His prosecutors claimed that those activities amounted to the crime of treason. The problem was that treason in England was a crime a subject committed against the king, not the king against his subjects. In order to try the king for this crime, his accusers had to construct a new theory of treason, according to which he had attacked his own political body, which they identified with the kingdom or the state.

The second problem was to make the court itself a legitimate tribunal. According to English constitutional law, the king possessed the highest legal authority in the land. He appointed his judges, and the courts represented his authority. Parliament could vote to erect a special court, but the bill authorizing it would become law only if the king agreed to it. In this case the House of Commons had set up the court by its own authority, and it had named 135 men, most of whom were army officers, to serve as its judges. The revolutionary nature of this tribunal was difficult to disguise, and Charles made its illegality the basis of his defense. When asked how he would plead, he refused, demanding to be told by what authority he had been brought into court.

The arguments presented by King Charles and John Bradshawe, the president of the court, regarding the legitimacy of the court reflected the main constitutional conflict in seventeenth-century England. On the one hand was the doctrine of divine-right absolutism, according to which the king received his authority from God. He was therefore responsible to God alone, not the people. His subjects could neither try him in a court of law nor fight him on the battlefield. "A king," said Charles, "cannot be tried by any superior jurisdiction on earth." On the other hand was the doctrine of popular sovereignty, which held that political power came from the people. As Bradshawe said in response to Charles's objection, "Sir, as the law is your superior, so truly Sir, there is something that is superior to the law, and that is indeed the parent or author of law, and that is the people of England." This trial, therefore, involved not only a confrontation between Charles and his revolutionary judges but an encounter between two incompatible political ideologies.

In 1649 the advocates of popular sovereignty triumphed over those of divine right. Charles was convicted as a "tyrant, traitor, murderer, and public enemy of the good people of this nation." The verdict was never in doubt, although only 67 of

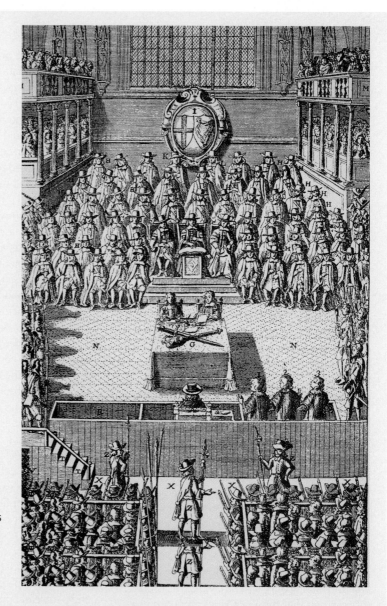

TRIAL OF CHARLES I AT WESTMINSTER HALL, JANUARY 1649

The king is sitting in the prisoner's box in the foreground, facing the commissioners of the High Court of Justice. His refusal to plead meant that a full trial could not take place.

the 135 men originally appointed as judges voted to convict the king, and a mere 59 signed the death warrant. The trial succeeded only to the extent that it facilitated the establishment of the new regime. With Charles gone, the revolutionaries move ahead with the abolition of the monarchy and the establishment of a republic. But in dramatic terms the trial was a complete failure. Charles, a small shy man with a nervous stammer, was expected to make a poor impression, but he spoke eloquently when he refused to plead, and he won support from spectators in the gallery. In the greatest show trial of the seventeenth century, the royal defendant stole the show.

When Charles's son, Charles II, was restored to the throne in 1660, Royalists finally had their revenge against the judges of this court. Those who could be found alive were hanged, disemboweled, and quartered. For those who were already dead, there was to be another type of justice. In 1661 Royalists exhumed the badly decomposed corpses of Bradshawe, Henry Ireton, and Oliver Cromwell, the three men who bore the largest responsibility for the execution of the king. The three cadavers were hanged and their skulls were placed on pikes on top of Westminster Hall. This macabre ritual served as the Royalists' way of vilifying the memory of the judges of this illegal and revolutionary trial, and their unpardonable sin of executing an anointed king.

For Discussion

1. The men who brought King Charles to trial often spoke about bringing him to "justice." How is justice best understood in this context?

2. How does this trial reveal the limitations of divine-right absolutism in England?

Taking It Further

Peacey, Jason (ed). *The Regicides and the Execution of Charles I.* 2001. A collection of essays on various aspects of this episode and the men who signed the death warrant.

Wedgewood, C. V. *The Trial of Charles I.* 1964. Presents a full account and analysis of the trial.

---

government was not creating a godly society, resulted in the army's dissolution of the Long Parliament in 1653 and the selection of a small legislative assembly consisting of zealous Puritans who were nominated by the army. When this "Parliament of the Saints" broke down later that year, Oliver Cromwell (1599–1658), the commander in chief of the army and the most prominent member of the republican government after 1649, assumed the title of Lord Protector. The protectorate, in which Cromwell shared legislative power with Parliament, represented an effort to return to a more traditional form of government. Cromwell however, relied primarily on the army to maintain power, thereby alienating many of the members of the landed class. After Cromwell's death in 1658, renewed tension between the army and Parliament led to a period of political chaos. In 1660 the army and Parliament decided to restore the monarchy by inviting Charles, the son of Charles I, to return from exile. When he returned, not only the monarchy but also the House of Lords and the Church of England were restored. The revolution had officially come to an end.

Later Stuart Absolutism and the Glorious Revolution

Charles II (r. 1660–1685) and his brother James II (r. 1685–1688) were both absolutists who admired the political achievement of their cousin, Louis XIV of France. They realized, however that they could never return to the policies of their father, much less adopt those of Louis. Neither of them attempted to rule indefinitely without Parliament, as Charles I had. Instead they sought to destroy the independence of Parliament by packing it with their own supporters and using the prerogative to weaken the force of the parliamentary statutes to which they objected.

The main political crisis of Charles II's reign was the attempt by a group of members of Parliament, headed by the Earl of Shaftesbury (1621–1683) and known by their opponents as Whigs, to exclude the king's brother, James, from the throne on the grounds that he was a Catholic. Charles opposed this strategy because it violated the theory of hereditary divine right, according to which God sanctioned the right of the king's closest heir to succeed him. Those members of Parliament who supported Charles on this issue, called Tories, thwarted the designs of the Whigs in three successive parliaments between 1679 and 1681.

An even more serious political crisis occurred after James II succeeded to the throne in 1685. James began to exempt his fellow Catholics from the penal laws, which prevented them from worshiping freely, and from the Test Act of 1673, which denied them the right to hold political office. James began appointing Catholics to positions in the army, the central administration, and local government. These efforts to grant toleration and political power to Catholics revived the traditional English fears of absolutism and "popery." Not only the Whigs but also the predominantly Anglican Tories became alarmed at the king's policies. The birth of a Catholic son to James by his second wife, the Italian princess Mary of Modena, in June 1688 created the fear that the king's religious policy might continue indefinitely. A group of seven Whigs and Tories, including the Bishop of London, invited William III of Orange, the captain-general of the military forces of the Dutch Republic and James's nephew, to come to England to defend their Protestant religion and their constitution. William was married to James's eldest daughter, the Protestant Princess Mary, and as the king's nephew he also had a claim to the throne himself.

Invading with an international force of 12,000 men, William gathered substantial support from the English population. When James's army defected, the king was forced to flee to France without engaging William's forces in battle. The Convention, a special parliament convened by William in 1689, offered the crown to William and Mary while at the same time securing their assent to the Declaration of Rights, a document that later became the parliamentary statute known as the Bill of Rights. This bill, which the English consider the cornerstone of their constitution, corrected many of the abuses of royal power at the hands of James and

Charles, especially the practice of exempting individuals from the penalties of the laws made by Parliament. By proclaiming William king and by excluding Catholics from the throne, the Bill of Rights also destroyed the theory of hereditary divine right.

The events of 1688–1689 were decisive in defeating once and for all the absolutist designs of the Stuart kings and in guaranteeing that Parliament would form a permanent and regular place in English government. The Glorious Revolution also prompted the publication of a political manifesto, John Locke's *Two Treatises of Government* (1690). Locke, a radical Whig, had written the *Treatises* in the early 1680s as a protest against the absolutist policies of Charles II, but only after the abdication and flight of James II could he safely publish his manuscript. Like Hobbes, Locke argued that people left the state of nature and agreed to form a political society mainly to protect their property Unlike Hobbes, however, Locke asserted that the people never relinquished their sovereignty and could replace a government that had violated the trust placed in it. Locke's treatises constituted an uncompromising attack on the system of royal absolutism, which he equated with slavery.

We have seen that the success of absolutism in continental European countries led to the expansion of state power. Paradoxically, the defeat of absolutism in England fostered the growth of the English state. As long as Parliament had remained suspicious of the Stuart kings, it had been reluctant to facilitate the growth of the state, which until 1688 was under direct royal control. Once the Glorious Revolution permanently restricted king's power, and Parliament emerged as the highest power within the country, Members of Parliament (MPs) had less to fear from the executive branch of government. The inauguration of a long period of warfare against France in 1689 required the development of a large army and navy, the expansion of the bureaucracy, government borrowing on an unprecedented scale, and an increase in taxes. By

1720 the kingdom of Great Britain, which had been created by the parliamentary union of England and Scotland in 1707, could rival the French state in military power, wealth, and diplomatic prestige.

The Dutch Republic

In many respects the United Provinces of the Netherlands, known as the Dutch Republic, forms the most striking exception to the pattern of state building in seventeenth-century Europe. Formally established in 1588 during its revolt against Spanish rule, the Dutch Republic was the only major European power to maintain a republican form of government throughout the seventeenth century. As a state it also failed to conform to the pattern of centralization and consolidation that became evident in virtually all European monarchies. Having successfully resisted the centralizing policies of a large multinational Spanish monarchy, the Dutch Republic never acquired much of a centralized bureaucracy of its own. The provinces formed little more than a loose confederation of sovereign republican states. Each of the provinces sent deputies to the States General, where unanimity was required on all important issues, such as the levying of taxes, the declaration of war, and the ratification of treaties.

Political power in the Dutch Republic lay mainly with the wealthy merchants and bankers who served as regents in the councils of the towns. The members of this bourgeois elite did not tend to seek admission to landed society in the way that successful English merchants often did. Nor were they lured into becoming part of an ostentatious court in the manner of the French nobility. Immersed in the world of commerce, they remained part of mercantile society and used their political power to guarantee that the Dutch state would serve the interests of trade.

The political prominence of Dutch merchants reflected the commercial character of the Dutch economy. Shortly after its truce with Spain in 1609, the Dutch cities, especially the port city of Amsterdam in Holland, began to dominate European and world trade. The Dutch served as middlemen and shippers for all the other powers of Europe, transporting grain from the Baltic, textiles from England, timber from Scandinavia, wine from Germany, sugar from Brazil and Ceylon, silk from Persia and China, and porcelain from Japan to markets throughout the world. The Dutch even served as middlemen for their archenemy Spain, providing food and manufactured goods to the Spanish colonies in the New World in exchange for silver from the mines of Peru and Mexico. As part of this process Dutch trading companies, such as the Dutch East India Company, began to establish permanent outposts in India, Indonesia, North America, the Caribbean, South America, and South Africa. Thus, a relatively small country with one-tenth the population of France became a colonial power.

To support their dynamic mercantile economy, Dutch cities developed financial institutions and techniques favorable to trade. An Exchange Bank in Amsterdam, which had a monopoly on the exchange of foreign currencies, eased international transactions. A stock market, also situated in Amsterdam, facilitated the buying and selling of shares in commercial ventures. Dutch merchants developed rational and efficient methods of bookkeeping. Even lawyers contributed to the success of Dutch commerce. In *The Freedom of the Sea* (1609), the great legal and political philosopher Hugo Grotius (1583–1645) defended the freedom of merchants to use the open seas for trade and fishing, thereby challenging the claims of European monarchs who wished to exclude foreigners from the waters surrounding their countries. Grotius, who also wrote *The Law of War and Peace* (1625), gained a reputation as the founder of modern international law.

One of the most striking contrasts between the Dutch Republic and the kingdom of France

THE AMSTERDAM STOCK EXCHANGE IN 1668
Known as the Bourse, this multipurpose building served as a gathering point for merchants trading in different parts of the world. The main activity was the buying and selling of shares of stock in trading companies during trading sessions that lasted for two hours each day.

in the seventeenth century lay in the area of religious policy. Whereas in France the revocation of the Edict of Nantes represented the culmination of a policy enforcing religious uniformity and the suppression of Protestant dissent, the predominantly Calvinist Dutch Republic gained a reputation for religious toleration. The Dutch Reformed Church did not always deserve this reputation, but secular authorities, especially in the cities, proved remarkably tolerant of different religious groups. Amsterdam, which attracted a diverse immigrant population during its period of rapid growth, contained a large community of Jews, including the philosopher Baruch Spinoza (1632–1677). The country became the center for religious exiles and political dissidents,

accommodating French Huguenots who fled their country after the repeal of the Edict of Nantes in 1685 as well as English Whigs (including the Earl of Shaftesbury and John Locke) who were being pursued by the Tory government in the 1680s.

This tolerant bourgeois republic also made a distinct contribution to European culture during the seventeenth century, known as its Golden Age. The Dutch cultural achievement was greatest in the area of the visual arts, where Rembrandt van Rijn (1606–1669), Franz Hals (ca. 1580–1666), and Jan Steen (1626–1679) belonged to an astonishing concentration of artistic genius in the cities of Amsterdam, Haarlem, and Leiden. Dutch painting reflected the

REMBRANDT, *SYNDICS OF THE CLOTHMAKERS OF AMSTERDAM* (1662)
Rembrandt's realistic portrait depicted wealthy Dutch bourgeoisie, who had great political as
well as economic power in the Dutch Republic.

religious, social, and political climate of this era. The Protestant Reformation had ended the tradition of devotional religious painting that had flourished during the Middle Ages, and the absence of a baroque court culture reduced the demand for royal and aristocratic portraiture and for paintings of heroic classical, mythological, and historical scenes. Instead the Dutch artists of the Golden Age produced intensely realistic portraits of merchants and financiers, such as Rembrandt's famous *Syndics of the Clothmakers of Amsterdam* (1662). Realism became one of the defining features of Dutch painting, evident in the numerous street scenes, still lifes, and landscapes that Dutch artists painted and sold to a largely bourgeois clientele.

In the early eighteenth century the Dutch Republic lost its position of economic superiority to Great Britain and France, which developed even larger mercantile empires of their own and began to dominate world commerce. The long period of war against France, which ended in 1713, took its toll on Dutch manpower and wealth, and the relatively small size of the country and its decentralized institutions made it more difficult for it to recover its position in European diplomacy and warfare. As a state it could no longer fight above its weight, and it became vulnerable to attacks by the French in the nineteenth century and the Germans in the twentieth. But in the seventeenth century this highly urbanized and commercial country showed that a small, decentralized republic could hold its own with the absolutist states of France and Spain as well as with the parliamentary monarchy of England.

CONCLUSION

The Western State in the Age of Absolutism

Between 1600 and 1715 three fundamental political changes helped redefine the West. The first was the dramatic and unprecedented growth of the state. During these years all Western states grew in size and strength. They became more cohesive as they brought the outlying provinces of kingdoms more firmly under central governmental control. The administrative machinery of the state became more complex and efficient. The armies of the state could be called upon at any time to take action against internal rebels and foreign enemies. The income of the state increased as royal officials collected higher taxes, and governments became involved in the promotion of trade and industry and in the regulation of the economy. By the beginning of the eighteenth century one of the most distinctive features of Western civilization was the prevalence of these large, powerful, bureaucratic states. There was nothing like them in the non-Western world.

The second change was the introduction of absolutism into these Western states. With the notable exception of Poland and Hungary, rulers aspired to complete and unrivaled power. These efforts achieved varying degrees of success, and in two states, England and the Dutch Republic, they ended in failure. Nevertheless, during the seventeenth and eighteenth centuries the absolutist state became the main form of government in the West. For this reason historians refer to the period of Western history beginning in the seventeenth century as the age of absolutism.

The third change was the conduct of a new style of warfare by Western absolutist states. The West became the arena where large armies, funded, equipped, and trained by the state, engaged in long, costly, and bloody military campaigns. The conduct of war on this scale threatened to drain the state of its financial resources, destroy its economy, and decimate its civilian and military population. Western powers were not unaware of the dangers of this type of warfare. The development of international law and the attempt to achieve a balance of power among European powers represented efforts to place restrictions on seventeenth-century warfare. These efforts, however, were not completely successful, and in the eighteenth and nineteenth centuries warfare in the West entered a new and even more dangerous phase, aided by the technological innovations that the Scientific and Industrial Revolutions made possible. To the first of those great transformations, the revolution in science, we now turn.

KEY TERMS

absolutism	baroque
divine right	balance of power
Estates General	mercantilism
Cortes	Junkers
diets	balance of power
standing armies	primogeniture
regency	prerogative
parlements	personal rule
intendants	

CHAPTER QUESTIONS

1. What did absolutism mean, both as a political theory and as a practical program, and how was absolutism related to the growth of the power of the state? (page 493)
2. How did France and Spain implement absolutism in the seventeenth century and how powerful did those states become? (page 495)
3. What was the nature of royal absolutism in central and eastern Europe, and how did the policies of the Ottoman Empire and Russia help to establish the boundaries of the West during this period? (page 506)

4. Why did absolutism fail to take root in England and the Dutch Republic during the seventeenth century? (page 516)

TAKING IT FURTHER

1. Absolutist rulers sought unrivalled power, but they frequently encountered resistance. Why were they often unable to achieve the power they desired?

2. The Thirty years' War was a major turning point in German and European history. What impact did it have on the development of absolutist theory and the development of modern states?

3. Many American notions of liberty originated in seventeenth-century England. How did developments in the two English Revolutions of the seventeenth century contribute to the ideology of religious liberty?

4. How would you define the political and cultural boundaries of the West by the beginning of the eighteenth century.

✔●─Practice on MyHistoryLab

17

The Scientific Revolution

- The Discoveries and Achievements of the Scientific Revolution
- The Search for Scientific Knowledge ■ The Causes of the Scientific Revolution
- The Intellectual Consequences of the Scientific Revolution
- Humans and the Natural World

IN 1609 GALILEO GALILEI, AN ITALIAN MATHEMATICIAN AT THE UNIVERSITY OF Padua, directed a new scientific instrument, the telescope, toward the heavens. Having heard that a Dutch artisan had put together two lenses in a way that magnified distant objects, Galileo built his own such device. Anyone who has looked through a telescope can appreciate his excitement. Objects that appeared one way to the naked eye looked entirely different when magnified by his new "spyglass," as he called it. The surface of the moon, long believed to be smooth, uniform, and perfectly spherical, now appeared full of mountains and craters. Galileo's spyglass showed that the sun, too, was imperfect, marred by spots that appeared to move across its surface. Such sights challenged traditional science, which assumed that "the heavens," the throne of God, were perfect and thus never changed. Traditional science was shaken even further, when Galileo showed that Venus, viewed over many months, appeared to change its shape, much as the moon did in its phases. This discovery provided evidence for the relatively new theory that the planets, including Earth, revolved around the sun rather than the sun and the planets around the Earth.

Galileo shared the discoveries he made not only with fellow scientists, but also with other educated members of society. He also staged a number of public demonstrations of his new astronomical instrument, the first of which took place on top of one of the city gates of Rome in 1611. To convince those who doubted the reality of the images they saw, Galileo turned the telescope toward familiar landmarks in the city. Interest in the new scientific instrument ran so high that a number of amateur astronomers acquired telescopes of their own.

Galileo's discoveries were part of what historians call the Scientific Revolution. This development changed the way Europeans viewed the natural world, the supernatural realm, and themselves. It led to controversies in religion, philosophy, and politics and changes in military technology, navigation, and business. It also set the West apart from the civilizations of the Middle East, Asia, and Africa and provided a basis for claims of Western superiority over the people in those lands.

The scientific culture that emerged in the West by the end of the seventeenth century was the product of a series of cultural encounters. It resulted from a complex interaction among scholars proposing different ideas of how nature operated. Some of these ideas originated in Greek philosophy. Others came from Christian sources. Still other ideas came from a tradition of late medieval science that had been influenced by the scholarship of the Islamic Middle East.

The main question this chapter seeks to answer is this: How did European scientists in the sixteenth and seventeenth centuries change the way in which people in the West viewed the natural world?

THE TELESCOPE

The telescope was the most important of the new scientific instruments that facilitated discovery. This engraving depicts an astronomer using the telescope in 1647.

THE DISCOVERIES AND ACHIEVEMENTS OF THE SCIENTIFIC REVOLUTION

■ What were the achievements and discoveries of the Scientific Revolution?

Unlike political revolutions, such as the English Revolution of the 1640s discussed in the last chapter, the Scientific Revolution developed gradually over a long period of time. It began in the mid-sixteenth century and continued into the eighteenth century. Even though it took a relatively long time to unfold, it was revolutionary in the sense that it transformed human thought, just as political revolutions have fundamentally changed systems of government. The most important changes in seventeenth-century science took place in astronomy, physics, chemistry, and biology.

Astronomy: A New Model of the Universe

The most significant change in astronomy was the acceptance of the view that the sun, not the Earth, was the center of the universe. Until the mid-sixteenth century, most natural philosophers—as scientists were known at the time—accepted the views of the ancient Greek astronomer Claudius Ptolemy (100–170 C.E.). Ptolemy's observations and calculations supported the cosmology of the Greek philosopher Aristotle (384–322 B.C.E.). According to Ptolemy and Aristotle, the center of the universe was a stationary Earth, around which the moon, the sun, and the other planets revolved in circular orbits. Beyond the planets a large sphere carried the stars, which stood in a fixed relationship to each other, around the Earth from east to west once every 24 hours, thus accounting for the rising and setting of the stars. Each of the four known elements—earth, water, air, and fire—had a natural place within this universe, with the heavy elements, earth and water, being pulled down toward the center of the Earth and the light ones, air and fire, hovering above it. All heavenly

a   b

TWO VIEWS OF THE PTOLEMAIC OR PRE-COPERNICAN UNIVERSE

(a) In this sixteenth-century engraving the Earth lies at the center of the universe and the elements of water, air, and fire are arranged in ascending order above the Earth. The orbit that is shaded in black is the firmament or stellar sphere. The presence of Christ and the saints at the top reflects the view that Heaven lay beyond the stellar sphere. (b) A medieval king representing Atlas holds a Ptolemaic cosmos. The Ptolemaic universe is often referred to as a two-sphere universe: The inner sphere of the Earth lies at the center and the outer sphere encompassing the entire universe rotates around the Earth.

bodies, including the sun and the planets, were composed of a fifth element, called ether, which unlike matter on Earth was thought to be eternal and could not be altered, corrupted, or destroyed.

This traditional view of the cosmos had much to recommend it, and some educated people continued to accept it well into the eighteenth century. The Bible, which in a few passages referred to the motion of the sun, reinforced the authority of Aristotle. And human observation seemed to confirm the motion of the sun. We do, after all, see the sun "rise" and "set" every day, so the idea that the Earth rotates at high speed and revolves around the sun contradicts the experience of our senses. Nevertheless, the Earth-centered model of the universe failed to explain many patterns that astronomers observed in the sky, most notably the paths followed by planets. Whenever ancient or medieval astronomers confronted a new problem as a result of their observations, they tried to accommodate the results to the Ptolemaic model. By the sixteenth century this model had been

modified or adjusted so many times that it had gradually become a confused collection of planets and stars following different motions.

Faced with this situation, a Polish cleric, Nicolaus Copernicus (1473–1543), looked for a simpler and more plausible model of the universe. In *The Revolutions of the Heavenly Spheres*, which was published shortly after his death, Copernicus proposed that the center of the universe was not the Earth but the sun. The book was widely circulated, but it did not win much support for the sun-centered theory of the universe. Only the most learned astronomers could understand Copernicus' mathematical arguments, and even they were not prepared to adopt his central thesis. In the late sixteenth century the great Danish astronomer Tycho Brahe (1546–1601) accepted the argument of Copernicus that the planets revolved around the sun but still insisted that the sun revolved around the Earth.

Significant support for the Copernican model of the universe among scientists began to

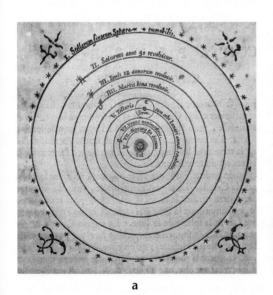

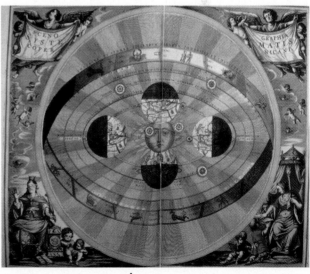

a   b

TWO EARLY MODERN VIEWS OF THE SUN-CENTERED UNIVERSE

(a) The depiction by Copernicus. Note that all the orbits are circular, rather than elliptical, as Kepler was to show they were. The outermost sphere is that of the fixed stars. (b) A late-seventeenth-century depiction of the cosmos by Andreas Cellarius in which the planets follow elliptical orbits. It illustrates four different positions of the Earth as it orbits the sun.

materialize only in the seventeenth century. In 1609 a German astronomer, Johannes Kepler (1571–1630), using data that Brahe had collected, confirmed the central position of the sun in the universe. In *New Astronomy* (1609) Kepler also demonstrated that the planets, including the Earth, followed elliptical rather than circular orbits and that physical laws governed their movements. Not many people read Kepler's book, however, and his achievement was not fully appreciated until many decades later.

Galileo Galilei (1564–1642) was far more successful in gaining support for the sun-centered model of the universe. Galileo had the literary skill, which Kepler lacked, of being able to write for a broad audience. Using the evidence gained from his observations with the telescope, and presenting his views in the form of a dialogue between the advocates of the two competing worldviews, Galileo demonstrated the plausibility and superiority of Copernicus's theory.

The publication of Galileo's *Dialogue Concerning the Two Chief World Systems— Ptolemaic and Copernican* in 1632 won many converts to the sun-centered theory of the universe, but it lost him the support of Pope Urban VIII, who had been one of his patrons. The character in *Dialogue* who defends the Ptolemaic system is named Simplicio (that is, a simple—or stupid—person). Urban wrongly concluded that Galileo was mocking him. In 1633 Galileo was tried before the Roman Inquisition, an ecclesiastical court whose purpose was to maintain theological orthodoxy. The charge against him was that he had challenged the authority of Scripture and was therefore guilty of heresy, the denial of the theological truths of the Roman Catholic Church. (See *Justice in History* in this chapter.)

As a result of this trial, Galileo was forced to abandon his support for the Copernican model of the universe, and *Dialogue* was placed on the Index of Prohibited Books, a list compiled by the papacy of all printed works containing heretical ideas. Despite this setback, by 1700 Copernicanism commanded widespread support

among scientists and the educated public. *Dialogue*, however, was not removed from the Index until 1822.

Physics: The Laws of Motion and Gravitation

Galileo made his most significant contributions to the Scientific Revolution in physics. In the seventeenth century the main branches of physics were mechanics (the study of motion and its causes) and optics (the study of light). Galileo formulated a set of laws governing the motion of material objects that challenged the accepted theories of Aristotle regarding motion and laid the foundation of modern physics.

According to Aristotle, whose views dominated science in the late Middle Ages, the motion of every object—except the natural motion of falling toward the center of the Earth—required another object to move it. If the mover stopped, the object fell to the ground or simply stopped moving. But this theory could not explain why a projectile, such as a discus or a spear, continued to move after a person threw it. Galileo's answer to that question was a theory of inertia, which became the basis of a new theory of motion. According to Galileo, an object continues to move or lie at rest until something external to it intervenes to change its motion. Thus, motion is neither a quality inherent in an object nor a force that it acquires from another object. It is simply a state in which the object finds itself.

Galileo also discovered that the motion of an object occurs only in relation to things that do not move. A ship moves through the water, for example, but the goods that the ship carries do not move in relationship to the moving ship. This insight explained to the critics of Copernicus how the Earth can move even though we do not experience its motion. Galileo's most significant contribution to mechanics was his formulation of a mathematical law of motion that explained how the speed and acceleration of a falling object are determined by the distance it travels during equal intervals of time.

The greatest achievements of the Scientific Revolution in physics belong to English scientist Sir Isaac Newton (1642–1727). His research changed the way future generations viewed the world. As a boy Newton felt out of place in his small village, where he worked on his mother's farm and attended school. Fascinated by mechanical devices, he spent much of his time building wooden models of windmills and other machines. When playing with his friends he always found ways to exercise his mind, calculating, for example, how he could use the wind to win jumping contests. It became obvious to all who knew him that Newton belonged at a university. In 1661 he entered Cambridge University, where, at age 27, he became a chaired professor of mathematics.

Newton formulated a set of mathematical laws to explain the operation of the entire physical world. In 1687 he published his theories in *Mathematical Principles of Natural Philosophy*. The centerpiece of this monumental work was the **universal law of gravitation,** which demonstrated that the same force holding an object to the Earth also holds the planets in their orbits. This law represented a synthesis of the work of other scientists, including Kepler on planetary motion and Galileo on inertia. Newton paid tribute to the work of these men when he said, "If I have seen farther, it is by standing on the shoulders of giants." But Newton went further than any of them by establishing the existence of a single gravitational force and by giving

SIR ISAAC NEWTON

This portrait was painted by Sir Godfrey Kneller in 1689, two years after the publication of *Mathematical Principles of Natural Philosophy.*

it precise mathematical expression. His book revealed the unity and order of the entire physical world and thus offered a scientific model to replace that of Aristotle.

CHRONOLOGY: DISCOVERIES OF THE SCIENTIFIC REVOLUTION

1543	Copernicus publishes *The Revolutions of the Heavenly Spheres*
1609	Johannes Kepler publishes *New Astronomy*
1628	William Harvey publishes *On the Motion of the Heart and Blood in Animals*
1632	Galileo publishes *Dialogue Concerning the Two Chief World Systems*
1638	Galileo publishes *Discourses on the Two New Sciences of Motion and Mechanics*
1659	Robert Boyle invents the air pump and conducts experiments on the elasticity and compressibility of air
1687	Newton publishes *Mathematical Principles of Natural Philosophy*

Chemistry: Discovering the Elements of Nature

At the beginning of the seventeenth century, the science today called chemistry was considered part of either medicine or **alchemy,** the magical art of attempting to turn base metals into gold or silver. The most famous chemist of the sixteenth century was the Swiss physician Paracelsus (1493–1541), who rejected the theory advanced by the ancient Greek physician Galen (129–200 C.E.) that an imbalance of the four "humors" or fluids in the body—blood, phlegm, black bile, and yellow bile—caused diseases. The medical practice of drawing blood from sick patients to cure them by correcting this alleged imbalance was based on Galen's theory. Instead, to cure certain diseases, Paracelsus began to treat his patients with chemicals, such as mercury and sulfur. Paracelsus is often dismissed for his belief in alchemy, but his prescription of chemicals helped give chemistry a respectable place within medical science.

During the seventeenth century chemistry became a legitimate field of scientific research, largely as the result of the work of Robert Boyle (1627–1691). Boyle destroyed the prevailing idea that all basic constituents of matter share the same structure. He contended that the arrangement of their components, which he identified as corpuscles or atoms, determined their characteristics. He also conducted experiments on the volume, pressure, and density of gas and the elasticity of air. Boyle's most famous experiments, undertaken with an air pump, proved the existence of a vacuum. Largely as a result of Boyle's discoveries, chemists won acceptance as legitimate members of the company of scientists.

Biology: The Circulation of the Blood

The English physician William Harvey (1578–1657) made one of the great medical discoveries of the seventeenth century by demonstrating in 1628 that blood circulates throughout the human body. Traditional science had maintained that blood originated in the liver and then flowed outward through the veins. A certain amount of blood

PORTRAIT OF ROBERT BOYLE WITH HIS AIR PUMP IN THE BACKGROUND (1664)
Boyle's pump became the center of a series of experiments carried on at the Royal Society in London.

flowed from the liver into the heart, where it passed from one ventricle to the other and then traveled through the arteries to different parts of the body. During its journey this arterial blood was enriched by a special *pneuma* or "vital spirit" that was necessary to sustain life. When this enriched blood reached the brain, it became the body's "psychic spirits," which influenced human behavior.

Through experiments on human cadavers and live animals in which he weighed the blood that the heart pumped every hour, Harvey demonstrated that rather than sucking in blood, the heart pumped it through the arteries by means of contraction and constriction. The only gap in his theory was the question of how blood went from the ends of the arteries to the ends of the veins. This question was answered in 1661, when scientists, using a new instrument known as a microscope, could see the capillaries connecting the veins and arteries. Harvey, however, had set the standard for future biological research.

THE SEARCH FOR SCIENTIFIC KNOWLEDGE

■ What methods did scientists use during this period to investigate nature, and how did they think nature operated?

The natural philosophers who made these scientific discoveries worked in different disciplines, and each followed his own procedures for discovering scientific truth. In the sixteenth and seventeenth centuries there was no "scientific method." Many natural philosophers, however, shared similar views about how nature operated and the means by which humans could acquire knowledge of it. In searching for scientific knowledge, these scientists observed and experimented, used deductive reasoning, expressed their theories in mathematical terms, and argued that nature operated like a machine. These features of scientific research ultimately defined a distinctly Western approach to solving scientific problems.

Observation and Experimentation

The most prominent feature of scientific research in sixteenth- and seventeenth-century Europe was the observation of nature, combined with the testing of hypotheses by rigorous experimentation. This was primarily a process of **induction,** in which theories emerged only after the accumulation and analysis of data. It assumed a willingness to abandon preconceived ideas and base scientific conclusions on experience and observation. This approach is also described as empirical: **empiricism** demands that all scientific theories be tested by experiments based on observation of the natural world.

In *New Organon* (1620), the English philosopher Francis Bacon (1561–1626) promoted this

DISSECTION

The English surgeon William Cheselden giving an anatomical demonstration to spectators in London around 1735. As medical science developed in the sixteenth and seventeenth centuries, the dissection of human corpses became a standard practice in European universities and medical schools. Knowledge of the structure and composition of the human body, which was central to the advancement of physiology, could best be acquired by cutting open a corpse to reveal the organs, muscles, and bones of human beings. The practice reflected the emphasis scientists placed on observation and experimentation in conducting scientific research.

empirical approach to scientific research. Bacon complained that all previous scientific endeavors, especially those of ancient Greek philosophers, relied too little on experimentation. In contrast, his approach involved the thorough and systematic investigation of nature, a process that Bacon, who was a lawyer and judge, compared to the interrogation of a person suspected of committing a crime. For Bacon, scientific experimentation was "putting nature to the question," a phrase that referred to questioning a prisoner under torture to determine the facts of a case.

Deductive Reasoning

The second feature of sixteenth- and seventeenth-century scientific research was the use of **deductive reasoning** to establish basic scientific truths or principles. From these principles other ideas or laws could be deduced logically. Just as induction is linked to empiricism, so deduction is connected to **rationalism.** Unlike empiricism—the idea that we know truth through what the senses can experience—rationalism insists that the mind contains rational categories independent of sensory observation.

Unlike the inductive experimental approach, which found its most enthusiastic practitioners in England, the deductive approach had its most zealous advocates on the European continent. The French philosopher and mathematician René Descartes (1596–1650) became the foremost champion of this methodology. In his *Discourse on the Method* (1637), Descartes recommended that to solve any intellectual problem, a person should first establish fundamental principles or truths and then proceed from those ideas to specific conclusions.

Mathematics, in which one also moves logically from certain premises to conclusions by means of equations, provided the model for deductive reasoning. Although rational deduction proved to be an essential feature of scientific methodology, the limitations of an exclusively deductive approach became apparent when Descartes and his followers deduced a theory of gravitation from the principle that objects could influence each other only if they actually touched. This theory, as well as the principle upon which it was based, lacked an empirical foundation and eventually had to be abandoned.

Mathematics and Nature

The third feature of scientific research in the sixteenth and seventeenth centuries was the application of mathematics to the study of the physical world. Scientists working in both the inductive and the deductive traditions used mathematics. Descartes shared with Galileo the conviction that nature had a geometrical structure and could therefore be understood in mathematical terms. The physical dimensions of matter, which Descartes claimed were its only properties, could of course be expressed mathematically. Galileo claimed that mathematics was the language in which philosophy was written in "the book of the universe."

Isaac Newton's work provided the best illustration of the application of mathematics to scientific problems. Newton used observation and experimentation to confirm his theory of universal gravitation, but he wrote his *Mathematical Principles of Natural Philosophy* in the language of mathematics. His approach to scientific problems, which became a model for future research, used examples derived from experiments and deductive, mathematical reasoning to discover the laws of nature.

The Mechanical Philosophy

Much of seventeenth-century scientific experimentation and deduction assumed that the natural world operated as if it were a machine made by a human being. This **mechanical philosophy** of nature appeared most clearly in the work of Descartes. Medieval philosophers had argued that natural bodies had an innate tendency to change, whereas artificial objects, that is, those constructed by humans, did not. Descartes, as well as Kepler, Galileo, and Bacon, denied that assumption. Mechanists argued that nature operated in a mechanical way, just like a piece of machinery. The only difference was that the operating structures of natural mechanisms could not be observed as readily as the structures of a machine.

Mechanists perceived the human body itself as a machine. Harvey, for example, described the heart as "a piece of machinery in which, though one wheel gives motion to another, yet all the wheels seem to move simultaneously." The only difference between the body and other machines was that the mind could move the body, although how it did so was controversial. According to Descartes, the mind was completely different from the body and the rest of the material world. Unlike the body, the mind was an immaterial substance that could be not be extended in space, divided, or measured mathematically, the way one could record the dimensions of the body. Because Descartes made this sharp distinction between the mind and the body, we describe his philosophy as **dualistic.**

Descartes and other mechanists argued that matter was completely inert or dead. It did not possess a soul or any innate purpose. Its only property was "extension," or the physical dimensions of length, width, and depth. Without a spirit or any other internal force directing its action, matter simply responded to the power of the other bodies with which it came in contact. According to Descartes, all physical phenomena could be explained by reference to the dimensions and the movement of particles of matter. He once claimed, "Give me extension and motion and I will construct the universe."[1]

The view of nature as a machine implied that it operated in a regular, predictable way in accordance with unchanging laws of nature. Scientists could use reason to discover what those laws were and thus learn how nature performed under any circumstances. The scientific investigations of Galileo and Kepler were based on those assumptions, and Descartes made them explicit. The immutability of the laws of nature implied that the entire universe was uniform in structure, an assumption that underlay Newton's formulation of the laws of motion and universal gravitation.

THE CAUSES OF THE SCIENTIFIC REVOLUTION

■ Why did the Scientific Revolution take place in western Europe at this time?

Why did the Scientific Revolution take place at this particular time, and why did it originate in western European countries? There is no simple answer to this question. We can, however, identify developments that inspired these scientific discoveries. Some of these developments arose out of earlier investigations conducted by natural philosophers in the late Middle Ages, the Renaissance, and the sixteenth century. Others emerged from the religious, political, social, and economic life of early modern Europe.

Developments Within Science

The three internal causes of the Scientific Revolution were the research into motion conducted by natural philosophers in the fourteenth century, the scientific investigations conducted by Renaissance humanists, and the collapse of the dominant conceptual frameworks, or paradigms, that had governed scientific inquiry and research for centuries.

LATE MEDIEVAL SCIENCE Modern science can trace some of its origins to the fourteenth century, when the first significant modifications of Aristotle's scientific theories began to emerge. The most significant of these refinements was the theory of impetus. Aristotle had argued that an object would stop as soon as it lost contact with the object that moved it. Late medieval scientists claimed that objects in motion acquire a force that stays with them after they lose contact with the mover. This theory of impetus questioned Aristotle's authority, and it influenced some of Galileo's early thought on motion.

Natural philosophers of the fourteenth century also began to recommend direct, empirical observation in place of the traditional tendency to accept preconceived notions regarding the operation of nature. This approach to answering scientific questions did not result in the type of rigorous experimentation that Bacon demanded three centuries later, but it did encourage scientists to base their theories on the facts that emerged from an empirical study of nature.

The contribution of late medieval science to the Scientific Revolution should not be exaggerated. Philosophers of the fourteenth century continued to accept Ptolemy's cosmology and Galen's anatomical theories. The unchallenged position of theology as the dominant subject in late medieval universities also guaranteed that new scientific ideas would receive little favor if they challenged Christian doctrine.

RENAISSANCE SCIENCE   Natural philosophers during the Renaissance contributed more than their late medieval predecessors to the rise of modern science. Many of the scientific discoveries of the late sixteenth and seventeenth centuries drew their inspiration from Greek scientific works that had been rediscovered during the Renaissance. Copernicus, for example, found the idea of his sun-centered universe in the writings of Aristarchus of Samos, a Greek astronomer of the third century B.C.E. whose work had been unknown during the Middle Ages. Similarly, the works of the ancient Greek philosopher Democritus in the late fifth century B.C.E. introduced the idea, developed by Boyle and others in the seventeenth century, that matter was divisible into small particles known as atoms. The works of Archimedes (287–212 B.C.E.), which had been virtually unknown in the Middle Ages, stimulated interest in the science of mechanics. The recovery and translation of previously unknown texts also made scientists aware that Greek scientists did not always agree with each other and thus provided a stimulus to independent observation and experimentation as a means of resolving their differences.

Renaissance revival of the philosophy of **Neoplatonism** (see Chapter 7) made an even more direct contribution to the birth of modern science. While most medieval natural philosophers relied on the ideas of Aristotle, Neoplatonists drew on the work of Plotinus (205–270 C.E.), the last great philosopher of antiquity who synthesized the work of Plato, other ancient Greek philosophers, and Persian religious traditions. Neoplatonists stressed the unity of the natural and spiritual worlds. Matter is alive, linked to the divine soul that governs the entire universe. To unlock the mysteries of this living world, Neoplatonists turned to mathematics, because they believed the divine expressed itself in geometrical harmony, and to alchemy, because they sought to uncover the shared essence that linked all creation. They also believed that the sun, as a symbol of the divine soul, logically stood at the center of the universe.

Neoplatonic ideas influenced seventeenth-century scientists. Copernicus, for example, took from Neoplatonism his idea of the sun sitting at the center of the universe, as "on a royal throne ruling his children, the planets which circle around him." From his reading in Neoplatonic sources Kepler acquired his belief that the universe was constructed according to geometric principles. Newton was fascinated by the subject of alchemy, and the original inspiration of his theory of gravitation probably came from his Neoplatonist professor at Cambridge, who insisted on the presence of spiritual forces in the physical world. Modern science resulted from an encounter between the mechanical philosophy, which held that matter was inert, and Neoplatonism, which claimed that the natural world was alive.

THE COLLAPSE OF PARADIGMS   The third internal cause of the Scientific Revolution was the collapse of the intellectual frameworks that had governed scientific research since antiquity. In all historical periods scientists prefer to work within an established conceptual framework, or what the scholar Thomas Kuhn has referred to as a **paradigm**, rather than introduce new theories. Every so often, however, the paradigm that has governed scientific research for an extended period of time can no longer account for many different observable phenomena. A scientific revolution occurs when the old paradigm collapses and a new paradigm replaces it.[2]

The revolutionary developments we have discussed in astronomy and biology were partly the result of the collapse of old paradigms. In astronomy the paradigm that had governed scientific inquiry in antiquity and the Middle Ages was the Ptolemaic model, in which the sun and the planets revolved around the Earth. By the sixteenth century, however, new observations had so confused and complicated this model that, to men like Copernicus, it no longer provided a satisfactory explanation for the material universe. Copernicus looked for a simpler and more plausible model of the universe. His sun-centered theory became the new paradigm within which Kepler, Galileo, and Newton all worked.

In biology a parallel development occurred when the old paradigm constructed by Galen, in which the blood originated in the liver and traveled from the heart through the arteries, also collapsed because it could not explain the findings of medical scholars. Harvey introduced a new paradigm, in which the blood circulated through the body. As in astronomy, Harvey's new paradigm served as a framework for subsequent biological research and helped shape the Scientific Revolution.

Developments Outside Science

Nonscientific developments also encouraged the development and acceptance of new scientific ideas. These developments include the spread of Protestantism, the patronage of scientific research, the invention of the printing press, and military and economic change.

PROTESTANTISM   Protestantism played a limited role in causing the Scientific Revolution. In the early years of the Reformation, Protestants were just as hostile as Catholics to the new science. Reflecting the Protestant belief in the literal truth of the Bible, Luther referred to Copernicus as "a fool who went against Holy Writ." Throughout the sixteenth and seventeenth centuries, moreover, Catholics as well as Protestants engaged in scientific research. Indeed, some of the most prominent European natural philosophers, including Galileo and Descartes, were devout Catholics. Nonetheless, Protestantism encouraged the emergence of modern science in three ways.

First, as the scientific revolution gained steam in the seventeenth century, Protestant governments were more willing than Catholic authorities to allow the publication and dissemination of new scientific ideas. Protestant governments, for example, did not prohibit the publication of books that promoted novel scientific ideas on the grounds

that they were heretical, as the papacy did in compiling the Index of Prohibited Books. The greater willingness of Protestant governments, especially those of England and the Dutch Republic, to tolerate the expression of new scientific ideas helps to explain why the main geographical arena of scientific investigation shifted from the Catholic Mediterranean to the Protestant North Atlantic in the second half of the seventeenth century. (See *Different Voices* in this chapter.)

Second, seventeenth-century Protestant writers emphasized the idea that God revealed his intentions not only in the Bible, but also in nature itself. They claimed that individuals therefore had a duty to study nature, just as it was their duty to read Scripture to gain knowledge of God's will. Kepler's claim that the astronomer was "as a priest of God to the book of nature" reflected this Protestant outlook.

Third, many seventeenth-century Protestant scientists believed that the millennium, a period of one thousand years when Christ would come again and rule the world, was about to begin. Millenarians believed that during this period knowledge would increase, society would improve, and humans would gain control over nature. Protestant scientists, including Boyle and Newton, conducted their research and experiments believing that their work would contribute to this improvement of human life after the Second Coming of Christ.

PATRONAGE   Scientists could not have succeeded without financial and institutional support. Only an organizational structure could give science a permanent status, let it develop as a discipline, and give its members a professional identity. The universities, which today support scientific research, were not the main source of that support in the seventeenth century. They remained predominantly clerical institutions with a vested interest in defending the medieval fusion of Christian theology and Aristotelian science. Instead of the universities, scientists depended on the patronage of wealthy and influential individuals, especially the kings, princes, and great nobles who ruled European states.

DIFFERENT VOICES COPERNICUS AND THE PAPACY

In dedicating his book, On the Revolution of the Heavenly Spheres *(1543), to Pope Paul II (r. 1464–1471), Copernicus explained that he drew inspiration from ancient philosophers who had imagined that the Earth moved. Anticipating condemnation from those who based their astronomical theories on the Bible, he appealed to the pope for protection while showing contempt for the theories of his opponents. Paul II neither endorsed nor condemned Copernicus's work, but in 1616, the papacy suspended the book's publication because it contradicted Scripture.*

Copernicus on Heliocentrism and the Bible

...I began to chafe that philosophers could by no means agree on any one certain theory of the mechanism of the Universe, wrought for us by a supremely good and orderly Creator...I therefore took pains to read again the works of all the philosophers on whom I could lay my hand to seek out whether any of them had ever supposed that the motions of the spheres were other than those demanded by the mathematical schools. I found first in Cicero that Hicetas had realized that the Earth moved. Afterwards I found in Plutarch that certain others had held the like opinion....

Taking advantage of this I too began to think of the mobility of the Earth; and though the opinion seemed absurd, yet knowing now that others before me had been granted freedom to imagine such circles as they chose to explain the phenomena of the stars, I considered that I also might easily be allowed to try whether, by assuming some motion of the Earth, sounder explanations than theirs for the revolution of the celestial spheres might so be discovered.

Thus assuming motions, which in my work I ascribe to the Earth, by long and frequent observations I have at last discovered that, if the motions of the rest of the planets be brought into relation with the circulation of the Earth and be reckoned in proportion to the circles of each planet...the orders and magnitudes of all stars and spheres, nay the heavens themselves, become so bound together that nothing in any part thereof could be moved from its place without producing confusion of all the other parts and of the Universe as a whole....

It may fall out, too, that idle babblers, ignorant of mathematics, may claim a right to pronounce a judgment on my work, by reason of a certain passage of Scripture basely twisted to serve their purpose. Should any such venture to criticize and carp at my project, I make no account of them; I consider their judgment rash, and utterly despise it.

This group included Pope Urban VIII, ruler of the Papal States.

Patronage, however, could easily be withdrawn. Scientists had to conduct themselves and their research to maintain the favor of their patrons. Galileo referred to the new moons of Jupiter that he observed through his telescope as the Medicean stars to flatter the Medici family that ruled

CHRONOLOGY: THE FORMATION OF SCIENTIFIC SOCIETIES

1603	Prince Cesi founds the Academy of the Lynx-Eyed in Rome
1657	Cosimo II de' Medici founds the Academy of Experiment in Florence
1662	Founding of the Royal Society of London under the auspices of Charles II
1666	Founding of the Academy of Sciences in Paris

Source: From Nicolaus Copernicus, *De Revolutionibus Orbium Coelestium* (1543), trans. by John F. Dobson and Selig Brodetsky in *Occasional Notes of the Royal Astronomical Society*, 2(10), 1947. Reprinted by permission of Blackwell Publishing.

Papal Decree against Heliocentrism, 1616

Decree of the Holy Congregation of his Most Illustrious Lord Cardinals especially charged by His Holiness Pope Paul V and by the Holy Apostolic See with the index of books and their licensing, prohibition, correction and printing in all of Christendom....

This Holy Congregation has also learned about the spreading and acceptance by many of the false Pythagorean doctrine, altogether contrary to the Holy Scripture, that the earth moves and the sun is motionless, which is also taught by Nicholaus Copernicus's *On the Revolutions of the Heavenly Spheres* and by Diego de Zuñiga's *On Job*. This may be seen from a certain letter published by a certain Carmelite Father, whose title is *Letter of the Reverend Father Paolo Antonio Foscarini on the Pythagorean and Copernican Opinion of the Earth's Motion and Sun's Rest and on the New Pythagorean World System*...in which the said Father tries to show that the above mentioned doctrine of the sun's rest at the center of the world and the earth's motion is consonant with the truth and does not contradict Holy Scripture. Therefore, in order that this opinion may not creep any further to the prejudice of Catholic truth, the Congregation has decided that the books by Nicholaus Copernicus (*On the Revolution of Spheres*) and Diego de Zuniga (*On Job*) be suspended until corrected; but that the book of the Carmelite Father Paolo Antonini Foscarini be completely prohibited and condemned; and that all other books which teach the same be likewise prohibited, according to whether with the present decree it prohibits condemns and suspends them respectively. In witness thereof this decree has been signed by the hand and stamped with the seal of the Most Illustrious and reverend Lord cardinal of St. Cecilia. Bishop of Albano, on March 5, 1616.

Source: From *The Galileo Affair: A Documentary History*, ed. and trans. by Maurice A. Finocchiaro, copyright © 1989 by The Regents of the University of California, is reprinted by permission of the University of Calfornia Press.

For Discussion

1. Why did the papal authorities prohibit and condemn the work by Antonini Foscarini but only suspend those of Copernicus and Diego de Zuñia?
2. How did Copernicus and the papal authorities differ about classical antiquity and the truth of Holy Scripture?

Florence. His publications were inspired as much by his obligation to glorify Grand Duke Cosimo II as by his belief in the sun-centered theory.

Academies in which groups of scientists could share ideas and work served as a second important source of patronage. One of the earliest of these institutions was the Academy of the Lynx-Eyed in Rome, named after the animal whose sharp vision symbolized the power of observation required by the new science. Founded in 1603 by Prince Cesi, the Academy published many of Galileo's works. In 1657 Cosimo II founded a similar institution in Florence, the Academy of Experiment. These academies offered a more regular source of patronage than scientists could acquire from individual positions at court, but they still served the function of glorifying their founders, and they depended on patrons for their continued existence. The royal academies established in the 1660s, however, especially the Royal Academy of Sciences in France and the Royal Society in England (1662), became in effect public institutions that operated with a minimum of royal intervention and made possible a continuous program of work.

the authors supplied. Illustrations, diagrams, tables, and other schematic drawings that helped to convey the author's findings could also be printed. The entire body of scientific knowledge thus became cumulative. Printing also made members of the nonscientific community aware of the latest advances in physics and astronomy and so helped to make science an integral part of the culture of educated Europeans.

THE FOUNDING OF THE FRENCH ACADÈMIE DES SCIENCES

Like the Royal Society in England, the French Academy of Sciences was dependent upon royal patronage. Louis XIV, seen sitting in the middle of the painting, used the occasion to glorify himself as a patron of the sciences as well as the arts. The painting also commemorates the building of the Royal Observatory in Paris, which is shown in the background.

The mission of the Royal Society in England was the promotion of scientific knowledge through experimentation. It also placed the results of scientific research at the service of the state. Members of the Royal Society, for example, did research on ship construction and military technology. These attempts to use scientific technology to strengthen the power of the state show how the growth of the modern state and the emergence of modern science were related.

THE PRINTING PRESS   Printing made it much easier for scientists to share their discoveries with others. During the Middle Ages, books were handwritten. Errors could creep into the text as it was being copied, and the number of copies that could be made of a manuscript limited the spread of scientific knowledge. The spread of printing ensured that scientific achievements could be preserved more accurately and presented to a broader audience. The availability of printed copies also made it much easier for other scientists to correct or supplement the data that

MILITARY AND ECONOMIC CHANGE The Scientific Revolution occurred at roughly the same time that both the conduct of warfare and the European economy were undergoing dramatic changes. As territorial states increased the size of their armies and arsenals, they demanded more accurate weapons with longer range. Some of the work that physicists did during the seventeenth century was deliberately meant to improve weaponry. Members of the Royal Society in England, for example, conducted extensive scientific research on the trajectory and velocity of missiles, and so followed Francis Bacon's recommendation that scientists place their research at the service of the state.

The needs of the emerging capitalist economy also influenced scientific research. The study of mechanics, for example, led to new techniques to ventilate mines and raise coal or ore from them, thus making mining more profitable. Some of the questions discussed at the meetings of the Royal Society suggest that its members undertook research to make capitalist ventures more productive and profitable. The research did not always produce immediate results, but ultimately it increased economic profitability and contributed to the English economy in the eighteenth century.

THE INTELLECTUAL CONSEQUENCES OF THE SCIENTIFIC REVOLUTION

- How did the Scientific Revolution influence philosophical and religious thought in the seventeenth and early eighteenth centuries?

The Scientific Revolution profoundly affected the intellectual life of educated Europeans. The discoveries of Copernicus, Kepler, Galileo, and Newton, as well as the assumptions on which their work was based, influenced what educated people in the West studied, how they approached intellectual problems, and what they thought about the supernatural realm.

Education

During the seventeenth and early eighteenth centuries, especially between 1680 and 1720, science and the new philosophy that was associated with it became an important part of university education. Outside academia, learned societies, public lectures, discussions in coffeehouses, and popular scientific publications spread the knowledge of science among the educated members of society. In this way science secured a permanent foothold in Western culture.

The spread of science did not go unchallenged. It encountered academic rivals committed not only to traditional Aristotelianism but also to Renaissance humanism. In the late seventeenth century, a conflict arose between "the ancients," who revered the wisdom of classical authors, and "the moderns," who emphasized the superiority of the new scientific culture. The most concrete expression of this conflict was the Battle of the Books, an intellectual debate that raged over the question of which group of thinkers had contributed more to human knowledge. No clear winner in this battle emerged, and the conflict between the ancients and the moderns was never completely resolved. The humanities and the sciences, while included within the same curriculum at many universities, are still often regarded as representing separate cultural traditions.

Skepticism and Independent Reasoning

The Scientific Revolution encouraged the habit of **skepticism,** the tendency to doubt what we have been taught and are expected to believe. This skepticism formed part of the method that seventeenth-century scientists adopted to solve philosophical problems. As we have seen, Descartes, Bacon, Galileo, and Kepler all refused to acknowledge the authority of classical or medieval texts. They preferred to rely upon the knowledge they acquired from observing nature and using their own rational faculties.

In *Discourse on the Method,* Descartes showed the extremes to which this skepticism could be taken. Descartes doubted the reality of his own sense perceptions and even his own existence until he realized that the very act of doubting proved his existence as a thinking being. As he wrote in words that have become famous, "I think, therefore I am."[3] Upon this foundation Descartes went on to prove the existence of God and the material world, thereby conquering the skepticism with which he began his inquiry. In the

CHRONOLOGY: THE IMPACT OF THE SCIENTIFIC REVOLUTION

1620	Francis Bacon argues for the necessity of rigorous experimentation
1633	Galileo tried by the Roman Inquisition
1637	René Descartes publishes *Discourse on the Method*
1670	Baruch Spinoza publishes *Treatise on Religion and Political Philosophy,* challenging the distinction between spirit and matter
1686	Bernard de Fontenelle publishes *Treatises on the Plurality of Worlds*

process, however, he developed an approach to solving intellectual problems that asked people to question authority and think clearly and systematically for themselves. The effects of this method became apparent in the late seventeenth century, when skeptics invoked Descartes' methodology to challenge both orthodox Judaism and Christianity. Some of the most radical of those opinions came from Baruch Spinoza (1632–1677), who grew up in Amsterdam in a community of Spanish and Portuguese Jews who had fled the Inquisition. Although educated as an Orthodox Jew, Spinoza also studied Latin and read Descartes and other Christian writers. From Descartes, Spinoza learned "that nothing ought to be admitted as true but what has been proved by good and solid reason." This skepticism and independence of thought led to his excommunication from the Jewish community at age 24.

Spinoza used Descartes' skepticism to challenge Descartes himself. He rejected Descartes' separation of the mind and the body and his radical distinction between the spiritual and the material. For Spinoza there was only one substance in the universe, which he identified with both God and nature. The claim that God and nature were two names for the same reality challenged not only the ideas of Descartes, but also the fundamental tenets of Christianity, including the belief in a personal God who had created the natural world by design and continued to govern it. In *A Treatise on Religion and Political Philosophy* (1670), Spinoza described "a universe ruled only by the cause and effect of natural laws, without purpose or design."

Spinoza's skeptical approach to solving philosophical and scientific problems revealed the radical intellectual potential of the new science. The freedom of thought that Spinoza advocated, as well as the belief that nature followed unchangeable laws and could be understood in mathematical terms, served as important links between the Scientific Revolution and the Enlightenment of the eighteenth century. We will discuss those connections more fully in Chapter 19.

Science and Religion

The new science presented two challenges to traditional Christian belief. The first involved the apparent contradiction between the sun-centered theory of the universe and biblical references to the sun's mobility. Because the Bible was considered the inspired word of God, the Church took everything it said, including any passages regarding the operation of the physical world, as literally true. The Bible's reference to the sun moving across the sky served as the basis of the papal condemnation of sun-centered theories in 1616 and the prosecution of Galileo in 1633.

The second challenge to traditional Christian belief was the implication that if the universe functioned as a machine, on the basis of unchanging

BARUCH SPINOZA

Spinoza was one of the most radical thinkers of the seventeenth century. His identification of God with nature made him vulnerable to charges of atheism. His followers in the Dutch Republic, who were known as freethinkers, laid the foundations for the Enlightenment in the eighteenth century.

natural laws, then God played little part in its operation. God was akin to an engineer, who had designed the perfect machine, and therefore had no need to interfere with its workings. This position, which thinkers known as **deists** adopted in the late seventeenth and eighteenth centuries, denied the Christian belief that God was constantly active in the operation of the world. More directly, it rejected the possibility of miracles. None of the great scientists of the seventeenth century were themselves deists, but their acceptance of the mechanical philosophy made them vulnerable to the charge that they denied Christian doctrine.

Although the new science and seventeenth-century Christianity appeared to be on a collision course, some scientists and theologians insisted that there was no conflict between them. They argued that religion and science had different concerns. Religion dealt with the relationship between humanity and God. Science explained how nature operated. As Galileo wrote in 1615, "The intention of the Holy Ghost is to teach us how one goes to heaven, not how heaven goes."[4] Scripture was not intended to explain natural phenomena, but to convey religious truths that human reason could not grasp.

Another argument for the compatibility of science and religion was the claim that the mechanical philosophy, rather than relegating God to the role of a retired engineer, actually manifested God's unlimited power. In a mechanistic universe God was still the creator of the physical world and the maker of the laws by which nature operated. He was still all-powerful and present everywhere. According to Boyle and Newton, moreover, God played a supremely active role in governing the universe. Not only had he created the universe, but as Boyle argued, he also continued to keep all matter constantly in motion. This theory served the purpose of redefining God's power without diminishing it in any way. Newton arrived at a similar position in his search for an immaterial agent who would cause gravity to operate. He proposed that God himself, who he believed "endures always and is present everywhere," made bodies move according to gravitational laws. Throughout the early eighteenth

century this feature of Newtonian natural philosophy served as a powerful argument for the active involvement of God in the universe.

As the new science became more widely accepted, many theologians, especially Protestants, accommodated scientific knowledge to their religious beliefs. Some Protestants welcomed the discoveries of science as an opportunity to purify the Christian religion by combating the superstition, magic, and ignorance that they claimed the Catholic Church had been promoting. Clergymen argued that because God worked through the processes of nature, scientific inquiry could lead to knowledge of God. Religion and science could illuminate each other.

Theologians and philosophers also began to expand the role that reason played in religion. The English philosopher John Locke (1632–1704) argued that reason should be the final judge of the existence of the supernatural and the true meaning of the Bible. This new emphasis on the role of reason in religion coincided with a rejection of the religious zeal that had prevailed during the Reformation and the wars of religion. Increasingly, political and ecclesiastical authorities condemned religious enthusiasm as dangerous and irrational.

The new emphasis on the reasonableness of religion and the decline of religious enthusiasm are often viewed as evidence of a trend toward the **secularization** of European life, a process in which religion gave way to more worldly concerns. In one sense this secular trend was undeniable. By 1700, theology had lost its dominant position at the universities and religion had lost much of its influence on politics, diplomacy, and economic activity.

Religion, however, had not lost its relevance. It remained a vital force in the lives of most Europeans. Many of those who accepted the new science continued to believe in a providential God and the divinity of Christ. Moreover, a small but influential group of educated people, following the lead of the French scientist and philosopher Blaise Pascal (1623–1662), argued that religious faith occupied a higher sphere of knowledge that reason and science could not penetrate. Pascal, the inventor of a calculating machine and the promoter of a system of public coach service in Paris, was an

JUSTICE IN HISTORY

The Trial of Galileo

The events leading to the trial of Galileo for heresy in 1633 began in 1616, when a committee of theologians reported to the Roman Inquisition that the sun-centered theory of Copernicus was heretical. Those who accepted this theory were declared to be heretics not only because they questioned the Bible itself, but because they denied the exclusive authority of the Catholic Church to interpret the Bible. The day after this report was submitted, Pope Paul V (r. 1605–1621) instructed Cardinal Robert Bellarmine (1542–16210, a theologian who was on good terms with Galileo, to warn him to abandon his Copernican views. Galileo had written extensively in support of the sun-centered thesis, especially in his *Letters on Sunspots* (1613) and his *Letter to the Grand Duchess Christina* (1615), although he had never admitted that the theory was proved conclusively. Then he was told not to hold, teach, or defend in any way the opinion that the sun was stable or the Earth moved. If he ignored that warning, he would be prosecuted as a heretic.

During the next 16 years Galileo published two books. The first, *The Assayer* (1623), attacked the views of an Italian philosopher regarding comets. The book won Galileo support, especially from the new pope, Urban VIII (r. 1623–1644), who was eager to be associated with the most fashionable intellectual trends. Urban took Galileo under his wing and made him the intellectual star of his court. Urban even declared that support for Copernicanism was rash but not heretical.

The pope's patronage may have emboldened Galileo to exercise less caution in writing his second book of this period, *Dialogue Concerning the Two Chief World Systems* (1632). Ostensibly an impartial presentation of the rival Ptolemaic and Copernican cosmologies, this book promoted Copernicanism in its own quiet way. Galileo sought proper authorization from ecclesiastical authorities to put the book in print, but he allowed it to be published in Florence before it received official approval from Rome.

The publication of *Dialogue* precipitated Galileo's fall from the pope's favor. Urban, accused of leniency with heretics, ordered the book taken out of circulation in the summer of 1632 and appointed a commission to investigate Galileo's activities. After receiving their report, he turned the matter over to the Roman Inquisition, which charged Galileo with heresy.

The Roman Inquisition had been established in 1542 to preserve the Catholic faith and prosecute heresy. Like the Spanish Inquisition, this Roman ecclesiastical court has acquired a reputation for being harsh and arbitrary, for administering torture, for proceeding in secrecy, and for denying the accused the right to know the charges before the trial. There is some validity to these criticisms, although the Inquisition did not torture Galileo or deny him the opportunity to defend himself. The most unfair aspect of the proceeding, and of inquisitorial justice in general, was that the same judges who had brought the charges against the accused and conducted the interrogation also decided the case. This meant that in a politically motivated trial such as Galileo's, the verdict was a foregone conclusion. To accept Galileo's defense would have been a sign of weakness and a repudiation of the pope.

Although the underlying issue in the trial was whether Galileo was guilty of heresy for denying the sun's motion and the Earth's immobility, the more technical question was whether by publishing *Dialogue* he had violated the prohibition of 1616. In his defense Galileo claimed he had only written *Dialogue* to present "the physical and astronomical reasons that can be advanced for one side or the other." He denied holding Copernicus's opinion to be true.

In the end the court determined that by publishing *Dialogue*, Galileo had violated the injunction of 1616. He had disseminated "the false opinion of

THE TRIAL OF GALILEO, 1633

Galileo is shown here presenting one of his four defenses to the Inquisition. He claimed that his book *Dialogue Concerning the Two Chief World Systems* did not endorse the Copernican model of the universe.

Source: Gérard Blot/Art Resource/Reunion des Musees Nationaux

the Earth's motion and the sun's stability," and he had "defended the said opinion already condemned." Even Galileo's efforts "to give the impression of leaving it undecided and labeled as probable" was still a serious error, because there was no way that "an opinion declared and defined contrary to divine Scripture may be probable." The court also declared that Galileo had obtained permission to publish the book in Florence without telling the authorities there that he was under the injunction of 1616.

Throughout the trial every effort was made to distance the pope from his former protégé. The papal court feared that because the pope had been Galileo's patron and had allowed him to develop his ideas, he himself would be implicated in Galileo's heresy. Information regarding the pope's earlier support for Galileo would not be allowed to surface during the trial. The court made sure, for example, that no one from the court of the Grand Duke of Tuscany in Florence, who had secured Galileo's appointment at the University of Padua and had defended him throughout this crisis, would testify for him. The trial tells us as much about Urban VIII's efforts to save face as about the Catholic Church's hostility to the new science.

The Inquisition required Galileo to renounce his views and avoid further defense of Copernicanism.

After making this humiliating submission to the court, he was sent to Siena and later that year was allowed to return to his villa near Florence, where he remained under house arrest until his death in 1642.

For Discussion

1. Galileo was silenced because of what he had printed. Why had he published these works, and why did the Church consider his publications a threat?

2. Should disputes between science and religion be resolved in a court of law? Why or why not?

Taking It Further

Finocchiaro, Maurice (ed). *The Galileo Affair: A Documentary History.* 1989. A collection of original documents regarding the controversy between Galileo and the Roman Catholic Church.

Sharratt, Michael. *Galileo: Decisive Innovator.* 1994. A study of Galileo's place in the history of science that provides full coverage of his trial and papal reconsiderations of it in the late twentieth century.

advocate of the new science. He endorsed the Copernican model of the universe and opposed the condemnation of Galileo. He introduced a new scientific theory regarding fluids that later became known as Pascal's law of pressure. But by claiming that knowledge of God comes from the heart rather than the mind, Pascal challenged the contention of Locke and Spinoza that reason was the ultimate arbiter of religious truth.

HUMANS AND THE NATURAL WORLD

■ How did the Scientific Revolution change the way in which seventeenth- and eighteenth-century Europeans thought of the place of human beings in nature?

The spread of scientific knowledge not only redefined the views of educated people regarding the supernatural, but also led them to reconsider their relationship to nature. This process involved three separate but related inquiries: to determine the place of human beings in a sun-centered universe, to investigate how science and technology had given human beings greater control over nature, and to reconsider the relationship between men and women in light of new scientific knowledge about the human mind and body.

The Place of Human Beings in the Universe

The astronomical discoveries of Copernicus, Kepler, and Galileo offered a new outlook about the position of human beings in the universe. The Earth-centered Ptolemaic cosmos that dominated scientific thought during the Middle Ages was also human-centered. Human beings inhabited the planet at the very center of the universe, and on that planet they enjoyed a privileged position. They were, after all, created in the image of God, according to Christian belief.

The acceptance of a sun-centered model of the universe began to change these views of

humankind. Once it became apparent that the Earth was not the center of the universe, human beings began to lose their privileged position in nature. The Copernican universe was neither Earth-centered nor human-centered. Scientists such as Descartes continued to claim that human beings were the greatest of nature's creatures, but their habitation of a tiny planet circling the sun inevitably reduced the sense of their own importance. Moreover, as astronomers began to recognize the incomprehensible size of the cosmos, the possibility emerged that there were other habitable worlds in the universe, calling into further question the unique status of humankind.

In the late sixteenth and seventeenth centuries a number of literary works explored the possibility of other inhabited worlds and forms of life. Kepler's *Somnium,* or *Lunar Astronomy* (1634), a book that combined science and fiction, described various species of moon dwellers, some of whom were rational and superior to humans. The most ambitious of these books on extraterrestrial life was Bernard de Fontenelle's *Conversations on the Plurality of Worlds* (1686). This fictional work by a dramatist and poet who was also well versed in scientific knowledge became immensely popular throughout Europe and was more responsible than any purely scientific achievement for leading the general reading public to call into question the centrality of human beings in Creation.

The Control of Nature

The Scientific Revolution strengthened the confidence human beings had in their ability to control nature. By disclosing the laws governing the operation of the universe, the new science gave humans the tools they needed to make nature serve them more effectively than it had in the past. Francis Bacon, for example, believed that knowledge of the laws of nature could restore the dominion over nature that humans had lost in the biblical Garden of Eden. Bacon thought that nature existed for human beings to control and exploit for their own benefit. His famous saying, "knowledge is power," conveyed his confidence that science would give human beings this type of control. This optimism regarding human control of nature found support in the belief that God permitted such mastery, first by creating a regular and uniform universe and then by giving humans the rational faculties by which they could understand nature's laws.

Many seventeenth-century scientists emphasized the practical applications of their research, just as scientists often do today. Descartes, who used his knowledge of optics to improve the grinding of lenses, considered how scientific knowledge could drain marshes, increase the velocity of bullets, and use bells to make clouds give rain. In his celebration of the French Academy of Sciences in 1699, Fontenelle wrote that "the application of science to nature will constantly grow in scope and intensity and we shall go on from one marvel to the next; the day will come when man will be able to fly by fitting on wings to keep him in the air...till one day we shall be able to fly to the moon."[5]

The hopes of seventeenth-century scientists for the improvement of human life by means of technology remained in large part unfulfilled until the eighteenth century. Only then did the technological promise of the Scientific Revolution begin to be realized, most notably with the innovations that preceded or accompanied the Industrial Revolution (see Chapter 21). By the middle of the eighteenth century, the belief that science would improve human life became an integral part of Western culture. Faith in human progress also became one of the main themes of the Enlightenment, which will be discussed in Chapter 19.

Women, Men, and Nature

The new scientific and philosophical ideas challenged ancient and medieval notions about women's physical and mental inferiority to men but not other traditional ideas about gender roles.

Until the seventeenth century, a woman's sexual organs were thought to be imperfect versions of a man's, an idea that made woman an inferior version of man and, in some respects, a freak of nature. During the sixteenth and seventeenth centuries, scientific literature advanced the new idea that women's sexual organs were perfect in their own right and served distinct functions in reproduction. Aristotle's view that men made a more important contribution to reproduction than women also came under attack. Semen was long believed to contain the form of both the body and the soul, while a woman only contributed the formless matter on which the semen acted. By 1700, however, most scholars agreed that both sexes contributed equally to the process of reproduction.

Some seventeenth-century natural philosophers also questioned ancient and medieval ideas about women's mental inferiority to men. In making a radical separation between the mind and the human body, Descartes, for example, found no difference between the minds of men and women. As one of his followers wrote in 1673, "The mind has no sex."[6] A few upper-class women provided evidence to support this revolutionary claim of female intellectual equality. Princess Elisabeth of Bohemia, for example, carried on a long correspondence with Descartes during the 1640s and challenged many of his ideas on the relationship between the body and the soul. The English noblewoman Margaret Cavendish (1623–1673) wrote scientific and philosophical works and conversed with leading philosophers. In early eighteenth-century France, small groups of women and men gathered in the salons or private sitting rooms of the nobility to discuss philosophical and scientific ideas. In Germany women helped their husbands run astronomical observatories.

Although seventeenth-century science laid the foundations for a theory of sexual equality, it did not challenge other traditional ideas that compared women unfavorably with men. Most educated people continued to ground female behavior in the humors, claiming that because women were cold and wet, as opposed to hot and dry, they were naturally more deceptive, unstable, and melancholic than men. They also continued to identify women with nature itself, which had always been depicted as female.

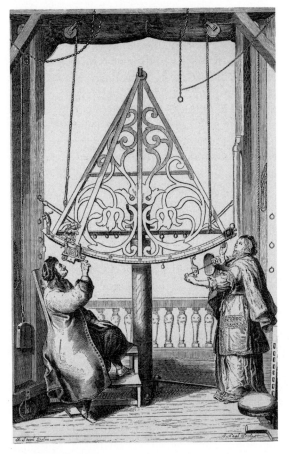

ASTRONOMERS IN SEVENTEENTH-CENTURY GERMANY

Elisabetha and Johannes Hevelius working together with a sextant in a German astronomical observatory. More than 14 percent of all German astronomers were female. Most of them cooperated with their husbands in their work.

Bacon's use of masculine metaphors to describe science and his references to "man's mastery over nature" therefore seemed to reinforce traditional ideas of male dominance over women. His language also reinforced traditional notions of men's superior rationality.[7] In 1664 the secretary of the Royal Society, which excluded women from membership, proclaimed that the mission of that institution was to develop a "masculine philosophy."[8]

The new science thus strengthened the theoretical foundations for the male control of women at a time when many men expressed concern over women's "disorderly" and "irrational" conduct. In a world populated with witches, rebels, and other women who refused to adhere to conventional standards of proper feminine behavior, the adoption of a masculine philosophy was associated with the reassertion of patriarchy.

CONCLUSION

Science and Western Culture

Unlike many of the cultural developments in the history of the West, the Scientific Revolution owes very little to Eastern influences. During the Middle Ages the Islamic civilizations of the Middle East produced a rich body of scientific knowledge that influenced the development of medieval science in Europe, but by the time of the Scientific Revolution, Middle Eastern science no longer occupied the frontlines of scientific research. Middle Eastern natural philosophers had little to offer their European counterparts as they made their contributions to the Scientific Revolution.

China and India had also accumulated a large body of scientific knowledge in ancient and medieval times. When Jesuit missionaries began teaching Western science and mathematics to the Chinese in the sixteenth and seventeenth centuries, they learned about earlier Chinese technological advances, including the invention of the compass, gunpowder, and printing. They also learned that ancient Chinese astronomers had been the first to observe solar eclipses and comets. By the time the Jesuits arrived, however, Chinese science had entered a period of decline. When those missionaries returned home, they introduced Europeans to many aspects of Chinese culture but very few scientific ideas that Europeans natural philosophers found useful.

None of these Eastern civilizations had a scientific revolution comparable to the one that occurred in the West in the late sixteenth and seventeenth centuries. For China the explanation probably lies in the absence of military and political incentives to promote scientific research at a time when the vast Chinese empire was relatively stable. In the Middle East the explanation is more likely that Islam during these years failed to give priority to the study of the natural world. In Islam nature was either entirely secular (that is, not religious) and hence not worthy of study on its own terms or so heavily infused with spiritual value that it could not be subjected to rational analysis. In Europe, however, religious and cultural traditions allowed scientists to view nature as both a product of supernatural forces and something that was separate from the supernatural. Nature could therefore be studied objectively without losing its religious significance. Only when nature was viewed as both the creation of God and at the same time as independent of God, could it be subjected to mathematical analysis and brought under human control.

Scientific and technological knowledge became a significant component of Western culture, and in the eighteenth century Western science gave many educated Europeans a new source of identity. These people believed that their knowledge of science, in conjunction with their Christian religion, their classical culture, and their political institutions made them different from, if not superior to, people living in the East.

The rise of Western science and technology played a role in the growth of European dominance over Africa, Asia, and the Americas. Science gave Western states the military and navigational technology that helped them gain control of foreign lands. Knowledge of botany and agriculture allowed Western powers to develop the resources of the areas they colonized and use these resources to improve their own societies. Some Europeans even appealed to science to justify their dominance of the people in the lands they settled and ruled. To this process of Western imperial expansion we now turn.

KEY TERMS

universal law of
  gravitation
alchemy
induction
empiricism
deductive reasoning
rationalism

mechanical philosophy
dualistic
Neoplatonism
paradigm
skepticism
deists
secularization

CHAPTER QUESTIONS

1. What were the achievements and discoveries of the Scientific Revolution? (page 529)
2. What methods did scientists use during this period to investigate nature, and how did they think nature operated? (page 535)
3. Why did the Scientific Revolution occur in Western Europe at this particular time? (page 537)
4. How did the Scientific Revolution influence philosophical and religious thought in the seventeenth and early eighteenth centuries? (page 543)
5. How did the Scientific Revolution change how Europeans thought about the place of human beings in nature? (page 548)

TAKING IT FURTHER

1. Were the changes in astronomy, physics, chemistry, and biology in the sixteenth and seventeenth centuries revolutionary? In which field were the changes most significant?
2. Scientists today often refer to the scientific method. Was there a scientific method in the seventeenth century or did scientists employ various methods?
3. Why did the scientific revolution occur at this time? Did it owe its development more to internal or external developments? Scientists today often refer to the scientific method. Was there a scientific method in the seventeenth century or did scientists employ various methods?
4. What does the conflict between the supporter of a sun-centered theory and the Catholic Church suggest about the compatibility of science and religion in the seventeenth century?

✔—Practice on MyHistoryLab

18

The West and the World: Empire, Trade, and War, 1650–1815

■ European Empires in the Americas and Asia ■ Warfare in Europe, North America, and Asia ■ The Atlantic World ■ Encounters Between Europeans and Asians ■ The Crisis of Empire and the Atlantic Revolutions

In 1789 OLAUDAH EQUIANO, A FREED SLAVE LIVING IN GREAT BRITAIN, wrote an account of his experiences in captivity. Equiano's narrative recounted his seizure in the Gambia region of Africa and his transportation on a slave ship to the British Caribbean colony of Barbados. He described the unmerciful floggings to which the Africans on his ship were subjected, the unrelieved hunger they experienced, and the insufferable heat and smells they endured in the hold of the ship. He witnessed the suicide of those who threw themselves into the sea to avoid further misery. He was terrified that his white captors would eat him, and he wished for a merciful death.

Once the ship had reached its destination the Africans were herded into pens where white plantation owners examined, purchased, and branded them. The most moving part of Equiano's narrative is his account of the cries he heard as family members were sold to different masters. "O you nominal Christians," wrote Equiano, "might not an African ask you, learned you this from your God? Is it not enough that we are torn from our country and friends to toil for your luxury and lust of gain? Must every tender feeling be sacrificed to your avarice?"[1]

Between 1650 and 1815 millions of African men and women took journeys similar to Equiano's. The forced emigration of black Africans from their homelands, their sale to white landlords, and their subjection to inhumane treatment number among the abiding horrors of Western civilization. To understand how these horrors could have occurred, especially at the hands of men who proclaimed a commitment to human freedom, we must study the growth of European empires during these centuries.

As European states grew in size, wealth, and military power in the sixteenth and seventeenth centuries, the most powerful of them acquired large overseas empires. By the end of the seventeenth century the British, French, and Dutch had joined the Portuguese and the Spanish as overseas imperial powers. As we discussed in Chapter 13, the first stage of empire-building, which lasted from 1500 until about 1650, had many different motives. The search for gold and silver, the mission to Christianize the indigenous populations, the desire of some colonists to escape religious persecution, the urge to plunder, the efforts of monarchs to expand the size of their dominions, and the desire to profit from international trade all

JEAN-BAPTISTE DEBRET, *PUNISHMENT OF A SLAVE*

This image of the flogging of a slave in Brazil conveys the brutality of Atlantic slavery. The French painter Jean Baptiste Debret included this engraving in his three-volume study, *A Pictureque and Historic Voyage to Brazil* (1834–1839).

Source: Biblioteca Nacional, Rio de Janiero Brazil/The Bridgeman Art Library

figured in the process. In 1625 the English government recognized many of these motives when it declared the purpose of the colony of Virginia to be "the propagation of the Christian religion, the increase of trade, and the enlarging of the royal empire."[2]

During the second stage of empire-building, which lasted from about 1650 to 1815, the economic motive for acquiring overseas possessions became dominant. More than anything else, the desire for profit within a world economy shaped imperial policy. In the eyes of western European governments, all colonies were economic enterprises. They supplied the parent country, often referred to as the **metropolis,** with agricultural products, raw materials, and minerals. Overseas colonies also provided the metropolis with markets for its manufactured goods.

The growth of these empires expanded the geographical boundaries of the West. It also resulted in the spread of Western ideas, political institutions, and economic systems to Asia and the Americas. At the same time, encounters between Europeans and non-Western peoples, especially those of Asia, changed the cultures of the West.

EUROPEAN EMPIRES IN THE AMERICAS AND ASIA

■ How did the composition and organization of European empires change during the seventeenth and eighteenth centuries?

The main political units in Europe during this long period of history are usually referred to as **states.** A state is a consolidated territorial area that has its own political institutions and recognizes no higher authority. Thus, we refer to France, England (which became Great Britain after its union with Scotland in 1707), Prussia, the Dutch Republic, and Portugal as states. As we have discussed in Chapter 16, most of these states acquired larger armies and administrative bureaucracies during the sixteenth and seventeenth centuries, mainly to meet the demands of war. Consequently, they became more highly integrated and cohesive political structures.

Many European states formed the center or core of much larger political formations known as **empires.** The main characteristic of empires in the seventeenth and eighteenth centuries was that they contained many different kingdoms or territorial possessions. The metropolis controlled these imperial territories, but did not fully integrate them into its administrative structure. Some of the territories that formed a part of these empires were located in Europe. The Austrian Habsburg monarchy, for example, had jurisdiction over a host of separate kingdoms and principalities in central and eastern Europe, including Hungary and Bohemia. The Spanish monarchy controlled many different kingdoms and provinces in the Iberian Peninsula as well as territories in southern Italy and the Netherlands. On the eastern and southeastern periphery of Europe lay two other empires: the Russian and

the Ottoman, which controlled vast expanses of land not only in eastern Europe, but also in Asia. As in previous centuries, the Russian and Ottoman empires marked the ever-shifting boundaries between East and West.

Beginning in the fifteenth century, as the result of transoceanic voyages of exploration and the establishment of overseas colonies, western European states acquired, settled, or controlled territories in the Americas, Africa, and Asia. Mastery of these lands came much more quickly in the New World than in Asia. The peoples of North and South America whom Europeans encountered when they arrived were able fighters, but diseases introduced by the Europeans drastically reduced their numbers. European settlers, who had the added advantage of superior military technology, were able to gain the upper hand in battle, seize or purchase their lands, and force those who survived to retreat to less inhabited areas.

When Europeans started to develop extensive trading routes in Asia, however, that continent was already highly developed politically and militarily. Three Muslim empires—the Ottoman, the Safavid (Persia), and the Mughal (India)—and the neighboring Chinese Empire in East Asia occupied the mass of land from the Balkans to the Pacific Ocean. Only when these Asian empires began to fall apart, giving greater autonomy to the smaller, subordinate states within their boundaries, were Europeans able to exploit the situation, secure favorable trading arrangements with provincial rulers in Asia, and ultimately gain control over some Asian territories.

The Rise of the British Empire

The fastest-growing of the new European overseas empires during this period was that of Great Britain. England had begun its overseas empire in the late twelfth century, when it conquered the neighboring island of Ireland, but only in the seventeenth century did it begin to acquire lands in the New World and Asia. By 1700 the English empire in the Americas included colonies on the eastern North American seaboard, a vast territory in the northern part of Canada, and a cluster of islands in the Caribbean, most notably Barbados, Jamaica, and the Bahamas.

These Caribbean or West Indian colonies developed an economy that used slave labor, and therefore black slaves brought there from Africa soon outnumbered Europeans by a significant margin. In the colonies on the mainland of North America, however, most of the colonists were white, even in the southern colonies, where black slaves accounted for less than half the population.

Many English settlers, especially in the northern colonies, emigrated so that they might practice their religion without legal restraint. During the 1630s communities of English Protestants known as Puritans settled in New England. They objected to the control of the English Church by bishops, especially during the period from 1633 to 1641, when William Laud served as archbishop of Canterbury. Their main complaint was that the church services authorized by Laud too closely resembled those of Roman Catholicism. During the same years small groups of English Catholics, who were denied the right to practice their religion, took refuge in Maryland. In the late seventeenth century a dissenting Protestant sect known as Quakers (so called because their founder, George Fox, told them to quake at the word of the Lord), smarting under legislation that denied them religious freedom and political power, emigrated to Pennsylvania.

During the seventeenth century the English also established trading posts, known as factories, along the coast of India. They settled at Surat in 1612, Madras in 1640, Bombay in 1661, and Calcutta in 1690. These mercantile depots differed markedly from the colonies in the Caribbean and on the North American mainland. The number of British settlers in India, who were mostly members of the East India Company (which had a monopoly of British trade with India), remained small, and they did not establish large plantations. Consequently, they did not introduce slave labor.

SAMUEL SCOTT, *A THAMES WHARF* (1750s)
British merchants conducted a brisk trade with Asia and the Americas in the eighteenth century.

As **Map 18.1** shows, the British also acquired influence and ultimately political control of the area from Southeast Asia stretching down into the South Pacific. In the late seventeenth century the British began to challenge the Dutch and the Portuguese for control of the trade with Indonesia, and in the second half of the eighteenth century British merchants established a thriving trade with the countries on the Malay Peninsula. In the late eighteenth century the British also began to explore the South Pacific, which remained the last part of the inhabited world that Europeans had not yet visited. (See *Justice in History* in this chapter.) In 1770 the British naval officer and explorer Captain James Cook (1728–1779) claimed the entire eastern coast of Australia for Britain, and in 1788 the British established a penal colony in the southeastern corner of the Australian continent at Botany Bay.

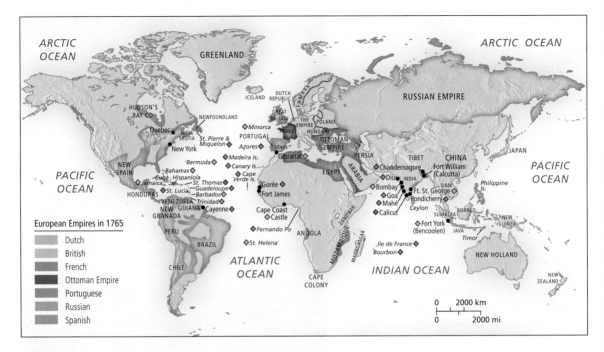

MAP 18.1

European Empires in 1763

This map shows the overseas possessions of Britain, France, the Dutch Republic, Spain, and Portugal. Russian overseas expansion into North America had not yet begun.

The Scattered French Empire

French colonization of North America and India paralleled that of Great Britain, but it never achieved the same degree of success. As the British were establishing footholds in the West Indies and the mainland of North America, the French acquired their own islands in the Caribbean and laid claim to large sections of Canada and the Ohio and Mississippi River valleys in the present-day United States. In the West Indies the French first drew their labor supply from servants indentured for periods of three years, but in the eighteenth century they began to follow the British and Spanish pattern of importing slaves to provide labor for the sugar plantations. In North America French settlers did not require a large labor supply, as their main economic undertakings were the fur trade and fishing, and so they did not introduce slaves to those areas.

The parallel between French and British overseas expansion extended to India, where in the early eighteenth century the French East India Company established factories at Pondicherry, Chandenagar, and other locations. Rivalry with the British also led the French to make alliances with native governors of Indian provinces, to assist them in a series of military conflicts with the British between 1744 and 1815. The British ultimately prevailed in this struggle, reducing the French presence in India to a few isolated factories by the early nineteenth century.

The waning of French influence in India coincided with a series of territorial losses in the New World. Defeats suffered at the hands of the British during the Seven Years' War (1756–1763) resulted in the transfer of French Canada and the territory east of the Mississippi River to Great Britain. During that conflict France also ceded the vast region of Louisiana between the Mississippi River and the Rocky Mountains to Spain. France regained Louisiana in 1801 but then promptly sold the entire territory to the United States in 1803. The following year the French Caribbean colony of Saint Domingue became independent, although France retained possession of its other West Indian colonies.

The Commercial Dutch Empire

The tiny Dutch Republic acquired almost all of its overseas possessions in the first half of the seventeenth century, at about the same time that the British and French were establishing their first colonies in Asia and the New World. The formation of the Dutch empire went hand in hand with the explosive growth of the Dutch economy in the seventeenth century. At that time the Dutch Republic became the center of a global economy, and its overseas colonies in the New World, Asia, and Africa helped the Dutch Republic maintain its commercial supremacy. Dutch overseas settlements, just like Dutch port cities in the metropolis, were dedicated almost exclusively to serving the interests of trade.

The Dutch were more eager than other European powers to use military and naval power to acquire and fortify trading depots. They seized two trading posts from the Portuguese on the West African coast in 1637, and in 1641 they also acquired from Portugal the African islands of São Tomé and Principe. In 1654 they seized two small West Indian islands and plantation colonies on the Guiana coast of South America, mainly in present-day Surinam. From these settlements in Africa and the Caribbean the Dutch carried on trade with the Spanish, Portuguese, French, and British colonies. Through these ports the Dutch brought more than 500,000 slaves to Brazil, the Spanish colonies, and the French and British West Indies.

In addition to their African and Caribbean possessions, the Dutch established a presence in three other parts of the world. In the early seventeenth century they settled a colony in the Hudson River valley on the North American mainland. They named the colony New Netherland and its main port, at the mouth of the river, New Amsterdam. In 1664 the Dutch lost the colony to the English, who renamed the colony and the port New York. The second area was in Asia, where the Dutch East India Company established a fort at Batavia (now Jakarta in Indonesia) and factories in India, China, and Japan. These possessions allowed the Dutch to engage in trade throughout Asia. In the eighteenth century, however, the British began to take control of Dutch trading routes.

THE DUTCH FACTORY OF BATAVIA IN INDONESIA, CA. 1665

The Dutch Republic dominated the Asian trade in the seventeenth century. Batavia (now Jakarta) was the most important of their settlements in Southeast Asia. The efforts of the Dutch to transplant their culture is evident in this building's Dutch style of architecture.

JUSTICE IN HISTORY

The Trial of the Mutineers on the *Bounty*

In December 1787 a British ship named the *Bounty,* under the captainship of William Bligh, left Portsmouth, England, on a momentous journey to Tahiti, an island in the South Pacific that Captain James Cook had first visited in 1769. The goal of the voyage of the *Bounty* was neither exploration nor colonial expansion, but to bring home breadfruit trees that Cook had discovered on his second trip to the island in 1773. The trees, so it was hoped, would be introduced to the West Indies as a source of food for the slaves and hence the survival of the plantation economy. The voyage of the *Bounty* was therefore part of the operation of the new global economy that European expansion had made possible. The total size of the crew, all of whom had volunteered for service, was 46. The master's first mate, who became the main leader of a mutiny against Bligh, was Fletcher Christian.

The mutiny did not take place until after the ship had remained at Tahiti for a number of months, loaded its cargo of more than one thousand breadfruit plants, and begun its return voyage. The main reason for the mutiny was Captain Bligh's abusive and humiliating language. Unlike many other officers who faced the task of maintaining order on their ships and commanding the obedience of their crews, Bligh did not flog his men. In that regard Bligh's behavior was mild. Instead he went into tantrums and verbally abused them, belittling them and calling them scoundrels. Just before the mutiny Bligh called Fletcher Christian a cowardly rascal and falsely accused him of stealing from him. On the morning of April 28, 1788, Christian arrested Bligh at bayonet point, tied his hands behind his back, and threatened him with instant death if he should speak a word. Claiming that "Captain Bligh had brought all this on himself," Christian and his associates put Bligh and 18 other members of the crew into one of the ship's small launch boats and set them adrift, leaving them to reach a nearby island by their own power.

The mutineers sailed on to the island of Tubuai, where after a brief stay they split into two groups. Nine of them, headed by Christian and accompanied by six Tahitian men and twelve women, established a settlement on Pitcairn Island, where their descendents still reside today. The remaining 16 mutineers returned to Tahiti. All but two of these men

THE MUTINEERS CASTING BLIGH ADRIFT IN THE LAUNCH, ENGRAVING BY ROBERT DODD (1790)

This was the central act in the mutiny led by Fletcher Christian. Captain Bligh is standing in the launch in his nightclothes. Some of the breadfruit trees loaded on the ship at Tahiti can be seen on the top deck.

were apprehended in 1791 by Captain Edwards of the H.M.S. *Pandora,* which had sailed to Tahiti to arrest and return them to England for trial. At the beginning of its return voyage the *Pandora* was shipwrecked, and four of the prisoners drowned. The rest reached England aboard another ship in 1792. They were promptly charged before a navy court-martial with taking the *Bounty* away from its captain and with desertion, both of which were capital offenses under the Naval Discipline Act of 1766.

The trial took place aboard a British ship, H.M.S. *Duke,* in Portsmouth harbor in September 1792. The proceeding had all the markings of a state trial, a proceeding initiated by the government for offenses against the Crown. Mutiny and desertion represented challenges to the state itself. During the second period of imperial expansion navies became major instruments of state power. Even when ships were used for purposes of exploration rather than naval combat, they served the interests of the state. The captain of the ship represented the power of the sovereign at sea. Because of the difficulty of maintaining order in such circumstances, the captain was given absolute authority. He could use whatever means necessary, including the infliction of corporal punishment, to preserve order. To disobey or challenge the captain was interpreted as an act of rebellion.

The trial was based on the assumption that the mutiny was illegal and seditious. The only question was the extent of individual involvement in the act itself. The degree of involvement was measured by evidence of one's co-operation with Christian or his loyalty to Bligh. The mere fact that some men had remained with Christian on the *Bounty* did not prove that they had supported the mutiny. Four of those men gave little evidence of having voluntarily cooperated with Christian, and those four men were eventually acquitted. The testimony of Captain Bligh, who declared that those four crew members had been reluctant to put him in the launch boat, was decisive in securing their not-guilty verdicts.

The remaining six men were convicted and sentenced to die by hanging. Three of those men were eventually spared their lives. Peter Heywood and James Morrison were well connected to influential people in the navy and the government and received royal pardons. William Muspratt, one of only three mutineers to hire a lawyer, entered a protest against the procedures of the court. In a court-martial, unlike a criminal trial at the common law, a prisoner could not call witnesses in his own defense. At the time of his conviction Muspratt protested that he had been "debarred calling witnesses whose evidence I have reason to believe would have tended to prove my innocence." The difference between the two systems of criminal justice, he claimed, "is dreadful to the subject and fatal to me." On this ground Muspratt was reprieved.

The three men who were executed died as model prisoners, proclaiming the illegality of their rebellion. By securing their conviction and dramatizing it with a widely publicized hanging, the government had upheld its authority and thus reinforced the power of the Crown.

For Discussion

1. How would you characterize the different ideals of justice adhered to by the mutineers on the *Bounty* and the British admiralty court that tried them?

2. What does the journey of the *Bounty* tell us about the role of the British navy in the process of imperial expansion? What problems were inherent in using British ships for these purposes?

Taking it Further

Rutter, Owen (ed.) *The Court-Martial of the "Bounty" Mutineers.* 1931. Contains a full transcript of the trial.

The third area was the southern tip of Africa, where in 1652 the Dutch settled a colony at the Cape of Good Hope, mainly to provide support for ships engaged in commerce with the East Indies. In this colony some 1,700 Dutch settlers, most of them farmers known as **boers,** developed an agricultural economy on plantations that employed slave labor. The loss of this colony to the British at the end of the eighteenth century reflected a more general decline of Dutch military and imperial strength.

The Vast Spanish Empire

Of the five western European overseas empires, the Spanish monarchy controlled the most land. At the height of its power in 1650, the Spanish Empire covered the western part of North America from California to Mexico and from Mexico down through Central America. It also included Florida and the Caribbean islands of Cuba, San Domingo, and Puerto Rico. It embraced almost all of South America except Brazil, which was under Portuguese control. In Asia the main Spanish possessions were the Philippine Islands, which served as the main base from which the Spanish engaged in trade with other Asian countries.

Spanish overseas possessions formed part of a much more authoritarian imperial system than those of the British. Like all mercantilist enterprises, the Spanish colonial empire served the purposes of trade. Until the eighteenth century a council known as the House of Trade, situated in Seville, exercised a monopoly over all colonial commerce. It funneled trade with the colonies from the southwestern Spanish port of Cadiz to selected ports on the eastern coasts of Spanish America, from which it was then redirected to other ports. The ships returned to Spain carrying the gold and silver from Mexican and Peruvian mines.

The Bourbon kings of Spain, who came to power in 1700, introduced political reforms that were intended to increase the volume of the colonial trade and prevent the smuggling that threatened to undermine it. On the one hand, they opened up the colonial trade to more Spanish and American ports and also permitted more trade within the colonies. On the other hand, the Bourbons, especially Charles III (r. 1759–1788), brought their overseas territories under more direct control of Spanish royal officials and increased the efficiency of the tax collection system. These **Bourbon reforms** made the empire more manageable and profitable, but they also created tension between the Spanish-born bureaucrats and the **creoles,** the people of Spanish descent who had been born in the colonies. These tensions eventually led in the early nineteenth century to a series of wars of independence from Spain that we shall discuss in a later section.

The Declining Portuguese Empire

The Portuguese had been the first European nation to engage in overseas exploration and colonization. During the late fifteenth and sixteenth centuries, they had established colonies in Asia, South America, and Africa (see Chapter 13). By the beginning of the eighteenth century, however, the Portuguese Empire had declined in size and wealth in relation to its rivals. The Portuguese continued to hold a few ports in India, most notably the small island of Goa. They also retained a factory at Macao off the southeastern coast of China. In the New World the major Portuguese plantation colony was Brazil, which occupied almost half the land mass of South America and supplied Europe with sugar, cacao (from which chocolate is made), and other agricultural commodities. Closely linked to Brazil were the Portuguese colonies along and off the West African coast. These possessions were all deeply involved in the transatlantic trade, especially in slaves. The Portuguese also had a series of trading stations and small settlements on the southeastern coast of Africa, including Mozambique.

A relatively weak European power, Portugal did not fare well in the fierce military conflicts that ensued in South America and Asia over control of the colonial trade. Portugal's main military and economic competition came from the Dutch, who seized many of its Asian, African, and South American colonies, thereby acquiring many Portuguese trading routes. Most of those losses took place in Asia between 1600 and 1670. The Portuguese Empire suffered further attrition when the crown relinquished Bombay and the northern African port of Tangier to the English as part of the dowry for the Portuguese princess Catherine of Braganza when she married King Charles II of Great Britain in 1661.

Brazil remained by far the most important of the Portuguese possessions during the late seventeenth and eighteenth centuries. The colony suffered from an unfavorable balance of trade with Portugal, but it expanded in population and wealth during this period, especially after the discovery of gold and diamonds led to large-scale mining in the interior. The slave trade increased in volume to provide additional labor in the mines and on the sugar plantations. In the first quarter of the nineteenth century, as the British slave trade declined and came to an end, Portuguese ships carried 871,600 slaves to Brazil. Between 1826 and 1850 the number increased to an astonishing 1,247,700. As a result of this massive influx of Africans, slaves accounted for approximately 40 percent of the entire Brazilian population in the nineteenth century.

Like most other European countries, Portugal tightened the control of its imperial possessions during the second half of the eighteenth century. During the ministry of the dictatorial Marquis of Pombal from 1755 to 1777, the Portuguese government increased its control over all aspects of colonial life. Like the Bourbon reforms in Spanish America, this legislation created considerable resentment among the creoles. As in Spanish America, these tensions led to demands for Brazil's autonomy in the nineteenth century.

The Russian Empire in the Pacific

The only eastern European state that established an overseas empire during the eighteenth century was Russia. Between the fifteenth and the early eighteenth centuries Russia had gradually acquired a massive overland empire stretching from St. Petersburg in the west across the frigid expanse of Siberia to the Pacific Ocean. The main impulse of Russian expansion had been the search for exotic furs that were in high demand in the colder climes of Russia and northern Europe. During the reign of the empress Catherine the Great (r. 1762–1796), Russia entered a period of further territorial expansion. On its western frontier it took part in the successive partitions of Poland between 1772 and 1795, while to the south it held the Crimean region within the Ottoman Empire between 1783 and 1792.

In the late eighteenth and early nineteenth centuries Russia extended its empire overseas. Russian traders and explorers undertook numerous expeditions to Hawaii and other islands in the Pacific Ocean, sailing as far south as Mexico. They did not, however, establish colonies in these locations. Further expeditions brought Russia across the northern Pacific, where they encroached upon the hunting grounds of the native Aleuts in Alaska. The Russian-American Company, established in 1789, built trading posts along the Pacific seaboard from Alaska down to Fort Ross in northern California. These claims led to a protracted territorial dispute with Spain, which had established a string of missions and settlements on the California coast as far north as San Francisco. In this way the two great European empires of Russia and Spain, advancing from opposite directions, confronted each other on the western coast of North America. Russian expansion into Alaska and California also led to territorial disputes with the United States, which was engaged in its own process of territorial expansion westward toward the Pacific during the nineteenth century.

WARFARE IN EUROPE, NORTH AMERICA, AND ASIA

■ In what ways did the wars waged by European powers during this period involve competition for overseas possessions and trading routes?

Until the middle of the seventeenth century, European states engaged each other in battle almost exclusively within their own continent.

The farthest their armies ever traveled was to the Near East to fight the Turks or to Ireland to conquer the native Celts. The acquisition of overseas empires and the disputes that erupted between European powers over the control of global trade brought those European conflicts to new and distant military theaters. Wars that began over territory in Europe were readily extended to America in one direction and to Asia in the other. The military forces that fought in these imperial battles consisted not only of metropolitan government troops but also colonists. These colonial forces were often supplemented by the troops drawn from the local population, such as when the French recruited Native Americans to fight with them against the British in North America. This pattern of recruiting soldiers from the indigenous population, which began in the eighteenth century, became the norm during the third and final phase of empire-building in the nineteenth and early twentieth centuries.

Wars fought overseas placed a premium on naval strength. Ground troops remained important, both in Europe and overseas, but naval power increasingly proved to be the crucial factor. All of the Western imperial powers either possessed or acquired large navies. Great Britain and the Dutch Republic rose to the status of world powers on the basis of sea power, while the French strengthened their navy considerably during the reign of Louis XIV. The Dutch used their naval power mainly against the Portuguese and the British, while the British directed theirs against the French and the Spanish and also the Dutch. The overwhelming success that the British realized in these conflicts resulted in the establishment of British maritime and imperial supremacy.

Mercantile Warfare

An increasingly important motive for engaging in warfare in the late seventeenth and eighteenth centuries was the protection and expansion of trade. The theory that underlay and inspired these imperial wars was mercantilism. As discussed in Chapter 16, mercantilists believed that the wealth of a state depended on its ability to import fewer commodities than it exported and thus acquire the largest possible share of the world's monetary supply. Mercantilists encouraged domestic industry and placed heavy customs duties or tariffs on imported goods. Mercantilism was therefore a policy of **protectionism,** the shielding of domestic industries from foreign competition. Mercantilists also sought to increase the size of the country's commercial fleet, establish colonies to promote trade, and import raw materials from the colonies to benefit domestic industry. The imperial wars of the seventeenth and eighteenth centuries, which were fought over the control of colonies and trading routes, thus formed part of a mercantilist policy.

The earliest of these mercantile wars took place between the emerging commercial powers of England and the Dutch Republic in the third quarter of the seventeenth century (1652–1654, 1664–1667, 1672–1675). The Dutch resented the passage of English laws, known as the Navigation Acts, which excluded them from trade with English colonies. The Dutch also claimed the right, denied to them by the English, to fish in British waters. Not surprisingly, many of the engagements in these Anglo-Dutch wars took place at sea and in the colonies. The most significant result of these conflicts was the Dutch loss of the port city of New Amsterdam, now renamed New York, to the English.

Shortly after the first Anglo-Dutch conflict, England went to war against Spain (1655–1657). Although this war pitted Protestants against a Catholic power, the two countries fought mainly over economic issues. The war resulted in the British acquisition of Jamaica, one of its most important Caribbean colonies, in 1655. When Britain tried to smuggle more goods than it was allowed by the Treaty of Utrecht (1713) into the Spanish trading post of Portobelo on the Isthmus of Panama, the Spanish retaliated by cutting off the ear of Robert Jenkins, an English captain. This incident led to the War of Jenkins' Ear in 1739. In 1762, during another war against Spain (as well as France), armed forces from Britain and the North American colonies seized the Cuban port of Havana, which Britain returned to Spain in exchange for Florida. Acquisition of Florida gave the British control of the entire North American eastern seaboard.

Anglo-French Military Rivalry

Anglo-Spanish conflict paled in comparison with the bitter commercial rivalry between Great Britain and France during the eighteenth century. Anglo-French conflict was one of the few consistent patterns of eighteenth-century European warfare. It lasted so long and had so many different phases that it became known as the second Hundred Years' War, a recurrence of the bitter period of warfare between England and France from the middle of the fourteenth century to the middle of the fifteenth century.

THE WARS OF THE SPANISH AND AUSTRIAN SUCCESSIONS, 1701–1748 This eighteenth-century Anglo-French rivalry had its roots in the War of the Spanish Succession (1701–1713). The war began as an effort to prevent France from putting Louis XIV's grandson, Philip, on the Spanish throne (see Chapter 16). By uniting French and Spanish territory the proposed succession would have created a massive French-Spanish empire not only in Europe, but in the Western Hemisphere as well. This combination of French and Spanish territory and military power threatened to eclipse the British colonies along the North American coast and deprive British merchants of much of their valuable trade.

The ensuing struggle in North America, known in the British colonies as Queen Anne's War, was settled in Britain's favor by the Treaty of Utrecht in 1713. Philip V (r. 1700–1746) was allowed to remain on the Spanish throne, but French and Spanish territories in Europe and America were kept separate. Even more important, the French ceded their Canadian territories of Newfoundland and Nova Scotia to the British. The treaty, which also gave Britain the contract to ship slaves to the Spanish colonies for 30 years, marked the emergence of Britain as Europe's dominant colonial and maritime power.

The next phase of Anglo-French warfare, the War of the Austrian Succession (1740–1748), formed part of a European conflict that engaged the forces of Austria, Prussia, and Spain in addition to those of Britain and France. In this conflict European dynastic struggles once again intersected with competition for colonial advantage overseas. The ostensible cause of this war was the impetuous decision by the new king of Prussia, the absolutist Frederick II, to seize the large German-speaking province of Silesia from Austria upon the succession of Maria Theresa (r. 1740–1780) as the ruler of the hereditary Habsburg lands (see **Map 18.2**). Frederick struck with devastating effectiveness, and by the terms of the treaty that ended the war he acquired most of the province.

CHRONOLOGY: A CENTURY OF ANGLO-FRENCH WARFARE

1701–1713	War of the Spanish Succession (Queen Anne's War in North America): Spain is allied with France
1740–1748	War of the Austrian Succession (Europe): France is allied with Spain and Prussia; Britain is allied with Austria and the Dutch Republic
1744–1748	King George's War (North America)
1754–1763	French and Indian War (North America): French and British are allied with different Indian tribes
1756–1763	Seven Years' War (Europe): France is allied with Austria; Britain is allied with Prussia
1775–1783	American War of Independence: France is allied with United States against Britain in 1778
1781–1783	Warfare in India
1792–1815	French Revolutionary and Napoleonic Wars: Britain is allied at various times with Austria, Prussia, Spain, and the Dutch Republic; warfare at times in the West Indies and India

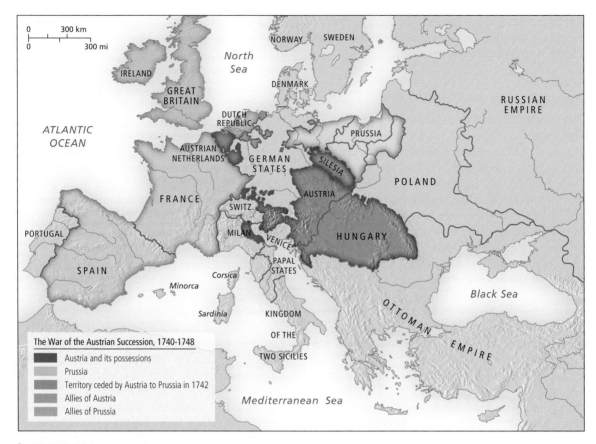

MAP 18.2

The War of the Austrian Succession, 1740–1748

Austria lost Silesia to Prussia during the War of the Austrian Succession in 1742. Maria Theresa's efforts to regain the province in the Seven Years' War were unsuccessful.

Frederick's aggression enticed other European powers to join the conflict. Eager to acquire Habsburg territories in different parts of Europe, France and Spain both declared war on Austria. Britain then entered the war against France, mainly to keep France from acquiring Austria's possessions in the Netherlands.

The colonial phase of this war, known in British North America as King George's War, opened in 1744, when the French supported the Spanish in a war that Spain had been waging against Britain since 1739 over the Caribbean trade. Clashes between French and British trading companies in India also began in the same

year. The main military engagement of this war was the seizure of the French port and fortress of Louisbourg on Cape Breton Island in Canada by 4,000 New England colonial troops and a large British fleet. At the end of the war, however, the British returned Louisbourg to the French in exchange for the factory of Madras in India, which the French had taken during the war.

THE SEVEN YEARS' WAR, 1756–1763 European and colonial rivalries became even more entangled in the next round of Anglo-French warfare, known as the Seven Years' War (1756–1763) in Europe and the French and Indian War (1754–1763) in

North America. In Europe the conflict arose as a result of Maria Theresa's eventually unsuccessful attempt to regain Silesia. In this encounter, however, she joined forces with her former enemies, France and Russia, after Great Britain signed a defensive alliance with Prussia. This "diplomatic revolution" of 1756 shifted all the traditional alliances among European powers, but it did not affect Anglo-French rivalry in the colonies, which continued unabated.

The fighting in North America was particularly brutal and inflicted extensive casualties. In their struggle to gain control of eastern port cities and interior lands, the British and the French secured alliances with different Indian tribes. Among the many victims were some of France's Indian allies who contracted smallpox when British-American colonists sold them blankets deliberately contaminated with the disease—the first known use of germ warfare in the West.

This colonial war also had an Asian theater, in which French and British forces, most of them drawn from the trading companies of their respective countries, vied for mercantile influence and the possession of factories along the coast of the Indian Ocean. This conflict led directly to the British acquisition of the Indian province of Bengal in 1765.

The Treaty of Paris of 1763 ended this round of European and colonial warfare. In Europe Prussia managed to hold on to Silesia, although its army incurred heavy casualties and its economy suffered from the war. In North America all of French Canada east of the Mississippi, including the entire province of Quebec, with its predominantly French population and French system of civil law, passed into British control (see **Map 18.3**). Even more important, the treaty secured British naval and mercantile superiority in the Atlantic, Caribbean, and Indian oceans. By virtue of its victories over France, Britain gained control of the lion's share of world commerce. This commercial superiority had profound implications for the economic development of Britain. Partly because of its ability to acquire raw materials from its colonies and to market its products throughout the world, Britain became the first country to experience the Industrial Revolution.

THE AMERICAN AND FRENCH REVOLUTIONARY WARS, **1775–1815** Despite the British victory over the French in 1763, the long conflict between the two countries continued into the early nineteenth century. During the American War of Independence (1775–1783), the North American colonists secured French military aid, a British fleet attacked the French colony of Martinique, and the French dispatched an expedition against the British at Savannah that included hundreds of Africans and **mulattos,** or people of mixed race, drawn from the population of the West Indies. In India further conflicts between the French and British occurred, mainly between 1781 and 1783. These simultaneous military engagements in various parts of the world turned this phase of Anglo-French conflict into the first truly global war.

Anglo-French rivalry entered yet another phase between 1792 and 1815, during the era of the French Revolution (see Chapter 20). The British were able to maintain their military and naval superiority, although once again it required an alliance with many European powers and the creation of a new balance of power against France. Even during this later phase of this French-British rivalry the British pursued imperial objectives. They expanded their empire in India and consolidated their territory there under the governorship of Richard Wellesley (1760–1842). In 1795, in the midst of the war against France, the British also acquired the Dutch colony at the Cape of Good Hope, giving them a base for their claims to much larger African territories in the nineteenth century.

THE ATLANTIC WORLD

■ How did European empires create an Atlantic economy in which the traffic in slaves was a major feature?

By the beginning of the eighteenth century, the territorial acquisitions of the five European

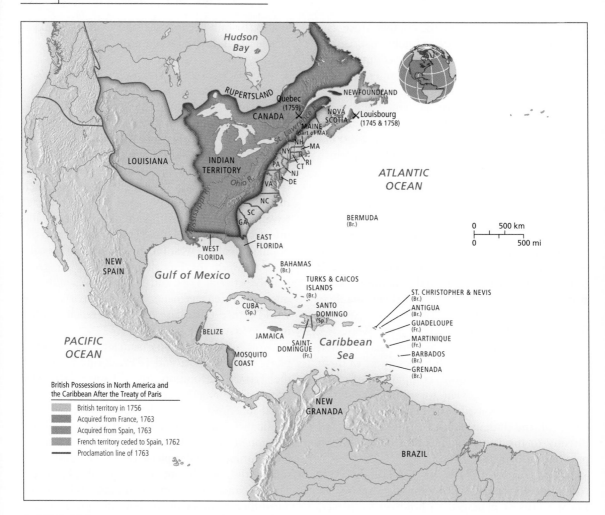

MAP 18.3

British Possessions in North America and the Caribbean After the Treaty of Paris, 1763

The British acquisition of French territory marked a decisive moment in the expansion of the British Empire.

maritime powers had moved the geographical center of the West from the European continent to the Atlantic Ocean itself. The Atlantic, rather than separating large geographical land masses, gave them a new unity. The boundaries of this new Western world were the four continents that bordered the Atlantic: Europe, Africa, North America, and South America. The main thoroughfares that linked them were maritime routes across the Atlantic and up and down its coasts. The main points of commer-

cial and cultural contact between the four continents, until the end of the eighteenth century, were the coastal areas and ports that bordered on the ocean. Within this Atlantic world arose new patterns of trade and economic activity, new interactions between ethnic and racial groups, and new political institutions. The Atlantic world also became the arena in which political and religious ideas were transmitted across the ocean and transformed within new environments.

The Atlantic Economy

The exchange of commercial goods and slaves between the western coasts of Europe, the African coasts, and the ports of North and South America created a major economic enterprise (see **Map 18.4**). The ships that brought the slaves from Africa to the Americas used the profits gained from their transactions to acquire precious metals

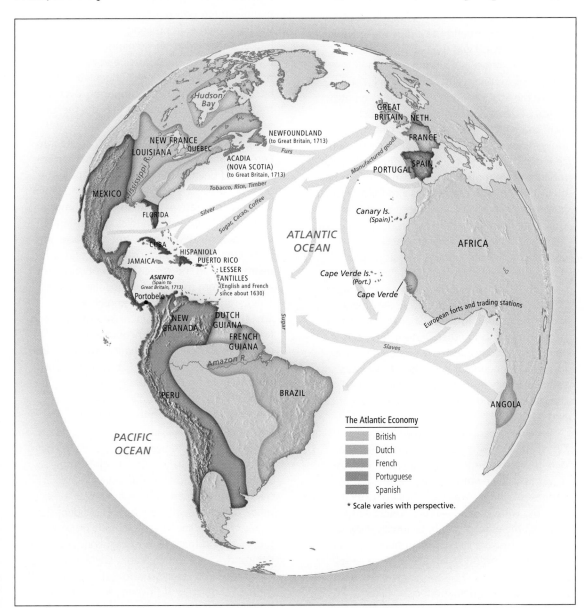

MAP 18.4

The Atlantic Economy in the Mid-Eighteenth Century

Commodities and African slaves were exchanged between the four continents of North America, South America, Europe, and Africa.

ENCOUNTERS AND TRANSFORMATIONS

Chocolate in the New World and the Old

One product of the encounters that took place between Spaniards and the indigenous people of the New World was the widespread consumption of chocolate among western Europeans in the seventeenth century. Long before the Spanish Conquest of the sixteenth century, Aztecs and Mayans produced chocolate from the seeds of the cacao tree, which was indigenous to South America. They consumed chocolate mainly as a beverage and used it, like tobacco (another native American plant), in religious and political ceremonies and for medicinal purposes. Spanish colonists received gifts of chocolate from Indians and soon began to enjoy the pleasurable physiological effects of this commodity, which contains chemical agents that act like amphetamines.

By the beginning of the seventeenth century, chocolate made its way from colonial America across the Atlantic to Spain. Shortly thereafter it became available in other western European countries. Its widespread use prepared the way for the introduction of two other stimulants that came originally from the Middle East and Asia in the latter half of the seventeenth century: coffee and tea.

Because chocolate was grown in non-Christian lands where Spaniards believed that demons inhabited the landscape, and because it was associated with sexual pleasure, it met with harsh disapproval. Clerics denounced it—together with tobacco—as an inducement to vice and the work of Satan. Gradually, however, chocolate came to be viewed in purely secular terms as a commodity, without any religious significance.

The European demand for chocolate contributed to three major transformations of Western life. The first was the growth of the Atlantic trade and a global economy. Among the products that were shipped from the Americas to Europe in exchange for slaves and manufactured goods, cacao was second only to sugar in volume. In preconquest America cacao had often served as an exchange currency. Now it was assigned a specific value in the world marketplace. As the price of chocolate escalated, Spain established a monopoly over the trade, and thus integrated it into the mercantilist system.

Second, the introduction of chocolate into Europe transformed Western drinking patterns. There had been nothing like chocolate in the diets of Europeans before its arrival, and when it was introduced, new rituals of consumption developed. Cups with handles were designed specifically for drinking the hot beverage, the same cups later used for coffee and tea. Europeans adopted the Aztec custom of scooping the foam from the top of a chocolate drink. The European desire to sweeten chocolate, and also coffee and tea, increased the demand for sugar, which in turn encouraged the growth of slavery on the sugar plantations in the West Indies. Sweetened chocolate eventually began to be served as a candy, and by the nineteenth century chocolate candy became the main form in which the commodity was consumed.

Finally, chocolate became a part of the emerging bourgeois sexual culture of eighteenth-century France and England. Just as in preconquest Spanish America, it began to play a role in rituals of sexual seduction. It is no accident that boxes of chocolate are popular gifts on Valentine's Day and that the most well-known chocolate candy in the United States, Godiva, features the English noblewoman who rode naked through the streets of Coventry in 1140. The sustained exchange of a delectable commodity between the New World and the Old World thus contributed to a transformation of Western culture.

THE CHOCOLATE HOUSE (1787)

Men and women drinking chocolate, tea, and coffee at the White Conduit House, Islington, London.

Source: Thomas Rowlandson (1756–1827), "The Chocolate House," 1787. HIP/Art Resource, NY

For Discussion

1. To what extent did the tastes of European consumers determine the nature of the Atlantic economy in the seventeenth and eighteenth centuries?

2. Why did political leaders and clerics differ in their views regarding the value of chocolate in the seventeenth and eighteenth centuries?

Taking it Further

Louis Grivetti and Howard-Yana Shapiro (eds.), *Chocolate: History, Culture, and Heritage*, 2009. A massive scholarly collection of 57 articles on all aspects of the subject.

and agricultural products for the European market. They then returned to western European Atlantic ports, where the goods were sold.

The Atlantic economy was fueled by the demand of a growing European population for agricultural products that were unavailable in Europe and were more costly to transport from Asia. Sugar was the most important of these commodities, but tobacco, cotton, rice, cacao,

and coffee also became staples of the transatlantic trade. (See *Encounters and Transformations* in this chapter.) For their part, North and South American colonists created a steady demand for manufactured goods, especially cutlery and metal tools produced in Europe.

Two of the commodities imported from the colonies, tobacco and coffee, were criticized for their harmful effects. "Tobacco, that outlandish weed," read one popular rhyme, "It spends the brain and spoils the seed." Critics also claimed that it had a hallucinatory effect. Coffee, a stimulant that originally came from the Middle East but later from Haiti and Brazil, was believed to encourage political radicalism, probably because the coffee-houses served as gathering places for political dissidents. Contemporaries also identified coffee's capacity to produce irritability and depression.

The Atlantic economy had its own rhythms but was also part of a global economy. As Europeans had expanded the volume of their imports from America, those markets were fully integrated into this world system. The system was capitalist in the sense that private individuals produced and distributed commodities for profit in a systematic way. European governments had an interest in this capitalist economy because as mercantilists they wanted their countries to acquire the largest possible share of world trade, but they did not control the actual operations of the marketplace. Their role was mainly to authorize individuals or trading companies to conduct trade in a particular geographical area.

The Atlantic Slave Trade

The slave trade became the linchpin of the Atlantic economy, and all five western European imperial powers—Britain, France, the Dutch Republic, Spain, and Portugal—participated in it. The trade arose to meet the demand of plantation owners in the New World for agricultural labor. In the seventeenth century this demand became urgent when disease ravaged the indigenous Indian population and when indentured whites who had emigrated from Europe in search of a more secure future gained their freedom. Slave labor possessed considerable advantages over free labor. Plantation masters could discipline slaves more easily and force them to work longer hours. Slaves became a vital part of a plantation economy in which one authority, the plantation master, directed the growing, harvesting, and processing of sugar and agricultural commodities. The use of slave labor also allowed the economies of European countries, especially

A SATIRE AGAINST COFFEE AND TOBACCO

A seventeenth-century satirical depiction of two European women smoking tobacco and drinking coffee. Turkey, represented by the figure to the right, was the main source of coffee in the seventeenth century. An African servant, to the left, pours the coffee. Tobacco came from the Americas.

Britain, to develop. Those who had invested in the colonial trade received attractive returns on their investment, while agricultural profits acquired from crops produced by slaves encouraged the growth of domestic manufacturing.

The slave trade formed the crucial link in the triangular pattern of commercial routes that began when European vessels traveled to ports along the western coast of Africa. There they exchanged European goods, including guns, for slaves that African merchants had captured in the interior and had marched to the sea. At these ports European slave traders branded the slaves with initials indicating to which nation they belonged. Traders then packed them into ships that transported them across the Atlantic to the coast of South America, to the Caribbean, or as far north as Maryland. This was the notorious **Middle Passage,** the second leg of the triangular journey, which was completed when the ships returned to their points of origin loaded with the plantation products of America. Once they had arrived in the Americas, the slaves were sold to the owners of plantations in the tropical areas of the Caribbean and the south Atlantic and in the more moderate climates of the North American mainland.

The African slave trade conducted by Europeans differed from other forms of slavery in world history in three respects. The first was its size: it was the largest involuntary, transoceanic transportation of human beings in world history. Between 1519 and 1867 more than eleven million slaves were shipped from Africa to the New World. Deaths at sea reduced the number of slaves who actually arrived in the Americas to about 9.5 million. Nine out of every ten of these slaves were sent to Brazil or the Caribbean region, including the northern coast of South America.

The second distinctive feature of African slavery in the Americas was its racial character. In this respect it differed from the forms of slavery that had existed in ancient Greece, Rome, and medieval Europe, where people of different races and ethnicities had been enslaved. It also differed from Muslim slavery, which involved the captivity of white European Christians as well as black Africans. As the slave trade brought millions of black Africans into the Americas, slavery came to be equated with being black, and Europeans referred to the color of the slaves' skin as evidence that they were inferior to white people.

The third distinctive feature of the Atlantic slave trade was its commercial character. Its sole function was to provide slave traders with a profit and slave owners with a supply of cheap labor. Europeans defended the right of slave masters to own their slaves as they would other pieces of property. The Atlantic slave trade turned African slaves into commercial commodities and treated them in a manner that deprived them of all human dignity. To justify such treatment their owners insisted that they "were beasts and had no more souls than beasts."[3]

One harrowing incident on the British slave ship *Zong* reveals the way in which financial calculations determined the fate of slaves. The *Zong* set sail in 1781 from Africa with 442 African slaves on board. When the slaves began to fall ill and die from malnutrition and disease, the captain of the ship, Luke Collingwood, feared that the owners of the ship would suffer a financial loss. If, however, the slaves were to be thrown overboard on the pretext that the safety of the crew was in jeopardy, those who had insured the voyage would absorb the loss. Accordingly Collingwood tied 132 slaves together, two by two, and flung them into the sea. When the ship owners went to court to collect the insurance, they argued that slaves were no different from horses and that they had a perfect right to throw the slaves overboard to preserve the safety of the ship.

The slave trade itself became the object of intense competition, as each country tried to establish a monopoly over certain routes. During the seventeenth century the British managed to make inroads into the French slave trade, and eventually the British surpassed the Portuguese and the Dutch as well. By 1700 British ships were transporting more than 50 percent of all slaves to the Americas. The dominance that Britain established in the slave trade reinforced its growing maritime and commercial strength. With an enormous merchant marine and a navy that could support it, the British came to dominate the slave trade in the same way they came to dominate the entire world economy. Both revealed how far mercantile capitalism had triumphed in Britain and its overseas possessions.

In the late eighteenth century, however, a movement arose in all European countries to end both the slave trade and the institution of slavery itself. (See *Different Voices* in this chapter.) The movement drew much of its inspiration from religious zeal, especially among evangelical Protestants in Britain and Jesuits in Spain and Portugal. The movement gradually acquired widespread support. In Britain more than 300,000 people

DIFFERENT VOICES THE ABOLITION OF THE SLAVE TRADE

In 1787 Quobna Ottobah Cugoano (1757–1791), a former slave, published a treatise calling for the abolition of the African slave trade. Like the narrative written by Olaudah Equiano quoted at the beginning of this chapter, Cugoano's book described the horrors of the African slave trade that he himself had experienced. In this passage Cugoano deplored the effect that the slave trade had on his native Africa. In Great Britain the politician and philanthropist William Wilberforce (1759–1833) spearheaded the campaign to abolish the slave trade in the late eighteenth and early nineteenth centuries. His was a lonely voice when he gave his first speech to parliament on this subject in 1789, 18 years before Britain ended the slave trade. Wilberforce also discussed the deleterious effects of the slave trade on Africa.

A former slave exposes the effects of the slave trade on Africa

That base traffic of kid-napping and stealing men was begun by the Portuguese on the coast of Africa, and as they found the benefit of it for their own wicked purposes, they soon went on to commit further depredations. The Spaniards followed their infamous example, and the African slave trade was thought most advantageous for them, to enable themselves to live in ease and affluence by the cruel subjection and slavery of others. The French and English, and some other nations in Europe, as they founded settlements or colonies in the West Indies or in America, went on in the same manner, and joined hand in hand with the Portuguese and Spaniards to rob and pillage Africa and desolate the inhabitants of the western continent. But the European depredators and pirates have not only robbed and pillaged the people of Africa themselves; but, by their instigation, they have infested the inhabitants with some of the vilest combinations of fraudulent and treacherous villains, even among their own people, and have set up their forts and factories as a reservoir of public and abandoned thieves and as a den of desperadoes, where they may ensnare, entrap and catch men. So that Africa has been robbed of its inhabitants, its freeborn sons and daughters have been stolen, and kid-napped and violently taken away and carried into captivity and cruel bondage. And it may be said in respect to that diabolical traffic which is still carried on by the European depredators, that Africa has suffered as much and more than any other quarters of the globe.

Source: Quobna Ottobah Cugoano, *Thoughts and Sentiments on the Evil and Wicked Traffic of the Slavery and Commerce of the Human Specie*s (London, 1787).

An English politician launches a campaign to end the slave trade Slave Trade in 1789

What should we suppose must naturally be the consequence of our carrying on a slave trade with Africa? With a country vast in its extent, not utterly barbarous, but civilized in a very small degree? Does one suppose a slave trade would

supported the cause of abolition by refusing to buy sugar—the largest consumer boycott the world had ever known. British capitalists also came to the conclusion that slavery was no longer economically advantageous. Goods produced by free labor, especially by machine, made slavery appear less cost-effective than in the past.

By the first decade of the nineteenth century opposition to slavery began to achieve limited

success. In 1807 the British parliament legislated an end to the trade within the British Empire, and in the following year the United States refused to allow any of its ports to accept slave ships. The Dutch ended their slave trade in 1814, the French in 1815, and the Spanish in 1838. The Portuguese continued to import slaves to Brazil until 1850.

Liberation of the slaves generally came later. The British dismantled the system within

help their civilization? Is it not plain that she must suffer from it?...that her barbarous manners must be made more barbarous; and that the happiness of her millions of inhabitants must be prejudiced with her intercourse with Britain? Does not everyone see that a slave trade, carried on around her coasts, must carry violence and desolation to her very center? That in a Continent just emerging from barbarism, if a trade in men is established, if her men are all converted into goods, and become commodities that can be bartered, it follows, they must be subject to ravage just as goods are; and this, too, at a period of civilization, when there is no protecting legislature to defend this their only sort of property, in the same manner as the rights of property are maintained by the legislature of every civilized country....In Africa it is the personal avarice and sensuality of their kings...[T]hese two vices we stimulate in all these African princes, and we depend upon these vices for the very maintenance of the slave trade....

I must speak of the transit of the slaves in the West Indies. This I confess, in my opinion, is the most wretched part of the whole subject. So much misery condensed in so little room is more than the human imagination had ever before conceived....Let anyone imagine to himself 6 or 700 of these wretches chained two and two, surrounded with every object that is nauseous and disgusting, diseased, and struggling under every kind of wretchedness! How can we bear to think of such a scene as this? One would think it had been

determined to heap upon them all the varieties of bodily pain, for the purposes of blunting the feelings of the mind....Exclusive of those who perish before they set sail, not less than $12\frac{1}{2}$ per cent perish in the passage. Besides these the Jamaica report tells you that not less than $4\frac{1}{2}$ per cent die on the shore before the day of sale, which is only a week or two from the time of landing. One third more die in the seasoning, and this in a country exactly like their own, where they are healthy and happy as some of the evidences would pretend....Upon the whole, however, there is a mortality of about 50 per cent, and this amongst negroes who are not bought unless healthy at first, and unless (as the phrase is with cattle) they are sound in wind and limb.

Source: From *Cobbett's Parliamentary History* 28, pp. 41–43

For Discussion

1. How did Cugoano and Wilberforce differ in their views of Africa?

2. The slave trade in Britain was not abolished until 1807, 20 years after the publication of Cugoana's treatise and 18 years after Wilberforce began his parliamentary campaign. Why might other legislators in Britain have resisted their efforts?

3. Why was the mortality rate of slaves transported to the West Indies higher than those shipped to other destinations?

their empire between 1834 and 1838. Slavery persisted until 1848 in the French Caribbean, 1863 in the southern United States, 1886 in Cuba, and 1888 in Brazil.

Ethnic Diversity in the Atlantic World

European countries had always possessed some ethnic diversity, but the emigration of people from many different parts of Europe and Africa to America, followed by their intermarriage, created societies of much greater complexity. Even white European communities in the colonies were more ethnically diverse than in the metropolis. The British colonies, for example, attracted not only English, Scottish, and Irish settlers, but also Germans, French, and Swiss.

***THE SLAVE SHIP* BY J. M. W. TURNER (1840)**

The English painter J. M. W. Turner captured the horror of the incident that took place aboard the slave ship *Zong,* when the crew threw 132 slaves overboard in 1781.

Source: Joseph Mallord William Turner (English 1775–1851), "Slave Ship (Slavers Throwing Overboard the Dead and Dying. Typhoon Coming On)." 1840. Oil on canvas. 90.8 × 122.6 (35 3/4 × 48 1/4 in). Henry Lillie Pierce Fund. 99.22. Courtesy, Museum of Fine Arts, Boston. Reproduced with permission. © 2006 Museum of Fine Arts, Boston. All Rights Reserved.

CHRONOLOGY: VOLUME OF THE TRANSATLANTIC SLAVE TRADE FROM AFRICA, 1519–1867

1519–1600	266,100
1601–1650	503,500
1651–1675	239,800
1676–1700	510,000
1701–1725	958,600
1725–1750	1,311,300
1751–1775	1,905,200
1776–1800	1,921,100
1801–1825	1,645,100
1826–1850	1,621,000
1851–1867	180,800
Total	11,062,500

Source: David Eltis, "The Volume and Structure of the Transatlantic Slave Trade: A Reassessment," *William and Mary Quarterly,* 3rd series, 58 (2001), Table II.6

The ethnicity of colonial populations was more varied in Latin America than in North America. The higher proportion of African slaves, more frequent intermarriage among different groups, and the free status achieved by many blacks and mulattos created highly stratified societies. In these colonies divisions arose not only between the recently arrived Europeans and the creoles, but also among the various groups that Europeans considered socially inferior.

The most complex social structure in the New World developed in Brazil. Portuguese bureaucrats stood at the top of the Brazilian social hierarchy, holding a social position just above a large and wealthy group of planter creoles. These two elite groups dominated a lower-class social hierarchy of **mestizos** (people of mixed white and Indian ancestry), indigenous people, mulattos, freed blacks, and slaves.

ENCOUNTERS BETWEEN EUROPEANS AND ASIANS

- How did cultural encounters between European and Asian peoples during this period of empire-building, change Western attitudes toward outsiders?

In Asia, European powers initially did not try to acquire and govern large territories and subjugate their populations, as they did in America. Europeans first came to Asia to trade, not to conquer or establish large colonies. Europeans did not engage in fixed battles with Asians, take steps to reduce the size of their populations, or force them to migrate, as they did in the New World. Nevertheless, during the period from 1650 to 1815 European powers established or greatly expanded their empires in Asia.

When Europeans used military force in Asia, it was almost always against rival European powers, not the indigenous population. When European countries did eventually use force against Asians, they discovered that victory was much more difficult than it had been in the New World. Indeed, Asian peoples already possessed or were acquiring sufficient military strength to respond to European military might. In China and Japan the possession of this military power prevented Europeans from even contemplating conquest or exploitation until the nineteenth century. Establishment of European hegemony in Asia, therefore, took longer and was achieved more gradually than in the Americas.

Political Control of India

Despite their original intentions, Europeans eventually began to acquire political control over large geographical areas in Asia and subject Asians to European rule. The first decisive steps in this process took place in India during the second half of the eighteenth century. Until that time the British in India, most of whom were members of the British East India Company, remained confined to the factories that were established along the Indian coast. We saw earlier that the main purpose of these factories was to engage in trade not only with Europe, but also with other parts of Asia. In conducting this trade the British had to deal with local Indian merchants and compete with the French, the Portuguese, and the Dutch, who had established factories of their own. They also found it advantageous to make alliances with the provincial governors, known as **nawabs,** who controlled the interior of the country. It became customary for each European power to have its own candidate for nawab, with the expectation that he would provide favors for his European patrons once he took office.

MILITARY CONFLICT AND TERRITORIAL ACQUISITIONS, 1756–1856 In 1756 this pattern of trading and negotiating resulted in armed military conflict in the city of Calcutta in the northeastern province of Bengal. The British had established a factory at Calcutta in 1690, and they continued to carry on an extensive trade there with Indian merchants, many of whom were Hindus. Bengal's nawab, the Muslim Siraj-ud-Daulah, had contempt for all Europeans, especially the British, and he was determined that he would not be beholden to any of them. In June 1756 he sent an army of 50,000 Muslims against Calcutta, burning and plundering the city and besieging the East India Company's Fort William, which was manned by 515 troops in the service of the company. The entire British population of the city, together with more than 2,000 Hindus, had taken refuge in the fort. After a long struggle, which resulted in the death of hundreds of Indians, the fort fell to the nawab's forces, and some of the British officers and magistrates, including the governor of Calcutta, fled by sea.

During this siege the shooting death of a Bengali guard led to an incident that became permanently emblazoned on the emerging imperial consciousness of the British people. In response to the shooting, officers in the nawab's army crammed the entire remaining British contingent, a total of 146 men and women, into the fort's lockup or prison, known as the Black Hole of Calcutta. Measuring 18' × 14', it was meant to hold only three or four prisoners overnight.

WARREN HASTINGS

Warren Hastings (1732–1818), who was appointed the first governor-general of India in 1773, represented the ambiguities of early British rule in that country. An officer in the British East India Company, he was sympathetic to Indian culture. He was, however, accused of gross misconduct in the management of Indian affairs. His impeachment by the British Parliament in 1786 for corruption in his administration and cruelty toward some of the native people in Bengal lasted 145 days but resulted in an acquittal in 1787.

Source: Thomas Gainsborough (1727–88), "Lord Hastings (1732–1818), Governor of India," 1780s, oil on canvas. Museu de Arte, Sao Paulo, Brazil/Giraudon/The Bridgeman Art Library

The stench was so bad that many prisoners vomited on the people squeezed next to them. The insufferable heat and lack of water and air were stifling. Only 22 men and one woman survived until the next morning, when the nawab released them. The remainder either had been trampled to death or had asphyxiated.

The deaths of these British men and women in the Black Hole of Calcutta led the British to seek swift and brutal retribution against the nawab. In 1757, under the direction of the British military officer Robert Clive, a force of 800 British troops and 2,000 native Indian soldiers known as **sepoys** retook Calcutta and routed Siraj-ud-Daulah's army at the Battle of Plassey. The British executed Siraj-ud-Daulah and replaced him with a nawab more amenable to their interests. A few years later the British East India Company secured the right to collect taxes and thus exercise political control over the entire province of Bengal. The enormous revenue from these taxes enabled the company to acquire a large army, composed mainly of sepoys. This force grew to 115,000 men by 1782. The British then used this army, equipped with Western military technology, to gain control of other provinces in India and defeat their French rivals in subsequent engagements during the early nineteenth century.

These further acquisitions of Indian territory led eventually to the establishment of British dominance throughout the South Asian subcontinent (see **Map 18.5**). New territories were brought under British control in the early years of the nineteenth century, and during the tenure of Lord Dalhousie as governor-general of India from 1848 to 1856 the British annexed eight Indian states, including the great Muslim state of Oudh in 1856. The expansion of British control went hand in hand with the introduction of Western technology and literature, the English language, and British criminal procedure. After suppressing a mutiny of sepoys against British rule in 1857, the British government abolished the East India Company and assumed direct control of the entire South Asian continent.

Changing European Attitudes Toward Asian Cultures

European imperialism in Asia played a crucial role in the formation of Western identity. Until the seventeenth century Europeans thought of "the East" mainly as the Near East, an area that was largely subsumed within the Ottoman Empire. The Far East, comprising South Asia (India), East Asia

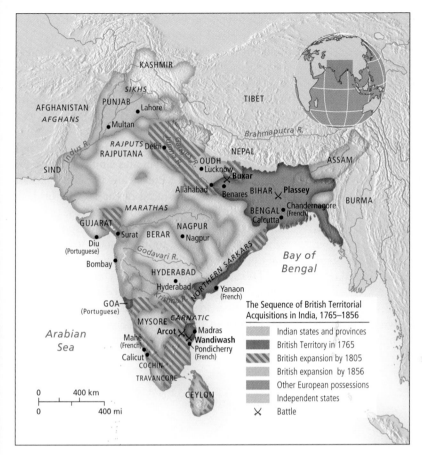

MAP 18.5

The Sequence of British Territorial Acquisitions in India, 1765–1856

British political control of large territories on the South Asian subcontinent began more than a century after the establishment of the first factories along the coast.

of those impressions were negative, especially when they dealt with the political power of Asian rulers, but many other characterizations of the East were positive. Interest in and admiration for Indian and Chinese culture were most widespread during the middle years of the eighteenth century. More and more European scholars committed themselves to the systematic study of Asian languages, especially Chinese and Sanskrit. European writers and thinkers used Asian comparisons to reinforce their criticisms of the West. The French writer Voltaire (1694–1778), for example, regarded Asian cultures as superior to those of Europe in many respects. Voltaire also found the East unaffected by the superstition and the fanaticism that characterized Western Christianity, which he loathed. To him, the main philosophical tradition of China, Confucianism, which embodied a strict moral code, was a more attractive

(China, Japan), and Southeast Asia (Burma, Siam, Indonesia), generally did not enter into European perceptions of "the Orient." Europeans had little contact with this part of the world, and much of what they knew about it was shrouded in mystery. During this period Europeans viewed the Far East mainly as an exotic land, rich in spices, silk, and other luxury commodities.

As Western missionaries and merchants made more frequent contacts with Asian society, Europeans developed more informed impressions of these distant lands and peoples. Some

alternative. Eastern religion, especially Hinduism, also won admiration for its ethical content and its underlying belief in a single deity.

This mid-eighteenth-century admiration of Asian culture even extended to Chinese and Indian political institutions. Voltaire transformed the despotic Chinese Empire into an enlightened monarchy, while the French Jesuit priest Guillaume Thomas Raynal (1713–1796) idealized the "purity and equity" of the ancient Indian political system. Comparison of contemporary Indian politics with the corruption of governments in Europe made native Asian political systems look good by comparison. In Britain there was more disrespect for the members of the East India Company, known as **nabobs,** than there was for native Indian officials.

This intellectual respect for Asian philosophy and politics coincided with a period of widespread Asian influences on Western art, architecture, and design. Eastern themes began to influence British buildings, such as in the Brighton Pavilion, designed by John Nash. Small cottages, known as bungalows, owed their inspiration to Indian models. French architects built pagodas (towers with the roof of each story turning upward) for their clients. Chinese gardens, which unlike classical European gardens were not arranged geometrically, became popular in England and France.

A new form of decorative art that combined Chinese and European motifs, known in French as **chinoiserie,** became highly fashionable. Wealthy French people furnished their homes with Chinese wallpaper and hand-painted folding screens. The demand for Chinese porcelain, known in English simply as china, was insatiable. Vast quantities of this porcelain, technically and aesthetically superior to the stoneware produced in Germany and England, left China for the ports of western Europe.

Asian styles also influenced styles of dress and types of recreation. Indian and Chinese silks were in high demand, and Europeans preferred Indian cotton over that produced in the New World. A style of Indian nightwear known as pajamas became popular in England. A new sport, polo, which had originated to India, made its entry into the upper levels of European society at this time.

During the late eighteenth and early nineteenth centuries the high regard in which many Europeans held Asian culture began to wane. As the European presence in Asia increased, as the British began to exercise more control in India,

BRIGHTON PAVILION

This building, designed by John Nash, reflected the incorporation of Eastern styles into English architecture, and was inspired by the description of Kubla Khan's palace in Samuel Taylor Coleridge's poem "Kubla Khan" (1816).

and as merchants began to monopolize the Asian trade, Western images of the East became more negative. Europeans now tended to view Chinese philosophy not as a repository of ancient ethical wisdom, but rather irrational when compared with that of the West. Confucianism fell out of favor, and Eastern religion in general came to be regarded as being inferior to Christianity. European thinkers ranked Asian political systems below those of the more "advanced" countries of Europe. English writers claimed that the Chinese did not deserve their reputation for industry, ingenuity, and technological innovation.

Western ideas of racial difference reinforced Europeans' belief in their superiority over Asians. European argued that differences in skin color and facial features reflected their superiority over the Chinese, dark-skinned South Asians, and Polynesians. Intellectual theories of race, which emerged in Europe during the late eighteenth century and were applied mainly to black Africans, provided a supposedly empirical and scientific foundation for these assumptions. Westerners used the color of South Asians' complexion, which had determined position of a person in the Hindu caste system, to identify them as "coloreds." Chinese people, previously described in the West as white, were now referred to as being nonwhite or yellow.

THE CRISIS OF EMPIRE AND THE ATLANTIC REVOLUTIONS

- Why did European powers begin to lose control of some of their colonies, especially those in the Americas, between 1775 and 1825?

During the period from 1780 to 1825, European empires experienced a crisis that marked the end of the second stage of European overseas expansion. As a result of this crisis, British, French, and Spanish governments lost large segments of their empires in the Americas. New states were carved out of the older sprawling empires.

The crisis was to some extent administrative. Having acquired large expanses of territory overseas, European states faced the challenging problem of governing them from a distance. They not only had to rule large areas inhabited by non-European peoples (Indians and African slaves), but they also faced the difficulty of maintaining the loyalty of people of European descent who were born in the colonies. These creoles became the main protagonists in the struggles that led to the independence of the North American colonies from Britain in 1776 and the South American colonies from Spain a generation later.

In the French colony of Saint Domingue and in Britain's European colony of Ireland, different stories unfolded. In Saint Domingue, the location of the only successful revolution in the Caribbean region, the revolution was led not by white creoles but by people of color, including the slaves who worked on the plantations. In Britain's European colony of Ireland, where an unsuccessful revolution against British rule took place in 1798, the urge for independence came both from settlers of British descent and the native Irish population.

The American Revolution, 1775–1783

The first Atlantic revolution began with the revolt of the 13 North American colonies in 1775 and resulted in the establishment of their independence from British rule in 1783. During the second half of the eighteenth century, tension arose between the British government and its transatlantic colonies. These overseas British colonies had developed traditions of self-government, but various governmental bodies responsible to the British Parliament continued to exercise control over their activities. The colonies had their own militias, but they also received protection from British troops when conflicts developed with the French.

The crisis that led to the American Revolution had its roots in the situation that emerged at the end of the French and Indian War. To maintain the peace of 1763, the British government stationed troops on the frontiers of the colonies.

It argued that because the troops were protecting the colonists, they should contribute financially to their own defense. To this end the government began imposing new taxes on the colonists. In 1765 the British Parliament passed the Stamp Act, which forced colonists to purchase stamps for almost anything that was printed. This piece of legislation raised the central constitutional issue of whether Parliament had the power to legislate for British subjects in lands that did not elect members of that Parliament. "Taxation without representation is tyranny" became the main rallying cry of the colonists. Opposition to the Stamp Act was so strong that Parliament repealed the act the following year, but it later passed a statute declaring that it had the authority to tax the colonists as it pleased. When the government imposed new taxes on the tea imported from Britain in 1773, colonists dressed as Indians threw the tea into Boston Harbor.

The government responded to this "Boston Tea Party" by passing a series of statutes, known in the colonies as the Intolerable Acts, in 1774. One of these acts specified that the port of Boston be closed until the colonists had repaid the cost of the tea. The Intolerable Acts led to organized resistance to British rule, and in the following year military conflict broke out at Lexington and Concord in Massachusetts. On July 4, 1776, 13 of the colonies on the North American mainland, stretching from New Hampshire to Georgia, approved a Declaration of Independence from Great Britain. A long revolutionary war, in which the colonists received assistance from France in 1778, ended with the defeat of British troops at Yorktown in 1781 and the recognition of the republic of the United States of America in the Treaty of Paris in 1783.

The case that the American colonists made for independence from Britain drew upon four distinct sources. First, the political theories of John Locke, who justified resistance against the Stuart monarchy at the time of the Glorious

THE BOSTONIANS' PAYING THE EXCISE-MAN OR TARRING & FEATHERING

THE BOSTONIANS' PAYING THE EXCISE MAN OR TARRING AND FEATHERING (1774)

This satirical engraving reflects the hatred of colonial Americans at the collection of taxes levied on them without their consent. The Boston Tea Party is depicted in the background. The colonists are forcing the tax collector to drink the tea on which he is trying to collect taxes.

Revolution and who placed limits on legislative as well as executive power, became the main inspiration of the Declaration of Independence. Second, the Revolution found support in the customs and traditions embodied in the English common law, especially the principle that governments could not encroach upon property rights. Third, republican ideas, drawn both from ancient Greece and Rome and revived at the time of the Renaissance, offered colonists a model of a community of virtuous men joined in a commitment to the body politic. Finally, the belief that all men had a natural right to life, liberty, and the pursuit of happiness, provided a philosophical inspiration to the colonists' cause (see Chapter 19).

The Haitian Revolution, 1789–1804

The second successful revolution in the Atlantic world took place in the French Caribbean colony of Saint Domingue, known later as Haiti, which occupied the western portion of the island of Hispaniola. This revolution resulted in the establishment of the colony's independence, but the revolt was directed not so much against French rule as against the island's white planters. Just like their counterparts in Spanish and British Caribbean colonies, these planters, known in Haiti as *colons*, had little desire for national independence. They wished to remain within the protective custody of the French state. Because they formed a distinct minority of the total population, they did not think of themselves as constituting a separate national community. Successful resistance to imperial rule, moreover, would have required them to arm their slaves, which would have threatened their control of the black population.

The Haitian revolution began in 1789 when the people defined legally as free coloreds, most of whom were mulattos, rose up in protest against the refusal of the white planters, who were creoles, to give them representation in the revolutionary French National Assembly as well as in local assemblies in Saint Domingue. This rebellion led directly to a massive slave revolt in 1791. At that time slaves constituted about 90 percent of the population. Their uprising took place after the French National Assembly voted to abolish slavery in France, but not in the French colonies. In this revolt 12,000 African slaves, armed with machetes and reacting to their brutal treatment by their masters, destroyed a thousand plantations and killed hundreds of whites. Their tactics, which included cutting white planters in half, raping their wives and daughters, and decapitating their children, were matched by those of the planters, who retaliated by torturing blacks and hanging them in the streets.

Spanish and British armies, frightened that this slave rebellion would spread to their colonies, occupied Saint Domingue and massacred thousands of slaves, many of them after they surrendered. In 1795, however, the Spanish withdrew from Saint Domingue and ceded their portion of the island of Hispaniola to France. The British were likewise forced to leave the colony in 1798, having lost as many as 40,000 soldiers, most of them from disease. The man who had assumed the leadership of the slave revolt, the freed slave Toussaint L'Ouverture, then proceeded to conquer the entire island in 1801, abolish slavery, and proclaim himself the governor-general of an autonomous province.

In 1801 a French army of 20,000 men occupied Saint Domingue. The purpose was to make the colony the centerpiece of a restored French Empire, which was to include Florida, Louisiana, French Guiana, and the French West Indies. The French secured the surrender of L'Ouverture, but when it was learned that the French were planning to reintroduce slavery, two black generals, Jean-Jacques Dessalines and Henri Christophe, whom the French had enlisted to suppress the revolt, united freed blacks and slaves against the French forces. In 1803 these united forces drove the French out of the colony, and in 1804 they established the independent state of Haiti.

This new state of Haiti was far different from the United States, in that it was governed entirely by people of color and it banned slavery. It proclaimed racial equality by defining all Haitians as black. Haiti's new government destroyed the plantation system, redistributed the land among free blacks, and forbade foreigners to hold property. Deciding upon the form of government took time, however, because the new rulers of the country were divided between those who wished to establish a monarchy and those who favored a republic. Those divisions led to a prolonged civil war from 1807 until 1822, when the warring northern and southern provinces were integrated into a single republic.

The Haitian revolution was the most radical and egalitarian of the Atlantic revolutions of the late eighteenth and early nineteenth centuries. Its unqualified declaration of human equality and its abolition of slavery served as an inspiration to abolitionist movements in other countries, including the United States, throughout the nineteenth century. The destruction of the plantation system, however, transformed the country's economy. As a French possession Saint Domingue was quite possibly the richest colony in the world, producing about two-fifths of the world's sugar and half of its coffee. After the revolution, with its economy severed from that of France, the country could no longer compete successfully in the Atlantic economy.

The Irish Rebellion, 1798–1799

The success of the American Revolution directly inspired a revolution in the kingdom of Ireland. Unlike the residents of the 13 colonies in North America, the Gaelic people of Ireland had long thought of themselves as a distinct nation. The English, however, had begun a conquest of this Irish nation in the twelfth century, and during the next 500 years had struggled to rule it effectively. One of their methods was to settle English landlords on Irish lands. They had done this in the Middle Ages by giving large estates to English feudal lords, but those old Anglo-Irish families had gradually begun to think of themselves as Irish, and after the Reformation they had remained Catholic, while most English people had become Protestant.

In the sixteenth century the English government began to settle colonies of English Protestants on plantations in various parts of Ireland. The purpose of this policy was to gain tighter control over the country and to promote the loyalty of Irish landowners to the English government. In the early seventeenth century James VI of Scotland (who had also become James I of England in 1603) had settled both Scottish Presbyterians, later known as the Scots Irish, and English Anglicans in the northern Irish province of Ulster. These Protestants of Scottish and English descent had become the core of the ruling establishment throughout Ireland, especially after

the failure of Catholic rebellions in 1641–1649 and again in 1689–1690.

In the eighteenth century these Irish Protestants began to resent their subservient relationship to the British government. Just like the American colonists, they recognized the way in which the Irish economy was serving British rather than Irish interests, and they resented the control that Britain had over the Irish parliament. A reform association known as the Society of United Irishmen, led by the Protestant Ulsterman Wolfe Tone, succeeded in building common ground between Protestants and Catholics. The United Irishmen demanded the repeal of the laws that denied Catholics the right to hold office and sit in the Irish parliament.

The ideals of the United Irishmen drew on many different sources. A long tradition of Presbyterian republican radicalism found reinforcement in the ideals of the American Revolution. The Irish objected to paying tithes to the established Church of England, and like the American colonists in the 1760s, they resented paying taxes to support the British war against the French during the 1790s.

In 1798 the United Irishmen aligned themselves with lower-class Catholic peasants known as **Defenders,** and these Irish groups staged a rebellion against British rule with the intention of establishing an Irish republic. Like the American colonists, the Irish revolutionaries sought French aid, but it came too little and too late, and the rebellion failed. The revolt, which featured atrocities on both sides, left 30,000 people dead.

The British government recognized that its arrangement for ruling Ireland, in which the nationalist republican movement had originated, could no longer work. It decided therefore to bring about a complete union between Great Britain and Ireland. By the terms of this arrangement, which took effect in 1801, Ireland's parliament ceased to meet. Instead, the Irish elected a limited number of representatives to sit in the British parliament. Ireland thus became a part of the United Kingdom, which had been formed when England and Scotland were united in 1707. The proximity of Ireland to Britain, which made the prospect of Irish independence much more dangerous, was a major factor in making the British determined to hold on to this "internal colony." The forces of Irish nationalism could not be contained, however, and during the nineteenth century new movements for Irish independence arose.

National Revolutions in Spanish America, 1810–1824

The final set of revolutions against European imperial powers occurred between 1810 and 1824 in six Spanish American colonies. These struggles, like the American Revolution, turned colonies into new states and led to the building of new nations. The first of these revolutions began in Mexico in 1810, and others soon arose in Venezuela, Argentina, Colombia, Chile, and Peru. In these revolutions creoles played a leading role, just as they had in the American War of Independence. The main sources of creole discontent were the Bourbon reforms, which ironically had sought to make the Spanish Empire more efficient and thus preserve it. The reforms had achieved this goal, however, by favoring commercial interests at the expense of the traditional aristocracy, thereby reversing or threatening the position of many creole elites. The creoles also faced increasingly heavy taxation, as the Spanish government sought to make them support the expenses of colonial administration.

CHRONOLOGY: THE ATLANTIC REVOLUTIONS, 1775–1824

1775–1783	United States of America
1789–1804	Haiti
1798–1799	Ireland
1810–1821	Mexico
1810–1819	Colombia
1810–1821	Venezuela
1810–1816	Argentina
1810–1818	Chile
1821–1824	Peru

During the late eighteenth century Spanish creole discontent had crystallized into demands for greater political autonomy, similar to the objectives of British American colonists. South American creoles began to think of themselves as Spanish Americans and sometimes simply as Americans. Like British American colonists, they also read and found inspiration in the works of French political philosophers. Nevertheless, the Spanish creole struggle against imperial rule did not commence until some 30 years after the North American colonies had won their independence. One reason for this slow development of revolutionary action was that Spanish American creoles still looked to the Spanish government to provide them with military support against the threat of lower-class rebellion. Faced with this threat, which continued to plague them even after independence, creoles were reluctant to abandon the military and police support provided by the metropolis.

The event that eventually precipitated these wars for national independence was the collapse of the Spanish monarchy after the French army invaded Spain in 1808 (see Chapter 20). This development left the Spanish Empire, which had always been more centralized than the British Empire, in a weakened position. In an effort to reconstitute the political order in their colonies, creoles sought to establish greater autonomy. Once the monarchy was restored, this demand for autonomy led quickly to armed resistance. This resistance began in Mexico, but it soon spread throughout Spanish America and quickly acquired popular support.

The man who took the lead in these early revolts against Spanish rule was the fiery Venezuelan aristocrat Símon Bolívar (1783–1830). Bolívar led uprisings in his homeland in 1811 and 1814 and eventually defeated the Spanish there in 1819. Unlike most creoles, Bolívar was not afraid to recruit free coloreds and blacks into his armies. His hatred of European colonial governors knew few boundaries. At one point he reportedly commanded his soldiers to shoot and kill any European on sight. He vowed never to rest until all of Spanish America was free. Bolívar carried the struggle for liberation to Peru, which became independent in 1824, and created the state of Bolivia in 1825. He was more responsible than any one individual for the liberation of Spanish America from Spanish rule. Independent states were established in Argentina in 1816, Chile in 1818, Colombia in 1819, and Mexico in 1821. By then the Spanish, who in the sixteenth century had the largest empire in the world, retained control of only two colonies in the Western Hemisphere: Puerto Rico and Cuba.

CONCLUSION

The Rise and Reshaping of the West

During the second period of European empire-building, the West not only expanded geographically, but also acquired a large share of the world's resources. By dominating the world's carrying trade, and by exploiting the agricultural and mineral resources of the Americas, Western states gained control of the world economy. The slave trade, with all its horrors, formed an important part of this economy and served as one of the main sources of Western wealth.

Western economic power laid the foundations for Western political control. In Asia European states assumed political control over territories slowly and reluctantly, as Britain's gradual and piecemeal acquisition of territory in India revealed. In the Americas, European powers acquired territory with relative ease, and European possessions in the New World soon became part of the West. By 1700, as we have seen, the geographical center of the West had become the Atlantic Ocean.

The American territories that were brought under European political control also became, at least to some extent, culturally part of the West. The European colonists who settled in the Americas preserved the languages, the religions, and many of the cultural traditions of the European countries from which they came. When some of the British and Spanish colonies in the Americas rebelled against European regimes in the late eighteenth and early nineteenth centuries, the identity of the colonists who led the resistance remained essentially Western. Even the political ideas that inspired national resistance to European regimes had their origins in Europe.

The assertion of Western political and economic power in the world cultivated a sense of Western superiority. The belief that Europeans, regardless of their nationality, were superior to those from other parts of the world originated in the encounters that took place between Europeans and both African slaves and the indigenous peoples in the Americas. In the late eighteenth century a conviction also developed, although much more slowly, that the West was culturally superior to the civilizations of Asia. This belief in Western superiority became even more pronounced when the economies of Western nations began to experience more rapid growth than those of Asia. The main source of this new Western economic strength was the Industrial Revolution, which will be the subject of Chapter 21.

KEY TERMS

metropolis	Middle Passage
states	mestizos
empires	nawabs
boers	sepoys
Bourbon reforms	nabobs
creoles	chinoiserie
protectionism	Defenders
mulattos	

CHAPTER QUESTIONS

1. How did the composition and organization of European empires change during the seventeenth and eighteenth centuries? (page 554)
2. In what ways did the wars waged by European powers during this period involve competition for overseas possessions and trading routes? (page 561)

3. How did European empires create an Atlantic economy in which the traffic in slaves was a major feature? (page 565)
4. How did cultural encounters between European and Asian peoples during this period of empire-building change Western attitudes toward outsiders? (page 575)
5. Why did European powers begin to lose control of some of their colonies, especially those in the Americas, between 1775 and 1825? (page 579)

TAKING IT FURTHER

1. Why did Britain become the major European imperial power by the beginning of the nineteenth century?

2. Why did wars between European powers in the eighteenth century spread to the Americas and Asia?
3. How could Europeans who professed to believe in the dignity of human beings justify placing Africans in slavery?
4. Which of the Atlantic Revolutions was the most radical and why?
5. How did the growth of European empires contribute to a redefinition of the West?

✓•⌐Practice on **MyHistoryLab**

19

Eighteenth-Century Society and Culture

■ The Aristocracy ■ Challenges to Aristocratic Dominance
■ The Enlightenment ■ The Impact of the Enlightenment

IN 1745 THOMAS BROWN AND ELEVEN OTHER MEN LIVING ON THE ESTATE OF the Earl of Uxbridge, an English nobleman, were jailed for up to one year for shooting deer and rabbits on the earl's land. All twelve defendants were poor. Brown eked out a living as a coal miner in the earl's mines and rented a cottage and five acres of land from him. Like many of his fellow villagers, Brown supplemented his family's diet by shooting game from time to time, usually as he was walking to work through the earl's vast estate. This poaching violated a set of English parliamentary statutes known as the game laws, which restricted the shooting or trapping of wild animals to wealthy landowners.

The earl and other noblemen defended the game laws on the grounds that they were necessary to protect their property. The laws, however, served an even more important purpose of maintaining social distinctions between landowners and the common people. Members of the landed class believed that only they should have the right to hunt game and to serve deer, pheasants, and hares at lavish dinners attended by their social equals. For a poor person like Thomas Brown, who was described in a court document as "a rude disorderly man and a most notorious poacher," to enjoy such delicacies was a challenge to the social order.

This mid-eighteenth-century encounter between the Earl of Uxbridge and his tenants reflected the tensions that simmered beneath the calm surface of eighteenth-century European society. These tensions arose between the aristocracy, a small but wealthy governing elite, and the masses of tenants and laborers who formed the overwhelming majority of the population. The aristocracy occupied a dominant position in eighteenth-century society and politics. They controlled an enormous portion of their countries' wealth, much of it in land. They staffed the state bureaucracies, the legislative assemblies, the military officer corps, and the judiciaries of almost all European states.

By 1800 the social and political dominance of the aristocracy had begun to wane. Their legitimacy as a privileged elite was increasingly called into question. In a few countries political power began to pass from them to other social groups. This change began during a period of political stability between 1750 and the outbreak of the French Revolution in 1789.

The decline of the aristocracy was the result of a series of cultural encounters. In the first, aristocratic landowners confronted peasants and agricultural laborers who resented the repressive features of upper-class rule. In the second increasingly literate, politically active people who

FIRST LECTURE IN THE SALON OF MADAME GEOFFRIN, 1755

The speaker is lecturing on Voltaire's *The Orphan of China* before a predominantly aristocratic audience of men and women.

Source: Lemonnier, Anicet Charles Gabriel (1743–1824), "Reading of Voltaire's tragedy 'L'orphelin de la Chine' at the salon of Madame Geoffrin". 1755. Oil on canvas, 129 × 196 cm. D. Arnaudet. Chateaux de Malmaison et Bois-Preau, Rueil-Malmaison, France. RMN Reunion des Musees Nationaux/Art Resource, NY

occupied the middle ranks of society, such as merchants and skilled artisans criticized the aristocracy and demanded political reform. The third set of encounters was the cultural and intellectual movement known as the Enlightenment. Even though many of the Enlightenment's most prominent thinkers came from the ranks of the aristocracy, they advanced a set of political, social, economic, and legal ideas that inspired the creation of a more egalitarian society. This chapter will explore the following question: How did these social and cultural encounters change the political and intellectual cultures of the West?

THE ARISTOCRACY

■ What social groups belonged to the aristocracy and how did they exercise their power and influence during the eighteenth century?

During the eighteenth century a relatively small, wealthy group of men dominated European society and politics. This social and ruling elite is often referred to as the **aristocracy,** a term derived from a Greek word meaning the men best fit to rule. In the eighteenth and nineteenth centuries the term *aristocracy* also referred to the wealthiest members of society, especially those who owned land.

Within the aristocracy those who received official recognition of their hereditary status, including their titles of honor and special legal privileges, were known as the **nobility.** In the Middle Ages the nobility consisted mainly of warriors who prided themselves on their courage and military skill. Over the course of many centuries these military functions became less important, although many noblemen, especially in central and eastern Europe, continued to serve as military officers in the armies of the state.

The aristocracy for the most part lived on their estates in the countryside, but they also spent time in the cities and towns, where many of them owned townhouses or even palaces. In cities that were centers of national government, such as Madrid and Berlin, aristocrats were prominent members of the royal court, and many of them served as royal judges. The aristocracy, therefore, maintained a visible and powerful presence in urban society.

By the eighteenth century most European aristocracies included a relatively small group of titled noblemen (such as dukes and counts) who possessed great wealth and political influence and a much larger group of lesser aristocrats, occasionally referred to as gentry, who did not necessarily have hereditary titles. In Spain a vast gulf separated a few hundred titled noblemen, the *titulos,* and thousands of sometimes poverty-stricken *hidalgos.* In Britain a few hundred titled noblemen, known as peers, took precedence over some 50,000 families that belonged to the gentry. In Poland the nobility, known as the *szlachta,* was divided between a tiny, powerful group of magnates and some 700,000 noblemen of more modest means who constituted more than ten percent of the entire population.

The aristocracy was not completely closed to outsiders. Commoners could gain entrance to it, especially its lower ranks, on the basis of acquired wealth or government service. Lawyers, wealthy merchants, or accomplished state servants might accumulate wealth during their careers, use that wealth to purchase land, and then acquire a title

of nobility. Many of the Russians who received titles of nobility in the early eighteenth century were commoners. In France many of the royal officials who belonged to the **nobility of the robe** in the eighteenth century could not trace their noble status back further than two generations.

Women of non-noble birth occasionally gained entry into aristocratic society by marriage. This usually occurred when a nobleman who was greatly in debt arranged to marry his son to the daughter of a wealthy merchant to secure the dowry from the father of the bride. The dowry became the price of the daughter's admission to the nobility.

In the sixteenth and seventeenth centuries the size of the aristocracy had grown faster than the general population as a result of economic prosperity and the expansion of the state bureaucracy. In the eighteenth century the size of the aristocracy stabilized and in many countries declined, as nobles took steps to restrict the number of newcomers from the lower orders. It was never a very large social group. The number of titled nobles was almost always less than one percent of the total population, and even when lesser nobles or gentry are taken into account, their total numbers usually amounted to no more than four percent. Only in Poland and Hungary did the percentages climb to more than ten percent.

Because of the small size of this social group, many members of the aristocracy knew each other, especially those who had seats in the same political assembly or served together at court. The aristocracy was, in fact, the only real **class** in European society before the early nineteenth century, in the sense that they formed a cohesive social group with similar economic and political interests, which they were determined to protect.

The Wealth of the Aristocracy

The aristocracy was the wealthiest social group in all European countries, and during the eighteenth century many of its members became even wealthier. The most prosperous aristocratic families lived in stupendous luxury. They built magnificent homes on their country estates and surrounded them with finely manicured gardens. In the cities, where service at court demanded more of their time, they built spacious palaces, entertained guests on a lavish scale, and purchased everything from expensive clothes to artistic treasures. This ostentatious display of wealth confirmed their social importance and status.

Most of the income that supported the lifestyle of the aristocracy came directly or indirectly from land. In all European countries the aristocracy owned at least one-third of all the land, and in some countries, such as England and Denmark, they owned more than four-fifths of it.

Even in the Italian states, where many of the nobility had come from families of merchants, they controlled large estates. Land provided the aristocracy with either feudal dues or rents from the peasants or laborers who lived and worked on their estates. Because noblemen did not engage in manual labor themselves, some social critics later condemned them as unproductive parasites living off the labor of others.

During the first half of the eighteenth century the collective wealth of the European aristocracy reached new heights. In eastern Europe that new wealth came mainly from the dramatic

MARRIAGE INTO THE NOBILITY

This painting by William Hogarth, in a series titled *Marriage à la Mode,* depicts the negotiation of a marriage contract between an English earl and a wealthy London merchant. The earl, seated to the left and pointing to his family tree, is negotiating with the merchant sitting across the table. The marriage will take place between the earl's vain son, sitting to the far right, and the distracted daughter of the merchant, sitting next to him. The two individuals who are about to be married have no interest in each other. The earl has incurred large debts from building the large mansion depicted in the rear, and he intends to use the dowry to recover financially. By virtue of this transaction the daughter will enter aristocratic society.

Source: © National Gallery, London/Art Resource, NY

increase in the size of the population. With more serfs under their control, the landed nobility could increase the wealth they gained from these poor people's labor and feudal dues. In western Europe, most notably Britain and France, the members of the aristocracy increasingly participated in other forms of economic activity. They operated rural industries such as mining and forestry. They entered the financial world by lending money to the government. They became involved in urban building projects and in the economic development of overseas colonies. Some members of old noble families considered such commercial pursuits to be beneath their status, but by investing at a distance, nobles could give the impression that they were not actually engaged in the sordid transactions of the marketplace.

Although some historians have argued that the members of the eighteenth-century aristocracy were social and economic conservatives who were unable or unwilling to act in an entrepreneurial manner, aristocratic involvement in financial and commercial projects suggests a different conclusion. Even on their agricultural estates, many members of the aristocracy, both titled and untitled, adopted capitalist techniques to make their lands more productive. In England a nobleman, Charles Townshend, became widely known as "Turnip Townshend" when he introduced a crop rotation that included the lowly turnip. This type of agricultural entrepreneurship accounts for the accumulation of many aristocratic fortunes.

The Political Power of the Aristocracy

The mid-eighteenth century also marked the apex of political power for the aristocracy in Europe. Having recovered from the economic and political turmoil of the mid-seventeenth century, when they experienced a temporary eclipse of their power, aristocrats pursued various strategies to increase or preserve their share of local and national political power. In England, where the Glorious Revolution had restricted royal power, the aristocracy gained political dominance. A small group of noblemen sat in the House of Lords, while the gentry formed the large majority of members of the House of Commons. After 1689 the English king could not rule without the cooperation of these two Houses of Parliament. The monarchy tried to control the proceedings of that assembly by creating parties of royal supporters within both houses. Because those parties were controlled by

SIZE OF THE ARISTOCRACY IN EUROPEAN STATES IN THE EIGHTEENTH CENTURY

Country	Date	Number of Nobles	Percent of the Population
Austria	1800	90,000	1.15%
France	1775	400,000	1.60
Great Britain and Ireland	1783	50,000	3.25
Hungary	1800	400,000	11.25
Poland	1800	700,000	11.66
Russia	1800	600,000	1.66
Spain	1797	402,000	3.80
Sweden	1757	10,000	0.50
Venice	1797	1,090	0.80

Sources: A. Corvisier, *Armies and Society in Europe, 1494–1789* (1976), 113, 115; J. Meyer, *Noblesses et pouvoirs dans l'Europe d'Ancien Régime* (1973); M. Reinard and A. Armenguard, *Histoire Générale de la Population Modiale* (1961); J. Dewald, *The European Nobility* (1996), 22–27.

the king's ministers, who were themselves members of the nobility, the system allowed the aristocracy to dominate.

In absolute monarchies members of the aristocracy exercised political power by dominating the institutions through which the monarchy exercised its power. As we saw in Chapter 16, absolute monarchs appeased the aristocracy by giving them control over provincial government and recruiting them to occupy positions in the central bureaucracy of the state. In France, for example, noblemen of the robe, a privileged group of approximately 2,000 officials, dominated the state bureaucracy. In Russia tsars granted the nobility privileges to secure their assistance in running local government.

The aristocracy also exercised political power through the judiciary. Members of the aristocracy often served as judges of the law courts of their kingdoms. In England noblemen and gentry served as the judges of almost all the common law courts, hearing cases both at the center of government at Westminster and in the provinces. In France noblemen staffed the nine regional *parlements* that registered royal edicts and acted as a court of appeal in criminal cases. The nobility controlled the central tribunals of the German kingdoms and principalities. At the local level the aristocracy exercised either a personal jurisdiction over the peasants who lived on their lands or an official jurisdiction as magistrates, such as the justices of the peace in each English county.

The Cultural World of the Aristocracy

During the eighteenth century aristocracies in western European countries adopted a lifestyle that emphasized their learning, refinement, and appreciation of the fine arts. It had not always been that way. As late as the fifteenth century the aristocracy had a reputation for their indifference or even hostility to learning, and their conduct was often uncouth if not boorish. In eastern Europe a tradition of aristocratic illiteracy persisted into the eighteenth century. In western and central Europe, however, the pattern began to change in the sixteenth century, when members of the aristocracy started providing for the education of their children either at universities or in private academies. Even more important, aristocratic families began to acquire the manners and social graces that would be acceptable at court. By the eighteenth century the aristocracy, especially its upper ranks, became the backbone of what was then called "polite society."

The aristocracy also developed a sophisticated appreciation of high culture. Their homes housed large private collections of artwork that occasionally rivaled those of contemporary European monarchs. They were the main participants in the cultural life of European cities, especially Paris, London, Rome, Vienna, and Berlin. They formed the audiences of musical recitals, attended plays and operas in large numbers, and frequented the art galleries that were established in all the capitals of Europe. They also became the patrons of musicians, writers, and artists.

The homes of the eighteenth-century aristocracy reflected their preference for **classicism**, a style in art, architecture, music, and literature that emphasized proportion, adherence to traditional forms, and a rejection of emotion and enthusiasm. The classicism of the eighteenth century marked a step away from the more dynamic, imposing baroque style, which had flourished in the seventeenth century. Classicism celebrated the culture of ancient Greece and Rome. The revival of that culture in the eighteenth century in art and architecture is often referred to as **neoclassicism**. The residences of the eighteenth-century aristocracy built in the classical style were perfectly proportioned and elegant without being overly decorated. Their Greek columns and formal gardens, lined with statues of classical figures, served as symbols of their cultural heritage. The classical architecture of the eighteenth century reflected the quiet confidence of the aristocracy that they, like their Greek and Roman forebears, occupied a dominant position in society.

CHISWICK HOUSE

This house was built by Lord Burlington as a library and reception hall on his estate near London about 1725. Symmetrical, balanced, and restrained, the building embodies many of the features of classicism. Chiswick House was modeled on the architecture of the Italian Andrea Palladio (1518–1580), who in turn drew his inspiration from the buildings of ancient Rome.

Eighteenth-century music, which is likewise referred to as classical, reflected a concern for formal design, proportion, and concise melodic expression. The two greatest composers of the eighteenth century, Franz Joseph Haydn (1732–1809) and Wolfgang Amadeus Mozart (1756–1791), whose music was played before predominantly aristocratic audiences, became the most famous composers in this tradition. Classical music appealed less to the emotions than either the baroque music of the seventeenth century or the romantic music of the nineteenth century. The dominance of classicism in music and architecture during the eighteenth century reflected broader cultural currents in European intellectual life, when science and philosophy placed the highest value on the rationality and order of all material and human life.

CHALLENGES TO ARISTOCRATIC DOMINANCE

■ How did subordinate social groups, most notably the rural peasantry and those who lived in the towns, challenge the aristocracy during the late eighteenth century?

Starting around the middle of the eighteenth century, the aristocracy endured increasingly acrimonious challenges to their power and criticisms of their values and lifestyles. They gradually lost the respect that they commanded from the lower ranks of society. By the end of the century many European aristocracies had suffered a loss of political power and an erosion of their privileges. A claim of nobility began to be viewed more as a sign of vanity than as a natural right to rule. The revolution that took place in France in the last decade of the eighteenth century, followed by the reform movements that developed in its wake throughout Europe in the early nineteenth century, brought the age of aristocracy to an end. Members of the aristocracy managed to regain some of what they had lost in the French Revolution, and they also showed their resourcefulness by accommodating themselves to the new order, but they never recovered the dominant position they had held in the eighteenth century.

Encounters with the Rural Peasantry

One set of challenges to the aristocracy came from the peasants and serfs who lived and worked on agricultural estates. This was the social group over whom the aristocracy exercised the most direct control. In central and eastern Europe, where the institution of serfdom persisted, aristocratic control over the rural masses was most oppressive. Landlords not only determined where serfs lived and when they married, but they also collected burdensome financial duties from the serfs. Royal edicts that eliminated some of the duties of serfdom in the late eighteenth century only partially relieved the plight of the rural masses.

In western Europe, where serfdom had for the most part given way to tenant ownership and leasehold tenure, the condition of the rural population was only marginally better than in Prussia, Austria, and Russia. After 1720, famines in western Europe became less common than in the late seventeenth century, making it possible for peasants to eke out an existence, but other economic pressures, including the elimination of common pasture rights and an increase in taxation, continued to weigh heavily on them. Over the course of the eighteenth century the number of peasants owning small plots of land declined. Many of those who leased land were forced to sell it as landowners consolidated their holdings. Consequently, the number of landless laborers who worked for wages increased. By 1789 almost half the peasants in France had no land at all.

Under these circumstances the relationship between peasants and aristocratic landowners continued to deteriorate. The realities of the marketplace gradually eroded the paternalistic concern that the nobility had traditionally shown for the welfare of their serfs or tenants. As the relationship between landlord and peasant became predominantly economic, visual and personal contact between lord and peasant became less frequent. Landlords built their mansions away from the local village, and by surrounding their homes with acres of parkland and gardens, they shielded themselves from the sight of the peasants working in the fields. The most direct contact a landlord made with the members of the lower classes was with the servants who worked in their homes.

As economic pressures on peasants mounted, conflicts between them and their landlords increased. In some countries, most notably France, peasants brought their grievances before village assemblies. These democratic institutions frequently succeeded in upholding peasants' demands, especially when royal officials in the provinces, who wished to collect their own taxes from the peasants, sided with them against the aristocracy.

Another option for the peasants was to file lawsuits against the lords, often with the assistance of the royal government. In Burgundy numerous peasant communities hired lawyers to take their **seigneurs** or lords to court to prevent the imposition of new financial dues or the confiscation of communal village land. In these lawsuits, which became common in the second half of the eighteenth century, peasants challenged not only the imposition of seigneurial dues but the very institution of aristocratic lordship. In 1765 one lawyer representing a peasant community argued that the rights claimed by landowners "derive from the violence of seigneurs" and had always been "odious." The language used in these cases inspired much of the rhetoric employed in the abolition of feudal privilege at the time of the French Revolution (see Chapter 20).

Peasants occasionally took more direct action against their landlords. In eastern France the number of incidents of rural violence against the property of seigneurs who tried to collect new financial exactions increased toward the end of the eighteenth century. In Ireland a group known as the Whiteboys maimed cattle and tore down fences when landowners denied tenants their common grazing rights. Other forms of peasant action included poaching on the lands of landowners who claimed the exclusive right to hunt or trap game on their estates. The hunting activities of the tenants of the Earl of Uxbridge discussed at the beginning of this chapter were just one example of this type of lower-class resistance to aristocratic privilege.

In eastern Europe the deteriorating economic condition of the peasantry led to large-scale rebellion. Bohemia, Hungary, and Croatia, all of which lay within the boundaries of the Austrian Habsburg monarchy, witnessed large peasant revolts in the 1780s. The bloodiest of these rebellions occurred in the province of Transylvania in 1784, when 30,000 peasants butchered hundreds of noblemen and their families after those landowners had raised the dues owed to them as much as 1,000 percent.

The largest eastern European rural rebellion took place in Russia between 1773 and 1774. Pretending to be the murdered Tsar Peter III (d. 1762), the Cossack Emelian Pugachev (1726–1775) set out to destroy the Russian government of Catherine the Great and the nobility that served it. Pugachev assembled an army of 8,000 men, which staged lightning raids against government centers in the southern Urals. The most serious phase of this uprising took place when these troops marched into the agricultural regions of the country and inspired as many as three million serfs to revolt. Pugachev promised to abolish serfdom, end taxation, and eliminate the lesser aristocracy. The rebellion took a heavy toll, as the serfs and soldiers murdered some 3,000 nobles and officials. The Russian upper class feared that the rebellion would spread and destroy the entire social order, but government troops prevented that from happening by brutally suppressing the rising. They locked Pugachev in an iron cage and carried him to Moscow, where he was hanged, quartered, and burned.

Neither Pugachev nor the serfs who joined his rebellion envisioned the creation of a new social order. They still spoke in conservative terms of regaining ancient freedoms that had been lost. But this massive revolt, like others that resembled it, reflected the depth of the tension that prevailed between landlord and peasant, between nobleman and serf, in the apparently stable world of the eighteenth century. That tension served as one of the most striking and ominous themes of eighteenth-century social history.

The Social Position of the Bourgeoisie

In the cities and towns the most serious challenges to the aristocracy came not from the urban masses, who posed an occasional threat to all urban authorities, but from the **bourgeoisie.** This social group was more heterogeneous than the aristocracy. It consisted of untitled people of property who lived in the cities and towns. Prosperous merchants and financiers formed the upper ranks of the bourgeoisie, while members of the legal and medical professions, second-tier government officials, and emerging industrialists occupied a social niche just below them. The bourgeoisie also included some skilled artisans and shopkeepers who were far more prosperous than the large mass of urban laborers. The size of the bourgeoisie grew as the urban population of Europe expanded during the eighteenth century, even before the advent of industrialization. This social group was far more numerous in the North Atlantic countries of France, the Dutch Republic, and Britain than in the states of central and eastern Europe. In England the bourgeoisie accounted for about 15 percent of the total population in 1800, whereas in Russia they constituted no more than three percent.

Because it was possible for some members of the bourgeoisie to achieve upward social mobility and join the ranks of the aristocracy, the social and economic boundaries separating wealthy townsmen from the lower aristocratic ranks were often blurred. In French towns it was often difficult to distinguish between wealthy financiers and noble bureaucrats. Although the two groups received their income from different sources, they both belonged to a wealthy, propertied elite. The middle and lower ranks of the bourgeoisie, however, gradually emerged as a social group that acquired its own social, political, and cultural identity, distinct from that of the aristocracy.

Bourgeois identity originated in the towns, which had their own political institutions and their own social hierarchies. The bourgeoisie also possessed the means of effectively communicating with each other and thus were capable of forming common political goals. Their high rates of literacy made them the core of the new political force of public opinion that emerged in the eighteenth century. The bourgeoisie were the main audience of the thousands of newspapers, pamphlets, and books that rolled off the presses. A "public sphere" of activity, in which politically conscious townsmen participated, became a peculiar feature of bourgeois society. During the eighteenth and early nineteenth centuries the bourgeoisie became the leaders of movements seeking political change. They organized and became the main participants in protests, demonstrations, petitioning drives, and efforts to overthrow established regimes.

The Bourgeois Critique of the Aristocracy

At the core of bourgeois identity lay a set of values that contrasted with those attributed to the aristocracy, especially the noblemen and noblewomen who gathered at court. Not all members of the bourgeoisie shared these values, nor did all members of the nobility embody those attributed to them. Nonetheless, the bourgeois critique of aristocratic society, which flourished mainly among the lower or middle bourgeoisie rather than the great merchants and financiers, contributed to the formation of bourgeois identity and helped to erode respect for the traditional aristocracy.

The bourgeois critique of the aristocracy consisted of three related claims. First, the bourgeoisie alleged that the aristocracy lived a life of luxury, hedonism, and idleness that contrasted with the values of the thrifty, sober, hardworking bourgeoisie. Unlike the aristocracy, the bourgeoisie did not display their wealth. Second, the bourgeoisie accused court nobles of sexual promiscuity and immorality and depicted their wives as vain flirts. There was some foundation to this charge, especially because the predominance of arranged marriages within the nobility had induced many noble husbands and wives to seek sexual partners outside marriage. By contrast, the bourgeoisie tended to enter into marriages in which both partners remained faithful to each

JOSHUA REYNOLDS, *MARY, DUCHESS OF RICHMOND* (CA. 1765)

At a time when most European noblewomen were attracting criticism for their luxury and vanity, this prominent English duchess was depicted as being engaged in the simple domestic task of needlepoint. Some members of the aristocracy were able to deflect criticism of their lifestyle by adopting the habits of the bourgeoisie.

Source: Sir Joshua Reynolds (1723–92), "Mary, Duchess of Richmond (1740–96)," 1746–67, oil on canvas. Private Collection/The Bridgeman Art Library

other. Third, the bourgeoisie considered the members of the aristocracy participants in a decadent international culture that often ignored or degraded their own wholesome, patriotic values.

This bourgeois critique of the aristocracy had profound political implications. It contributed to bourgeois demands for the right to participate fully in the political process. These demands came not from wealthy financiers, merchants, and capitalists who had the opportunity to ascend into the ranks of the nobility, but from men of more modest means: holders of minor political offices, shopkeepers, and even skilled artisans. Criticism of aristocratic values and the demands for an expansion of the franchise received support from intellectuals who are usually identified with the movement known as the **Enlightenment.** Not all of these thinkers and writers came from the middle ranks of society. Many of them were, in fact, members of the aristocracy or the beneficiaries of aristocratic patronage. Nevertheless, their goal was to bring about the reform of society, and that inevitably led to a critique of aristocratic values and behavior.

THE ENLIGHTENMENT

- What were the main features of Enlightenment thought and how did it present a threat to the old order?

The Enlightenment was the defining intellectual and cultural movement of the eighteenth century. Contemporaries used the word *enlightenment* to describe their own intellectual outlook and achievements. For Immanuel Kant (1724–1804), the renowned German philosopher and author of *Critique of Pure Reason* (1781), enlightenment was the expression of intellectual maturity, the attainment of understanding solely by using one's reason without being influenced by dogma, superstition, or another person's opinion. For Kant, enlightenment was both the process of thinking for oneself and the knowledge of human society and human nature that one achieved as a result. His

famous exhortation, "Have the courage to know!" could serve as a slogan for the entire Enlightenment.

The Enlightenment is often referred to as a French movement, and it is true that the most famous of the European writers and thinkers of the Enlightenment, known as **philosophes,** were French. But French philosophes found inspiration in seventeenth-century English sources, especially the writings of Isaac Newton (1647–1727) and John Locke (1632–1704), while German, Scottish, Dutch, Swiss, and Italian writers made their own distinctive contributions to Enlightenment thought. The ideas of the Enlightenment also spread to the Americas, where they inspired movements for political reform and national independence. The men and women of the Enlightenment thought of themselves not so much as French, British, or Dutch, but as members of an international **Republic of Letters,** not unlike the international community of scholars that had arisen within the ancient Roman Empire and again at the time of the Renaissance. This cosmopolitan literary republic knew no geographical boundaries, and it was open to ideas from all lands (see **Map 19.1**). Its literary achievements, however, bore a distinctly Western stamp, and the ideas its members promoted became essential components of Western civilization.

Themes of Enlightenment Thought

Because the Enlightenment spanned the entire European continent and lasted for more than a century, it is difficult to establish characteristics that all its participants shared. The Enlightenment was more a frame of mind, an approach to obtaining knowledge, as Kant claimed, than a set of clearly defined beliefs. Enlightenment writers, however, emphasized several intellectual themes that gave the entire movement a certain degree of unity and coherence.

REASON AND THE LAWS OF NATURE   The first theme that Enlightenment thinkers emphasized was the elevation of human reason to a position of paramount philosophical importance. Philosophes

MAP 19.1

The European Enlightenment

The map shows the birthplaces and birthdates of thinkers and writers of the Enlightenment. The greatest number came from France and Britain, but all European countries were represented. The map does not draw sharp distinctions between the territorial boundaries of European states because the men and women of the Enlightenment thought of themselves as belonging to an international "Republic of Letters" that knew no political boundaries.

placed almost unlimited confidence in the ability of human beings to understand how the world operated. In previous ages philosophers had always found a place for human reason, but they also placed limits on it, especially when it came into conflict with religious faith. In the eighteenth century, however, philosophes placed greater emphasis on reason alone, which they believed to be superior to religious faith and the final arbiter of all philosophical and theological disputes.

Confidence in human reason underlay the effort of Enlightenment thinkers to discover

ENCOUNTERS AND TRANSFORMATIONS

The Enlightenment, Pacific Islanders, and the Noble Savage

When European explorers visited the Pacific islands for the first time in the late eighteenth century, they encountered peoples who had had no previous contact with the West. Enlightenment thinkers, who delighted in studying cultures that were different from their own, seized upon the descriptions of these people, especially the natives of Tahiti, as evidence of the real nature of human beings, before the advent of civilization. From this commentary emerged a picture of the noble savage, who was viewed as being closer to nature than contemporary Europeans. The most positive assessment of the primitive culture of the Pacific islanders appeared in Denis Diderot's *Supplement to the Voyages of Bougainville*, written in 1772 and published in 1796. Regarding the Tahitians, Diderot wrote:

> The life of savages is so simple, and our societies are such complicated machines! The Tahitian is close to the origin of the world, while the European is closer to its old age...they understand nothing about our manners or our laws, and they are bound to see in them nothing but shackles disguised in a hundred different ways. These shackles could only provoke the indignation and scorn of creatures in whom the most profound feeling is a love of liberty.

Diderot (1713–1784) admired these islanders' natural religion, their lack of sexual inhibitions, and their superior sense of morality and justice. His depiction of Tahitian society provided support for the argument of Jean-Jacques Rousseau in *Discourse on Inequality* (1754) that civilization itself had a profoundly negative effect on human society.

Western encounters with the noble savages in the "New World" of the Pacific presented an unprecedented challenge to the dominant Western view of the natural state of human beings. Neither Thomas More, who contrasted the evils of European society with the virtues of a fictional

island society in *Utopia* (1516), nor Bartolome las Casas, the Spanish priest who condemned conquistadors for their brutal treatment of Native Americans, idealized human beings in a natural, uncivilized state. The Christian belief that all people are born in a state of original sin prevented them from taking this position. Even John Locke, who described a peaceful state of nature in *Two Treatises of Government* (1690), referred to "the viciousness of man" in that state and contended that the inconveniences of the state of nature necessitated the formation of government. Only when Enlightenment thinkers, with their emphasis on natural

DENIS DIDEROT

Diderot's *Encyclopedia*, which he co-authored with D'Alembery, stands as a classic statement of the range and themes of Enlightenment thought. In *Supplement to the Voyages of Bougainville,* Diderot presented his radical ideas regarding religion and sexuality morality.

law and their hostility to traditional Christianity, encountered Pacific peoples who were untouched by Western civilization did the image of the noble savage fully emerge. Interest in these uncivilized people was so great that Tahitian natives were transported to Paris and London where they became the darlings of literate society.

The idealization of primitive Pacific Islanders by Enlightenment thinkers gave Westerners a standard by which they could gain a clearer sense of their own identity. As we saw in Chapter 16, the boundaries of the West became blurred in the early eighteenth century, as both the Ottoman Empire and Russia became more closely tied to Europe. Eighteenth-century descriptions of "uncivilized" Pacific islanders who had radically different customs from those of the West made it possible for Westerners to determine who they were by observing who they were not. For those philosophes who believed that these islanders were noble savages, this self-evaluation was not very favorable. It transformed earlier appeals for reform,

such as those urged by More and Las Casas, into demands for a fundamental restructuring of society.

For Discussion

1. In what ways did Diderot's idealization of the culture of Pacific islanders challenge traditional Christianity?

2. How might a person who did not subscribe to the ideas of the Enlightenment have criticized Diderot's argument regarding the noble savage?

Taking it Further

Denis Diderot, *Rameau's Nephew and D'Alembert's Dream*, 1976. These two works by Diderot, unpublished during his lifetime, provide further insights into Diderot's criticism of conventional morality, society, and religion.

scientific laws that governed not only the operation of the natural world, but also the functioning of human society. The belief that scientific laws governed human behavior was the most novel feature of Enlightenment thought. For example, the Scottish philosopher David Hume (1711–1776) proposed a science of the human mind in his *Treatise of Human Nature* (1739–1740) and a science of politics in *Political Discourses* (1752). The Scottish economist Adam Smith (1723–1790), who described the operation of economic life in *The Wealth of Nations* (1776), believed that the economy followed inviolable laws, just like those that governed the movement of the heavens. The Enlightenment thus gave birth to modern social science. Economics, political science, sociology, anthropology, and psychology all trace their origins as intellectual disciplines to this time. They are all based on the

premise that reason can discover the laws or principles of human nature.

The search for natural laws governing all human life provides an explanation for the unprecedented interest of eighteenth-century writers in non-European cultures. During the Enlightenment, European writers subjected the peoples of the world to detailed description, classification, and analysis. The first thorough, scholarly studies of Indian, Chinese, and Arab cultures appeared in print during the middle and late eighteenth century. Egypt, which had been isolated from the West since the sixteenth century, became the subject of an extensive literature, especially after the French occupied the country in 1798. Books on societies that Europeans were encountering for the first time, including the indigenous peoples of northwestern Canada, Australia, and Tahiti, also became readily available in the bookshops of Paris and London.

RELIGION AND MORALITY   The spread of scientific knowledge in the eighteenth century gave the thinkers of the Enlightenment a new understanding of God and his relationship to humankind. The Christian God of the Middle Ages and the Reformation period was an all-knowing, personal God who often intervened in the life of human beings. He could be stern and severe or gentle and merciful, but he was always involved in the affairs of humankind, which he governed through Providence. The gradual recognition that the universe was of unfathomable size and that it operated in accordance with natural laws made God appear more remote. Most philosophes believed that God was still the creator of the universe and the author of the natural laws that governed it, but they did not believe that he was still actively involved in its operation. God was the playwright of the universe, but not its director. This belief that God had created the universe, given it laws, and then allowed it to operate in a mechanistic fashion is known as **deism.** In deism there was no place for the traditional Christian belief that God became human to redeem humankind from original sin.

Enlightenment thinkers, especially those who were deists, believed that human beings could use reason to discover the natural laws God had laid down at the time of creation. This inquiry included the discovery of the principles of morality, which no longer were to be grounded in the Bible. To observe the laws of God now meant not so much keeping his commandments, but discovering what was natural and acting accordingly. In a certain sense God was being remade in a human image and was being identified with the natural instincts of human beings. Religion had become equated with the pursuit of human happiness.

Because Enlightenment thinkers believed that God established natural laws for all humanity, doctrinal differences between religions became less important. In the Enlightenment view, all religions were valid to the extent that they led to an understanding of natural law. This denial of the existence of one true religion led to a demand for toleration of all religions, including those of non-Western peoples.

Enlightenment thinkers were highly critical of the superstitious and dogmatic character of contemporary Christianity, especially Roman Catholicism. French philosophes in particular had little use for priests, whom they castigated relentlessly in their letters and pamphlets. They minimized the importance of religious belief in the conduct of human life and substituted rational for religious values. They had little respect for the academic discipline of theology. The German-born Parisian writer Barond'-Holbach (1723–1789), one of the few philosophes who could be considered an atheist (one who denied the existence of God), dismissed theology as a "pretended science." He claimed that its principles were "only hazardous suppositions, imagined by ignorance, propagated by enthusiasm or knavery, adopted by timid credulity, preserved by custom which never reasons, and revered solely because not understood."[1]

In *An Enquiry Concerning Human Understanding* (1748), David Hume epitomized the new religious outlook of the Enlightenment. Hume challenged the claim of the seventeenth-century rationalist philosopher René Descartes that God implants clear and distinct ideas in our minds, from which we are able to deduce other truths. Hume argued instead that our understanding derives from sense perceptions, not innate ideas. Even more important, he denied that there was any certain knowledge, thereby calling into question the authority of revealed truth and religious doctrine.

Hume's writing on religion reflected his skepticism. Raised a Presbyterian, he nevertheless rejected the revealed truths of Christianity on the ground that they had no rational foundation. The concept of Providence was completely alien to his philosophical position. An avowed agnostic, he expressed contempt for organized religion, especially Catholicism in France and Anglicanism in England. Organized religion, according to Hume, "renders men tame and submissive, is acceptable to the magistrate, and seems inoffensive to the people; till at last the priest, having firmly established his

WILLIAM HOGARTH, *CREDULITY, SUPERSTITION, AND FANATICISM* (1762)

Hogarth was a moralist who embodied the rationalism and humanitarianism of the Enlightenment. In this engraving he exposes the effects of fanatical religion, witchcraft, and superstition. The sermon has whipped the entire congregation into a highly emotional state. The woman in the foreground is Mary Tofts, who was believed to have given birth to rabbits. The boy next to her, allegedly possessed by the Devil, vomits pins. The Protestant preacher's wig falls off, exposing the shaven head of a Roman Catholic monk. An unemotional Turk observes this scene from outside the window.

Source: William Hogarth (1697–1764), "Credulity, Superstition and Fanaticism," 1762, engraving. The Israel Museum, Jerusalem, Israel/Vera & Arturo Schwarz Collection of Dada and Surrealist Art/The Bridgeman Art Library

the eighteenth century the very notion of progress was alien to even the most highly educated Europeans. Programs of reform were almost always associated with the restoration of a superior golden age rather than the realization of something new and different. If movement took place, it was cyclical rather than progressive. In the eighteenth century, however, the possibility of improvement began to dominate philosophical and political discussion. The Enlightenment was largely responsible for making this belief in progress, especially toward the attainment of social justice, a prominent feature of modern Western culture.

Another source of the Enlightenment's belief in progress was the conviction that corrupt institutions could be reformed. State bureaucracies, established churches, and the institution of monarchy itself all became the targets of Enlightenment reformers. The judicial institutions of government were particularly susceptible to this type of reforming zeal. Campaigns arose to eliminate the administration of judicial torture and capital punishment. Philosophes hoped that these reforms would lead to the creation of a more humane, civilized society.

The Italian jurist Cesare Beccaria (1738–1794) provided the intellectual inspiration of the movement for legal reform. In his *Essay on Crimes and Punishments* (1764), Beccaria argued that punishment should be used not to exact retribution for crimes, but to rehabilitate the criminal and to serve the interests of society. "In order that every punishment may not be an act of violence committed by one or by many against a private member of society," wrote Beccaria, "it should be above all things public, immediate, and necessary, the least possible in the case given, proportioned to the crime, and determined by the laws."[3] Beccaria called for the abolition of capital punishment and the imprisonment of convicted felons. The prison, which prior to the eighteenth century had been little more than a jail or holding facility, now became a symbol of the improvement of society.

authority, becomes the tyrant and disturber of human society."[2]

PROGRESS AND REFORM Theories regarding the stages of human development, coupled with the commitment of philosophes to the improvement and ultimate transformation of society, contributed to the Enlightenment belief in the progress of civilization. (See *Different Voices* in this chapter.) Until

DIFFERENT VOICES THE ENLIGHTENMENT DEBATE OVER PROGRESS

*The Enlightenment produced two radically differ-
ent views of the course of human development.
The more optimistic of these, expressed most
clearly by the French mathematician and political
reformer the Marquis de Condorcet (1743–1794),
envisioned human beings gradually progressing
toward perfection. The more pessimistic view,
exemplified by the Swiss born philosopher and
political theorist Jean-Jacques Rousseau, saw civilization as inherently corrupting and degenerative.
Rousseau developed this pessimistic view in his
historical analysis of the causes of social and economic inequality. His description of the state of
nature offered a philosophical foundation for
the Enlightenment's ideal of the noble savage.
(See* Encounters and Transformations *in this chapter.)*

The Marquis of Condorcet Celebrates the Progress of the Human Mind

All these causes of the improvement of the
human species, all these means that assure it,
will by their nature act continuously and acquire
a constantly growing momentum....[W]e could
therefore already conclude that the perfectibility
of man is unlimited, even though, up to now, we
have only supposed him endowed with the same
natural faculties and organization. What then
would be the certainty and extent of our hopes
if we could believe that these natural faculties
themselves and this organization are also susceptible of improvement? This is the last question
remaining for us to examine.

The organic perfectibility or degeneration of
races in plants and animals may be regarded as
one of the general laws of nature. This law extends
to the human species; and certainly no one will
doubt that progress in medical conservation [of
life], in the use of healthier food and housing, a
way of living that would develop strength through
exercise without impairing it by excess, and finally
the destruction of the two most active causes of
degradation—misery and too great wealth—will
prolong the extent of life and assure people more
constant health and a more robust constitution.
We feel that the progress of preventive medicine
as a preservative, made more effective by the
progress of reason and social order, will eventually
banish communicable or contagious illnesses and
those diseases in general that originate in climate,
food, and the nature of work. It would not be difficult to prove that this hope should extend to
almost all other diseases, whose more remote
causes will eventually be recognized. Would it be
absurd now to suppose that the improvement of
the human race should be regarded as capable of
unlimited progress? That a time will come when
death would result only from extraordinary accidents or the more and more gradual wearing out
of vitality, and that, finally, the duration of the
average interval between birth and wearing out
has itself no specific limit whatsoever? No doubt
man will not become immortal, but cannot the
span constantly increase between the moment he
begins to live and the time when naturally, without illness or accident, he finds life a burden?

Voltaire and the Spirit of the Enlightenment

The philosophe who captured all the main
themes and the spirit of the Enlightenment was
the writer and philosopher François Marie
Arouet (1694–1778), known universally by his
pen name, Voltaire. Born into a French bourgeois family, Voltaire became one of the most
prominent and prolific writers of the eighteenth century. Although he wrote for a fairly
broad, predominantly bourgeois audience, and
although he decried the injustices of aristocratic society, he was comfortable in the homes
of the nobility and at the courts of European
monarchs. Voltaire's main career was as an
author. He wrote plays, novels, poems, letters,
essays, and history. These writings revealed
commitment to scientific rationality, contempt

Source: Marie Jean Antoine Nicolas Caritat, Marquis de Condorcet, *Esquisse d'un tableau historique des progrès de l'esprit humain* (Paris: Masson et Fils, 1822), pp. 279–285, 293–294, 303–305.

Rousseau on the Degeneration of Humankind (1754)

Many writers have hastily concluded that man is naturally cruel and requires civil institutions to make him more mild; whereas nothing is more gentle than man in his primitive state, as he is placed by nature at an equal distance from the stupidity of brutes and the fatal ingenuity of civilized man. Equally confined by instinct and reason to the sole care of guarding himself against the mischiefs which threaten him, he is restrained by natural compassion from doing any injury to others, and is not led to do such a thing even in return for injuries received.... The example of savages, most of whom have been found in this state, seems to prove that men were meant to remain in it, that it is the real youth of the world, and that all subsequent advances have been apparently so many steps towards the perfection of the individual, but in reality towards the decrepitude of the species.

Before the invention of signs to represent riches, wealth could hardly consist in anything but lands and cattle, the only real possessions men can have. But, when inheritances so increased in number and extent as to occupy the whole of the land, and to border on one another, one man could aggrandize himself only at the expense of another.... Thus, as the most powerful or the most miserable considered their might or misery as a kind of right to the possessions of others, equivalent, in their opinion, to that of property, the destruction of equality was attended by the most terrible disorders. Usurpations by the rich, robbery by the poor, and the unbridled passions of both, suppressed the cries of natural compassion and the still feeble voice of justice, and filled men with avarice, ambition and vice. Between the title of the strongest and that of the first occupier, there arose perpetual conflicts, which never ended but in battles and bloodshed. The new-born state of society thus gave rise to a horrible state of war; men thus harassed and depraved were no longer capable of retracing their steps or renouncing the fatal acquisitions they had made, but, laboring by the abuse of the faculties which do them honor, merely to their own confusion, brought themselves to the brink of ruin.

Source: Jean-Jacques Rousseau, *Discourse on Inequality* (1754).

For Discussion

1. What is the basis of Condorcet's optimism that human beings are progressing toward perfection?

2. What is the basis of Rousseau's contention that the human species was degenerating?

3. Do you think modern Western society is progressing or deteriorating?

for established religion, and unflagging pursuit of liberty and justice.

Like many men of the Enlightenment, Voltaire developed a deep interest in science. He acquired much of his scientific knowledge from a learned noblewoman, Madame du Châtelet (1706–1749), a scientist and mathematician who translated the works of Newton into French. Madame du Châtelet became Voltaire's mistress, and the two lived together with her tolerant husband in their country estate in eastern France. The sexual freedom they experienced was characteristic of many Enlightenment figures, who rejected the Christian condemnation of sexual activity outside marriage and who justified their behavior on the basis of natural law and the pursuit of happiness. From Madame du Châtelet, Voltaire acquired not only an understanding of

JUSTICE IN HISTORY

A Case of Infanticide in the Age of the Enlightenment

A mid-eighteenth-century trial of a young French woman charged with killing her newborn child provides a window into the life of women who occupied the lower rungs of French society, in contrast to those who frequented the court and met in salons. The trial also raises the larger question, debated during the Enlightenment, whether the punishments prescribed for infanticide were proportionate to the crime.

In August 1742 Marie-Jeanne Bartonnet, a 21-year-old unmarried woman from a small French village in Brie, moved to Paris, where she took up residence with Claude le Queux, whom she had known in her youth, and Claude's sister. At that time Bartonnet was seven months pregnant. On October 22 Bartonnet caused a ruckus in the middle of the night when she went to the toilet and began groaning loudly and bleeding profusely. When her neighbors found her, and when she asked for towels for the blood, they suspected that she had had a miscarriage and called for a midwife. By the time the midwife arrived, it was clear that the delivery had already taken place and that the infant had fallen down the toilet to the cesspool five stories below. Suspecting that Bartonnet had killed the baby, the proprietress of the building reported her to the nearest judicial officer. The next day authorities returned to the building and found the dead infant in the cesspool. An autopsy revealed that either a blunt instrument or a fall had dented the child's skull. After a medical examination of Bartonnet revealed the signs of having just delivered a baby, she was arrested and imprisoned for the crime of infanticide.

Bartonnet came very close to being executed, but the strict procedures of French justice saved her from paying the ultimate price for her apparent crime. In the seventeenth and eighteenth centuries French criminal justice had established clear criteria for determining the guilt or innocence of a person accused of a crime. These procedures involved a systematic interrogation of the accused (only rarely under torture), the deposition of witnesses, the evaluation of physical evidence, and the confrontation of the accused with the witnesses who testified against

A WOMAN ACCUSED OF MURDER IN THE EIGHTEENTH CENTURY

With the exception of infanticide—the crime for which Marie-Jeanne Bartonnet was tried and convicted—few women were tried for capital crimes in the eighteenth century. One exception was Sarah Malcolm, a 22-year-old Englishwoman, shown here in a portrait by William Hogarth (1733). Malcolm was executed for slitting the throat of a wealthy lady in London.

her. There also was a mandatory review of the case, which involved a further interrogation of the defendant, before the Parlement of Paris, the highest court in northern France.

The interrogations of Bartonnet did not give her judges much evidence on which they could convict her. When asked the name of the village where she had lived in Brie, she told her interrogators, "It's none of your business." She denied that she had even known she was pregnant, refused to name the man with whom she had had intercourse, and claimed that she had mistaken her labor pains for colic or diarrhea. She denied picking her baby off the floor of the toilet after the delivery and throwing it into the cesspool. When presented with the baby's corpse, she claimed she did not recognize it.

After this interrogation, Bartonnet was given the opportunity to challenge the testimony of the witnesses who had seen her the night of the delivery. The most damning testimony came from Madame Pâris, the wife of the proprietor, who had found Bartonnet on the toilet and thus could verify the circumstances of the clandestine delivery. Bartonnet's inability to challenge the testimony of Madame Pâris led directly to her initial conviction. After reviewing the entire dossier of evidence, the king's attorney recommended conviction for concealing her pregnancy, hiding her delivery, and destroying her child. French criminal procedure entrusted the decision of guilt or innocence to the judges themselves, and on November 27 they voted that Bartonnet should be executed by hanging.

Marie-Jeanne Bartonnet's fate, however, was not yet sealed. When her case was appealed to the Parlement of Paris, Bartonnet repeated her statement that she had gone to the toilet but did not know whether she had given birth. Even though her execution was warranted by terms of a law of 1557 that defined the crime of infanticide, the judges of this court voted to commute her sentence to a public whipping, banishment from the jurisdiction of the Parlement of Paris, and confiscation of her property. The basis of this decision appears to have been the absence of any proof that she had

deliberately killed her baby. Indeed, its injuries could have been caused by its fall down the drain pipe into the cesspool. There was also the persistent refusal of the defendant to make a confession. She may have been lying, but it is equally possible that once she had delivered the baby, which happened very quickly, she convinced herself that it had not happened.

Bartonnet's trial for infanticide stands at the end of a long period of intense prosecution of this crime. Trials of this sort declined as cities built foundling hospitals for abandoned infants and as moral criticism of illegitimacy was redirected from the pregnant mother to the father. The new legal values promoted at the time of the Enlightenment, moreover, made it less likely that any woman or man would be executed for this or any other crime.

For Discussion

1. As in many trials, the facts of this case can be used to support different claims of justice. If you had been the prosecutor in this trial, what position would you have taken to prove the crime of infanticide? If you had been defending Marie-Jeanne Bartonnet, what arguments would you have used in her defense?

2. In his *Essay on Crimes and Punishments* (1764), Beccaria recommended that punishments be determined strictly in accordance with the social damage committed by the crime. What would Beccaria have said about the original sentence of death in this case? What would he have said about the modified sentence handed down by the Parlement of Paris?

Taking It Further

Michael Wolfe (ed.) *Changing Identities in Early Modern France.* 1997. Gives a full account of Marie-Jeanne Bartonnet's trial for infanticide.

Mark Jackson (ed.) *Infanticide: Historical Perspectives on Child Murder and Concealment, 1550–2000.* (Ashgate, 2002). A collection of essays on infanticide in various countries.

Newton's scientific laws, but also a commitment to women's education and equality. Voltaire lived with her until she died in 1749 while giving birth to a child that neither Voltaire nor her husband had fathered.

Voltaire's belief in a Newtonian universe—one governed by the universal law of gravitation—laid the foundation for his deism and his attacks on contemporary Christianity. In his *Philosophical Dictionary* (1764), he lashed out at established religion and the clergy, Protestant as well as Catholic. In a letter to another philosophe attacking religious superstition he pleaded, "Whatever you do, crush the infamous thing." In Voltaire's eyes Christianity was not only unreasonable, but also vulgar and barbaric. He condemned the Catholic Church for the slaughter of millions of indigenous people in the Americas on the grounds that they had not been baptized, as well as the executions of hundreds of thousands of Jews and heretics in Europe. All of these people were the victims of "barbarism and fanaticism."[4]

Voltaire's indictment of the Church for these barbarities was matched by his scathing criticism of the French government for a series of injustices, including his own imprisonment for insulting the regent of France. While living in England for three years, Voltaire became an admirer of English legal institutions, which he considered more humane and just than those of his native country. A tireless advocate of individual liberty, he became a regular defender of victims of injustice. One of the victims he defended was Jean Calas, a Protestant shopkeeper from Toulouse who had been tortured and executed for allegedly murdering his son because he had expressed a desire to convert to Catholicism. The boy had, in fact, committed suicide.

Voltaire showed a commitment to placing his knowledge in the service of humanitarian causes. In his most famous novel, *Candide* (1759), the character by that name challenged the smug confidence of Dr. Pangloss, the tutor who repeatedly claimed that they lived in "the best of all possible worlds." At the end of the novel Candide responded to this refrain by saying that "we must cultivate our garden." Voltaire, instead of being content with the current condition of humankind, was demanding that we work actively to improve society.

Enlightenment Political Theory

Enlightenment thinkers are known most widely for their political theories, especially those that supported the causes of liberty and reform. They did not share a common political ideology or agree on the most desirable type of political society, but they did share a belief that politics was a science that had its own natural laws. They also thought of the state in secular rather than religious terms. There was little place in Enlightenment thought

MADAME DU CHÂTELET

In her *Institutions de physique* (1740) this French noblewoman, the mistress of Voltaire, made an original and impressive attempt to give Newtonian physics a philosophical foundation.

for the divine right of kings. Nor was there a place for the Church in the government of the state. On other issues, however, there was little consensus. Three thinkers in particular illustrate the range of Enlightenment political thought: Montesquieu, Rousseau, and Paine.

BARON DE MONTESQUIEU: THE SEPARATION OF POWERS The most influential political writer of the Enlightenment was the French philosophe Charles-Louis de Secondat, Baron de Montesquieu (1689–1755). The son of a nobleman of the robe from Bordeaux, Montesquieu had a legal education and also developed an interest in science, history, and anthropology. In *Spirit of the Laws* (1748), Montesquieu argued that there were three forms of government: republics, monarchies, and despotisms, each of which had an activating or inspirational force. In republics that force was civic virtue, in monarchies it was honor, and in despotisms it was fear. In each form of government there was a danger that the polity could degenerate: The virtue of republics could be lost, monarchies could become corrupt, and despotisms could lead to repression. The key to maintaining moderation and preventing this degeneration of civil society was the law of each country.

Montesquieu used his knowledge of the British political system, which he had studied firsthand while living in England for two years, to argue that the key to good government was the separation of executive, legislative, and judicial power. He was particularly concerned about the independence of the judiciary. Montesquieu was unaware that legislative and executive powers actually overlapped in eighteenth-century Britain, but his emphasis on the importance of a separation of powers became the most durable of his ideas. It had a profound influence on the drafting of the Constitution of the United States of America in 1787.

CHRONOLOGY: LITERARY WORKS OF THE ENLIGHTENMENT

1687	Isaac Newton, *Mathematical Principles of Natural Philosophy*
1690	John Locke, *An Essay Concerning Human Understanding*
1721	Baron de Montesquieu, *The Persian Letters*
1738	Voltaire, *Elements of the Philosophy of Newton*
1738	David Hume, *Treatise of Human Nature*
1748	Baron de Montesquieu, *Spirit of the Laws*
	David Hume, *An Enquiry Concerning Human Understanding*
1751	First volume of Diderot and d'Alembert's *Encyclopedia*
1755	Jean-Jacques Rousseau, *Discourse on the Origin of Inequality Among Men*
1759	Voltaire, *Candide*
1762	Jean-Jacques Rousseau, *The Social Contract* and *Emile, or On Education*
1763	Voltaire, *Treatise on Toleration*
1764	Cesare Beccaria, *Essay on Crimes and Punishments*
	Voltaire, *Philosophical Dictionary*
1776	Adam Smith, *The Wealth of Nations*
1781	Immanuel Kant, *Critique of Pure Reason*
1791	Thomas Paine, *The Rights of Man*
1792	Mary Wollstonecraft, *A Vindication of the Rights of Woman*
1795	Marquis de Condorcet, *Progress of the Human Mind*

JEAN-JACQUES ROUSSEAU: THE GENERAL WILL Also influential as a political theorist was the Swiss philosophe Jean-Jacques Rousseau (1712–1778), who as a young man moved from Geneva to Paris and became a member of a prominent intellectual circle. Rousseau did not conform to the model of the typical Enlightenment thinker. His distrust of human reason and his emotionalism separated him from Hume, Voltaire, and Diderot. That distrust laid the foundations for the romantic reaction against the Enlightenment in the early nineteenth century (see Chapter 22). Instead of celebrating the improvement of society as it evolved into higher forms, Rousseau had a negative view of the achievements of civilization. He idealized the uncorrupted condition of human beings in the state of nature, supporting the theory of the "noble savage." Human beings could never return to that original natural state, but Rousseau held out the hope of recreating an idealized golden age when they were not yet alienated from themselves and their environment.

Rousseau's political theories were hardly conventional, but they appealed to some segments of the reading public. In his *Discourse on the Origin of Inequality Among Men* (1755) and *The Social Contract* (1762), he challenged the existing political and social order with an uncompromising attack on aristocracy and monarchy. He linked absolute monarchy, which he referred to as despotism, with the court and especially with the vain, pampered, conceited, and over-decorated aristocratic women who wielded political influence with the king and in the salons. As an alternative to this aristocratic, monarchical, and feminized society, Rousseau proclaimed the sovereignty of the people. Laws were to be determined by the General Will, by which he meant the true and inherent interest of the community, not the vote of the majority.

As a result of his writings, Rousseau became associated with radical republican and democratic ideas that flourished at the time of the French Revolution. One indication of that radicalism was the fact that *The Social Contract* was banned not only in absolutist France, but also in the republics of the Netherlands and Switzerland.

DIFFERENCES AMONG THE PHILOSOPHERS

This satirical print shows Rousseau, to the left, and Voltaire engaged in heated debate. The two men were both major figures in the Enlightenment, but they differed widely in temperament and in their philosophical and political views. Rousseau was very much the rebel; unlike Voltaire, he distrusted reason and articulated highly egalitarian political principles.

Source: Bibliotheque Nationale de France

Rousseau was also criticized for justifying authoritarian rule. His argument that the General Will placed limits on individual civil liberty encouraged autocratic leaders, such as the radical Maximilien Robespierre at the time of the French Revolution, to claim that their dictatorial rule embodied that General Will.

THOMAS PAINE: THE RIGHTS OF MAN Of all the Enlightenment political theorists, the English publicist and propagandist Thomas Paine (1737–1809) was arguably the most radical. Paine was influenced by Rousseau, Diderot, and Voltaire, but his radicalism developed mainly as a result of his intense involvement in the political world of revolutionary America. In *Common Sense* (1776), Paine presented the case for American independence from Britain. This included a passionate statement of human freedom, equality, and rationality. It also involved a trenchant attack on hereditary monarchy and an eloquent statement for the sovereignty of the law. At the time of the French Revolution, Paine continued to call for the establishment of a republic in France and in his native country. In his most widely circulated work, *The Rights of Man* (1791), he linked the institution of monarchy with the aristocracy, which he referred to as "a seraglio of males, who neither collect the honey nor form the hive but exist only for lazy enjoyment."

The title of *The Rights of Man* established a theme that appeared in much Enlightenment writing. Like Diderot and Rousseau, Paine spoke the language of natural rights. Until the Enlightenment, rights were considered legal privileges acquired by royal charter or by inheritance. One had a right, for example, to a particular piece of land or to elect representatives from one's county or town. Those rights could be surrendered under certain circumstances, such as when a person sold land. The new emphasis on natural law, however, led to the belief that simply by being a human being one acquired natural rights that could never be taken away. The American Declaration of Independence (1776), drafted by Thomas Jefferson, presented an eloquent statement of these God-given inalienable rights, which included "life, liberty and the pursuit of happiness."

Women and the Enlightenment

The emphasis that Enlightenment thinkers placed on natural law led to two very different views regarding the position of women in society. A large number of philosophes, including Diderot and Rousseau, argued that because women are different in nature from men, they should be confined to an exclusively domestic role as wives and mothers. Rousseau also insisted on the separate education of girls. This patriarchal argument supported the emerging theory of **separate spheres,** which held that men and women should conduct their lives in different social and political environments. The identification of women with the private, domestic sphere laid the foundation for the ideology of female domesticity, which became popular in bourgeois society in the nineteenth century. This ideal denied women the freedom that aristocratic women in France had acquired during the eighteenth century, especially those who belonged to polite society. It also continued to deny them civil rights. Eighteenth-century women could not vote and could not initiate lawsuits. They were not full members of civil society.

A small minority of Enlightenment thinkers rejected this theory of the separate spheres, demanding the full equality of men and women. The first of these appeals came from the Marquis de Condorcet, who published *On the Admission of Women to the Rights of Citizenship* in 1789. In this pamphlet Condorcet proposed that all women who owned property be given the right to vote. He later called for universal suffrage for all men and women on the grounds that they shared a common human nature.

Condorcet's English contemporary, Mary Wollstonecraft (1759–1797), also made an eloquent appeal for extending civil and political rights to women. In *A Vindication of the Rights of Woman* (1792), Wollstonecraft argued that girls should receive the same education as boys and learn how to support themselves. Only in this way could women take control of their lives and become the social and political equals of men. Thus, Wollstonecraft challenged the belief of Rousseau and other male Enlightenment thinkers that cultural and social differences between men and women were "natural."

The Enlightenment and Sexuality

One facet of Enlightenment thought that had a profound effect on the position of women in society was the appeal for greater sexual permissiveness. Many philosophes, including Voltaire, Diderot, and Holbach, remained openly critical of the strict standard of sexual morality enforced by Christian churches. The basic argument of the philosophes was that sexual activity should not be restricted because it was pleasurable and a source of happiness. The arbitrary prohibitions imposed by the Church contradicted human nature. Enlightenment thinkers used European encounters with pagan natives of the South Pacific, who were reported to enjoy great sexual permissiveness, to reinforce this argument. Diderot appealed to the sexual code of the Tahitians in his attack on Christian sexual morality.

Many philosophes, including Voltaire, practiced what they preached and lived openly with women out of wedlock. Other members of wealthy society adopted an even more libertine lifestyle. The Venetian adventurer and author Giacomo Casanova (1725–1798), who was expelled from a seminary for his immorality, gained fame for his life of gambling, spying, and seducing hundreds of women. To one young Spanish woman, who resisted his advances to protect her virginity, he said: "You must abandon yourself to my passion without any resistance, and you may rest assured I will respect your innocence." Casanova's name soon became identified with sexual seduction.

The violent excesses to which this type of eighteenth-century sexual permissiveness could lead can be seen in the career of the Marquis de Sade (1740–1814). The author of licentious libertine narratives, including his own memoirs and an erotic novel, *Justine* (1793), de Sade described the use of violence in sexual encounters and thus gave rise to the word *sadism* to describe the pleasurable administration of pain. He spent 27 years in prison for his various sexual offenses.

It makes sense that noblemen like Casanova and de Sade would have adopted the libertine values of the Enlightenment thinkers. Somewhat more remarkable was the growth of public sexual permissiveness among all social groups, including the rather prim and proper bourgeoisie and the working poor. Erotic literature, such as John Cleland's *Memoirs of a Woman of Pleasure* (1749), and pornographic prints achieved considerable popularity in an increasingly commercialized society, while prostitution became more open and widespread. Voltaire and Diderot might not have approved of this literature or these practices, but the libertine, anti-Christian, materialist outlook of these philosophes helped to prepare the ground for their acceptance.

THE IMPACT OF THE ENLIGHTENMENT

■ What impact did the Enlightenment have on Western culture and politics?

The ideas of the Enlightenment spread to every country in Europe and the Americas. They inspired programs of reform and radical political movements. Enlightenment thought, however, did not become the property of the entire population. It appealed mainly to the educated and the relatively prosperous, and it failed to penetrate the lower levels of society.

The Spread of Enlightened Ideas

The ideas of the Enlightenment spread rapidly among the literate members of society, mainly by means of print. During the eighteenth century, print became the main medium of formal communication. The technology of printing allowed for the publication of materials on a scale unknown a century before. Pamphlets, newspapers, and books rolled off presses not only in the major cities, but in provincial towns as well. Literacy rates increased dramatically throughout western Europe. By 1750 more than half the male population of France and England could read basic texts. The foundation of public libraries in all the major cities of western Europe made printed materials more widely available. In many bookshops, rooms were set aside for browsing in the hope that readers would eventually purchase the books they consulted.

One of the most widely circulated publications of the Enlightenment was the *Encyclopedia* compiled by Denis Diderot and the mathematician Jean le Rond d'Alembert. This massive 17-volume work, which was published between 1751 and 1765, contained thousands of articles on science, religion, politics, and the economy. The entries in the *Encyclopedia* were intended not only to promote knowledge, but also to advance the ideas of the Enlightenment. Included, for example, were two entries on natural law, which was described as being "perpetual and unchangeable." Other articles praised the achievements of science and technology and gave special attention to industrial crafts and trades. Underlying the entire enterprise was the belief that knowledge was useful, that it could contribute to the improvement of human life. In these respects, the *Encyclopedia* became the quintessential statement of the worldview of the Enlightenment, and its publication stands as a crowning achievement of the entire movement.

Encyclopedias, pamphlets, newspapers, and novels were not the only means by which the ideas of the Enlightenment spread. Literary societies and book clubs, which proliferated in the major cities of western Europe, encouraged the public reading and discussion of the latest publications. Scientific societies sponsored lectures on developments in physics, chemistry, and natural history. One of the most famous of these lectures demonstrated the power of electricity by charging a young boy, suspended from the ground, with static electricity. This "electrified boy," who was not harmed in the process, attracted objects from a stool placed below him. Lectures like this one attracted large crowds.

Equally important in the spread of the scientific and cultural ideas of the Enlightenment were museums, where an increasingly curious and educated public could view scientific and cultural artifacts, many of them gathered from around the world. The museums often sponsored exhibits and lectures. Paris became home to many of these museums in the 1780s, and they could be found in all the major cities of Europe by the end of the eighteenth century.

Enlightenment ideas also spread, although more informally, in the coffeehouses that sprang up in cities across Europe. These commercial establishments were open to everyone who could pay the fare, and therefore they proved immensely successful in facilitating the spread of ideas within the bourgeoisie. Newspapers were often read aloud at coffeehouses, and political debates often took place there.

Another set of institutions that promoted the ideas of the Enlightenment were the secret societies of men and women known as **freemasons.** Committed to the principles of liberty and equality, freemasons strove to create a society based on reason and virtue. Freemasonry first appeared in England and Scotland in the seventeenth century and then spread to France, the Dutch Republic, Germany, Poland, and Russia during the eighteenth century. Some of the most famous figures of the Enlightenment, including Voltaire, belonged to masonic lodges. In the 1770s there were more than 10,000 freemasons in Paris alone. In the lodges philosophes interacted with merchants, lawyers, and government leaders. The pope condemned the freemasons in 1738, and many civil authorities considered their ideas subversive.

The most famous informal cultural institutions of the Enlightenment were the **salons,** the private sitting rooms or parlors of aristocratic women where discussions of philosophy, science, literature, and politics took place. The salons of Madame Geoffrin and Madame du Deffand in Paris won international fame. The women who hosted these meetings invited the participants, entertained those who attended, and used their conversational skills to direct and facilitate the conversation. They also used their influence to secure aristocratic patronage of the young male writers and scientists whom they cultivated

Most of the prominent male figures of the French Enlightenment participated in these meetings, at least during the early years of their careers.

The salons became the target of contemporary criticism because they allowed women a place in public life and because they epitomized aristocratic culture. What mattered most in the salons, however, was not gender or social status, but quickness of wit, conversational skill, and intellectual appeal. Thus, the salon contributed to the creation of a society based on merit rather than birth alone.

The Limits of the Enlightenment

The ideas of the Enlightenment spread rapidly across Europe, but their influence was limited. The market for books by philosophes such as Voltaire and Rousseau was quite small. Diderot and d'Alembert's *Encyclopedia* sold a remarkable 25,000 copies by 1789, but that was exceptional, and libraries purchased a large number of them. Paine's *The Rights of Man* also reached a fairly broad audience, mainly because it was written in a simple direct style and its price was deliberately kept low. Most books on social and political theory and scholarly works on science did not sell very well. Rousseau's *Social Contract* was a commercial failure.

Books on other topics had much better sales. Inspirational religious literature continued to be immensely popular, indicating the limits of Enlightenment secularism. Novels, a relatively new genre of fiction that appealed to the bourgeoisie, were almost as successful. Rousseau and Voltaire both used novels to advance their radical social views. In France, books that were banned because of their pornographic content or their satirical attacks on the monarchy, the clergy, or ministers in the government also proved to be best-sellers in the huge underground French book market.

Pseudoscientific popular literature also led the limited influence of the Enlighten-The reading public did not show much in genuinely scientific books, but they chase thousands of copies of publications

on such technological developments as hot-air balloons, which became a new fad in the 1780s, and on the monsters supposedly sighted in distant lands. They also bought books on **mesmerism.** The Viennese physicist and physician Franz Anton Mesmer (1734–1815), who moved to Paris in 1778, claimed that he had discovered a fluid that permeated and surrounded all bodies and was the source of heat, light, electricity, and magnetism. Sickness was caused by the obstruction to the flow of this fluid in the human body. To restore this flow patients were massaged, hypnotized, or "mesmerized" with the intention of producing a convulsion or crisis that restored health. Mesmerism developed into a form of spiritualism in which its patients engaged in séances with spirits, and its practitioners dabbled in the occult. This pseudoscience, which the French Academy of Science rejected as a hoax, became the subject of numerous pamphlets and newspaper articles that fascinated the reading public.

Those who read books about mesmerism had only a tenuous connection with the learned world of the Enlightenment. Among those who were illiterate or barely literate, Enlightenment ideas made even fewer inroads. Throughout the eighteenth century, for example, uneducated villages continued to believe in magic and witchcraft and occasionally lynched neighbors suspected of causing misfortune by such means. Philosophes considered the belief in magic and witchcraft as superstitious and ignorant, but they were unable to change popular mentality.

More physical manifestations of popular culture included cockfighting and baiting bulls, bears, and badgers by tying them down and allowing dogs to attack them. These blood sports, which could attract thousands of spectators at a single event, resulted in the serious injury or death of the animals. Enlightenment thinkers and many others condemned this activity for its cruelty and barbarism and argued that just like the torture and execution of criminals, these pastimes had no place in polite society. Popular sports, however, could not be easily eradicated. They did not begin to disappear until the nineteenth century, often as the result of campaigns conducted by clergymen.

The Political Legacy of the Enlightenment

When we turn to Enlightened political ideas, we confront an even more difficult task of determining the extent of their impact. The main figures of the Enlightenment were intellectuals—men of letters who did not occupy positions of great political importance and who did not devote much thought to the challenging task of putting their theories into practice. Rulers often treated Enlightenment thinkers with suspicion, if only because they criticized established authority. Nevertheless, Enlightenment thought did make its mark on eighteenth-century politics in two strikingly different ways.

Enlightened Absolutism

The first was through the reforms enacted by rulers known as **enlightened despots,** although the term *despot* is misleading because these enlightened rulers were rarely despotic in the sense of exercising power cruelly and arbitrarily. Enlightened absolutists, as these monarchs are more properly called, used royal power to implement reforms that Enlightenment thinkers had proposed. The connection between Enlightenment and royal absolutism is not as unnatural as it might appear. It is true that philosophes tended to be critical of the **Old Regime,** the eighteenth-century political order dominated by an absolute monarch and a privileged nobility and clergy. But many of them, including Voltaire, had little sympathy with democracy, which they identified with irrational mob rule. These philosophes preferred to entrust absolute monarchs with the implementation of the reforms they advocated.

Rulers of central and eastern European countries were particularly receptive to Enlightenment thought. These monarchs had read widely in the literature of the Enlightenment and introduced Western intellectuals to their courts. The most famous of the enlightened absolutists was King Frederick II of Prussia, known as Frederick the Great (r. 1740–1786). A deist who wrote poetry and played the flute, Frederick was enamored of all things French. When the French philosophe d'Alembert visited his court, the king hosted a dinner at which he spoke only French, leaving many of the Prussian guests to sip their soup in stunned silence. Frederick corresponded extensively with Voltaire and invited him to take up residence at his French-style royal palace, "Sans Souci," at Potsdam. The relationship between king and philosopher, however, was often stormy, and when Frederick publicly burned a publication in which Voltaire had lampooned a royal favorite, Voltaire left Potsdam.

The departure of Voltaire did not weaken Frederick's determination to implement policies that reflected the ideals of the Enlightenment. The most noteworthy of these was the introduction of religious toleration throughout his predominantly Lutheran kingdom. Protestants of all denominations and Catholics (but not Jews) received the protection of the law and even benefited from royal patronage. Frederick also introduced legal reforms with the intention of realizing the Enlightenment ideal of making the law both rational and humane. He authorized the codification of Prussian law (an undertaking that was completed after his death in 1794), abolished judicial torture, and eliminated capital punishment. To provide for the training of future servants of the state, he began a system of compulsory education throughout the country. Like most enlightened rulers, Frederick never abandoned his commitment to absolute rule, which he strengthened by winning the support of the nobility. He also remained committed to the militaristic and expansionist policies of his father, Frederick William I. For him there was no contradiction between his style of rule and his commitment to Enlightenment ideals.

In neighboring Austria two Habsburg rulers, Maria Theresa (r. 1740–1780) and her son

Joseph II (r. 1780–1790), pursued reformist policies that gave them the reputation of being enlightened monarchs. Most of Maria Theresa's reforms were of an administrative nature. Stunned by the Prussian invasion and occupation of the Habsburg province of Silesia in 1740, Maria Theresa set out to strengthen the Habsburg monarchy by gaining complete control over taxation and by reorganizing the military and civil bureaucracy. She also took steps to make the serfs more productive, mainly by restricting the work they performed on their lords' lands and by abolishing the feudal dues they paid.

These efforts won the applause of philosophes, but the policies of Maria Theresa that most clearly bore the stamp of the Enlightenment were her legal reforms. Inspired by Beccaria and Montesquieu, she established a commission to reform the entire corpus of Austrian law. She promulgated a new code of criminal law in 1769, and seven years later she issued an edict abolishing judicial torture. Joseph continued this program of legal reform by reorganizing the entire central court system and by eliminating capital punishment. He also revealed the influence of the Enlightenment by granting religious toleration, first to Protestants and eastern Orthodox Christians in 1781, and then to Jews in 1782. With respect to social issues, he completed his mother's work of abolishing serfdom altogether.

The efforts of Catherine II of Russia (r. 1762–1796) to implement the ideas of the Enlightenment followed a different course from those of Maria Theresa and Joseph. The daughter of a German prince, Catherine received an education grounded in a traditional curriculum of history, geography, and Lutheran theology. In 1745 she was married to a distant cousin, Peter, who was in line to inherit the Russian throne from his aunt, the childless Empress Elizabeth (r. 1741–1762). After arriving in St. Petersburg Catherine not only studied Russian language, literature, and religion, but also read widely in western

European sources, including the works of Enlightenment thinkers. She later corresponded with Voltaire and d'Alembert and employed the famous salon hostess Madame Geoffrin at her court. At Catherine's invitation Diderot visited St. Petersburg for six months.

Early in her reign, Catherine embarked on a program of reform similar to those of other enlightened absolutists. In 1767 she appointed a commission to codify Russian law on the basis of western European principles. Her

CATHERINE THE GREAT

Catherine II of Russia on the day she succeeded in taking the throne from her husband, Peter III, at Peterhof in 1762. Catherine, who despised her husband, joined a conspiracy against him right after his accession to the throne. Catherine, like Peter, had several lovers, and her two children, including the future emperor Paul, were reputedly conceived by members of the nobility.

Source: Vigilius Erichsen (1722–82), "Equestrian Portrait of Catherine II (1729–96), the Great of Russia," oil on canvas. Musee des Beaux-Arts, Chartres, France/The Bridgeman Art Library

recommendations to the commission included the abolition of torture and inhumane punishment and the establishment of religious toleration. She was eventually forced to disband the commission, whose members could not agree on a new code, but she later abolished torture and capital punishment on her own authority. Like Maria Theresa, she instituted administrative and educational reforms, including the introduction of primary schooling in the provinces. Catherine, who became known as Catherine the Great, also tried unsuccessfully to provide for the education of girls.

Catherine gained a reputation for being an enlightened European monarch, but she never fully embraced the ideals of the Enlightenment. She admitted that it was easier to subscribe to those ideals than to implement them. On the issue of serfdom, which most Enlightenment thinkers wished to see abolished, she would not yield. Catherine not only preserved that social system to secure the loyalty of the Russian nobility, but also extended it to Ukraine and parts of Poland after Russia incorporated those regions into the empire. Some philosophes called for the dissolution of large imperial structures, but Catherine expanded the Russian Empire by acquiring vast territories in Eastern Europe, East Asia, and Alaska.

Eventually Catherine disavowed the ideals of the Enlightenment altogether. After putting down the Pugachev rebellion in 1774, she began to question the desirability of social reform. The experience of the French Revolution in the 1790s (see Chapter 20) led her to repudiate Enlightenment reformism.

The Enlightenment and Revolution

While Enlightenment thought led to enlightened absolutism, it also led in the opposite direction. The second mark that Enlightenment thought made on eighteenth-century politics was the inspiration it gave to movements for reform and revolution in western Europe and the Americas. The emphasis placed by Enlightenment thinkers on individual liberty, natural rights, and political reform pressured monarchs and the traditional nobility either to make concessions or to relinquish power altogether. Very few philosophes were themselves revolutionaries, but their ideas contributed to the creation of a new political order.

The towering reputation of Voltaire during the French Revolution in 1789, as well as the anger of conservatives who exhumed and burned his bones after the revolution had ended, suggests that this philosophe's passionate criticisms of the Old Regime and his pleas for human freedom played a significant role in the revolutionary developments of the 1790s. The same is true of the radical Rousseau, whose concept of the General Will served as the basis of a revolutionary ideology. Rousseau's democratic and republican ideas were used to justify some of the most important changes that took place during the revolution. Contemporaries either glorified or attacked him, depending on their political philosophy, for having actually caused the revolution. One book published in 1791 was titled *On Jean-Jacques Rousseau Considered as One of the First Authors of the Revolution.*

Yet another application of enlightened ideas to politics took place in the Americas. The advocates of colonial independence from their mother countries, such as Thomas Jefferson in Virginia and Símon Bolívar in Venezuela and Colombia, were all deeply influenced by the Enlightenment concepts of natural law, natural rights, liberty, and popular sovereignty. The Declaration of Independence, which was written by Jefferson, betrayed its debt to the Enlightenment in its reference to the inalienable rights of all men and to the foundation of those rights in "the law of nature and Nature's God." As discussed in Chapter 18, the American Revolution cannot be explained solely in terms of these Enlightenment ideas. The colonists found inspiration in many different sources, including English common law. But the American colonists did wish to create an entirely new world order, just as did many

Enlightenment thinkers. They also adopted some of the most radical political ideas of the Enlightenment, which identified the people as the source of political power.

CONCLUSION

The Enlightenment and Western Identity

The Enlightenment was a distinctly Western phenomenon. It arose in the countries of western Europe and then spread to central and eastern Europe and to the Americas. Many traditions identified today as "Western values" either had their origin or received their most cogent expression in the Enlightenment. In particular, the commitment to individual liberty, civil rights, toleration, and rational decision making all took shape during this period.

It would be misleading to make a simple equation between the ideas of the Enlightenment and the Western intellectual tradition. The ideals of the Enlightenment have never been fully accepted within Western societies. Ever since the original formulation of Enlightenment ideas, conservatives have challenged those ideas on the grounds that they would lead to the destruction of religion and the social order. Those conservative criticisms became most vocal at the time of the French Revolution and during the early years of the nineteenth century.

Even though the values of the Enlightenment have never met with universal approval, they gave many Europeans a clear sense of their own identity with respect to the rest of the world. Educated people who prided themselves on being enlightened knew that their scientific, rational worldview was not shared by Asians, Africans, indigenous Americans, or South Pacific islanders. It did not matter whether Enlightenment thinkers had a positive view of those other cultures, like Voltaire or Rousseau, or a negative one, like Montesquieu. What mattered was that they shared a similar mental outlook and a commitment to individual liberty, justice, and the improvement of civilization. For all of them religious faith was less important, both as an arbiter of morality and as a source of authority, than it was in these other cultures. The men and women of the Enlightenment all looked to the law of their country as a reflection of natural law and as the guardian of civil liberty. Their writings helped their European and colonial audiences think of themselves as even more distinct from non-Western people than they had in the past.

KEY TERMS

aristocracy	Republic of Letters
nobility	deism
nobility of the robe	separate spheres
classicism	freemasons
neoclassicism	salons
seigneurs	mesmerism
bourgeoisie	enlightened despots
Enlightenment	Old Regime
philosophes	

CHAPTER QUESTIONS

1. What social groups belonged to the aristocracy and how did they exercise their power and influence during the eighteenth century? (page 587)
2. How did subordinate social groups, most notably the rural peasantry and those who lived in the towns, challenge the aristocracy during the late eighteenth century? (page 592)
3. What were the main features of Enlightenment thought and how did it present a threat to the old order? (page 596)
4. What impact did the Enlightenment have on Western culture and politics? (page 610)

TAKING IT FURTHER

1. How might a nobleman in the eighteenth century have defended himself from the critiques leveled by members of the bourgeoisie?
2. In what ways did Enlightenment thinkers contribute to the decline of the aristocracy in the late eighteenth century?
3. What were the main issues over which philosophes disagreed? What were the issues that led Rousseau to disagree with Voltaire, Condorcet, and Mary Wollstonecraft?
4. How did the Enlightenment help to define the geographical limits of the West in the late eighteenth century?

✓•⎯Practice on MyHistoryLab

20

The Age of the French Revolution, 1789–1815

- The First French Revolution, 1789–1791 ■ The French Republic, 1792–1799
■ Cultural Change in France during the Revolution ■ The Napoleonic
Era, 1799–1815 ■ The Legacy of the French Revolution

ON JULY 12, 1789, THE FRENCH JOURNALIST CAMILLE DESMOULINS addressed an anxious crowd of Parisian citizens gathered outside the Palais-Royal, where public debate often took place. Playing upon fears that had been mounting during the past two months, Desmoulins claimed that the government of Louis XVI was preparing a massacre of Parisians. "To arms, to arms," Desmoulins cried out, as he roused the citizens to their own defense. That night Parisians responded to his call by invading arsenals in the city in anticipation of the violence they thought was about to descend upon them. The next day they continued to seize weapons and declared themselves members of the National Guard, a volunteer militia of propertied citizens.

On the morning of July 14, crowds of Parisians moved toward an ancient fortress known as the Bastille, where royal troops were stationed. The Parisians feared that the troops in the Bastille would take violent action against them, and they also wanted to capture the ammunition stored inside the building, which served as an arsenal and a prison. Negotiations with the governor of the Bastille were interrupted when some of the militia, moving into the courtyard of the fortress, demanded the surrender of the troops. Both sides fired shots, and the

exchange led to a full-scale assault upon the Bastille by the National Guard.

After three hours of fighting and the death of 83 people, the governor surrendered. His captors, bearing the arms they had seized, then led him to face charges before the officers of the city government. The crowd, however, crying for vengeance against their oppressors, attacked the soldiers and crushed some of them underfoot. The governor was stabbed hundreds of times, hacked to pieces, and decapitated. The chief magistrate of the city suffered the same fate for his reluctance to issue arms to its citizens. The crowd then placed the heads of the two men on pikes and paraded through the city.

The storming of the Bastille was the first of many violent episodes that occurred during the sequence of events called the French Revolution. That revolution brought about some of the most fundamental changes in European political life since the end of Roman rule. It heralded the destruction of the Old Regime, the eighteenth-century political order that had been dominated by an absolute monarch and a privileged nobility and clergy. It led to the submission of the Catholic Church to state control. A more radical phase of the revolution, beginning in 1792, resulted in the

THE STORMING OF THE BASTILLE, JULY 14, 1789

Parisian citizens attacked the Bastille not because it was a symbol of the Old Regime, but because it contained weapons that they needed to protect themselves from royalist troops.

destruction of the French monarchy and the declaration of a republic. It also led to a period of state-sponsored terrorism in 1793 and 1794, during which one group of revolutionaries engaged in a brutal campaign to eliminate their real and imagined enemies.

The excesses of the revolution led to a conservative reaction, and after a long period of rule by Napoleon Bonaparte between 1799 and 1815,

the French monarchy was restored, marking the end of the revolutionary period. The ideas of the revolution, however, especially its commitment to democratic republicanism and its concept of the nation, continued to dominate politics in the West for the next two hundred years. This chapter will address this question: How did the French Revolution permanently change the political culture of the West?

THE FIRST FRENCH REVOLUTION, 1789–1791

■ Why did the Old Regime in France collapse in 1789, and what revolutionary changes took place in French government and society during the next two years?

The French Revolution consisted of two distinct revolutions. The first, which began in 1789, resulted in a destruction of royal absolutism and the drafting of a constitution. The second and more radical revolution began in 1792 with the abolition of the monarchy and the formation of the French Republic.

The Beginning of the Revolution

The immediate cause of the revolution was a financial crisis that bankrupted the monarchy and deprived it of its authority. The government of Louis XVI (r. 1774–1792) had inherited considerable debts as a result of protracted periods of warfare with Great Britain. The opening of a new phase of this warfare in 1778, when France intervened in the American War of Independence on the side of the United States, pushed the government further into debt and strained the entire French economy. As the crisis deepened the king proposed a direct tax on all landowners. The nobility, however, objected to this plan, which would have perpetuated the absolutist policies of the royal government.

The deterioration of the government's financial condition finally forced the king to yield. When tax returns dried up as the result of an agricultural crisis in the summer months of 1788, the government could no longer pay its creditors. In a desperate effort to save his regime, Louis announced that he would convene the Estates General, a national representative assembly that had not met since 1614.

The meeting of the Estates General was set for May 1789, and during the months leading up to its opening, public debates arose over how the delegates should vote. The Estates General

CHRONOLOGY: THE FIRST FRENCH REVOLUTION, 1789–1791

1788

August 8	Announcement of the meeting of the Estates General
1789	
May 5	The Estates General opens at Versailles
June 17	The Third Estate adopts the title of the National Assembly
June 20	Oath of the Tennis Court
July 14	The storming of the Bastille
Late July	The Great Fear in rural areas
August 4	Abolition of feudalism and privileges
August 26	*Declaration of the Rights of Man and Citizen*
October 5	March to Versailles; Louis XVI and National Assembly move to Paris
November 2	Church property is nationalized
1790	
July 12	Civil Constitution of the Clergy
November 27	Decree requiring oath of loyalty from the clergy
1791	
June 20	Royal family flees to Varennes, is apprehended by the National Guard
October 1	Newly elected Legislative Assembly opens

consisted of representatives of the three orders or social groups, known as **estates,** which made up French society: the clergy, the nobility, and the **Third Estate.** The Third Estate technically contained all the commoners in the kingdom (about 96 percent of the population), ranging from the wealthiest merchant to the poorest peasant. The elected representatives of the Third Estate were propertied non-noble elements of lay society, including many lawyers and military officers.

Before the meeting a dispute arose among the representatives over whether the three groups would vote by estate, in which case the first two estates would dominate the assembly, or by head, in which case the Third Estate would have about the same number of representatives as the other two estates. Each side claimed that it was the best representative of the "nation," a term meaning the entire body of French people.

After the king indicated that he would side with the clergy and the nobility, the Third Estate took the dramatic step of declaring itself a National Assembly and asked members of the other estates to vote with them. When the king locked the Third Estate out of their meeting place without explanation, the outraged members went to a nearby indoor tennis court and took a solemn oath (known as the Oath of the Tennis Court) that they would not disband until the country had been given a constitution. One week later the king ordered the nobility and the clergy to join the National Assembly.

As this political crisis was reaching a climax, a major social crisis, fueled by the high price of bread, caused a breakdown of public order. For many years French agriculture had experienced difficulty meeting the demands of an expanding population. A widespread harvest failure in 1788 reduced the supply even further. As the price of

JACQUES-LOUIS DAVID, *THE OATH OF THE TENNIS COURT*
The oath taken by the members of the Third Estate not to disband until France had a constitution led to the creation of the National Assembly and the legislation that destroyed royal absolutism and feudalism.

bread soared, demand for manufactured goods shrank, thus causing widespread unemployment among artisans. An increasing number of bread riots, peasant revolts, and urban strikes contributed to a sense of panic at the very time that the government's financial crisis deepened. In Paris the situation reached a critical point in June 1789.

At that point the king, a man with little political sense, made the ill-advised decisions to send 17,000 royal troops to Paris to restore order. The arrival of the troops gave the impression that the government was planning to attack the people of the city. In this atmosphere of public paranoia Parisians formed the National Guard and stormed the Bastille.

The fall of the Bastille unnerved the king. When he asked one of his aides, "Is it a revolt?" the aide replied, "No, sire, it is a revolution." The revolution had just begun. It moved into high gear two weeks later when the National Assembly responded to the outbreak of social unrest in the provinces. The scarcity of grain in the countryside gave rise to false rumors that the nobles were engaged in a plot to destroy crops and starve the people into submission. Peasants armed themselves and prepared to fight off the hired agents of the nobility. A widespread panic, known as the "Great Fear," gripped many parts of the country. Townspeople and peasants amassed in large numbers to defend themselves and save the harvest. In response to this panic, which reached its peak in the last two weeks of July, the National Assembly began to pass legislation that destroyed the Old Regime and created a new political order.

The Creation of a New Political Society

Between August 1789 and September 1790 the National Assembly took three revolutionary steps. First, it eliminated noble and clerical privileges. In August the assembly abolished the feudal dues that peasants paid their lords, the private legal jurisdictions of noblemen, the collection of tithes by the clergy, and the exclusive right of noblemen to hunt game on their lands. Ten months later the nobility lost their titles. Instead of a society divided into various corporate groups, each with its own privileges, France would now have only citizens, all of them equal at law. Social distinctions would be based on merit rather than birth.

The second step, taken on August 26, was the promulgation of the *Declaration of the Rights of Man and Citizen*. This document revealed the main influence of the Enlightenment on the revolution. It declared that all men, not just Frenchmen, had a natural right to liberty, property, equality before the law, freedom from oppression, and religious toleration. The statement that the "law is the expression of the general will" reflected the influence of Rousseau's *The Social Contract* (1762), while the statement that every citizen has the right to participate in the formation of that law either personally or through a representative embodied the basic principle of democracy. (See *Different Voices* in this chapter.)

The third step in this revolutionary program was a complete reorganization of the Church. To solve the problem of the national debt, the National Assembly placed land owned by the Church (about ten percent of all French territory) at the service of the nation. The Civil Constitution of the Clergy of July 1790 in effect made the Church a department of the state, with the government paying the clergy directly. To retain their positions, the clergy were required to take an oath of loyalty to the nation.

In 1791 a newly elected Legislative Assembly—replacing the National Assembly—confirmed and extended many of these changes. A constitution, put into effect in October, formalized the end of royal absolutism. The king became a constitutional monarch, retaining only the power to suspend legislation, direct foreign policy, and command the armed forces.

The new constitution formally abolished hereditary legal privileges, thus providing equality of all citizens before the law. Subsequent legislation

THE FRENCH REPUBLIC, 1792–1799

■ How did a second, more radical revolution, which began with the establishment of the Republic in 1792, create a regime that used the power of the state to institute the Reign of Terror?

Beginning in 1792 France experienced a second revolution that was much more radical than the first. During this revolution France was transformed from a constitutional monarchy into a republic. The state claimed far greater power than it had acquired in 1789, and it used that power to bring about a radical reform of French society.

The Establishment of the Republic, 1792

During the first two years of the revolution it appeared that the building of a new French nation would take place within the framework of a constitutional monarchy. There was little sentiment among the members of the Legislative Assembly, much less among the general population, in favor of abolishing the institution of monarchy. The only committed republicans—those supporting the establishment of a republic—in the Legislative Assembly belonged to a party known as the **Jacobins**, who found support in political clubs in Paris and in other parts of the country. By the late summer of 1792 this group of radicals, drawing upon the support of militant Parisian citizens known as **sans-culottes** (literally, those without breeches, the pants worn by noblemen), succeeded in bringing about the second, more radical revolution.

King Louis himself was in part responsible for this destruction of the monarchy. The success of constitutional monarchy depended on the king's willingness to play the new role assigned to him. In October 1789 Louis had agreed, under considerable pressure, to move his residence from Versailles to Paris, where the National Assembly

TRICOLOR COCKADE
Louis XVI wearing the red liberty bonnet with the tricolor cockade on October 20, 1792. Refusing to be intimidated by a crowd of 20,000 people outside the royal palace, he donned the cap and proclaimed his loyalty to the constitution.

granted Jews and Protestants full civil rights and toleration. A law eliminating primogeniture (inheritance of the entire estate by the eldest son) gave all heirs equal rights to inherited property. The establishment of marriage as a civil contract and the right to end a marriage in divorce supported the idea of the husband and wife as freely contracting individuals.

This body of legislation destroyed the Old Regime and promoted a revolutionary view of French society as a nation composed of equal citizens possessing natural rights. Contemporaries recognized the significance of these changes. The Portuguese ambassador to France, who witnessed the events of 1789 firsthand, reported back to his government, "In all the world's annals there is no mention of a revolution like this."

DIFFERENT VOICES THE RIGHTS OF MAN AND WOMAN

The French Revolution gave rise to formal demands for the recognition and enforcement of the rights of man, but it also led to some of the earliest appeals for the equal rights of women. These two documents present the proclamation of the rights of man by the National Assembly and a parallel statement by a female writer who called for fundamental changes in the relations between men and women.

The passage of the Declaration of the Rights of Man and Citizen *by the National Assembly on August 26, 1789, was one of the earliest and most enduring acts of the French Revolution. A document of great simplicity and power, it was hammered out during many weeks of debate. Its concern with natural rights and equality before the law reflected the ideas of the Enlightenment.*

For Olympe de Gouges, the Declaration of the Rights of Man and Citizen *did not guarantee women the same rights as men nor address existing inequalities between the sexes. In a pamphlet titled* Declaration of the Rights of Women and the Female Citizen (1791), *which is a founding document of modern feminism, de Gouges offered a set of principles that paralleled the rights claimed in the National Assembly's demand for universal human rights.*

Declaration of the Rights of Man and Citizen (1789)

1. Men are born free and remain free and equal in rights. Social distinctions may be founded only on the common good.
2. The aim of all political association is the preservation of the natural and imprescriptible rights of man. These rights are liberty, property, security and resistance to oppression.
3. The principle of all authority rests essentially in the nation. No body nor individual may exercise any authority which does not emanate expressly from the nation.
4. Liberty consists in the freedom to do whatever does not harm another; hence the exercise of the natural rights of each man has no limits except those which assure to the other members of society the enjoyment of the same rights. These limits can only be determined by law....
6. Law is the expression of the general will. Every citizen has the right to participate personally or through his representative in its formation. It must be the same for all, whether it protects or punishes. All citizens, being equal in the eyes of the law, are equally eligible to all dignities and to all public positions and occupations, according to their abilities, and without distinction except that of their virtues and talents.
7. No man may be indicted, arrested, or imprisoned except in cases determined by the law and according to the forms prescribed by law....
10. No one should be disturbed for his opinions, even in religion, provided that their manifestation does not trouble public order as established by law.
11. The free communication of thoughts and opinions is one of the most precious of the rights of man. Every citizen may therefore speak, write, and print freely, but shall be responsible for any abuse of this freedom in the cases set by the law....
17. Property being an inviolable and sacred right, no one may be deprived of it except when public necessity, determined by law, obviously requires it, and then on the

had also relocated. The pressure came mainly from women, who formed the large majority of 10,000 demonstrators who marched from Paris to Versailles demanding a reduction in the price of bread. The king yielded to their demands and came to Paris. As he entered the city, accompanied by soldiers, monks, and women carrying guns and pikes, he reluctantly agreed to wear the tricolor cockade (a badge) to symbolize his acceptance of the revolution. Louis, however,

condition that the owner shall have been previously and equitably compensated.

Source: From P.-J.-B. Buchez and P.-C. Roux, *Histoire parlementaire de la Révolution française* (Paris, 1834).

Olympe de Gouges, *Declaration of the Rights of Women and the Female Citizen* (1791)

1. Woman is born free and lives equal to man in her rights. Social distinctions can be based only on common utility.

2. The purpose of any political association is the conservation of the natural and impre-scriptible rights of woman and man; these rights are liberty, property, security, and especially resistance to oppression.

3. The principle of all sovereignty rests essen-tially with the nation, which is nothing but the union of woman and man; no body and no individual can exercise any authority which does not come expressly from it [the nation].

4. Liberty and justice consist of restoring all that belongs to others; thus, the only limits on the exercise of the natural rights of woman are perpetual male tyranny; these limits are to be reformed by the laws of nature and reason....

6. The laws must be the expression of the gen-eral will; all female and male citizens must contribute either personally or through their representatives to its formation; it must be the same for all: male and female citizens, being equal in the eyes of the law, must be equally admitted to all honors, positions, and public employment according to their capacity and without other distinctions besides those of their virtues and talents.

7. No woman is an exception: she is accused, arrested, and detained in cases determined by law. Women, like men, obey this rigorous law....

10. No one is to be disquieted for his very basic opinions; woman has the right to mount the scaffold; she must equally have the right to mount the rostrum, provided that her demonstrations do not disturb the legally established public order.

11. The free communication of thoughts and opinions is one of the most precious rights of woman, since this liberty assures the recognition of children by their fathers. Any female citizen thus may say freely, I am the mother of your child, without being forced by a barbarous prejudice to hide the truth; as long as she accepts responsibility for any abuse of this liberty [by lying about thee paternity of the child] in cases determined by law....

17. Property belongs to both sexes whether united or separated; for each it is an invio-lable and sacred right; no one can be deprived of it, since it is a true patrimony of nature, unless public necessity, determined by law, requires it, and then only with a just compensation, settled in advance.

Source: Olympe de Gouges, *Les Droits de la femme* (Paris, 1791).

For Discussion

1. What is the basis of Olympe de Gouges's demand for equal rights for women?

2. Did the two declarations differ in their views of the nation? Did they differ in their view of the proper function of law?

could not disguise his opposition to the revolu-tion, especially the ecclesiastical legislation of 1789. His opposition led many people to suspect that he was encouraging the powers of Europe to invade France to restore the Old Regime.

Louis XVI had few personal resources upon which he might draw to win the confidence of his subjects. He was not as intelligent as his grandfa-ther, Louis XV, nor did he have the skills necessary to dispel his subjects' growing distrust of him.

La Femme du sans Culotte

SANS-CULOTTES

Male and female dress of the *sans-culottes,* the armed Parisian radicals who supported the Republic. The men did not wear the breeches (*culottes*) that were in style among the members of the French nobility.

Neither Louis nor his Austrian wife, Marie Antoinette, commanded much respect among the people. For many years the royal couple had been the object of relentless, sometimes pornographic satire. Critics lampooned the king for his rumored sexual inadequacies and the queen for a series of alleged infidelities with the king's brother and a succession of female partners. Whatever confidence Parisian citizens might have retained in the royal couple evaporated in June 1791, when the king and queen attempted to flee the country. The National Guard apprehended them at Varennes, close to the eastern French border, and forced them to return to Paris, where they were kept under guard at the palace of the Tuileries.

The development that actually precipitated the downfall of the monarchy and led to the establishment of a republic was the decision by the Legislative Assembly to go to war. After the flight to Varennes and the capture of the royal family, Frederick William II of Prussia and Emperor Leopold II of Austria, the brother of Marie Antoinette, signed an alliance and called upon the other European monarchs "to restore to the king of France complete liberty and to consolidate the bases of monarchical government." In response to this threat a small group of republicans, headed by the eloquent orator Jacques-Pierre Brissot (1754–1793), convinced the assembly that an international conspiracy against the revolution would end in an invasion of their country. Brissot and his supporters also believed that France could be lured into a foreign war, the king and queen would be revealed as traitors, and the monarchy would be destroyed. Exploiting xenophobic and revolutionary sentiment, and claiming that the strength of a citizen army would win a quick and decisive victory, Brissot and his allies won the support of the entire assembly. They also appealed to the international goals of the revolution, claiming that the French army would inspire revolution against "the tyrants of Europe" everywhere they went.

The Legislative Assembly declared war on Austria in April 1792. Instead of a glorious victory, however, the war resulted in a series of disastrous defeats at the hands of the Austrians and their Prussian allies. This military failure contributed to a mood of paranoia in France, especially in Paris. Fears arose that invading armies, in alliance with nobles, would undermine the revolution and destroy the assembly itself. In July the assembly officially proclaimed the nation to be in danger, calling for all citizens to rally against the enemies of liberty at home and abroad. Women petitioned for the right to bear arms. When the Austrians and Prussians threatened to torch the entire city of Paris and slaughter its population if anyone laid a hand on the royal family, Parisian citizens immediately demanded that the king be deposed.

On August 10 a radical republican committee overthrew the Paris commune, the city government that had been installed in 1789, and set up a new, revolutionary commune. A force of about 20,000 men, including volunteer troops from various parts of the kingdom, invaded the Tuileries, which was defended by about 900 Swiss guards. When the members of the royal bodyguard fled, members of the Paris crowds pursued them, stripped them of their red uniforms and hacked 600 of them to death with knives, pikes, and hatchets. The attack on the Tuileries forced the king to take refuge in the nearby Legislative Assembly. The assembly promptly suspended the monarchy and turned the royal family over to the commune, which imprisoned them in the Temple, a medieval fortress in the northeastern part of the city. The Assembly then ordered its own dissolution and called for the election of a new legislative body that would draft a new constitution.

The fall of the monarchy did nothing to allay the siege mentality of the city, especially after further Prussian victories in early September escalated fears of a Prussian invasion. The foreign invasion never materialized. On September 20, 1792 a surprisingly well-disciplined and well-trained army of French citizens, inspired by dedication to France and the revolution, repulsed the Prussian army at Valmy. This victory saved the revolution. Delegates to a new National Convention, elected by **universal male suffrage,** had already arrived in Paris to write a new constitution. On September 22 the Convention declared that the monarchy was formally abolished and that France was a republic. France had now experienced a second revolution, more radical than the first, but dedicated to the principles of liberty, equality, and fraternity, which soon became the motto of the revolution.

The Jacobins and the Revolution

By the time the Republic had been declared, the Jacobins had become the major political party in the Legislative Assembly. Soon, however, factional divisions began to develop within Jacobin ranks. The main split occurred between the followers of Brissot, known as **Girondins,** and the radicals known as Montagnards, or **"the Mountain."** The latter acquired their name because they occupied the benches on the side of the Convention hall, where the floor sloped upward. The Girondins occupied the lower side of the hall, while the uncommitted deputies, known as "the Plain," occupied the middle.

Both the Mountain and the Girondins claimed to be advancing the goals of the revolution, but they differed widely on which tactics to pursue. The Mountain took the position that as long as internal and external enemies threatened the state, the government needed to centralize authority in the capital. The Mountain thought of themselves as the representatives of the common people, especially the sans-culottes in Paris. Many of their leaders, including Georges-Jacques Danton (1759–1794), Jean-Paul Marat (1743–1793), and Maximilien Robespierre (1758–1794), were in fact Parisians. Their mission was to make the revolution even more egalitarian and to establish a republic characterized by civic pride and patriotism, which Robespierre referred to as the **Republic of Virtue.**

The Girondins, known as such because many of their leaders came from the southwestern department of Gironde, took a more conservative position than the Mountain on these issues. Favoring the economic freedom and local control desired by merchants and manufacturers, they were reluctant to support further centralization of state power. They believed that the revolution had advanced far enough and should not become more radical. They were also afraid that the egalitarianism of the revolution, if unchecked, would lead to a leveling of French society and result in social anarchy.

The conflict between the Girondins and the Mountain became apparent in the debate over what to do with the deposed king. Louis had been suspected of conspiring with the enemies of the revolution, and the discovery of his correspondence with the Austrian government led to his trial for treason against the nation. The Girondins had originally expressed reluctance to bring him to trial, preferring to keep him in prison. Once the trial began, they joined the entire National Convention in voting to convict him, but they opposed his execution. This stance led the Mountain to accuse the Girondins of being secret collaborators with the monarchy. By a narrow vote the Convention decided to put the king to death, and on January 21, 1793, Louis was executed at the Place de la Révolution, formerly known as the Place de Louis XV. (See *Justice in History* in this chapter.)

The instrument of death was the guillotine, an efficient and merciful but nonetheless terrifying decapitation machine first pressed into service in April 1792. It took its name from Dr. Joseph-Ignace Guillotin, who had the original idea for such a device, although he did not invent it. The guillotine was inspired by the conviction that all criminals, not just those of noble blood, should be executed in a swift, painless manner. The new device was to be put to extensive use during the next 18 months, and many Girondins fell victim to it.

The split between the Mountain and the Girondins became more pronounced as the republican regime encountered increasing opposition from foreign and domestic enemies. Early in 1793 Great Britain and the Dutch Republic allied with Prussia and Austria to form the First Coalition against France, and within a month Spain and the Italian kingdoms of Sardinia and Naples joined them. The armies of these allied powers defeated French forces in the Austrian Netherlands in March of that year, and once again an invasion seemed imminent. At the same time internal rebellions against the revolutionary regime took place in various outlying provinces, especially in the district of the Vendée in western France. Noblemen and clerics led these uprisings, but they also had popular support, especially from tenant farmers who resented the increased taxation imposed by the new revolutionary government.

In the minds of Robespierre and his colleagues, the Girondins were linked to these provincial rebels, whom they labeled as *federalists* because they opposed the centralization of the French state and thus threatened the unity of the nation. In June 1793, 29 Girondins were expelled from the Convention for supporting local officials accused of hoarding grain. This purge made it apparent that any political opponent of the Mountain, even those with solid republican credentials, could now be identified as an enemy of the revolution.

The Reign of Terror, 1793–1794

To deal with its domestic enemies, the French republican government claimed powers that far exceeded those exercised by the monarchy in the age of absolutism. The Convention passed laws that set up special courts to prosecute enemies of the regime and authorized procedures that deprived those accused of their legal rights. These laws laid the legal foundation for the **Reign of Terror,** a campaign to rid the state of its internal enemies. A Committee of Public Safety, consisting of twelve members entrusted with the executive power of the state, superintended this process. Although technically subordinate to the

CHRONOLOGY: THE FRENCH REPUBLIC AND THE TERROR, 1792–1794

1792

April 20	Declaration of war against Austria
August 10	Attack on the Tuileries; monarchy is suspended
September 20	French victory at the Battle of Valmy
September 21	National Convention meets
September 22	Abolition of the monarchy and establishment of the Republic

1793

January 21	Execution of Louis XVI
February 1	Declaration of war against Great Britain and the Dutch Republic
March 11	Beginning of rebellion in the Vendée
June 2	Purge of Girondins from the Convention
June 24	Ratification of a republican constitution
October 16	Execution of Marie Antoinette

1794

July 28	Tenth of *Thermidor*; execution of Robespierre
November 12	Jacobin clubs closed

Convention, the Committee of Public Safety became, in effect, a revolutionary dictatorship.

The man who emerged as the main figure on the Committee of Public Safety was Maximilien Robespierre. A brilliant student as a youth, Robespierre had taken offense when the royal carriage splashed him with mud as he was waiting to read an address to the king. A man with little sense of humor, he was passionate in his quest for justice. As a lawyer who defended indigent clients, Robespierre was elected to the Third Estate in 1789 and became a favorite of the *sans-culottes,* who called him "The Incorruptible." That he may have been, but he was also susceptible to the temptation to abuse power for partisan political purposes. Like Rousseau, whose work he admired, he was also willing to sacrifice individual liberty in the name of the General Will. He reasoned that because the General Will was indivisible, it could not accommodate dissent. Robespierre was primarily responsible for pushing the revolution to new extremes by establishing the program of state repression that began in the autumn of 1793.

The most intense prosecutions of the Terror took place between October 1793 and June 1794,

but they continued until August 1794. By that time the revolutionary courts had executed 17,000 people, while 500,000 had suffered imprisonment. Another 20,000 either died in prison or were killed without any form of trial. Among the victims of the Terror were substantial numbers of clergy and nobility, but the overwhelming majority were artisans and peasants. One Parisian stableboy was guillotined for having said "f . . the Republic," while a baker from Alsace lost his head for predicting that "the Republic will go to hell with all its partisans."[1] Many of the victims came from the outlying regions of the country, especially the northeast, where foreign armies threatened the Republic, and the west, where a brutal civil war between the French army and Catholics and royalists was raging. Special surveillance committees identified these provincial enemies of the regime, and revolutionary tribunals tried them. The guillotine was by no means the only method of execution. In November and December 1793, about 1,800 rebels captured during the uprising in the Vendée were tied to other prisoners, placed in sinking boats, and drowned in the chilly waters of the Loire River.

JUSTICE IN HISTORY

The Trial of Louis XVI

After the abolition of the monarchy and the proclamation of the French Republic in September 1792, the National Convention considered the fate of the deposed king. There was a broad consensus that Louis was guilty of treason against the nation and that he should answer for his crimes, but how he should do so became a subject of heated debate. The Convention was divided between the Girondins and the Mountain. Of the two, the Girondins were more inclined to follow due process, whereas the Mountain considered themselves to be acting as a revolutionary tribunal that had no obligation to adhere to existing French law. The Convention thus became a forum where Louis's accusers expressed competing notions of revolutionary justice.

The most divisive and revealing issue was whether there should be a trial at all. The Mountain originally took the position that because the people had already judged the king on August 10, when the monarchy had fallen and the king was taken prisoner, there was no need for a second judgment. They believed the death sentence should have been carried out immediately. Robespierre argued that a trial would have been counterrevolutionary, for it would have allowed the revolution itself to be brought before the court to be judged. A centrist majority, however, decided that the king had to be charged with specific offenses in a court of law and found guilty by due process before being sentenced.

A second issue, closely related to the first, was the technical legal question of whether Louis could be subject to legal action. Even in a constitutional monarchy, such as had been established in 1789, the legislative branch of the government did not possess authority over the king. The Convention based its decision to try Louis, however, on the revolutionary principle that he had committed crimes against the nation, which the revolutionaries claimed was a higher authority than the king. Louis, moreover, was no longer king but was now a citizen and, therefore, subject to the law in the same way as anyone else.

The third issue was Louis's culpability for the specific charges in the indictment. These crimes included refusing to call the Estates General, sending an army to march against the citizens of Paris, and conducting secret negotiations with France's enemies. The journalist and deputy Jean-Paul Marat added that "he robbed the citizens of their gold as a subsidy for their foes" and "caused his hirelings to hoard, to create famine, to dry up the sources of abundance that the people might die from misery and hunger." The king, who appeared personally to hear the indictment and then respond to the charges, based his defense on the laws in force at the times he was supposed to have committed his crimes. Thus, he defended his sending of troops to Paris on the grounds that in June and July 1789 he could order troops wherever he wanted. In the same vein, he argued that he had used force solely in response to illegal intimidation. These legalisms, however, only made the members of the Convention more contemptuous of the king. His defense failed to persuade a single convention deputy. He was convicted of treason by a vote of 693–0.

The unanimous conviction of the king did not end the factional debates over the king's fate. Knowing that there was extensive support for the king in various parts of the country, the Girondins asked that the verdict be appealed to the people. They argued that the Convention, dominated by the Mountain and supported by militants in Paris, had usurped the sovereignty of the people. A motion to submit the verdict to the people for ratification lost by a vote of 424–283.

EXECUTION OF LOUIS XVI, JANUARY 21, 1793

Although the king was convicted of treason by a unanimous vote, the vote to execute him carried by a slender majority of only 27 votes.

The last vote, the closest of all, determined the king's sentence. Originally, it appeared that a majority might vote for noncapital punishment. The Marquis de Condorcet, for example, argued that although the king deserved death on the basis of the law of treason, he could not bring himself to vote for capital punishment on principle. The radical response to this argument came from Robespierre, who appealed to the "principles of nature" that justified the death penalty in such cases, "where it is vital to the safety of private citizens or of the public." Robespierre's impassioned oratory carried the day. By a vote of 361–334 the king was sentenced to "death within 24 hours" rather than the alternatives of imprisonment followed by banishment after the war or imprisonment in chains for life. The following day Louis was led to the guillotine.

All public trials, especially those for political crimes, are theatrical events, in that the various parties play specific roles and seek to convey certain messages to their audiences. The men who voted to put Louis XVI on trial wanted to create an educational spectacle in which the already deposed monarch would be stripped of any respect he might still have commanded among the people. Louis was to be tried like any other traitor, and he was to suffer the same fate, execution by the guillotine. The attempt to strip him of all privilege and status continued after his death. His corpse, with his head placed between his knees, was taken to a cemetery, placed in a wooden box, and buried in the common pit. The revolutionaries were determined to guarantee that even in death the king would have the same position as the humblest of his former subjects.

For Discussion

1. How would you describe the standard of justice that the members of the National Convention upheld in voting to execute the king? How did this standard of justice differ from the standard to which King Louis XVI appealed?

2. Evaluate the argument of Robespierre that the death penalty can be justified only in cases of public safety. Compare his argument to that of Enlightenment thinkers such as

Cesare Beccaria that capital punishment was an unjust, unnecessary, and uncivilized punishment.

Taking It Further

Jordan, David P. *The King's Trial: The French Revolution vs. Louis XVI.* 1979. The most thorough account of the trial.

Walzer, Michael (ed.) *Regicide and Revolution: Speeches at the Trial of Louis XVI.* 1974. A valuable collection of speeches with an extended commentary.

Some of the most prominent figures of the Enlightenment fell victim to this paranoia. Among them was the Marquis de Condorcet, who believed passionately that all citizens, including women, had equal rights. Having campaigned against capital punishment, he committed suicide in a Parisian prison, just before he was to be executed. Another figure of the Enlightenment, the famous chemist Antoine Lavoisier (1743–1794), who had devoted himself to improving social and economic conditions in France, was executed at the same time. So too was the feminist Olympe de Gouges, who had petitioned for the equal rights of women. Many French revolutionaries, including Robespierre, used the political ideas of the Enlightenment to justify their actions, but the Terror struck down some of the most distinguished figures of that movement. In that sense the Terror marked the end of the Enlightenment in France.

The Committee of Public Safety then went after Danton and other so-called Indulgents who had decided that the Terror had gone too far. Danton's execution made everyone, especially moderate Jacobins, wonder who would be the next victim of a process that had spun completely out of control. In June 1794 the Terror reached a climax as 1,300 people went to their deaths. To stop the process, a group of Jacobins

in the Convention organized a plot against Robespierre. Calling him a tyrant, they arrested him and more than 100 of his followers and guillotined them in late July 1794. In the provinces members of the White Terror, so named for the white Bourbon flag they displayed, executed leaders of local revolutionary tribunals. With these reprisals the most violent and radical phase of the French revolution came to an end.

The Reign of Terror had ended, but its memory would never be extinguished. Its horrors served as a constant warning against the dangers inherent in revolutionary movements. The guillotine, the agent of a dysfunctional and indiscriminate state terrorism, became just as closely identified with the French Revolution as its famous slogan of "Liberty, Equality, Fraternity." The contrast between those two symbols, each of them emblematic of a different stage of the revolution, helps to explain how both conservatives and liberals in the nineteenth century would be able to appeal to the experience of the revolution to support their contradictory ideologies.

The Directory, 1795–1799

A desire to end the violence of the Terror allowed moderates in the National Convention to regain control of the state apparatus that Robespierre and his allies had used to such devastating effect. They dismantled the Paris Commune and stripped the Committee of Public Safety of most of its powers. In November 1794 they closed Jacobin clubs throughout the country, which had provided support for the Terror. The moderates who now controlled the government still hoped to preserve the gains of the revolution, while returning the country to more familiar forms of authority. A new constitution of 1795 bestowed executive power on a five-man Directorate, while an assembly consisting of two houses, the Council of Elders and the Council of Five Hundred, proposed and voted on all legislation. The franchise was limited to property holders, allowing only two million men out of an adult male population of seven million to vote. A system of indirect election, in which a person voted for electors who then selected representatives, guaranteed that only the wealthiest members of the country would sit in the legislative councils.

Some of the wealthier and more entrepreneurial citizens of Paris welcomed the new regime, but opposition soon arose, mainly from Jacobins and sans-culottes. When the government relaxed the strict price controls that had been in effect under the Jacobins, the soaring price of bread and other commodities caused widespread social discontent among the populace. The continuation of the interminable war against the foreign powers only aggravated the situation. Wherever French troops went, their constant need of food and other goods resulted in serious shortages of these commodities.

By the end of 1798 conditions had grown even worse. Inflation was running out of control. The collection of taxes was intermittent at best. The paper money known as *assignats*, first issued by the government in 1791 and backed by the value of confiscated church lands, had become almost worthless. Late in 1797 the Directory, as the new regime was called, had to cancel more than half the national debt, a step that further alienated wealthy citizens who had lent money to the government. Military setbacks in 1798 and 1799 brought the situation to a critical point. The formation of a Second Coalition of European powers in 1799, which included Britain, Austria, Russia, Naples, and Turkey, presented a formidable challenge to French power and ensured that the war would not end soon. These military events produced a swing to the political left and raised the specter of another Jacobin coup.

CHRONOLOGY: THE DIRECTORY, 1795–1799

1795

August 22	The National Convention approves a new constitution
October 5	Napoleon suppresses a royalist insurrection in Paris
October 26	End of the Convention; beginning of the Directory

1796

February 19	The issuing of *assignats* halted
April 12	Beginning of a series of victories by Napoleon in Italy

1798

May 13	Napoleon's expedition departs for Egypt
May	Second Coalition (Britain, Austria, Russia, Naples, and Turkey) is formed against Napoleon
July 21	Napoleon wins the Battle of the Pyramids
August 1	Nelson destroys the French fleet at the Battle of the Nile

1799

November 9–10	Napoleon's coup; Consulate established

In the face of this instability, Emmanuel-Joseph Sieyès, who had been elected as one of the directors two years earlier, decided to overthrow the government. Sieyès provided a link between the early years of the revolution, when he had defended the Third Estate, and the government of the Directory. Unlike many other prominent political figures, he had managed to avoid prosecution as the revolution had become more radical. When asked what he had done during the Reign of Terror, Sieyès replied, "I survived." Now he sought to provide the country with strong government, its greatest need in a period of political, economic, and social instability. The person Sieyès selected as his partner in this enterprise, who immediately assumed leadership of the coup, was Napoleon Bonaparte (1769–1821), a 30-year-old general who in 1795 had put down a royalist rebellion in Paris with a "whiff of grapeshot."

Napoleon had already established impressive credentials as a military leader. In 1796 and 1797 he had won major victories in Italy, leading to the Treaty of Campo Formio with Austria in 1797. Those victories and his short-lived success at the Battle of the Pyramids in Egypt had made him enormously popular in Paris, where he was received as a hero when he assumed command of the armed forces in the city in 1799. (See *Encounters and Transformations* in this chapter.) His popularity, his demonstrated military leadership, and his control of a large armed force made this "man on horseback" appear to have the best chance to replace the enfeebled civilian regime of the Directory.

On November 9, 1799, Napoleon addressed the two legislative councils. He reported the discovery of another Jacobin conspiracy and called for a new constitution to give the executive branch of the government more authority. Napoleon encountered resistance from some members of the Council of Five Hundred, who demanded that he be declared an outlaw. At this stage the president of the council, Napoleon's brother Lucien, intervened and called in troops to evict the members who opposed him. The following day France had a new government, known as the Consulate.

Executive power in the new government was to be vested in three consuls. It soon became clear, however, that Napoleon would dominate this trio. In the new constitution of December 1799, which the electorate ratified by **plebiscite** (a vote to accept or reject a proposal), Napoleon was named First Consul. This appointment made him the most powerful man in France and, for all practical purposes, a military dictator. The dictatorship became more apparent in 1802, when Napoleon was named Consul for Life.

CULTURAL CHANGE IN FRANCE DURING THE REVOLUTION

■ In what ways did the political events of the revolution change French culture?

The French Revolution was primarily a political revolution, but it also brought about profound changes in French culture. It destroyed the cultural institutions of the Old Regime and created a new revolutionary culture.

The Transformation of Cultural Institutions

Between 1791 and 1794 many of the cultural institutions of the Old Regime were either destroyed or radically transformed, and new institutions under the control of the state took their place.

ACADEMIES The Parisian scientific and artistic academies established by Louis XIV (see Chapter 16) had a monopoly over the promotion and transmission of knowledge in the sciences and the visual arts. The academies were the epitome of privilege. They controlled their own membership, determined the recipients of their prizes, and monopolized their particular branches of knowledge. They were also heavily aristocratic institutions. As many as three-quarters of their members were nobles or clergy.

During the revolution the academies were abolished as part of a general attack on corporate bodies, and various government committees replaced them. For example, the Commission on Weights and Measures, which had been part of the Academy of Science, became an independent commission. Its task was to provide uniform weights and measures for the entire kingdom. In 1795 it established the meter, calculated as one ten-millionth of the distance from the North Pole to the equator, as the standard measure of distance. Like the decimal system, which was introduced at the same time, the metric system was subsequently adopted as a universal standard in all European countries.

The Popular and Republican Society of the Arts replaced the Royal Academy of Arts. The inspiration for this new republican society, which was open to artists of all social ranks, was Jacques-Louis David (1748–1825), the greatest painter of his generation. Employed at the court of Louis XVI, David became a vocal critic of the academy at the time of the revolution. He painted some of the most memorable scenes of the revolution, including the oath taken at the tennis court by the members of the National Assembly in 1789. During the Republic David depicted heroes of the revolution, such as Jean-Paul Marat (see the illustration on page 638), and he was later appointed First Painter to Napoleon. David presided over a revival of classicism in French painting, employing Greek and Roman motifs and exhibiting a rationalism and lack of sentiment in his work.

LIBRARIES Shortly after the revolution had begun, thousands of books and manuscripts from the libraries of monasteries, royal castles, residences of the nobility, and academies came into the possession of the state. Many of these became part of the Royal Library, which was appropriately renamed the National Library. The government also intended to catalog all the books held in libraries throughout the country. This effort to create the General Bibliography of France was never completed, and while the books were being cataloged, the government decided to get rid of those that dealt with "theology, mysticism, feudalism, and royalism" by sending them to foreign countries. This decision initiated a frenzy of book sales, mainly to private individuals. Altogether about five million books were lost or sold during these years.

MUSEUMS AND MONUMENTS The day after the abolition of the monarchy the Legislative Assembly created a Commission of the Museum, whose charge was "to collect paintings, statues and other precious objects" from royal residences, churches, and houses of émigrés. The museum was to be located in the Louvre, a royal palace that also served as an art gallery. When it opened in August 1793 the Louvre included a majority of paintings with religious themes. These religious works of art remained in the collection even though they appeared to be incompatible with the republican rejection of Christianity. The revolutionaries justified this decision on the grounds that this museum was intended to be entirely historical and have no relevance to contemporary culture.

The revolutionaries did not have the same respect for the bodies of their former kings. On August 10, 1793, the first anniversary of the deposition of Louis XVI, the National Convention ordered the destruction of all the tombs of past French kings. One by one the tombs were opened and the corpses, embalmed in lead, were removed. Metals and valuables were melted down for use in the war effort. The corpses were either left to disintegrate in the atmosphere or dragged unceremoniously to the cemetery, where they were thrown into the common pit. The corpse of Louis XIV landed on top of that of Henry IV. This disrespectful treatment of the remains of France's former kings was intended to erase the memory of monarchy.

The Creation of a New Political Culture

As the state was taking over and adapting the cultural institutions of the Old Regime, revolutionaries engaged in a much bolder and original undertaking: the production of a new, revolutionary political culture. Its sole purpose was to legitimize and glorify the new regime. This culture was almost entirely political; all forms of cultural expression were subordinated to the realization of a pressing political agenda.

The main political doctrine of the revolution was popular sovereignty: the claim that the people were the highest political power in the state. The new political culture was also popular in the sense that the entire populace, not simply the literate elite, adopted it. The people who embraced the new culture most enthusiastically were the *sans-culottes*—the radical shopkeepers, artisans, and laborers of Paris. The dress of these people influenced a change in fashion among the wealthier segments of society. A simple jacket replaced the ruffled coat worn by members of the upper classes, their powdered wigs gave way to natural hair, and long trousers replaced the shorter breeches. They also donned the red liberty cap, to which a tricolor cockade was affixed. The tricolor, which combined the red and blue colors of Paris with the white symbol of the Bourbon monarchy, identified the adherents of the revolution.

Symbols of revolution could be found everywhere. The commercialization of the revolution guaranteed that the tricolor flag, portraits of revolutionary figures, and images of the Bastille appeared on household objects as constant reminders of the public's support for the revolution. An order of the government in 1792 required all men to wear the tricolor cockade. Liberty trees, first planted by peasants as protests against local landlords, became a symbol of the revolution. By May 1792 more than 60,000 trees had been planted throughout the country.

The press, no longer tightly controlled by the government and the printers' guild, became a crucial agent of revolutionary propaganda and a producer of the new culture. Pamphlets, newspapers, brochures, and posters all promoted a distinctive revolutionary language, which became one of the permanent legacies of the revolution. Political leaders used the same rhetoric in their political speeches. *Sans-culottes* sang satirical songs and ballads, many of them to tunes well known in the Old Regime. The most popular of the songs of the revolutionary period was the *Marseillaise,* first sung by soldiers preparing for battle against the Austrians, but soon adopted by the civilian population and sung at political gatherings.

Much of this new political culture stemmed from the conviction that the doctrine of popular sovereignty should be practiced in everyday life. *Sans-culottes* did this by joining the political clubs organized by different factions within the National Assembly, by addressing others as citizens, and by using the more familiar form of the pronoun *you* (*tu* rather than *vous*) in all conversations. They also participated in the revolution by taking public oaths. On the first anniversary of the fall of the Bastille, as many as 350,000 people, many of them members of the "federations" of National Guards throughout the country, gathered on the royal parade ground outside Paris to take an oath "to the Nation, to the Law, to the King." Direct democracy was not possible in a society of 27 million people, but these cultural practices allowed people to believe that they were participating actively in the political process.

The new revolutionary culture was emphatically secular. In its most extreme form, it was blatantly anti-Christian. In September 1793 the radical Jacobin and former priest Joseph Fouché inaugurated a program of **de-Christianization.** Under his leadership, radical Jacobins closed churches and removed religious symbols such as crosses from cemeteries and public venues. In an effort to establish a purely civic religion, they forbade the public practice of religion and renamed churches "temples of reason." In their public pronouncements the architects of de-Christianization avoided reference to the Christian period of French history, which covered the entire national past.

This de-Christianization campaign became the official policy of the Paris Commune and the National Convention. The program, however, did not win widespread support, and even some Jacobins claimed that in rejecting Christianity it had undermined a belief in God and the afterlife. In 1794 Robespierre attempted to modify the excesses of de-Christianization by launching the

OATH TAKING

On July 14, 1790, the first anniversary of the fall of the Bastille, as many as 350,000 people gathered on a field outside Paris to take an oath of loyalty to the new French nation. The event was referred to as the Feast of the Federation, because most of the oath takers were members of the regional federations of National Guards. The oath taking, which had many characteristics of a religious gathering, was led by the king himself, and it marked the most optimistic period of the revolution.

Cult of the Supreme Being. He promoted a series of festivals acknowledging the existence of a deity and the immortality of the soul. This new cult paid lip service to traditional religious beliefs, but it still served secular purposes. The cult was designed to direct the spiritual yearnings of the French people into patriotic undertakings and promote republican virtue.

In an effort to destroy all vestiges of the Old Regime, the government also instituted a new calendar in October 1793. The dates on the calendar began with September 22, 1792, the day the Republic was established. That became the first day of the year I, while the weeks now had ten days instead of seven. The new months were given names to evoke the different seasons, such as *Brumaire* for the first month of wintry weather, *Germinal* for the season of planting, and

Thermidor for the warmest month of the summer. Hostile British contemporaries gave their own humorous renditions of these names, translating them as Freezy, Flowery, Heaty, and so on. The new calendar was intended to make the revolution a part of people's everyday consciousness. It remained in effect until the last day of 1805.

The new revolutionary culture was disseminated widely, but it was always contested. Royalists trampled on the tricolor cockade, refused to adopt the new style of dress, and pulled up the liberty trees. During the Directory many wealthy members of society donned fancy and opulent clothes and revived the high social life of the capital. This resistance from counterrevolutionary forces guaranteed that when the revolution was reversed, much of the new political culture would disappear. Napoleon did little to perpetuate it in

JACQUES-LOUIS DAVID, *THE DEATH OF MARAT* (1793)

The Jacobin journalist Jean-Paul Marat was stabbed to death in his bathtub by a noblewoman, Charlotte Corday, in July 1793. Marat holds the letter from his murderer that gave her entrance to his residence. The painting depicts the slain victim in the manner of the dead Christ in Michelangelo's *Pietà*. The painting thus shows how new secular culture of the revolution incorporated many elements of the Christian culture that had prevailed before the revolution began.

the first decade of the nineteenth century, and the restored monarchy was openly hostile to it. Like the political revolution, however, some elements of revolutionary culture, such as the tricolor and the rhetoric of the revolutionary press, could never be suppressed. Not only did these cultural innovations inspire revolutionaries for the next 100 years, but they also became part of the mainstream of Western civilization.

THE NAPOLEONIC ERA, 1799–1815

- Did the authoritarian rule of Napoleon Bonaparte from 1799 to 1814 confirm or betray the achievements of the French Revolution, and what impact did his military conquests have on Europe and the world?

The coup d'état on November 9, 1799, or the eighteenth of *Brumaire* on the revolutionary calendar, marked a turning point in the political history of France. The Consulate ushered in a period of authoritarian rule. Liberty was restricted in the interest of order; republicanism gave way to dictatorship. The French Revolution had apparently run its course. But the period between 1799 and 1815 was also a time of considerable innovation, especially in the realm of politics and diplomacy. Those innovations were primarily the work of one man, Napoleon Bonaparte, who controlled the French government for the next 15 years.

Napoleon's Rise to Power

Napoleon Bonaparte was born on the Mediterranean island of Corsica. His father, Charles-Marie de Buonaparte, was an attorney who had supported the cause of winning Corsica's independence from the Italian state of Genoa. His mother, Letizia, came from an old noble family in the northern Italian region of Lombardy. In 1770 the new French government, which had gained control of the island the previous year, accepted the Buonaparte family as nobility. In 1779 the young Napoleon, whose native language was Corsican, received an appointment to a French military school. He survived both the rigors of the course of study and the taunting of his classmates, who mocked him for his accent and his poverty. Displaying a natural gift for military science, he won a position in the artillery section of the national military academy in Paris.

The events of the French Revolution made possible Napoleon's rapid ascent to military prominence and political power. When the revolution broke out, Napoleon returned to Corsica, where he organized the National Guard and petitioned the government to grant full rights of citizenship to his people. After becoming a Jacobin, he was commissioned to attack federalist and royalist positions in the south of France. Unlike many of his fellow Jacobins, he found favor with the Directory. In 1796 Napoleon was given command of the Army of Italy, at which time he abandoned the Italian spelling of his name for Bonaparte. His decisive victories against the

Austrians and his popularity in Paris attracted the attention of Sieyès and others who wished to give the country strong, charismatic leadership.

Napoleon's personality was ideally suited to the acquisition and maintenance of political power. A man of unparalleled ambition, he was driven by an extraordinarily high assessment of his abilities. After one of his military victories he wrote, "I realized I was a superior being and conceived the ambition of performing great things." To the pursuit of his destiny he harnessed a determined and stubborn will and enormous energy. Temporary setbacks never seemed to thwart his single-minded pursuit of glory. He brought enormous energy to his military and political pursuits. He wrote more than 80,000 letters during his life, many of them transmitting orders to his officers and ministers. Authoritarian by nature, he used both intimidation and paternalism to cultivate the loyalty of his subordinates. Like many authoritarian leaders, he had difficulty delegating authority, a trait that weakened his regime. Finally, in an age dominated by high-minded causes, he exhibited an instinctive distrust of ideology and the doctrinaire pronouncements of philosophes such as Rousseau. Napoleon's military training led him to take a pragmatic, disciplined approach to politics, in which he always sought the most effective means to the desired end.

Napoleon's acquisition of power was systematic and shrewd. Playing on the need for a strong leader, and using the army as his main political tool, he maneuvered himself into the position of first consul in 1799. In 1802 he became consul for life, and two years later he crowned himself emperor of the French and his wife Josephine empress. The title of emperor traditionally denoted the height of monarchical power.

EMPEROR NAPOLEON CROWNING HIS WIFE, JOSEPHINE, EMPRESS OF THE FRENCH IN THE CATHEDRAL OF NOTRE DAME, 1804

This painting by Jacques-Louis David depicts secular and religious figures gathered around Napoleon not as members of privileged orders, but as representatives of the nation. Pope Pius VII remains seated as Napoleon places the crown on Josephine's head. Napoleon had already crowned himself emperor of the French.

Source: Jacques Louis David (1748–1825), "Consecration of the Emperor Napoleon I and Coronation of Empress Josephine," 1806–07. Louvre, Paris. Bridgeman-Giraudon/Art Resource, NY

It is ironic that Napoleon, while continuing to hunt down and execute royalists, accepted a title of royalty himself and made his position, just like the French kingship, hereditary. As one royalist declared in 1804, "We have done more than we hoped. We meant to give France a king, and we have given her an emperor." Napoleon's coronation also made a negative impression outside France. The great German composer Ludwig van Beethoven, having dedicated his *Third Symphony* (1803) to Napoleon for overthrowing tyranny in France, scratched the emperor's name from the dedication after he assumed his new title the following year.

Napoleon and the Revolution

What was the relationship between Napoleon's rule and the French Revolution? Did Napoleon consolidate the gains of the revolution or destroy them? Did he simply redirect the revolutionary commitment to liberty, equality, and fraternity into more disciplined channels of expression after 1799? Or did he reverse the political trends that had prevailed from 1789 to 1799, crushing liberty in all its forms and establishing a ruthless, authoritarian dictatorship?

Napoleon always thought of himself as the heir of the revolution rather than its undertaker. He used the radical vocabulary of the revolution to characterize his domestic programs and his military campaigns. He presented himself as the ally of the common man against entrenched aristocratic privilege. He proclaimed a love for the French people and gave his support to the doctrine of popular sovereignty. He often referred to the rulers of other European countries as tyrants and presented himself as the liberator of their subjects.

Yet Napoleon's commitment to liberty was almost entirely rhetorical. Behind the appeals to the slogans of the revolution lurked a domineering will that was stronger than that of any eighteenth-century absolute monarch. Napoleon used the language of liberty and democracy to disguise a thoroughgoing authoritarianism, just as he used the rhetoric of republicanism to legitimize his own dictatorial regime. He orchestrated and controlled elections to make it appear that his rule reflected the will of the people. When the empire was established he told his troops that they had the freedom to vote for or against the new form of government, but that if they voted against it, they would be shot.

We can make a stronger case for Napoleon's egalitarianism. He demonstrated a commitment to providing equality of opportunity in the service of the state, and he supported the equality of all Frenchmen (but not Frenchwomen) before the law. This egalitarianism laid the foundation for the support he received from peasants, soldiers, and workers. He brought equality and political stability to France in exchange for political liberty. He synthesized the egalitarianism of the revolution with the authoritarianism of the Old Regime.

Napoleon was the heir of the revolution in two other ways. First, he continued the centralization and growth of state power and the rational organization of the administration that had begun in 1789. Each of the successive regimes between 1789 and 1815, even the Directory, had contributed to this pattern of state-building, and Napoleon's contribution was monumental. Second, he continued and extended France's military mission to export the revolution to its European neighbors. The two achievements are related to each other because the war effort necessitated the further growth and centralization of state power.

Napoleon and the French State

Once Napoleon had gained effective control of the French state, he sought to make it more efficient, organized, and powerful. In addition to turning the government into a de facto dictatorship, Napoleon settled the long struggle between Church and state, laid down a new law code that imposed legal uniformity on the entire country, and made the civil bureaucracy more centralized and uniform. He did all this with the intention of making the state an effective instrument of social and political control.

CONCORDAT WITH THE PAPACY Napoleon's first contribution to the development of the French state, achieved during the Consulate, was to resolve the bitter struggle between Church and state. A committed secularist, Napoleon was determined to bring the Church under the direct control of the state. This had been the main purpose of the Civil Constitution of the Clergy of 1790. Napoleon also realized, however, that the Civil Constitution had divided the clergy between those who had taken an oath to the nation and those who had refused. Clerical independence had also become a major rallying cry of royalists against the new regime, thereby threatening the stability of the country.

The death of Pope Pius VI (r. 1775–1799), an implacable foe of the revolution, gave Napoleon the opportunity to address this problem. The new pope, Pius VII (r. 1800–1823), who was more sympathetic to liberal causes, was eager to come to terms with the French government. The Concordat, which Napoleon and Pope Pius agreed to in 1801, gave something to both sides, although Napoleon gained more than he conceded. The pope agreed that all the clergy who refused to swear their loyalty to the nation would resign their posts, thus ending the bitter divisions of the past twelve years. The pope would appoint new bishops, but only with Napoleon's prior approval. The state would pay all clerical salaries, and the Church would abandon its claims to the ecclesiastical lands seized by the state at the beginning of the revolution.

These provisions represented formidable concessions to state power, and many French bishops found the terms of the Concordat too unfavorable to the Church. But the pope did manage to secure a statement that Roman Catholicism was the religion of the majority of citizens, and Napoleon agreed to scrap the secular calendar introduced in 1793, thereby restoring Sundays and holy days. Church attendance, having reached historic lows during the period of the Republic, began to rise. The Church regained respect and the freedom to function in French society, and more young recruits joined the clergy. Napoleon did not make many concessions to the Church, but they were significant enough to alienate a group of liberal philosophers and writers known as the Ideologues, who objected to what they saw as the return of "monkish superstition."

With the pope somewhat appeased, Napoleon took unilateral steps to regulate the administration of the French church. In a set of regulations known as the Organic Articles, which were added to the Concordat in 1802, the French church became a department of state, controlled by a ministry, just like any other bureaucratic department. Pronouncements from the pope required prior government approval, and the clergy were obliged to read government decrees from the pulpit. The state also gained control of Protestant congregations, which were given freedom of worship, and their ministers were also paid by the state. Jews received the protection of the state, but the government did not pay the salaries of rabbis.

THE CIVIL CODE Napoleon's most enduring achievement in the realm of state building was the promulgation of a new legal code, the Civil Code of 1804. A legal code is an authoritative and comprehensive statement of the law of a particular country. The model for modern legal codes in Europe was the *Corpus Juris Civilis* of the Roman Empire, which Justinian decreed at Constantinople between 529 and 534 C.E. That code had replaced the thousands of constitutions, customs, and judicial decisions that had been in effect during the Roman Republic and Empire. In compiling the new French code Napoleon, who had just proclaimed himself emperor of the French, imitated Justinian's legal achievement.

The Civil Code also met a long-standing set of demands to reform the confusing and irregular body of French law. Ever since the Middle Ages, France had been governed by a multiplicity of laws. In the southern provinces of the country, those closest to Italy, the law had been influenced by Roman law. In the north, the law was based on local or provincial customs. France needed a common law for all its people. Efforts to produce an authoritative written law code for all parts of the country had begun during the revolution, but Napoleon completed the project and published the code.

The Civil Code, which consisted of more than 2,000 articles, reflected the values of Napoleonic France. Articles guaranteeing the rights of private property, equality before the law, and freedom of religion enshrined key revolutionary ideas. The values promoted by the Civil Code, however, did not include the equality of the sexes. It granted men control of all family property. Women could not buy or sell property without the consent of their husbands. All male heirs were entitled to inherit equal shares of a family estate, but daughters were excluded from the settlement.

The Civil Code, which dealt only with the rights and relationships of private individuals, was the first and most important of six law codes promulgated by Napoleon. Others dealt with civil procedure (1806), commerce (1807), and criminal law (1811). Renamed the **Napoleonic Code** in 1806, the Civil Code had an impact on the law of several countries outside France. It became the basis for the codification of the laws of Switzerland, northern Italy, Poland, and the Netherlands, and it served as a model for the codes of many German territories controlled by France during the Napoleonic period. The Napoleonic Code also influenced the law of French-speaking North America, including the civil law of the state of Louisiana, which bears signs of its influence even today.

Administrative Centralization   Napoleon laid the foundation of modern French civil administration, which acquired the characteristics of rational organization, uniformity, and centralization. All power emanated from Paris, where Napoleon presided over a Council of State. This body consisted of his main ministers, who handled all matters of finance, domestic affairs, and war and oversaw a vast bureaucracy of salaried, trained officials. The central government also exercised direct control over the provinces. In each of the departments, the administrative

divisions of France organized in 1790, an official known as a *prefect,* appointed by the central government, enforced orders coming from Paris (see **Map 20.1**). Paid the handsome annual salary of 20,000 francs, the prefects were responsible for the maintenance of public order. They enforced conscription, collected taxes, and supervised local public works, such as the construction and improvement of roads.

The men who served in the government of the French Empire belonged to one of two elaborate, hierarchical institutions: the civil bureaucracy and the army officer corps. The two were closely related, because the main purpose of the administrative bureaucracy was to prepare for and sustain the war effort. Both institutions were organized hierarchically, and those who held positions in them were trained and salaried. Appointment and promotion were based primarily on talent rather than birth.

The idea of "a career open to all talents," as Napoleon described it, ran counter to the tradition of noble privilege. This was one of the achievements of the revolution that Napoleon perpetuated during the empire. The new system did not amount to a **meritocracy**, in which advancement depends solely on ability and performance, because Napoleon himself made or influenced many appointments on the basis of friendship or kinship. The system did, however, allow people from the ranks of the bourgeoisie to achieve upward social mobility. To recognize their new status, Napoleon created a new order of nonhereditary noblemen, known as *notables.* Instead of inheriting status, these men acquired their titles by governmental service. Napoleon created more than 3,500 notables during his rule, thereby encouraging service to the state and strengthening loyalty to it.

Napoleon, the Empire, and Europe

Closely related to Napoleon's efforts to build the French state was his creation of a sprawling European empire. This empire was the product of a series of military victories against the armies of Austria, Prussia, Russia, and Spain between

MAP 20.1

French Departments during the Revolution

In 1790 France was divided into the 83 departments, each roughly equal in population. A preoccupation with uniformity, a product of the Enlightenment, became a major feature of French revolutionary culture. Note the departments of Vendée, a major center of counterrevolution in 1793, and Gironde, from which the Girondins, the moderate Jacobin party, took its name.

1797 and 1809. The instrument of these victories was the massive army that Napoleon assembled. With more than one million men under arms, it was the largest military force controlled by one man up to this time in European history.

Napoleon's victories against Austria in 1797 and 1800 resulted in territorial gains in Italy and control over the southern Netherlands, now called Belgium. A temporary peace with Britain in 1802 gave Napoleon free rein to reorganize

CHRONOLOGY: THE CONSULATE AND THE EARLY YEARS OF THE EMPIRE, 1799–1806

1799
December 15 | Proclamation of the Constitution of the Consulate
1801
July 15 | Concordat with the Papacy
1804
March 21 | The Civil Code promulgated
December 2 | Napoleon crowned emperor of the French
1805
August | Third Coalition (Britain, Austria, and Russia) formed against France
1806
October 14 | French victories at the battles of Jena and Auerstädt
August 6 | Formal dissolution of the Holy Roman Empire

the countries that bordered on France's eastern and southeastern boundaries. In Italy he named himself the president of the newly established Cisalpine Republic, and he transformed the cantons of Switzerland into the Helvetic Republic. Victories over Prussian forces at Jena and Auerstädt in 1806 gave him the opportunity to carve a new German kingdom of Westphalia out of Prussian territory in the Rhineland and to install his brother Jerome as its ruler. In the east Napoleon created the duchy of Warsaw out of Polish lands he seized from Prussia and Austria. In 1806 he formally dissolved the ancient Holy Roman Empire and replaced it with a loose association of 16 German states known as the Confederation of the Rhine (see **Map 20.2**).

Napoleon's final step in his effort to achieve mastery of Europe was the invasion and occupation of Spain. This campaign began as an effort to crush Portugal, an ally of Britain. In May 1808, as French armies marched through Spain en route to Lisbon, the Portuguese capital, a popular insurrection against Spanish rule occurred in Madrid. This spontaneous revolt, which led to the abdication of King Charles IV and the succession of his son Ferdinand VII, was the first of many developments that caused the collapse of the Spanish Empire in America. In Europe it led to the absorption of Spain into the French Empire. Sensing that he could easily add one more territory to his list of conquests, Napoleon forced Ferdinand to abdicate and summoned his own brother, Joseph Bonaparte, to become king of Spain.

Joseph instituted some reforms in Spain, but the abolition of the Spanish Inquisition and the closing of two-thirds of the Spanish convents triggered a visceral reaction from the Spanish clergy and the general populace. Fighting for Church and king, small bands of local guerillas subjected French forces to intermittent and effective sabotage. An invasion by British forces under the command of Arthur Wellesley, later the Duke of Wellington (1769–1852), in what has become known as the Peninsular War (1808–1813), strengthened Spanish and Portuguese resistance.

The Downfall of Napoleon

The turning point in Napoleon's personal fortunes and those of his empire came in 1810. After securing a divorce from Josephine in late 1809 because she had not borne him an heir, he married Marie-Louise, the daughter of the Habsburg emperor. This diplomatic marriage, which produced a son and heir to the throne the following year, should have made the French Empire

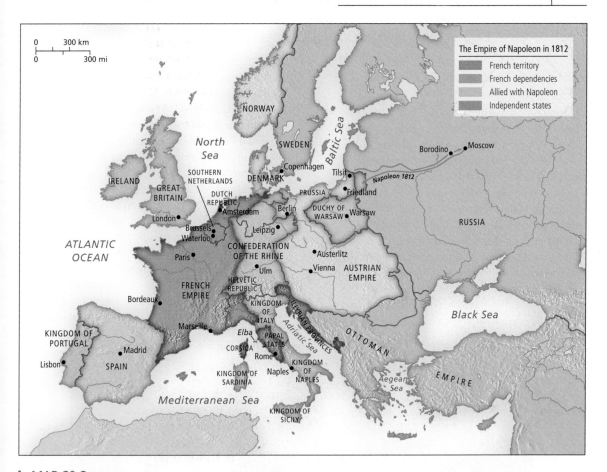

MAP 20.2

The Empire of Napoleon in 1812

At its peak the official French Empire had 44 million inhabitants. The population of dependent states in Spain, Italy, Germany, and Poland brought the population of the "Grand Empire" to 80 million people.

more secure, but it had the opposite effect. For the first time during his rule, Napoleon faced dissent from both the right and the left, provoked in part by his negotiations with the Austrian Habsburgs. Despite the most stringent efforts at censorship, royalist and Jacobin literature poured off the presses. The number of military deserters and those evading conscription increased. Relations with the papacy reached a breaking point when Napoleon annexed the Papal States, at which point Pope Pius VII, who had negotiated the Concordat of 1801, excommunicated him.

Dissent at home had the effect of driving the megalomaniacal emperor to seek more glory and

further conquests. In this frame of mind Napoleon made the ill-advised decision to invade Russia. The motives for engaging in this overly ambitious military campaign were not completely irrational. Victory over Russia promised to give France control of the Black Sea, and that in turn could ultimately have led to the control of Constantinople and the entire Middle East. More immediately, defeating Russia would have been necessary to enforce the French blockade of British goods, which Russia had refused to support.

The problem with a Russian invasion was that it stretched Napoleon's lines of communication

ENCOUNTERS AND TRANSFORMATIONS

The French Encounter the Egyptians, 1798–1801

Napoleon's expedition to Egypt in 1798 marked one of the few times during the revolutionary period that the French came in direct contact with non-Western peoples. The expedition resulted in the military occupation of the country for three years and set the stage for the first extensive encounters between Egyptians and Europeans since the Ottoman conquest of Egypt in the sixteenth century. At that time Egypt had become a semiautonomous province of the Ottoman Empire and had very little contact with the West. Egypt's isolation from the West meant that it had little exposure to the scientific and technological discoveries that had

taken place in western Europe during the previous 300 years.

In addition to 38,000 soldiers, Napoleon brought with him 165 scholars who were organized in a Commission of Science and Arts. These men came from virtually every branch of learning: surveyors, cartographers, civil engineers, architects, botanists, physicians, chemists, and mineralogists. The commission also included artists, archaeologists, writers, and musicians. Their purpose was to give Napoleon information on the people and the resources of the country so that he could more easily subject it to French domination. A small group of these scholars set up an Institute of Egypt, whose mission was to propagate the Enlightenment and to undertake

JEAN CHARLES TARDIEU, *THE FRENCH ARMY HALTS AT SYENE, UPPER EGYPT, ON FEBRUARY 2, 1799*

This painting depicts a cultural encounter between French soldiers and Egyptians in the city of Syene (now Aswan) during the Egyptian campaign of 1798–1799. The soldiers are scribbling on the ruins of ancient Egypt, indicating a lack of respect for Egyptian culture.

Source: Jean-Charles Tardieu (1765–1830), "Troops Halted on the Banks of the Nile, 2nd February 1812", oil on canvas. Chateau de Versailles, France/Lauros/Giraudon/The Bridgeman Art Library

research on the history, people, and the economy of the country. This involved the scholarly study of Egyptian antiquities, including the pyramids.

This work of the institute ushered in a long period in which many artifacts of Egyptian antiquity were taken from the country and transported to European museums and palaces. Members of the institute encouraged this cultural plundering, arguing that these Egyptian additions to the collections of the Louvre would embellish the glory of France. This ransacking of native Egyptian antiquities represented a form of cultural imperialism that continued unabated during the nineteenth century.

A description of Egypt, *Travels in Upper and Lower Egypt* (1802), written by a member of the institute, Dominique-Vivant Denon, reflected a different sort of French cultural imperialism. In this two-volume work Vivant Denon described the different "races" of Egyptians whom he had encountered in the port town of Rosetta. He described the Copts, the most ancient Egyptians, as "swarthy Nubians" with flat foreheads, high cheekbones, and short broad noses and tendencies toward "ignorance, drunkenness, cunning, and finesse." He described the physical and personal characteristics of the Arabs and the Turks in more appealing terms, but they too were often reduced to the "degraded state of animals."

Expressions of French cultural superiority permeated other contemporary accounts of Napoleon's expedition. A multivolume work, *The Description of Egypt,* claimed that Napoleon wanted to procure for Egyptians "all the advantages of a perfected civilization." It praised him for bringing modern knowledge to a country that had been "plunged into darkness." These attitudes provided a justification for the subsequent economic exploitation of Egypt, first by the French and later by the British, during the nineteenth century.

For Discussion

In what ways did Vivant Denon's work reflect the values that were cultivated during the Enlightenment?

---

too far and his resources too thin. Even before the invasion it was becoming increasingly difficult to feed, equip, and train the huge army he had assembled. The Grand Army that crossed from Poland into Russia in 1812 was not the efficient military force that Napoleon had commanded in the early years of the empire. Many of his best soldiers were fighting in the guerilla war in Spain. Casualties and desertions had forced Napoleon to call up new recruits who were not properly trained. Half the army, moreover, had been recruited from the population of conquered countries, making their loyalty to Napoleon uncertain.

The tactics of the Russians contributed to the failure of the invasion. Instead of engaging the Grand Army in combat, the Russian army kept retreating, pulling Napoleon further east toward Moscow. On September 7 the two armies clashed at Borodino, suffering a staggering 77,000 casualties in all. The Russian army then continued its retreat eastward. When Napoleon reached Moscow he found it deserted, and fires deliberately set by Muscovites had destroyed more than two-thirds of the city. Napoleon, facing the onset of a dreaded Russian winter and rapidly diminishing supplies, began the long retreat back to France. Skirmishes with the Russians along the way, which cost him 25,000 lives just crossing the Beresina River, conspired with the cold and hunger to destroy his army. During the entire Russian campaign his army lost a total of 380,000 men to death, imprisonment, or desertion. In the midst of this horror Napoleon, oblivious to the suffering of his troops, reported back to Paris, "The health of the emperor has never been better."

Not to be discouraged, Napoleon soon began preparing for further conquests. Once again his enemies formed a coalition against him, pledging to restore the independence of the countries that had become his satellites or dependents. Napoleon scored a few victories in the late summer of 1813, but in October allied forces inflicted a crushing defeat on him in the Battle of the Nations at Leipzig. Austrian troops administered another blow to the French in northern

FRANCISCO GOYA, *THE THIRD OF MAY 1808*

This painting of the suppression of the popular revolt in Madrid in 1808 captures the brutality of the French occupation of Spain. A French unit executes Spanish citizens, including a monk in the foreground. Goya was a figure of the Enlightenment and a Spanish patriot.

Italy, and the British finally drove them out of Spain. Napoleon's army was pushed back into France. A massive allied force advanced into Paris and occupied the city. After extensive political maneuvering, including a vote by the Senate to depose him, Napoleon abdicated on April 6, 1814. The allies promptly exiled him to the Mediterranean island of Elba. As he made the journey to the coast, crowds surrounding his coach shouted "Down with the tyrant!" while some villagers hanged him in effigy.

This course of events led to the restoration of the Bourbon monarchy. By the terms of the first Treaty of Paris of May 1814, the allies restored the brother of Louis XVI, the Count of Provence, to the French throne as Louis XVIII (r. 1814–1824). An implacable foe of the revolution, Louis strove to undermine its achievements. The white Bourbon flag replaced the revolutionary tricolor. Catholicism was once again recognized as the state religion. Exiled royalists returned to their high-ranking positions in the army. Nonetheless, Louis accepted a Constitutional Charter that incorporated many of the changes made between 1789 and 1791. Representative government, with a relatively limited franchise, replaced the absolutism of the Old Regime. The Constitutional Charter reaffirmed equality before the law, freedom of religion, and freedom of expression. Even more important, the powers of the state that the National Assembly and the Directory had extended and Napoleon had enhanced were maintained. The administrative division of France into departments continued, and the Napoleonic Code remained in force.

France had experienced a counterrevolution in 1814, but it did not simply turn the political clock back to 1788. Some of the political achievements of the previous 25 years were preserved.

Despite his disgrace and exile, Napoleon still commanded loyalty from his troops and large segments of the population. While in power he had constructed a legend that drew on strong patriotic sentiment. Supporters throughout France continued to promote his cause in the same way that royalists had maintained that of the Bourbon monarchy since 1792. The strength of the Napoleonic legend became apparent in March 1815, when Napoleon escaped from Elba and landed in southern France. Promising to rid the country of the exiled royalists who had returned and thereby save the revolutionary cause, he won over peasants, workers, and soldiers. Regiment after regiment joined him as he marched toward Paris. By the time he arrived, Louis XVIII had gone into exile once again, and Napoleon found himself back in power.

CHRONOLOGY: THE DOWNFALL OF NAPOLEON, 1810–1815

1810

April 2	Marriage of Napoleon to Marie-Louise

1812

September 7	Battle of Borodino
September 14	Napoleon enters Moscow
October	Retreat from Moscow begins

1813

October 16–19	Battle of the Nations at Leipzig

1814

April 6	Abdication of Napoleon
May 30	First Treaty of Paris
September	Congress of Vienna assembles

1815

March	Napoleon escapes from Elba
June 18	Battle of Waterloo
November 20	Second Treaty of Paris

But not for long. The allied European powers quickly began to assemble yet another coalition. Fearing that the allies would launch a massive invasion of France, Napoleon decided to strike first. He marched an army of 200,000 men into the Austrian Netherlands, where the allies responded by amassing 700,000 troops. Near the small village of Waterloo, south of Brussels, Napoleon met the British forces of the Duke of Wellington, who had turned the tide against him during the Peninsula War. Reinforced by Prussian troops, Wellington inflicted a devastating defeat on the French army, which lost 28,000 men and went into a full-scale retreat. Napoleon abdicated once again and was exiled to the remote South Atlantic island of St. Helena, from which escape was impossible. He died there in 1821.

Even before the Battle of Waterloo, the major powers of Europe had gathered in Vienna to redraw the boundaries of the European states that had been created, dismembered, or transformed during the preceding 52 years (see **Map 20.3**). Under the leadership of the Austrian foreign minister, Prince Klemens von Metternich (1773–1859), this conference, known as the **Congress of Vienna,** worked out a settlement that was intended to preserve the balance of power in Europe and at the same time uphold the principle of dynastic legitimacy. By the terms of a separate Treaty of Paris (the second in two years) the boundaries of France were scaled back to what they had been in 1790, before it had begun its wars of expansion. To create a buffer state on the northern boundary of France, the Congress annexed the Austrian Netherlands to the Dutch Republic, which now became the Kingdom of the Netherlands with William I, a prince of the House of Orange, as its king. The treaty ceded territory along the Rhineland to Prussia, while Austria, now named the Austrian Empire, gained territory in Italy. In place of the defunct Holy Roman Empire, the Congress established a new German Confederation, a loose coalition of 39 separate territories with a weak legislative assembly. The duchy of Warsaw, established in 1807 and renamed the Kingdom of

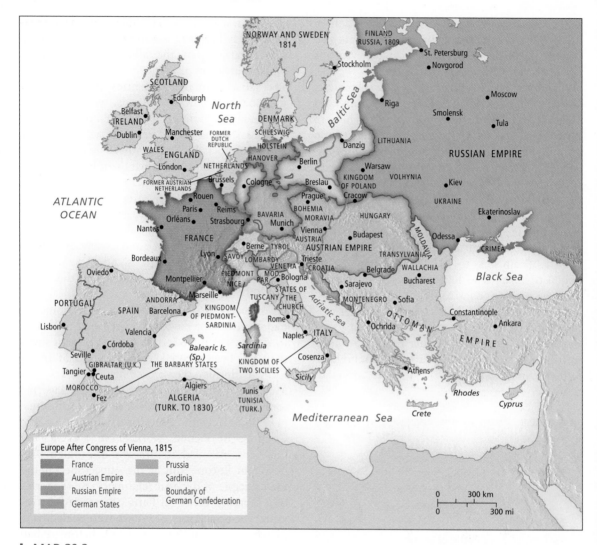

MAP 20.3

Europe After the Congress of Vienna, 1815

The Congress scaled back the boundaries of France to their status in 1790, ceded territory to Austria in western and northeastern Italy; created the kingdom of the Netherlands, a new German Confederation, and a new Kingdom of Poland ruled by Russia. The western part of Poland was ceded to Prussia.

Poland in 1812, was partitioned between Prussia and Russia. The five major powers that had drawn this new map of Europe—Britain, Austria, Prussia, Russia, and France—agreed to meet annually to prevent any one country, especially France but also Russia, from achieving military dominance of the European Continent.

THE LEGACY OF THE FRENCH REVOLUTION

■ What did the French Revolution ultimately achieve and in what ways did it change the course of European and Western history?

With the conclusion of the Congress of Vienna a tumultuous period of European and Western history finally came to an end. Not only had France experienced a revolution, but every country in Europe and America had felt its effects. Governments were toppled in countries as far apart as Poland and Peru. Added to this turbulence was the experience of incessant warfare. France was at war for more than 20 years during the Republic and the Empire, and it had involved almost all European powers in the struggle. With armies constantly in need of provisions and supplies, high taxation, galloping inflation, and food shortages inflicted economic hardship on a large portion of the European population.

The cost of all this instability and warfare in terms of human life was staggering. Within the space of one generation almost two million European soldiers were killed in action, wasted by disease, or starved or frozen to death. In France alone just under 500,000 soldiers died during the revolutionary wars of 1792–1802 and another 916,000 during the wars of the Empire. Internal political disturbances took the lives of hundreds of thousands of civilians from all ranks of society, not only in France, but throughout Europe. Unprecedented fears of internal and external subversion fed the violence at all levels. Government officials, collaborators, counterrevolutionaries, and imagined enemies of the state were all executed. This spate of violence and death—much of it in the name of liberty—occurred almost entirely at the hands of the state or its enemies.

What was achieved at this extraordinary price? How did the France of 1815 differ from the France of 1788? What on balance had changed? Historians once argued that as a result of the revolution the bourgeoisie, composed of merchants, manufacturers, and other commoners of substantial wealth, had replaced the nobility as the dominant social and political class in France. This argument can no longer be sustained. The nobility certainly lost many of their privileges in 1789, and many of them went into exile during the revolutionary period, but the position they had in French society in 1815 did not differ greatly from what it had been under the Old Regime. In both periods there was considerable blurring of the distinctions between nobility and bourgeoisie. Nor did the revolutionary period witness the emergence of a new class of industrial entrepreneurs. The only group that definitely profited from the revolution in the long run were men of property, regardless of their membership in any social category or "class." Wealthy men emerged triumphant in the Directory, found favor during the Napoleonic period, and became the most important members of political society after the monarchy was restored.

It would be difficult to argue that *women* of any social rank benefited from the revolution. During the early years of the revolution, women participated actively in public life. They were involved in many demonstrations in Paris, including the storming of the Bastille and the march to Versailles. But women never achieved the position of equality with men for which the Marquis de Condorcet and Olympe de Gouges had hoped. The radical Jacobins dealt that goal a major setback when they banned all women's clubs and societies on the grounds that female participation in public life would harm the institution of the family. This action ended the extensive participation of women in political life, which had begun during the eighteenth century, especially in the salons. During the nineteenth century French women exercised influence in the private sphere of the home, but not in the public sphere of politics.

It is even more difficult to identify permanent economic changes as a result of the revolution. The elimination of the remnants of feudalism may have made France marginally more capitalist than it had been before the revolution, but agricultural and mercantile capitalism had long been entrenched in French society. Nor did the Continental System, the blockade of British goods from all European ports initiated in 1806, allow French industry to catch up with that of Great Britain. Whatever economic gains were made under the protective shield of the state were offset by the adverse economic effects of 22 years of nearly continuous warfare. In the long run the revolutionary period delayed the process of industrialization that had entered its preliminary stages in France during the 1780s and retarded the growth of the French economy for the remainder of the nineteenth century.

The permanent legacy of the French Revolution lies in the realm of politics. First, the period from 1789 to 1815 triggered an enormous growth in the competence and power of the state. This trend had begun before the revolution, but the desire of the revolutionaries to transform every aspect of human life in the service of the revolution, coupled with the necessity of utilizing all the country's resources in the war effort, gave the state more control over the everyday life of its citizens than ever before. Fifteen years of Napoleonic rule only accentuated this trend, and after 1815 many of those powers remained with the government.

A second permanent political achievement of the French Revolution was the promotion of the doctrine of popular sovereignty. The belief that the people constituted the highest political authority in the state became so entrenched during the revolution that it could never be completely suppressed, either in France or in the other countries of Europe. Napoleon recognized its power when he asked the people to approve political changes he had already made by his own authority. After the restoration of the monarchy the doctrine of popular sovereignty was promoted mainly by the press, which continued to employ the new revolutionary rhetoric to keep alive the high ideals and aspirations of the revolution. The doctrine also contributed to the formation of two nineteenth-century ideologies, liberalism and nationalism, which will be discussed in Chapter 22.

CONCLUSION

The French Revolution and Western Civilization

The French Revolution was a central event in the history of the West. It began as an internal French affair, reflecting the social and political tensions of the Old Regime, but it soon became a turning point in European and Western history. Proclamations of the natural rights of humanity gave the ideals of the revolution widespread appeal, and a period of protracted warfare succeeded in disseminating those ideals outside the boundaries of France.

Underlying the export of French revolutionary ideology was the belief that France had become the standard-bearer of Western civilization. French people believed they were *la grande nation*, the country that had reached the highest level of political and social organization. They did not believe they had acquired this exalted status by inheritance. Unlike the English revolutionaries of the seventeenth century, the French did not claim that they were the heirs of a medieval constitution. French republicans of the 1790s attributed none of their national preeminence to the monarchy, whose memory they took drastic steps to erase. They considered the secular political culture that emerged during the French Revolution to be entirely new.

The export of French revolutionary political culture during the Republic and the Empire led to widespread changes in the established order. Regimes were toppled, French puppets acquired political power, boundaries of states were redrawn, and traditional authorities were challenged. Liberal reforms were enacted, new constitutions were written, and new law codes were promulgated. The Europe of 1815 could not be mistaken for the Europe of 1789.

The ideas of the French Revolution, like those of the Enlightenment that had helped to inspire them, did not go unchallenged. From the very early years of the revolution they encountered determined opposition, both in France and abroad. As the revolution lost its appeal in France, the forces of conservatism and reaction gathered strength. At the end of the Napoleonic period, the Congress of Vienna took steps to restore the legitimate rulers of European states and to prevent revolution from recurring. It appeared that the revolution would be completely reversed, but that was not the case. The ideas born of the revolution continued to inspire demands for political reform in Europe during the nineteenth century, and those demands, just like those in the 1790s, met with fierce resistance.

KEY TERMS

estates
Third Estate
Jacobins
sans-culottes
universal male suffrage
Girondins
The Mountain
Republic of Virtue

Reign of Terror
plebiscite
de-Christianization
Napoleonic Code
departments
meritocracy
Congress of Vienna

CHAPTER QUESTIONS

1. Why did the Old Regime in France collapse in 1789, and what revolutionary changes took place in French government and society during the next two years? (page 620)
2. How did a second, more radical revolution, which began with the establishment of the Republic in 1792, lead to the creation of a regime that used the power of the state to institute the Reign of Terror? (page 623)
3. In what ways did the political events of the revolution change French culture? (page 634)
4. Did the authoritarian rule of Napoleon Bonaparte from 1799 to 1814 confirm or betray the achievements of the French Revolution, and what impact did his military conquests have on Europe and the world? (page 638)
5. What did the French Revolution ultimately achieve and in what ways did it change the course of European and Western history? (page 650)

TAKING IT FURTHER

1. Did the events of 1789 constitute a revolution in the sense that they brought about a fundamental change in the system of government? In what sense did the establishment of the Republic in 1792 represent a more radical change in French politics?
2. To what extent did the ideas of the Enlightenment inspire the events of the French Revolution?
3. How did the Jacobin commitment to equality lead to the Reign of Terror?
4. Did the French Revolution end in 1799 or did Napoleon perpetuate it in any significant ways?
5. Why did Napoleon fail to realize his diplomatic and military objectives?

✓●─┤Practice on MyHistoryLab

absolutism (p. 492)   A form of government in the seventeenth and eighteenth centuries in which a ruler possessed unrivalled power.

acropolis (p. 79)   The defensible hilltop around which a polis grew. In classical Athens, the Acropolis was the site of the Parthenon (Temple of Athena).

Aeneid (p. 182)   Written by Virgil (70–19 B.C.E.), this magnificent epic poem celebrates the emperor Augustus by linking him to his mythical ancestor, Aeneas, the Trojan refugee who founded the Roman people. Considered by many to be the greatest work of Latin literature, the poem has had enormous influence in the West.

agora (p. 79)   An open area in the town center of a Greek polis that served as a market and a place for informal discussion.

agricultural revolution (p. 300)   Refers to technological innovations that began to appear during the eleventh century, making possible a dramatic growth in population. The agricultural revolution came about through harnessing new sources of power with water and wind mills, improving the pulling power of animals with better collars, using heavy plows to better exploit the soils of northern Europe, and employing a three-field crop rotation system that increased the amount and quality of food available.

agricultural societies (p. 65)   Settled communities in which people depend on farming and raising livestock as their sources of food.

alchemy (p. 534)   A form of learned magic that was intended to turn base metals into precious ones.

aldeias (p. 414)   Settlements for natives who had converted to Christianity in Brazil. In these settlements the Jesuit fathers protected the natives from enslavement.

Alexandrianism (p. 130)   A style of Hellenistic poetry that demonstrated a command of meter and language and appealed more to the intellect than the emotions.

Allies (p. 785)   During World War I, the states allied against the Central Powers of Germany and Austria-Hungary. During World War II, the states allied against the regimes of Nazi Germany, fascist Italy and imperial Japan.

Amarna Letters (p. 44)   A collection of over 370 cuneiform tablets discovered at Tell El-Amarna in 1887 that contains the diplomatic and imperial correspondence of the pharaohs from the mid-fourteenth century B.C.E.

Amarna Period (p. 39)   Time of religious ferment during the reign of Amenhotep IV (1351–1334 B.C.E.) in New Kingdom Egypt.

Anabaptism (p. 447)   Meaning "to rebaptize;" refers to those Protestant radicals of the sixteenth century who rejected infant baptism and adopted adult baptism. Anabaptists treated the Bible as a blueprint for reforming not just the church but all of society, a tendency that led them to reject the authority of the state, to live in self-governing "holy communities," and in some cases to practice a primitive form of communism.

anarchism (p. 737)   Ideology that views the state as unnecessary and repressive and rejects participation in parliamentary politics in favor of direct, usually violent, action.

anticlericalism (p. 765)   Opposition to the political influence of the Roman Catholic Church.

Antonine Decree (p. 180)   In 212 C.E. the emperor Aurelius Antoninus, called Caracalla, issued a decree that granted citizenship to all the free inhabitants of the Roman Empire. The decree enabled Roman law to embrace the entire population of the empire.

apartheid (p. 904)   System of racial segregation and discrimination put into place in South Africa in 1948.

appeasement (p. 860)   British diplomatic and financial efforts to stabilize Germany in the 1920s and 1930s and so avoid a second world war.

Arians (p. 213)   Christians who believe that God the Father is superior to Jesus Christ his Son. Most of the Germanic settlers in western Europe in the fifth century were Arians.

aristocracy (p. 587)   A term that originally applied to those who were considered the most fit to rule and later identified the wealthiest members of society, especially those who owned land.

asceticism (p. 215)   The Christian practice of severely suppressing physical needs and daily desires in an effort to achieve a spiritual union with God. Asceticism is the practice that underlies the monastic movement.

Auschwitz (p. 880)   Technically Auschwitz-Birkenau; death camp in Poland that has become the symbol of the Holocaust.

auto-da-fé (p. 466)   Meaning literally a "theater of faith," an *auto* was practiced by the Catholic Church in early modern Spain and Portugal as an extended public ritual of penance designed to cause physical pain among the sinful and promote fear of God's judgment among those who witnessed it.

Babylonian Captivity of the Church (p. 354)   Between 1305 and 1378 seven consecutive popes voluntarily chose to reside in Avignon, France, in order to escape anarchy in the streets of Rome. During this period the popes became subservient to the kings of France.

Babylonian Exile (p. 67)   The period of Jewish history between the destruction of Solomon's temple in Jerusalem by Babylonian armies in 587 B.C.E., and 538 B.C.E, when Cyrus of Persia permitted Jews to return to Palestine and rebuild the temple.

balance of power (p. 501)   An arrangement in which various countries form alliances to prevent any one state from dominating the others.

Balfour Declaration (p. 817)   Declaration of 1917 that affirmed British support of a Jewish state in Palestine.

barbarians (p. 108)   A term used by Greeks to describe people who did not speak Greek and who were therefore considered uncivilized.

baroque (pp. 126, 498)   A dynamic style in art, architecture, and music that was intended to elicit an emotional response. Baroque buildings were massive, imposing structures with sweeping façades. The baroque style represented a development of Greek classicism in the Hellenistic period. In the seventeenth century the baroque style was closely associated with royal absolutism.

Berlin Wall (p. 908)   Constructed by the East German government, the wall physically cut the city of Berlin in two and prevented East German citizens from access to West Germany; stood from 1961 to 1989.

Big Three (p. 892)   Term applied to the British, Soviet, and U.S. leaders during World War II: until 1945, Winston Churchill, Joseph Stalin, and Franklin Roosevelt; by the summer of 1945, Clement Atlee, Joseph Stalin, and Harry Truman.

Black Death (p. 332)   An epidemic disease, possibly Bubonic plague, that struck Europe between 1348

and the 1350s killing at least one-third of the total population.

blitzkrieg (p. 861)   "Lightning war;" offensive military tactic making use of airplanes, tanks, and motorized infantry to punch through enemy defenses and secure key territory. First demonstrated by the German army in World War II.

Bolsheviks (p. 809)   Minority group of Russian socialists, headed by Vladimir Lenin, who espoused an immediate transition to a socialist state. It became the Communist Party in the Soviet Union.

boule (p. 83)   A council of 400 male citizens established by Solon in Greece in the sixth century B.C.E. It served as an advisory body for the general assembly of all male citizens.

Bourbon reforms (p. 560)   Measures introduced by the Bourbon Kings of Spain in the eighteenth century to make the Spanish empire more manageable and profitable.

bourgeoisie (p. 594)   A social group, technically consisting of those who were burghers in the towns, that included prosperous merchants and financiers, members of the professions, and some skilled craftsmen known as "petty bourgeoisie."

boyars (p. 488)   Upper-level nobles who dominated Russian society until the tsars began to supplant them in the fifteenth and sixteenth centuries.

Bretton Woods Agreement (p. 894)   Agreement signed in 1944 that established the post-World War II economic framework in which the U.S. dollar served as the world's reserve currency.

brinkmanship (p. 905)   Style of Cold War confrontation in which each superpower endeavored to convince the other that it was willing to wage nuclear war.

bronze (p. 36)   An alloy of tin and copper that produces a hard metal suitable for weapons, tools, ornaments, and household objects. Bronze production began about 3200 B.C.E.

Byzantine Empire (p. 225)   The eastern half of the Roman Empire, which lasted from the founding of Constantinople in 324 to its conquest by the Ottoman Turks in 1453.

caliphate (p. 250)   The Islamic imperial government that evolved under the leadership of Abu Bakr (r. 632–634), the successor of the prophet Muhammad. The sectarian division within Islam between the Shi'ites and Sunni derived from a disagreement over how to determine the hereditary succession from Muhammad to the caliphate, which combined governmental and some religious responsibilities.

calling (p. 442) The Calvinist doctrine that God calls the Elect to perform his will on earth. God's calling gave Calvinists a powerful sense of personal direction.

canon law (p. 276) The collected laws of the Roman Catholic Church. Canon law applied to cases involving the clergy, disputes about church property, and donations to the Church. It also applied to the laity for annulling marriages, legitimating bastards, prosecuting bigamy, protecting widows and orphans, and resolving inheritance disputes.

capital (p. 663) All the physical assets used in production, including fixed capital, such as machinery, and circulating capital, such as raw materials; more generally the cost of these physical assets.

caravels (p. 397) Hybrid three-masted ships developed about 1450 in the Iberian peninsula by combining the rigging of square with triangular lateen sails. These ships could be sailed in a variety of winds, carry large cargoes, be managed by a small crew, and be defended by guns mounted in the castle superstructure.

Carolingian Renaissance (p. 275) The "rebirth" of interest in ancient Greek and Latin literature and language during the reign of the Frankish emperor Charlemagne (r. 768–814). Charlemagne promoted the intensive study of Latin to promote governmental efficiency and to propagate the Christian faith.

Catholic Reformation (p. 450) A series of efforts during the sixteenth century to purify the Church that evolved out of late medieval spirituality and that included the creation of new religious orders, especially the Society of Jesus.

Central Powers (p. 785) Germany and Austria-Hungary in World War I.

Chalcedonians (p. 213) Christians who followed the doctrinal decisions and definitions of the Council of Chalcedon in 451 C.E. stating that Christ's human and divine natures were equal, but entirely distinct and united in one person "without confusion, division, separation, or change." Chalcedonian Christianity came to be associated with the Byzantine Empire and is called Greek Orthodoxy. In western Europe it is known as Roman Catholicism.

Chartists (p. 702) A British group of workers and middle-class radicals who drafted a People's Charter in 1837 demanding universal male suffrage and other political reforms.

chinoiserie (p. 578) A French word for an eighteenth-century decorative art that combined Chinese and European motifs.

Christian Democracy, Christian Democratic parties (p. 916) Conservative and confessionally based (Roman Catholic) political parties that dominated much of western European politics after World War II.

Christian humanists (p. 430) During the fifteenth and sixteenth centuries these experts in Greek, Latin, and Hebrew subjected the Bible to philological study in an attempt to understand the precise meaning of the founding text of Christianity.

Church Fathers (p. 220) Writers in Late Antiquity from both the Greek and Latin-speaking worlds who sought to reconcile Christianity with classical learning.

circuit court (p. 321) Established by King Henry II (r. 1154–1189) to make royal justice available to virtually anyone in England. Circuit court judges visited every shire in England four times a year.

civic humanism (p. 378) A branch of humanism introduced by the Florentine chancellor Leonardo Bruni who defended the republican institutions and values of the city. Civic humanism promoted the ethic of responsible citizenship.

civilization (p. 12) The term used by archaeologists to describe a society differentiated by levels of wealth and power, and in which religious, economic, and political control are based in cities.

civil society (p. 935) Public organizations and activities separate from the state, commerce, or the family that help to create community life.

clans or kin groups (p. 267) The basic social and political unit of Germanic society consisting of blood relatives obliged to defend one another and take vengeance for crimes against the group and its members.

class consciousness (p. 674) The awareness of people from different occupations that they belonged to a class.

classicism (p. 591) A style in art, architecture, music, and literature that emphasizes proportion, adherence to traditional forms, and a rejection of emotion and enthusiasm.

Cluny (p. 306) A monastery founded in Burgundy in 910 that became the center of a far-reaching movement to reform the Church that was sustained in more than 1,500 Cluniac monasteries, modeled after the original in Cluny.

Cold War (p. 892)   Struggle for global supremacy between the United States and the Soviet Union, waged from the end of World War II until 1990.

collectivization (p. 840)   The replacement of private and village farms with large cooperative agricultural enterprises run by state-employed managers. Collectivization was a key part of Joseph Stalin's plans for modernizing the Soviet economy and destroying peasant opposition to communist rule.

colons (p. 581)   White planters in the French Caribbean colony of Saint Domingue (Haiti).

Columbian exchange (p. 418)   The trade of peoples, plants, animals, microbes, and ideas between the Old and New Worlds that began with Columbus.

Columbian question (p. 420)   The debate among historians and epidemiologists about whether syphilis or its ancestor disease originated in the Americas and was brought to the Old World after Columbus's voyages.

Common Market (p. 917)   Originally comprising West Germany, France, Italy, Belgium, Luxembourg, and the Netherlands, the Common Market was formed in 1957 to integrate its members' economic structures and so foster both economic prosperity and international peace. Also called the European Economic Community (EEC). Evolved into the European Union (EU).

communes (p. 303)   Sworn defensive associations of merchants and workers that appeared in north-central Italy after 1070 and that became the effective government of more than a hundred cities. The communes evolved into city-states by seizing control of the surrounding countryside.

communism (p. 690)   The revolutionary form of socialism developed by Karl Marx and Friedrich Engels that promoted the overthrow of bourgeois or capitalist institutions and the establishment of a dictatorship of the proletariat.

Companions (p. 110)   Elite regiments of cavalrymen armed with heavy lances formed by Philip of Macedon.

Concert of Europe (p. 696)   The joint efforts made by Austria, Prussia, Russia, Britain, and France during the years following the Congress of Vienna to suppress liberal and nationalist movements throughout Europe.

Conciliar Movement (p. 354)   A fifteenth-century movement that advocated ending the Great Schism and reforming church government by calling a general meeting or council of the bishops, who would exercise authority over the rival popes.

confessions (p. 456)   The formal sixteenth-century statements of religious doctrine: the Confession of Augsburg for Lutherans, the Helvetic Confessions for Calvinists, the Thirty-Nine Articles for Anglicans, and the decrees of the Council of Trent for Catholics.

Congress of Vienna (p. 649)   A conference of the major powers of Europe in 1814–1815 to establish a new balance of power at the end of the Napoleonic Wars.

conquistadores (p. 408)   Spanish adventurers in the Americas who explored and conquered the lands of indigenous peoples, sometimes without legal authority but usually with a legal privilege granted by the king of Spain who required that one-fifth of all things of value be turned over to the crown. The conquistadores extended Spanish sovereignty over new lands.

conservatism (p. 686)   A nineteenth-century ideology intended to prevent a recurrence of the revolutionary changes of the 1790s and the implementation of liberal policies.

containment (p. 896)   Cold War policy of blocking communist expansion; inaugurated by the Truman Doctrine in 1947.

corporatism (p. 834)   The practice by which committees (or "corporations") made up of representatives of workers, employers, and the state direct the economy.

Corpus Juris Civilis (pp. 143, 226)   The body of Roman law compiled by the emperor Justinian in Constantinople in 534. The Corpus became a pillar of Latin-speaking European civilization.

Cortes (p. 494)   Legislative assemblies in the Spanish kingdoms.

cosmology (p. 134)   A theory concerning the structure and nature of the universe such as those proposed by Aristotle in the fourth century B.C.E. and Copernicus in the sixteenth century.

counties (p. 275)   Territorial units devised by the Carolingian dynasty during the eighth and ninth centuries for the administration of the empire. Each county was administered by a count who was rewarded with lands and sent to areas where he had no family ties to serve as a combined provincial governor, judge, military commander, and representative of the king.

courtly love (p. 326)   An ethic first found in the poems of the late twelfth- and thirteenth-century troubadours that portrayed the ennobling possibilities of the love between a man and a woman. Courtly love formed the basis for the modern idea of romantic love.

creoles (p. 560) People of Spanish descent who had been born in Spanish America.

Crusades (p. 288) Between 1095 and 1291, Latin Christians heeding the call of the pope launched eight major expeditions and many smaller ones against Muslim armies in an attempt to gain control of and hold Jerusalem.

Cubism (p. 763) Modernist artistic movement of the early twentieth century that emphasized the fragmentation of human perception through visual experiments with geometric forms.

cultural relativism (p. 422) A mode of thought first explored during the sixteenth century to explain why the peoples of the New World did not appear in the Bible. Cultural relativism recognized that many (but not necessarily all) standards of judgment are specific to particular cultures rather than the fixed truths established by natural or divine law.

culture (p. 12) The knowledge and adaptive behavior created by communities that helps them to mediate between themselves and the natural world through time.

cuneiform (p. 24) A kind of writing in which wedge-shaped symbols are pressed into clay tablets to indicate words and ideas. Cuneiform writing originated in ancient Sumer.

curia (p. 309) The administrative bureaucracy of the Roman Catholic Church.

Cynics (p. 132) Followers of the teachings of Antisthenes (ca. 445–360 B.C.E.) who rejected pleasures, possessions, and social conventions to find peace of mind.

Darwinian theory of evolution (p. 753) Scientific theory associated with nineteenth-century scientist Charles Darwin that highlights the role of variation and natural selection in the evolution of species.

Decembrists (p. 697) Russian liberals who staged a revolt against Tsar Nicholas I on the first day of his reign in December 1825.

de-Christianization (p. 636) A program inaugurated in France in 1793 by the radical Jacobin and former priest Joseph Fouché that closed churches, eliminated religious symbols, and attempted to establish a purely civic religion.

decolonization (p. 904) The retreat of Western powers from their imperial territories.

deduction, deductive reasoning (pp. 24, 536) The logical process by which ideas and laws are derived from basic truths or principles.

Defenders (p. 582) Irish Catholic peasants who joined the United Irishmen in the rebellion against Britain in 1798.

deists (p. 545) Seventeenth- and eighteenth-century thinkers who believed that God created the universe and established immutable laws of nature but did not subsequently intervene in the operation of nature or in human affairs.

Delian League (p. 92) The alliance among many Greek cities organized by Athens in 478 B.C.E. in order to fight Persian forces in the eastern Aegean Sea. The Athenians gradually turned the Delian League into the Athenian Empire.

demand (p. 664) The desire of consumers to acquire goods and the need of producers to acquire raw materials and machinery.

democracy (p. 82) A form of government in which citizens devise their own governing institutions and choose their leaders; began in Athens, Greece, in the fifth century B.C.E.

de-Stalinization (p. 912) Nikita Khrushchev's effort to decentralize political and economic control in the Soviet Union after 1956.

détente (p. 930) During the 1970s, a period of lessened Cold War hostilities and greater reliance on negotiation and compromise.

dialectic (p. 688) The theory that history advanced in stages as the result of the conflict between different ideas or social groups.

dialectical materialism (p. 689) The socialist philosophy of Karl Marx according to which history advanced as the result of material or economic forces and would lead to the creation of a classless society.

Diaspora (p. 195) Literally "dispersion of population;" usually used to refer to the dispersion of the Jewish population after the Roman destruction of the Temple in Jerusalem in 70 C.E.

diets (p. 494) Legislative assemblies in German territories.

divination (p. 24) The practice of discerning the future by looking for messages imprinted in nature.

divine right (p. 494) The theory that rulers received their power directly from God.

division of labor (p. 660) The assignment of one stage of production to a single worker or group of workers to increase efficiency and productive output.

domestication (p. 13)   Manipulating the breeding of animals over many generations in order to make them more useful to humans as sources of food, wool, and other byproducts. Domestication of animals began about 10,000 years ago.

domestic system (p. 660)   An economic arrangement developed in the sixteenth century in which capitalist entrepreneurs employed families in rural areas to spin and weave cloth and make nails and cutlery.

Dreyfus Affair (p. 730)   The trials of Captain Alfred Dreyfus on treason charges dominated French political life in the decade after 1894 and revealed fundamental divisions in French society.

dualistic (pp. 88, 537)   A term used to describe a philosophy or a religion in which a rigid distinction is made between body and mind, good and evil, or the material and the immaterial world.

Dutch Revolt (p. 479)   The rebellion against Spanish rule of the seven northern provinces of the Netherlands between 1579 and 1648, which resulted in the independence of the Republic of the United Provinces.

Edict of Nantes (p. 477)   Promulgated by King Henry IV in 1598, the edict allowed the Huguenots to build a quasi-independent state within the kingdom of France, giving them the right to have their own troops, church organization, and political autonomy within their walled towns, but banning them from the royal court and the city of Paris. King Louis XIV revoked the edict in 1685.

Einsatzgruppen (p. 879)   Loosely translated as strike force or task force; SS units given the task of murdering Jews and Communist Party members in the areas of the Soviet Union occupied by Germany during World War II.

empires (pp. 20, 554)   Large political formations consisting of different kingdoms or territories outside the boundaries of the states that control them.

empiricism (p. 535)   The practice of testing scientific theories by observation and experiment.

enclosure (p. 663)   The consolidation of scattered agricultural holdings into large, compact fields which were then closed off by hedges, bushes, or walls, giving farmers complete control over the uses of their land.

encomienda (p. 410)   The basic form of economic and social organization in early Spanish America, based on a royal grant awarded to a Spaniard for military or other services that gave the grantee and

his successors the right to gather tribute from the Indians in a defined area.

English Parliament (p. 321)   King Edward I (r. 1272–1307) began to call the English Parliament in order to raise sums of money for his foreign wars. The English Parliament differed from similar assemblies on the Continent. It usually included representatives of the "commons," which consisted of townsmen and prosperous farmers who lacked titles of nobility, but whom the king summoned because he needed their money. As a result, a broader spectrum of the population joined Parliament than in most other medieval kingdoms.

enlightened despots (p. 613)   The term assigned to absolute monarchs who initiated a series of legal and political reforms in an effort to realize the goals of the Enlightenment.

Enlightenment (p. 596)   An international intellectual movement of the eighteenth century that emphasized the use of reason and the application of the laws of nature to human society.

Epicureans (p. 131)   Followers of the teachings of the philosopher Epicurus (341–271 B.C.E.). Epicureans tried to gain peace of mind by choosing pleasures rationally.

Estates General (p. 494)   The legislative assembly of France in the Old Regime.

ethnic cleansing (p. 948)   A term introduced during the wars in Yugoslavia in the 1990s; the systematic use of murder, rape, and violence by one ethnic group against members of other ethnic groups in order to establish control over a territory.

Etruscans (p. 139)   A people of unknown origin who maintained a loose confederation of independent cities in central Italy and who strongly influenced the culture of ancient Rome.

Eucharist (p. 318)   Also known as Holy Communion or the Lord's Supper, the Eucharistic rite of the Mass celebrates Jesus' last meal with his apostles when the priest-celebrant consecrates wafers of bread and a chalice of wine as the body and blood of Christ. In the Middle Ages the wafers of bread were distributed for the congregation to eat, but drinking from the chalice was a special privilege of the priesthood. Protestants in the sixteenth century and Catholics in the late twentieth century began to allow the laity to drink from the chalice.

eugenics (p. 832)   The effort to improve the physical and intellectual capacities of the population by encouraging individuals with "desirable" traits to reproduce and/or by discouraging those individuals designated as "undesirable" from reproducing.

Euro-Islam (p. 956)   The identity and belief system being forged by European Muslims who argue that Islam does not contradict or reject European values.

European Economic Community (EEC) (p. 917) Originally comprising West Germany, France, Italy, Belgium, Luxembourg, and the Netherlands, the EEC was formed in 1957 to integrate its members' economic structures and so foster both economic prosperity and international peace. Also called the Common Market.

European Union (EU) (p. 949)   A successor organization to the EEC; the effort to integrate European political, economic, cultural, and military structures and policies.

excommunication (p. 309)   A decree by the pope or a bishop prohibiting a sinner from participating in the sacraments of the Church and forbidding any social contact whatsoever with the surrounding community.

existentialism (p. 822)   Twentieth-century philosophy that emerged in the interwar era and influenced many thinkers and artists after World War II. Existentialism emphasizes individual freedom in a world devoid of meaning or coherence.

Expressionism (p. 763)   Modernist artistic movement of the early twentieth century that used bold colors and experimental forms to express emotional realities.

factories (p. 416)   Trading posts established by European powers in foreign lands.

fanatic (p. 474)   Originally referring to someone possessed by a demon, during the sixteenth century a fanatic came to mean a person who expressed immoderate enthusiasm in religious matters or who pursued a supposedly divine mission, often to violent ends.

fascism (p. 833)   Twentieth-century political ideology that rejected the existing alternatives of conservatism, communism, socialism, and liberalism. Fascists stressed the authoritarian power of the state, the efficacy of violent action, the need to build a national community, and the use of new technologies of influence and control.

federalists (p. 628)   The name assigned by radical Jacobins to provincial rebels who opposed the centralization of the state during the French Revolution.

feminism, feminist movement (p. 741)   International movement that emerged in the second half of the

nineteenth century and demanded broader political, legal, and economic rights for women.

Fertile Crescent (p. 13)   Also known as the Levantine Corridor, this twenty-five mile wide arc of land stretching from the Jordan River to the Euphrates River was the place where food production and settled communities first appeared in Southwest Asia (the Middle East).

feudalism (p. 281)   A term historians use to describe a social system common during the Middle Ages in which lords granted fiefs (tracts of land or some other form of income) to dependents, known as vassals, who owed their lords personal services in exchange. Feudalism refers to a society governed through personal ties of dependency rather than public political institutions.

fief (p. 281)   During the Middle Ages a fief was a grant of land or some other form of income that a lord gave to a vassal in exchange for loyalty and certain services (usually military assistance).

Final Solution (p. 879)   Nazi term for the effort to murder every Jew in Europe during World War II.

fin-de-siecle (p. 757)   French term for the "turn of the century;" used to refer to the cultural crisis of the late nineteenth century.

First Triumvirate (p. 163)   The informal political alliance made by Julius Caesar, Pompey, and Crassus in 60 B.C.E. to share power in the Roman Republic. It led directly to the collapse of the Republic.

Forms (p. 103)   In the philosophical teachings of Plato, these are eternal, unchanging absolutes such as Truth, Justice, and Beauty that represent true reality, as opposed to the approximations of reality that humans encounter in everyday life.

Forum (p. 138)   The political and religious center of the city of Rome throughout antiquity. All cities in the empire had a forum in imitation of the capital city.

Fourteen Points (p. 814)   The principles outlined by U.S. President Woodrow Wilson as the basis for a new world order after World War I.

franchise (p. 602)   The right to vote; also called suffrage.

freemasons (p. 611)   Members of secret societies of men and women that flourished during the Enlightenment, dedicated to the creation of a society based on reason and virtue and committed to the principles of liberty and equality.

French Wars of Religion (p. 475)   A series of political assassinations, massacres, and military engagements between French Catholics and Calvinists from 1560 to 1598.

friars (p. 315) "Brothers" who wandered from city to city and throughout the countryside begging for alms. Unlike monks who remained in a cloister, friars tried to help ordinary laypeople with their problems by preaching and administering to the sick and poor.

Gaullism (p. 923) The political ideology associated with twentieth-century French political leader Charles DeGaulle. Gaullism combined the advocacy of a strong, centralized state with social conservatism.

genocide (p. 807) The murder of an entire people.

German-Soviet Non-Aggression Pact (p. 859) Signed by Joseph Stalin and Adolf Hitler in 1939, the agreement publicly pledged Germany and the Soviet Union not to attack each other and secretly divided up Poland and the Baltic states between the two powers.

Girondins (p. 627) The more conservative members of the Jacobin party who favored greater economic freedom and opposed further centralization of state power during the French Revolution.

glasnost (p. 937) Loosely translated as openness or honesty; Gorbachev's effort after 1985 to break with the secrecy that had characterized Soviet political life.

globalization (p. 964) The process by which global systems of production, distribution, and communication link together the peoples of the world.

Gnostic, Gnosticism (p. 197) Religious doctrine that emphasizes the importance of *gnosis*, or hidden truth, as a way of releasing spiritual reality from the prison of the essentially unreal or evil material world.

Gothic (p. 327) A style in architecture in western Europe from the late twelfth and thirteenth centuries, characterized by ribbed vaults and pointed arches, which drew the eyes of worshipers upward toward God. Flying buttresses, which redistributed the weight of the roof, made possible thin walls pierced by large expanses of stained glass.

grand jury (p. 321) In medieval England after the judicial reforms of King Henry II (r. 1154–1189), grand juries were called when the circuit court judge arrived in a shire. The sheriff assembled a group of men familiar with local affairs who constituted the grand jury and who reported to the judge the major crimes that had been committed since the judge's last visit.

Great Depression (p. 834) Calamitous drop in prices, reduction in trade, and rise in unemployment that devastated the global economy in 1929.

Great Persecution (p. 207) An attack on Christians in the Roman empire begun by the emperor Galerius in 303 C.E. on the grounds that their worship was endangering the empire. Several thousand Christians were executed.

Great Purge (p. 842) Period of mass arrests and executions particularly aimed at Communist Party members. Lasting from 1934 to 1939, the Great Purge enabled Joseph Stalin to consolidate his one-man rule over the Soviet Union.

Great Schism (p. 354) The division of the Catholic Church (1378–1417) between rival Italian and French claimants to the papal throne.

Green movement, Green politics (p. 932) A new style of politics and set of political ideas resulting from the confluence of environmentalism, feminism, and anti-nuclear protests of the 1970s.

guilds (p. 345) Professional associations devoted to protecting the special interests of a particular trade or craft and to monopolizing production and trade in the goods the guild produced.

haciendas (p. 411) Large landed estates that began to be established in the seventeenth century replaced encomiendas throughout much of Spanish America.

habiru (p. 55) Peasants who existed outside the palace system of the Late Bronze Age; often seen as bandits.

Hallstatt (p. 122) The first Celtic civilization in central Europe is called Halstatt. From about 750 to about 450 B.C.E., Hallstatt Celts spread throughout Europe.

Hellenistic (p. 108) The word used to describe the civilization, based on that of Greece, that developed in the wake of the conquests of Alexander the Great.

helots (p. 82) The brutally oppressed subject peoples of the Spartans. Tied to the land they farmed for Spartan masters, they were treated little better than beasts of burden.

hetairai (p. 97) Elite courtesans in ancient Greece who provided intellectual as well as sexual companionship.

hieroglyphs (p. 32) Ancient Egyptian system of writing that represented both sounds and objects.

Holocaust (p. 877) Adolf Hitler's effort to murder all the Jews in Europe during World War II.

Homo sapiens sapiens (p. 13) Scientific term meaning "most intelligent people" applied to physically and intellectually modern human beings that first appeared between 200,000 and 100,000 years ago in Africa.

hoplites (p. 81)   Greek soldiers in the Archaic Age who could afford their own weapons. Hoplite tactics made soldiers fighting as a group dependent on one another. This contributed to the internal cohesion of the polis and eventually to the rise of democracy.

Huguenots (p. 474)   The term for French Calvinists, who constituted some 10 percent of the population by 1560.

humanists (p. 376)   During the Renaissance humanists were writers and orators who studied Latin and sometimes Greek texts on grammar, rhetoric, poetry, history, and ethics.

Hundred Years' War (p. 346)   Refers to a series of engagements (1337–1453) between England and France over England's attempts to assert its claims to territories in France.

hyperinflation (p. 827)   Catastrophic price increases and currency devaluation, such as that which occurred in Germany in 1923.

iconoclasm (p. 241)   The destruction of religious images in the Byzantine empire in the eighth century.

icons (p. 240)   The Christian images of God and saints found in Byzantine art.

ideologies (p. 684)   Theories of society and government that form the basis of political programs.

induction (p. 535)   The mental process by which theories are established only after the systematic accumulation of large amounts of data.

indulgences (p. 354)   Certificates that allowed penitents to atone for their sins and reduce their time in purgatory. Usually these were issued for going on a pilgrimage or performing a pious act, but during the Babylonian Captivity of the Church (1305–1378) popes began to sell them, a practice Martin Luther protested in 1517 in an act that brought on the Protestant Reformation.

industrial capitalism (p. 671)   A form of capitalism characterized by the ownership of factories by private individuals and the employment of wage labor.

intendants (p. 496)   French royal officials who became the main agents of French provincial administration in the seventeenth century.

interdict (p. 309)   A papal decree prohibiting the celebration of the sacraments in an entire city or kingdom.

Investiture Controversy (p. 308)   A dispute that began in 1076 between the popes and the German emperors over the right to invest bishops with their offices. The most famous episode was the conflict between Pope Gregory VII and Emperor Henry IV.

The controversy was resolved by the Concordat of Worms in 1122.

"Iron Curtain" (p. 892)   Metaphor for the Cold War division of Europe after World War II.

Islamism (p. 952)   Islamic radicalism or *jihadism*. The ideology that insists that Islam demands a rejection of Western values and that violence in this struggle against the West is justified.

Jacobins (p. 623)   A French political party supporting a democratic republic that found support in political clubs throughout the country and dominated the National Convention from 1792 until 1794.

Jim Crow (p. 777)   Series of laws mandating racial segregation throughout the American South.

Junkers (pp. 509, 705)   The traditional nobility of Prussia.

justification by faith (p. 432)   Refers to Martin Luther's insight that humanity is incapable of performing enough religious good works to earn eternal salvation. Salvation is an unmerited gift from God called grace. Those who receive grace are called the Elect.

Keynesian economics (p. 846)   Economic theories associated with the British economist John Maynard Keynes that advocate using the power of the democratic state to ensure economic prosperity.

knight (p. 281)   During the Middle Ages a knight was a soldier who fought on horseback. A knight was a vassal or dependent of a lord, who usually financed the knight's expenses of armor and weapons and of raising and feeding horses with a grant of land known as a fief.

Koine (p. 124)   The standard version of the Greek language spoken throughout the Hellenistic world.

La Tène (p. 122)   A phase of Celtic civilization that lasted from about 450 to 200 B.C.E. La Tène culture became strong especially in the regions of the Rhine and Danube Rivers.

laissez-faire (p. 686)   The principle that governments should not regulate or otherwise intervene in the economy unless it is necessary to protect property rights and public order.

late antiquity (p. 202)   The period between about 250 and 600, which bridged the classical world and the Middle Ages.

Latin Christendom (p. 214)   The parts of medieval Europe, including all of western Europe, united by Christianity and the use of Latin in worship and intellectual life. Latin served as an international language among the ruling elites in western Europe, even though they spoke different languages in their daily lives.

Latin War (p. 144)   A war that the Latin peoples of Italy waged against the Roman Republic between 340 and 338. B.C.E.

Law Code of Hammurabi (p. 25)   The world's oldest complete surviving compendium of laws, promulgated during the reign of Hammurabi (1792–1750 B.C.E.) of Babylon.

lay investiture (p. 307)   The practice of nobles, kings, or emperors installing churchmen and giving them the symbols of office.

League of Nations (p. 814)   Association of states set up after World War I to resolve international conflicts through open and peaceful negotiation.

Lend-Lease Act (p. 869)   Passed in March 1941, the act gave Britain access to U.S. industrial products during World War II, with payment postponed for the duration of the war.

Levantine Corridor (p. 13)   Also known as the Fertile Crescent, this arc of land stretching from the Jordan River to the Euphrates River was the place where food production and settled communities first appeared in Southwest Asia (the Middle East).

liberalism (p. 686)   An ideology based on the conviction that individual freedom is of supreme importance and the main responsibility of government is to protect that freedom.

"Linear B" (p. 47)   The earliest written form of Greek, used by the Mycenaeans.

linear perspective (p. 384)   In the arts the use of geometrical principles to depict a three-dimensional space on a flat, two-dimensional surface.

liturgy (p. 262)   The forms of Christian worship, including the prayers, chants, and rituals to be said, sung, or performed throughout the year.

lord (p. 276)   During the Middle Ages a lord was someone who offered protection to dependents, known as vassals, who took an oath of loyalty to him. Most lords demanded military services from their vassals and sometimes granted them tracts of land known as fiefs.

ma'at (p. 30)   Ancient Egyptian concept of the fundamental order established by the gods.

Macedonian Renaissance (p. 242)   During the Macedonian dynasty's rule of Byzantium (867–1056), aristocratic families, the Church, and monasteries devoted their immense riches to embellishing Constantinople with new buildings, mosaics, and icons.

The emperors sponsored historical, philosophical, and religious writing.

Mafia (p. 711)   Organizations of armed men who took control of local politics and the economy in late nineteenth-century Sicily.

magic (p. 469)   Learned opinion described two kinds of magic: natural magic, which involved the manipulation of occult forces believed to exist in nature, and demonic magic, which called upon evil spirits to gain access to power. Widely accepted as a reality until the middle of the seventeenth century.

Magisterial Reformation (p. 440)   Refers to Protestant churches that received official government sanction.

Magna Carta (p. 321)   In 1215 some English barons forced King John to sign the "great charter," in which the king pledged to respect the traditional feudal privileges of the nobility, towns, and clergy. Subsequent kings swore to uphold it, thereby accepting the fundamental principle that even the king was obliged to respect the law.

Malthusian population trap (p. 670)   The theory of Thomas Malthus (1766–1834) that the natural tendency of population to grow faster than the food supply would eventually drive the size of populations back to sustainable levels and end periods of economic expansion that usually accompany the growth of population.

Manhattan Project (p. 875)   Code name given to the secret Anglo-American project that resulted in the construction of the atom bomb during World War II.

manor (p. 301)   A medieval unit of agricultural management in which a lord managed and served as the presiding judge over peasants who worked the land.

marches (p. 275)   Territorial units of the Carolingian empire for the administration of frontier regions. Each march was ruled by a margrave who had special powers necessary to defend vulnerable borders.

Marshall Plan (p. 896)   The use of U.S. economic aid to restore stability to Europe after World War II and so undercut the appeal of communist ideology.

mass politics (p. 725)   A political culture characterized by the participation of non-elites.

matriarchy (p. 47)   A social or cultural system in which family lineage is traced through the mother and/or in which women hold significant power.

metropolis (p. 553).   The "mother state" that controlled an empire.

mechanical philosophy (p. 536)   The seventeenth-century philosophy of nature, championed by René

Descartes, holding that nature operated in a mechanical way, just like a machine made by a human being.

megalith (p. 000)   A very large stone used in prehistoric European monuments in the second millennium B.C.E.

mercantilism (p. 499)   The theory that the wealth of a state depended on its ability to import fewer commodities than it exported and thus acquire the largest possible share of the world's monetary supply. The theory encouraged state intervention in the economy and the regulation of trade.

meritocracy (p. 642)   The practice of appointing people to office solely on the basis of ability and performance rather than social or economic status.

mesmerism (p. 612)   A pseudoscience developed by Franz Anton Mesmer in the eighteenth century that treated sickness by massaging or hypnotizing the patient to produce a crisis that restored health.

mestizos (p. 574)   People of mixed white and Indian ancestry.

metropolis (p. 553)   The parent country of a colony or imperial possession.

Middle Passage (p. 571)   The journey taken by European ships bringing slaves from Africa to the Americas.

Modern Devotion (p. 355)   A fifteenth-century religious movement that stressed individual piety, ethical behavior, and intense religious education. The Modern Devotion was promoted by the Brothers of the Common Life, a religious order whose influence was broadly felt through its extensive network of schools.

modernism (p. 757)   Term applied to artistic and literary movements from the late nineteenth century through the 1950s. Modernists sought to create new aesthetic forms and values.

monastic movement (p. 215)   In Late Antiquity, Christian ascetics organized communities where men and women could pursue a life of spirituality through work, prayer, and asceticism. Called the monastic movement, this spiritual quest spread quickly throughout Christian lands.

Monophysites (p. 214)   Christians who do not accept the Council of Chalcedon (see Chalcedonians). Monophysites believe that Jesus Christ has only one nature, equally divine and human.

monotheism (p. 39)   The belief in only one god, first attributed to the ancient Hebrews. Monotheism is the foundation of Judaism, Christianity, Islam, and Zoroastrianism.

Montagnards (p. 627)   Members of the radical faction within the Jacobin party who advocated the centralization of state power during the French Revolution and instituted the Reign of Terror.

mosque (p. 247)   A place of Muslim worship.

Mountain, the (p. 627)   The radical faction of Jacobins in the National Convention during the French Revolution.

mulattos (p. 565)   People of mixed white and black race.

Munich Agreement (p. 859)   The agreement in 1939 between the governments of Nazi Germany, Britain, and France that granted Germany sovereignty over the Sudetenland; part of the effort to appease the Nazi government and avoid a second total war in Europe.

nabobs (p. 578)   Members of the British East India Company who made fortunes in India and returned to Britain, flaunting their wealth.

Napoleonic Code (p. 642)   The name given to the Civil Code of 1804, promulgated by Napoleon, which gave France a uniform and authoritative code of law.

nation (p. 690)   A large community of people who possess a sense of unity based on a belief that they have a common homeland and share a similar culture.

national consciousness (p. 691)   The awareness or belief of people that they belong to a nation.

nationalism (p. 690)   The belief that the people who form a nation should have their own political institutions and that the interests of the nation should be defended and promoted at all costs.

national self-determination (p. 690)   The doctrine advanced by nationalists that any group that considers itself a nation has the right to be ruled only by the members of their own nation and to have all members of the nation included in that state.

nation-state (p. 690)   A political structure sought by nationalists in which the boundaries of the state and the nation are identical, so that all the members of a nation are governed by the same political authorities.

natural law (p. 143)   A law that is believed to be inherent in nature rather than established by human beings.

nawabs (p. 575)   Native provincial governors in eighteenth-century India.

Nazism (p. 835)   Twentieth-century political ideology associated with Adolf Hitler that adopted many fascist ideas but with a central focus on racism and particularly anti-Semitism.

neoclassicism (p. 591)   The revival of the classical art and architecture of ancient Greece and Rome in the eighteenth century.

Neolithic Age (p. 10)   The New Stone Age, characterized by the development of agriculture and the use of stone tools.

Neoplatonism (pp. 221, 538)   A philosophy based on the teachings of Plato and his successors that flourished in Late Antiquity, especially in the teachings of Plotinus. Neoplatonism influenced Christianity in Late Antiquity. During the Renaissance Neoplatonism was linked to the belief that the natural world was charged with occult forces that could be used in the practice of magic.

New Conservatism (p. 932)   Political ideology that emerged at the end of the 1970s combining the free market approach of nineteenth-century liberalism with social conservatism.

New Economic Policy (NEP) (p. 824)   Vladimir Lenin's economic turnaround in 1921 that allowed and even encouraged small private businesses and farms in the Soviet Union.

new feminism (p. 931)   Reemergence of the feminist movement in the 1970s.

new imperialism (p. 766)   The third phase of modern European imperialism, that occurred in the late nineteenth and early twentieth centuries and extended Western control over almost all of Africa and much of Asia.

New Left (p. 926)   Leftwing political and cultural movement that emerged in the late 1950s and early 1960s; sought to develop a form of socialism that rejected the over-centralization, authoritarianism, and inhumanity of Stalinism.

New Testament (p. 197)   The collection of texts that together with the Hebrew Bible, or Old Testament, comprise the Christian Bible. New Testament texts include the Epistles (letters of Paul of Tarsus to early Christians), the Gospels (stories of Jesus Christ's life, death, and resurrection), and other early Christian documents.

95 theses (p. 434)   Propositions about indulgences Martin Luther announced he was willing to defend in debate. The publication of the 95 theses in 1517 started the Protestant Reformation.

nobility (p. 588)   Members of the aristocracy who received official recognition of their hereditary status, including their titles of honor and legal privileges.

nobility of the robe (p. 588)   French noblemen whose families acquired their status by appointment to office.

no-man's-land (p. 793)   The area between the combatants' trenches on the Western Front during World War I.

North Atlantic Treaty Organization (NATO) (p. 897)   Defensive anti-Soviet alliance of the United States, Canada, and the nations of western Europe established in 1949.

northern Renaissance (p. 430)   A movement in northern Europe that built on the foundations of the Italian Renaissance, especially to subject the Bible and the sources of Christianity to critical scrutiny.

Nuremberg trials (p. 874)   Post-World War II trials of members of the Nazi Party and German military; conducted by an international tribunal.

Old Regime (p. 613)   The political order of eighteenth-century France, dominated by an absolute monarch and a privileged nobility and clergy.

oligarchy (p. 82)   A government consisting of only a few people rather than the entire community.

Olympic Games (p. 79)   Greek athletic contests held in Olympia every four years between 776 B.C.E and 217. C.E.

Oppian Law (p. 147)   A law of the Roman Republic passed in 217 B.C.E. to help pay the cost of war. The law restricted the amount of gold or silver a single woman or widow could hold and restricted the articles of clothing they could wear.

Ottonian Renaissance (p. 285)   Under the patronage of the Saxon Emperor Otto I (936–973) and his brother Bruno, learned monks, Greek philosophers from Byzantium, and Italian scholars gathered at the imperial court, stimulating a cultural revival in literature and the arts. The writers and artists enhanced the reputation of Otto.

pagan (p. 211)   The Christian term for polytheist worship (worshiping more than one god). In the course of Late Antiquity, the Christian church suppressed paganism, the traditional religions of the Roman empire.

palace system (p. 52)   Late Bronze Age social system that concentrated religious, economic, political, and military power in the hands of an elite, who lived apart from most people in monumental fortified compounds.

pan-Arabism (p. 849)   Nationalist ideology that called for the political unification of all Arabs, regardless of religious affiliation.

panhellenic (p. 79)   This word means covering all Greek communities. It applies, for example, to the Olympic Games, in which competitors came from all over the Greek world.

papacy (p. 209)   The bishop of the city of Rome is called the Pope, or Father. The papacy refers to the administrative and political institutions controlled by the Pope. The papacy began to gain strength in the sixth century in the absence of Roman imperial government in Italy.

papal infallibility (p. 765)   The doctrine of the Roman Catholic Church proclaimed at the First Vatican Council in 1870 that the pope could not err when making solemn declarations regarding faith or morals.

paradigm (p. 538)   A conceptual model or intellectual framework within which scientists conduct their research and experimentation.

parlements (p. 496)   The highest provincial courts in France, the most important of which was the Parlement of Paris.

patriarchy (p. 28)   A social or cultural system in which men occupy the positions of power; in a family system, a father-centered household.

patricians (p. 140)   In ancient Rome, patricians were aristocratic clans with the highest status and the most political influence.

patrons and clients (p. 156)   In ancient Roman society, a powerful man (the patron) would exercise influence on behalf of a social subordinate (the client) in anticipation of future support or assistance.

Pax Romana (p. 168)   Latin for "Roman Peace," this term refers to the Roman Empire established by Augustus that lasted until the early third century C.E.

Pentateuch (p. 72)   The first five books of the Hebrew Bible.

perestroika (p. 939)   Loosely translated as "restructuring;" Gorbachev's effort to decentralize, reform, and thereby strengthen Soviet economic and political structures.

personal rule (p. 517)   The period from 1629 to 1640 in England when King Charles I ruled without Parliament.

phalanx (p. 81)   The military formation favored by hoplite soldiers. Standing shoulder to shoulder in ranks often eight men deep, hoplites moved in unison and depended on one another for protection.

pharaoh (p. 36)   Title for the Egyptian king, used during the New Kingdom period.

philology (p. 376)   A method reintroduced by the humanists during the Italian Renaissance devoted to the comparative study of language, especially to understanding the meaning of a word in a particular historical context.

philosophes (p. 596)   The writers and thinkers of the Enlightenment, especially in France.

pilgrimages (p. 219)   Religious journeys made to holy sites in order to encounter relics.

Pillars of Islam (p. 248)   The five basic principles of Islam as taught by Muhammad.

plantation colony (p. 399)   First appearing in the Cape Verde Islands and later in the tropical parts of the Americas, these colonies were established by Europeans who used African slave labor to cultivate cash crops such as sugar, indigo, cotton, coffee, and tobacco.

plebeians (p. 140)   The general body of Roman citizens.

plebiscite (p. 634)   A popular vote for or against a form of government or rule by a particular person.

pogroms (p. 740)   An organized and often officially encouraged riot or attack to persecute a particular ethnic or religious group, especially associated with eastern European attacks against Jews.

polis (p. 79)   A self-governing Greek city-state

polytheistic (p. 23)   Refers to polytheism, the belief in many gods.

pop art (p. 920)   Effort by artists in the 1950s and 1960s both to utilize and to critique the material plenty of post-World War II popular culture.

Popular Front (p. 846)   A political coalition of liberals, socialists, and communists to defeat fascist and racist-nationalist political rivals.

popular sovereignty (p. 636)   The claim that political power came from the people and that the people constituted the highest political power in the state.

positivism (p. 692)   The philosophy developed by August Comte in the nineteenth century according to which human society passed through a series of stages, leading to the final positive stage in which the accumulation of scientific data would enable thinkers to discover the laws of human behavior and bring about the improvement of society.

positivist (p. 756)   The emphasis on the use of the scientific method to reach truth; a stress on observable fact.

postindustrialism, postindustrial society (p. 962)   A service rather than manufacturing-based economy characterized by an emphasis on marketing and information and by a proliferation of communications technologies.

postmodernism (p. 957)   Umbrella term covering a variety of artistic styles and intellectual theories and practices; in general, a rejection of a single, universal, Western style of modernity.

Potsdam Conference (p. 895)   The meeting in July 1945 of the Allied leaders of Britain, the Soviet Union, and the United States in the German city of Potsdam.

Pragmatic Sanction of Bourges (p. 390)   An agreement in 1438 that guaranteed the virtual autonomy of the French Church from papal control, enabling the French king to interfere in religious affairs and exploit Church revenues for government purposes.

Prague Spring (p. 915)   Short-lived popular effort in 1968 to reform Czechoslovakia's political structures; associated with the phrase "socialism with a human face."

predestination (p. 442)   The doctrine promoted by John Calvin that since God, the all-knowing and all-powerful being, knew everything in advance and caused everything to happen, then the salvation of any individual was predetermined.

prerogative (p. 517)   The set of powers exercised by the English monarch alone, rather than in conjunction with Parliament.

Price Revolution (p. 462)   After a long period of falling or stable prices that stretched back to the fourteenth century, Europe experienced sustained price increases between about 1540 and 1640, causing widespread social and economic turmoil.

priesthood of all believers (p. 434)   Martin Luther's doctrine that all those of pure faith were themselves priests, a doctrine that undermined the authority of the Catholic clergy over the laity.

primogeniture (p. 514)   The legal arrangement by which the eldest son inherits the entire estate upon the death of the father.

proletariat (p. 690)   The word used by Karl Marx and Friedrich Engels to identify the class of workers who received their income from wages.

prophetic movement (p. 70)   An important phase in the development of what became Judaism. In the ninth century B.C.E., Hebrew religious reformers, or prophets, demanded the transformation of religious and economic practices to reflect ideals of social justice and religious purity.

protectionism (p. 562)   The policy of shielding domestic industries from foreign competition through a policy of levying tariffs on imported goods.

Protestant Reformation (p. 426)   Dominated European affairs between 1517 and 1560 when the movement for religious reform begun by Martin Luther led Germany, Britain, and most of northern Europe to break away from the Catholic Church.

Radical Reformation (p. 440)   Refers to Protestant movements that failed to gain official government recognition and were at best tolerated, at worst persecuted, during the sixteenth century.

rationalism (p. 536)   The theory that the mind contains rational categories independent of sensory observation; more generally that reason is the primary source of truth.

Realpolitik (p. 712)   The adoption of political tactics based solely on their realistic chances of success.

redistributive economies (p. 18)   Type of economic system characteristic of ancient Mesopotamian societies. The central political authority controls all agricultural resources and their redistribution.

regency (p. 496)   Rule by relative of a monarch during a period when the monarch was too young to rule or otherwise incapacitated.

Reign of Terror (p. 628)   A purging of alleged enemies of the French state between 1793 and 1794, superintended by the Committee of Public Safety, that resulted in the execution of 17,000 people.

Reinsurance Treaty (p. 787)   Treaty of 1887 in which the governments of Germany and Russia agreed to remain neutral if either was attacked.

relics (p. 219)   In Christian belief, relics are sacred objects that have miraculous powers. They are associated with saints, biblical figures, or some object associated with them. They served as contacts between Earth and Heaven and were verified by miracles.

Religious Peace of Augsburg (p. 439)   In 1555 this peace between Lutherans and Catholics within the Holy Roman Empire established the principle of *cuius regio, eius religio*, which means "he who rules determines the religion of the land." Protestant princes in the Empire were permitted to retain all church lands seized before 1552 and to enforce Protestant worship, but Catholic princes were also allowed to enforce Catholic worship in their territories.

Renaissance (p. 364) A term meaning "rebirth" used by historians to describe a movement that sought to imitate and understand the culture of antiquity. The Renaissance generally refers to a movement that began in Italy and then spread throughout Europe from about 1350 to 1550.

reparations (p. 814) Payments imposed upon Germany after World War I by the Versailles Treaty to cover the costs of the war.

republic (p. 139) A state in which political power resides in the people or their representatives rather than in a monarch.

republicanism (p. 366) A political theory first developed by the ancient Greeks, especially the philosopher Plato, but elaborated by the ancient Romans and rediscovered during the Italian Renaissance. The fundamental principle of republicanism as developed during the Italian Renaissance was that government officials should be elected by the people or a portion of the people.

Republic of Virtue (p. 628) The ideal form of government proposed by Maximilien Robespierre and other Jacobins during the French Revolution. Its proponents wished to make the republic established in 1792 more egalitarian and secular and inspire civic pride and patriotism in the people.

requerimiento (p. 408) A document read by conquistadores to the natives of the Americas before making war on them. The document briefly explained the principles of Christianity and commanded the natives to accept them immediately along with the authority of the pope and the sovereignty of the king of Spain. If the natives refused, they were warned they would be forced to accept Christian conversion and subjected to Spain anyway.

Resistance, the (p. 883) Label given to the many different underground political and partisan movements directed against Nazi rule in German-occupied Europe during World War II.

revisionism, socialist revisionism (p. 736) The belief that an equal society can be built through participation in parliamentary politics rather than through violent revolution.

rhetoric (p. 376) The art of persuasive or emotive speaking and writing, which was especially valued by the Renaissance humanists.

Roman Forum (p. 136) The central area in the city of Rome between the Palatine hill and the Capitoline hill.

Roman Republic (p. 137) The name given to the Roman state from about 500 B.C.E., when the last king of Rome was expelled, to 31 B.C.E., when Augustus established the Roman Empire.

Romanesque (p. 327) A style in architecture that spread throughout western Europe during the eleventh and the first half of the twelfth centuries and characterized by arched stone roofs supported by rounded arches, massive stone pillars, and thick walls.

Romanization (p. 177) The process by which conquered peoples absorbed aspects of Roman culture, especially the Latin language, city life, and religion.

romanticism (p. 693) An artistic and literary movement of the late eighteenth and nineteenth centuries that involved a protest against classicism, appealed to the passions rather than the intellect, and emphasized the beauty and power of nature.

Rome-Berlin Axis (p. 859) Alliance between Benito Mussolini's Italy and Adolf Hitler's Germany formed in 1936.

salons (p. 611) Private sitting rooms or parlors of aristocratic French women where discussions of philosophy, science, littérature, and politics took place in the eighteenth century.

sans-culottes (p. 623) The militant citizens of Paris who refused to wear the pants worn by noblemen and provided support for the Jacobins during the French Revolution; literally, those without breeches.

satraps (p. 115) Persian provincial governors who collected taxes and oversaw the bureaucracy.

Schlieffen Plan (p. 788) German military plan devised in 1905 that called for a sweeping attack on France through Belgium and the Netherlands.

scholasticism (p. 324) A term referring to a broad philosophical and theological movement that dominated medieval thought and university training. Scholasticism used logic learned from Aristotle to interpret the meaning of the Bible and the writings of the Church Fathers, who created Christian theology in its first centuries.

Scramble for Africa (p. 773) The frenzied imposition of European control over most of Africa that occurred between 1870 and 1914.

scriptorium (p. 271) The room in a monastery where monks copied books and manuscripts.

Sea Peoples (p. 54) Name given by the Egyptians to the diverse groups of migrants whose attacks helped bring the International Bronze Age to an end.

Second Industrial Revolution (p. 723) A new phase in the industrialization of the processes of production and consumption, underway in Europe in the 1870s.

Second Triumvirate (p. 165) In 43 B.C.E. Octavian (later called Augustus), Mark Antony, and Lepidus made an informal alliance to share power in Rome while they jockeyed for control. Octavian emerged as the sole ruler of Rome in 31 B.C.E.

secularization (p. 545) The reduction of the importance of religion in society and culture.

seigneur (p. 593) The lord of a French estate who received payments from the peasants who lived on his land.

separate spheres (p. 609) The theory that men and women should conduct their lives in different social and political environments, confining women to the domestic sphere and excluding them from the public sphere of political involvement.

sepoys (p. 576) Indian troops serving in the armed forces of the British East India Company.

Septuagint (p. 125) The Greek translation of the Hebrew Bible (Old Testament).

serfs (p. 301) During the Middle Ages serfs were agricultural laborers who worked and lived on a plot of land granted them by a lord to whom they owed a certain portion of their crops. They could not leave the land, but they had certain legal rights that were denied to slaves.

settler colony (p. 399) A colony authorized when a private person obtained a license from a king to seize an island or parcel of land and occupied it with settlers from Europe who exported their own culture to the new lands. Settler colonies first appeared among the islands of the eastern Atlantic and portions of the Americas.

simony (p. 307) The practice of buying and selling church offices.

skepticism (p. 543) A tendency to doubt what one has been taught or is expected to believe.

Social Darwinism (p. 755) The later-nineteenth-century application of the theory of evolution to entire human societies.

social democracy (pp. 843, 887) Political system in which a democratically elected parliamentary government endeavors to ensure a decent standard of living for its citizens through both economic regulation and the maintenance of a welfare state.

socialism (p. 687) An ideology calling for the ownership of the means of production by the community with the purpose of reducing inequalities of income, wealth, opportunity and economic power.

socialist revisionism (p. 736) The belief that an equal society can be built through participation in parliamentary politics rather than through violent revolution.

Social War (p. 159) The revolt of Rome's allies against the Republic in 90 B.C.E. demanding full Roman citizenship

Solidarity (p. 935) Trade union and political party in Poland that led an unsuccessful effort to reform the Polish communist state in 1981; survived to lead Poland's first non-communist government since World War II in 1989.

Sophists (p. 102) Professional educators who traveled throughout the ancient Greek world, teaching many subjects. Their goal was to teach people the best ways to lead better lives.

soviets (p. 808) Workers' and soldiers' councils formed in Russia during the Revolution of 1917.

Spanish Armada (p. 478) A fleet of 132 ships, which sailed from Portugal to rendezvous with the Spanish army stationed in the Netherlands and launch an invasion of England in 1588. The English defeated the Armada as it passed through the English Channel. The defeat marked a shift in the power balance from Spain to England.

Spanish Reconquest (p. 260) Refers to the numerous military campaigns by the Christian kingdoms of northern Spain to capture the Muslim-controlled cities and kingdoms of southern Spain. This long, intermittent struggle began with the capture of Toledo in 1085 and lasted until Granada fell to Christian armies in 1492.

spiritualists (p. 448) A tendency within Protestantism, especially Lutheranism, to emphasize the power of personal spiritual illumination, called the "inner Word," a living form of the Scriptures written directly on the believer's soul by the hand of God.

stagflation (p. 930) Term coined in the 1970s to describe an economy troubled by both high inflation and high unemployment rates.

standing armies (p. 495) Trained and equipped military forces that were not disbanded after the conclusion of war. Standing armies often helped maintain order and enforce governmental policy at home.

states (p. 554) Consolidated territorial areas that have their own political institutions and recognize no higher political authority.

Stoics (p. 132) Followers of the philosophy developed by Zeno of Citium (ca. 335–ca. 263 B.C.E.) that urged acceptance of fate while participating fully in everyday life.

structuralism (p. 920)   Influential post-World War II social theory that explored the common structures of language and thought.

Struggle of the Orders (p. 140)   The political strife between patrician and plebeian Romans beginning in the fifth century B.C.E. The plebeians gradually won political rights and influence as a result of the struggle.

suffragettes (p. 746)   Feminist movement that emerged in Britain in the early twentieth century. Unlike the suffragists, who sought to achieve the national vote for women through rational persuasion, the suffragettes adopted the tactics of violent protest.

suffragists (p. 745)   Feminists who sought to achieve the national vote for women through rational persuasion and parliamentary politics.

supply (p. 664)   The amounts of capital, labor, and food that are needed to produce goods for the market as well as the quantities of those goods themselves.

syncretism (p. 69) The practice of equating two gods and fusing their cults was common throughout the Roman Empire and helped to unify the diverse peoples and religions under Roman rule.

syndicalism (p. 737)   Ideology of the late nineteenth and early twentieth century that sought to achieve a working-class revolution through economic action, particularly through mass labor strikes.

Talmud's (p. 217)   Commentaries on Jewish law. Rabbis completed the Babylonian Talmud and the Jerusalem Talmud by the end of the fifth century C.E.

tetrarchy (p. 205)   The government by four rulers established by the Roman emperor Diocletian in 293 C.E. that lasted until 312. During the tetrarchy many administrative and military reforms altered the fabric of Roman society.

Third Estate (p. 621)   The component of the Estates General in Old Regime France that technically represented all the commoners in the kingdom.

Third Reich (p. 864)   Term for Adolf Hitler's Germany; articulates the Nazi aim of extending German rule across Europe.

Third World (p. 909)   Term coined in 1955 to describe nations that did not align with either the Soviet Union or the United States; commonly used to describe the industrially underdeveloped nations.

Thomism (p. 325)   A branch of medieval philosophy associated with the work of the Dominican thinker,

Thomas Aquinas (1225–1274), who wrote encyclopedic summaries of human knowledge that confirmed Christian faith.

Time of Troubles (p. 489)   The period from 1604 to 1613 when Russia fell into chaos, which ended when the national assembly elected Tsar Michael Romanov, whose descendants ruled Russia until they were deposed in 1917.

Torah (p. 72)   Most commonly, the first five books of the Hebrew Bible; also used to refer to the whole body of Jewish sacred writings and tradition.

total war (p. 784)   A war that demands extensive state regulation of economic production, distribution, and consumption; and that blurs (or erases entirely) the distinction between civilian and soldier.

trading posts (p. 401)   Built by European traders along the coasts of Africa and Asia as a base for trade with the interior. Trading posts or factories were islands of European law and sovereignty, but European authority seldom extended very far beyond the fortified post.

transubstantiation (p. 318)   A doctrine promulgated at the Fourth Lateran Council in 1215 that explained by distinguishing between the outward appearances and the inner substance how the Eucharistic bread and wine changed into the body and blood of Christ.

Treaty of Brest-Litovsk (p. 797)   Treaty between Germany and Bolshevik-controlled Russia, signed in March, 1918, that ceded to Germany all of Russia's western territories.

trial by jury (p. 321)   When disputes about the possession of land arose after the late twelfth century in England, sheriffs assembled a group of twelve local men who testified under oath about the claims of the plaintiffs, and the circuit court judge made his decision on the basis of their testimony. The system was later extended to criminal cases.

Triple Alliance (p. 787)   Defensive alliance of Germany, Austria-Hungary, and Italy, signed in 1882.

Triple Entente (p. 787)   Informal defensive agreement linking France, Great Britain, and Russia before World War I.

triremes (p. 90)   Greek warships with three banks of oars. Triremes manned by the poorest people of Athenian society became the backbone of the Athenian empire.

troubadours (p. 326)   Poets from the late twelfth and thirteenth centuries who wrote love poems, meant to be sung to music, which reflected a new sensibility, called courtly love, about the ennobling possibilities of the love between a man and a woman.

Truman Doctrine (p. 896)   Named after U.S. president Harry Truman, the doctrine that in 1947 inaugurated the Cold War policy of resisting the expansion of communist control.

Twelfth-Century Renaissance (p. 325)   An intellectual revival of interest in ancient Greek philosophy and science and in Roman law in western Europe during the twelfth and early thirteenth centuries. The term also refers to a flowering of vernacular literature and the Romanesque and Gothic styles in architecture.

tyrants (p. 81)   Rulers in Greek city-states, usually members of the aristocracy, who seized power illegitimately rather than acquiring it by heredity or election. Tyrants often gained political support from the hoplites and the poor.

Unitarians (p. 449)   A religious reform movement that began in the sixteenth century and rejected the Christian doctrine of the Trinity. Unitarians (also called Arians, Socinians, and Anti-Trinitarians) taught a rationalist interpretation of the Scriptures and argued that Jesus was a divinely inspired man, not God who became a man as did other Christians.

universal law of gravitation (p. 533)   A law of nature established by Isaac Newton in 1687 holding that any two bodies attract each other with a force that is directly proportional to the product of their masses and indirectly proportional to the square of the distance between them. The law was presented in mathematical terms.

universal male suffrage (p. 627)   The granting of the right to vote to all adult males.

vassals (p. 281)   During the Middle Ages men voluntarily submitted themselves to a lord by taking an oath of loyalty. Vassals owed the lord certain services—usually military assistance—and sometimes received in exchange a grant of land known as a fief.

Vatican II (p. 922)   Popular term for the Second Vatican Council that convened in 1963 and introduced a series of changes within the Roman Catholic Church.

vernacular languages (p. 480)   The native spoken languages of Europe, which became literary languages and began to replace Latin as the dominant form of learned expression during the sixteenth century.

Versailles Treaty (p. 814)   Treaty between Germany and the victorious Allies after World War I.

Vichy, Vichy regime, Vichy government (p. 864)   Authoritarian state established in France after defeat by the German army in 1940.

Vulgate (p. 214)   The Latin translation of the Bible produced about 410 by the monk Jerome. It was the standard Bible in western Christian churches until the sixteenth century.

Wahhabism (p. 850)   A religious reform and revival movement founded by Muhammad Abd al-Wahhab (1703–1787) in the eighteenth century to purify Islam by returning to a strict interpretation of the *Sharia*, or Islamic law. Revived during the 1920s in Saudi Arabia.

Warsaw Pact (p. 897)   Military alliance of the Soviet Union and its eastern European satellite states in the Cold War era.

Weimar Republic (p. 825)   The democratic German state constructed after defeat in World War I and destroyed by the Nazis in 1933.

wergild (p. 267)   In Germanic societies the term referred to what an individual was worth in case he or she suffered an injury. It was the amount of compensation in gold that the wrongdoer's family had to pay to the victim's family.

witch-hunt (p. 469)   Refers to the dramatic increase in the judicial prosecution of alleged witches in either church or secular courts from the middle of the sixteenth to the middle of the seventeenth centuries.

Yalta Conference (p. 894)   Meeting in 1945 of the leaders of the Allied states of Britain, the Soviet Union, and the United States to devise plans for postwar Europe.

ziggurat (p. 23)   Monumental tiered or terraced temple characteristic of ancient Mesopotamia.

Zionism (p. 741)   Nationalist movement that emerged in the late nineteenth century and sought to establish a Jewish political state in Palestine (the Biblical Zion).

Zoroastrianism (p. 88)   The monotheistic religion of Persia founded by Zoroaster that became the official religion of the Persian Empire.

CHAPTER 1. THE BEGINNINGS OF CIVILIZATION, 10,000–1150 BCE.

Andrews, Anthony P. *First Cities*. 1995. An excellent introduction to the development of urbanism in Southwest Asia, Egypt, India, China, and the Americas.

Crawford, Harriet. *Sumer and the Sumerians*. 2004. A comprehensive study of the interplay between the physical environment, emerging political structures, and technological change. Clearly illustrated.

Dalley, Stephanie. *Mari and Karana: Two Old Babylonian Cities*. 1984. Despite the rather forbidding title, a delightful exploration of daily life in the eighteenth century B.C.E., using excavations of two small kingdoms in northwest Mesopotamia.

Fagan, Brian. *People of the Earth: An Introduction to World Prehistory*. 1998. A comprehensive textbook that introduces basic issues with a wealth of illustrations and explanatory materials.

Hornung, Erik. *History of Ancient Egypt: An Introduction*, trans. David Lorton. 1999. A concise and lucid overview of Egyptian history and life.

Kuhrt, Amélie. *The Ancient Near East, ca. 3000–330 B.C.*, 2 vols. 1995. A magisterial overview, with an excellent bibliography. The place to start for a continuous historical narrative of the region.

Redford, Donald B. *Egypt, Canaan, and Israel in Ancient Times*. 1993. A distinguished Egyptologist discusses 3,000 years of uninterrupted contact between Egypt and southwestern Asia.

Sasson, Jack M, ed. *Civilizations of the Ancient Near East*, Vol. 2. 1995. Contains a number of very helpful essays, particularly on Egypt.

Schmandt-Besserat, Denise. *How Writing Came About*. 1996. A highly readable and groundbreaking argument that cuneiform writing developed from a method of counting with tokens.

Schulz, Regine, and Matthias Seidel, eds. *Egypt: The World of the Pharaohs*. 1999. A sumptuously illustrated collection of essays on all aspects of Egyptian society and life by leading experts.

Snell, Daniel C. *Life in the Ancient Near East*. 1997. A concise account of the major developments over 5,000 years.

Spindler, Konrad. *The Man in the Ice: The Discovery of a 5,000-Year-Old Body Reveals the Secrets of the Stone Age*. 1994. A leader of the international team of experts interprets the corpse of a Neolithic hunter found in the Austrian Alps.

Stiebing, William H. *Ancient Near Eastern History and Culture*. 2008. Clear and comprehensive survey of important political and cultural events.

Trigger, Bruce G. *Early Civilizations: Ancient Egypt in Context*. 1995. A leading cultural anthropologist examines Old and Middle Kingdom Egypt through comparison with the early civilizations of China, Peru, Mexico, Mesopotamia, and Africa.

Van De Mieroop, Marc. *A History of the Ancient Near East ca. 3000–323 B.C.* 2007. Authoritative and up to date.

Wenke, Robert J. *Patterns in Prehistory: Humankind's First Three Million Years*. 4th ed. 1999. An often witty, highly readable account.

CHAPTER 2. THE AGE OF EMPIRES: THE INTERNATIONAL BRONZE AGE AND ITS AFTERMATH, CA. 1500–550 BCE.

Bryce, Trevor. *Life and Society in the Hittite World*. 2002. A lively look at Hittite customs, laws, and social structures.

Bryce, Trevor. *The Letters of the Great Kings of the Ancient Near East: The Royal Correspondence of the Late Bronze Age*. 2003. Bryce explores the Club of the Great Powers through their surviving correspondence.

Bryce, Trevor. *The Trojans and Their Neighbors*. 2005. An up-to-date examination of the historical Troy.

Cohen, Raymond, and Raymond Westbrook, eds. *Amarna Diplomacy: The Beginnings of International Relations*. 2000. An intriguing collaboration of archaeologists, linguists, and specialists in international diplomacy, this book looks at the

Amarna Letters from the context of modern international relations.

Dever, William G. *What Did the Biblical Writers Know and When Did They Know It?: What Archaeology Can Tell Us about the Reality of Ancient Israel.* 2001. A clear and often entertaining account of the writing of the Hebrew Bible.

Dever, William G. *Who Were the Early Israelites and Where Did They Come From?* 2003. A clear and lively account that takes the reader step-by-step through the various historical, archaeological, and political controversies that bedevil the study of ancient Israel.

Dickinson, Oliver. *The Aegean Bronze Age.* 1994. Now the standard treatment of the complex archaeological data.

Dothan, Trude, and Moshe Dothan. *People of the Sea: The Search for the Philistines.* 1992. A survey of the archaeological material, written for non-specialists.

Finkelstein, Israel, and Neil Asher Silberman. *David and Solomon: In Search of the Bible's Sacred Kings and the Roots of the Western Tradition.* 2006. An important, if controversial archaeological interpretation that views David and Solomon as tribal chieftains and the "United Monarchy" as a fiction, this elegantly written study also explores the impact of the biblical story on Western identity.

Fitton, J. Lesley. *Minoans: Peoples of the Past.* 2002. Accessible account of recent research and conclusions.

Fitton, J. Lesley. *The Discovery of the Greek Bronze Age.* 1996. A lucid and well-illustrated study of the archaeologists who brought the Greek Bronze Age to light in the nineteenth and early twentieth centuries.

Kuhrt, Amélie. *The Ancient Near East, ca. 3000–330 B.C.,* 2 vols. 1995. A magisterial overview, with an excellent bibliography. The place to start for a continuous historical narrative of the region.

Latacz, Joachim. *Troy and Homer: Towards a Solution of an Old Mystery.* 2004. One of the most recent efforts to solve the puzzle of the historicity of Homer's account of the Trojan War.

Markoe, Glenn. *Phoenicians.* 2000. An important treatment of Phoenician society by a noted expert.

Miller, Patrick D. *Chieftains of the Highland Clans: A History of Israel in the 12th and 11th Centuries B.C.* 2003. Uses not only archaeological and textual evidence but also anthropological methodology to explore the history of the early Israelites.

Redford, Donald B. *Egypt, Canaan and Israel in Ancient Times.* 1992. An excellent, detailed synthesis of textual and archaeological evidence that emphasizes interconnections among cultures.

Stiebing, William H. *Ancient Near Eastern History and Culture.* 2008. A comprehensive survey that also pays close attention to historiographical and archaeological controversies. The chapter on the end of the International Bronze Age is particularly well done.

Van De Mieroop, Marc. *A History of the Ancient Near East ca. 3000–323 BC.* 2007. An excellent survey, with clear maps and useful time lines.

Walker, Christopher, ed. *Astronomy Before the Telescope.* 1996. A fascinating collection of essays about astronomy in the premodern period, which makes clear Western civilization's enormous debt to the Babylonians.

CHAPTER 3. GREEK CIVILIZATION

Boardman, John. *Persia and the West: An Archaeological Investigation of the Genesis of Achaemenid Art.* 2000. A brilliantly illustrated study that stresses intercultural influences in every aspect of Persian art.

Boyce, Mary. *A History of Zoroastrianism,* Vol. 2. 1975. This authoritative examination provides a masterful overview of the religion of the Persian Empire.

Burkert, Walter. *The Orientalizing Revolution: Near Eastern Influence on Greek Culture in the Early Archaic Age,* trans. Margaret Pinder and Walter Burkert. 1993. Explains how the Semitic East influenced the development of Greek society in the Archaic Age.

Cohn, Norman. *Cosmos, Chaos, and the World to Come: The Ancient Roots of Apocalyptic Faith.* 1993. Expert critical analysis of apocalyptic religions in the West, including Zoroastrianism, ancient Judaism, Christianity, and other faiths.

Finkelstein, Israel, and Neil Asher Silberman. *The Bible Unearthed: Archaeology's New Vision of Ancient Israel and the Origin of the Sacred Texts.* 2001. An important archaeological interpretation that challenges the narrative of the Hebrew Bible and offers a reconsideration of biblical history.

Gottwald, Norman K. *The Hebrew Bible: A Socio-Literary Introduction.* 1985. Combines a close reading of the Hebrew Bible with the latest archaeological and historical evidence.

Just, Roger. *Women in Athenian Law and Life.* 1989. Provides an overview of the social context of women in Athens.

Kuhrt, Amélie. *The Ancient Near East, ca. 3000–330 B.C.,* Vol. 2. 1995. This rich and comprehensive bibliography is a remarkably concise and readable account of Persian history with excellent discussion of ancient textual evidence. Many important passages appear in fluent translation.

Lindberg, David C. *The Beginnings of Western Science: The European Scientific Tradition in Philosophical, Religious, and Institutional Context, 600 B.C. to A.D. 1450.* 1992. This highly readable study provides an exciting survey of the main developments in Western science.

Markoe, Glenn. *Phoenicians.* 2000. The best and most up-to-date treatment of Phoenician society by a noted expert.

Murray, Oswyn. *Early Greece.* 1983. A brilliant study of all aspects of the emergence of Greek society between the Dark Age and the end of the Persian Wars.

Osborne, Robin. *Greece in the Making, 1200–479 B.C.* 1996. An excellent narrative of the development of Greek society with special regard to the archaeological evidence.

Stewart, Andrew. *Art, Desire, and the Body in Ancient Greece.* 1997. A provocative study that examines Greek attitudes toward sexuality and art.

Walker, Christopher, ed. *Astronomy Before the Telescope.* 1996. A fascinating collection of essays about astronomy in the premodern period, which makes clear our enormous debt to the Babylonians.

Wieshöfer, Josef. *Ancient Persia from 550 B.C. to A.D. 650,* trans. Azizeh Azodi. 1996. A fresh and comprehensive overview of Persian cultural, social, and political history that relies on Persian evidence more heavily than on biased Greek and Roman sources.

CHAPTER 4. HELLENISTIC CIVILIZATION

Auatin, Michel. *The Hellenistic World from Alexander to the Roman Conquest: A Selection of Ancient Sources in Translation,* 2nd ed. 2006. A major collection of more than 325 documents from this period.

Boardman, John, Jasper Griffin, and Oswyn Murray, eds. *Greece and the Hellenistic World. The Oxford History of the Classical World.* 1988. A synthesis of all aspects of Hellenistic life, with excellent illustrations and bibliography.

Bosworth, A. B. *Alexander and the East: The Tragedy of Triumph.* 1997. A negative interpretation of Alexander as a totalitarian ruler.

Bugh, Glenn R., *The Cambridge Companion to the Hellenistic World.* 2006. A collection of essays on 15 different aspects of Hellenistic politics and culture.

Cartledge, Paul, Peter Garnsey, and Erich Gruen, eds. *Hellenistic Constructs: Essays in culture, history and historiography.* 1997.

Cohen, Getzel M. *The Hellenistic Settlements in Europe, the Islands, and Asia Minor.* 1996. The standard reference work on the cities founded in these areas during the Hellenistic period.

Cohn, Norman. *Cosmos, Chaos, and the World to Come: The Ancient Roots of Apocalyptic Faith.* 1993. This brilliant study explains the development of ideas about the end of the world in the cultures of the ancient world.

Cunliffe, Barry. *The Ancient Celts.* 1997. This source analyzes the archaeological evidence for the Celtic Iron Age, with many illustrations and maps.

Cunliffe, Barry, ed. *The Oxford Illustrated Prehistory of Europe.* 1996. A collection of well-illustrated essays on the development of European cultures from the end of the Ice Age to the Classical period.

Fox, Robin Lane. *Alexander the Great.* 1994. Shows that the myth Alexander created is as influential today as it was in the ancient world.

Green, Peter. *Alexander to Actium: The Historical Evolution of the Hellenistic Age.* 1990. A vivid interpretation of the world created by Alexander until the victory of Augustus.

Gruen, Erich S. *The Hellenistic World and the Coming of Rome.* 1984. An important study of how Rome entered the eastern Mediterranean world.

Kuhrt, Amélie, and Susan Sherwin-White, eds. *Hellenism in the East: The Interaction of Greek and Non-Greek Civilizations from Syria to Central Asia After Alexander.* 1987. These studies help us understand the complexities of the interaction of Greeks and non-Greeks in the Hellenistic world.

Momigliano, Arnaldo. *Alien Wisdom: The Limits of Hellenization*. 1975. A study of Greek attitudes toward the contemporary civilizations of the Romans, Celts, Jews, and Persians.

Onians, John. *Art and Thought in the Hellenistic Age: The Greek World View, 350–50 BC*. 1979.

Pollitt, J. J. *Art in the Hellenistic Age*. 1986. A brilliant interpretation of the development of Hellenistic art. Discusses the freedom of aristocratic Greek women in Egypt during this period.

Pomeroy, Sarah B. *Women in Hellenistic Egypt: From Alexander to Cleopatra*. 1984.

Steele, James. *Hellenistic Architecture in Asia Minor*. 1992. Challenges the belief that Hellenistic architecture represented a degradation of the Greek classical style.

CHAPTER 5. THE ROMAN REPUBLIC

Bringmann, Klaus. *A History of the Roman Republic*. 2007. A useful survey that not only provides a detailed narrative but also challenges some of the traditional interpretations.

Cornell, T. J. *The Beginnings of Rome: Italy and Rome from the Bronze Age to the Punic Wars (ca. 1000–264 B.C.)*. 1996. A synthesis of the latest evidence with many important new interpretations.

Crawford, Michael, *The Roman Republic*, 2nd ed. 1992. An overview by a leading scholar.

Flower, Harriet I., ed. *The Cambridge Companion to the Roman Republic*. 2004. Includes essays on political and military history, Roman society, republican territorial expansion, culture, and the influence of the Republic on the French and American revolutions.

Gardner, Jane F. *Women in Roman Law and Society*. 1986. Explains the legal position of women in the Roman world.

Goldsworthy, Adrian. *The Fall of Carthage: The Punic Wars, 265–146 B.C.* 2003.

Gruen, Erich S. *The Last Generation of the Roman Republic*. 1995. An exhaustive study of a crucial period of the republic.

Lintott, Andrew. 2003. *The Constitution of the Roman Republic*. An authoritative and well-written treatment of the subject.

Orlin, Eric. *Temples, Religion and Politics in the Roman Republic*. 2002.

Pocock, J. G. A. *The Machiavellian Moment*. 1975. An immense scholarly discussion of the use of republican thought in Renaissance Europe, late seventeenth century England and eighteenth-century British America.

Pomeroy, Sarah B. *Goddesses, Whores, Wives, and Slaves: Women in Classical Antiquity*. 1995.

Sherwin-White, A. N. *Roman Citizenship*. 1980. A comprehensive treatment of the subject. A general study of women in the ancient world.

Stein, Peter. *Roman Law in European History*. A superb overview, beginning with the Law of the Twelve Tables.

CHAPTER 6. ENCLOSING THE WEST: THE EARLY ROMAN EMPIRE AND ITS NEIGHBORS: 31 BCE-235 CE.

Barrett, Anthony A. *Livia: First Lady of Imperial Rome*. 2002. Recent biography of one of the most intriguing figures in the Roman Empire.

Beard, Mary, John North, and Simon Price. *Religions of Rome*. 1995. The first volume contains essays on polytheist religions, and the second contains translated ancient sources.

Chancey, Mark. *Greco-Roman Culture and the Galilee of Jesus*. 2005. A concise but broad-ranging survey of the title topic.

Crossan, J. D. *The Birth of Christianity*. 1998. Lively account of the Roman context of this new religious force.

Futrell, Alison. *Blood in the Arena: The Spectacle of Roman Power*. 1997. Explores the role of violent spectacle in creating and sustaining Roman rule.

Gardner, Jane F. *Women in Roman Law and Society*. 1987. Discusses issues pertaining to women in Rome.

Garnsey, Peter, and Richard Saller. *The Roman Empire: Economy, Society, and Culture*. 1987. Stresses the economic and social foundations of the Roman Empire.

Isaac, Benjamin. *The Creation of Racism in Classical Antiquity*. 2004. A highly readable discussion of ancient social prejudices and discriminatory stereotypes that influenced the development of modern racism.

Nickelsburg, George W. E. *Ancient Judaism and Christian Origins. Diversity, Continuity, and Transformation*. 2003. Innovative study of the emergence of Christianity from Judaism.

Ramage, Nancy H., and Andrew Ramage. *Roman Art,* 4th ed. 2005. An excellent, beautifully illustrated introduction to Roman art and architecture.

Romm, James. *The Edges of the Earth in Ancient Thought: Geography, Exploration, and Fiction.* 1992. An exciting introduction to the Roman understanding of real and imaginary peoples.

Scott, Sarah, and Jane Webster, eds. *Roman Imperialism and Provincial Art.* 2003. A collection of essays that explores new approaches to the cultural interconnections between the Romans and the peoples they ruled.

Talbert, Richard, ed. *The Barrington Atlas of the Classical World.* 2000. This atlas contains the best maps available.

Webster, Graham. *The Roman Imperial Army,* 3rd ed. 1985. Discusses military organization and life in the empire.

Wells, Peter S. *The Battle That Stopped Rome.* 2003. A lively account of the Battle of Teutoberg Forest that provides a clear and comprehensive demonstration of the way archaeological evidence helps shape our understanding of the past.

Wolfram, Herwig. *The Roman Empire and Its Germanic Peoples.* 1997. Examines the interrelation of Romans and Germans over several centuries.

Woolf, G., ed. *The Cambridge Illustrated History of the Roman World.* 2003. Richly illustrated and comprehensive.

Woolf, Greg. *Becoming Roman: The Origins of Provincial Civilization in Gaul.* 1998. The best recent study of Romanization.

CHAPTER 7. LATE ANTIQUITY: THE AGE OF NEW BOUNDARIES, 250-600

Bowersock, G. W. *Hellenism in Late Antiquity.* 1990. Explains the important role of traditional Greek culture in shaping late antiquity.

Bowersock, G. W., Peter Brown, and Oleg Grabar, eds. *Late Antiquity: A Guide to the Postclassical World.* 1999. An indispensable handbook containing synthetic essays and shorter encyclopedia entries.

Brown, Peter. *The Cult of the Saints: Its Rise and Function in Late Antiquity.* 1981. A brilliant and highly influential study.

Brown, Peter. *The Rise of Western Christendom: Triumph and Diversity.* 1997. An influential and highly accessible survey.

Brown, Peter. *The World of Late Antiquity.* 1971. A classic treatment of the period.

Cameron, Averil. *The Later Roman Empire.* 1993. *The Mediterranean World in Late Antiquity.* 1997. Excellent textbooks with bibliography and maps.

Clark, Gillian. *Women in Late Antiquity: Pagan and Christian Life-Styles.* 1993. The starting point of modern discussion; lucid and reliable.

Harries, Jill. *Law and Empire in Late Antiquity.* 1999. Explores the presence and practice of law in Roman society.

Lee, A. D. *Information and Frontiers: Roman Foreign Relations in Late Antiquity.* 1993. An exciting and original investigation.

Maas, Michael. *The Cambridge Companion to the Age of Justinian.* 2005. A collection of 20 chapters by different experts on all aspects of the Mediterranean world in the sixth century.

Maas, Michael. *Readings in Late Antiquity: A Sourcebook.* 2000. Hundreds of ancient sources in translation illustrating all aspects of late antiquity.

Markus, Robert. *The End of Ancient Christianity.* 1995. Excellent introduction to the transformation of Christianity in late antiquity.

Rich, John, ed. *The City in Late Antiquity.* 1992. Important studies of changes in late antique urbanism.

Thompson, E. A. *The Huns,* rev. Peter Heather. 1997. The best introduction to major issues.

CHAPTER 8. MEDIEVAL EMPIRES AND BORDERLANDS: BYZANTIUM AND ISLAM

Bowersock, Glen, Peter Brown, and Oleg Grabar, eds. *Late Antiquity: A Guide to the Post-Classical World.* 1999. Interpretive essays combined with encyclopedia entries make this a starting point for discussion.

Brown, Thomas S. *Gentlemen and Officers: Imperial Administration and Aristocratic Power in Byzantine Italy,* A.D. *554–800.* 1984. The basic study of Byzantine rule in Italy between Justinian and Charlemagne.

Bulliet, Richard W. *The Camel and the Wheel.* 1990. A fascinating investigation of the importance of the camel in history.

Cook, Michael. *Muhammad.* 1996. A short, incisive account of Muhammad's life that questions the traditional picture.

Cormack, Robin. *Writing in Gold: Byzantine Society and Its Icons.* 1985. An expert discussion of icons in the Byzantine world.

Donner, Fred M. *The Early Islamic Conquests.* 1981. Discusses the first phases of Islamic expansion

Fletcher, Richard. *Moorish Spain.* 1992. Highly readable.

Franklin, Simon, and Jonathan Shepard. *The Emergence of Rus: 750–1200.* 1996. The standard text for this period.

Hawting, G. R. *The first dynasty of Islam: the Umayyad caliphate, AD 661–750.* 2000. The most up-to-date study of the Umayyads.

Herrin, Judith. *The Formation of Christendom.* 2001. An exceptionally learned and lucid book; Herrin sees Byzantium as crucial both for the development of Christianity and Islam.

Hourani, George. *Arab Seafaring in the Indian Ocean in Ancient and Early Medieval Times.* 1995. The standard discussion of Arab maritime activity.

King, Charles. *The Black Sea: A History.* 2004. A comprehensive history of the Black Sea region from antiquity to the present. It is especially useful for anyone interested in this borderland among cultures.

Moorhead, John. *The Roman Empire Divided, 400–700.* 2001. A reliable and up-to-date survey of the period.

Robinson, Francis, ed. *The Cambridge Illustrated History of the Islamic World.* 1978. Many excellent and well-illustrated articles that will be useful for beginners.

Treadgold, Warren. *A History of the Byzantine State and Society.* 1998. A reliable narrative of Byzantine history.

Treadgold, Warren T. *A Concise History of Byzantium.* 2001. A reliable and insightful short survey.

CHAPTER 9. MEDIEVAL EMPIRES AND BORDERLANDS: THE LATIN WEST

Bachrach, Bernard S. *Early Medieval Jewish Policy in Western Europe.* 1977. A significant revisionist view of the history of the Jews in Latin Christian Europe.

Bartlett, Robert. *The Making of Europe: Conquest, Colonization and Cultural Change: 950–1350.* 1993. The best, and often greatly stimulating, analysis of how Latin Christianity spread in post-Carolingian Europe.

Brown, Peter. *The Rise of Western Christendom: Triumph and Diversity* A.D. *200–1000.* 2001. A brilliant interpretation of the development of Christianity in its social context.

Cohen, Jeremy. *Living Letters of the Law: Ideas of the Jew in Medieval Christianity.* 1999.

A masterful investigation of early medieval Judaism.

Geary, Patrick J. *The Peoples of Europe in the Early Middle Ages.* 2002. Discusses the emergence of the new kingdoms of Europe, stressing the incorporation of Roman elements.

Hollister, C. Warren. *Medieval Europe: A Short History.* 1997. This concise, crisply written text presents the development of Europe during the Middle Ages by charting its progression from a primitive rural society, sparsely settled and impoverished, to a powerful and distinctive civilization.

Jones, Gwyn. *A History of the Vikings.* 2001. A comprehensive, highly readable analysis.

Keen, Maurice, ed. *Medieval Warfare: A History.* 1999. Lucid specialist studies of aspects of medieval warfare.

Lawrence, C. H. *Medieval Monasticism.* 2001. A fine introduction to the phenomenon of Christian monasticism.

Maalouf, Amin. *The Crusades through Arab Eyes.* 1984. Based on the works of Arab chroniclers, this book depicts a culture nearly destroyed both by internal conflicts and the military threat of the alien Christian culture.

Mayr-Harting, Henry. *The Coming of Christianity to Anglo-Saxon England.* 1991. How a Germanic people were converted to Christianity.

McKitterick, Rosamond. *The Early Middle Ages.* 2001. The best up-to-date survey for the period 400–1000. It is composed of separate essays by leading specialists.

Moorhead, John. *The Roman Empire Divided, 400–700.* 2001. The best recent survey of the period.

Reuter, Timothy. *Germany in the Early Middle Ages, c. 800–1056.* 1991. A lucid explanation of the complexities of German history in this period.

Reynolds, Susan. *Fiefs and Vassals: The Medieval Evidence Reinterpreted.* 1994. The most important reexamination of the feudalism problem.

Riché, Pierre. *Education and Culture in the Barbarian West, Sixth Through Eighth Centuries,* translated from the third French edition. by John J. Contreni. 1975. Demonstrates the rich complexity of learning during this period, once thought to be the Dark Ages of education.

Riché, Pierre. *The Carolingians: A Family Who Forged Europe.* 1993. Translated from the 1983 French edition, this book traces the rise, fall, and revival of the Carolingian dynasty, and shows how it molded the shape of a post-Roman Europe that still prevails today. This is basically a family history, but the family dominated Europe for more than two centuries.

Riley-Smith, Jonathan Simon Christopher. *The Crusades: A Short History.* 1987. Exactly what the title says.

Riley-Smith, Jonathan Simon Christopher. *The Oxford Illustrated History of the Crusades.* 2001. An utterly engaging, comprehensive study.

Stenton, Frank M. *Anglo-Saxon England.* 2001. This classic history covers the period ca. 550–1087 and traces the development of English society from the oldest Anglo-Saxon laws and kings to the extension of private lordship.

Strayer, Joseph B., ed. *Dictionary of the Middle Ages.* 1986. An indispensable reference work.

Webster, Leslie, and Michelle Brown, eds. *The Transformation of the Roman World, A.D. 400–900.* 1997. A well-illustrated synthesis with maps and bibliography.

Wickham, Chris. *Early Medieval Italy: Central Government and Local Society, 400–1000.* 1981. Examines the economic and social transformation of Italy.

CHAPTER 10. MEDIEVAL CIVILIZATION: THE RISE OF WESTERN EUROPE

Bony, Jean. *French Gothic Architecture of the Twelfth and Thirteenth Centuries.* 1983. With many beautiful illustrations, this is a good way to begin an investigation of these magnificent buildings.

Colish, Marcia L. *Medieval Foundations of the Western Intellectual Tradition, 400–1400.* 1997. The best general study.

Gimpel, Jean. *The Medieval Machine: The Industrial Revolution of the Middle Ages.* 1976. A short, lucid account of the power and agricultural revolutions.

Keen, Maurice. *Chivalry.* 1984. Readable and balanced in its coverage of this sometimes misunderstood phenomenon.

Lambert, Malcolm. *Medieval Heresy: Popular Movements from the Gregorian Reform to the Reformation,* 2nd ed. 1992. The best general study of heresy.

Lawrence, C. H. *The Friars: The Impact of the Early Mendicant Movement on Western Society.* 1994.

The best general study of the influence of Dominicans and Franciscans.

Moore, R. I. *The Formation of a Persecuting Society: Power and Deviance in Western Europe, 950–1250.* 1987. A brilliant analysis of how Europe became a persecuting society.

Morris, Colin. *The Papal Monarchy: The Western Church from 1050 to 1250.* 1989. A thorough study that should be the beginning point for further investigation of the many fascinating figures in the medieval Church.

Mundy, John H. *Europe in the High Middle Ages, 1150–1309,* 3rd ed. 1999. A comprehensive introduction to the period.

Peters, Edward. *Europe and the Middle Ages.* 1989. An excellent general survey.

Strayer, Joseph R. *On the Medieval Origins of the Modern State.* 1970. Still the best short analysis.

CHAPTER 11. THE MEDIEVAL WEST IN CRISIS

Carmichael, Ann G. *Plague and the Poor in Renaissance Florence.* 1986. An innovative study that both questions the traditional theory of the bubonic plague as the cause of the Black Death and examines how fear of the disease led to regulation of the poor.

Cohn, Samuel. *The Black Death Transformed: Disease and Culture in Early Renaissance Europe.* 2003. A well-argued case that the Black Death was not caused by the bubonic plague.

Duby, Georges. *France in the Middle Ages, 987–1460: From Hugh Capet to Joan of Arc.* 1991. Traces the emergence of the French state.

Gordon, Bruce, and Peter Marshall, eds. *The Place of the Dead: Death and Remembrance in Late Medieval and Early Modern Europe.* 2000. A collection of essays that shows how the placing of the dead in society was an important activity that engendered considerable conflict and negotiation.

Herlihy, David. *The Black Death and the Transformation of the West.* 1997. A pithy, readable analysis of the epidemiological and historical issues surrounding the Black Death.

Holmes, George. *Europe: Hierarchy and Revolt, 1320–1450.* 1975. Excellent examination of rebellions.

Huizinga, Johan. *The Autumn of the Middle Ages,* trans. Rodney J. Payton and Urlich Mammitzsch. 1996. A new translation of the classic study of France and the Low Countries during the fourteenth and fifteenth centuries. Dated and perhaps too pessimistic, Huizinga's lucid prose and broad vision still make this an engaging reading experience.

Imber, Colin. *The Ottoman Empire, 1300–1481.* 1990. The basic work that establishes a chronology for the early Ottomans.

Jordan, William C. *The Great Famine: Northern Europe in the Early Fourteenth Century.* 1996. The most comprehensive book on the famine.

Lambert, Malcolm. *Medieval Heresy: Popular Movements from the Gregorian Reform to the Reformation.* 1992. Excellent general study of the Hussite and Lollard movements.

Le Roy Ladurie, Emmanuel. *Times of Feast, Times of Famine: A History of Climate Since the Year 1000,* trans. Barbara Bray. 1971. The book that introduced the idea of the Little Ice Age and promoted the study of the influence of climate on history.

Lynch, Joseph H. *The Medieval Church: A Brief History.* 1992. A pithy, elegant survey of ecclesiastical institutions and developments.

Morgan, David O. *The Mongols.* 1986. Best introduction to Mongol history.

Nirenberg, David. *Communities of Violence: Persecution of Minorities in the Middle Ages.* 1996. An important analysis of the persecution of minorities that is deeply rooted in Spanish evidence.

Scott, Susan, and Christopher Duncan. *Biology of Plagues: Evidence from Historical Populations.* 2001. An analysis by two epidemiologists who argue that the Black Death was not the bubonic plague but probably a virus similar to Ebola.

Sumption, Jonathan. *The Hundred Years' War: Trial by Battle.* 1991. First volume goes only to 1347. When it is completed, it will be the best comprehensive study.

Swanson, R. N. *Religion and Devotion in Europe, c. 1215–c. 1515.* 1995. The best up-to-date textbook account of late medieval religious practice.

CHAPTER 12. THE ITALIAN RENAISSANCE AND BEYOND: THE POLITICS OF CULTURE

Baxandall, Michael. *Painting and Experience in Fifteenth Century Italy: A Primer in the Social History of Pictorial Style.* 1988. A fascinating study of how the daily social experiences of Florentine bankers and churchgoers influenced how these individuals saw Renaissance paintings and how painters responded to the viewers' experience. One of the best books on Italian painting.

Brown, Howard M. *Music in the Renaissance.* 1976. Dated but still the best general study of Renaissance music.

Brown, Patricia Fortini. *Art and Life in Renaissance Venice.* 1997. A delightful study about how art fit into the daily lives and homes of the Venetian upper classes.

Brucker, Gene. *Florence: The Golden Age, 1138–1737.* 1998. A brilliant, beautifully illustrated history by the most prominent American historian of Florence.

Burke, Peter. *The Italian Renaissance.* 1999. A concise and readable synthesis of the most recent research.

Hale, J. R. *Renaissance Europe, 1480–1520.* 2000. A witty, engaging, and enlightening study of Europe during the formation of the early modern state system. Strong on establishing the material and social limitations of Renaissance society.

King, Margaret L. *Women of the Renaissance.* 1991. The best general study of women in Renaissance Europe. It is especially strong on female intellectuals and women's education.

Kohl, Benjamin G., and Alison Andrews Smith, eds. *Major Problems in the History of the Italian Renaissance.* 1995. A useful collection of articles and short studies of major historical problems in the study of the Renaissance.

Martines, Lauro. *Power and Imagination: City-States in Renaissance Italy.* 1988. An excellent general survey that is strong on class conflicts and patronage.

Najemy, John M. *A History of Florence, 1200–1575.* 2006. The best and most up-to-date history of the home of the Renaissance.

Nauert, Charles G., Jr. *Humanism and the Culture of Renaissance Europe.* 1995. The best survey of humanism for students new to the subject. It is clear and comprehensive.

Skinner, Quentin. *Machiavelli: A Very Short Introduction.* 2000. This is the place to begin in the study of Machiavelli. Always clear and precise, this is a beautiful little book.

Stephens, John. *The Italian Renaissance: The Origins of Intellectual and Artistic Change Before the Reformation.* 1990. A stimulating analysis of how cultural change took place.

Vasari, Giorgio. *The Lives of the Artists.* 1998. Written by a sixteenth-century Florentine who was himself a prominent artist, this series of artistic biographies captures the spirit of Renaissance society.

CHAPTER 13. THE WEST AND THE WORLD: THE SIGNIFICANCE OF GLOBAL ENCOUNTERS, 1450–1650

Chaudhuri, K. N. *Trade and Civilization in the Indian Ocean: An Economic History from the Rise of Islam to 1750.* 1985. Arguing for the long-term unity of trade routes, the book lays out the importance of Asian merchants to maritime trade networks from the South China Sea to the Mediterranean.

Clendinnen, Inga. *Aztecs: An Interpretation.* 1991. A provocative, sometimes disturbing book that directly confronts the implications of human sacrifice and cannibalism among the Aztecs and offers an explanation for it by analyzing Aztec religion.

Crosby, Alfred W., Jr. *The Columbian Exchange: Biological and Cultural Consequences of 1492.* 1973. The most significant study on the implications of the biological exchanges for the cultural history of both the Old and New Worlds. It has the benefit of being an exciting book to read.

Curtin, Philip D. *African History: From Earliest Times to Independence.* 1995. An excellent survey by one of the most distinguished comparative historians.

Elvin, Mark. *The Pattern of the Chinese Past: A Social and Economic Interpretation.* 1973. An excellent overview of Chinese history that covers Chinese responses to Western encounters.

Fernández-Armesto, Felipe. *Before Columbus: Exploration and Colonization from the Mediterranean to the Atlantic, 1229–1492.* 1987. Engagingly written and original in scope, this is the best single account of early European colonization efforts.

Fernández-Armesto, Felipe. *Columbus.* 1991. The 500th anniversary of Columbus's voyage in 1492 provoked a wide-ranging reappraisal of his motives and career. This pithy, engaging book is by far the most convincing in revising Columbus's image, but it deflated much of the Columbus myth and caused considerable controversy.

Oliver, Roland. *The African Experience from Olduvai Gorge to the 21st Century.* 2000. A highly readable general survey.

Pagden, Anthony. *European Encounters with the New World: From Renaissance to Romanticism.* 1993. A fascinating examination of how Europeans interpreted their encounters with America.

Parry, J. H. *The Age of Reconnaissance.* 1982. An analysis of European shipping technology and the causes behind European explorations. It covers all the major voyages.

Parry, J. H. *The Spanish Seaborne Empire.* 1990. The standard study on the subject. It brings together an enormous range of material and presents it clearly and cogently.

Phillips, William D., Jr., and Carla Rahn Phillips. *The Worlds of Christopher Columbus.* 1992. A balanced analysis of Columbus's attempts to find financing for his voyage that pays equal attention to his personal ambition, Christian zeal, and navigational skills.

CHAPTER 14. THE REFORMATIONS OF RELIGION

Bireley, Robert. *The Refashioning of Catholicism, 1450–1700: A Reassessment of the Counter Reformation.* 1999. A fair reappraisal of the major events by one of the most prominent historians of Catholicism in this period.

Bossy, John. *Christianity in the West, 1400–1700.* 1985. A short study not of the institutions of the Church but of Christianity itself, this book explores the Christian people, their beliefs, and their way of life. The book demonstrates considerable continuities before and after the Reformation and is especially useful in understanding the attitudes of common lay believers as opposed to the major reformers and Church officials.

Cameron, Euan. *The European Reformation.* 1995. The most comprehensive general survey, this bulky book covers all the major topics in considerable detail. It is excellent in explaining theological issues.

Hsia, R. Po-chia. *The World of Catholic Renewal, 1540–1770.* 1998. An excellent survey of the most recent research.

Koenigsberger, H. G., George L. Mosse, and G. Q. Bowler. *Europe in the Sixteenth Century,* 2nd ed. 1989. A good beginner's survey. Strong on political events.

McGrath, Alister E. *Reformation Thought: An Introduction,* 3rd rev. ed. 1999. Indispensable introduction for anyone seeking to understand the ideas of the European Reformation. Drawing on the most up-to-date scholarship, McGrath offers a clear explanation of these ideas, set firmly in their historical contexts.

Muir, Edward. *Ritual in Early Modern Europe*, 2nd ed. 2005. A broad survey of the debates about ritual during the Reformation and the implementation of ritual reforms.

Oberman, Heiko A. *Luther: Man Between God and the Devil*, trans. Eileen Walliser-Schwarzbart. 1992. First published to great acclaim in Germany, this book argues that Luther was more the medieval monk than history has usually regarded him. Oberman claims that Luther was haunted by the Devil and saw the world as a cosmic battleground between God and Satan. A brilliant, intellectual biography that is sometimes challenging but always clear and precise.

O'Malley, John. *Trent and All That: Renaming Catholicism in the Early Modern Era*. 2000. O'Malley works out a remarkable guide to the intellectual and historical developments behind the concepts of Catholic reform and, in his useful term, Early Modern Catholicism. The result is the single best overview of scholarship on Catholicism in early modern Europe, delivered in a pithy, lucid, and entertaining style.

Ozment, Steven. *The Age of Reform, 1250–1550: An Intellectual and Religious History of Late Medieval and Reformation Europe*. 1986. Firmly places the Protestant Reformation in the context of late medieval spirituality and theology; particularly strong on pre-Reformation developments.

Reardon, Bernard M. G. *Religious Thought in the Reformation*, 2nd ed. 1995. A good beginner's survey of the intellectual dimensions of the Reformation.

Scribner, R. W. *For the Sake of the Simple Folk: Popular Propaganda for the German Reformation*. 1994. An innovative and fascinating study of the Lutheran use of visual images.

Scribner, R. W. *The German Reformation*. 1996. A short and very clear analysis of the appeal of the Reformation by the leading social historian of the period. Pays attention to what people actually did rather than just what reformers said they should do.

CHAPTER 15. THE AGE OF CONFESSIONAL DIVISION

Anderson, M. S. *The Origins of the Modern European State System, 1494–1618*. 1998. The best

short study for students new to the subject of the evolution of the confessional states in Europe. This book is very good at establishing common patterns among the various states.

Burke, Peter. *Popular Culture in Early Modern Europe*. 1994. This wide-ranging book includes considerable material from eastern Europe and Scandinavia, as well as the more extensively studied western European countries. Extraordinarily influential, it practically invented the subject of popular culture by showing how much could be learned from studying festivals and games.

Davies, Norman. *God's Playground: A History of Poland*. Rev. ed., 2 vols. 1982. By far the most comprehensive study of Polish history, this is particularly strong for the sixteenth and seventeenth centuries. Davies offers a Polish-centered view of European history that is marvelously stimulating even if he sometimes overstates his case for the importance of Poland.

Dukes, Paul. *A History of Russia: Medieval, Modern, Contemporary, ca. 882–1996*, 3rd ed. 1998. A comprehensive survey that synthesizes the most recent research.

Dunn, Richard S. *The Age of Religious Wars, 1559–1715*, 2nd ed. 1980. An excellent survey for students new to the subject.

Evans, R. J. W. *Rudolf II and His World: A Study in Intellectual History, 1576–1612*. 1973. A sympathetic examination of the intellectual world Rudolf created. Evans recognizes Rudolf's mental problems but lessens their significance for understanding the period.

Holt, Mack P. *The French Wars of Religion, 1562–1629*. 1996. A lucid short synthesis of the events and complex issues raised by these wars.

Hsia, R. Po-chia. *Social Discipline in the Reformation: Central Europe, 1550–1750*. 1989. An excellent, lucid, and short overview of the attempts to discipline the people in Germany.

Huppert, George. *After the Black Death: A Social History of Early Modern Europe*. 1986. Engaging, entertaining, and elegantly written, this is the best single study of European social life during the Early Modern period.

Levack, Brian P. *The Witch-Hunt in Early Modern Europe*, 2nd ed. 1995. The best and most up-to-date short examination of the complex problem of the witch-hunt. This is the place to begin for students new to the subject.

Ozment, Steven E. *Ancestors: The Loving Family in Old Europe*. 2001. This comprehensive study of family life demonstrates that families were actually far more loving than the theory of patriarchy would suggest.

Parker, Geoffrey. *The Dutch Revolt*, rev. ed. 1990. The classic study of the revolt by one of the most masterful historians of the period. This study is especially adept at pointing to the larger European context of the revolt.

Parker, Geoffrey. *The Grand Strategy of Philip II*. 1998. Rehabilitates Philip as a significant strategic thinker.

Wiesner, Merry E. *Women and Gender in Early Modern Europe*. 1993. The best short study of the subject. This is the best book for students new to the subject.

CHAPTER 16. ABSOLUTISM AND STATE BUILDING, 1618–1715.

Aylmer, G. E. *Rebellion or Revolution*. 1986. A study of the nature of the political disturbances of the 1640s and 1650s.

Beik, William. *Louis XIV and Absolutism: A Brief Study with Documents*. 2000. An excellent collection of documents.

Collins, James B. *The State in Early Modern France*. 1995. The best general study of the French state.

Elliott, J. H. *Richelieu and Olivares*. 1984. A comparison of the two contemporary absolutist ministers and state builders in France and Spain.

Goffman, Daniel. *The Ottoman Empire and Early Modern Europe*. 2002. A broad survey that challenges many of the Western stereotypes of Ottoman politics and culture, including the belief that Ottoman government was tyrannical.

Harris, Tim. *Politics Under the Later Stuarts*. 1993. The best study of Restoration politics, including the Glorious Revolution.

Hughes, Lindsey. *Russia in the Age of Peter the Great*. 1998. A comprehensive study of politics, diplomacy, society, and culture during the reign of the "Tsar Reformer."

Israel, Jonathan. *The Dutch Republic: Its Rise, Greatness and Fall, 1477–1806*. 1996. A massive and authoritative study of the Dutch Republic during the period of its greatest global influence.

Lincoln, W. Bruce. *Sunlight at Midnight: St. Petersburg and the Rise of Modern Russia*. 2000. The best study of the building of Peter the Great's new capital city.

Parker, David. *The Making of French Absolutism*. 1983. A particularly good treatment of the early seventeenth century.

Parker, Geoffrey. *The Military Revolution*. 1988. Deals with the impact of the military revolution on the world as well as European history.

Rabb, Theodore K. *The Struggle for Stability in Early Modern Europe*. 1975. Employs visual as well as political sources to illustrate the way in which Europeans responded to the general crisis of the seventeenth century.

Schama, Simon. *The Embarrassment of Riches: An Interpretation of Dutch Culture in the Golden Age*. 1987. Contains a wealth of commentary on Dutch art and culture during its most influential period.

Wilson, Peter H. *Absolutism in Central Europe*. 2000. Analyzes both the theory and the practice of absolutism in Prussia and Austria.

CHAPTER 17. THE SCIENTIFIC REVOLUTION

Biagioli, Mario. *Galileo, Courtier: The Practice of Science in the Culture of Absolutism*. 1993. Argues that Galileo's desire for patronage determined the type of research he engaged in and the scientific questions he asked.

Campbell, Mary Blaine. *Wonder and Science, Imagining Worlds in Early Modern Europe*. 1999. Explores the conceptual and celestial worlds opened by science as well as the geographical worlds found in voyages of discovery.

Cohen, H. Floris. *The Scientific Revolution: A Historiographical Inquiry*. 1995. A thorough account of all the different interpretations of the causes and significance of the Scientific Revolution.

Dear, Peter. *Discipline and Experience: The Mathematical Way in the Scientific Revolution*. 1995. Explains the importance of mathematics in the development of seventeenth-century science.

Debus, Allen G. *Man and Nature in the Renaissance*. 1978. Deals with the early history of the Scientific Revolution and develops many of its connections with the Renaissance.

Drake, Stillman, ed. *Discoveries and Opinions of Galileo*. 1957. Includes four of Galileo's most important writings, together with a detailed commentary.

Feingold, Mordechai. *The Newtonian Moment: Isaac Newton and the Making of Modern Culture.* 2004. A richly illustrated volume that contains valuable material on the reception of Newtonian ideas in the eighteenth century as well as a chapter on Newtonian women.

Grayling, A. C. Descartes: *The Life and Times of a Genius.* 2006. A biography that places Descartes in his proper historical context and suggests that he may have served as a spy.

Huff, Toby. *The Rise of Early Modern Science: Islam, China and the West*, 2003. Adresses the question why modern science arose only in the West despite the fact that non-Western science was more advanced in the Middle Ages.

Kuhn, Thomas S. *The Copernican Revolution.* 1957. The most comprehensive and authoritative study of the shift from an Earth-centered to a sun-centered model of the universe.

Needham, Joseph. *The Grand Titration: Science and Society in East and West.* 1979. Discusses the weaknesses and strengths of Chinese science.

Popkin, Richard. *The History of Scepticism from Erasmus to Spinoza.* 1979. Discusses skepticism as a cause as well as an effect of the Scientific Revolution.

Schiebinger, Londa. *The Mind Has No Sex? Women in the Origins of Modern Science.* 1989. Explores the role of women in all aspects of scientific endeavor.

Shapin, Steven. *The Scientific Revolution.* 1996. A study of the origins of the modern scientific worldview that emphasizes the social influences on the production of knowledge and the social purposes for which scientific knowledge was intended.

Shapin, Steven, and Simon Schaffer. *Leviathan and the Air Pump.* 1989. Discusses the difference between Robert Boyle and Thomas Hobbes regarding the value of experimentation.

Shea, William R., and Mariano Artigas. *Galileo in Rome: The Rise and Fall of a Troublesome Genius.* 2004. Attributes some of Galileo's troubles to his tactlessness and headstrong behavior.

Stewart, Matthew. *The Courtier and the Heretic: Leibniz, Spinoza, and the Fate of God in the Modern World.* 2006. Illuminates the conflicting philosophical ideas of Wilhelm Leibniz and Baruch Spinoza, arguing that Spinoza anticipated

later philosophical and scientific developments by two and sometimes three centuries.

Thomas, Keith. *Man and the Natural World: A History of the Modern Sensibility.* 1983. A study of the shifting attitudes of human beings toward nature during the period from 1500 to 1800.

Webster, Charles. *The Great Instauration: Science, Medicine and Reform, 1626–1660.* 1975. Explores the relationship between Puritanism and the Scientific Revolution in England.

Westfall, Richard S. *Never at Rest: A Biography of Isaac Newton.* 1980. A superb biography of the most influential scientist in the history of the West.

CHAPTER 18. THE WEST AND THE WORLD: EMPIRE, TRADE, AND WAR, 1650–1815

Bailyn, Bernard. *Ideological Origins of the American Revolution.* 1967. A probing analysis of the different intellectual traditions upon which the American colonists based their arguments for independence.

Blackburn, Robin. *The Making of New World Slavery: From the Baroque to the Modern, 1492–1800.* 1997. Places European slavery in a broad world perspective.

Boxer, C. R. *The Dutch Seaborne Empire, 1600–1800.* 1965. A thorough account covering the entire period of Dutch expansion.

Brown, Christopher L. *Moral capital: Foundations of British Abolitionism.* 2006. Establishes the popular campaign as well as the work of parliamentary reformers like William Wilberforce.

Elliott, J. H. *Empires of the Atlantic World: Britain and Spain in America 1492–1830.* 2006. A superb comparative study of the two largest overseas empires in the early modern period.

Eltis, David. *The Rise of African Slavery in the Americas.* 2000. An analysis of the different dimensions of the slave trade based on a database of slave ships and passengers.

Goody, Jack. *The East in the West.* 1996. Challenges the idea that Western cultures are more rational than those of Asia.

Greene, Jack P. *Peripheries and Center: Constitutional Development in the Extended Polities of the British Empire and the United States, 1607–1788.* 1986. A study of the composition of the British Empire and its disintegration in North America.

Kamen, Henry. *Empire: How Spain Became a World Power.* 2003. Explains how Spain established the most extensive empire the world had ever known.

Langley, Lester D. *The Americas in the Age of Revolution, 1750–1850.* 1996. A broad comparative study of revolutions in the United States, Haiti, and Latin America.

Liss, Peggy K. *The Atlantic Empires: The Network of Trade and Revolutions, 1713–1826.* 1983. Places the American Revolution in a broader comparative setting and includes material on early Latin American independence movements.

Mungello, D. E. *The Great Encounter of China and the West, 1500–1800.* 1999. Studies China's acceptance and rejection of Western culture as well as the parallel Western reception of China.

Pagden, Anthony. *Lords of All the World: Ideologies of Empire in Spain, Britain and France, ca. 1500–ca. 1800.* 1996. Discusses the theoretical foundations of the Atlantic Empires.

Said, Edward. *Orientalism.* 1979. A study of the way in which Western views of the East have assumed its inferiority.

CHAPTER 19. EIGHTEENTH-CENTURY SOCIETY AND CULTURE

Alexander, John T. *Catherine the Great: Life and Legend.* 1989. A lively biography of the remarkable "enlightened despot."

Beckett, J. V. *The Aristocracy in England, 1660–1914.* 1986. A comprehensive study of this landholding and governing elite. Makes the important distinction between the aristocracy and the nobility.

Darnton, Robert. *The Forbidden Best-Sellers of Pre-Revolutionary France.* 1995. A study of the salacious, blasphemous, and subversive books that sold more copies than those of the philosophes in eighteenth-century France.

Dewald, Jonathan. *The European Nobility, 1500–1800.* 1996. A comprehensive study of this social class that emphasizes its adaptability.

Doyle, William. *The Old European Order, 1660–1800,* 2nd ed. 1999. The best general study of the period.

Houston, R. A. *Literacy in Early Modern Europe: Culture and Education.* 1991. The best survey of the subject for the entire period.

Israel, Jonathan. *Radical Enlightenment: Philosophy and the Making of Modernity 1650–1750.* 2001. Emphasizes the influence of the radical philosophical ideas of the followers of Benedict Spinoza on the Enlightenment.

Knott, Sarah, and Barbara Taylor, eds. *Women, Gender and the Enlightenment.* 2005. A valuable collection of 39 essays that reflect the influence of feminist scholarship on the study of the Enlightenment.

Lugee, Carolyn. *Le Paradis des Femmes: Women, Salons and Social Stratification in 17th-Century France.* 1976. A social study of the women of the salons.

Outram, Dorinda. *The Enlightenment.* 1995. A balanced assessment of the major historiographical debates regarding the Enlightenment.

Robertson, John. *The Case for Enlightenment: Scotland and Naples, 1680–1760.* 2005. Argues that the main unifying theme of the Enlightenment throughout Europe was not its philosophical ideas but the determination to achieve "human betterment" and material improvement.

Root, Hilton. *Peasants and King in Burgundy: Agrarian Foundations of French Absolutism.* 1979. A study of peasant communal institutions and their relationship with the crown as well as the nobility.

Smith, Adam. Introduction to *The Wealth of Nations.* 1776.

Williams, David, ed. *The Enlightenment.* 1999. An excellent collection of political writings with a long introduction.

CHAPTER 20. THE AGE OF THE FRENCH REVOLUTION, 1789–1815

Andress, David. *The French Revolution and the People.* 2004. Focuses on the role played by the common people of France—the peasants, craftsmen and those living on the margins of society—in the revolution.

Blanning, T. C. W. *The French Revolutionary Wars, 1787–1802.* 1996. An authoritative political and military narrative that assesses the impact of the wars on French politics.

Chartier, Roger. *The Cultural Origins of the French Revolution.* 1991. Explores the connections between the culture of the Enlightenment and the cultural transformations of the revolutionary period.

Cobban, Alfred. *The Social Interpretation of the French Revolution.* 1964. Challenges the Marxist interpretation of the causes and effects of the revolution.

Doyle, William. *The Oxford History of the French Revolution.* 1989. An excellent synthesis.

Ellis, Geoffrey. *Napoleon.* 1997. A study of the nature and mechanics of Napoleon's power and an analysis of his imperial policy.

Furet, François. *The French Revolution, 1770–1814.* 1992. A provocative narrative that sees Napoleon as the architect of a second, authoritarian revolution that reversed the gains of the first.

Hardman, John. *Louis XVI: The Silent King.* 2000. A reassessment of the king that mixes sympathy with criticism.

Higonnet, Patrice. *Goodness Beyond Virtue: Jacobins During the French Revolution.* 1998. Explores the contradictions of Jacobin ideology and its descent into the Terror.

Hunt, Lynn. *Politics, Culture and Class in the French Revolution.* 1984. Analyzes the formation of a revolutionary political culture.

Kennedy, Emmet. *The Culture of the French Revolution.* 1989. A comprehensive study of all cultural developments before and during the revolution.

Landes, Joan B. *Women and the Public Sphere in the Age of the French Revolution.* 1988. Explores how the new political culture of the revolution changed the position of women in society.

Lefebvre, Georges. *The Great Fear of 1789: Rural Panic in Revolutionary France.* 1973. Shows the importance of the rural unrest of July 1789 that provided the backdrop of the legislation of August 1789.

Schama, Simon. *Citizens: A Chronicle of the French Revolution.* 1989. Depicts the tragic unraveling of a vision of liberty and happiness into a scenario of hunger, anger, violence, and death.

CHAPTER 21. THE INDUSTRIAL REVOLUTION

Ashton, T. A. *The Industrial Revolution,* reprint edition with preface by P. Hudson. 1992. The classic statement of the optimist position, identifying the benefits of the revolution.

Berg, Maxine. *The Age of Manufactures, 1700–1820: Industry, Innovation and Work in Britain.* 1994. A study of the process and character of specific industries, especially those employing women.

Brinley, Thomas. *The Industrial Revolution and the Atlantic Economy: Selected Essays.* 1993. Essays

challenging the view that Britain's Industrial Revolution was a gradual process.

Deane, Phyllis. *The First Industrial Revolution.* 1967. The best study of technological innovation in Britain.

Gutmann, Myron. *Toward the Modern Economy: Early Industry in Europe, 1500–1800.* 1988. A study of cottage industry, especially in France.

Hobsbawm, E. J. *Industry and Empire.* 1968. A general economic history of Britain from 1750 to 1970 that analyzes the position of Britain in the world economy.

Jacob, Margaret. *Scientific Culture and the Making of the Industrial West.* 1997. An exploration of the spread of scientific knowledge and its connection with industrialization.

Morris, R. J. *Class and Class Consciousness in the Industrial Revolution, 1780–1850.* 1979. A balanced treatment of the link between industrialization and class formation.

Pollard, Sidney. *Peaceful Conquest: The Industrialization of Europe, 1760–1970.* 1981. Links coal supplies to economic development.

Rule, John. *The Vital Century: England's Developing Economy, 1714–1815.* 1992. A general economic history establishing the importance of early eighteenth-century developments.

Stearns, Peter. *The Industrial Revolution in World History,* 2nd ed. 1998. The best study of industrialization in a global context.

Teich, Mikulas, and Roy Porter, eds. *The Industrial Revolution in National Context: Europe and the USA.* 1981. Essays illustrating similarities as well as national differences in the process of industrialization.

Wrigley, E. A. *Continuity, Chance and Change: The Character of the Industrial Revolution in Britain.* 1988. Includes the best discussion of the transition from an advanced organic economy to one based on minerals.

CHAPTER 22. IDEOLOGICAL CONFLICT AND NATIONAL UNIFICATION, 1815–1871

Anderson, Benedict. *Imagined Communities: Reflections on the Origin and Spread of Nationalism.* 1991. A discussion of the ways in which people conceptualize the nation.

Clark, Martin. *The Italian Risorgimento.* 1999. A comprehensive study of the social, economic, and religious context of Italian unification as well as its political and diplomatic dimensions.

Gellner, Ernest. *Nations and Nationalism.* 1983. An interpretive study that emphasizes the social roots of nationalism.

Holmes, Richard. *The Age of Wonder: How the Romantic Generation Discovered the Beauty and Terror of Nature.* 2009. Argues that science inspired the romantic imagination.

Hamerow, Theodore S. *Restoration, Revolution, Reaction: Economics and Politics in Germany, 1815–1871.* 1966. An investigation of the social basis of ideological encounters in Germany.

Honour, Hugh. *Romanticism.* 1979. A comprehensive study of romantic painting.

Hunczak, Tara, ed. *Russian Imperialism from Ivan the Great to the Revolution.* 1974. A collection of essays that illuminate Russian nationalism as well as imperialism over a long period of time.

Lichtheim, George. *A Short History of Socialism.* 1970. A good general treatment of the subject.

Nipperdey, Thomas. *Germany from Napoleon to Bismarck, 1800–1866.* 1996. An exploration of the creation of German nationalism as well as the failure of liberalism.

Onuf, Peter S. *Jefferson's Empire: The Language of American Nationhood.* 2000. A study of Jefferson's expansionary nationalism.

Pflanze, Otto. *Bismarck and the Development of Germany: The Period of Unification, 1815–1871.* 1963. The classic study of both Bismarck and the unification movement.

Pinckney, David. *The French Revolution of 1830.* 1972. The best treatment of this revolution.

Seton-Watson, Hugh. *Nations and States.* 1977. A clearly written study of the nation-state.

Sperber, Jonathan. *The European Revolutions, 1848–1851.* 1994. The best study of the revolutions of 1848.

Tombs, Robert. *The War Against Paris, 1871.* 1981. A narrative history of the Paris Commune.

CHAPTER 23. THE COMING OF MASS POLITICS: INDUSTRIALIZATION, EMANCIPATION, AND INSTABILITY, 1870–1914

Clyman, Toby W., and Judith Vowles, eds. *Russia through Women's Eyes: Autobiographies from Tsarist Russia.* 1999. Fascinating collection that allows us to see both women's history and Russian history in new ways.

Crossik, Geoffrey, and Serge Jaumin, eds. *Cathedrals of Consumption: The European Department Store, 1850–1939.* 1999. A set of essays exploring the impact of the retail revolution.

Hoerder, Dirk. *Cultures in Contact: World Migrations in the Second Millennium.* 2002. Wide-ranging study of the causes and consequences of human migration.

Kern, Stephen. *The Culture of Time and Space, 1880–1918.* 1983. An innovative work that explores the cultural impact of technological change.

Lidtke, Vernon. *The Alternative Culture: Socialist Labor in Imperial Germany.* 1985. Looks beyond the world of parliamentary politics to assess the meaning and impact of working-class socialism.

Lindemann, Albert. *Esau's Tears: Modern Anti-Semitism and the Rise of the Jews.* 1997. A comprehensive and detailed survey that challenges many assumptions about the roots and nature of modern anti-Semitism.

Mayer, Arno. *The Persistence of the Old Regime: Europe to the Great War.* 1981. Argues that landed elites maintained a considerable amount of economic and political power throughout the nineteenth century.

Maynes, Mary Jo. *Taking the Hard Road: Life Course in French and German Workers' Autobiographies in the Era of Industrialization.* 1995. Fascinating study of the "life course" of industrial workers.

Milward, A. S., and S. B. Saul. *The Development of the Economies of Continental Europe, 1850–1914.* 1977. A helpful survey.

Nord, Philip. *The Republican Moment: Struggles for Democracy in Nineteenth-Century France.* 1996. Illuminates the struggle to define and redefine France.

Pilbeam, Pamela. *The Middle Classes in Europe, 1789–1914: France, Germany, Italy, and Russia.* 1990. A comparative approach that helps clarify the patterns of social change.

Rendall, J. *The Origins of Modern Feminism: Women in Britain, France, and the United States.* 1985. A comprehensive comparative study.

Richards, Thomas. *The Commodity Culture of Victorian England: Advertising and Spectacle, 1851–1914.* 1990. Fascinating study of the manufacturing of desire.

Slezkine, Yuri. *The Jewish Century*. 2004. A good companion volume to Lindemann's *Esau's Tears*.

Steenson, Gary P. *After Marx, Before Lenin: Marxism and Socialist Working-Class Parties in Europe, 1884–1914*. 1991. Examines both ideology and political practice within Europe's socialist parties.

Weber, Eugen. *Peasants into Frenchmen: The Modernization of Rural France, 1870–1914*. 1976. A very important work that helped shape the way historians think about "nation making."

CHAPTER 24. THE WEST AND THE WORLD: CULTURAL CRISIS AND THE NEW IMPERIALISM, 1870–1914

Adas, Michael. *Machines as the Measure of Men: Science, Technology, and Ideologies of Western Dominance*. 1989. A superb study of the way in which the ideology of empire was inextricably connected with cultural and intellectual developments within the West.

Barnes, David S. *The Great Stink of Paris and the Nineteenth-Century Struggle against Filth and Germs*. 2005. Important study of developing attitudes toward public health.

Butler, Christopher. *Early Modernism: Literature, Music, and Painting in Europe, 1900–1916*. 1994. Wide-ranging and nicely illustrated

Crews, Robert. *For Prophet and Tsar: Islam and Empire in Russia and Central Asia*. 2006. Important study of an often-overlooked aspect of imperialism.

Dijkstra, Bram. *Idols of Perversity: Fantasies of Feminine Evil in* Fin-de-Siècle *Culture*. 1986. This richly illustrated work shows how anxiety over the changing role of women permeated artistic production at the end of the nineteenth century.

Dodge, Ernest. *Islands and Empires: The Western Impact on the Pacific and East Asia*. 1976. A useful study of Asian imperialism.

Ellis, John. *The Social History of the Machine Gun*. 1975. Lively, nicely illustrated, and informative.

Gould, Stephen Jay. *The Mismeasure of Man*. 1996. A compelling look at the manipulation of scientific data and statistics to provide "proof" for racist and elitist assumptions.

Headrick, Daniel R. *The Tools of Empire: Technology and European Imperialism in the Nineteenth Century*. 1981. Highlights the important role played by technology in determining both the timing and success of Western imperialism.

Hochschild, Adam. *King Leopold's Ghost*. 1998. Blistering account of Leopold's imperialist rule in the Congo.

Pick, Daniel. *Faces of Degeneration: A European Disorder, c. 1848–1918*. 1993. Argues that concern over degeneration formed a central theme in European culture in the second half of the nineteenth century.

Showalter, Elaine. *Sexual Anarchy: Gender and Culture at the* Fin de Siècle. 1990. An illuminating look at the turbulence that characterized gender relations in the *fin-de-siècle*.

Sperber, Jonathan. *Popular Catholicism in Nineteenth-Century Germany*. 1984. A look at the religious dimensions of popular culture.

Vandervort, Bruce. *Wars of Imperial Conquest in Africa, 1830–1914*. 1998. An up-to-date study by a military historian.

Weeks, Theodore. *Nation and State in Late Imperial Russia: Nationalism and Russification on the Western Frontier*. 1966. Important study of Russian imperialism and nation-making.

Weiner, Jonathan. *The Beak of the Finch: The Story of Evolution in Our Time*. 1994. Prize-winning study of Darwin's theory and its impact.

Wesseling, H. L. *Divide and Rule: The Partition of Africa, 1880–1914*. 1996. A solid survey of complex developments.

CHAPTER 25. THE FIRST WORLD WAR

Cooper, John Milton. *Breaking the Heart of the World: Woodrow Wilson and the Fight for the League of Nations*. 2001. Examines the failure of Wilson's new world order.

Ferguson, Niall. *The Pity of War*. 1999. A bold reconsideration of many accepted interpretations of the origins and experience of the war.

Cork, Richard. *A Bitter Truth: Avant-Garde Art and the Great War*. 1994. A beautifully illustrated work that looks at the cultural impact of the war.

Davis, Belinda. *Home Fires Burning: Food, Politics, and Everyday Life in World War I Berlin*. 2000. An important look at the German home front.

Figes, Orlando. *A People's Tragedy: A History of the Russian Revolution*. 1997. Award-winning, gripping account of the revolutionary years.

Fitzpatrick, Sheila. *The Russian Revolution, 1917–1932.* 1994. As the title indicates, Fitzpatrick sees the revolutions of 1917 as the opening battle in a more than ten-year struggle to shape the new Russia.

Gilbert, Martin. *The First World War: A Complete History.* 1994. A comprehensive account, packed with illuminating detail.

Higonnet, Margaret. *Lines of Fire: Women's Visions of World War I.* 1998. An important study of women's experiences.

Joll, James. *The Origins of the First World War.* 1984. One of the best and most carefully balanced studies of this complicated question.

Keegan, John. *The First World War.* 1999. Military history at its best.

Read, Christopher. *From Tsar to Soviets: The Russian People and Their Revolution, 1917–1921.* 1996. An up-to-date study of the popular revolution and its fate.

Steinberg, M. D. *Voices of Revolution, 1917.* 2001. The Russian Revolution in the words of the ordinary people who made and experienced it.

Winter, J. M. *The Experience of World War I.* 1989. Despite the title, this richly illustrated work not only covers the war itself but also explores the factors that led to its outbreak and outlines its chief consequences

Zuckerman, Larry. *The Rape of Belgium: The Untold Story of World War I.* 2004. Corrective account that takes a hard look at German atrocities.

CHAPTER 26. RECONSTRUCTION, REACTION, AND CONTINUING REVOLUTION—THE 1920s AND 1930s

Balderston, Theo, ed. *The World Economy and National Economics in the Interwar Slump.* 2003. Collections of essays exploring the impact of the Great Depression.

Berend, Ivan T. *Decades of Crisis: Central and Eastern Europe before World War II.* 2001. Surveys the complex history of these crucial regions.

Blinkhorn, Martin. *Fascism and the Right in Europe 1919–1945.* 2000. A clear and concise historical and historiographical survey, with a selection of key primary documents.

Bookbinder, Paul. *Weimar Germany: The Republic of the Reasonable.* 1996. An innovative interpretation.

Bosworth, R. J. B. *Mussolini's Italy: Life under the Fascist Dictatorship.* 2007. Crucial study of a crucial place and time.

Brendon, Piers. *The Dark Valley: A Panorama of the 1930s.* 2000. Fast-paced but carefully researched and comprehensive overview of the histories of the United States, Germany, Italy, France, Britain, Japan, Russia, and Spain.

Fischer, Conan. *The Rise of the Nazis.* 1995. Summarizes recent research and includes a section of primary documents.

Fitzpatrick, Sheila. *Everyday Stalinism. Ordinary Life in Extraordinary Times: Soviet Russia in the 1930s.* 1999. Explores the daily life of the ordinary urban worker in Stalinist Russia.

Fitzpatrick, Sheila. *Stalin's Peasants: Resistance and Survival in the Russian Village After Collectivization.* 1995. A superb history from the bottom up.

Getty, J. Arch, and Oleg V. Naumov. *The Road to Terror: Stalin and the Self-Destruction of the Bolsheviks, 1932–1939.* 1999. Interweaves recently discovered documents with an up-to-date interpretation of the Great Purge.

Gilbert, Bentley Brinkerhoff. *Britain 1914–1945: The Aftermath of Power.* 1996. Short, readable overview, designed for beginning students.

Jackson, Julian. *The Popular Front in France: Defending Democracy, 1934–1938.* 1988. A political and cultural history.

Kershaw, Ian. *Hitler.* 1991. A highly acclaimed biography.

Kitchen, Martin. *Nazi Germany: A Critical Introduction.* 2004. Short, clearly written, up to date. An excellent introduction and overview.

Lewis, Bernard. *The Shaping of the Modern Middle East.* 1994. Concise but comprehensive analysis.

Mack Smith, Denis. *Mussolini: A Biography.* 1983. An engaging read and a now-classic account.

Pedersen, Susan. *Family, Dependence, and the Origins of the Welfare State: Britain and France, 1914–1945.* 1993. Shows how welfare policy was inextricably linked to demographic and eugenic concerns.

Thomas, Hugh. *The Spanish Civil War.* 1977. An authoritative account.

Wolpert, Stanley. *Gandhi's Passion: The Life and Legacy of Mahatma Gandhi.* 2001. An intellectual and spiritual biography by one of the foremost historians of modern India.

CHAPTER 27. WORLD WAR II

Alperovitz, Gar. *Atomic Diplomacy: Hiroshima and Potsdam. The Use of the Atomic Bomb and the*

American Confrontation with Soviet Power. 1994. The first edition of this book, published in 1965, sparked an ongoing scholarly debate over whether or not U.S. fears about Soviet power influenced the decision to use the atomic bombs against Japan..

Browning, Christopher. *Ordinary Men: Reserve Police Battalion 101 and the Final Solution in Poland.* 1992. A powerful account of the participation of a group of "ordinary men" in mass murder.

Calder, Angus. *The People's War: Britain, 1939–1945.* 1969. Lengthy—but worth the effort for students wishing to explore the war's impact on British society. (Those who want a shorter account can turn to Robert Mackay, *The Test of War: Inside Britain 1939–45* [1999].)

Frayn, Michael. *Copenhagen.* 1998. A remarkable play in which Frayn dramatizes a meeting (that actually did occur) between the German atomic physicist Werner Heisenberg and his Danish anti-Nazi colleague Niels Bohr. Contains both extremely clear explanations of the workings of atomic physics and a provocative exploration of the moral issues involved in the making of the atom bomb.

Friedlander, Saul. *Nazi Germany and the Jews, 1933–1939.* 1998. An important study of the evolution of Nazi anti-Semitic policy before the war.

Hilberg, Raul. *Perpetrators, Victims, Bystanders: The Jewish Catastrophe, 1933–1945.* 1992. As his title indicates, Hilberg looks at the three principal sets of participants in the Holocaust.

Iriye, Akira. *The Origins of the Second World War in Asia and the Pacific.* 1987. Part of Longman's "Origins of Modern Wars" series aimed at university students, this short and readable study highlights the major issues and events.

Keegan, John. *The Second World War.* 1989. Provides clear explanations of military technologies and techniques; packed with useful maps and vivid illustrations.

Kitchen, Martin. *Nazi Germany at War.* 1995. A short and nicely organized survey of the German home front.

Marrus, Michael R. *The Holocaust in History.* 1987. A clearly written, concise account of historians' efforts to understand the Holocaust. Highly recommended.

Maudsley, Evan. *Thunder in the East: The Nazi-Soviet War 1941–1945.* 2005. A wide-ranging account that looks at social and political contexts as well as military strategy and technology.

Merridale, Catherine. *Ivan's War: Life and Death in the Red Army, 1939–1945.* 2007. "From-the-bottom-up" military history, this account looks at the often harrowing experiences of ordinary soldiers.

Moore, Bob, ed. *Resistance in Western Europe.* 2000. A collection of essays that explores recent research on this controversial topic.

Overy, Richard. *Russia's War: A History of the Soviet War Effort, 1941–1945.* 1997. A compelling account, written to accompany the television documentary *Russia's War.*

Paxton, Robert. *Vichy France: Old Guard and New Order, 1940–1944.* 1972. A now-classic study of the aims and evolution of France's collaborationist government.

Rees, Laurence. *WWII Behind Closed Doors: Stalin, the Nazis and the West.* 2008. Winner of the British Book Award for History and companion volume to the BBC Television series, this account uses recently revealed archival documents and interviews to explore the morally complex issues involved in the strange alliance between Stalin and Western democracy.

Rhodes, Richard. *Masters of Death: The SS-Einsatzgruppen and the Invention of the Holocaust.* 2002. Compelling account of the Einsatzgruppen actions during the German invasion of the Soviet Union.

Rhodes, Richard. *The Making of the Atomic Bomb.* 1986. A lengthy but very readable account; very good at explaining the complicated science involved.

Rock, William R. *British Appeasement in the 1930s.* 1977. A balanced and concise appraisal.

Weinberg, Gerhard. *A World at Arms: A Global History of World War II.* 1994. Places the war within a global rather than simply a European context.

CHAPTER 28. REDEFINING THE WEST AFTER WORLD WAR II

Ansprenger, Franz. *The Dissolution of Colonial Empires.* 1989. A clear and comprehensive account (that unfortunately includes no maps).

Castles, Stephen, et al. *Here for Good: Western Europe's New Ethnic Minorities.* 1984. A useful exploration of the impact of postwar immigration, despite the rather rigid Marxist analysis.

Crampton, R. J. *Eastern Europe in the Twentieth Century—And After.* 1997. Detailed chapters on the 1950s and 1960s, including a substantial discussion of the Prague Spring.

De Grazia, Victoria. *Irresistible Empire: America's Advance through Twentieth-Century Europe.* 2005. A study of the Americanization of Europe.

Elkins, Caroline. *Imperial Reckoning: The Untold Story of Britain's Gulag in Kenya.* 2005. This controversial work won the Pulitzer Prize for Non-Fiction.

Fineberg, Jonathan. *Art Since 1940: Strategies of Being.* 1995. A big, bold, lavishly illustrated volume that makes the unfashionable argument that individuals matter.

Fink, Carole, et al. *1968: The World Transformed.* 1998. A collection of essays that explores both the international and the domestic political context for the turmoil of 1968.

Gaddis, John Lewis. *The Cold War: A New History.* 2005. A comprehensive overview by a prominent Cold War historian.

Gillingham, John. *European Integration, 1950–2003: Superstate or New Market Economy?* 2003. An important interpretive history of the European Union.

Gross, Jan T., ed. *The Politics of Retribution in Europe: World War II and Its Aftermath.* 2000. This series of essays makes clear that war did not end in Europe in May 1945.

Judge, Edward, and John Langdon. *A Hard and Bitter Peace: A Global History of the Cold War.* 1999. An extremely useful survey for students. Excellent maps.

Judt, Tony. *Postwar: A History of Europe since 1945.* 2005. An important interpretive survey.

Keep, John. *Last of the Empires: A History of the Soviet Union, 1945–1991.* 1995. Looks beyond the Kremlin to explore social, cultural, and economic developments.

Madara'z, Jeannette. *Working in East Germany: Normality in a Socialist Dictatorship, 1961–1979.* 2006. Examines ordinary life in an extraordinary society.

Poiger, Uta. *Jazz, Rock, and Rebels: Cold War Politics and American Culture in a Divided Germany.* 2000. Explores the interplay among youth culture, Americanization, and political protest.

Rees, Laurence. *WWII Behind Closed Doors: Stalin, the Nazis and the West.* 2008. Winner of the British Book Award for History and companion volume to the BBC Television series, this account uses recently revealed archival documents and interviews to explore the compromises that created Cold War Europe.

de Senarclens, P. *From Yalta to the Iron Curtain: The Great Powers and the Origins of the Cold War.* 1995. A look at the diplomatic, political and military concerns that created the Cold War.

Steege, Paul. *Black Market Cold War: Everyday Life in Berlin, 1946–1949.* 2007. History "from the bottom up" that explores the ways Berlin became the symbolic center of the Cold War and its impact on the people of Berlin.

Stromberg, Roland. *After Everything: Western Intellectual History Since 1945.* 1975. A swiftly moving tour through the major intellectual developments.

Taylor, Frederick. *The Berlin Wall: A World Divided, 1961–1989.* 2007. Uses the dramatic history of the Berlin Wall to explore the global impact of the Cold War.

Westad, Odd Arne. *The Global Cold War: Third World Interventions and the Making of Our Time.* 2007. Highly recommended study of the Cold War's globalization.

Wyman, Mark. *DPs: Europe's Displaced Persons, 1945–1951.* 1989. An important study of an often-neglected topic.

CHAPTER 29. THE WEST IN THE CONTEMPORARY ERA: NEW ENCOUNTERS AND TRANSFORMATIONS

NOTE: Many of the readings recommended for Chapter 28 supplement this chapter as well.

Ardagh, John. *Germany and the Germans: The United Germany in the Mid-1990s.* 1996. A snapshot of a society in the midst of social and economic change.

Kavanagh, Dennis. *Thatcherism and British Politics: The End of Consensus?* 1987. Kavanagh answers the question posed in his title with a convincing "yes."

Kenney, Padraic. *The Burdens of Freedom: Eastern Europe since 1989.* 2006. In only 160 pages, Kenney offers a lucid and very helpful account of postrevolutionary developments.

Lewis, Jane, ed. *Women and Social Policies in Europe: Work, Family and the State.* 1993. A series of essays exploring the position of women in western Europe. Packed with statistics and useful tables.

Lovell, Stephen. *Destination in Doubt: Russia Since 1989.* 2006. A clear and succinct account.

McNeill, John. *Something New Under the Sun: An Environmental History of the Twentieth Century.* 2000. Argues that twentieth-century human economic activity has transformed the ecology of the globe—an ongoing experiment with a potentially devastating outcome.

Ost, David. *Solidarity and the Politics of Anti-Politics: Opposition and Reform in Poland Since 1968.* 1990. Although the bulk of this account was written before the Revolution of 1989, it provides a compelling study of Solidarity's emergence, impact, and ideology.

Rogel, Carole. *The Breakup of Yugoslavia and the War in Bosnia.* 1998. Designed for undergraduates, this work includes a short but detailed historical narrative, biographies of the main personalities, and a set of primary documents.

Rosenberg, Tina. *The Haunted Land: Facing Europe's Ghosts After Communism.* 1995. Winner of the Pulitzer Prize, this disturbing account focuses on the fundamental moral issues facing postcommunist political cultures.

Sandler, Irving. *Art of the Postmodern Era: From the Late 1960s to the Early 1980s.* 1996. Much more broad-ranging than the title suggests, this well-written, blessedly jargon-free work sets both contemporary art and the theories of the postmodern within the wider historical context.

Stokes, Gale. *The Walls Came Tumbling Down: The Collapse of Communism in Eastern Europe.* 1993. A superb account, firmly embedded in history.

Young, John W. *Cold War Europe, 1945–1991: A Political History.* 1996. A solid survey.

NOTES

CHAPTER 1

1. Robert J. Wenke, *Patterns in Prehistory: Humankind's First Three Million Years* (1999), 404.
2. Ibid.
3. Marc van de Mieroop, *A History of the Ancient Near East, ca 3000–323 B.C.E.* (2007), 23.
4. Wenke, *Patterns in Prehistory,* 404.
5. Quoted in Stephen Bertman, *Handbook to Life in Ancient Mesopotamia* (2003), 65.
6. Ibid., 179.
7. Quoted in van de Mieroop, *A History of the Ancient Near East,* 113.
8. Ibid.
9. Quoted in Bertman, *Handbook to Life in Ancient Mesopotamia,* 172–173.
10. Jean Bottero, *Mesopotamia: Writing, Reasoning, and the Gods.* Translated by Zainab Bahrani and Mac Van De Mieroop (1992), 33, 127, 129.
11. *Code of Hammurabi,* trans. J. N. Postgate, 55–56. Cited in Postgate, *Early Mesopotamia: Society and Economy at the Dawn of History* (1992), 160.
12. Samuel Greengus, "Legal and Social Institutions of Ancient Near Mesopotamia," in *Civilizations of the Ancient Near East,* ed. Jack M. Sasson, vol. 1 (1995), 471.
13. Ibid., 474.
14. *A Dispute of a Man with His Ba,* probably composed ca. 2180–2040 B.C.E. Quoted in W. Stiebing, *Ancient Near Eastern History and Culture* (2008), 153.
15. *The Admonitions of Ipuwer,* quoted in Stiebing, *Ancient Near Eastern History and Culture,* 164.

CHAPTER 2

1. Quoted in Carlo Zaccagnini, "The Interdependence of the Great Powers," in *Amarna Diplomacy: The Beginnings of International Relations,* eds. Raymond Cohen and Raymond Westbrook (2000), 149.
2. Quoted in Michael Roaf, *Cultural Atlas of Mesopotamia and the Ancient Near East* (2004), 136.

3. Quoted in Trevor Bryce, *Life and Society in the Hittite World* (2002), 113.
4. Quoted in William H. Stiebing, Jr., *Ancient Near Eastern History and Culture* (2008), 229.
5. Quoted in Marc Van De Mieroop, *A History of the Ancient Near East ca. 3000–323 B.C.* (2007), 194.
6. Ibid., 195.
7. A. Kirk Grayson, in *Assyrian and Babylonian Chronicles* (1975).
8. Quoted in Stiebing, *Ancient Near Eastern History and Culture,* 281.
9. Micah 6: 6–8, Revised Standard Version.
10. Ezekiel 34: 15–20. Revised Standard Version.

CHAPTER 3

1. Demosthenes, *Orations,* 59.122.
2. From Euripides, *The Trojan Women.* Translated by Peter Levi, in John Boardman, Jasper Griffith, and Oswyn Murray, eds., *The Oxford History of the Classical World* (1986), 169.
3. Plato, *Phaedo,* 1.118.

CHAPTER 4

1. Athenaios, 253 D; cited and translated in J. J. Pollitt, *Art in the Hellenistic Age* (1986), 271.

CHAPTER 5

1. From *Selected Works* by Cicero, translated by Michael Grant (Penguin Classics 1960, second revised edition 1971). Copyright © Michael Grant 1960, 1965, 1971. Reproduced by permission of Penguin Books Ltd.

CHAPTER 7

1. John Helgeland, *Christians in the Military: The Early Experience* (1985), 64–65.

CHAPTER 8

1. Al-Tabari, *The History of Al-Tabari,* Vol. 17: *The First Civil War,* trans. and annotated by G. R. Hawting (1985), 50.
2. Quoted in Jane S. Gerber, *The Jews of Spain: A History of the Sephardic Experience* (1992), 28.

CHAPTER 9

1. Willibald, *The Life of Boniface,* in Clinton Albertson, trans., *Anglo-Saxon Saints and Heroes* (1967), 308–310.
2. Quoted in Edward Peters, *Europe and the Middle Ages* (1989), 159.

CHAPTER 10

1. Cited in Emmanuel Le Roy Ladurie, *Montaillou: Promised Land of Error.* Translated by Barbara Bray (1978), 130.
2. Ibid., 56.
3. Ibid., 63.

CHAPTER 11

1. Quoted in William Bowsky, "The Impact of the Black Death." In Anthony Molho (ed.), *Social and Economic Foundations of the Italian Renaissance* (1969), 92.
2. Cited in Philip Ziegler, *The Black Death* (1969), 20.
3. Giovanni Boccaccio, *The Decameron.* Translated by Richard Aldington (1962), 30.
4. Ibid.
5. Quoted in Mark C. Bartusis, *The Late Byzantine Army: Arms and Society, 1204–1453* (1992), 133.
6. Trial record as quoted in Marina Warner, *Joan of Arc* (1981), 122.
7. Ibid., 127.
8. Ibid., 143.
9. *The Trial of Joan of Arc.* Translated W. S. Scott (1956), 134.
10. Ibid., 106.
11. Ibid., 135.
12. Johan Huizinga, *The Autumn of the Middle Ages.* Translated Rodney J. Payton and Ulrich Mammitzsch (1996), 156.
13. Quoted in Barbara W. Tuchman, *A Distant Mirror: The Calamitous 14th Century* (1978), 505–506. Translation has been slightly modified by the authors.
14. Cited in Bartlett, *The Making of Europe,* 238.

CHAPTER 12

1. Baldesar Castiglione, *The Book of the Courtier.* Translated by Charles S. Singleton (1959), 43.
2. Giovanni Villani, *Cronica* vol. 7, (1823), 52. Translation by the authors.
3. Agostino di Colloredo, "Chroniche friulane, 1508–18," *Pagine friulane* 2 (1889), 6. Translation by the authors.

4. Francesco Petrarca, "Letter to the Shade of Cicero." In Kenneth R. Bartlett (ed.), *The Civilization of the Italian Renaissance: A Sourcebook* (1992), 31.
5. Quoted in Margaret L. King, *Women of the Renaissance* (1991), 197.
6. "Laura Cereta, "Bibulus Sempronius: Defense of the Liberal Instruction of Women." In Margaret King and Alfred Rabil (eds.), *Her Immaculate Hand: Selected Words by and About the Women Humanists of Quattrocento Italy* (1983), 82.

CHAPTER 13

1. Christopher Columbus, quoted in Felipe Fernández-Armesto, *Columbus* (1991), 6.
2. Ibid., 154.
3. *The Life of The Admiral Christopher Columbus by his Son Ferdinand.* Translated and Annotated by Benjamin Keen (1959), 222.
4. Sir Arthur Helps, *The Spanish Conquest in America,* vol. 1 (1900), 1, 264–267.
5. *The Book of Chilam Balam of Chumayel,* edited and translated Ralph L. Roy (1933), 83.
6. *The Conquistadores: First-Person Accounts of the Conquest of Mexico,* edited and translated Patricia de Fuentes (1963), 159.
7. Quoted in Margaret T. Hodgen, *Early Anthropology in the Sixteenth and Seventeenth Centuries* (1964), 9.
8. Quoted in Ibid., 207. Spelling has been modernized.
9. Quoted in Ibid., 369.
10. Quoted in Ibid., 373–374. Spelling and syntax have been modernized.

CHAPTER 14

1. Quoted in Gordon Rupp, *Luther's Progress to the Diet of Worms* (1964), 29.
2. Ibid., 33.
3. Quote from an anonymous caricature reproduced in A. G. Dickens, *Reformation and Society in Sixteenth-Century Europe* (1966), Figure 46, 61.
4. Quoted in Roland H. Bainton, *Here I Stand: A Life of Martin Luther,* (1950), 166, 181–185.
5. Translated and quoted in Thomas Head, "Marie Dentière: A Propagandist for the Reform." In Katharina M. Wilson (ed.), *Women Writers of the Renaissance and Reformation* (1987), 260.

6. Quoted in Peter Blickle, "The Popular Reformation." In *Handbook of European History 1400–1600: Late Middle Ages, Renaissance and Reformation*, Vol. 2: *Visions, Programs and Outcomes*, Thomas A. Brady, Jr., Heiko A. Oberman, and James D. Tracy (eds.), (1995), 171.
7. Quoted in Heiko A. Oberman, *Luther: Man Between God and the Devil*. Translated by Eileen Walliser-Schwarzbart (1989), 240.
8. Quoted in Dickens, *Reformation and Society*, 134

CHAPTER 15

1. Quoted in R. Po-Chia Hsia, *Social Discipline in the Reformation: Central Europe, 1550–1750* (1989), 147–148.
2. Quoted in Norbert Elias, *The Civilizing Process*, vol. 1: *The History of Manners*. Translated by Edmund Jephcott (1978), 119.
3. Quoted in R. J. Knecht, *The French Wars of Religion, 1559–1598*, 2nd ed. (1996), 13.
4. Michel de Montaigne, *Essays and Selected Writings*. Translated and edited by Donald M. Frame (1963), 219–221.

CHAPTER 16

1. Thomas Hobbes, *Leviathan*, C. B. Macpherson (ed.) (1968), 186.
2. Marshall Poe, "The Truth about Muscovy," *Kritika* 3 (2002), 483.
3. Quoted in Lindsey Hughes, *Russia in the Age of Peter the Great* (1998), 92.

CHAPTER 17

1. René Descartes, *Le Monde*, Book VI.
2. Thomas S. Kuhn, *The Structure of Scientific Revolutions* (1970).
3. René Descartes, *Discourse on the Method and Meditations on First Philosophy*, edited by David Weissmann (1996), 21.
4. Galileo, "Letter to the Grand Duchess Christina." In Stilman Drake (ed.), *Discoveries and Opinions of Galileo* (1957), 186.
5. Quoted in W. Hazard, *The European Mind, 1680–1715* (1964), 362.
6. François Poullain, *De l'égalite des deux sexes* (1673), 85.
7. Francis Bacon, *The Works of Francis Bacon*, vol. 3, J. Spedding (ed.) (1857–1874), 524–539.
8. Henry Oldenburg, "To the Reader." In Robert Boyle (ed.), *Experiments and Considerations in Touching Colours* (1664).

CHAPTER 18

1. Olaudah Equiano, *The Interesting Narrative of the Life of Olaudah Equiano, or Gustavus Vassa the African* (1789).
2. Thomas Rymer (ed.), *Foedera* vol. 18 (1704–1735), 72.
3. Quoted in Robin Blackburn, *The Making of New World Slavery* (1997), 325.

CHAPTER 19

1. Baron d'Holbach, *Good Sense* (1753).
2. David Hume, *Essays Moral, Political, and Literary* (1742), Essay 10: "Of Superstition and Enthusiasm."
3. Cesare Beccaria, *An Essay on Crimes and Punishments* (1788), Chapter 47.
4. Voltaire, "Religion," *The Philosophical Dictionary* (1802).

CHAPTER 20

1. H. Wallon, *Histoire du tribunal révolutionnaire de Paris* vol. 4 (1880–1882), 511.

CHAPTER 21

1. Lord Ashley's Commission on Mines, *Parliamentary Papers*, Vols. 15–17 (1842), Appendix 1, Note 26.
2. Sir James Kay-Shuttleworth (1832), quoted in John Rule, *The Labouring Classes in Early Industrial England* (1986).
3. John Richardson, *The Friend: A Religious and Literary Journal*, 30 (1856), 97.
4. "Report of the Select Committee on the Factories Bill," *Parliamentary Papers*, Vol. 20 (1833).
5. John O'Rourke, *The History of the Great Irish Famine of 1847* (1902).
6. David Gillard, ed., *British Documents on Foreign Affairs*, Vol. 1: *The Ottoman Empire in the Balkans, 1856–1875* (1984–1985), 20.

CHAPTER 23

1. Leslie Moch, *Moving Europeans: Migration in Western Europe Since 1650* (1992), 147.
2. Quoted in Eugen Weber, *Peasants into Frenchmen: The Modernization of Rural France, 1870–1914* (1976), 332–333.
3. Norman Kleeblatt, *The Dreyfus Affair: Art, Truth, and Justice* (1987), 96.

4. Quoted in Eric Cahm, *The Dreyfus Affair in French Society and Politics* (1994), 167.
5. Quoted in Robert Gildea, *Barricades and Borders: Europe, 1800–1914* (1987), 317.
6. Eugen Weber, *France*, Fin-de-Siècle (1986), 126.
7. Albert Lindemann, *Esau's Tears: Modern Anti-Semitism and the Rise of the Jews* (1997).
8. Maria Desraismes, "La Femme et Le Droit," *Eve dans l'humanite* (1891), 16–17.

CHAPTER 24

1. Winston Churchill, *The River War: An Account of the Re-Conquest of the Sudan* (1933); quoted in Daniel Headrick, *The Tools of Empire: Technology and European Imperialism in the Nineteenth Century* (1981), 118.
2. Quoted in Anne McClintock, *Imperial Leather: Race, Gender, and Sexuality in the Colonial Contest* (1995), 50.
3. From Rider Haggard, *She* (1887).
4. Quoted in H. Stuart Hughes, *Consciousness and Society* (1958), 296.
5. Quoted in Shearer West, *Fin de Siècle* (1993), 24.
6. Stephen Kern, *The Culture of Time and Space, 1880–1918* (1983), 195.
7. From *Elementary Forms*. Quoted in Hughes, *Consciousness and Society*, 284–285.
8. Quoted in William Schneider, *An Empire for the Masses: The French Popular Image of Africa, 1870–1900* (1982), 72.
9. Heinrich von Treitschke, *Politics* (1897).
10. Yves-Alain Bois, "Painting as Trauma," in Christopher Green, *Picasso's Les Demoiselles d'Avignon* (2001), 49.
11. Brassaï, *Conversations with Picasso*, trans. Jane Marie Todd (1999), 32.
12. John Golding, "*Les Demoiselles D'Avignon* and the Exhibition of 1988," in Green, *Picasso's Les Demoiselles*, 29.
13. Mary Kingsley, in *West African Studies* (1901), 329–330.
14. Rudyard Kipling, *Verse* (1920).
15. Headrick, *The Tools of Empire*, 101. Headrick is the historian who identified the crucial role of the steamship, the quinine prophylaxis, and the breech-loading, repeating rifle in the conquest of Africa.
16. Quoted in Thomas Pakenham, *The Scramble for Africa, 1876–1912* (1991), 22.
17. Quoted in F. K. Crowley (ed.), *A New History of Australia* (1974), 6.
18. Ibid., 207.
19. Quoted in W. G. Beasley, *Japanese Imperialism, 1894–1945* (1987), 31–33.

CHAPTER 25

1. Quoted in Niall Ferguson, *The Pity of War* (1999), 152.
2. Quoted in Eric Leeds, *No Man's Land: Combat and Identity in World War I* (1979), 17.
3. Allister Horne, *The Price of Glory: Verdun, 1916* (1967), 27.
4. Siegfried Sassoon, *Memoirs of an Infantry Officer* (1937), 228.
5. Ernst Lessauer, "Hymn of Hate" (1914), in *Jugend* (1914). Translated by Barbara Henderson, *New York Times*, October 15, 1914.
6. Quoted in W. Bruce Lincoln, *Red Victory: A History of the Russian Civil War* (1989), 32.
7. Quoted in Edvard Radzinsky, *The Last Tsar*, trans. Marian Schwartz (1993), 336.
8. From the written account of Yakov Yurovsky, quoted in Radzinsky, *The Last Tsar*, 355.
9. Quoted in William Henry Chamberlin, *The Russian Revolution, 1917–1921, Vol. 2: From the Civil War to the Consolidation of Power* (1987), 91.
10. Quoted in Lincoln, *Red Victory*, 151.
11. Ibid., 155.
12. Quoted in Radzinsky, *The Last Tsar*, 326.
13. Richard Pipes et al. (eds.), *The Unknown Lenin* (1999), 6.
14. Ibid., Document 59.
15. Quoted in Richard Cork, *A Bitter Truth* (1994), 198.

CHAPTER 26

1. Quoted in Peter Gay, *Weimar Culture* (1970), 99.
2. Martin J. Sherwin, *A World Destroyed: Hiroshima and the Origins of the Arms Race* (1987), 17.
3. Quoted in Michael Burleigh, *The Third Reich: A New History* (2000), 36.
4. Quoted in Ibid., 52.
5. Quoted in Joachim Fest, *Hitler* (1973), 190–193.
6. Ibid., 192, 218.
7. Quoted in Wendy Goldman, *Women, the State, and Revolution: Soviet Family Policy and Social Life, 1917–1936* (1993), 5.
8. Quoted in Claudia Koonz, *Mothers in the Fatherland* (1987), 130.
9. Quoted in Fest, *Hitler*, 445.
10. Quoted in Koonz, *Mothers in the Fatherland*, 194.
11. Ibid., 178.

12. Ibid., 56; Victoria DeGrazia, *How Fascism Ruled Women: Italy, 1922–1945* (1992), 234.
13. Quoted in Mark Mazower, *Dark Continent: Europe's Twentieth Century* (1998), 123.
14. Quoted in Sheila Fitzpatrick, *Everyday Stalinism* (1999), 68.
15. See Stephen G. Wheatcroft, "More Light on the Scale of Repression and Excess Mortality in the Soviet Union in the 1930s," in J. Arch Getty and Roberta Manning, *Stalinist Terror: New Perspectives* (1993), 275–290.
16. "Appendix 1: Numbers of Victims of the Terror," in J. Arch Getty and Oleg V. Naumov, *The Road to Terror: Stalin and the Self-Destruction of the Bolsheviks, 1932–1939* (1999), 587–594.
17. Quoted in Felix Gilbert, *The End of the European Era* (1991), 162.
18. Mohandas K. Gandhi, *An Autobiography: The Story of My Experiments with Truth* (1957), 120.
19. Quoted in Tyler Stovall, *Paris Noir: African Americans in the City of Light* (1996), 32.

CHAPTER 27

1. Quoted in Robert H. Abzug, *Inside the Vicious Heart: Americans and the Liberation of Nazi Concentration Camps* (1985), 19.
2. Quoted in Gordon Horwitz, *In the Shadow of Death: Living Outside the Gates of Mauthausen* (1991), 167.
3. Quoted in Piers Brendon, *The Dark Valley: A Panorama of the 1930s* (2000), 282.
4. Quoted in Richard Overy, *Russia's War* (1998), 95.
5. Quoted in Mark Mazower, *Dark Continent: Europe's Twentieth Century* (1999), 157.
6. Quoted in Peter Clarke, *Hope and Glory: Britain, 1900–1990* (1996), 204.
7. Quoted in Joachim Fest, *Hitler* (1973), 665.
8. Quoted in Richard Rhodes, *The Making of the Atomic Bomb* (1988), 474.
9. Elie Wiesel, *Night* (1960), 39.
10. Gideon Hausner, *Justice in Jerusalem* (1966), 291.
11. Ibid., 323–324.
12. From Hausner's opening statement; quoted in Moshe Pearlman, *The Capture and Trial of Adolf Eichmann* (1963), 149.
13. Ibid., 463–465.
14. Ibid., 603; Hausner, *Justice in Jerusalem*, 422.
15. Quoted in Ulrich Herbert, *Hitler's Foreign Workers* (1997), 306.

CHAPTER 28

1. Stalin to Maxim Litvinov, cited in Vladislav Zubok and Constantine Pleshakov, *Inside the Kremlin's Cold War: From Stalin to Khrushchev* (Cambridge, 1996), 37–38.
2. Leo Crowley, director of the Foreign Economic Administration under Roosevelt and Truman; quoted in William Appleman Williams, *The Tragedy of American Diplomacy* (New York, 1972), 241.
3. Lawrence Rees, *World War II Behind Closed Doors: Stalin, the Nazis, and the West* (2008), 221, 236.
4. Quoted in William Hardy McNeill, *America, Britain, and Russia: Their Cooperation and Conflict 1941–1946* (New York, 1970), 700, note 2.
5. Quoted in Karel Kaplan, *Report on the Murder of the General Secretary* (1990), 159.
6. Ibid., 242.
7. Ibid., 231.
8. Quoted in John Hargreaves, *Decolonization in Africa* (1996), 113.
9. Quotation from *Time* magazine, 1950; quoted in Martin Walker, *The Cold War and the Making of the Modern World* (1993), 66–67.
10. Quoted in Walker, *The Cold War*, 83.
11. Quoted in Stephen Ambrose, *Rise to Globalism* (1971), 225.
12. Quoted in Donald White, *The American Century* (1999), 286.
13. Quoted in John L. H. Keep, *Last of the Empires: A History of the Soviet Union, 1945–1991* (1995), 79.
14. Quoted in Michael Scammell, *From Gulag to Glasnost: Nonconformist Art in the Soviet Union*, eds. Alla Rosenfeld and Norton T. Dodge (1995), 61.
15. Quoted in Walker, *The Cold War*, 105.
16. Quoted in Robert Paxton, *Europe in the Twentieth Century* (1997), 578.
17. Quoted in Jonathan Fineberg, *Art Since 1940: Strategies of Being* (1995), 144.
18. Ibid., 89.
19. Quoted in Adrian Hastings, *Modern Catholicism: Vatican II and After* (1991), 29.
20. Reinhold Wagnleitner, *Coca-Colonization and the Cold War: The Cultural Mission of the United States in Austria After the Second World War* (1994).
21. Quoted in Felix Gilbert, *The End of the European Era, 1890 to the Present* (1991), 429.
22. Quoted in Richard Kuisel, *Seducing the French: The Dilemma of Americanization* (1993), 147.

CHAPTER 29

1. Quoted in Robert Paxton, *Europe in the Twentieth Century* (1997), 613.
2. Kenneth Boulding, "The Economics of the Coming Spaceship Earth," first published in 1966, reprinted in *Toward a Steady-State Economy*, ed. Herman Daly (1973).
3. Quoted in D. J. Peterson, *Troubled Lands: The Legacy of Soviet Environmental Destruction* (1993), 12.
4. Quoted in Archie Brown, *The Gorbachev Factor* (1996), 125.
5. Stephen Lovell, *Destination in Doubt: Russia Since 1989* (2006), 99.
6. Salman Rushdie, "Please, Read *Satanic Verses* Before Condemning It," *Illustrated Weekly of India* (October 1988). Reprinted in M. M. Ahsan and A. R. Kidwai, *Sacrilege Versus Civility: Muslim Perspectives on The Satanic Verses Affair* (1991), 63.
7. Quoted in Malise Ruthven, *A Satanic Affair: Salman Rushdie and the Wrath of Islam* (1991), 562.
8. Quoted in Ruthven, *A Satanic Affair,* 100.
9. *Bookseller,* London (February 24, 1989). Quoted in Lisa Appignanesi and Sara Maitland, *The Rushdie File* (1990), 103–104.
10. *The Sunday Telegraph* (June 24, 1990). Quoted in Ahsan and Kidwai, *Sacrilege Versus Civility,* 80.
11. Quoted in Irving Sandler, *Art of the Postmodern Era* (1996), 4.

PHOTO CREDITS

Carnavalet, Paris, France; **page 460:** Jan the Elder Brueghel, Velvet, 1568–1625, "Flooded Road and Windmill in the Countryside", 1614, oil on copper, 23.6 × 33 cm. Bildarchiv Preussischer Kulturbesitz/Art Resource, NY; **page 465:** Pieter de Hooch (Dutch 1629–1684), "The Bedroom". ca. 1658/1660. Oil on Canvas. 20" × 23 ½" (51.0 × 60.0 cm). Widener Collection. 1942.9.33. Photograph © Board of Trustees, National Gallery of Art, Washington, D.C; **page 467:** AKG-Images; **page 468:** Coll. Duke of Northumberland, Alnwick Castle, Northumberland, Great Britain; **page 471:** Private Collection/The Bridgeman Art Library; **page 477:** Getty Images/De Agostini Editore Picture Library; **page 482:** The Bridgeman Art Library International; **page 484:** Giuseppe Arcimboldo (1527–93), "Vertumnus (Emperor Rudolf II)," 1590. Oil on wood, 70.5 × 57.5 cm. Stocklosters Slott, Sweden. Erich Lessing/Art Resource, NY; **page 487:** Piotr Jamski © Dorling Kindersley; **page 488:** Wojtek Buss/AGE Fotostock America, Inc; **page 493:** British Library, London, Great Britain; **page 496:** National Gallery, London, UK/The Bridgeman Art Library International; **page 498:** Chateaux de Versailles et de Trianon, Versailles, France; **page 502:** Chateaux de Versailles et de Trianon, Versailles, France; **page 504:** Museo del Prado, Madrid, Spain; **page 507:** Kunstbibliothek, Staatliche Museen zu Berlin, Berlin, Germany; **page 516:** Private Collection/The Stapleton Collection/The Bridgeman Art Library; **page 520:** Trial of Charles I, 4th January 1649 (engraving), English School, (17th century)/Private Collection/The Stapleton Collection/The Bridgeman Art Library International; **page 524:** Museum Boijmans Van Beuningen, Rotterdam; loan Stichting Willem van der Vorm 1972; **page 525:** Hermann Buresch/Art Resource, NY; **page 529:** Salmer Imagen ID, SL; **page 530 (from left to right):** Library of Congress; Whipple Museum of the History of Science, University of Cambridge; **page 531 (from left to right):** British Library, London, UK/Bridgeman Art Library; Courtesy of the Library of Congress; **page 533:** Godfrey Kneller (1646–1723). Bust-length portrait of Sir Isaac Newton (1641–1723). Academie des Sciences, Paris, France. Art Resource, New York; **page 534:** Courtesy of the Library of Congress; **page 535:** William Cheselden giving an anatomical demonstration to six spectators in the anatomy-theatre of the Barber-Surgeons' Company, London, ca. 1730/1740. Oil painting attributed to Charles Phillips. Oil, early 1730s. Size: canvas 79.7 × 60.5 cm. Library reference no.: ICV No 48699"/Wellcome Library, London; **page 542:** Chateau de Versailles, France/The Bridgeman Art Library; **page 544:** Herzog August Bibliothek, Wolfenbuttel, Germany/The Bridgeman Art Library; **page 547:** Gérard Blot/Art Resource/Reunion des Musees Nationaux; **page 550:** © Bettmann/CORBIS All Rights Reserved; **page 553:** Biblioteca Nacional, Rio de Janiero Brazil/The Bridgeman Art Library; **page 555:** Scott Samuel (c.1702–72). A Thames Wharf. Victoria & Albert Museum, London/Art Resource NY; **page 557:** Courtesy Instructional Resources Corporation; **page 558:** National Maritime Museum, Greenwich, Great Britain; **page 569:** Thomas Rowlandson (1756–1827), "The Chocolate House", 1787. HIP/Art Resource, NY; **page 570:** Private Collection/The Bridgeman Art Library; **page 574:** Joseph Mallord William Turner (English 1775–1851), "Slave Ship (Slavers Throwing Overboard the Dead and Dying. Typhoon Coming On)". 1840. Oil on Canvas. 90.8 × 122.6 (35 ¾ × 48 ¼ in). Henry Lillie Pierce Fund. 99.22. Courtesy, Museum of Fine Arts, Boston. Reproduced with permission. © 2006 Museum of Fine Arts, Boston. All Rights Reserved; **page 576:** Thomas Gainsborough (1727–88), "Lord Hastings (1732–1818), Governor of India", 1780s, oil on canvas. Museu de Arte, Sao Paulo, Brazil/Giraudon/The Bridgeman Art Library; **page 578:** British Museum, London, UK/The Bridgeman Art Library; **page 580:** The Granger Collection; **page 587:** Lemonnier, Anicet Charles Gabriel (1743–1824), "Reading of Voltaire's tragedy 'L'orphelin de la Chine' at the salon of Madame Geoffrin". 1755. Oil on Canvas, 129 × 196 cm. Photo: D. Arnaudet. Chateaux de Malmaison et Bois-Preau, Rueil-Malmaison, France. RMN Reunion des Musees Nationaux/Art Resource, NY; **page 589:** © National Gallery, London/Art Resource, NY; **page 592:** John Bethell/The Bridgeman Art Library International; **page 595:** Sir Joshua Reynolds (1723–92), "Mary, Duchess of Richmond (1740–96), 1746–67, oil on canvas. Private Collection/The Bridgeman Art Library; **page 598:** Louvre, Paris, France/Erich Lessing/Art Resource, NY; **page 601:** William Hogarth (1697–1764), "Credulity, Superstition and Fanaticism", 1762, engraving. The Israel Museum, Jerusalem, Israel/Vera & Arturo Schwarz Collection of Dada and Surrealist Art/The Bridgeman Art Library; **page 604:** William Hogarth, Sarah Malcolm in Prison. 1733. Oil on canvas. 48.80 × 38.70 cm (framed: 56.20 × 46.40 × 9.00 cm). National Galleries of Scotland, Scottish National Gallery of Modern Art; **page 606:** Private Collection/The Bridgeman Art Library; **page 608:** Bibliotheque Nationale de France; **page 614:** Vigilius Erichsen (1722–82), "Equestrian Portrait of Catherine II (1729–96), the Great of Russia", oil on canvas. Musee des Beaux-Arts, Chartres, France/The Bridgeman Art Library; **page 619:** Chateau de Versailles, France/Giraudon/The Bridgeman Art Lirary Nationality; **page 621:** Musee Carnavalet, Paris, France/ The

Bridgeman Art Library, London/New York; **page 623:** Snark/Art Resource, NY/Art Resource, NY; **page 626** (**from left to right**): The Art Archive/Musee Carnavalet Paris/Dagli Orti; The Art Archive/Private Collection/Marc Charmet; **page 631:** Bibliotheque Nationale, Paris, France/The Bridgeman Art Library; **page 637:** Musee de la Ville de Paris, Musee Carnavalet, Paris, France/The Bridgeman Art Library; **page 638:** Giraudon/Musees Royaux des Beaux-Arts de Belgique, Brussels/Art Resource, NY; **page 639:** Jacques Louis David (1748–1825), "Consecration of the Emperor Napoleon I and Coronation of Empress Josephine," 1806–07. Louvre, Paris. Bridgeman-Giraudon/Art Resource, NY; **page 646:** Jean-Charles Tardieu (1765–1830), "Troops Halted on the Banks of the Nile, 2nd February 1812", oil on canvas. Chateau de Versailles, France/Lauros/Giraudon/The Bridgeman Art Library; **page 648:** Francisco de Goya, (Spanish, 1746–1828). "The Third of May, 1808". 1814–1815. Oil on canvas, approx. 8'8" × 11'3". Derechos reservados © Museo Nacional Del Prado-Madrid. Photo Oronoz; **page 655:** Library of Congress; **page 656:** Guildhall Library, City of London/The Bridgeman Art Library; **page 657:** © RCAHMS. Reproduced courtesy of J R Hume. Licensor www.rcahms.go.uk; **page 659:** Science Museum London/Bridgeman Art Library; **page 661:** Private Collection/The Bridgeman Art Library; **page 668:** Archiv/Photo Researchers, Inc; **page 673:** Getty Images Inc. Hulton Archive Photos; **page 676:** The Image Works; **page 678:** The Bridgeman Art Library International; **page 679:** Joseph Mallord William Turner, 1775–1851, "Rain, Steam, and Speed—The Great Western Railway." Oil on canvas, 90.8 × 121.9. © The National Gallery, London; **page 685:** Eugene Delacroix (1798–1860) "July 28th, 1830; Liberty Guides the People", oil on canvas, 260 × 325 cm. Louvre, Dept. des Peintures, Paris, France. © Photograph by Erich Lessing/Art Resource, NY; **page 690:** The Granger Collection, New York; **page 693:** Hamburger Kunsthalle, Hamburg, Germany/The Bridgeman Art Library; **page 697:** Getty Images/De Agostini Editore Picture Library; **page 701:** The Illustrated London News Picture Library, London, UK/The Bridgeman Art Library; **page 705:** Ullstein Bild/The Granger Collection, New York; **page 707:** Image Works/Mary Evans Picture Library Ltd; **page 711:** © Hulton-Deutsch Collection/CORBIS; **page 714:** Art Resource/Bildarchiv Preussischer Kulturbesitz; **page 718:** Bildarchiv Preussischer Kulturbesitz/Art Resource, NY; **page 721:** Pierre Auguste Renoir. Le Moulin de la Galette, 1876. Oil on canvas. © 2004 Artists Rights Society (ARS), New York. Louvre Museum/Art Resource, NY; **page 722:** Getty Images; **page 725:** Private Collection/Roger Perrin/The Bridgeman Art Library Nationality; **page 727:** The Children's Class, 1889 (oil on canvas) by Henry Jules Jean Geoffroy (1853–1924). Ministere de L'Education Nationale, Paris, France/Archives Charmet/The Bridgeman Art Library Nationality; **page 728:** Getty Images Inc.—Hulton Archive Photos; **page 732:** Getty Images Inc.—Hulton Archive Photos; **page 734:** Sovfoto/Eastfoto; **page 737:** Getty Images/De Agostini Editore Picture Library; **page 740:** The Black Banner (Czarny Sztandar), 1905. Oil on canvas, 30 × 81". Gift of the Estate of Rose Mintz, JM 63–67a. Photo by Richard Goodbody, The Jewish Museum, New York, NY, U.S.A; **page 743:** Réunion des Musées Nationaux/Art Resource, NY; **page 751:** Giraudon/Art Resource, NY; **page 752:** Adalbert Franz Seligmann "Allgemeines Krankenhaus" (General Hospital) 19th Century Painting, canvas. "Professor Theodor Billroth lectures at the General Hospital, Vienna. 1880". Erich Lessing/Art Resource, NY; **page 754:** National History Museum, London, UK/Bridgeman Art Library; **page 758:** Edgar Degas, "The Glass of Absinthe," 1876. Oil on canvas, 36 × 27 in. Musee d'Orsay, Paris. Scala/Art Resource, NY; **page 759:** Erich Lessing/Art Resource, NY; **page 761:** The Granger Collection, New York; **page 763:** Egon Schiele (1890–1918), "Standing Nude, Facing Front (Self Portrait)," 1910. Graphische Sammlung Albertina, Vienna, Austria/The Bridgeman Art Library; **page 764:** William Holman Hunt (1827–1910), "The Light of the World", c. 1852, oil on canvas. © Manchester Art Gallery, UK/The Bridgeman Art Library; **page 767:** Bodleian Library, University of Oxford, Shelfmark 2523; **page 768:** Pablo Picasso, "Les Demoiselles d'Avignon". 1907. Oil on Canvas. 8' × 7'8" (2.44 × 2.34 m). Acquired through the Lillie P. Bliss Bequest. Digital Image © The Museum of Modern Art/Licensed by Scala-Art Resource, NY. © 2008 ARS Artists Rights Society, NY; **page 780:** Hulton Archive/Getty Images; **page 785:** British Topical Committee for War Films/Picture Desk, Inc./Kobal Collection; **page 786:** UPI/CORBIS-NY; **page 792:** Getty Images; **page 793:** The Art Archive/Imperial War Museum; **page 796:** Private Collection/The Stapleton Collection/The Bridgeman Art Library; **page 798:** Getty Images; **page 799:** Brooks Ernest (Lt)/Imperial War Museum, London; **page 805:** Courtesy of the Library of Congress; **page 806:** Getty Images; **page 808:** Sovfoto/Eastfoto; **page 810:** Bettmann/Corbis; **page 821:** Bildarchiv Preussischer Kulturbesitz/Art Resource, NY; **page 823:** Getty Images Inc.—Hulton Archive Photos; **page 828:** George Grosz (1893–1959), "Stuetzen der Gesellschaft (Pillars of Society)". 1926. Oil on canvas, 200,0 × 108,0 cm. Inv.: NG 4/58. Photo: Joerg P. Anders. Nationalgalerie,

Staatliche Museen zu Berlin, Berlin, Germany. Art © Estate George Grosz/Licensed by VAGA, New York, New York; **page 830:** Library of Congress; **page 831:** Roger Viollet/The Image Works; **page 832:** Hoover Institution Archive Library; **page 839:** Art Resource/Bildarchiv Preussischer Kulturbesitz; **page 841:** Hoover Institution Archive Library; **page 847:** Robert Capa © 2001 by Cornell Capa/Magnum Photos; **page 852:** © Bettmann/CORBIS All Rights Reserved; **page 853:** Walery/Getty Images Inc. Hulton Archive Photos; **page 857:** Getty Images, Inc; **page 858:** Corbis RF; **page 867:** © Dimitri Baltermants/The Dimitri Baltermants Collection/CORBIS. All Rights Reserved; **page 868:** Sovfoto/Eastfoto; **page 874:** Retna Ltd; **page 876:** Getty Images Inc.—Hulton Archive Photos; **page 879:** AKG-Images; **page 881:** © Bettmann /CORBIS. All Rights Reserved; **page 885:** Marius Meijboom/Nederlands Fotomuseum; **page 887:** Topham/The Image Works; **page 891:** Retna Ltd; **page 894:** Franklin D. Roosevelt Library; **page 899:** CTK Photobank/Czech News Agency CTK; **page 904:** © CORBIS All Rights Reserved; **page 913:** Getty Images Inc.—Hulton Archive Photos; **page 918:** Alberto Giacometti (1901–1966), "Man Pointing". 1947. Bronze, 70 $\frac{1}{2}$ × 40 $\frac{3}{4}$ × 16 $\frac{3}{8}$", at base, 12 × 13 $\frac{1}{4}$". Gift of Mrs. John D. Rockefeller 3rd. (678.1954) The Museum of Modern Art, New York, NY, U.S.A. Digital Image The Museum of Modern Art/Licensed by SCALA/Art Resource, NY. © 2010 ARS Artists Rights Society, NY; **page 919 (from left to right):** Francis Bacon, English, born Ireland, 1909–1992, Figure with Meat, 1954. Oil on canvas, 129.9 × 121.9 cm (51 1/8 × 48 in.) Unframed, Harriott A. Fox Fund, 1956.1201. Photograph Bob Hashimoto. The Art Institute of Chicago. All Rights Reserved. Diego Rodriguez Velasquez (1599–1660), "Portrait of Innocent X", 1650. Araldo De Luca © ADP Management Fratelli Alinari/Art Resource, NY; **page 920:** Digital Image © The Museum of Modern Art/Licensed by SCALA/Art Resource, NY; **page 921:** Richard Hamilton (English, b. 1922), "Just what is it that makes today's homes so different, so appealing?", 1956. Collage. Kunsthalle, Tubingen, Germany. The Bridgeman Art Library International © 2005 Artists Rights Society (ARS), New York/DACS, London; **page 924:** Getty Images; **page 929:** Lionel Cironneau/AP Wide World Photos; **page 933:** Getty Images; **page 934:** AP Wide World Photos; **page 936:** Getty Images; **page 939:** Jiri Bednar/Sovfoto/Eastfoto; **page 940:** Sovfoto/Eastfoto; **page 942:** Hoover Institution Archive Library; **page 954:** Getty Images; **page 956:** Getty Images; **page 958:** Marco Ventura, "Mona Lisa Contemplating the Bust of Nefertiti as God Creates Order out of Chaos on a Starry Night on the Island of La Grande Jatte as the Infanta Margarita Looks On", 1993, oil on gessoed paper, 10"w × 8-$\frac{1}{2}$"h. Painting by MARCO VENTURA 1993; **page 959:** Chad Ehlers/Stock Connection.

INDEX